American 1

Personal Documentary

The publisher gratefully acknowledges the generous support of the
Ahmanson Foundation Humanities Endowment Fund of the
University of California Press Foundation.

The publisher also gratefully acknowledges the
generous support of the Humanities Endowment Fund of the
University of California Press Foundation, the LEF Foundation, and
Hamilton College.

American Ethnographic Film and Personal Documentary

The Cambridge Turn

Scott MacDonald

UNIVERSITY OF CALIFORNIA PRESS

Berkeley   Los Angeles   London

University of California Press, one of the most distinguished university presses in the United States, enriches lives around the world by advancing scholarship in the humanities, social sciences, and natural sciences. Its activities are supported by the UC Press Foundation and by philanthropic contributions from individuals and institutions. For more information, visit www.ucpress.edu.

University of California Press
Berkeley and Los Angeles, California

University of California Press, Ltd.
London, England

The author gratefully acknowledges the generous support of the Academy of Motion Picture Arts and Sciences in the form of an Academy Film Scholars grant.

Library of Congress Cataloging-in-Publication Data

MacDonald, Scott, 1942–
    American ethnographic film and personal documentary : the Cambridge turn / Scott MacDonald.
        pages   cm
    Includes bibliographical references and index.
    ISBN 978-0-520-27561-4 (hardback) — ISBN 978-0-520-27562-1 (paper) — ISBN 978-0-520-95493-9 (ebook)
    1. Documentary films—United States—History and criticism.
    2. Ethnographic films—United States—History and criticism.
    I. Title.
    PN1995.9.D6M315   2013
    070.1′8—dc23

                                                2012045799

22   21   20   19   18   17   16   15   14   13
10   9   8   7   6   5   4   3   2   1

*For Jordan Belson, Robert Breer, Chick Callenbach,
Mani Kaul, George Kuchar, Chris Marker, Robert Nelson,
Anne Charlotte Robertson, and Amos Vogel.*

*Your passing will not dim your accomplishments
or our gratitude for them.*

CONTENTS

Introduction

Knowledge of sensible realities thus comes to life inside the tissue of experience. It is made; and made by relations that unroll themselves in time.
WILLIAM JAMES, *ESSAYS IN RADICAL EMPIRICISM*[1]

A TENTATIVE OVERVIEW OF BOSTON-AREA DOCUMENTARY FILMMAKING

Over the years, particular forms of filmmaking have been identified with particular cities: Hollywood, with commercial melodrama, obviously; Mumbai, with a certain form of Indian musical; and New York and San Francisco with American avant-garde filmmaking. And in his remarkable book, *The Most Typical Avant-Garde: History and Geography of Minor Cinemas in Los Angeles* (Berkeley: University of California Press, 2005), David James argues convincingly for the Los Angeles area's centrality not simply in the history of commercial filmmaking but in the histories of a wide range of alternative cinemas. One of James's accomplishments is to recognize that the makeup of a particular urban area can facilitate the production of specific forms of cinematic art and particular kinds of cinematic critique.

During the past fifty years, the Boston area has been the fountainhead of American documentary filmmaking.[2] Much of the most interesting and influential nonfiction filmmaking of recent decades has been made in and around Boston, or by men and women who have had significant connections with the Boston area. And filmmakers working in Cambridge at the MIT "Film Section" and at Harvard have made formative changes in how documentary is understood and in what kinds of documentaries get made. Surprisingly, however, relatively little attention has been accorded this phenomenon. Even in the Boston area itself, at least until very recently, very few have seemed to recognize the city's significance for this crucial dimension of film history.[3]

1

To some extent, the Boston area's emergence as a producer of documentary film had to do with the expansion of technological options available to nonfiction film-makers beginning in the early 1960s. The availability of lightweight, sync-sound film rigs (Ricky Leacock, who would team up with Ed Pincus in 1968 to establish the Film Section at MIT, was a central figure in the development of this equip-ment) made new forms of "cinema verite" filmmaking possible.[4] The result was a new set of options for documentary. The increasing mobility, flexibility, and sensi-tivity of recording equipment facilitated a wide range of innovative approaches to representing reality. Filmmakers recording image and sound from within the flux of events could now act as "flies on the wall," observing what they saw and heard with little interference, or they could instigate new situations and record the results as they unfolded.[5]

Observational documentary has substantial roots in the Boston area. In 1960 Robert Drew, who studied new editorial approaches for candid film reporting while on a Nieman Fellowship at Harvard, assembled a group of filmmakers—Leacock, Albert Maysles, D. A. Pennebaker—to document the Wisconsin Demo-cratic primary race between John F. Kennedy and Hubert H. Humphrey. The result, *Primary* (1960), was a breakthrough, providing viewers with an insider's view of the American political process; this in-close depiction of American poli-tics at work continued in Drew Associates' later films, including *Crisis: Behind a Presidential Commitment* (1963), a documentation of the desegregation of the Uni-versity of Alabama by John Kennedy and his attorney general, Robert Kennedy, in the face of Governor George Wallace's resistance.[6] Several of the Drew Associates were soon making their own contributions to the observational mode: after film-ing what became a television show about the strange scene that surrounded the birth of the Fischer quintuplets in Aberdeen, South Dakota, in 1963, Leacock made *Happy Mother's Day* (1963, co-directed by Joyce Chopra), his own satirical version of the experience. At MIT from 1968 on, Leacock would continue to explore the possibilities of observational filmmaking, to work toward the development of increasingly lightweight and inexpensive sync-sound equipment, and to nurture a younger generation of filmmakers. Albert Maysles and his brother David (both were born in Boston and raised in Brookline, and both were graduates of Boston University: Albert earned an M.A. in psychology and taught at B.U. for three years; David, a B.A. in psychology), made their breakthrough feature, *Salesman,* in 1968, documenting four Bible salesmen who were working out of Boston.

The most prolific and independent of Cambridge documentary filmmakers working in the observational mode is Frederick Wiseman. Since 1967 and *Titicut Follies,* his controversial film about inmates at the Massachusetts Correctional Institution in Bridgewater (shot by John Kennedy Marshall), Wiseman has been recognized as the quintessential observational filmmaker. Accomplished and often brilliant, Wiseman has focused on a wide range of American institutions—

institutions in a broad sense of the term—in dozens of feature films, including such cine-landmarks as *High School* (1968), *Law & Order* (1969), *Hospital* (1969), *Welfare* (1975), *Near Death* (1989), and *Belfast, Maine* (1999). Wiseman's work, a staple of American public television for a generation, has provided, and continues to provide, a remarkable panorama of contemporary institutional life. Wiseman's films are distributed by Zipporah Films, Wiseman's distribution company in Cambridge.

Another major Boston area contribution, or really a continuing series of contributions, to modern documentary has resulted from the long-term commitment of Boston's television station WGBH to well-crafted informational documentaries. Since *The Negro and American Promise* (1963), WGBH has been a pioneer in television programming about race. One of WGBH's signal series, of course, is *Eyes on the Prize*, produced by Henry Hampton, who moved to Boston in 1961, where he founded Blackside Productions. For the two *Eyes on the Prize* series—the first, *Eyes on the Prize: America's Civil Rights Years (1954–1965)*, which premiered in 1987 on PBS; the second, *Eyes on the Prize II: America at the Racial Crossroads (1965–1985)*; it premiered in 1990—Hampton assembled a group of researchers and filmmakers, many of them African Americans, who compiled a wealth of documentation of the civil rights movement and interviewed many of the individuals who had participated in or witnessed crucial events in this history. The fourteen programs in the two series provide the most extensive and gripping cinematic record of one of the major social transformations in American history. Among the most powerful of the *Eyes on the Prize* episodes is the thirteenth program, *The Keys to the Kingdom (1974–1980)*, which was produced, directed, and written by Harvard graduate Paul Stekler and the late Jacqueline Shearer, a lifelong Bostonian: this episode chronicles the clash in Boston over school busing. Boston University graduate Orlando Bagwell, who directed the third and fifth episodes of *Eyes on the Prize*, has gone on to make a series of documentaries about African American history, including the four-part, six-hour, WGBH-produced *Africans in America* (1998).

ETHNOGRAPHIC FILM AND
PERSONAL DOCUMENTARY

The Boston area continues to be a remarkably active center for nonfiction filmmaking, though the modern development of two particular genres of documentary seems more precisely a product of Cambridge, and in particular of the MIT Film Section and the Peabody Museum, the Film Study Center and the Department of Visual and Environmental Studies at Harvard. One of these genres has come to be called "ethnographic film": originally, the term designated the use of film to document information about preindustrial cultures, particularly cultures on the verge of collapse or transformation. During recent years, "ethnographic film" has come to have a much broader cinematic application.

The other genre of documentary Cambridge has nurtured is what has come to be called "personal documentary": the cinematic chronicling of the filmmaker's personal and/or family life. This genre of documentary needs to be understood, at least for the purposes of this study, as distinct from the various forms of "personal filmmaking" that have been developed by "avant-garde" filmmakers since the 1940s. These include the "psychodrama"—dramatizations of disturbed states of mind: for example, Maya Deren and Alexander Hammid's *Meshes of the Afternoon* (1943) and Kenneth Anger's *Fireworks* (1947); the personally expressive cinema of Stan Brakhage, Bruce Baillie, and Nathaniel Dorsky; and the diaristic work of Jonas Mekas. In this study, "personal documentary" is used to refer to those explorations and depictions of the personal lives of the filmmakers during which family members, friends, and others are recorded in sync sound, or with the illusion of sync sound, interacting conversationally with the filmmakers.

On one level, ethnographic documentary and personal documentary might seem the antithesis of each other: one has traditionally involved the travels of anthropologists to far-flung locations to observe people very different from themselves; the other, the self-conscious investigations by filmmakers of their personal lives. But for all their apparent differences, the two approaches are fundamentally two sides of the same cinematic coin, the inverse of each other. Robert Gardner has said that "going to distant cultures leads to self-examination which in turn refines sensibilities for detecting meaning in the lives of others."[7] By the early 1970s, the use of cinema to explore the exotic Other had not only revealed aspects of the Self to particular ethnographic filmmakers, it—along with a variety of other cultural developments—was instigating what soon became a major new avenue for documentary: the cinematic exploration of the patterns and nuances of the filmmakers' own culture, as exemplified by their personal lives.

Prime movers in the development of ethnographic cinema were Lorna Marshall, her son John Marshall, and Robert Gardner. Once she and her family had decided to travel to the Kalahari Desert in southwest Africa, longtime Cambridge resident Lorna Marshall studied anthropology at Harvard; she went on to write *The !Kung of Nyae Nyae* (Harvard University Press, 1975) and *Nyae Nyae !Kung Belief and Rites* (Peabody Museum Press, 1999). She also produced *First Film* (shot in 1951; final form 1995), a breakthrough depiction of the lives of gatherer-hunters in the Kalahari Desert. John Marshall began documenting the lives of these same groups on expeditions sponsored by the Peabody Museum and the Smithsonian Institution, and in later years, worked to help those he had filmed maintain some vestige of their culture. *The Hunters: A !Kung Bushmen Film* (1957) was the first of John Marshall's dozens of films about these people—a body of work that reveals a wide range of experimentation.

Robert Gardner, another major figure in the evolution of ethnographic documentary, graduated from Harvard, then, after some years on the West Coast, where he made several short films, returned for graduate study in anthropology. In 1957 the Peabody Museum established the Film Study Center to assist in the management of the Marshall family's African footage and named Gardner the center's first director. For several years Gardner worked with Marshall on the editing of *The Hunters*. In 1963 Gardner finished his own ethnographic classic, *Dead Birds*, which premiered in Cambridge at Harvard's Loeb Drama Center. Like John Marshall, Gardner would continue to make important contributions to documentary filmmaking for decades. *Dead Birds* and *The Hunters* were the first modern ethnographic films to be included in the Library of Congress's National Film Registry, in 1998 and 2003, respectively.[8]

A third crucial figure in the history of ethnographic cinema was Timothy Asch, who got his M.A. in African Studies at Boston University (with a concentration in anthropology at Harvard). For a time, Asch worked at the Peabody Museum as a production assistant on several of John Marshall's films, and he reviewed and cataloged the material Gardner sent back from New Guinea during the shooting of *Dead Birds*. In the late 1960s Asch teamed up with anthropologist Napoleon Chagnon to begin what became a remarkable (and in the end controversial) series of films focusing on the Yanomami people living near the headwaters of the Orinoco River in southern Venezuela. Several of these films, including the landmark *The Ax Fight* (1975), were finished in Cambridge, while Asch was teaching at Harvard.

In 1968 John Marshall and Asch teamed up to found Documentary Educational Research, which in 1971 incorporated as Documentary Educational Resources (DER), a nonprofit distribution organization whose mission, as set forth in its certificate of incorporation, was to serve the "needs of educational institutions and of education, in general, in respect of the fields of anthropology, ethnology, ethnography, sociology and all related disciplines and science." Asch and Marshall hoped to "stimulate, discover, develop, foster, coordinate, plan, improve and encourage all aspects of educational instruction," specifically, by having the new organization distribute their own films—and in time, films by others committed to using film to explore the diversity of world culture. For some years, Marshall and Asch *were* DER, and Marshall remained in close touch with the organization until his death; but working within the parameters the two filmmakers had set up, Sue Cabezas, hired as administrative manager in 1974, and Cynthia Close, who became DER's executive director in 1993 when Cabezas left, developed DER into an effective distributor. Currently based in Watertown, Massachusetts, DER now distributes hundreds of films by nearly three hundred filmmakers, and its collections of John Marshall and Timothy Asch films and papers are the core of the Smithsonian Institution's Human Studies Film Archive.

Other accomplished ethnographic filmmakers have visited Harvard and have taught there over the decades: Jean Rouch, for several years during the early 1980s, for example, and more recently, David McDougall. And by the end of the first decade of the new millennium, the Cambridge tradition of ethnographic film production had been revived by Lucien Castaing-Taylor at Harvard's Sensory Ethnography Lab. Along with his partner, Ilisa Barbash (currently a curator of visual anthropology at the Peabody Museum), Castaing-Taylor studied visual anthropology at the University of Southern California with Asch, then earned his Ph.D. in anthropology at Berkeley. At Harvard, he and Barbash completed a feature film (*Sweetgrass,* 2009), documenting the final moments of a century-old practice of herding sheep into Montana's Absaroka-Beartooth mountains for summer pasture, and in 2006 Castaing-Taylor established the Sensory Ethnography Lab, which has nurtured a cadre of accomplished and adventurous filmmakers interested in using cinema to provide sensory experiences of other cultures or cultural practices that are in the process of transformation—experiences that cannot be encoded within written anthropological texts.

A prime mover in the development of personal documentary was Ed Pincus, whose *Diaries: 1971–1976* (1980) reveals the struggles of maintaining a marriage during an era of social experimentation. At MIT, Pincus had considerable influence on a younger generation of filmmakers. Miriam Weinstein, for example, explored her relationship with her father in *My Father the Doctor* (1972), her marriage with Peter Feinstein in *Living with Peter* (1973) and *We Get Married Twice* (1973); and during the 1970s and 1980s, Jeff Kreines, Ann Schaetzel, Robb Moss, Michel Negroponte, Mark Rance, John Gianvito, and other veterans of the MIT Film Section explored a variety of approaches to using their personal experiences as the subject of documentary. The best-known filmmaker to come out of the MIT program is Ross McElwee, whose chronicling of his own life and family—in *Backyard* (1984), *Sherman's March* (1986), *Time Indefinite* (1994), *Six O'Clock News* (1996), *Bright Leaves* (2003), *In Paraguay* (2009), and *Photographic Memory* (2012)—is well known and has become widely influential.

At Harvard, Alfred Guzzetti began making his own contributions to the development of personal documentary first with *Family Portrait Sittings* (1975), which explores the ways in which families construct mythic versions of their histories, and subsequently with films about his children. In 2012 he returned to the personal mode in *Time Exposure,* a video homage to his parents' support of his filmmaking. Joined at Harvard first by McElwee in 1986 and soon after by Robb Moss, Guzzetti and his colleagues have been inspirational to a generation of younger filmmakers, some of whom have explored the personal documentary (Nina Davenport, Alexander Olch), while others have incorporated dimensions of personal documentary into other forms: Andrew Bujalski's influential "Mumblecore" films, for example, while fictional, owe a good deal to the personal documentary approach.[9]

PRAGMATISM: LEARNING FROM EXPERIENCE

What is it about the Boston area, and Cambridge in particular, that can account for a continuing preeminence in the production of documentary? Certainly, the area's remarkable cluster of educational institutions has created not only a context for the production of films that serve the purposes of education but also academic programs that have nurtured prospective filmmakers: Boston University, Emerson College, the Massachusetts College of Art, MIT, and Harvard, in particular, have long served filmmaking students. Further, the steady production of independent documentaries in the Boston area has also been fueled by the strong presence of nonprofit media organizations. In addition to WGBH, the Center for Independent Documentary, Filmmakers Collaborative, the former Boston Film and Video Foundation, and more recently the LEF Foundation have all played important roles by facilitating the production and exhibition of independent nonfiction film. This network of academic and nonprofit organizations remains a key part of Boston–Cambridge's documentary tradition. Also, the area has long been served by independent cinemas—the Brattle Theater in Cambridge, the Harvard Film Archive, the Coolidge Corner Theatre in Brookline—as well as independent film series offered by colleges and universities: Fred Camper's MIT film series in the late 1960s and early 1970s, for example, and Saul Levine's ongoing series at Massachusetts College of Art, and the nomadic Balagan Film Series initiated and curated by Alla Kovgan and Jeff Silva.[10] The estimable work done by these and many other individuals and institutions has kept a vital film culture alive in the Boston area.

And how might one account for the particular emergence of ethnographic filmmaking and personal documentary in Cambridge? Here, conjecture is a bit foolhardy: so many factors are at play in urban environments. However, one intellectual tradition that seems as fully identified with Cambridge as ethnographic filmmaking and personal documentary may at least offer a way of thinking about this phenomenon. For Charles Peirce and William James, the creators of Pragmatism, coming to know the truth, or what truth there is, involves looking carefully at lived experience in order to become aware of its process and its principles. In the minds of the Pragmatists, a priori reasoning may produce intellectual ideas of remarkable complexity and brilliance, but firsthand experience of real events produces knowledge and the ground for reasoning itself.

Early documentary film, including much of American documentary from Robert Flaherty through the 1950s, was focused on explaining ideology and providing information conditioned by ideology: that is, on applying ideas already arrived at to a variety of social realities, from the nature of the Inuit struggle for survival in northern Canada to the reasons why Americans needed to fight the Nazis. The advent of new filmmaking technologies during the 1950s and 1960s made it possible for filmmakers to make different kinds of documentaries. The emergence of cinema verite shooting transformed ethnographic filmmaking and made personal documentary possible—in both cases, allowing filmmakers to record lived experience as it unfolded and to provide cinematic experiences from which audiences must draw their own conclusions. The types of documentary most fully identified with Cambridge do not primarily report findings or offer polemics; rather, they attempt to cinematically observe and reconstitute real experience so that the filmmakers and their audiences can come to understand the process of human life more completely.

In *Art as Experience,* his landmark Pragmatist treatise on aesthetics (based on lectures he delivered as the first William James Lecturer at Harvard in 1932), John Dewey explores the relationship between works of art and lived experience in considerable detail. For Dewey, "an experience" is distinct from "experience" in general by virtue of the fact that an experience is understood by the experiencer as having a shape: a beginning, middle, and end. An aesthetic experience is a particular instance of this shaped experience. For Dewey, "That which distinguishes an experience as esthetic is conversion of resistance and tensions, of excitations that in themselves are temptations to diversion, into a movement toward an inclusive and fulfilling close"; an aesthetic experience occurs only "when the factors that determine anything which can be called an experience are lifted high above the threshold of perception and are made manifest for their own sake."[11] Works of cinema, and in particular, the forms of cinema produced by the filmmakers explored in this book, are manifestations of the process of transforming the experiences witnessed and lived by the filmmakers, experiences full of tensions and resistance, into particular cinematic experiences that are, if not conclusive (no one film, or set of films, can be entirely conclusive about any particular or general experience), at least fulfilling, in Dewey's sense of the term.

Dewey distinguishes between the delivery of intellectual conclusions and the perception of lived reality in a manner that is relevant for this discussion:

> An intellectual statement is valuable in the degree in which it conducts the mind to many things all of the same kind. It is effective in the extent to which, like an even pavement, it transports us easily to many places. The meaning of an expressive object, on the contrary, is individualized. The diagrammatic drawing that suggests grief does not convey the grief of an individual person; it exhibits the *kind* of facial "expression" persons in general manifest when suffering grief. The esthetic portrayal of grief manifests the grief of a particular individual in connection with a particular event. It is *that* state of sorrow which is depicted, not depression unattached. It has a *local* habitation.[12]

In general, the tradition of documentary up until the late 1950s and early 1960s was intellectual, in the sense Dewey describes, or at least "intellectual" (I'm thinking here of the jingoistic logic used in most war propaganda). Even if the conclusions early documentaries presented to viewers were based on lived experience, they were presented primarily as facts that viewers needed to understand and affirm, not in a form that can be called experiential in any sense beyond the basic fact that all films are experienced perceptually.

What distinguishes the forms of observational and interactive cinema made possible by cinema verite shooting, and ethnographic film and personal documentary in particular, from the earlier tradition of documentary is the filmmakers' commitment to lived experience, on several levels. Most obviously, these films reveal how things happened to certain people at a particular time. This experience occurs on two levels simultaneously: we understand that the subjects in the film are going through specific experiences that we are in some measure witness to, *and* we, as members of an audience, are *experiencing* these cinematic versions of the subjects' experiences. Whatever conclusions the subjects might draw from what has happened to them, we, as spectators, must decide not only what their experiences, as rendered through cinema, might have meant to them and to the filmmakers, but what they do mean to us.

In ethnographic film and personal documentary, we also become aware of the experience of the filmmaker as he or she develops the experience of the film we are seeing. Sometimes the filmmaker's experiences are implicit (as they are in many of Marshall's and Gardner's films); at other times they're explicit, as they usually are in personal documentaries and as they are in some of the films coming out of the Sensory Ethnography Lab. But always, in the films that are discussed in the following chapters, there are three levels of experience that must be taken into account: the experiences of the subjects as rendered in film, the experiences of the filmmakers who have created the cinematic links between their subjects and audiences, and the experiences of the individuals in the audiences that assemble for these films.[13]

As this introduction is written (summer–winter 2011–12), I am unaware of any specific evidence that directly connects Pragmatism with the emergence of Harvard's Film Study Center or MIT's Film Section. It does seem clear, however, that the formation of the Film Study Center grew out of the decision of J. O. Brew of the Peabody Museum to support the work of the Marshall family, and John Marshall in particular, in their attempt to record the lived experience of the nomadic peoples of the Kalahari Desert. According to John Marshall, when Laurence Marshall went to the Peabody Museum to see whether a planned expedition to the Kalahari might be useful to the museum, Brew suggested they look for "wild Bushmen," and made it clear that "if you could [find them] in the plains of Africa, you had a window on the Pleistocene that nobody ever dreamed of."[14] Presumably, Brew's hope was that cinematic records of the lived experience of the !Kung might offer clues to the nature of human history and of the human experience in our own time. The

MIT Film Section was established by then-MIT provost (later president) Jerome Wiesner as part of the School of Architecture and Planning, again presumably as a means of adding cinema's ability to record and present lived experience to the university's academic mission: Wiesner's original hires were Ed Pincus and Ricky Leacock, both, at the time, accomplished observational filmmakers.[15]

Each of the following chapters explores different dimensions of how particular filmmakers have learned from their experiences and of how we can learn from the experiences of their films, but I'm sure it will be obvious to readers who find their way into *American Ethnographic Film and Personal Documentary: The Cambridge Turn* that I am less interested in defending an argument that these filmmakers and films are "Pragmatic" than I am in demonstrating the richness of the experiences made available in the work I explore. Particular "themes" will be evident—most obviously, the ways in which the personal lives of filmmakers factor into the ethnographic films and personal documentaries they've created—but here too, I am less concerned with proving a point about the personal than in revealing what individual filmmakers and films can offer to thoughtful audiences. To paraphrase what Harvard philosopher Stanley Cavell said, long ago—about books—in "Film in the University," I know that the films I discuss here are better than anything I say about them, but I also believe it is one, perhaps after all the fundamental, value of a scholar-teacher to put such films before possible viewers to show that this adult human being takes them with whatever seriousness is at his disposal.[16]

It should be mentioned, of course, that Cavell's fascination with movies and moviegoing as a subject for philosophy was deeply influential in the development of a filmmaking community in Cambridge and on the thinking and work of Robert Gardner and Alfred Guzzetti, in particular—as well as on William Rothman, who was Cavell's student at Harvard, then taught at Harvard, and has made important scholarly contributions to thinking about documentary films produced in Cambridge. Of those who have explored the accomplishments of Cambridge documentary filmmakers, Rothman has been the most alert both to particular contributions and to the nature of the filmmaking community that has nurtured them.[17]

THE MISSION OF *AMERICAN ETHNOGRAPHIC FILM AND PERSONAL DOCUMENTARY: THE CAMBRIDGE TURN*

Scholarship on documentary cinema has proliferated during recent decades in the wake of Erik Barnouw's still estimable *Documentary* (Oxford University Press, 1974) and the prolific work of Bill Nichols, beginning with *Ideology and the Image* (Indiana University Press, 1981) and *Representing Reality* (Indiana University Press, 1991). The establishment of the annual Visible Evidence Conference by Jane Gaines and Michael Renov in 1993 was instrumental in establishing a community of scholars interested in exploring both the long history of documentary and the burgeoning production of new documentaries and new documentary forms around the world; these scholars have produced, under the guidance of Gaines and Renov, the Visible Evidence series of books on documentary, published by the University of Minnesota Press. If for many years, little substantive commentary could be found on documentary in general and/or on particular documentary films, it has become a considerable task to keep up with new work in the field. Of course, any number of scholarly explorations of documentary filmmaking have been important for the discussions in *American Ethnographic Film and Personal Documentary: The Cambridge Turn* . The inventive selection of films discussed in Catherine Russell's *Experimental Ethnography: The Work of Film in the Age of Video* (Duke University Press, 1999), and in Barry Keith Grant and Jeannette Slo-niowski's *Documenting the Documentary* (Wayne State University Press, 1998), for example, confirmed my growing interest in moving beyond my interest in avant-garde film to explore more fully the variety of nonfiction film practices.

More specifically and more recently, Stella Bruzzi's *New Documentary: A Critical Introduction* (Routledge, 2000) has been useful in drawing my attention to the fact "that documentaries are inevitably the result of the intrusion of the filmmaker onto the situation being filmed, that they are performative because they acknowledge the construction and artificiality of even the non-fiction film and propose, as the underpinning truth, the truth that emerges through the encounter between filmmakers, subjects and spectators."[18] And Dai Vaughan in *For Documentary* (University of California Press, 1999), a collection of essays based on Vaughan's experiences working as a documentary cinematographer, has helped me understand that, while fiction cannot lie ("How would you set about telling a lie in fiction?"), our experience of documentary film is defined by our assumption that documentary *can* lie, can betray our expectation that an image represents "what, within its given context, it may reasonably be taken as representing."[19] Both Bruzzi and Vaughan recognize that whatever distortions of "reality" are inevitable in the process of representation, sometimes "it seems necessary to remind writers on documentary that reality does exist and that it can be represented without such a representation either invalidating or having to be synonymous with the reality that preceded it."[20] Without a sense that the experience of documentary film can reveal something worth knowing about "reality," we cannot learn from it—and yet, clearly we do learn from these experiences, even if what we learn is that we cannot be sure of what we understand, that all truth is tentative and evolving.

Documentary has become theorized in recent decades, and as a result we have come to more clearly understand the many issues raised in attempts to represent reality, but a good many of the most interesting contributions to documentary history have remained underappreciated. The fundamental mission of this volume is not to engage in the ongoing debate about the potentials and limitations of documentary in general, but to bring long overdue attention to specific Cambridge-based filmmakers who have made major contributions to ethnographic filmmaking and personal documentary and to explore what seem to me their most interesting films. Both genres have received some critical and scholarly attention (this will be evident in subsequent chapters), but for the most part commentary on particular films has been constricted by their categorization as "documentary": to treat the films discussed in *The Cambridge Turn* solely as instances of traditional and ongoing debates about documentary filmmaking is to miss much of what the films have to offer as contributions to the history of film art.

In certain instances my approach will seem to fly in the face of filmmakers' own senses of themselves. Both John Marshall and Timothy Asch resisted thinking of their work as "artistic." Their conscious goal was education, not the production of works of film art. And yet, looking at their films now, it is clear that whatever the educational value of their work (and in some cases it is considerable), their films *are* in fact interesting aesthetically, and they themselves can be, and in my view should be, understood as visual artists whose work relates in a variety of ways to the work of filmmakers who *are* generally regarded, and who have regarded themselves, as visual artists. My discussions of particular filmmakers and films offer what I hope are new and useful insights into the accomplishments of particular films and the shapes of individual careers; and in general *American Ethnographic Film and Personal Documentary: The Cambridge Turn* is an attempt to situate the considerable achievements of these filmmakers and their work within a larger sense of film history and in some instances the histories of literature and painting. Of course, given my decades-long fascination with what (for better or worse) continues to be called "avant-garde" cinema, it is probably inevitable that I see a good many intersections between the films I discuss here and films usually identified with that category.

The overall trajectory of my discussions is meant both to suggest how ethnographic filmmaking and personal documentary have evolved during the past half-century and to reveal some of the ways in which what originally may have seemed quite different approaches to filmmaking have influenced each other, sometimes becoming imbricated with each other. While John Marshall initially attempted to provide what he understood as a detached, objective depiction of the lives of the !Kung, his developing awareness of how the lives of these people were transforming—indeed, how his family's involvement with these people had hastened this transformation—caused Marshall to become *personally* involved in the !Kung struggle to retain something of their culture and their dignity as a people. Conversely, while Ross McElwee's films about the American South seem to focus on his own family and his filmmaking, the resulting films provide viewers with a considerable panorama of southern life during a particular era—not a formal ethnography, of course, but a fascinating and engaging set of cultural insights.

The extent of my commentary on individual filmmakers and films has depended both on my sense of the longevity of particular careers and contributions and on the complexity of specific films. Early chapters of *The Cambridge Turn* are focused on careers that have evolved over a period of sometimes more than half a century. Later chapters focus on selected contributions by often-younger makers. In some instances, important but limited accomplishments—*limited* meaning either that a filmmaker made one specific contribution to Cambridge filmmaking, or that a particular contribution is historically important but less than remarkable aesthetically—by individual filmmakers are included within overviews of longer careers. Of course, I have tended to write in more detail about films that I have found especially complex, enlightening, and useful.

A note on terminology: throughout this project I have used *film* to refer to moving-image art and document, whether the individual "films" were shot or are available on 35mm, 16mm, or 8mm celluloid, or as video in the ever-proliferating digital forms. When a "film" was produced or is available in a digital format, I make that clear—but since the filmmakers discussed generally call themselves "filmmakers" and their films and videos "films," I have not attempted to maintain a distinction between *film* and *video* except when the difference is germane to a particular discussion. Also, I use the terms *personal documentary* and *autobiographical filmmaking* interchangeably.

SUBJECTS FOR FURTHER RESEARCH

My focus on ethnographic film and personal documentary precludes my dealing in depth with a good many facets of Boston-area and even Cambridge filmmaking. In a few instances, I was unable to access films that I know are relevant to my discussions of personal documentary. I could not find a way to see either Jeff Kreines's *The Plaint of Steve Kreines as Recorded by His Younger Brother Jeff* (1974) or Mark Rance's *Death and the Singing Telegram* (1983), as well as other early work by Kreines, Rance, and Joel DeMott—all three of whom were students at the MIT Film Section.[21] This counts as a considerable limitation to *American Ethnographic Film and Personal Documentary: The Cambridge Turn* , one that I am embarrassed by. Filmmaker-teacher John Terry should also have been part of these discussions, but by the time I was aware of his connection with the MIT Film Section and began to learn about his films, this volume was already too extensive and too far along in the publishing process: I must be satisfied to come to grips with Terry's work and influence at a later time.

The two most famous documentary filmmakers living in Cambridge as this is written—Fred Wiseman and Errol Morris—receive no attention here. Wiseman's films do provide a kind of ethnography of institutional life in modern America. Nevertheless, his films are not ethnographic in the usual sense of the term, and, beyond the implications of Wiseman's choices of subject, they are some of the least personally revealing films in the documentary canon. And while Wiseman's home base has been Cambridge since the beginning of his career, he does not seem to see himself as part of the community of filmmakers that has developed in Cambridge over the decades and has functioned in a wide range of ways as a mutual support system for independent work:

> MacDonald: Fred, was there something in the Boston area, or in Cambridge in particular, that helped you move in the direction of documentary filmmaking or that helped you become the kind of filmmaker that you've become?
>
> Wiseman: Nothing that I can think of.[22]

Errol Morris's expressionist approach to often bizarre, nearly surreal subject matter is distinct from the development of ethnographic documentary (though clearly there are ethnographic dimensions to a number of his early films: *Gates of Heaven* [1981], for example, and *Vernon, Florida* [1978]) and from the evolution of personal documentary (though Morris's voice in some films—*The Fog of War* [2003], for example—reveals a good bit about his personal passions). My commitment in *American Ethnographic Film and Personal Documentary: The Cambridge Turn* is to bring attention to underrecognized and/or less understood filmmakers and films. Like Wiseman, Morris does not lack for attention from reviewers, critics, and even scholar-filmmakers: Charles Musser and Carina Tautu's *Errol Morris: A Lightning Sketch* [2011] is an engaging feature-length interview with the filmmaker.

The many accomplishments of documentary filmmakers who have worked under the auspices of WGBH must also be the subject of another scholar's investigation. The same is true of the contributions of a variety of individuals, including John Terry, who worked with Pincus and Leacock at MIT (*Made in Milwaukee*, 1979, and many other films); Richard Broadman (*Mission Hill and the Miracle of Boston*, 1978; *The Collective Fifteen Years Later*, 1985; *Brownsville Black and White*, 2002), Abraham Ravett (*The North End*, 1977; *Haverhill High*, 1979), Jane Gillooly (*Leona's Sister Gerri*, 1994; *Today the Hawk Takes One Chick*, 2008; *Suitcase of Love and Shame*, 2012), Juan Mandelbaum (*Our Disappeared/Nuestros desaparecidos*, 2008), and Alla Kovgan (*Nora*, 2008).

This study also largely ignores many forms of filmmaking and electronic media arts that have been produced at MIT and Harvard. I know nothing about the MIT Media Laboratory, which came into being in 1980 after the demise of the Film Section. Nor do I discuss the many accomplished animators who have been connected with the Carpenter Center (Robert Gardner claims that "almost every animator of moment in American and European animation has taught at Harvard").[23] And the Visual and Environmental Studies filmmaking program at Harvard has produced many accomplished filmmakers who are not discussed here—instances include Darren Aronofsky, Andrew Bujalski, Mira Nair, and Jehane Noujaim—despite my having considerable interest in some of them.

Finally, with one important exception, I say almost nothing about avant-garde cinema, a dimension of film history that much of my earlier writing has explored, even when filmmakers have had some connection with Cambridge, including, for example, Radcliffe graduate Abigail Child, who began her career as a documentary filmmaker and has become a prolific avant-garde filmmaker and video artist and a member of the senior faculty at the School of the Museum of Fine Arts, Boston. There is also Cambridge resident Rebecca Meyers, who has worked at the Harvard Film Archive and more recently for Robert Gardner's Studio7Arts—Meyers's exquisite depictions of the subtleties of daily experience have obvious documentary elements. Of course, my not writing about these (and other) Cambridge- and Boston-area filmmakers (prolific diarist, Anne Charlotte Robertson; Robert Todd, Luther Price, teacher-filmmaker Saul Levine) means no disrespect for their work. I have written about some of their accomplishments elsewhere and hope to explore others in the future.[24]

The exception is Alfred Guzzetti. In addition to *Family Portrait Sittings,* his pioneering contribution to the personal documentary, Guzzetti has collaborated on ethnographic films, on films about the Nicaraguan revolution; and his *Two or Three Things I Know about Her: Analysis of a Film by Godard* was published in 1981 by Harvard University Press. During all this time, however, Guzzetti has been making contributions to avant-garde film and video, beginning with *Air* (1971) and continuing into the 1990s, when he began producing a remarkable series of video works that combine documentary elements with personal revelation in a manner more in tune with the avant-garde traditions of personal film than with personal documentary. I have included a full chapter on this dimension of Guzzetti's work because attention to it is long overdue and because the unusual breadth of his career has allowed him to have considerable impact on his filmmaker colleagues and on filmmaking students at Harvard for forty years.

Perhaps it goes without saying that the following chapters are a function of my personal admiration of the filmmakers and films I do discuss. While I try to be an honest and painstaking and reasonably thorough scholar, at least within the parameters set up by this book, I cannot pretend to be a *detached* scholar. I am not, and have no desire to be, merely an observer or an analyst of what has gone on in documentary during a particular time in a specific place. Cinemagoing and the process of developing some sense of the history of the wide world of cinema have invigorated my life, providing me with experiences that have been not merely pleasurable, but formative—and as the years have gone by, re-formative—in my thinking about cinema, myself, and the world. Many of the films I discuss here have had and continue to have—to use William James's provocative term—

immense "cash value" for my work as a film history teacher. It will be obvious that my admiration of the filmmakers I discuss and of their particular films is not unalloyed; nevertheless, the writing in this volume—and this has been true of all of my writing—is essentially an ongoing act of gratitude.

ACKNOWLEDGMENTS

Any long-term project in film history requires the assistance of many individuals and organizations. My designation as an Academy Scholar for 2012 by the Academy of Motion Picture Arts and Sciences came at a most opportune time, providing both financial and moral support for the completion of this project. But *American Ethnographic Film and Personal Documentary: The Cambridge Turn* required an extensive period of germination.

In order to see the films I've written about, I depended on the consistent generosity of Documentary Educational Resources, and in particular of Cynthia Close, executive director at DER during most of the time when I was researching and writing. Thanks also to current Executive Director Alice Apley and Director of Design & Media Frank Aveni. A good many films by filmmakers I wanted to explore are not in distribution, and the Harvard Film Archive was very helpful in making many of these films available for study. Thanks to Haden Guest, Clayton Mattos, Mark Johnson, and Elizabeth Coffey for their assistance.

The filmmakers themselves were remarkably generous in sharing their work with me. I am deeply grateful to Robert Gardner, Ed Pincus, Jane Pincus, Alfred Guzzetti, Miriam Weinstein, Robb Moss, Ann Schaetzel, Ross McElwee, Michel Negroponte, Steve Ascher and Jeanne Jordan, Valerie Lalonde, John Gianvito, Nina Davenport, Amie Siegel, Jeff Silva, Lucien Castaing-Taylor, Ilisa Barbash, Stephanie Spray, J. P. Sniadecki, and Véréna Paravel for their kindness, generosity, and patience with me.

During early moments in the development of this project, the LEF Foundation, that stalwart supporter of New England filmmakers and filmmaking, involved me in public events that allowed me to test the thinking that has led to *The Cambridge Turn*. Lyda Kuth engaged me to assist LEF with their exhibition program, Facing Realities, arranging for me to interview Robert Gardner and Jane Gillooly at a public event at the Museum of Fine Arts, Boston. During the summer of 2010, LEF asked me to interview Fred Wiseman after a screening of *Hospital* at the Brattle Theater in Cambridge. These experiences helped me to develop the confidence to pursue this study.

My sense that the development of Pragmatism was relevant to the cinema history this volume explores was nurtured by Robert Huot, Ian MacDonald, Rutgers professor James Livingston, my Hamilton College colleague Katheryn Doran, and by the writing of Harvard professor Louis Menand.

In trying to understand how ethnographic film and personal documentary developed in Cambridge, I had the assistance of several organizations. Ilisa Barbash helped me make contact with the Peabody Museum, and with the help of Reference Archivist Patricia H. Kervick, I was able to explore the origins of the Marshall project and the founding of the Film Study Center at Harvard. In July 2010, I was able to spend several days researching the Marshalls and Timothy Asch at the Human Studies Archive at the Smithsonian Institution in Washington, D.C., where I was assisted by Karma Foley. Robert Gardner made the resources of his Studio7Arts studio available to me several times, and Rebecca Meyers assisted my work there.

The Visual and Environmental Studies Department at Harvard asked me to teach the history of documentary filmmaking during the fall of 2007 and again during the winter of 2009 and fall of 2012, when I focused on Cambridge's role in documentary history. This opportunity was very helpful, and I am grateful to David Rodowick, Dominique Bluher, J. P. Sniadecki, Stephanie Spray, Robb Moss, Lucien Castaing-Taylor, Heidi Bliss, Haden Guest, Julie Knippa, Clayton Mattos, Rebecca Meyers, Jeff Silva, and Jason Steeves—and of course to the students, including Che Salazar, Lili Erlinger, Stephanie Lam, and several Nieman Fellows (Kael Alford, Thorne Anderson, Rosita Boland, Sapiyat Dakhshukaeva, Jake Hooker, Andrea Simakis, and Chris Vognar), who were part of what was a wonderful learning experience for me.

My opportunities to teach at Hamilton College and at Colgate University during the years when this project was researched and written provided me with opportunities to test out my ideas, to travel when necessary for my research, and of course, to maintain economic stability. I am particularly grateful to my Hamilton colleagues Patricia O'Neill, Nancy Rabinowitz, Peter Rabinowitz, Marilyn Huntley, Timothy Hicks, Bret Olsen, Heather Johnsen, Deborah Pokinski, and Terri Viglietta; and to John Knecht and Lynn Schwarzer at Colgate University. Thanks too, to the Office of the Dean of the Faculty at Hamilton—and to Dean Patrick Reynolds and Associate Dean Margaret Gentry—for their willingness to support *American Ethnographic Film and Personal Documentary: The Cambridge Turn* with a generous subvention.

For many years I taught at Utica College of Syracuse University (now Utica College) and had the good fortune to team-teach courses in ethnographic cinema with anthropologist John Johnsen. These were formative learning experiences for me, and I am grateful to Johnsen for his knowledge and his ongoing collegiality.

Many other individuals, including a good many scholars and teachers, have made important contributions to my thinking, have supported my various attempts to garner financial support for this project, and have offered other forms of assistance. Thanks in particular to Jay Ruby, David James, Linda Williams, Tom Gunning, John Terry, Jane Weiner, Perle Møhl, Clayton Mattos, Fred Camper, Haden Guest, Jim Lane, Kenneth Eisenstein, and Rebecca Meyers.

Lorna and John Marshall

At the outset, the Marshall family expeditions to the Kalahari Desert from 1950 to 1961 to find and learn something about the San peoples living there were conceived as a means to the end of a more intensive, engaged experience of family life—an upscale version of the family camping trips that would become ubiquitous across the country during the following decades. Laurence Marshall's determination that his family's experiences with the San be useful in producing valuable insights into an ancient way of life led (along with his willingness to finance the project) to the Peabody Museum's sponsorship of the Marshalls' early expeditions, which did in fact produce impressive results, including several significant contributions to the written anthropological discourse about the San and a wealth of photographic and cinematic documentation.

John Marshall's particular excitement about the men and women he grew to know during these expeditions had a good deal to do with his wonder at how much his new friends had come to understand about their environment through their long experience with it, but this early fascination was merely the first stage of what became a lifelong process of learning not only about the people he befriended in the Kalahari but about how much his early excitement about being with them had blinded him to the realities of their lives. Indeed, during the following years, as he came to see how quickly San life was transforming and to feel that his family's expeditions into the Kalahari had contributed to the destruction of the way of life that had so impressed him, Marshall transformed his approach to documenting the San over and over. His hope was that each new contact he had with the "Ju/'hoansi" (Marshall came to use *Ju/'hoansi* to refer to the group of !Kung San he grew to know, since this is how they referred to themselves),[1] and each new film that resulted from it might bring him and his viewers toward a clearer sense of what the experience of the Ju/'hoansi actually was and what their struggles might mean for those who were coming to know something of them.

BEGINNINGS: LORNA MARSHALL AND *FIRST FILM*

When Laurence Kennedy Marshall retired from Raytheon, the electronics company he had founded in 1922, he and Lorna Marshall agreed that they needed to break away from their routines in Cambridge in order to focus on their children. Laurence and Lorna had visited South Africa in 1949, where they met Dr. E. Van Zyl, who was planning an expedition to find "The Lost City of the Kalahari." Laurence decided to join the expedition and to take John with him. As John Marshall would explain later, "After years of war and absence from his family, Laurence wanted to take a trip to get to know his son. One of my hobbies was reading accounts of explorers like Livingstone, Stanley and Grant. I was enthralled by *Jock of the Bushveld* by Percy Fitzpatrick, and mesmerized by the films of Osa and Martin Johnson."[2] This first expedition, in 1950, led to a series of visits to Nyae Nyae. In 1951 Lorna Marshall and daughter Elizabeth joined Laurence and John; and the family continued to visit the region together for the next decade—a total of eight expeditions: 1950, 1951, 1952–53, 1955, 1956, 1957–58, 1959, 1961.[3] And John Marshall would continue to visit Nyae Nyae into the 1980s.

The Marshalls were not tourists. From the beginning, Laurence and Lorna believed that these should be working visits, and they were immediately in touch with Lauriston Ward and J. O. Brew, anthropologists at Harvard. By the time of the 1951 expedition, the Marshalls had developed a system for serious study of what was one of the last hunter-gatherer groups in Africa:

> We tried to find an ethnographer or a graduate student who wanted to go and study daily life of hunter-gatherers on the plains of Africa. We couldn't find one. Isn't that incredible? We went through Harvard, Yale, Princeton, Chicago, and a couple of other places that Dad called up and said, "Who wants to start this study?" Dad said he'd back them for a long time, for an in-depth, long-term study because he thought that would be unique, and nobody responded. . . . So the result was that Dad said, "Okay, Lorna, you're going to do the ethnography; Elizabeth, you're going to write a book; John, you're going to do the movies." And he handed me a camera and said "Shoot the films."[4]

The first three expeditions were sponsored by the Peabody Museum of Harvard University; the expeditions from 1955 through 1961 (the "Peabody Museum Kalahari Expeditions") by the Peabody, the Smithsonian Institution, and the Transvaal Museum of Pretoria. These expeditions produced Lorna Marshall's *The !Kung of Nyae Nyae* (Cambridge: Harvard University Press, 1976), a substantial, early

FIGURE 1. Lorna Marshall with Ju/'hoansi mother and children in the 1950s. Courtesy
Documentary Educational Resources.

ethnographic study of the San of the Kalahari; Elizabeth Marshall Thomas's *The
Harmless People* (New York: Vintage, 1958), a beautifully written reminiscence of
her and her family's experiences with the San during the 1951, 1952–53, and 1955
expeditions; and a considerable series of films, beginning with *!Kung Bushmen of
the Kalahari*, which John Marshall says was edited by "my mother, my father, and
filmmaker Jerry Ballantine"; and *First Film*, which Lorna edited from the same
footage in 1951 (fig. 1).[5]

   While *The Hunters* is usually considered the first important Marshall film about
the !Kung and the instigation of the long series of !Kung films that followed, this is
unfair to the accomplishments of *First Film*. While the Marshalls' visit to Gautscha
in Nyae Nyae in 1951 was only six weeks (Lorna Marshall has indicated that the
1952–53 expedition was "the most productive period of our study"),[6] it was long
enough to produce footage that not only served as warm-up and précis for the
long saga of films that would follow, but was at some point edited into a film that
has remained remarkably underappreciated. Shot in a very functional manner—
Laurence had told John, "Don't try to be artistic. Just film what you see people

doing naturally. I want a record, not a movie"[7]—what became *First Film* was edited so as to provide an information-filled overview of !Kung life at Nyae Nyae.

After a bit of indigenous music and a map locating Gautscha, a group of !Kung arrive and set up their temporary village. During the hour-long film, we see men making karosses (the cloaks made from animal skin that women wear), men and women getting and sharing water, women gathering foods ("women's principal work"), a child dancing (the earliest imagery of N!ai, who would become a central character in John Marshall's films about the Ju/'hoansi), boys setting snares for guinea fowl, men hunting for spring hare, the making of bows and poison arrows, men hunting gemsbok and wildebeest and the distribution of meat, eating and cooking, women making beads and a man playing music on his bow, boys playing, the group dancing and singing, a man falling into trance and coming out of it, children dancing, the group smoking, talking, and laughing; then, packing up and leaving to walk to the next temporary village. A bit of indigenous music ends the film. John Marshall's later films would focus in on many of the particulars of Lorna Marshall's overview, often using virtually the same language in his voice-overs as she uses in hers.

It is the nature of Lorna Marshall's voice-overs in *First Film* that makes this film distinctive and memorable—probably more distinctive and memorable than it seemed in 1951, precisely because of the way in which voice-over in documentary has been debated during the past sixty years. It is not clear precisely when this voice-over was married to the imagery (Cynthia Close, director of Documentary Educational Resources [DER], suspects that it was in the 1970s, but John Bishop, who worked with the Marshall materials at the Peabody Museum, has suggested that, whenever the soundtrack was recorded, the comments that became the voice-over had had a history in advance of their inclusion on the soundtrack of *First Film*: "I imagine John cut it [the first version of *First Film*] for her soon after their return so she could use it to illustrate a lecture, or possibly to be used for multiple performances of the lecture, a popular use of documentary footage in the 1950s."[8] As Bishop suggested to me, the tone of the narration "is as if she was projecting to a large audience."

What seems noteworthy now about Lorna Marshall's voice-over on *First Film* is the degree to which she seems to have avoided many of the problems of conventional documentary voice-overs, including those in early ethnographic films. She is certainly not a "voice of god" or even a "voice of goddess." While the imagery John Marshall recorded and put together for his mother (presumably under her direction) must have seemed exotic to the original audiences, and still may seem exotic to audiences unfamiliar with ethnographic filmmaking, the voice-over commentary in *First Film* reveals not merely Lorna Marshall's familiarity with the people gathered at Gautscha, but her unpretentious empathy with them, as a parent. There are statements that seem to mean to protect the San from stereotyping by the audience—"We observed no theft nor aggression; we observed impressive honesty, cooperation, and integration among this far away and independent group"—and comments that remind us of the physical difference between the San and the viewer: as one woman cuts meat with a knife close to her face, Marshall comments, "A good way to eat if one belongs to a short-nosed race."

The overall tone of the voice-over is quite informal, something like the comments of a good teacher telling a class about some people she knows (Marshall, who graduated from the University of California at Berkeley with a B.A. degree in English, had taught English at Mt. Holyoke College before meeting Laurence Marshall). When Old Gaú is smoking, she comments, "Like every good bushman, he passes the pipe around," and a moment later, as we see Old Gaú with his grandson, "Little ≠Gao. . . loves his grandfather and, I think, wants to be just like him. The grandfather adores this child." As we see young N!ai dancing, Marshall notes, "She is a blithe child," and as we see a widow, Marshall comments that she "sometimes looked lonely. Not always, but sometimes."

In one instance Marshall engages gender relations in a manner that suggests a kind of insight that goes beyond, or beneath, detached scholarly observation: within a composition where the "head man" is in the left foreground and his wife and several other women are sitting in a circle in the right background, Marshall indicates that the head man "rarely gives orders, but . . . ," then says, "Watch his wife!" The wife makes a gesture with her hand as if to say, "Leave us alone, mind your own business," after which Marshall says, "But they do what he says." Marshall adds that the head man "watches over his people," and that his wife is a "lively woman": "One felt she would not be easily imposed upon." Throughout Lorna Marshall's voice-over in *First Film,* and despite what seem to be moments of humor meant to amuse the audience, one can feel Marshall's immense, unpatronizing respect and affection for the people she is introducing to us; these people, she suggests, are not simply types, generic representatives of a way of life, but individuals that she is coming to know and working to know better.

JOHN MARSHALL: *THE HUNTERS*

John has 6000 feet of film—He created a documentary—to be called The Water Hole. I yearn to see it. He will edit it. He has 2 more sequences to make. How he has opened to this and taken hold! At last his creative powers are geared to achievement. Laurence and I are deeply happy. Laurence and John are planning to order more film, so John can feel an abandon of creation, not worry about using or wasting some footage.

LORNA MARSHALL'S DIARY[9]

The filmmaker's response is in many ways the reverse of that of other viewers. For the filmmaker, the film is an extract from all the footage shot for it, and

> *a reminder of all the events that produced it. It reduces the experience onto a
> very small canvas. For the spectator, by contrast, the film is not small but
> large: it opens onto a wider landscape. If the images evoke for the filmmaker
> a world that is largely missing, in the spectator they induce endless extrapola-
> tions from what is actually seen. . . . But for the filmmaker the same images
> only reaffirm that the subject existed. Instead of imagining, there is remem-
> bering; instead of discovery, there is recognition; instead of curiosity, there is
> foreknowledge and loss.*
>
> DAVID MACDOUGALL[10]

The Hunters (1957), shot and edited by John Marshall (with some postproduction assistance by Robert Gardner),[11] remains, by far, the best-known film in the Marshall family's saga of Ju/'hoansi life, and among the best-known of all ethnographic films. Indeed, in the United States *The Hunters* seems to have revived a tradition of representing far-flung cultures that was begun by Edward Curtis in *In the Land of the Head-Hunters* (also known as *In the Land of the War Canoes*) (1914) and Robert Flaherty in *Nanook of the North* (1921) and *Moana* (1926). In some senses, of course, *The Hunters* has much in common with *Nanook* and *Moana,* and over the years, it has been critiqued in much the same way. While all three films communicate a level of reality that Flaherty and Marshall understood as basic to the Inuit , the Samoans, and the Ju/'hoansi at the time when they shot these films, the Flaherty films and *The Hunters* are not simply candid records of events as they unfolded. As most everyone who is introduced to these films now knows, the events we see were constructed in the editing—even though the editing in all three films allows many viewers to believe they are seeing events unfold precisely as they unfolded in reality at the time of the shooting. This, it seems to me, has always said more about the hunger of film audiences to believe in the candidness of what they see than it does about any attempt on the part of the filmmakers to fool anyone; indeed, the current generation of college students seems convinced that candid recording *is* documentary and that any fabrication subtracts from reality—despite the obvious fact that simply turning on a camera and recording what is going on and presenting the results is revealing of almost nothing at all.

The feeling of betrayal on the part of some critics of *The Hunters* seems particularly naïve, since from the beginning of the film Marshall is at pains to make clear that he is not simply providing information about a far-flung cultural group but is artistically constructing a tale. Of course, in 1957, when *The Hunters* was completed and first shown, it was such a departure from the lecture-documentaries that had dominated nonfiction filmmaking for a quarter century that, by comparison, it must have seemed astonishingly candid.

The Hunters opens with a brief montage of nineteen shots of the Kalahari environment and its flora and fauna. The first three shots (10, 8, and 7 seconds, respectively) draw immediate attention to the filmmaker as visual artist, in that the tiny sequence is sutured together on the basis of subtle movements: in the first two shots, of a bush moving in the breeze, and in the third, by the slightly unsteady movement of the handheld camera as it records a long shot of a vulture (?) in a distant tree. After a brief shot of a lizard, at first still, then moving, we see, through some brush, a tree underneath which we gradually realize are at least two antelope. These first five shots are silent, but the longer sixth shot introduces a wide-angle shot of two men walking through a field, hunting (this image is carefully composed so that one man walks at the right edge of the frame; the other man at the left edge; the shot is accompanied by phrases of what we assume is a bit of music indigenous to this environment). Once the men are visible, our sense of the earlier shots takes on another level: we realize that our carefully noting the tiny movements in this environment has been an evocation of what these hunters must do as they search for game. This conflation of our sensitivity to Marshall's composition and editing and the hunters' sensitivity to their environment is maintained through the remaining thirteen shots, and concludes with a 14-second close-up of one hunter, which fades out just as the title of the film is presented.

After the title, Marshall places *The Hunters* within the tradition established by *Nanook* and *Grass:* a map guides us to the Nyae Nyae region of the Kalahari Desert, after which Marshall's voice-over introduces the place and the people who live there: "The northern Kalahari is a hard, dry land. In this bitter land live a quiet people who call themselves !Kung or Ju/'hoansi." In his introduction, and during the brief survey of !Kung life that follows, Marshall's comments are not so different from those of the voices-of-god narrators so familiar from informational and polemical documentaries of the 1940s and early 1950s, but once he has provided some context for what will become his focus on the hunters—the distinction between women's gathering work and men's hunting, the process through which boys become hunters, the poison that allows the !Kung arrows to kill large animals—the nature of Marshall's narration turns increasingly literary and evocative not merely of earlier films and *Nanook* but of epic literature. His introductions of the four hunters who will form the nucleus of the hunt constructed for the film are heroic in content, and poetic in diction and rhythm; for example:

≠Toma, the leader,
≠Toma, the vigorous and able,
He was a man of many words and a lively mind,
One who had traveled to the edges of his world.

and

Tao, the beautiful,
Tao was a natural hunter,
Taking great pleasure in the chase.

His arrows were keen and each point was shaped in his own fashion. . . .
On the day he consummated his marriage, Tao shot five wildebeest out of a herd of
    thirty and found and killed four of them and brought home the meat.
From this he got his name . . . Tao Wildebeest.

The introductions of the four hunters are followed by the hunt itself. Bill Nichols has suggested that Marshall was using San culture as a pretext for a universal story with an implicit message: "Men will venture into a dangerous world to bring back food for people who might otherwise starve. They will show us knowledge, skill, patience, humor. Their success in the face of adversity commands respect; their qualities are qualities of enduring value. We must celebrate them."[12] At the time, Marshall might have said that the film was less a pretext than a demonstration of a traditional way of life, the source of myth, that he felt he had found, still alive, in the present-day real world.

Once the hunters have wounded the giraffe, Marshall constructs the adventure of tracking the animal by intercutting between the hunters following her trail and the giraffe, as she tries and increasingly fails to keep up with the other giraffes and ultimately succumbs to the hunters. The very invisibility of Marshall's camera within the diegesis of this story is the best evidence of the fact that this *is* a story, and Marshall's intercutting between hunters and giraffe (if the hunters haven't been able to find the giraffe, how has Marshall located her!) confirms the fabrication. Of course, the unusual nature of this story and its reliance on real !Kung in a real environment, clearly killing a real giraffe, provides sufficient interest so that a consciousness of Marshall's construction of what we see tends to disappear for most viewers, just as it does in commercial fiction films successful enough to engage viewers.

After the giraffe has been killed, slaughtered, and "the meat spread across the werft as a ripple across water," the group gathers to hear the story of the hunt, and Marshall provides a concluding reminder of the conflation of his storytelling with theirs: "and old men remembered, and young men listened, and so the story of the hunt was told." These final words are closely matched to imagery of an old man sleeping and a young man listening, and at the very end, of the group getting up to go to bed and a final fade-out. The story of the hunt, told around the fire in Nyae Nyae, concludes simultaneously with the end of Marshall's film and (one can imagine) his audience getting up to leave the theater.

While the artistry of *The Hunters* is apparent in Marshall's composition and editing and in the poetry of his narration, and is compromised only by the somewhat strident tone of his narrating voice, the film's very artistic success quickly became a problem for Marshall himself: "Dad didn't like . . . *The Hunters*. He thought it was an art film."[13] In subsequent years Marshall would turn away from the kinds of artistry evident in *The Hunters* and would account for that film as a product of youthful indulgence. While he would claim that he didn't regret making *The Hunters,* he came to feel that "Laurence was right," and that "*The Hunters* was a romantic film by an American kid and revealed more about me than about Ju/'hoansi."[14] Specifically, what it revealed was that "I was a kid, and I got captivated by hunting, so I went hunting. . . . I was eighteen, nineteen—the best years of my life, the happiest I've ever been, without any question. It was a pretty wonderful experience for a kid of that age in a place like that with people like Tshumkwe, damned decent, good-to-be-with people."[15] What it failed to reveal was the true nature of Ju/'hoansi life: *The Hunters* gave "the impression of people spending enormous amounts of energy and time hunting"; "And the real economy is the other way around. Not only the economy is based on gathering, but all concepts of land ownership, all the rules of land ownership, all the basis of the social organization of the people, groups, bands, all flow from gathering, and from stable, fixed, reliable sources of food and water."[16]

We might remind Marshall that obviously no single film can tell the whole story about any people or any dimension of their lives, and that *The Hunters was* about an important facet of Ju/'hoansi life. In the National Geographic special *Bushmen of the Kalahari* (1974; shot and directed by Robert M. Young), Marshall himself did say, referring to the more efficient means of hunting employed by a !Kung horseman with a rifle, depicted in that television show, "Killing so efficiently seemed to rob hunting of its symbolic quality, making it a simple act of subsistence, instead of a larger act of kinship, biding the people together." Nevertheless, Marshall would remain embarrassed about his indulgence in art, and this embarrassment would increasingly characterize his assumptions about what he should be filming and how he should be filming it—especially once he began to realize, indeed to personally *experience,* what the history of the Ju/'hoansi would become during the thirty years following the first Marshall expeditions. However, while he turned increasingly away from the particularly obvious art-film dimensions of *The Hunters* in the following decades, he did for a moment find a way of making film art that did not seem to embarrass him, indeed that did not immediately declare itself as *art* at all—though the unusual artistry of some of the resulting films has become increasingly obvious and admirable as the decades have passed.

IDYLLS OF THE !KUNG

In his essay, "Filming and Learning," Marshall offers two observations that were fundamental in his approach to filming the Ju/'hoansi. First, "What the people I am filming actually do and say is more interesting and important than what I think about them"; and second, "When I filmed people from a distance, they were easy to understand. If their actions were not obvious, I could explain what they were doing with a few words of narration. The closer I got to people with my camera, the more interesting they seemed, and the more surprised I was by what they did and said."[17] The two earliest films Marshall finished after *The Hunters—A Group of Women* (1961) and *A Joking Relationship* (1962)—represent an aesthetic break-through and, perhaps, to some degree a missed opportunity. These two films embody Marshall's observations far more effectively than *The Hunters*.

In a sense, nothing happens in *A Group of Women*. It is a 5-minute montage made up of twenty-three shots focusing on several women and a baby lying together under a baobab tree (Marshall's camera is generally so close that it is dif-ficult to be entirely sure how many women are present, but his focus is on three). During the film, the women talk about what appears to be an imminent move for one of the women and her band to Gautscha in order to gather berries; she isn't interested in moving, and one of the other women suggests she "just refuse it," and later tells her, "You shouldn't go south." They also discuss nursing children, and the mother of the baby—she refers to her daughter in one instance as "little seed pod"—wants the child to nurse, though the child doesn't seem interested. At one point, a woman walking by addresses the women lying under the baobab, trying to get one or all of them to go with her to get water, but they refuse, and at the end of the film they seem to have drifted off to sleep.

While there are close-ups in *The Hunters,* they function as close-ups normally do within a developing action-adventure narrative, but *A Group of Women* is almost entirely constructed of close-ups, and sometimes extreme close-ups (fig. 2). The only exceptions are the film's first and last shots, both of them revealing the larger scene under the baobab tree, and the two medium shots of the woman who asks the friends to accompany her to the water hole (these two shots are presented from a ground-up angle, suggesting that the woman is an intruder, perhaps even a jealous intruder: she interrupts the conversation, saying, "Lazy creatures! If I lie down will you tickle me?"). At the beginning of the film, each shot moves us closer to the women, until, in the seventh shot, an extreme close-up reveals the mother's nipple, centered in the frame. The pacing of Marshall's editing reflects the utter tranquility of this moment among friends; the shots range from 4 seconds to 54, and are organized so as to maintain the quiet mood of this "non-action" scene: the editing builds to no climax, and in general, extended shots interrupt whatever velocity begins to develop in shorter shots.[18]

In *A Group of Women* conversation *is* the action. Marshall offers no voice-over explanation of what he is showing us, though he does, for the first time, provide subtitles that propose to translate what the women are saying (according to David MacDougall, this was a first, a *transformative* first, not only for Marshall, but for ethnographic film in general).[19] As is true in the other films about the Ju/'hoansi Marshall made during the 1960s, the sound in *A Group of Women* is not synchro-nized, but, to quote the text that precedes most of these films, "was recorded at the time of filming and reconstructed during editing. Translations are from both tapes and notes."[20] Our ability to hear the voices of the women, who talk very quietly,

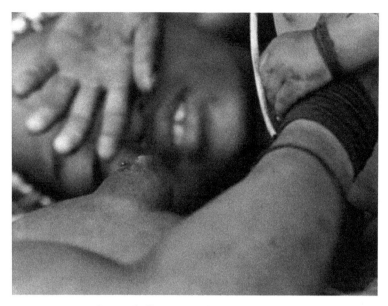

FIGURE 2. From John Marshall's *A Group of Women* (1961). Courtesy
Documentary Educational Resources.

adds an audio component to the intimacy established by the in-close cinematography, and our reading the subtitles—while it does interrupt our view on the
women—engages us within this quiet moment in a way that Marshall's voice-over
in *The Hunters* does not.

Marshall's films have nearly always been subsumed within the category of
ethnographic film, the assumption being that their primary, if not only, function
is to provide a useful adjunct to anthropological investigations of an indigenous
group, and particularly, an indigenous group whose way of life is under threat
from modernity—as represented, of course, by the camera itself. But *A Group of
Women* only seems an ethnographic film if one thinks of it within the meta-
sequence of Marshall's Ju/'hoansi project. Understood outside of this project, the
film represents, on one hand, a young man's fascination with several young
women, with their physicality, their friendship, and the realities of young motherhood. On the other hand, the film demonstrates how intimate Marshall had
become with this band of Ju/'hoansi—he seems to hover quite close to the
women in order to make the shots he uses (it may also be that the very difference
represented by Marshall's filming makes him, for all practical purposes, invisible
to these women). *A Group of Women* seems to go beneath any scholarly ethnographic pretensions to a level of friendship and interchange that defies
cultural distinction, even as Marshall refuses to present the women as anything

but Ju/'hoansi. The differences between young women in American culture and these Ju/'hoansi women will be obvious to anyone seeing their clothing, the decorative marks on their skin, their comfort with the desert dirt and the ubiquitous flies (the first sound heard in the film is a fly buzzing). And yet, the way in which these young women relate to one another feels instantly familiar and understandable.

A useful cinematic reference here is not another ethnographic film, but Stan Brakhage's *Blood's Tone,* the second part of the trilogy *3 Films: Bluewhite, Blood's Tone, Vein,* completed in 1965. In *Blood's Tone* Brakhage hovers close to his nursing child and uses his zoom lens to suggest that he is, through cinema, participating in the child's suckling: his short zooms in and out echo the baby's taking the nipple into her mouth and sucking on Jane Brakhage's breast (we never see more of Jane than this breast). *Blood's Tone* seems to have been filmed at night (the baby is distracted by the camera, sometimes seeming to wonder what this strange being so nearby is doing with all this light and, presumably, noise—*Blood's Tone* is silent), and Brakhage's lighting causes the little scene to be golden, an allusion not only to this golden moment of childhood and parenthood, but perhaps to the ubiquitous Renaissance and pre-Renaissance paintings of Mary and the baby Jesus that were often decorated with gold leaf.[21]

Like *Blood's Tone, A Group of Women* takes us inside an intimate moment, a moment that for Marshall, as for Brakhage—both of them American men who grew up during an era when nudity was forbidden from the commercial cinema and when birth and nursing were kept relatively secret—must have seemed both fascinating and exciting. As in *Blood's Tone,* but rather less obviously, the camera movement in *A Group of Women,* as well as the pacing of Marshall's editing, is of a piece with what is filmed: as the women lie still, Marshall's handheld shots are still; when the women reposition themselves and move the baby, Marshall's camera makes subtle adjustments that reflect the motion of the women. Throughout the film, the serenity of the editing echoes this quiet conversation, this moment of interchange and affection before the imminent trek to Gautscha. And at the end, as the women drift off to sleep and out of their intimate moment, the camera moves away from the scene. The home-movie dimension of *Blood's Tone,* the desire by the filmmaker father to hold on to this amazing, but inevitably fleeting moment, is similar to Marshall's desire to record and reconstruct the loveliness of this quiet sensual moment of friendship and of the miracle of his own apparent acceptance into this space by these women.

A similar level of intimacy, in this case between a mature man and a girl, as well as between Marshall and his subjects, is evident in *A Joking Relationship,* though in many ways this short film (13 minutes) is quite different in tone from *A Group of Women. A Joking Relationship* focuses on N!ai and her great uncle, /Ti!kay, as they banter and wrestle under a baobab tree. Again, and more obviously here, the

Now don't watch me!

FIGURE 3. N!ai in John Marshall's *A Joking Relationship* (1962).
Courtesy Documentary Educational Resources.

dialogue—and this film too is largely dialogue—is not synchronized, though presumably it was recorded during the same extended moment as the imagery, and Marshall provides us with subtitled translations (fig. 3). As commentators on *A Joking Relationship* have often noted, what gives this film its energy is Marshall's depiction of the complex emotions at work in the scene. N!ai is a beautiful, confident girl: when near the opening of the film /Ti!kay teases her for refusing to gather food for him, saying, "You're a lazy wife" (N!ai had become, against her own wishes, the wife of young /Gunda), N!ai responds, "I'm not a wife and it's too hot to gather." Though she is betrothed to /Gunda, N!ai has refused to live with him or to consummate the marriage (N!ai's marriage to /Gunda is a central issue in Marshall's 1980 film, *N!ai: The Story of a !Kung Woman,* as is N!ai's history of defiance of social convention).

What Marshall captures in *A Joking Relationship* is both the open affection of an uncle and a niece, a relationship rarely accorded attention in cinema of any kind, and the underlying sexual dimension of this, and perhaps any, relationship between mature men and their young relatives. Here, this sexual pull, which seems to go both ways, is continually evident, even as the two parties are redirecting an urge that could cause them problems within the small community in which they live into good-humored banter and nonsexual (but sensual) physical interchange.[22] In general, their interaction is presented in a series of pulses; N!ai and /Ti!kay wrestle around, then separate, then wrestle around some more, then separate . . . all the while bantering with each other: /Ti!kay calls N!ai a snake and an insect, tells her to "come here to be cooked and eaten!" and at one point conjoins his literal hunger and his sexual hunger: he takes out his knife, opens it, and says he'll "nip a bud to eat"—meaning N!ai's nipple (her breasts have just begun to show). A moment later, after his mock attack and her mock resistance, Marshall provides a close-up of /Ti!kay's hands folding up the knife in front of his wrinkly belly—in clear contradistinction to N!ai's young breasts. N!ai says, "Let's stay together," then "No, let's stay together really," but she soon stops playing, puts her beads back on, and despite /Ti!kay's urging her to stay, says, "You're a silly old man," and walks off.

Marshall's composition and use of sound function as a kind of cinematic participation in this extended moment of uncle–niece interchange. When /Ti!kay and N!ai are wrestling, Marshall is in close, often focusing on a calf, a breast, an arm with bracelets, half a face; when N!ai and /Ti!kay momentarily separate, the camera moves back as well and we see N!ai and /Ti!kay in long shot and alone. Further, as the sexual tension becomes increasingly evident to the viewer (we might imagine that it was increasingly felt by young John Marshall as he was shooting), a repeated bird sound seems to speak the hidden sexual-romantic urge underlying the banter and wrestling. Whereas in *A Group of Women,* there are usually sounds of distant conversations in the background, *A Joking Relationship* seems an isolated moment, interrupted only by the presence of Marshall, which is always implicit, and for at least one moment, quite explicit. Marshall's close-ups of N!ai's and /Ti!kay's faces, often seem to capture not just good-humored fun but subtle embarrassment, possibly a function of the girl's and man's unspoken recognition of their attraction being witnessed, and in the case of /Ti!kay, some bemusement at Marshall's fascination with what might seem to /Ti!kay this nonevent. Near the middle of the film, /Ti!kay tells N!ai to come down from the crotch of the baobab where she is standing: "He [meaning Marshall] wants to take your picture while I tumble you." And N!ai responds, "He wants to take me gathering in the truck." And N!ai slides down the tree to /Ti!kay to wrestle around some more, for both the fun of it and for John Marshall and his camera.

A different sort of idyll, though related to *A Group of Women* and *A Joking Relationship* in both form and implication, is *Baobab Play* (1974), finished twelve years after these films. Here again, a baobab tree is the location of the action, or really a kind of nonaction, and here too, Marshall forgoes voice-over, and even subtitles, since what is happening is quite clear without verbal intervention. All we see during the 8 minutes of *Baobab Play* is several boys playing around and in the baobab: the boys in the tree throw sticks, leaves, berries down at the group on the ground, and the boys on the ground respond in kind. It is the sort of good-humored "war" that seems endemic to male childhood in widely different cultures and geographies—which may have been Marshall's fascination with this scene.

The end credits of *Baobab Play* indicate that Marshall produced and directed the film (it was edited by Frank Galvin, who edited many of Marshall's films of the 1960s and 1970s; Timothy Asch was a production assistant), and it is clear throughout the film that Marshall must have directed the boys to play, presumably in their normal manner, while ignoring, insofar as possible, his presence with them under the tree and up in its branches. The film intercuts between the two "warring" groups from within each group. The cinematography and sound in *Baobab Play* provide an idyllic context for this depiction of childhood: the light in the tree is lovely, as is the sound of the breeze blowing through the tree, which continually transforms the lightscape of the film.

Marshall's meditation on male childhood in *Baobab Play* is deeply poignant, coming as it does near the end of the editing of the material shot during the Peabody Museum Kalahari Expeditions. By the time he edited *Baobab Play,* Marshall had moved through several phases of filmmaking, and his understanding of his project was radically changing. But here, for a moment, he seems to meditate not simply on the innocence of these boys, and not merely on childhood in general as represented by this group, but on what he came to think of, what perhaps he already felt were "the best years of my life, the happiest I've ever been, without any question"—that is, not on his own childhood, but on his *filmmaking* childhood, which had produced so much footage and the increasing dexterity with the camera so evident in *Baobab Play.* As in *A Group of Women, A Joking Relationship,* and in other 1960s and 1970s films, in *Baobab Play* Marshall is able simultaneously to record lovely moments in the lives of some Ju/'hoansi and to document his immersion within this culture and implicitly his pleasure in being accepted by these people he so admires, in being allowed to be part of their lives. In these films the baobab tree becomes a symbol of the fragile cultural Eden the Marshalls felt their expeditions had revealed to them and the Eden of John Marshall's engagement with the !Kung as (cinematic) hunter and gatherer.[23]

Of course, it is precisely the Marshalls' apparent assumption that what they had seen in the Kalahari was a way of life unchanged since the Pleistocene Era, a vestige of an original culture unaffected by more modern developments, within which peacefulness and cooperation were the rule—in other words, a kind of Eden—that came to be understood within the anthropological community as a fundamental problem with the films that came out of the Marshall family expeditions. The assumption that the !Kung had lived in the Kalahari, precisely the way that the Marshalls had "found" them—even the subsequent contention by both John Marshall and Elizabeth Marshall Thomas that the family's presence had led to the problematic transformation of this ancient way of life—soon came to be seen as a naïve sense of the history of southern Africa. Subsequent research revealed that many changes had probably occurred to the San peoples as migrations of other ethnic populations into southwest Africa from other areas caused the San to move into the Kalahari. What the Marshalls "found" may have seemed Edenic to them, but it wasn't an original Eden for the !Kung. Indeed, in their research into the 700,000 feet of footage accumulated during the years when John Marshall was filming the San, Keyan G. Tomaselli and John P. Homiak discovered that Marshall himself was well aware of a variety of inroads into San culture, but simply eliminated them from his early depictions of the particular group of !Kung he got to know.[24]

That during his early decades as a filmmaker, John Marshall would become attached to the idea that he had discovered an Eden, what at least for *him* was an Eden, is hardly surprising. It is one of the central conceits of my book, *The Garden in the Machine,* that within the rapidly transforming America of the late twentieth century, American cinema (filmmaking and filmgoing) became an arena not, of course, for experiencing an actual Eden, but for producing cinematic experiences that provided Edenic moments.[25] In a world recovering from a century of warfare, and from the psychic shock of learning the true extent of the Holocaust (an event that seemed to render all ideas of innocence in modern society absurd), any number of filmmakers came to understand that their mission was to recover some sense of innocence, some sense of the world before the Fall. Without even the idea of innocence, how could more humane societies be developed? Marshall's idylls of the !Kung have come to seem untenable ethnographically, but they are understandable both psychologically and aesthetically—and they remain moving and in their own ways revealing.

PEDAGOGY

Making and poisoning arrows is an ingenious application of collected knowledge. There is nothing obvious about the use of the particular grubs in the particular way. The combination of accident and invention that produced the technique would be impossible to reconstruct. Furthermore, the ammount [sic] those people know about their world is phenomenal. They have names for almost every kind of mouse that lives in Nyae Nyae (there are a great many species). They recognize more sub-species of plants than botanists commonly do. Men's knowledge of the behavior of animals is extraordinary; not all men, of course, but the masters of their profession are masters indeed. Somehow all this knowledge gets, or did get, passed from one generation to another. It is not, however, passed on only as an integrated body of specific knowledge wrapped up in a forgone conclusion. Each man's experience with his profession is different and no two mixtures of poison that I ever saw had the same ingredients. Also, no two men spoor quite alike. They seem to operate on a few principles which they modify constantly.

JOHN MARSHALL, "THE ARROW MAKERS"[26]

John Marshall's filmmaking career developed in three distinct phases and reflects three different kinds of experience. During the 1950s, he learned to shoot film and found his way into !Kung practices and rituals with his camera. Beginning in 1957 with *The Hunters,* he began to edit the material he had collected (first with Robert

Gardner at the Peabody Museum, later with Timothy Asch), fashioning individual films, and during the following seventeen years, produced sixteen short films about the Ju/'hoansi. In these short films (Marshall called them "sequence films" and the term has come to mean usually short ethnographic films about particular dimensions of a culture) we can see him trying one, then another editing strategy for presenting !Kung culture to the audience. And finally, developments within !Kung culture that had already begun during the 1950s, though they were not particularly evident to the Marshalls when they arrived in the Kalahari, accelerated during the 1960s and 1970s, forcing Marshall to reconsider his earlier work and, as a media maker, to move in new directions. *N!ai, the Story of a !Kung Woman* (1980) represented a radically different approach that Marshall continued to develop through his capstone work, *A Kalahari Family* (2001). The evolution of Marshall's career also offers *viewers* three different kinds of experience, related to Marshall's own development, but also distinct from it—more on this later.

This second phase of Marshall's career has its own contours, determined by Marshall's quest to find what was most valuable for an audience in the footage he had shot during the 1950s. For a time, he seems to have assumed, as Flaherty apparently did, that, given the widespread stereotyping of indigenous peoples, film experiences that provided an informed but friendly window into indigenous worlds might work to confront stereotypes and to help audiences see these peoples (and themselves) more fully as part of a larger humanity. Certainly *Nanook* represented a radically different sense of Native Americans than most films offered during the first decades of film history; and from the beginning, the Marshalls' films revealed the "bushmen" not simply as interesting, but exemplary. As John Marshall says in his voice-over at the beginning of *Playing with Scorpions,* "!Kung people by and large are not excited by the thought of dangerous encounters with each other or their environment. They do not respect the warrior or admire the struggle against nature. Such follies, they believe, are provoked by the senseless and characterize the red people (Europeans) and the animals without hooves (the Bantu)." What Marshall felt he had witnessed during the 1950s in Nyae Nyae must have seemed all the more remarkable in the late 1960s and early 1970s during the throes of the war in Vietnam. Indeed, there has been some conjecture that the Marshall family's involvement with the !Kung was originally instigated by Laurence Marshall's feeling of complicity with the bombing of Hiroshima and Nagasaki: at Raytheon he had overseen the production of the trigger mechanism used in the original atom bombs. According to John Marshall, the elder Marshall "went into a kind of shock when atomic bombs were used against Japan."[27]

I see *A Group of Women, A Joking Relationship,* and *Baobab Play* as personal films, not in the sense of the "personal documentary" explored later in this volume, but in the sense that Stan Brakhage made personal films about his family and as a means of expressing his personal concerns and ecstasies. But within the canon of Marshall's films about the Ju/'hoansi, these three films are anomalies, precisely in their refusal to be openly *instructive*. Laurence Marshall's assumption that "truth could be discovered by objective means in any field" and that "most art was mushy" had a lasting impact on John, even once he had learned new ways of seeing from his friend ≠Toma and other Ju/'hoansi.[28] Laurence's influence, when combined with the fact that John's shooting had been done under the auspices of the Peabody Museum and the Smithsonian, resulted in a decision to work with the footage he had recorded so that it might be useful in academic contexts, and in the 1960s and early 1970s, this meant within the traditional conventions of documentary cinema: that is, Marshall came to feel that his sequence films needed to provide, insofar as feasible, teachable *information* about the !Kung and about hunter-gatherers—though the resulting films do offer moments that evoke the earlier, more personal films.

After *A Group of Women* and *A Joking Relationship*, which forgo narration entirely, Marshall returned to voice-over, sometimes using it in a manner not very different from the pervasive commentary in *The Hunters*—this is the case in *Bitter Melons* (1971), *A Rite of Passage* (1972), and *Debe's Tantrum* (1972)—but more often, employing a general formula that seems to have been a compromise between the desire to let his interaction with the Ju/'hoansi generate his films and the need to make the material he had collected usable within an academic context. Beginning in 1969–70 with *N/um Tchai: The Ceremonial Dance of the !Kung Bushmen* (1969), *An Argument about a Marriage* (1969) and *N!owa T'ama: The Melon Tossing Game* (1970), and continuing through *The Wasp Nest* (1972), *Playing with Scorpions* (1972), *Men Bathing* (1973), and *The Meat Fight* (1974), Marshall opens each film with a précis, a voice-over introduction providing information about a certain event or ritual, supplemented with still images of the people and actions Marshall describes. After this précis, the body of the film is presented without voice-over. This strategy allows Marshall to offer information about the Ju/'hoansi but also demonstrates an implicit commitment to careful looking and listening on the part of the audience. Marshall's resistance to transforming the complex San culture into *information* is sometimes evident in the way he speaks of this two-part structure within the films. In *N/um Tchai: The Ceremonial Dance of the !Kung Bushmen*, for example, the informational précis is not preceded by a formal title, and Marshall makes clear that the longer body of the film that follows is "the film proper"; only once the précis is complete do we see the film's formal title.[29]

N/um Tchai: The Ceremonial Dance of the !Kung Bushmen and *N!owa T'ama: The Melon Tossing Game,* as their similarly arranged titles imply, can be understood as a diptych, not only in the sense that both focus on San rituals, but because Marshall's way of depicting these activities reveals a variety of parallels and interrelationships. Both films focus on dancing and singing, in *N/um Tchai* as part of a curing ceremony that includes men moving into trance (the Ju/'hoansi call it "half-death"), and in *N!owa T'ama* as part of symbolic game that women play, which can also cause a participant or an observer to enter trance. In both films women sing and clap, creating energy for the ceremonies. Both films provide an extended review of events that take place over a period of time, and that include some of the same characters, most notably N!ai and /Gunda, whose betrothal is a subject in *N!ai, the Story of a !Kung Woman* (and is referred to in *A Joking Relationship*).

Indeed, in retrospect, we can see that the two films play out a bit of marital melodrama, though this was not clear for audiences until 1980, when *N!ai, the Story of a !Kung Woman* was finished. During the section of *N/um Tchai* focusing on /Gunda's movement into trance (both in the précis and in the film proper), we see close-ups of N!ai, who seems either bored or unhappy. Since N!ai is a recognizable figure, her facial expressions seem noteworthy, if obscure in this case. In *N!ai, the Story of a !Kung Woman* we learn that N!ai was frightened of /Gunda's going into trance ("Your face looked so crazy," she says to /Gunda, then to Marshall, "I was so scared of this man"). Her fear comes into play during the latter part of *N!owa T'ama:* when an older woman is inspired to go into trance by /Gunda's dancing, N!ai harasses the woman—as if to demonstrate her fear and resistance to trance in general and to /Gunda's involvement in it.

Marshall's manner of depicting the two rituals confirms the thematic and implicitly narrative relationships between the two films, and it suggests that while he was trying to make films that would have practical pedagogical value, he had not foresworn the personal and aesthetic engagement that characterizes *A Group of Women* and *A Joking Relationship*. In both *N/um Tchai* and *N!owa T'ama* the move from précis to film proper (and this is true of other films using this two-part structure) is essentially a move *from* Marshall's observing events from the outside *to* his cinematically joining in the rituals. In *N/um Tchai* the précis is presented in live action, but generally in long shot and especially at the beginning, using downward angles: that is, we see the Ju/'hoansi literally from a distance and below us. As soon as the "film proper" begins, the camera is closer and at a ground level, looking up or across at the participants. In *N!owa T'ama* the précis is presented differently, but to the same effect. As we hear Marshall in voice-over, explaining the melon-tossing game, we are seeing freeze frames of moments in the ritual. As David MacDougall has suggested, freezing the moving image "returns film to the status of still photography, from which cinema was born. Seized out of the flow of events, the photograph excludes us from the film and bears us away from the story. . . . "[30] But once the film proper begins, we are seeing live action, and we feel instantly more involved.

In *N/um Tchai* Marshall's black-and-white cinematography, especially at the beginning of the film proper, is elegant and evocative. The men dancing are seen in silhouette from a position slightly below; this evokes morning (Marshall has explained that the dancing has continued all night and into the morning) and implicitly suggests the mythic beauty of this event and its power for him. The changing chiaroscuro of the cinematography throughout the day functions as a clock. As the curing ritual becomes more involved, Marshall's camera movement expresses the participants' growing excitement and his own—essentially he is dancing with his camera in conjunction with the ritual; and the pace of the editing speeds up as the ritual grows more intense and slows down as the ritual concludes: a final 54-second shot concludes the film. A similar strategy is evident in *N!owa T'ama,* where in the film proper (here, the title comes at the very beginning, before the précis) Marshall's color cinematography records the women throwing the melon not simply from a detached distance, but from within the dance and in a manner that expressionistically communicates the excitement of the game. In several sequences Marshall positions the camera so that when one woman throws the little melon to the next woman, the melon stays roughly in the center of the frame, while the first woman runs out of the frame, and the next runs in. The movement of women and men running and dancing quickly into and through the frame expresses the ritual as a kind of controlled wildness. When the men momentarily interrupt the ritual, Marshall interrupts his focus on the game and uses intercutting to emphasize the friendly collision of genders. Both films use sound in much the same way; the singing and clapping of the !Kung women, and in *N/um Tchai,* the rhythm of the men's stamping feet, provide a continual background for the action; the singing dies out near the end of each film, signaling the conclusion of both the !Kung ritual and the cinematic ritual that allows us to engage it.

In other films Marshall's combination of teaching and artistic expression works in somewhat different ways. In *An Argument about a Marriage,* for example, the précis combines live action and freeze frame. As Marshall explains how members of a group of Ju/'hoansi who had been captured by white farmers were reunited with other members of the group (several of whom had escaped soon after capture), in part through the Marshalls' intervention, we see a truck wending its way through the trees and the moment when the groups are reunited. Then, when he explains the complex situation that has resulted from /Qui's having a child with Baou during captivity, we see the relevant parties in freeze frame. Then once the film proper begins, we are back in live action, and as usual, *inside* the events: much of the ongoing action is in close-up, sometimes extreme close-up, generally filmed so that we are looking slightly up at the participants: Marshall and his filmmaking are in a submissive position with regard to the experience of the !Kung. More fully than any other of the sequence films, *An Argument about a Marriage* communicates the complexity, indeed the near-chaos, of this moment in the lives of the Ju/'hoansi. During the film proper, Marshall uses subtitles to translate, but often so many people are speaking at once that it is clear that we're getting only a fraction of what is being said. The forced interplay of the !Kung and the white farmers has thrown these lives into crisis: as ≠Toma says, near the close of the film, "When we act like ourselves, these things don't happen." The film ends with a freeze frame on

≠Toma, who has negotiated a momentary stalemate, as Marshall explains how this volatile situation resolved itself.

Marshall's strategy for presenting information about the !Kung allows for a wide range of moods. *Men Bathing,* for example, could not be more different from *An Argument about a Marriage* either in tone or in presentation. The précis of *Men Bathing* begins in live action and with John Marshall's voice-over, as we see several men arrive at a lovely pan on a gorgeous day. Then the film shifts to freeze frame as Marshall explains who these men are and how they are related to each other. A return to live action and the increased volume of environmental sounds signal the beginning of the film proper, during which little happens: the men bathe, make jokes,[31] and enjoy the moment; and Marshall's camera meditates on this idyllic scene, on the gorgeous landscape, and on the bodies of these men. *Men Bathing* is the most serene of all Marshall's films and one of the most beautiful—a final vestige, perhaps, of the filmmaker's fast-fading innocence.

EXPULSION FROM EDEN: *BITTER MELONS* AND *N!AI, THE STORY OF A !KUNG WOMAN*

But things had changed; it came out that . . . two entire bands of Bushmen whom we had known at Gautscha, and many Bushmen from Gam, including the husband of Beautiful Ungka, had been taken away by Europeans to work on the farms. Three times European farmers had come, having followed in the tire tracks we ourselves had left behind the last time. They came all the way to Gam, where they had found the Bushmen, no longer shy of Europeans, and had "offered to take them for a ride on their trucks but had promised to bring them back." The Bushmen had believed them, had gone for the ride, and of course were never seen again.

ELISABETH MARSHALL THOMAS, *THE HARMLESS PEOPLE*[32]

Seen as a whole, however, John's "Bushmen" films reveal the expanding of a sensitive consciousness not only to a gestalt of life but to the complexity of filmic (re)presentation and to the limitations of audiences to comprehend what is presented. He alone of the 1950s–'60s recorders of "Bushmen" has expressed his changed views in uncompromising terms; he deserves applause for this. Collectively, his films constitute important ethnographic documents. They are not, however, dependable documents of the objectified peoples made subjects in the films, but faithful documents of the filmmaker/ethnographer situated in the discourse of a distorted modernity at the time they were made.

EDWIN N. WILMSEN[33]

I first became aware of John Marshall in 1972 at a summer film institute organized by Peter Feinstein in conjunction with what was called the University Film Study Center and presented at Hampshire College.[34] Among the many opportunities available to those who enrolled in the institute was a course in ethnographic cinema taught by Marshall. My most vivid memories of this course include his beginning the week's first screening with Peter Kubelka's flicker film, *Arnulf Rainer* (1960) and his presentation of his own film, *Bitter Melons* (1971), which I taught regularly for a number of years. *Bitter Melons,* like *First Film,* is a general introduction to the San of the Kalahari, focusing on a band of Khwe San living at /Ei hxa o, in what is now Botswana. While Lorna Marshall organized *First Film* roughly in accordance with the way written anthropological studies, including her own *The !Kung of Nyae Nyae,* are arranged, John Marshall organized *Bitter Melons* around music, and in particular, around the blind musician Oukwane, whose compositions are a motif during much of the film (Oukwane's "Bitter Melons," his favorite composition according to Marshall, is the source of the title).[35]

During roughly the first third of the (30-minute) film, we hear a series of songs Oukwane has learned, some of them his own, others passed onto him by other musicians; Marshall provides information about the songs in voice-over. The second third of the film briefly reviews general aspects of Kalahari San life: gathering food and water, planting melons, hunting, the etiquette of sharing or not sharing various foods, the slaughtering of meat. During the final third of the film, a distant grass fire is spotted, and two men walk to the fire in the hope of meeting their relatives and bringing them back to their camp; their journey is accompanied by relevant songs played by Oukwane. After a cutaway to several boys performing traditional animal songs and playing the musical porcupine game, the two men return with the visitors and the film climaxes with men and boys dancing to various tunes. The film ends with the bands dispersing; Oukwane and his wife Kutera decide to stay where they are, being "old and finished."

Bitter Melons is a lovely and engaging film, in large measure because of Marshall's obvious respect for and refusal to patronize Oukwane's music and the traditional musics of the Khwe San: "I wanted to celebrate the wealth of music, musical traditions and games which the people supported with their marginal economy."[36] Oukwane's songs are a pleasure to hear, and the young boys' enjoyment of their songs and games and the dancing of the men and boys near the end makes for a high-spirited experience. The landscape imagery, especially during the walk to the distant grass fire, is reminiscent of *Nanook of the North;* here too, we see men tiny against vast spaces, working to create a subsistence and a life against considerable odds. In general, *Bitter Melons* is an idyll—poignant because of Oukwane and Kutera's decision to remain behind, alone, at the end of the film, adding a final emphasis to the challenges of the Kalahari from which all this music and enjoyable social interplay has come. Marshall's affection and admiration for these people are evident in the general functionality of his editing and in his use of extended shots during the dancing, one of them nearly two-and-a-half-minutes long. Like

Flaherty in much of *Nanook,* Marshall makes himself invisible as an act of respect; *their* art is what is interesting to Marshall, not his own.

For anyone who has enjoyed *Bitter Melons,* the fact that Marshall later discredited the film might come as a surprise. But his experience in first making *Bitter Melons* and then coming to terms with what he saw as its failures models the central trajectory of his career from the early 1970s on. Like *The Hunters, Bitter Melons* is an attempt to create a general view of a people and inevitably can be faulted for leaving out as much as it includes, both in the specifics of the activities it reveals (in *The Harmless People* Elizabeth Marshall Thomas explains that the dance seen at the end of *Bitter Melons* was part of a far more complex ritual than is evident in the film),[37] and in a more general sense: whatever sense we have of Khwe life from the film doesn't include the kinds of complex interaction Marshall's Nyae Nyae films reveal.[38] Further, Marshall echoes Flaherty in not including those aspects of the activities we see that were affected by the filming itself: for example, Elizabeth Marshall Thomas explains, "Dances are usually held at night, but this time, out of consideration for us, they agreed to hold it [the dance we see in *Bitter Melons*] during the day so we could film it."[39] And Marshall himself has indicated that when the visitors came to visit Oukwane, "we gave everybody water. . . . Before and after the final dance in the film everybody had a good drink. No one would, or could, have danced in the sun with only *tsama* melons to relieve their thirst. Everybody's stay at /Ei hxa o was strictly limited by the water supply."[40]

John Marshall's discrediting of *Bitter Melons,* however, has less to do with these issues than with how the poignant idyll he so carefully created, and that we viewers enjoy, turned out to falsify the historical realities that occurred after the film was shot and the Marshalls had left. He has explained:

> In 1972, while working on *Bushmen of the Kalahari,* I searched the Ghanzi farms for Oukwane's people.[41] I found !Gai, whom I called "the fulcrum of the little band" in *Bitter Melons,* and Oukwane's youngest son, /Gaiamakwe. !Gai was staying on a farm where an exceptional white farmer allowed a few Khwe to drink water and gather bushfoods. !Gai told me what happened when our expedition pulled out of /Ei hxa o in 1955. Of course Oukwane and his wife, Kutera, did not stay at /Ei hxa o as my narration suggests. The group lived on roots and melons for as long as possible, then they tried to get back to their permanent waters at Ghanzi.
>
> Oukwane died of thirst somewhere between /Ei hxa o and Ghanzi. When the group reached the farms, they were driven off. /Twikwe and Da si n!a, another old woman, died of thirst along the fences. The survivors reached Ghanzi. In the town commons, the people could drink water from a municipal tap but there was nothing to eat. Kutera died of hunger. The two older boys, Wi!abe and Wi!e, disappeared. While trying to beg for corn meal, !Gai's wife Tsetchwe was raped. She got syphilis and died. The disease had already killed their small son, N!oakwe, and riddled !Gai.

> I found /Giamakwe, the other survivor, failing to get a job on another farm. I asked him if he remembered his father's music. He said, "What music?" . . . In 1955 it did not occur to me to find out what would actually happen to the people I filmed at /Ei hxa o.[42]

For Marshall, whatever satisfaction the artistry of *Bitter Melons* (or for that matter, the artistry of Oukwane and the other musicians and dancers in the film) gave him, and whatever pleasure audiences might take from his film, were rendered pointless, once one understood the historical realities within which this film was made. And, rather than ignore those historical realities any further, Marshall committed the remainder of his filmmaking life, or at least that portion of his filmmaking life that had to do with the peoples of the Kalahari, to a direct engagement with them. The result was a series of films that not only have a very different function from the films of the 1950s through the 1970s, but that re-present material from earlier films in ways that provide this material with the context that was beyond the frame during the shooting and unacknowledged during the editing. This new context allows those of us who know Marshall's early films to reexperience them in new ways.

N!ai, the Story of a !Kung Woman, at 59 minutes, was the longest film about the !Kung that Marshall had finished since *The Hunters*. It was made following Marshall's long exile from Nyae Nyae; in 1958 the government of South Africa refused to renew his visa, and as a result, he was denied contact with the !Kung for twenty years, including the entire period during which he was editing the !Kung films that followed *The Hunters*. In retrospect, we can imagine that working with the footage that recorded what he considered the happiest experiences of his life was a way of revisiting his friends during the first years of his exile.

Like a modern-day Rip Van Winkle, Marshall returned to the Kalahari in 1978, to the village of Tshumkwe on the border of Botswana and what in 1990 would become the independent nation of Namibia, now the administrative center of a reservation established in 1970 for the !Kung. Here, he discovered the dramatic changes that had occurred in his absence. He also discovered that a feature film, *The Gods Must Be Crazy* (1980), was being shot in the area, and that N!ai, among the most frequent participants in his films, had a role in Jamie Uys's feature. N!ai became the focus of Marshall's shooting (fig. 4).

N!ai, the Story of a !Kung Woman opens with a sequence revealing the inhumane conditions on the reservation: the Ju/'hoansi can no longer gather or hunt and are sustained only by "mealy meal" (a kind of cornmeal porridge). Further, their health has deteriorated; N!ai says, "We're all TB people [people with tuberculosis]." Marshall uses close-ups of N!ai, who is still very beautiful, speaking to the camera, as a visual motif (her comments are presented in voice-over translation by Letta Mbulu). During the first third of the film, N!ai reviews

FIGURE 4. N!ai in John Marshall's
N!ai, the Story of a !Kung Woman
(1980). Courtesy Documentary
Educational Resources.

the experiences that have brought her, and her neighbors, to their current situation. N!ai's memories are interwoven with voice-overs by Marshall, and their dual commentary is illustrated with sequences from earlier Marshall films. We see imagery of N!ai as a young girl in *The Hunters* and helping to gather berries in *First Film;* and Marshall reviews the action in *The Hunters* as we see moments from that film.

As N!ai's reminiscence continues, we also learn information not in the earlier films about the marriage of N!ai and /Gunda and see footage of N!ai and /Gunda not included in earlier films: details of the marriage ritual that betrothed N!ai to /Gunda, for example. N!ai also recalls the events recorded in *A Curing Ceremony* (1969), where a woman gives birth to a stillborn baby; and we see a moment from *A Joking Relationship* when /Ti!kay chides N!ai for teasing /Gunda; and finally, moments from *N/um Tchai,* when /Gunda is in trance, learning to be a healer (in *N!ai, the Story of a !Kung Woman* these moments are presented in color). And N!ai and /Gunda comment on these past events themselves. N!ai talks about resisting the marriage ("I just didn't want a husband"), and /Gunda, in good humor, remembers, "You gave me such a hard time!" Both remember how N!ai left /Gunda for other men: "My husband did not know for years. . . . I tormented him." We find out that they did come to live as man and wife and had several children together.

Seeing imagery of N!ai and /Gunda's past while they comment on the events from twenty-plus years later is, on one level, amusing and engaging, particularly because of their apparent good humor about their youthful struggles—indeed, the sequence of N!ai and /Gunda together is reminiscent of the couples talking about how they met and came to marry in Rob Reiner's *When Harry Met Sally* (1989)! Further, as suggested earlier, this information allows us to understand details of both *N/um Tchai: The Ceremonial Dance of the !Kung Bushmen* and *N!owa T'ama: The Melon Tossing Game* that were not yet clear in those films: the meta-narrative of Marshall's career moves chronologically through the years *and,* for those familiar with the various segments of this meta-narrative, back in time: we learn what's new, but also have an opportunity to revise our understanding of the past. Of course, the conditions at Tshumkwe in 1978 seem all the more appalling when contrasted with the imagery from the past, which is quite gorgeous. Indeed, the beauty of this footage from the 1950s and 1960s suggests a golden age, a time when, as N!ai explains, the !Kung went where they wanted to and were not poor, and when Marshall could take unabashed pleasure as a filmmaker in what he understood as an independent and beautiful way of life that, as he explains in his voiceover, had endured in the western Kalahari for twenty thousand years.[43]

The review of the past, conveyed by N!ai's story, Marshall's voice-over, and the footage from the 1950s ends with a dramatic cut from the text, "Tshum!kwi 1958," superimposed over a shot of a giant baobab tree, to a second text, "Tshum!kwi 1978," superimposed over a shot of a (white) man and woman, sitting in their living room.[44] What follows is a more detailed investigation of the current situation at Tshumkwe. N!ai continues to address the camera, but from here on it's mostly in song (as though the pain of the present is being redirected into art), and Marshall intervenes in voice-over from time to time to situate particular sequences. The imagery, however, is all from the present—though in several instances current activities echo images we've seen in the earlier part of the film. The structure of this section of the film is designed to demonstrate the ways in which the various kinds of white intervention into !Kung life are failing the !Kung.

The man and woman, presumably the administrators of the reservation, complain about how lazy the "bushmen" are, how they don't earn the money they are given. This is juxtaposed with a !Kung servant cleaning their home. The local game warden explains government policy about hunting; his comments on the fact that the giraffe are disappearing are intercut with shots of Tsamko, ≠Toma's son, chasing a giraffe on horseback, despite the new rules (the giraffe's fall to the ground echoes the giraffe falling near the end of *The Hunters*). The game warden then reviews the South African budget for dealing with the San on the reservation ("development of human potential," including school: 2,000 rand; social services, medical clinic: 2,500 rand; administration: 200,000 rand!), as we see images of the results. A white doctor treats N!ai but doesn't believe anything is wrong with a baby who has been ill since birth. This is juxtaposed with the !Kung performing a curing ceremony (echoing N!ai's earlier memory of /Ti!kay's attempt to assist Sha//ge, documented in *A Curing Ceremony*) for this baby who, in the end, dies—in the background white tourists are enjoying the scene, taking pictures. Some soldiers arrive to trade tins of meat for !Kung artifacts and to urge !Kung men to join the South African army; this is juxtaposed with a !Kung man working on a painting.

The most surreal aspect of this survey is Marshall's record of Jamie Uys shooting what would become the final shot of *The Gods Must Be Crazy*. If I read it correctly, this sequence offers an implicit statement of Marshall's critique of what is usually called film "art." Marshall records a series of retakes of a moment when Xi (played by a !Kung, N!xau)[45] is supposedly returning to his home and family (N!ai plays his wife): his little son runs to him and he lifts the son up, then puts him down and greets the rest of his band. Uys wants the man to lift the boy just once, then put him down; but each time, the man lifts the boy twice before lowering him to the ground. The absurdity of Uys's apparent preference of a single lift, juxtaposed with N!xau's seemingly automatic double lift, subtly demonstrates the way in which this white director ignores what seems to be an automatic (and thus comparatively natural) action on the part of N!xau, in the interest of a vague aesthetic preference—an emblem presumably for the film's failure, for all its possible good intentions, to do anything like justice to !Kung life at the time of the filming.[46]

Marshall's record of Uys's creating an idyllic scene for *The Gods Must Be Crazy* is followed by a sequence of N!ai and the other !Kung on the reservation that reveals the bitterness and conflict that has been created by N!ai's earning money as an actress: even /Qui, who in *The Hunters* is described as "a simple, kindly man and an optimist, who tended to remember only the better times of his life," bitterly complains to N!ai, demanding she buy him blankets and shoes. !Kung society seems to be falling apart.[47] One of the many ironies here is that, despite N!ai's charisma and charm, her role in *The Gods Must Be Crazy* is minor; she is not credited on Uys's film. Another is that the Coke bottle that seduces the bushmen away from their communal Eden in *The Gods* could be seen in retrospect to emblemize the process of filmmaking itself, both Uys's and Marshall's.

N!ai, the Story of a !Kung Woman ends first with a visit of a white minister and his black translator to the reservation, then with a sequence of army recruits. The minister's telling the story of Jesus and the Samaritan woman at the well comes across as vague and confusing, and N!ai sees the story as a moral offense to her !Kung ways of doing things. The officer in charge of the recruits assumes that the San believe in the whites, but it's clear that joining the South African military to fight SWAPO (the guerrilla army fighting for the independence of what was then a South African colony) is the only way of earning a living. In the final sequence, /Qui, now a soldier, says good-bye—we can see it's probably forever—to his friends, including ≠Toma and N!ai, and N!ai sings, "Death mocks me, Death dances with me." The !Kung have been expelled from Marshall's Eden into time, because over time Eden has disappeared around them.

THE PITTSBURGH POLICE FILMS AND
BRAKHAGE'S *EYES*

Within the meta-narrative of John Marshall's career, it is interesting to remember that, during the same period when he was editing the films I've been discussing, he was involved in the other two projects on which his reputation rests: his collaboration with Frederick Wiseman, *Titicut Follies* (1967), and the series of Pittsburgh Police films that were sponsored by the Lemberg Center for the Study of Violence at Brandeis University. Marshall shot most of *Titicut Follies* (Timothy Asch also did some shooting) and was involved, early on, in the editing, though at a certain point Wiseman told Marshall he wanted to finish the film himself. While this has led to speculation that Wiseman in some sense stole the film from Marshall (early on, the credits listed Marshall as a co-director; this is no longer the case), Marshall seems to have been ambivalent about the experience. While he says that from the beginning he and Wiseman agreed that they would be co-directors and that later he was "kicked out" of the editing room, he also admits that "it was his [Wiseman's] movie"; "I thought of it as Fred's movie."[48] Of course, Marshall's contributions to *Titicut Follies* as cinematographer have never been in doubt, and his in-close shooting is often reminiscent of his early !Kung films.

While the working relationship between Marshall and Wiseman deteriorated once the shooting of *Titicut Follies* was completed, the two men seem to have worked well together during the shooting. When he was asked whether he and Wiseman developed "some kind of direction system," Marshall responded, "We didn't need to. We clicked. We were in tune with each other, we hit it off."[49] Their being in tune is also suggested by the fact that both were working on films about police work during the years 1968–69. Wiseman completed *Law and Order,* his exploration of police work in Kansas City, Missouri, in 1969 (William Brayne shot *Law and Order* and would shoot nine more films for Wiseman), and Marshall was shooting his Pittsburgh Police films in 1968–69: *Inside/Outside Station 9* was released in 1970; *Three Domestics* and *Vagrant Woman* in 1971; *Investigation of a Hit and Run* and *901/904* in 1972; and the remaining fifteen titles in 1973.[50] The longer films—*Inside/Outside Station 9* and *901/904* include films subsequently released, often in slightly different edits, as shorts.[51] The structure of the longest of the Pittsburgh Police films, *Inside/Outside Station 9* (78 minutes)[52] bears some relationship to the structure of *Law and*

Order, though in general, the Wiseman film is more finished and more visceral and is shaped to appeal to a television audience, whereas *Inside/Outside Station 9*, and the other Marshall films, feel more raw, partly because Marshall was often shooting at night, in situations when lighting was difficult to control. Also, Wiseman seems more detached from the events, Marshall more intimate with them.

As was true of Marshall's earlier films, the police films were made not as art films—though in many senses, of course, they are artful—but in the hope that the results would be useful in a specific practical sense, as aids in helping to improve police work and as part of courses in law schools. Indeed, although the Pittsburgh Police films were shown to the police, they were not shown to the general public for years. *Investigation of a Hit and Run* (1972) was followed by *A Legal Discussion of a Hit and Run* (1973, co-shot with Timothy Asch), in which a Harvard Law School class discusses legal aspects of what is revealed by the earlier film. *The 4th & 5th & the Exclusionary Rule* (1973) includes sequences from Pittsburgh Police films intercut with a panel discussion moderated by Professor James Vorenberg of Harvard Law School (filmmaker Jacqueline Shearer was a member of this panel).

The Pittsburgh films formally echo the !Kung films after *The Hunters* and before *N!ai* in that they are, in Marshall's terminology, "sequence films"—that is, they are, or are made up of, short films documenting what John Dewey would call particular "experiences." The differences between the Pittsburgh films and the films shot in the Kalahari are as noteworthy as the similarities, however. The police films include no voice-over or extradiagetic explanation; they were shot in black and white, probably because of the limitations of color film stocks; the result is a gritty, journalistic feel. Most important, the police films are not simply "thick" films (Marshall designates films as "thin" or "thick," depending on how effectively they reflect the complexity of social interaction),[53] they are more ambiguous than the !Kung films: while Marshall came to feel close to the police he traveled with ("Getting to know them is what the film is about. We lived with them. Some of us became very fond of each other"),[54] neither they nor the citizens they come into contact with represent anything like the idealized community we see in so many of the early !Kung films. Indeed, one might conjecture that the complexity and immensity of the social issues at play in the police films helped to maintain a nostalgia in Marshall for the "small town" innocence, not so much of the Ju/'hoansi (by the early 1970s, he was well aware of what was happening to their traditional way of life), but of his own youthful experiences with them, innocence evoked in *A Group of Women* and *A Joking Relationship* and more generally expressed in the lovely color of the early films shot in the Kalahari.

As he was shooting and editing the Pittsburgh Police films, Marshall took a personal interest in sharing the work with the police themselves:

I filmed events of policework for about nine months over the two-year period. On my own, I used the sequences as case studies for discussion with the cops in the loft of Station 9. A number of us would foregather with some six-packs after the four to midnight shift. . . .

Discussion was lively. . . . Many of my sequences showed "domestics" [that is, domestic disputes between marital or live-in partners]. The cops in Station 9 had all three schools of thought: get involved and try to help the family; arrest the man, or everybody; do nothing and maybe call the welfare department. The sequences of real events and specific officers motivated and grounded the discussions. The police appreciated the reality . . . and all said they benefited from arguing their views and airing their feelings.[55]

All in all, Marshall's personal involvement with the police he worked with to make the Pittsburgh Police Films provides an interesting contrast to another "personal" film about police work shot in Pittsburgh in 1970 and finished in 1971: Stan Brakhage's *Eyes*, one of the three films that have become known as The Pittsburgh Trilogy (*The Act of Seeing with One's Own Eyes* and *Deus Ex*, both 1971, are the other parts of the trilogy; *The Act* was filmed in the Pittsburgh morgue; *Deus Ex*, in a Pittsburgh hospital).

Marshall's Pittsburgh films and Brakhage's *Eyes* emblemize two radically different approaches to independent filmmaking, to documentary, and to personal filmmaking that were developing during the 1960s and early 1970s. Both projects are radically anticommercial, implicit critiques of standard Hollywood fare. In both cases, there was no scripting: Marshall and Brakhage immersed themselves in the experience of police work, then edited what they'd shot to reflect what they had come to understand so that we could experience their impressions in cinematic form and draw our own conclusions.

Except for the fact that both filmmakers used handheld 16mm cameras, however, the films are formally quite distinct. *Eyes* is silent and in color, and reflects Brakhage's fascination with the visual accoutrements of police work: the various symbols (badges, uniforms, name tags) and characteristic gestures of the police he travels with. Marshall's fascination is with the human interactions between Pittsburgh citizens and the police, especially as these interactions are expressed vocally. While Brakhage demonstrates his feelings for the situations he witnesses (some of them quite graphic: a dead body in the street, an old man whose face has been battered) in his gestures with the camera and in his freeform editing, Marshall works at remaining invisible but within the development of events; in interior shots, his lighting makes his presence obvious, and from time to time a citizen reveals some discomfort with, or at least interest in, his presence—but in general Marshall's films are as self-effacing as *Eyes* is self-expressive.

Together, however, the two projects provide a fascinating reflection on Pittsburgh and on the ways in which independent film artists were attempting to engage the urban experience during the early 1970s. Despite the obvious formal distinctions between the work of the two filmmakers, it is clear that certain problems are endemic to Pittsburgh: in both films the police are dealing with homelessness, with young people who have nothing to do; and in both, the police are working across racial lines during an era when racial issues were especially volatile (though this remains mostly implicit in both films). In *Eyes* and in Marshall's films the police are nominally, and to some extent actually, the guardians of order, but they also seem a bit at sea in dealing with the complexities of the society evolving around them.

The early responses to the films reflect these complexities. When Marshall's films were shown at the Lemberg Center for the Study of Violence at Brandeis, the reactions to the police work depicted varied widely, as is clear in Marshall's *The 4th, 5th, & Exclusionary Rule;* and Brakhage remembers that while the police "loved *Eyes* . . . , felt that their dignity had been restored," and used the film "to show how kind and gentle they are," Black Panthers in Chicago "used *Eyes* to show what pigs the police are."[56] Of course, the fact that these two cinematically radical projects were shot in Pittsburgh at roughly the same time suggests something about both the openness of the city's police department and the prestige of independent cinema in Pittsburgh at that moment.[57]

PUTTING DOWN THE CAMERA AND
PICKING UP THE SHOVEL

The journey from the subsistence to the commercial world has often been devastating, but I think few black people want to reverse the clock. Most Ju/'hoansi, at any rate, would rather go forward in the mixed economy even if it were possible to turn back.

JOHN MARSHALL, "FILMING AND LEARNING"[58]

After his return to the Kalahari and the Ju/'hoansi, and *N!ai, the Story of a !Kung Woman,* Marshall's documentaries of the !Kung saga take a very different form. Indeed, when I contacted Documentary Educational Resources to ask for DVD copies of *Pull Ourselves Up or Die Out* (1985) and *To Hold Our Own Ground: A Field Report* (1991), DER director Cynthia Close sent me the following e-mail: "I can send you *N!ai* [I had also requested *N!ai*], but John never considered those other two titles 'films'—some of the footage from both those 'reports' was used throughout A KALAHARI FAMILY and the final chapter there, DEATH BY MYTH, really tells this whole aspect of the story."[59] Whatever one calls *Pull Ourselves Up or Die Out* and *To Hold Our Own Ground: A Field Report* (and other related works from the 1980s that are not in distribution), they are certainly parts of Marshall's meta-film of Kalahari life, which, as Close suggests in her e-mail, concludes with the epic, five-part series, *A Kalahari Family* (2001).[60] And if we can see them not only as "field reports," but also as video works by an accomplished film artist, it becomes evident that through their form and style, as well as their apparent content, they provide a postmodern reflection on the role of filmmaking in the transformation of a way of life.

Especially in *Pull Ourselves Up or Die Out* but also in *To Hold Our Own Ground: A Field Report* the video imagery is fuzzy and washed out, inferior to what one had come to expect from Marshall. But it is obvious in both videos that image quality and other "artistic" dimensions of cinema are irrelevant; composition and editing are entirely functional in these tapes. Marshall's concern is with the developing crisis faced by the Ju/'hoansi. I'm reminded here of Joris Ivens's *The Spanish Earth* (1937), where Ivens sometimes chose to sacrifice conventional concerns with film aesthetics in the hope that the film might make a positive contribution within a flow of events that constituted a political and human emergency. What *is* visible in *Pull Ourselves Up* is John Marshall himself, not as an artist documenting what is going on but as an active participant in the events. This is signaled in the titles of both field reports: "Pull *Ourselves* Up or Die Out" and "To Hold *Our* Own Ground."[61]

As is standard in Marshall's !Kung films, we hear his voice-over, and he translates what various men and women say; here, however, he is visible physically, first, arriving in a truck, bringing cattle feed for the kral at N!am Tchoa in 1982 and, cigarette hanging from his mouth (rather like Sigourney Weaver's character in *Avatar*), helping to unload the heavy bags.[62] In the final section of the video, Marshall is visible again, this time in December 1984, at //Xaru pan, where, he explains, "We're piling rocks around the borehole to hopefully hurt elephants' feet and keep them off" (a magnificent elephant hovers in the distance). Marshall is then seen among a group of Ju/'hoansi who are installing a water pump. The work is interrupted by government officials who tell the group that they must have written authority to install a pump, and Marshall is heard arguing that traditional water rights in the Kalahari do not require written permission. Tsamko (the eldest son of ≠Toma) tells the officials, "This pump is our business; we just asked John to help"; and later, after an official indicates that Marshall is testing his patience, Tsamko says, "It's us Ju/'hoansi that are doing this pump, not John Marshall" (a Ju/'hoan Bushman Development Foundation, set up by Marshall with a gift from Laurence Marshall just before his death in 1980, has bought the pump and hired the contractor to install it—though this is not made clear in *Pull Ourselves Up*). The video ends with the officials leaving, the installation complete, and the pump working— and a final series of informational texts.

The very tenuous optimism of water being pumped in the final shot of the video (optimism immediately tempered by the final texts, which chart the devastating effects of reservation life on those Ju/'hoansi who have not set up their own farms and ranches) is the inverse of a subtle dimension of the review of Ju/'hoansi history that begins the video. In order to contexualize *Pull Ourselves Up* for those who have not followed his work, Marshall recycles a shot of a column of !Kung walking through the desert, shot in the 1950s; then, several shots from *N!ai, the Story of a !Kung Woman* of activities around the reservation offices at Tshumkwe: Jamie Uys shooting *The Gods Must Be Crazy,* U! going for mealy meal, /Qui marching with the soldiers and leaving. For anyone familiar with Marshall's earlier work, this recycled imagery is at once familiar and de-familiarized by our recognition that it is faded and fuzzy—not surprisingly, since these shots are from earlier generations of film and video that have been re-recorded with video technology that substitutes convenience (and sync sound) for image quality.

In the early !Kung films, Marshall always remained outside the frame. Even though he felt personally at one with the Ju/'hoansi, and even when he was directly involved in the action (he was part of the group that shoots the giraffe in *The Hunters*), as a *filmmaker* he felt obliged to seem detached from their lives. This was, I assume, an act of respect, similar to Flaherty's suppressing his own physical presence in *Nanook of the North,* as Marshall made clear even as late as the 1990s:

> The problem is to let the audience meet the people in the film instead of just the film-maker. The films that could help achieve the goal will have to try to show what people do and say, not what filmmakers feel, think and want their audience to know.
>
> Robert Gardner, Fred Wiseman, Ricky Leacock and John Marshall are not particularly interesting. Ju/'hoansi pulling themselves up from the depths of dispossession are interesting.[63]

Pull Ourselves Up, however, reveals a new kind of presence that signals fundamental changes in Marshall's thinking as media maker. Our consciousness of the (literal) decay of Marshall's concern with aesthetic issues, at least as conventionally conceived, in both the film footage shot for *N!ai* and in that canonical shot of the !Kung walking into the desert (a shot that can be read as an index of Marshall's idealistic youth), provides a historical context for Marshall's entering the frame both in body and in voice (not simply in voice-*over,* but as a voice within the diegesis of the action). Here he is, for the first time in his moving image work, part of a "we": not exactly the "we" of the Ju/'hoansi, but the "we" of a transcultural group made up of Ju/'hoansi and others working in the present for political change in the Kalahari.

The shifts in Marshall's position with regard to filmmaking and the Ju/'hoansi continue in *To Hold Our Own Ground,* which takes roughly the same form as *Pull Ourselves Up.* Again, Marshall begins with a map and in voice-over reviews the changes in how southern African territory has come to be divided up: "The following visual report shows the Ju/wa struggle to hold on to their last fragment of land and farm for their lives." Tsamko, who has emerged as a leader of the Ju/'hoansi

FIGURE 5. Ju/'hoansi on the move, in a Marshall photograph. Courtesy Documentary Educational Resources.

(this is already evident in *Pull Ourselves Up*) is seen walking toward the camera, and Marshall's revelation of Tsamko's thoughts makes clear that he will be a focus of this video. The appearance of Tsamko leads into a review of the past, conducted both in voice-over ("I first met Tsamko in 1951") and through recycled imagery from earlier work.

Once again, we see the canonical shot of a column of !Kung walking into the desert, here even less true to the original than the version of the shot seen in *Pull Ourselves Up* (fig. 5). This is followed by imagery of Tsamko learning to hunt by shooting a beetle with arrows, from *The Hunters,* then by imagery of the hunters shooting the giraffe and of women gathering roots (this imagery is quite faded and breaks down), and then—after a bit more information about the present political situation—imagery from *N!ai* (the presence of the South African soldiers at Tshumkwe) and from *Pull Ourselves Up,* including, in its entirety, the sequence focusing on the way in which alcohol consumption has accelerated the transformation of Ju/'hoansi life on the reservation. Here, the fight between several men and women (with /Gunda trying to calm things down) is horrific, in part because when one man is brutally knocked to the ground, he falls on a puppy whose screams of pain express what this moment means for this formerly peaceful people. Marshall's review concludes with imagery from the attempt to keep elephants away from the waterhole and the confrontation over the installation of the water pump from *Pull Ourselves Up:* the recycled scenes from the earlier field report are second-generation video and the decay in quality emphasizes the "past-ness" of even these comparatively recent events.

The present in *To Hold Our Own Ground* was recorded in much-improved video technology that, especially in the outdoor shots revealing Tsamko's effective leadership and the development of the Nyae Nyae Farmers Cooperative, presents these developments as a new "golden moment," or at least as evidence of the possibility that the Ju/'hoansi, through their own efforts (and with the collaboration of others who are committed to the justice of their desire for a homeland) may overcome the many challenges still facing them. Marshall is quite clear about these challenges: among them, the myth that the Ju/'hoansi are incapable of rising above animal status; the opening of eastern Bushmanland to trophy hunting (illustrated with shots of the carcasses of dead elephants being dismembered with chainsaws); and the resistance of the neighboring Herero who spread false rumors about Tsamko's activities and goals.

But we also see that Tsamko and the other Ju/'hoansi continue to develop their organization in ways that may be successful, and Marshall himself is again visible, not filming, but taking minutes at a meeting of the cooperative and translating for the Ju/'hoansi. The film ends with some real hope: water is flowing from a new borehole (again, evocative of *The Spanish Earth,* where the final scenes reveal Spanish peasants irrigating their land) and Tsamko is seen marching in support of SWAPO and an independent Namibia (there is some indication that a SWAPO victory might assist the Ju/'hoansi in their struggle). Even the video's final credits indicate the change in Marshall's sense of his filmmaking. Instead of the usual hierarchical designation of roles, the credits indicate that the video was "produced by DER for the Nyae Nyae Farmers Cooperative," and that it's "a film by Peter Baker, Cliff Bestall, John Bishop, Sue Cabezas, John Marshall, Claire Ritchie, Pitchie Rommelaere, John Terry"—that is, the cooperative nature of the Ju/'hoansi struggle is reflected in the collaborative production of the video.

THE ROAD TAKEN: *A KALAHARI FAMILY*

The five-part television series, *A Kalahari Family,* finished in 2002, is the capstone of the Marshalls' Kalahari saga; and it moved John Marshall's approach to filmmaking, and his understanding of his early work, into a final phase. In the opening, 90-minute episode, "A Far Country," Marshall reviews the history of his family's arrival in Nyae Nyae as well as the previous history of that area of southwest Africa; and, recycling footage from many of the !Kung films (in this case in gorgeous reproductions of that early footage), he recalls his experiences with the Ju/'hoansi in the 1950s, up through Laurence Marshall's reuniting the band by interceding with the South African authorities to broker the release of those who had been working as forced labor on white farms (the resulting friction between /Ti!kay and /Qui is documented in *An Argument about a Marriage*).[64] "A Far Country" begins in 2002, when Marshall and several Ju/'hoansi men are erecting a monument to ≠Toma, who died in 1988, under a baobab tree (the text is in Ju/'hoansi and English; the English reads "He stopped our feet/He taught us").

"A Far County" presents two kinds of imagery from the 1950s: footage not previously released (for example, Lorna Marshall's making Polaroids of the Ju/'hoansi and her own family during the first Marshall family expedition to help explain what the family was doing in Nyae Nyae) and recycled moments from *First Film* and *The Hunters* through *Men Bathing* and *Baobab Play*. After this historical introduction, Marshall intercuts among Lorna Marshall, ≠Toma, !U, Tsamko, N!ai, /Gunda, and Marshall himself reminiscing about their lives in the 1950s and imagery from the experiences they describe. The bulk of these reminiscences were recorded during Marshall's return to Nyae Nyae after his twenty-year exile, as he and his friends were becoming reacquainted and remembering their previous lives together. The reminiscences also function to explain Ju/'hoansi life to those who are unfamiliar with the earlier Marshall films.

For those who do know the earlier Marshall films, Marshall's return to Nyae Nyae is, of course, also their return, and it is fascinating and moving to see the changes in the people remembered from those films (moving, in part, because we know their changes are reflected by our own: we're all Rip Van Winkles, returning to a place we thought we knew). The mood of "A Far Country" is generally nostalgic, though as the episode evolves, Marshall reminds viewers that what may have seemed Edenic to him was disappearing even as it was being recorded, and in part *because* it was recorded: "While we were home in America, white ranchers followed our tracks into Nyae Nyae to round up the Ju/'hoansi by persuasion or force." The later Marshall expedition, during which Laurence Marshall was able to see to the reuniting of the band, may seem to have mended this wound to the community, but, near the end of "A Far Country," just after we see a final shot of Marshall at the ≠Toma memorial in 2002, imagery from *Men Bathing* is accompanied by Marshall's voice-over: "Looking back, I'm struck by how naïve we all were about the future"; "On our last winter morning together, as we enjoyed a bath in Nama waters, we had no idea how soon or how willingly most people would give up the hunting-gathering life." "A Far Country" concludes with the men laughing uproariously and then sleeping in the sun—a perfect metaphor for the naïveté (their own, Marshall's, and perhaps, ours) that was part of the experience of those earlier films.

Marshall's recycling of the *Men Bathing* imagery at the conclusion of "A Far Country" also makes explicit his own presence at this event as well as his participation in the bathing ("as *we* enjoyed a bath in Nama waters") and, presumably, in the joking and laughing (somewhat less in the resting, perhaps, since he is filming the men). The disappearance of the detachment of Marshall-as-filmmaker in his films, already evident in *Pull Ourselves Up or Die Out* and *To Hold Our Own Ground: A Field Report,* is here extended, in the sense that we are now becoming aware of the implicit fiction of Marshall's (however well-intentioned) invisibility in his early films: Marshall is entering the frame of an earlier film, at least conceptually, in retrospect.

As time has passed, Marshall has come to accept that he was, for a time, a member of the !Kung band—in one instance, forcibly separated from them, as they were from each other—and in a sense a part of an extended family that includes many !Kung as well as his own parents and sister. Indeed, this seems to be implied by the use of the singular in *A Kalahari Family.* His decision to use five Ju/'hoansi narrators (actually, we see ≠Toma, !U, Tsamko, N!ai, and /Gunda speaking and hear English translations of their memories by voice-over actors Sello Sabotsane, Lucia Mthiyane, Jerry Mofokeng, Letta Mbulu, and Michael Sishange, respectively) announces this "we" as part of the filmmaking strategy of *A Kalahari Family.*

In the following three, hour-long episodes of *A Kalahari Family*—"End of the Road," "Real Water," and "Standing Tall"—Marshall returns to the period recorded in *Pull Ourselves Up or Die Out* and *To Hold Our Own Ground: A Field Report,* this time in more detail, both in terms of what we learn about these events and literally in how the events are seen. After a brief review of Marshall's history in Nyae Nyae, ending with !U's saying, "You never thought about us!"—deeply ironic for anyone aware of Marshall's immersion in his 1950s footage from the time his visa was revoked into the 1970s—he recycles earlier imagery of Nama Pan in 1958 in order to contrast the idyllic moment there with what he found when he returned to Nyae Nyae in 1978 and what had become the ghetto of poverty at Tshumkwe, the headquarters of the Nyae Nyae reservation. Marshall's tour of "downtown" Tshumkwe is followed by a series of recyclings of imagery from the 1950s, so that viewers can be clear about how dramatically !Kung life has changed for Tsamko, N!ai, /Gunda, G≠kao Dabe, and the others, in part because "my family's expeditions had played a part in the South African occupation of Nyae Nyae." As G≠kao Dabe says, "It was the roads you and your father made that brought us kadi [a cheap local corn liquor, which was doing serious damage to the !Kung community—I'm not sure about the spelling].... When you and your father left, you left behind those ugly things: roads."

The real focus of "End of the Road," however, is Marshall's attempt to make amends for the damage his family's visits helped to instigate by forming a foundation with Claire Ritchie to help the Ju/'hoansi learn a new way of life. Since gathering-hunting could no longer support the Ju/'hoansi, Marshall and Ritchie, and some of the Ju/'hoansi, too, have come to believe that the only chance for a decent life is to move away from Tshumkwe and back to Gautscha Pan and learn to garden and raise cattle. The episode ends on the morning of Christmas Eve, when Marshall, who is "pissed in more ways than one" (angry that *talk* of moving out of Tshumkwe has seemed to be all that was happening, and drunk), discovers that the group left Tshumkwe for Gautscha while he was sleeping. As he stands alone in Tshumkwe, looking lost and befuddled, we understand that Marshall-as-film-maker is celebrating the initiative of the Ju/'hoansi and recognizing that it is *their* efforts that make change; he and his foundation can only follow them.

"Real Water" and "Standing Tall" reveal the struggles and successes of the !Kung group at Gautscha, first to get their farms up and going and then to develop a place where the diaspora of bushmen spread across southern Africa can return to and build a new life. Tsamko and G≠kao Dabe become increasingly important figures during these episodes, when wells are drilled, farms started, and as Tsamko and his colleagues work to ensure the political viability of eastern Bushmanland by resisting first a wildlife preserve, then the luring of lions and elephants to the area for trophy hunting. At the conclusion of "Real Water," we see the Gautscha Farm-ers Cooperative meeting under a tree—evoking that Edenic tree in *Baobab Play* and the other early films, but within a new, politically aware, progressive context.

"Standing Tall" is a road movie, focusing on Marshall, Tsamko, G≠kao Dabe, and N!xau, the star of *The Gods Must Be Crazy*, venturing into Hereroland and Ghobabi in a van (Marshall drives) to locate members of !Kung families and let them know that there is now an option for them, other than the near-slavery of their lives on white farms and their destitution in Hereroland. During their travels, they meet /Ui Chapman, who seems particularly excited about the prospect of having his own place. "Standing Tall" ends with the celebration of the victory of SWAPO and Namibian independence in 1989 and with /Ui Chapman leaving a white farm and coming home to Gautscha with his family to start his own farm.

The look, as well as the overall mood, of the middle episodes of *A Kalahari Family* could hardly be more different from what we see in *Pull Ourselves Up or Die Out* and *To Hold Our Own Ground: A Field Report*. As mentioned earlier, the frag-ile optimism evident in those field reports is reflected in their tenuous image quality, but by the end of the 1990s, as Marshall looked back on how events had developed, once his foundation had been established and a group of Ju/'hoansi had come to believe that gardening and ranching (combined with local gathering and hunting) could provide them with a subsistence and move them away from dependent desperation in Tshumkwe, a sense of the rightness and excitement of this moment and these developments seems to have allowed him to see that all was not lost, that the Ju/'hoansi might still recover from the unfortunate cultural trans-formation exacerbated by his family's arrival in Nyae Nyae in 1951. In general, the beauty and emotional power of *A Kalahari Family*, at least up through "Standing Tall," reflect this new hope and excitement.

During "Standing Tall" we also see Marshall and his Ju/'hoansi colleagues returning to the films of the 1950s, not simply to provide a contrast between a comparatively idyllic past and a desperate present and not to reconfirm Marshall's earlier naïveté about filmmaking. Marshall and his colleagues look at early !Kung films on a tiny television in order to determine who of those seen in the films might still be alive and where they might be found. As the lives of the Ju/'hoansi are transforming, so is Marshall's (and our) understanding of the significance of the early films. Instead of being accidental contributors to the demise of a culture, they have become an important resource for those trying to create a new, healthy Ju/'hoansi way of life on a resettled homeland. That the group is watching the films on a tiny black-and-white television is a final confirmation that while these films may be valuable as artful, often gorgeous records of a lost past—as is evident throughout *A Kalahari Family*—they have also become, even in their most degraded form, a potential force for positive change.

Amid these signs of hope in "Standing Tall," there are also what, during the final episode of *A Kalahari Family*, "Death by Myth," are premonitions of problems to come. Marshall and Claire Ritchie retire as directors of the Nyae Nyae Development Foundation and are replaced by Dr. Marguerite Biesele; and when Tsamko goes to a Herero-DTA rally during the buildup to the vote on Namibian independence, we learn more of what is only hinted at during *To Hold Our Own Ground: A Field Report*. Marshall himself is attacked by a speaker at the rally: "John, what are you doing to the Ju/'hoansi? You are meddling in my people and their concerns. Does the money from John's father help everyone? Or a chosen few, including John himself?" It is after this speech that Tsamko tries to access the microphone but is denied the opportunity to refute these charges. The sequence ends with Marshall arguing with a Herero man and asserting that Nyae Nyae is, and has always been, Ju/'hoansi territory: "I was a kid here; I saw with my own eyes!"

Later in "Death by Myth," Marshall returns to Nyae Nyae after a two-year absence to discover that things have not developed as he had hoped—in large measure because various constituencies in the region, white and black, have been promoting the bushman myth in order to profit from it. The myth, as Marshall explains it and as demonstrated in the film by a considerable range of men and women, is that the bushmen are "natural hunters and gatherers" who remain capable of supporting themselves if they adhere to their traditional ways, and that efforts to assist the bushmen in developing a new way to maintain themselves are misguided: as a people they are more beautiful as nature made them, in their original, primitive, hunting-gathering state. Of course, this is the myth promoted by *The Gods Must Be Crazy*, which has been a motif in Marshall's !Kung saga since *N!ai, the Story of a !Kung Woman;* but in "Death by Myth" we hear the same ideas expressed by those who want to remake the region as a nature conservancy and/or to promote trophy hunting (and in the case of the Herero, to annex the land for their herds). During Marshall's absence, assistance to farmers has ceased to be a priority for the Nyae Nyae Development Foundation, which has allocated the funds coming in from donors to building offices at a new town called Baraka, buying trucks, and hiring experts who do studies of the region and produce books

about it—an echo of those earlier whites who established Tshumkwe as the political center of Bushmanland and allocated government aid primarily to facilities for
the whites. All the decisions relevant to Nyae Nyae are now made in Windhoek by
a German administrator and those who answer to him.

During Marshall's 1994 and 1995 visits, it is clear that the Ju/'hoansi struggle for
their Nyae Nyae territory and a practical means of subsistence is failing. Even the
baobab tree in the center of Tshumkwe has collapsed as a result of an infection.
The original leaders are no longer listened to, and elephants have destroyed many
farms. The German administrator is ultimately fired by the Nyae Nyae Farmers'
Coop, but Tsamko, who in earlier films was the leading proponent of the new
farming communities, has been persuaded to support the Nature Conservancy,
which has promised the Ju/'hoansi money from hunters and from filmmakers; in
1995 Tsamko, furious at whites who have once again taken over Nyae Nyae, refuses
to be filmed by Marshall ("You make money from your film!"). Near the end of
"Death by Myth," we learn that the annual payment to each Ju/'hoansi from the
conservancy is $10.50 American.

The main body of the episode ends with tourists visiting a fake bushman village, where a group of Ju/'hoansi pretend to be living a traditional way of life.
"Epilogue 2000," which concludes *A Kalahari Family*, provides a tiny spark of
hope: G≠kao Dabe has started farming again; Tsamko is a leader again, settling
disputes between his fellow Ju/'hoansi the way his father once did; Tsamko's sister
Bao has become a health worker and the first Ju/'hoan woman to have a driver's
license; and Baraka and its fleet of vehicles has fallen apart. Still, the local road
signs are hidden so as not to interfere with the tourists' fantasies, and !U makes
jewelry to sell to them. "Death by Myth," and *A Kalahari Family* and the entire
Marshall !Kung saga, conclude with a return to the monument to ≠Toma and with
the narrator's indication that in 2001 six members of ≠Toma's family continue to
live at Gautscha. This ambiguous ending is entirely appropriate to this remarkable
project and a final demonstration of Marshall's no longer naïve but always hopeful
approach to cinema.

A PROCESS IN TIME

According to my view, experience as a whole is a process in time, whereby
innumerable particular terms lapse and are superseded by others that follow
upon them by transitions which, whether disjunctive or conjunctive in con-
tent, are themselves experiences, and must in general be accounted at least as
real as the terms which they relate.

WILLIAM JAMES, *ESSAYS IN RADICAL EMPIRICISM*[65]

To see John Marshall's fifty-year career as a filmmaker as significant primarily
because of his pioneering contribution to ethnographic cinema and his production

of several canonical films—*The Hunters* and *N!ai, the Story of a !Kung Woman,* most obviously—is to undervalue one of the signal accomplishments of modern documentary cinema and to ghettoize an accomplished and inventive film artist. Most of those who come into contact with Marshall's work have been anthropology students learning about indigenous, preindustrial cultures, but Marshall's achievement as a film artist is fully evident only to those who have experienced his many films and videos about the Ju/'hoansi and have understood them as a single ever-evolving meta-work. While most film artists are satisfied with producing individual, discrete films, Marshall never seems to have thought of filmmaking this way—except perhaps momentarily at the very dawn of his career.

For Marshall, filmmaking was an ongoing, pragmatic process that went well beyond learning enough to produce films that audiences might feel they were learning from. He himself continued to engage the people he had filmed and had made films about, and as his awareness expanded, he rethought the earlier conclusions about them that were evident in those films and demonstrated this revised understanding in new work. Instead of abandoning the group of Ju/'hoansi who were recorded in his early footage and moving on to other subjects, Marshall revisited the Ju/'hoansi as often as he could (altogether Marshall made fifteen visits to Nyae Nyae), exploring their efforts to adjust to the changing world of which his presence in Nyae Nyae was a crucial part. And instead of abandoning his earlier films once he became aware of the limitations and failures of his representations of the Ju/'hoansi, he continued to revisit these films, recycling them into new works that reflected both the ongoing history of Nyae Nyae and the surrounding region, and his own expanding, continually revised awareness of this history and his attempts to honestly represent the people most affected by it.

Marshall's !Kung films have long been understood as a record of a particular cultural group, just as the films of Timothy Asch and Napoleon Chagnon are understood as a record of the Yanomami in southern Venezuela. Here too, however, this traditional understanding has failed to recognize the accomplishment of Marshall's saga. The transformation we see in the Ju/'hoansi between Marshall's early 1950s footage through his final visits to Nyae Nyae chronicled in *A Kalahari Family* do, of course, document the experiences of a very specific group, but, as is implicit in Marshall's ongoing saga, these experiences are emblematic of one of the fundamental transformations that has been taking place across the globe for several centuries. If the original remoteness of the Ju/'hoansi living in the central Kalahari kept their gathering-hunting way of life more or less intact well into the twentieth century, the transformation of their lives during the past fifty years recalls the struggles of indigenous societies around the world. For an American it is difficult not to see the near-destruction of the Ju/'hoansi community through economic dependence, alcohol, and broken promises as parallel to the transformation of Native America wrought by the arrival of Europeans and the establishment of the American nation. Nyae Nyae is just one of those Other worlds that were sacrificed, that continue to be sacrificed, to make modern life seem "normal."

In "The Regional Writer" Flannery O'Connor argues that for her to declare herself a Georgia writer is "to declare a limitation, but one which, like all limitations, is a gateway to reality. It is perhaps the greatest blessing a writer can have, to find at home what others have to go elsewhere seeking."[66] Marshall, of course, went elsewhere seeking, but he found in that elsewhere a kind of home for himself, and, over a period of half a century of visits to this new home, he transformed the limitations of his own cultural background and his own assumptions about cinema into a gateway to reality: specifically, the reality that life for "us" and for "them" (and for the relations between "us" and "them") is always a process of personal and social transformation. And this is true if the "us" means Americans from Cambridge and "them," the Ju/'hoansi in Nyae Nyae, and if "us" means filmmakers and "them," their subjects, and if "us" means film audiences and "them," filmmakers and/or their subjects.

Robert Gardner

While John Marshall spent much of his filmmaking life rethinking and revisiting his earlier filmmaking experiences in the Kalahari Desert, learning what he could from the ongoing transformations of San life and from what he saw as his limited understanding and his filmmaking mistakes, Robert Gardner's career has been focused on an expansive engagement with the ways in which the human need to make life meaningful and beautiful despite the inevitability of physical death has been expressed both in far-flung cultures and by artists working in cultural environments closer to home. Gardner's important, if controversial, contributions to ethnographic cinema have taken him to various parts of Africa (in one instance into the Kalahari with the Marshalls), to New Guinea, to the Andes, and to the Indian subcontinent. In each instance, he has thrown himself into the experience of recording what has seemed of interest to him in these cultures, not simply because the events he films are crucial within the lives of those he has documented, but also because of the relationships he sees between these events and transformations in his own culture and his own life.

Throughout his long career, Gardner has braided his fascination with exotic cultural practices that seem unusual but are sometimes surprisingly relevant to the lives of most film audiences with a fascination with artistic sensibility in general and with the particular accomplishments of writers, painters, sculptors, as well as other film artists. The result is a panorama of image making and writing within which Gardner has attempted, again and again, to confirm his commitment to the ritual of art and the art of ritual as a means of negotiating the passages of human experience.

EAST COAST/WEST COAST: EARLY EXPERIMENTS

Robert Gardner is a formative figure in the evolution of Cambridge documentary and in the emergence of Cambridge as a center of film activity. An accomplished and influential filmmaker in his own right, he was crucial in the development of the Film Study Center at Harvard, and in 1964, when the Film Study Center moved from the Peabody Museum to the new Carpenter Center, which Gardner helped to design, he managed the Film Study Center, assisting filmmakers in producing films and overseeing the programming of events at the Harvard Film Archive's cinematheque. He was, so far as I am aware, the first to teach courses in film production and film history/theory at Harvard (in what, early on, he called the Department of Light and Communications), and over the years his teaching nurtured a number of filmmakers. Beginning in 1972 and continuing for ten years, he hosted *Screening Room* on channel 5 in Boston, for which he interviewed major contributors to independent filmmaking—animators, documentary filmmakers, and film artists identified with the avant-garde—and broadcast their films to the local television audience.

Gardner was director of the Carpenter Center from 1975 to 1994 and continued to teach in what had become the Visual and Environmental Studies Department until 1997, when he retired from his formal connection with the university. He has continued to contribute to film culture and the arts at Harvard, and in 2003 he established Studio7Arts, which offers monetary support and facilities to individual artists working to mine the potential of still and moving images to provide "visible evidence that testifies to our shared humanity."[1] The 2000s saw Gardner turn his attention to writing, in particular to the journals he compiled during the making of his films: *The Impulse to Preserve: Reflections of a Filmmaker* (New York: Other Press) appeared in 2006; *Making Dead Birds: Chronicle of a Film* (Cambridge: Peabody Museum), in 2007; and *Just Representations* (Cambridge: Peabody Museum/Studio7Arts) in 2010.

Gardner's diverse career has been punctuated with the production of independent documentary films, though his original interest in cinema was more conventional. As a Harvard undergraduate, and a sometime college roommate of Jack Lemmon, he was drawn to theater; he and Lemmon acted together in *The Proof of the Pudding* at the Hasty Pudding Theatrical Society. Upon graduation, the two friends traveled together to Hollywood to seek fame and fortune, neither of which was immediately forthcoming for either man, though Gardner was offered the part of Mark Trail in a proposed TV serial based on the famous comic strip. Returning to Cambridge, Gardner became an assistant to Thomas Whittemore of Harvard's Fogg Museum and traveled to Turkey to assist with conservation work on mosaics in Istanbul's Church of the Chora (Karije Jami): "These were transformative experiences during which I learned, among other things, that I knew nothing and that I had little time to lose correcting that appalling truth."[2]

FIGURE 6. Sidney Peterson and Robert Gardner in Kwakiutl outfits
sometime in the early 1950s. Courtesy Robert Gardner.

In 1949 Gardner moved to Seattle and for a time taught medieval history at the
College of Puget Sound in Tacoma. Reading Ruth Benedict's *Patterns of Culture*
moved Gardner toward anthropology, which he studied briefly at the University of
Washington and later on at Harvard. During his years in Seattle, Gardner became
involved with the film society at the University of Washington's Henry Gallery, and
in 1951–52, made his first foray into filmmaking, working for a time with avant-
garde surrealist Sidney Peterson on a feature about an interracial romance between
a Kwakiutl princess and a white man (fig. 6). While Gardner and Peterson did do
some shooting on Vancouver Island, nothing came of their work. However, Gardner's visit to Vancouver Island's Blunden Harbour would soon instigate his first
two films: *Blunden Harbour* (1951) and *Dances of the Kwakiutl* (1951).

Gardner's Kwakiutl films seem to have been inspired by the lyrical documentaries he was seeing at the Henry Gallery, and especially Henry Watt and
Basil Wright's *Night Mail* (1936), which Gardner remembers watching about

twenty-five times.[3] Watt and Wright's combination of image and spoken poetry (by W. H. Auden) also seem to have influenced Gardner's third film, an evocation of the person and work of painter Mark Tobey, with whom Gardner became friends while in the Northwest. For both *Blunden Harbour* and *Mark Tobey* Gardner wrote poetic narrations; the text in *Blunden Harbour* was spoken by poet Richard Selig; the texts in *Mark Tobey* by Gardner and Tobey (Tobey contributed some of his lines). *Blunden Harbour* and *Mark Tobey* seem generally representative of film society films of the 1950s, in their interest in other cultures and in art, in their use of poetic imagery and narration, even in the ways in which Gardner worked with sound and image in the years before sync sound was an option for independents.

Blunden Harbour is an effective portrait of a place. Heinck's and Jacquemin's cinematography is lovely, evocative sometimes of Frank Stauffacher's *Sausalito* (1948) and Bruce Baillie's *To Parsifal* (1963), and Gardner's editing is capable, and sometimes powerful: for instance, a shot of one older man doing painstaking work on a mask is followed via a direct cut by a shot of the same man during a Kwakiutl ceremony; for a moment we don't realize that this is the same person, though once we do, we are reminded how participation in a traditional ceremony can transform an individual. The voice-over is carefully controlled, limited to four instances when poetic lines are spoken by Selig; each of the four stanzas of the voice-over vary or build on the original phrase, "From the water: food; from the wood: a way of life," until we hear "A way of life, a way of death, a way of dreams, and a way to remember" at the beginning of the ceremony (the cut from the man as craftsman to participant in the ceremony occurs just at the phrase "a way to remember," foregrounding the idea of ceremony as cultural memory).[4]

Dances of the Kwakiutl is a more straightforward document of Kwakiutl dancers performing in part for the camera, introduced with Gardner's voice-over: "Fifty years ago, the Kwakiutl Indians of British Columbia held their winter ceremonial in order to bring back the youth who were staying with the supernatural protector of their society. The songs and dances which belonged to this ritual were vital to the success of the ceremony. Lately, both the intention and performance of the winter ceremonial have been substantially altered. The dances are no longer significant within the ceremonial complex and their performance depends now on an individual and spontaneous will to recreate a very old, syncopated dance form." In the voice-over, one can sense Gardner's disappointment with the changes he describes, but the dancing and the enthusiasm of the dancers are effectively documented.

Mark Tobey was of special importance to Gardner in two ways. First, he did his own (color) cinematography for the first time, and this portrait of Tobey and his Seattle environment is visually impressive. Second, in *Mark Tobey* Gardner's fascination with art and his own poetic urge is unbridled: while the poetic voice-over is rather overwhelming—these days it feels strident and pretentious—one can feel Gardner's enthusiasm for his subject and his excitement that this important artist has trusted him fully enough to be an active participant in the film. If the two Kwakiutl films are early premonitions of the films that would, beginning a decade later, establish Gardner's reputation as a pioneer in ethnographic filmmaking, *Mark Tobey* seems a premonition not only of Gardner's subsequent films about artists (including a second film about Tobey), but of the focus and approach that would dominate his better-known features about the Dani, the Hamar, the Bororo (Gardner spells the name of this group "Borroro") Fulani, and the Ika. For Gardner the making of art is a fundamental, perhaps *the* fundamental, function of culture; and the job of filmmaking, especially nonfiction filmmaking within *our* culture, is to sing the variety of art making across the globe and the ways in which particular art objects and ritual performances have functioned within particular groups as a form of cultural memory and as a spiritual basis for daily life.

GARDNER AND THE MARSHALLS

Between the completion of *Mark Tobey* and the release of *Dead Birds* in 1964, Gardner studied anthropology at Harvard, immersed himself in the community of poets and artists in Cambridge, and became involved with the Marshall family's project of documenting the !Kung, assisting John Marshall with the editing of *The Hunters* (1957). Gardner was in touch with Laurence Marshall as early as 1953. When J. O. Brew sent the elder Marshall a copy of a seminar talk on film that Gardner had given, Marshall wrote back to Brew, expressing his appreciation of Gardner's talk: "As to the use of film in anthropology, I still feel that it ought somehow to be essential in any study of man. . . . I think my feeling is based on some of the ideas that Bob brings out; the importance of sight in perception, the ability of film to represent the eye and to portray events in actual time so that one can perceive interaction and tempo, and not least in importance, the fact that film can be studied repeatedly and by many people."[5] However, Marshall remains a bit dubious about the significance of the films that have come out of the expedition and assures Brew that the costs of the film that John Marshall has been shooting would not be paid for with the money Harvard had granted the expedition, but by the Marshalls themselves.

Brew apparently shared Laurence Marshall's letter with Gardner, who responded, on April 16, 1953, with a seven-page letter, exploring more fully his ideas about cinema: "Through very complicated psysio-psychic processes involving principles of identification, association and learning, the net effect possible with film is to impart a credible experience to a spectator."[6] Defining *experience* as "the acquiring of knowledge by the use of one's own perceptions of sense and judgment," Gardner (basically paraphrasing John Dewey's ideas about experiential learning) goes on to explore "what is meant by learning and experience":

> In a larger sense it could also be thought to be an experiment in the use of one's per-
> ceptions in the process of learning. In this light the old saw about experience being
> the best teacher gains a little luster. . . . It may already be clear that what I wish to
> make is a distinction between two kinds of learning, one kind which is the result of
> rote memorization which has a minimal participation of perceptual organs, and the
> other which involves multiple senses and promotes experimental participation
> within the learning process. Although the relative value of these two general types of
> learning situations depends on the individual learning and the reasons for learning
> at all, in a broad sense the advantages of what might be called "experience learning"
> have been dramatically attested in such contexts as training for war. It is now general
> practice, I am told, to subject trainees to maneuvers under actual fire, the supposi-
> tion being that out of this experience will result a more dependable . . . soldier than
> the one who reads in a manual that someday he may be shot at. . . . It might seem that
> the point which should be brought in here as justification for the use of films in
> anthropology is that a film can provide a close approximation to otherwise unavail-
> able field experiences.

Ultimately, Gardner argues that since experiential learning requires considerable integration of information from various senses, "the film which best achieves the 'experience' type learning effect must be left in the hands of creative artists."

By 1954, when Gardner began working with John Marshall on the editing of what would become *The Hunters,* he had had some experience in producing, directing, and editing film; he had developed his thinking about documentary filmmaking as a creative enterprise; he had earned the confidence of the administration at the Peabody Museum; and he had been in touch with the Marshall family for more than a year. Especially given that Gardner was seven years John Marshall's senior when they began working together (Gardner was twenty-nine; Marshall, twenty-two), it would not be surprising if Gardner had substantial input into *The Hunters,* though over the decades there has been some question about the nature and extent of this input (fig. 7). According to Gardner, his contribution was to collaborate with Marshall at the Peabody's Film Study Center (the !Kung footage was the original *film* to be *studied* at the center) in expanding a 45-minute edit that Marshall had produced into the 75-minute film that was released in 1957.

In his description of the process, however, Marshall claims that "*The Hunters* was edited on the third floor of our family home on Bryant Street in Cambridge, Massachusetts between 1954 and 1956," and he would later seem to express frustration with the presumption that Gardner had had a major role in the film: when asked about his sense of the way "*The Hunters* was being taken up" during the years following its release, he comments, "Yes, well, we got an award. They

FIGURE 7. John Kennedy Marshall (left foreground) and Robert Gardner during the early days at Harvard's Film Study Center. Courtesy Robert Gardner.

gave Bob an award for it."[7] In what remains the most critical essay on Gardner's filmmaking, Jay Ruby questions what he sees as Gardner's tendency to take excessive credit for some of the projects he has been involved in: "John Marshall's name does not even appear in the 1957 article Gardner wrote discussing the activities of the Film Study Center. Unless you knew otherwise, the article would lead you to believe that Robert Gardner made *The Hunters* by himself."[8] In *The Impulse to Preserve* (2006) Gardner claims only "a minor role [in] collaborating with John Marshall" on *The Hunters;* and in his introduction to *Making Dead Birds* (2007), Gardner calls Marshall "*The Hunters'* principal and talented young author."[9]

The Peabody Museum's accession of the !Kung footage and Gardner's collaboration with Marshall on *The Hunters,* whatever the precise nature of this collaboration, established the Film Study Center; and despite the fact that Marshall and Gardner parted ways after *The Hunters* was finished, it seems likely that Gardner's collaboration with John and his participation in the 1958 Marshall expedition to Nyae Nyae (an experience he found frustrating),[10] helped to confirm a desire to produce his own film about a far-flung cultural group and to assemble the Harvard-Peabody expedition to the Baliem region of western New Guinea in 1961. This expedition, led by Gardner, included Dutch anthropologist Jan Broekhuyse; Harvard anthropology graduate student Karl G. Heider; photographer and sound technician Michael Rockefeller; and writer Peter Matthiessen, whose *Under the Mountain Wall: A Chronicle of Two Seasons in Stone Age New Guinea* (New York: Viking, 1962) was, along with Gardner's *Dead Birds,* the best-known and most widely admired product of the expedition.

DEAD BIRDS

Along with *The Hunters, Dead Birds,* which premiered at Harvard in 1963, confirmed the Peabody Museum as the primary sponsor of ethnographic filmmaking in this country; and together, the two films came to epitomize what has become a genre of documentary filmmaking. As different as Marshall's and Gardner's overall attitudes and approaches to making documentary turned out to be, and may already have been in 1957 and 1963, the two films that established their reputations have a great deal in common. Both films focus on peoples and ways of life that seem unaffected by the onslaught of modern life and modern technology (except, of course, by implication, filmmaking); in this, both filmmakers are children of Flaherty—though both *The Hunters* and *Dead Birds* are more thorough in their suppression of the realities of contemporary life than Flaherty was in *Nanook of the North:* early in *Nanook,* after all, the Inuit family visits the trading post, where Nanook is introduced to the phonograph. *Moana* is the more relevant Flaherty film here (though Gardner has indicated that of the Flaherty films, he most admires *Man of Aran*).

Both filmmakers were faced with two challenges, one of them impossible to meet, the other difficult. Since no previous feature film had been made about either the !Kung or the Dani, both filmmakers had to decide how much and what to reveal to audiences about these groups: that is, how to depict a people in a single film; and, especially since both filmmakers were coming to cinema at a time when the idea of cinema seemed to necessitate entertainment, both wanted to find a way of being interesting as they presented the wealth of new information they decided on. Not surprisingly, both *The Hunters* and *Dead Birds* are organized according to a storytelling logic, and in both, the filmmakers provide relatively continual narration that contextualizes and interprets what we see. Further, both films feature expansive landscapes, sometimes reminiscent of the landscapes the earlier Flaherty films and in classic Hollywood westerns as well as unusually intimate looks at family and social life. Both *The Hunters* and *Dead Birds* were filmed beautifully in color; and both are reasonably effective in approximating the feeling of sync sound.

Seeing *The Hunters* and *Dead Birds* now, viewers may forget how different the experience of these films would have been fifty years ago. In 1957 and 1963 the nudity in both films was radical: it was not until 1965 that the first moment of female frontal nudity, in Sidney Lumet's *The Pawnbroker*, would challenge the Hays Office rules. According to Stan Brakhage, his *Window Water Baby Moving* (1959) could cause moviegoers to faint;[11] and Jack Smith's *Flaming Creatures* (1963) could get its exhibitors arrested. Both *The Hunters* and *Dead Birds* also include moments of "violence" that would have shocked most moviegoers of the era, even those studying anthropology in college classes: the death and butchering of the giraffe in *The Hunters* and, especially, the killing of pigs and the corpse of a dead child being prepared for cremation in *Dead Birds*. The deaths of the animals remain powerful even for jaded contemporary audiences.

Further, both films reflect an attitude that must have seemed surprising to many of those who saw *The Hunters* and *Dead Birds* during the 1950s and 1960s. Both Marshall and Gardner present aspects of !Kung and Dani culture that would have seemed strange, even bizarre, to most Americans, but without indulging in disparaging comments about them. In *Bitter Melons,* for example, Marshall shows how the !Kung collect water from the rumen of certain antelope, and in *The Hunters,* we see the men drink the blood of the dead giraffe. The voice-over presentation of these events is entirely matter-of-fact, even though Marshall had to have experienced surprise, perhaps even disgust, when he first saw these things done and would know how his viewers could be expected to react.

This same matter-of-fact delivery of information is evident in both filmmakers' presentation of the belief systems of the !Kung and Dani. In *Dead Birds,* when Weyak's lookout tower is repaired, Gardner tells us, "Weyak magically cleans the hands that have done the potent work with the feather of a parrot," as we see a close-up of Weyak's hands brushing another man's hands with a small feather. Gardner frequently describes the Dani's consistent concern about the ghosts of the departed: as a warrior is carried back from the front, we learn that he will not have to walk, "but he must be covered to protect him from the gaze of ghosts which wounded men are careful to avoid." And during a religious ceremony, we learn that "of great importance is the little fenced enclosure, put up as a resting place for wandering ghosts." Nothing in Gardner's manner of delivering any of this information suggests that he finds these ideas and activities absurd, illogical, "exotic." It is clear that he and Marshall mean for us to see these activities and beliefs as legitimate ways of dealing with life and death. I am surprised that the combination of nudity, visceral violence, and what would have seemed a complete lack of outrage and disapproval at cultural practices that many Americans would have found repugnant did not earn both films entries in Amos Vogel's canonical *Film as a Subversive Art*.[12]

There are also significant differences between *The Hunters* and *Dead Birds* that have to do not only with the very different peoples represented but also with differences in attitude between the two filmmakers. These differences are signaled by the two titles. "The Hunters" is a straightforward indication of Marshall's focus in the film, a focus that, later on, would embarrass him because of its overemphasis on the importance of hunting to the !Kung. "Dead Birds" refers to the ancient fable presented during the opening of Gardner's film. As we watch a continuous, elegant, 36-second shot of a hawk in flight, Gardner's voice-over tells of a contest between a snake and a bird to decide whether men would be like snakes, who shed their skins and have eternal life, or birds, who die: "The bird won, and from that time, all men, like birds, must die." This opening (both the beauty of the shot of the hawk and the poetic phrasing of the fable) makes clear that Gardner sees himself as a film artist and storyteller, fascinated not simply with what this particular group does but with the idea of culture in general: Gardner is producing not simply an informational film about Dani ways of facing death but a cultural artifact, a work of art, about the idea of confronting death. After all, it is not simply the Dani who die, but all of us; and we all deal with this reality by producing the artifacts of the cultures that simultaneously distinguish and unite us.

Both *The Hunters* and *Dead Birds* are structured in ways familiar from narrative literature and earlier cinema. Marshall's film is framed as an epic quest narrative that leads finally to the killing of a giraffe and the reinvigoration of the hunters' band through the distribution of the meat. Gardner chooses a different, more expansive strategy: he provides a panorama of what he had come to understand about the Willihiman-Wallalua clan of the Dani by focusing on the activities of two very different characters: the distinguished warrior Weyak and the young swineherd Pua. In general, *Dead Birds* intercuts between Weyak and Pua, whose days are spent in very different sectors of Dani daily life, but Gardner brings them into proximity during moments when the band or several bands join together in celebration or mourning.

Throughout *Dead Birds*, Gardner's attempt at expansiveness is reflected in his use of intercutting. He intercuts not simply between Weyak and Pua but in a variety of circumstances: between scenes where men are doing battle and women are climbing to a salt lick to bring salt back to the village; between warriors attending to a comrade's wounds and a group of younger warriors, still at the front, shouting humorous insults at the enemy; between Weyak weaving and participating in battle; even, during the preparation for a cremation, between wood being piled for the fire and wind blowing the leaves of trees—a suggestion, perhaps, that the burning of the body will free the soul to wander on its own. In general, Gardner's voice-over confirms the transitions between one activity and another (from time to time, these vocal confirmations seem both awkward and a bit too rote; Gardner has admitted that his reading of the text in *Dead Birds* was not what he had hoped for: "In fact, in recent years I have been greatly tempted to both rewrite the text and 're-voice' the narration"),[13] though at times the imagery and the soundtrack diverge.

As depicted in *Dead Birds,* virtually the entirety of Dani life is focused on the ritual warfare carried on between the men of the Willihiman-Wallalua clan and the men of the Wittaia clan (women garden and tend to home and children); and the consistency with which Gardner frames his shots so that the Warabara (the small mountain near which the ritual battles are fought) is visible expresses this: the visual motif of the Warabara suggests the clan members' continuing conscious-ness of the current state of the warfare. In fact, the most dramatic moment *Dead Birds* occurs during the religious ceremony called "Pig Treasure," which brings several neighboring villages together for a feast—a rare moment in Willihiman-Wallalua life when the war seems momentarily forgotten. As the feast culminates, news arrives that a young boy, Weaké, has been killed near the Aikhé River by the Wittaia, transforming the balance of power in the war. The arrival of this news is dramatized by a 26-second, nine-shot montage that interrupts the previous steady flow of the depiction of the feast and leads into the extended funeral ceremony for the boy. The remainder of *Dead Birds* focuses on the various effects of Weaké's death: the victory celebration of the enemy, the sacrifice of two joints on the fin-gers of several young girls; Weyak's and Pua's ritual ways of coming to terms with their loss; and finally, on this group's restoring momentary balance by killing an enemy and mounting their own celebration, which is presented in considerable detail at the conclusion of the film.

While John Marshall's focus in *The Hunters* is on the hunters' skill in tracking and killing the giraffe and on the democracy represented by their careful distribu-tion of the meat among their band, Gardner's focus in *Dead Birds* involves a kind of double consciousness: he is committed to representing the Dani as distinct and separate from his own world—paradoxically so that he can suggest general parallels between their lives and ours. As the phrase, "the impulse to preserve," the title of an early essay and of his recent book, suggests, Gardner means to create a vision of a culture before its (by then, inevitable) transformation by modern life and modern technology: he means to preserve at least a cinematic memory of a culture that has endured for many centuries. In the preface to *Under the Mountain Wall,* Peter Matthiessen, who shares Gardner's attitude, puts the purpose of the Harvard-Peabody Expedition of 1961 this way: "Its purpose was to live among the people as unobtrusively as possible and to film and record their wars, rituals, and daily life with a minimum of interference, in order that a true picture of a Stone Age culture . . . might be preserved."[14]

Gardner goes even further than Matthiessen, however, in suppressing the degree to which Dani culture was already in a process of transformation. Though *Under the Mountain Wall* focuses on traditional Dani culture, and indeed, depicts many of the specific events recorded in *Dead Birds,* it is framed very differently from Gardner's film. The first words in Matthiessen's text are "One morning in April, in the year when the old history of the Kurelu came to an end . . ."; and his chronicle concludes with Weyak (in *Under the Mountain Wall,* his name is "Weak-lekek") climbing into his watch tower and seeing "a strange smoke" drifting on the wind "from down the valley," where "the remnants of Wako Aik's Mokoko tribe clustered for protection around the village of the Waro; this people had come out of the sky to live on the Mokokos' abandoned lands": "The first Waro had come to the Kurelu just after the last mauwe, through the land of the Wittaia. He had white skin, and he was accompanied by black men dressed like himself. The strangers had been stopped at the frontier, and a warrior named Awulapa, brother of Tamugi, had been shot down and killed by a Waro weapon with a noise that echoed from the mountains. . . . The Waro had not left the valley; already they were building huts among the river tribes throughout the valley."[15] The only evidence in *Dead Birds* that the transformation of Dani life is already occurring is implicit: the film could not have been shot had modern life not already arrived in New Guinea. Further, the final celebration sequences in Gardner's film seem clearly performed for the camera, so perhaps Gardner means to end the film by drawing attention to the intersection of two ways of life.

Both Gardner and Matthiessen participate in what now seems a presumptive brand of historicizing by assuming that the Willihiman-Wallalua and Wittaia clans have been in a kind of stasis since the Stone Age, and that no fundamental change in their history has occurred until very recently, that is, until the arrival of Western white men. The very diversity of lifestyles on New Guinea would seem to give the lie to this assumption: surely, there have been a variety of historical developments on the island, some of them considerable enough to produce a range of subcultures—though the absence of a written record keeps these changes from being more than conjectural, at least for these white visitors. Of course, the idea that Matthiessen and Gardner are depicting Stone Age people was probably useful in promoting the book and film, but I think Gardner's determination to depict the life of the Willihiman-Wallalua clan as a form of cultural integrity, not yet affected by modern history, has two particular functions.

First, Gardner's commitment to the depiction of a way of life that, on the surface, seems radically, even shockingly different from our own allows him to raise a deeper question, a question that is suggested by what Gardner has called "a certain despair" about his own culture: "I grew up thinking that much of what America

FIGURE 8. Robert Gardner with New Guinea men, during the shooting of *Dead Birds* (1964). Courtesy Robert Gardner.

stood for was not particularly noble or uplifting. These feelings were exaggerated by events like the war in Viet Nam, various assassinations and so on. Going far away was cowardly but attractive in that it offered the prospect of refuge."[16] The expedition to New Guinea might have begun as an escape from American culture (fig. 8), but Gardner's exploration and witnessing of the lives of the Willihiman-Wallalua revealed fundamental patterns that seemed increasingly to speak to the life he had escaped: Was not the United States involved in its own forms of periodic ritual warfare; did not men determine the national agenda; were we not at pains to assuage our own "ghosts"; and did not some of our nation's most widely held beliefs—the virgin birth of Jesus Christ, for instance—challenge simple logic and common sense?

Second, Gardner's interest in the commonalities implicit within disparate cultural practices is evident in a particular motif in *Dead Birds:* one of the first things we learn about Weyak is that, when he is not standing guard in his tower or actively at war with the Wittaia, he entertains himself by weaving a shell band, a long woven strip on which shells are mounted at regular intervals. Indeed, weaving is the first thing we see Weyak doing, and Gardner returns to this weaving periodically (the narration makes clear that these shell bands have a ritual function: they are used to commemorate birth, marriage, and death). During the final minutes of *Dead Birds,* Gardner intercuts between the Willihiman-Wallalua dancing and chanting and Weyak's finishing the shell band he has been working on and then rolling it up. The shell band is clearly a metaphor for filmmaking and for Gardner's film in particular. Both the shell band and *Dead Birds* commemorate moments of death, and both are means, as Gardner's final voice-over in the film suggests, "to ease the burden of knowing what birds will never know, and what . . . [the Dani], as men, who have forever killed each other, cannot forget": the inevitability of death itself. For Gardner, the fundamental human issue is mortality, and what unites all men and women, across the globe and from the Stone Age until the present, is their production of cultural artifacts and rituals—jewelry, dances, music, films—as a means of simultaneously distracting them from the inevitability of mortality and of materially transcending it.[17]

THE EXPERIENCE OF FILMMAKING
AS THOUGHT PROCESS

What can I possibly mean by saying that going to the ends of the world has been a way for me to understand myself better? Hidden in the answer are ideas such as it is presumptuous to try and explain other people without bothering to explain oneself.

ROBERT GARDNER[18]

During the twenty years that followed the release and reception of *Dead Birds,* which was widely admired and won the Robert Flaherty Award in 1963, Gardner's career moved in a variety of directions. His first project was a cinema verite film made for local television: *Marathon* (1965), co-directed with Joyce Chopra, a still-engaging half-hour film on the Boston Marathon. Stylistically, with its in-close engagement with three individuals (Erich Segal, the author of *Love Story,* then a Harvard professor; a Harvard student, and an African American pastor) within a public event, its black-and-white cinematography (some of it provided by D. A. Pennebaker), and its conventional narrating voice (Gardner himself), *Marathon* recalls such breakthroughs as *Primary* (1960) and *Crisis: Behind a Presidential Commitment* (1963). *Marathon* remains an engaging film, though what seems most obvious now is the growth of distance running as a participant and spectator sport over the past fifty years: as depicted in *Marathon,* the Boston Marathon seems quaint. Gardner has never been enthusiastic about this kind of sync-sound observational cinema, usually preferring to construct his films as extended montages without assuming sync sound as an essential, but *Marathon* demonstrates his ability to work in what had become, by 1965, an important new direction in non-fiction filmmaking.

Beginning in 1966 Gardner's attention alternated between films on artists and art making and further filmmaking adventures in far-flung cultures. *The Great Sail* (1966) documents the installation of a large Alexander Calder sculpture at MIT. Gardner's fascination with Calder himself and the workers assembling his *La Grande Voile* is in counterpoint with his wry depiction of the smug complaints about the non-artistry of the piece on the part of (mostly student) onlookers; the film seems a premonition of the Maysles brothers' films about Christo's projects, and particularly *Christo's Valley Curtain* (1973) and *Running Fence* (1978). In Gardner's depiction of the event as a kind of American ritual, in this case around the public presence of modern art, the film recalls Ricky Leacock and Joyce Chopra's *Happy Mother's Day* (1963).

In February 1968, Gardner was in Ethiopia, contributing cinematography to what would become Hillary Harris's *The Nuer* (1971), a feature on a group of nomadic cattle herders with, as Gardner would later describe them, "arresting cultural expressiveness," who were famous in anthropological literature but virtually unknown beyond those confines.[19] Approaching this project as part of a larger, Film Study Center–sponsored survey of three forms of indigenous life: hunter-gatherers (*The Hunters*), warrior farmers (*Dead Birds*), and pastoralists (*The Nuer*), Gardner asked Harris to direct the film. Gardner was back in Africa in June 1968 to begin working with the Hamar, another pastoralist group—work that would eventually produce his next feature, *Rivers of Sand* (1974). In between the shooting for *The Nuer* and *Rivers of Sand* and the editing of the latter, Gardner returned to the subject of art, and in particular to Mark Tobey, for *Mark Tobey Abroad* (1973), a lovely portrait of the painter in his later years (Robert Fulton contributed much of the cinematography) and one of Gardner's finest films. *Mark Tobey Abroad* alternates between interviews with Tobey and montage explorations of the painter's Basel apartment and his walks in town—a structure that predicts the organization of *Rivers of Sand,* completed the following year.[20]

Gardner has always been reasonably astute about the cultural currents evolving around him, and the emergence of a powerful feminist transformation in American society in general, and in American academe in particular, during the 1970s is reflected in *Rivers of Sand*. Indeed, Gardner's decision to focus on the Hamar seems to have reflected his own developing gender awareness. *Rivers of Sand* is basically an 85-minute montage, organized according to three general principles, the most basic of which has been described by Gardner himself: "The film was intentionally conceived as a collection of impressions of a frequently fragmentary nature threaded together to comment on the notion of sexual injustice."[21] In this, *Rivers of Sand* echoes Peter Kubelka's *Unsere Afrikareise* (*Our Trip to Africa*, 1966), a Gardner favorite, without that film's exhilarating and brilliant terseness; Bruce Conner's *A Movie* (1959), which recycles a wide range of moving-image material to create a reflection on modern life; and the Russian Artavazd Peleshian's *Nash Vek*

FIGURE 9. Omali Inda addresses the camera in *Rivers of Sand* (1974). Courtesy Robert Gardner.

(*Our Age,* 1982, 1990). Gardner works with something like what Peleshian calls "distance montage," where particular images or sequences and specific sounds and sound sequences are repeated in changing contexts, so that they accumulate meaning as the film develops.[22]

The most obvious organizational principle in *Rivers* is Gardner's intercutting between an extended interview with Omali Inda, a mature Hamar woman who speaks candidly and eloquently about gender relations among the Hamar (fig. 9), and a general survey of Hamar life (Gardner's translators were Ivo Strecker, Jean Lydall (Strecker), who also functioned as anthropologist-advisors, and Eric Berinas). Omali is filmed in close-up (indeed, as she speaks, Gardner often includes a stylistic flourish; he begins in close-up and then zooms in to a closer view of her face). Like N!ai in John Marshall's *N!ai: the Story of a !Kung Woman,* Omali is beautiful and charismatic; indeed, Gardner was later to say "that was more than just an interview. She was an actress in the film, in the sense that she took it over in many ways. I wish I'd let her take it over more."[23] A final organizational principle echoes Flaherty's *Moana:* after Gardner's survey of Hamar life during the first hour or so of the film, *Rivers of Sand* culminates with a major celebration among the Hamar, when young men and young women are initiated into adulthood, and when many of the elements we've grown familiar with during the film come together.

Jay Ruby has reviewed the controversy over *Rivers of Sand* within anthropological literature, reporting that the Streckers were upset with that "the artistic vision of

Gardner as auteur dominated the project with little competent ethnographic assistance."[24] The assumption of the film's critics, however, is that *Rivers* was meant to be a film primarily in service to the field of anthropology. While it is true that all of Gardner's early features were originally understood under this rubric, and while Gardner often represented himself as an ethnographic filmmaker, the elements that seem to define *Rivers of Sand* this way—its look at the cultural practices of a group unfamiliar to most in the industrialized world, Gardner's narrative commentary about particular elements of the culture—are simply major elements in a film that is quite different in tone and purpose, even from *The Hunters* or *Dead Birds*.

I see *Rivers* as an amalgam of feminism and surrealism. Gardner is less interested in providing an ethnographic analysis of Hamar culture (though it would be foolish to pretend that we don't learn anything about the Hamar from the way they look and move, from their living spaces, and from the evidence of the cultural practices we do see) than in using what he believed he had seen in two visits to the Hamar as a way of considering, on the one hand, the nature of gender relations between men and women in most of the world, and on the other, the surreality of "normal" life, regardless of where it is lived.

The Hamar women, as portrayed in *Rivers of Sand*, are second-class citizens: they seem to do a majority of the work (though Gardner does seem to undervalue the labor of men, who tend the herds; we see the men at work from time to time, but there is little emphasis on whatever challenges they must face); they own nothing; they do not choose their marital partners; and they are married for life, even if their husbands die. Most obviously, the women must put up with a variety of forms of physical abuse, some of them ritualized. Gardner focuses in particular on the women's job of grinding grain, which is both a part of everyday life and symbolic of gender relations: at the very beginning of *Rivers of Sand* Omali says, "A time comes when a Hamar woman leaves her father's house to live with her husband. It's like smoothing the grindstone with a piece of quartz. The quartz is his hand, his whip, and you are beaten and beaten." We see and hear women at work grinding millet as a motif throughout the film, and in each instance, we are reminded of what Gardner sees as its larger implications. A second, related motif is the ritual whipping of women, which we get hints of early in *Rivers* and then see in some detail during the ceremonies that conclude the film. From what Gardner shows us, a woman ritually requests a man to whip her, and when she is struck, she is expected to act as if the whipping, which is powerful enough to create open wounds, has not fazed her.[25] A third, related motif is the decoration of women with ankle and wrist bracelets: seen as status symbols of beauty by the Hamar, they evoke the shackles of slaves.

In many ways, the gender relations Omali describes echo those Gardner would have been familiar with from his own society, and from his own life. As he told Ilisa Barbash:

Indeed, *Rivers of Sand* does owe something to the climate of thought about the situation of women in the late 60s, but it also owes something to what was happening in my own life as a father and husband. Here I would like to say I think this film is not just about how women feel or behave but also about what happens to men as they make their lives with women. I made the film at a time when my own long-standing marriage was coming to an end and when there were accusations, if not good evidence, of certain kinds of abuses—I don't mean physical abuses—I mean troubling circumstances which were distorting our life together. I would go off for a long time to make a film. For example, I left everyone at home for six or seven months when I went to do the shooting for *Dead Birds*. And that's not fair. It caught up with me and it seemed quite natural and helpful to be going about the making of *Rivers of Sand* at that particular time.[26]

It seems clear that for Gardner, shooting and editing *Rivers* was both an experience in itself and a way of using the film production process as a way of coming to terms with the transformations occurring within his personal life. As an audience, our experience of *Rivers* occurs on both levels: we explore Omali's version of her own experiences as a Hamar woman, as contextualized by Gardner; and we experience Gardner's wrestle with the question of how fully what seem to be the gender experiences of Hamar women and men match the experiences of American women and men, including his own.

For much of *Rivers of Sand* Omali seems to echo the American feminists of the late 1960s and early 1970s—indeed, her testimony evokes the many feminist films of the 1970s and 1980s in which women testified about their cultural oppression—but near the conclusion of the film, her narration takes what feels like a surprising turn. Omali describes to us, and speaks to Hamar girls about, the ritual of removing the two central incisors from the lower jaws of girls—theoretically to demonstrate Hamar girls' courage and provide what the Hamar consider a beautiful look. Omali indicates that removal of the teeth is not required, but it is clearly preferred, and her comments are supportive of the ritual. Omali's apparent approval of what seems to us still another form of oppression is confirmed at the conclusion of *Rivers of Sand* when she says, "Beating is our custom; we were born with it. . . . So how can it be bad?" Although on one level, this seeming acceptance of oppression as normal—something to be complained about, perhaps, but not eliminated—is reminiscent of a similar pattern of self-abnegation and acceptance of lower status that feminists have challenged in many Western countries in recent decades, it is also an instance of what Gardner sees as a larger reality, and not just for the Hamar.

All organized social life seems to involve strange combinations of logic and absurdity. This is clear in *Dead Birds,* where ritual war seems to have no particular function other than to provide an organizational framework for two Dani groups; it is clear in *Rivers of Sand,* where women seem to accept forms of oppression that seem to do little but provide a form of social continuity; and it is clear in American society, where we build ever-more-expensive new forms of weaponry to maintain peace and where each generation seems to find new ways of colonizing the body in order to create societal standards of "beauty." In *Rivers* Gardner frequently shows several male elders spraying coffee with their lips, seemingly in order to maintain the spiritual health of their community. As presented in *Rivers,* this ritual is rather comic, though when it is juxtaposed with the continual labor of women, which it always is in the film, this all-male "spiritual" activity seems a further confirmation of the gender inequity of Hamar society. The coffee ritual is also representative of religious rituals around the world that depend on what seem (at least to nonbelievers, and perhaps even to some of those who profess their faith in these religions) to be utterly absurd activities—eating a wafer and drinking a bit of grape juice and "believing" it's the body and blood of Jesus Christ; wearing a beard and a particular form of *payot* (sidelock) in order to conform to a book of the Old Testament; refusing to use electricity or automobile transportation in a culture where they are ubiquitous—as a means of maintaining a sense of community and continuity. Indeed, the more obvious the apparent absurdity of these activities, the more commitment they require, the more faith they seem to demonstrate, and the more respect they demand, both from believers and nonbelievers. This strange surreality of social life has been explored by a number of filmmakers over the decades: Buñuel, most obviously of course, but Gardner too, especially in *Dead Birds, Rivers of Sand,* and *Deep Hearts* (1981).

Like *Rivers of Sand, Deep Hearts* seems, at least to current audiences, focused on the issue of gender—though in a different sense. During the 1970s the feminist project of rethinking gender relations between men and women was increasingly interwoven with what we have come to understand as "Queer," and particularly the Queer understanding of gender as a form of performance, a set of distinctions and practices not determined by sex (or not entirely by sex), but largely by cultural assumptions and societal expectations, and reflective of the complexity and contradictions of personal identity. Few scenes in any motion picture demonstrate this idea more effectively than the opening moments of *Deep Hearts,* when a large group of men is seen in a long line, moving sensuously in unison and chanting a dirge, outfitted in facial makeup and dress that, from our perspective, seem obviously feminine (fig. 10). These are the Bororo Fulani, a nomadic society located in the central Niger Republic, at "the Gerewol, an occasion during the rainy season when two competing lineages come together to choose the most 'perfect' Borroro male. It is something of a physical and moral beauty contest in which the winner, selected by a maiden of the opposing lineage, is acclaimed the 'bull.'"[27]

It seems clear that in both *Dead Birds* and *Rivers of Sand* Gardner chose the Dani and the Hamar as subjects because the nature of these cultures resonated with issues he himself was working through; making these films was his way of

FIGURE 10. Two Bororo Fulani men, looking beautiful, in Robert
Gardner's *Deep Hearts* (1981). Courtesy Robert Gardner.

personally coming to terms with warfare and with gender relations between the
sexes. The opening of *Deep Hearts* foregrounds Gardner's fascination with the
"cross-dressing" Fulani men and presumably his interest in coming to terms with
a deeper cultural questioning of gender assumptions. While this theme does not
seem to have been foremost in his consciousness during the month he spent
shooting in the Sahel region of sub-Saharan Africa—a month that, judging from
Gardner's journal entries, was almost entirely unpleasant—Gardner's journal
does make clear that what most powerfully caught his eye about the Gerewol was
seeing "accomplished males applying rouge and lipstick under a full moon."[28] And
like other cinematic contributions to the evolution of Queerness—Jean Genet's
Un Chant d'amour (1952), Kenneth Anger's *Inauguration of the Pleasure Dome*
(1954), Jack Smith's *Flaming Creatures* (1963)—the finished film destabilizes gender, in this case by revealing that these men, who live in a nomadic culture that
faces considerable challenges from its desert environment, define themselves in
part by competing to see which of them can be the supreme exemplar of sensual
beauty. For an American filmgoer, it is difficult not to think of Jennie Livingston's
Paris Is Burning (1991)—despite the obvious differences in cultural contexts of the
Black and Latino transgender ball culture documented in the Livingston film and
the Gerewol—or the Gerewol's surreal inverse in American culture: the Miss
America pageant.

The overall structure of *Deep Hearts* evokes that of *Rivers of Sand,* though in this instance the dancing of the men is the central motif: Gardner intercuts between this dancing and other aspects of Bororo Fulani life, many of which provide a clearer context for the dancing: early in the film a woman is scouring what look like golden pots, which, later in the film, are revealed to be decorative tubes worn on one woman's legs during that part of the Gerewol ceremony when several women indicate who the "bull" is. Like *Rivers of Sand, Deep Hearts* culminates in a large-scale celebration, and it concludes with the ritual activities that allow the various Bororo Fulani clans to leave the large gathering and move back into their nomadic lives.

Gardner's decision to collaborate with Robert Fulton on *Deep Hearts* seems to have had a considerable impact on the compositional style of the film. The camera is a good bit more mobile in *Deep Hearts* than it is in any previous Gardner film; in the catalog produced for an Anthology Film Archives retrospective of Gardner's work in 1995, Thomas W. Cooper describes Fulton's camera work as full of "moving point-of-view shots taken from irregular heights and angles while Fulton was running, speed-walking, or 'dancing' with his camera. . . . Fultonian motion images propel us across sand, under camels, and close to the earth, as if from a running child's perspective."[29]

While Fulton's camerawork is often engaging as camerawork, it does not seem particularly relevant to the events portrayed, but despite Cooper's contention that Gardner has normally added visible cinematic effects "only when they best served the film's intentions,"[30] I see this gap between content and style as less than unusual in Gardner's early films. In *Dead Birds, Rivers of Sand,* and *Deep Hearts* Gardner sometimes includes moments of stop-action and other formal devices that are not motivated by anything in the action. These devices seem to me little more than affectations—"arty," rather than artful—and I suspect they are a product of Gardner's decades-long wrestle with the idea of being both documentarian and poetic filmmaker. This struggle has also been reflected in Gardner's use of narration. Film by film, at least in those of his films that Gardner seems to take most seriously, narration has become less pervasive.[31] Early in his career, Gardner was under the influence of the poetic voice-overs of such films as *Night Mail* and Basil Wright's *Song of Ceylon* (1934) and presumably of Marshall's narration for *The Hunters;*[32] but in part as a result of his own increasing dissatisfaction with his own voice-overs in *Dead Birds* and *Rivers of Sand,* and perhaps because of the increasing prestige of detached observational cinema and its proponents' hostility toward the overdeterminism of narration of any kind, Gardner has used voice-over less and less. *Deep Hearts* is less fully narrated than *Dead Birds* and *Rivers of Sand;* nevertheless, the voice-over Gardner does include is often less than persuasive—it too seems something of an affectation. It would not be until *Forest of Bliss* (1986) that Gardner would finish a feature devoid of visual or poetic affectations.

ROBERT FULTON: *REALITY'S INVISIBLE*—
"SERIOUS PLAYING AROUND"

In 1971 Gardner hired Robert Fulton (the great grandson of the inventor of the steam-boat), to teach filmmaking at the Carpenter Center for the 1971–72 year; and during his brief tenure, Fulton produced *Reality's Invisible,* one of the remarkable experimental documentaries of the era—and (as is true of Fulton's entire oeuvre) one of the most underappreciated. Fulton would go on to make a substantial body of work—though as yet, no one has compiled anything like a definitive Fulton filmography—and to make major contributions to films by others, including Gardner: Fulton contributed cinematography to *Mark Tobey Abroad* (1972) and to both *Deep Hearts* (1981) and *Ika Hands* (1988). He taught at the School of the Art Institute of Chicago from 1974 to 1976, where he vied with Stan Brakhage for the most remarkable commute (like Brakhage, Fulton commuted from Colorado, but unlike Brakhage, who traveled by train, Fulton flew his own plane). Filmmaker and longtime Canyon Cinema director Dominic Angerame, then a student at the Art Institute School, remembers Fulton as a powerful influence.[33] Until his death in 2002, Fulton remained a productive film artist, working both on personal films and on sponsored projects, and he was widely known as an accomplished aerial cinematographer. Indeed, Fulton died when his Cessna crashed during a storm near Scranton, Pennsylvania.

Reality's Invisible was Fulton's eighth film (if we trust his own informal filmography). By the time he produced it, he had won Cine Golden Eagles for his cinematography on *Outward Bound* (1968), *Portrait of Paul Soldner* (1969), *The Great Ski Chase* (1969), and *Nzuri: East Africa* (1970);[34] and his television commercial for Eastern Airlines, *The Wings of Man* (1971; narrated by Orson Welles), was, according to Fulton, "estimated to have been seen by over four hundred million people and is considered the longest running commercial in the history of television."[35] According to Fulton's filmography, *Path of Cessation,* completed in 1972, is the first film he produced and directed (he also did the cinematography and the editing). It is an evocative portrait of Tibetan religion, beginning with an 8-minute, black-and-white shot of a Nepalese monastery waking up, framed inventively so that we see individuals from a distance through windows and doorways as the morning's mundane events begin to unfold. The second and third sections of the film are in color: a sequence of mountain imagery leads to a shot of a bridge that provides a transition into a montage of color superimpositions of mountains, a stream, animals, people, time-lapsed clouds . . . *Path of Cessation* ends with a group of monks chanting, superimposed with imagery of mountains. Fulton's fascination with Buddhism continued to inform his filmmaking in the following years, including the hour-long *Reality's Invisible,* his portrait of life and creativity at the Carpenter Center, the facility designed by Le Corbusier and completed in 1963 (it is the only Le Corbusier building in North America).

FIGURE 11. Robert Fulton in motion, filming. Courtesy Robert Gardner.

In keeping with the Carpenter Center itself, which is described on the Center's website as a reflection of Le Corbusier's belief that "a building devoted to the visual arts must be an experience of freedom and unbound creativity" and must represent a "'synthesis of the arts,' a union of architecture with painting, sculpture," Fulton's film provides a cinematic experience as far from the conventional as the Carpenter Center is from the Harvard buildings that surround it. Indeed, the experience of *Reality's Invisible* often verges on the overwhelming; it combines myriad kinds of imagery and approaches to shooting with dizzying editing to provide a phantasmagoria of life in and around the building and a paean to unbounded cinematic freedom (fig. 11). *Reality's Invisible* has the celebratory energy of Dziga Vertov's *The Man with a Movie Camera* (1929) but without the structure provided by that City Symphony's composite day—though as *Reality's Invisible* unfolds, we do begin to recognize a variety of motifs in addition to the Carpenter Center building itself: particular individuals (including Robert Gardner), kinds of activities, editing rhythms.

Fulton begins the film with a series of brief shots—in a small stream with light flickering on the surface, a flattened Budweiser can floats by; this is followed by several flecks of light, then by a lovely color shot of sunrise; then a brief passage of light flickering through a woods, apparently filmed (in black and white) from a moving vehicle—and with this halting statement, spoken by Fulton himself: "I just feel like there's a lot that I have to say, and I haven't been able to say it yet. And it won't be . . . and I don't want to write it, because I'm . . . and I try to paint it, but maybe I could, maybe I could film it" ("could film it" is matched with the flickering light through the trees). Again, as in *Path of Cessation,* Fulton signals that this is the "morning" of his personal filmmaking.

Fulton's montage in *Reality's Invisible* combines three forms of dense editing. First, any particular strand of visual investigation tends to be made up of constant shifts in subject and method—and often includes wildly unpredictable camera movements as well as analogously edited sound. Second, Fulton works with a variety of forms of split screen. In a good many instances the film frame is divided into four separate images (and sometimes into three or two), within each of which a different image is visible; sometimes, the imagery in one or more of these inner frames is heavily edited. There are also instances where a single frame-within-the-frame is revealing one activity, while the full-frame image around the frame-within-the-frame is revealing another.

Third, *Reality's Invisible* is full of multilayered imagery: we are regularly seeing one image and one kind of image through others. Fulton uses more, and more complex, layers of superimposition than any other filmmaker I am aware of, with the possible exception of Brakhage, whose *Dog Star Man* (1964) seems a particularly important influence on Fulton. Since each layer of Fulton's superimposition is made up of quickly shifting imagery, or is interrupted by split screen imagery of one design or another, the effect of *Reality's Invisible* is something like a cine-kaleidoscope. To use a phrase of one of the students, Fulton's epic celebration of the Carpenter Center is a form of "serious playing around": it reflects on and embodies the high-spirited, deeply serious work and play that the building represents to him.

Reality's Invisible includes on-the-street sync-sound interviews with students in, around, and passing by the Carpenter Center, many of whom question Fulton about what he is doing (in one instance we hear a student say, "Reality's invisible"); and statements by men and women who were teaching in the center or who had considerable connections with it, including then-young filmmakers Richard P. Rogers and Alfred Guzzetti, theorist Rudolf Arnheim, and Gardner, then director of the Carpenter Center, whose presence expands during the final section of the film. Sometimes, the faculty talk directly to Fulton; in other cases, we see them speaking to classes or offering individual students one-on-one critiques. *Reality's Invisible* also documents a very wide range of art projects—in architecture, painting, drawing, sculpture, design, filmmaking—that were underway as Fulton was shooting; these include a variety of forms of experimental animation: passages of visuals and sounds scratched directly into dark leader, colorful sequences of imagery painted directly onto clear leader, cutout animation, "light writing" (that is, filming lights at night with a gestural camera so that streaks and curlicues of color fill the screen—it is unclear to me whether these sequences were filmmaking experiments that Fulton conducted himself or works by Carpenter Center students that he recycled into his film (my guess is the latter). And of course, the Carpenter Center itself is featured as an artwork; Fulton visually explores and documents every facet of the building, seemingly in every way he can think of.

The soundtrack is analogous to the image track, a mix of sync-sound statements by individuals, moments of silence, and passages of music, especially jazz (Fulton features jazz saxophone played by a musician we see several times during the film). In several instances the combination of freeform jazz and Fulton's wild montage results in a kind of freeform "visual music." And from time to time, Fulton includes sequences of several different speakers saying bits of what become constructed meta-statements: for example, a series of voices say "gradual narrowing down"/"two-dimensional experience"/"no continuity, no connection"/"live with it"/"my image"/"just exploded." These meta-statements are prescient of language experiments that Abigail Child would include in her multipartite *Is This What You Were Born For?* (1981–89).[36]

From time to time we hear Fulton speaking behind the camera. When one young man asks what kind of picture is going to be on the screen when Fulton is done with his film, Fulton replies, "You tell me"; and when a young woman asks, "Can you tell me anything more about this?," Fulton says, "Not much." And in a few instances we hear Fulton in voice-over, presumably commenting on the filmmaking process he's involved in: "Correlating what you see with what you do with your hands. Considering what's important and what isn't. Flowing with the movement of the universe as opposed to against it. All the natural movements. You can't talk about a beginning because everything is circular, but all those things interrelate. It doesn't begin without any of those." In his editing, Fulton does maximize "flow"; indeed he positions his exploration of the Carpenter Center and those who are studying and working there within a much larger context, so that their activities are seen as part of "the movement of the universe." Not only does Fulton include views of the larger Harvard campus, including the green areas that lie near the Carpenter Center, but in frequent instances he embeds his imagery of art and artists within a much broader panorama: he films mountains from a plane; there are frequent shots of a woods, and of ocean surf, and imagery of a stream running, and of a field of grain. What goes on in this center of artistic creativity is seen as an extension of the larger world of natural forces.

One can hope that *Reality's Invisible*—and Fulton's work in general—will become more widely known and appreciated. At the moment, the film exists in a single 16mm print housed at the Harvard Film Archive. Fortunately, it is also available, in a reasonably good version, as part of a discussion with Robert Gardner in April 1973 that was recorded for a new television experiment, *Screening Room.*

SCREENING ROOM: MIDNIGHT MOVIES

In the late 1960s, Gardner was part of a group of Boston area businessmen and educators who took over Boston's channel 5, an ABC affiliate, in order to offer the region a more educationally engaging alternative to standard television programming. After the takeover, Gardner initiated and hosted the long-running interview show, *Screening Room,* which presented films by independent filmmakers, contextualized by discussions with the filmmakers (and sometimes visiting scholars). The first *Screening Room* episode was an interview with John Whitney Sr., aired in November 1972; the series lasted until 1981. Around a hundred episodes were aired, and thirty of them are currently available on DVD from Studio7Arts. *Screening Room* was dedicated to a reasonably wide range of independent cinema; and Gardner's selection of *Screening Room* programs for the original Documentary Educational Resources release reflected this: included were independent and experimental animators Robert Breer, George Griffin, Faith and John Hubley, Derek Lamb, Caroline Leaf and Mary Beams, Jan Lenica, Suzan Pitt; documentarians Les Blank, Emile de Antonio, Hillary Harris, Ricky Leacock, Alan Lomax, Richard P. Rogers, and Jean Rouch; and a range of avant-garde filmmakers: Bruce Baillie, Stan Brakhage, James Broughton, Ed Emshwiller, Hollis Frampton, Robert Fulton, Peter Hutton, Standish Lawder, Jonas Mekas, Yvonne Rainer, and Michael Snow.[37] Each *Screening Room* episode intercuts between the presentation of short films or excerpts from longer films and Gardner and the filmmaker (and sometimes other guests), sitting in chairs around a coffee table, talking about the work.[38]

Screening Room remains interesting on a number of levels—some of these, I assume, not originally anticipated. As educational entertainments, the best episodes tend to be those during which complete short films were shown—especially when these films are reasonably well served by presentation on television—and when the filmmaker guests were comfortable speaking about their work. The inaugural episode, with John Whitney Sr., is an excellent introduction to his work. The first Derek Lamb program (June 1973) is an informative introduction to animation in general and to Lamb's engaging teaching style. The James Broughton and Robert Breer shows (April 1977 and November 1976, respectively) remain enjoyable, in large measure because Broughton and Breer were articulate and comfortable speaking about their films. The Jean Rouch *Screening Room* (July 1980) provides a rare and valuable moment with a major force in the development of provocational filmmaking and of ethnographic documentary. And the first Stan Brakhage *Screening Room* (June 1973; Brakhage returned in June 1980) is an excellent record of Brakhage's legendary passion and clarity about his work; indeed, his reaction to the broadcast of *Window Water Baby Moving* (1959) remains poignant: immediately after the film is aired, Brakhage comments, "My god, isn't that wonderful that that can finally be shown on television. I'm so happy about that."

To Gardner's credit, *Screening Room* aired a good many films—*Window Water Baby Moving* and Jean Rouch's *Les Maîtres Fous* (*Mad Masters*, 1954)—that, even today, are often considered outrageous and would be unlikely to find their way to television audiences. This was possible in large measure because *Screening Room* was aired at midnight, though in 1970s Boston, this did not mean no one was watching: the *Screening Room* audience was estimated at a quarter of a million people, many of them students at the Boston area's many colleges and universities. Indeed, Brakhage's excitement at having *Window Water Baby Moving* aired is poignant not only because Brakhage had waited fourteen years to see the film reach a television audience, but because his implicit assumption that the film could now reach a wider public via broadcast has not been confirmed; these days, *Window Water Baby Moving* is still seen almost exclusively in educational institutions; and even its release on the *By Brakhage* DVD hardly guarantees a large public audience.

Demanding in a very different sense, the excerpts from Michael Snow's *"Rameau's Nephew" by Diderot (Thanx to Dennis Young) by Wilma Schoen* (1974) that were the focus of a March 1977 *Screening Room* would confound most any viewer not familiar with Snow's earlier work; and one passage from that film, of a nude man and a nude woman, each standing and peeing into a bucket, was the only moment from a *Screening Room* episode that was censored: a black rectangle was superimposed over the offending body parts, though, despite this, the shot remains effective and amusing because of the sound of the urine hitting the buckets: the focus of *"Rameau's Nephew,"* after all, is sound's relationship to image in cinema! Gardner remembers "getting called around two o'clock in the morning from the head of the station: 'Jesus, Gardner, are you trying to get our license taken away! A movie with somebody peeing in a bucket!' I said, 'It's a work of art!' He thought that was a big joke."[39]

From our perspective in the 2010s, we can forget that during the 1960s and 1970s, filmmakers often needed to develop their own technology for making the films they were interested in producing. Few independents had access to sound studios or to high-grade equipment. The result was that individuals jerry-rigged a variety of systems, some of which proved quite effective. During the early years of *Screening Room*, Gardner often asked filmmaker guests to bring their filmmaking equipment to Boston and to demonstrate its uses. Standish Lawder demonstrated his homemade optical printer in the January 1973 episode; in the March 1973 episode, Hillary Harris showed how he created a variety of effects with a 36-inch, 1000mm lens (a camera was mounted onto the lens) and how his time-lapse shooting was done; and in June 1973 Ricky Leacock, with the assistance of Jon Rosenfeld and Al Meklenberg, demonstrated the Super-8mm, sync-sound, cableless rig he had designed for student film courses and hoped to market widely, including in underdeveloped areas of the world. Robert Fulton's first visit to

Screening Room in April 1973 was largely dedicated to his film *Reality's Invisible,* an homage to the Carpenter Center, but Fulton also demonstrated the unusual approach to camera movement, partly balletic and partly athletic, that characterizes much of his work. Gardner's interest in the do-it-yourself aspects of independent filmmaking in the early 1970s, as film was working its way into academe, have become a useful historical resource, in some cases, perhaps, the only motion picture documentation of this dimension of some filmmakers' activities.

Some *Screening Room* episodes are interesting not because they are effective or entertaining television programs, but because, forty years later, they provide an index of the kinds of challenges that so many of us faced during the 1970s as we were first coming to terms with radically new approaches to cinema; and because they provide a glance at the ways in which independent filmmakers understood and related to media exposure during a complex and volatile decade. While Gardner plays the knowledgeable, worldly host, it is obvious as he engages Michael Snow and Yvonne Rainer (March 1977) that he has no clear idea of what they mean to accomplish in their work; his questions and comments are quietly desperate attempts to relate their films to filmmaking approaches with which he is familiar. The same is true of his second Brakhage show in 1980, where Brakhage's increasingly abstract approach seems to stymie Gardner. Even in the case of the Hollis Frampton *Screening Room* (January 1977), an excellent record of Frampton as theorist and raconteur, it is evident that Gardner remains wedded to the idea of cinema as the production of well-crafted meaningful or beautiful artifacts and/or of autobiographical expressions of the artist. The idea that cinema itself can be a theoretical enterprise in which film artists explore their fascinations with little regard for the immediate reactions of audiences, seems foreign to Gardner. At the same time, his persistence in inviting filmmakers whose work was a challenge both to him and to his audiences reveals a commitment to a broad sense of film history, a commitment honored by Anthology Film Archives in 2008 with one of that year's Film Preservation Honors awards.

During the 1970s a good many independent filmmakers, and particularly avant-garde filmmakers, were suspicious of both the commercial media and academe; and some filmmakers were resistant to speaking about their work. This sometimes produced *Screening Room* episodes that can only have frustrated the host. Despite Gardner's obvious admiration of the Polish animator Jan Lenica, Lenica was a difficult, largely unresponsive guest. Even Robert Fulton, a Gardner favorite and lifelong close friend, seems awkward during his 1973 visit to *Screening Room.* And the Bruce Baillie episode (April 1973) begins without Baillie, who is late for the show—a bit defiantly, one assumes: when Baillie does arrive, he barely utters a word (Gerald O'Grady, who Gardner had asked to participate in the episode, works at speaking for Baillie, but comes across as stuffy and pretentious). Adding insult to injury, at the end of the show Baillie critiques *Screening Room* itself and his co-hosts: "Without this kind of classroom obligation to surround the thing itself [by "thing itself" Baillie means filmmaking], maybe we in this country can lead to some good broadcasting. I am thinking about TV a lot." Despite Baillie's critique, however, *Screening Room* was, all in all, a worthy experiment in television: Gardner's willingness to include an unusually broad range of cinematic accomplishment; his willingness to pay filmmakers for their appearances on the show; and his courage in airing films that few others would have brought to public audiences make it a distinctive contribution to the history of independent cinema.[40]

That the first major film Gardner completed after the nearly ten-year run of *Screening Room* was *Forest of Bliss* (1986) seems no accident. Like most filmmakers of his generation, Gardner had entered filmmaking without professional training and without anything like a coherent immersion in film history. Nevertheless, by the end of the 1960s he found himself in a position of some responsibility with regard to the production and exhibition of film as director of Harvard's Film Study Center and of film operations at the Carpenter Center. *Screening Room* was, on one hand, an outgrowth of his professional life at Harvard, and, on the other, a form of self-education. If he couldn't always make sense of what some of the filmmakers he hosted were doing, he clearly learned from their commitment to their own ways of doing things and to the films they wanted to make, regardless of what others might think about these films and regardless of how these new cinematic forms might conflict with traditional expectations. Early on, Gardner's own films were weakened by his sense that to be a film artist he needed to imitate what a poet might do or what an accomplished film artist might have done, and the result was a tendency toward affectation. Gardner seems to have approached *Forest of Bliss* with a new kind of confidence and from within a more complete awareness of film history. The film would become a landmark contribution to an important genre—a genre claimed by both documentary and avant-garde film.

CITY SYMPHONY: *FOREST OF BLISS*

The City Symphony—the cinematic depiction of a composite day in the life of a major city—has become one of the most recognizable and prolific forms of independent cinema. After a series of premonitions, including many Lumière films about Lyon and Paris and much documentation of Manhattan during the 1890s as well as, two decades later, Charles Sheeler's and Paul Strand's *Manhatta* (1921), the form emerged with a triad of European features: Alberto Cavalcanti's *Rien que les heures* (*Nothing but Time*, 1926); Walther Ruttmann's *Berlin: Sinfonie einer Grosstadt* (*Berlin: Symphony of a Big City*, 1927), the film that gave the form its name; and Dziga Vertov's *The Man with a Movie Camera* (*Cheloveks kinoapparatom*, 1929). Each of these films focuses on the life of a modern city—respectively,

Paris, Berlin, and the post–Revolutionary Russian "city," a composite of Moscow, Kiev, and Odessa—as it unfolds from before dawn until night (or the following dawn); and in each instance, the city chosen is understood as the quintessential city of a particular culture: France, Germany, communist Russia. Within this general formal contour, however, the films vary a good deal. While *Rien que les heures* seems ambivalent about the modern metropolis, *Berlin* and *The Man with a Movie Camera* reveal a fascination with industrialization, and Vertov's film in particular is an all-out celebration of modernization and cinema's crucial place within modernization's transformation of a traditional culture. By the end of the 1920s, the City Symphony had become one of the two major forms of nonfiction filmmaking, the other being its inverse: the depiction of preindustrial cultures and ways of life: *Nanook of the North* (1921) and *Moana* (1926), Merian C. Cooper's and Ernest B. Schoedsack's *Grass* (1925).

The City Symphony soon became a mainstay in American independent cinema. The early 1930s saw the completion of Jay Leyda's *A Bronx Morning* (1931), Irving Browning's *City of Contrasts* (1931), and Herman G. Weinberg's *Autumn Fire* (1933), all of them focusing on New York; and during the 1940s, Rudy Burckhardt began what was to become a long series of New York City films. The following decades added Frank Stauffacher's City Symphony of San Francisco, *Notes on the Port of St. Francis* (1952); *Weegee's New York* (c. 1952), by Weegee (Arthur Fellig) and Amos Vogel; Francis Thompson's *N.Y., N.Y.* (1957); Marie Menken's *Go! Go! Go!* (1964); and Hilary Harris's *Organism* (1975), as well as a wide range of other forms of city film. More recent years have seen the appearance of a series of remarkable feature-length City Symphonies that, in scope and accomplishment, compare favorably with the European films of the 1920s: most notably, Pat O'Neill's pop surrealist depiction of Los Angeles, *Water and Power* (1989); Spike Lee's day in the life of a Bedford-Stuyvesant neighborhood in Brooklyn, *Do the Right Thing* (1989); and Robert Gardner's *Forest of Bliss*. These last two radically revise our sense of what the City Symphony can do.

Ruttmann and Vertov firmly established the City Symphony form by celebrating the modern city as culmination of the industrial revolution, and whatever reservations Ruttmann had about the problems that industrial progress might also be creating (Vertov seems to have had none) were minor compared with the excitement of the speed and power of the new, mechanized society.[41] This attitude has characterized nearly all subsequent city films. I have argued elsewhere that Spike Lee's fiction feature is the finest American City Symphony—though to be fair, *Forest of Bliss* is equally deserving of this designation. While Lee's insight was to see that the intermixture of people that the mechanized city had produced was of more interest than the mechanical wonders of industry themselves, Gardner's approach in *Forest of Bliss* is to question the very notion that energy and excitement are products of industrial transformation by delving into a very particular cultural tradition and embodying it within a spectacular and beautiful form. While other filmmakers who have contributed to the City Symphony have documented their own cities or the cities they see as emblematic of their own cultures, Gardner focuses on Benares (Vāranāsi), India, a city utterly distinct from either Boston or any other American metropolis. However, what we find familiar is determined by what we find strange, and one can also understand Gardner's fascination with Benares, which he sees as wildly different from any city he has known, as fully a reflection of his American-ness as is Lee's depiction of Brooklyn.

Forest of Bliss is exciting and full of energy (and it produced an energized response from the academic anthropological community)[42]—but not because of the transformations of modern life. Indeed, Gardner is at pains to eliminate evidence of modern technology from his vision of Benares. He cannot do this entirely, of course (and perhaps wouldn't if he could): early in the film, in the background of several shots, we see a major bridge with automobile traffic, and in a few instances the film depicts street scenes that include some automobile traffic or the sound of distant traffic. In general, however, Gardner's fascination is with the way in which Benares has continued to emblemize tradition: this city may be the quintessence of a culture, but it is interesting precisely because of those elements that are *not* modern and do *not* adhere to modern assumptions about what a city should be (fig. 12). While nearly all City Symphonies celebrate life, *Forest of Bliss* celebrates a culture's ways of dealing with mortality and with the dead themselves: the focus of Benares (or at least Gardner's Benares) is the burning of bodies and/ or the disposal of the dead in the Ganges: that is, on the city's cremation grounds, which are sometimes called the "Forest of Bliss" in sacred texts.[43] In the end, however, the film's very distinctiveness from other city films allows *Forest of Bliss* to function as a metaphor for the inevitability of mortality and the ways in which human beings come to terms with it.

The focus of *Forest of Bliss* is the many rituals that surround the disposal of corpses; in fact, the daily round of Benares is depicted as an ongoing meta-ritual, made up of countless ritualized activities. This meta-ritual is depicted in an immense montage, held together in three of ways: by the temporal trajectory of dawn to dawn, by the repetition of particular details of image and sound; and by the presence of three men. As in other City Symphonies, *Forest of Bliss* creates the illusion of a single day, clearly a composite day, filmed over a period of months during 1984 when Gardner lived in Benares on a Fulbright Fellowship. The daily cycle is most evident at the beginning and end of the film, though it is clear that particular activities occur during specific moments throughout the day.

Within the structure provided by the movement from morning to night and the arrival of another morning, Gardner develops a wealth of image and sound motifs: dogs, marigolds, men carrying corpses, stairways, birds flying, boats passing on the river, men transporting wood and sand onto and off of boats, people sweeping

FIGURE 12. Man rowing along the Ganges, from Robert Gardner's *Forest of Bliss* (1986). Courtesy Robert Gardner.

with small brooms, and the sounds that accompany these tasks: men chanting, the loads of wood crashing onto cement, hammering, the ritual ringing of bells and striking of gongs, the squeak of oars on wooden boats—*Forest of Bliss* is truly a City *Symphony:* its sound montage is as complex and as memorable as its imagery. These visual and auditory motifs accumulate and often intersect and interact (various animals eat marigolds and spiritual men use them in ritual activities), so that, over the 90 minutes of the film, a powerful sense of being inside this strange city evolves. Earlier in this chapter, I mentioned Artavazd Peleshian's "distance montage" in conjunction with *Rivers of Sand,* but *Forest of Bliss* is an even better example of the approach; indeed, it exemplifies distance montage as well as Peleshian's own films.

A final structuring device involves three men, each of whom is seen periodically through *Forest of Bliss,* though none of them is identified within the film. On Gardner's website, they are described as "a healer of great geniality who attends the pained and troubled [this is Mithai Lal]"; "a baleful and untouchable King of the Great Cremation Ground who sells the sacred fire [the Dom Raja]"; and an unusually conscientious priest who keeps a small shrine on the banks of the Ganges

[Ragul Pandit]." As Gardner indicates in his book-length conversation with Ákos Östör, these three "main figures are never portrayed in any depth. In fact, they are never even named. But they do get sufficient attention to emerge as fairly well-rounded individuals."[44] The men and their various activities through the day become another set of motifs that also intersect at times: the class difference between Mithai Lal and the Dom Raja is sometimes emphasized in the editing.

Gardner's compositional strategy in *Forest of Bliss* contributes much to the epic quality of the film. Gardner's Benares is a complex maze of tiny, crowded streets that open onto the broad river, the many architectural approaches to the shore, and the myriad activities taking place on and near the river. As *Forest of Bliss* develops, each of these activities grows increasingly familiar, and we understand them more and more fully in their multileveled relation to one another. One particularly obvious instance is the early images of the making of what look to be ladders; why would the men be making ladders? Soon it becomes clear that in fact these are devices on which dead bodies are carried—though the original assumption that these are ladders remains implicitly relevant, suggesting the near-universal desire for transcendence of mortality. A typical composition late in *Forest of Bliss* involves activities taking place in close-up and at various distances from the camera simultaneously, as well as implicit intellectual intersections of multiple motifs. In this, Gardner's City Symphony is reminiscent of Warren Sonbert's montage films, where each image is a nexus of motif and implication.

As is true in *Dead Birds, Forest of Bliss* is punctuated by moments of shock value. The précis before the opening title and director credit concludes with a horrifying moment when several dogs attack, and presumably kill, another dog (the impact of this moment comes from the screams of the dying dog). And at various times, we see decaying corpses floating in the Ganges (a dog eating one; another, ass-up in the water), a dead donkey and a dead dog being dragged down the steps to the river, a dog seemingly so weak it can barely climb stairs, another lying dead among garbage—this in addition to the many corpses being burned and the bones collected, an old woman in a hospice on the verge of death (we see her a few moments later, dead, on her way to the cremation ground), the bodies of two children launched into the river. . . . These shots create a nervous attention and a kind of dread.

This dread is, no doubt, the residue of Gardner's confrontations of death and dying in Benares. In the conversation between Gardner and Stan Brakhage, an extra on the most recent DVD edition of *Forest of Bliss*, Brakhage, who claims to have seen the film fifty or sixty times, invokes *The Act of Seeing with One's Own Eyes* (1971), his shocking film of autopsies performed in a Pittsburgh morgue, in commending Gardner on having the courage and stamina to make his film, courage presumably not only to shoot on and around the cremation grounds in

FIGURE 13. Men barely visible, rowing on the Ganges in early morning fog, from Robert Gardner's *Forest of Bliss* (1986). Courtesy Robert Gardner.

Benares, but in owning the imagery and shaping it into a feature film.[45] Of course, the dread created by this imagery is *our* confrontation of mortality within the film experience, though throughout *Forest of Bliss* this shock value is carefully balanced by the film's many remarkably beautiful shots: boats in the mist, a field of marigolds, a gorgeous sunset . . . moments reminiscent of the work of Peter Hutton, Bruce Baillie, and James Benning (fig. 13).

The unusual balance of the horrifying and the gorgeous in *Forest of Bliss* is itself a kind of metaphor. It reflects the reality of Gardner's Benares, and it offers a theoretical perspective on the art of cinema. Throughout his filmmaking, Gardner's primary fascination has been with what he sees as the two ways in which individuals and societies come to terms with mortality: through ritual and the making of art. The emphasis in Gardner's depiction of Benares is, of course, ritual. From what we see, the industry of the entire city is in service of the various rituals surrounding death. Further, the daily cycle evoked in this film, and in all City Symphonies, foregrounds the idea that the very existence of cities requires that they function as immense, complex rituals that render what may at first look like chaos into a precise and productive order. In other words, Benares itself *is* a daily ritual, and the only way in which it differs from other cities—and for that matter from other social units of whatever density—is that its primary industry is (or at least in *Forest of Bliss* seems to be) a continual direct confrontation with the materiality of death itself. Wherever we are and whoever we are, our daily round is our way of ignoring and avoiding mortality and the implication that in the long run death renders everything meaningless. Gardner's Benares is a holy city because its denizens have the courage to face the fact of mortality while simultaneously transcending its implications: they continue to live and work and to demonstrate, day after day, that the fact of death instigates the passion of life.

On another level, our cinematic experience of Benares is also, as Gardner himself has suggested, "a kind of ceremony."[46] Of course, it is not merely *Forest of Bliss* that is a ritual, but both filmmaking and cinemagoing. Both have been ritualized experiences fundamental to our society for more than a century. And both filmmaking and cinemagoing share with all rituals the fundamental goal of helping us to come to terms with mortality. If the overwhelming majority of commercial films repress the fear of mortality by redirecting it into heroes and superheroes who transcend mortality or who conquer the representatives of mortality; and, more fundamentally, into the conflict resolution pattern nearly all Hollywood films employ, *Forest of Bliss* reminds us that the inevitability of death has always been the basic motor of all culture and all art. *Forest of Bliss* celebrates both the daily cycle of "the holiest city in the world" and (implicitly) the daily labor of the filmmaker documenting this place; and through its power and beauty, the finished film celebrates the way the art of cinema can transform even a subject terrifying to most of us into an engaging, illuminating, even transcendent—of place, of time, of death itself—experience, a *literally* transcendent experience of death, because the life of the film can be reincarnated, over and over, merely by rewinding the film or starting the DVD again.

THE RETURN OF THE REPRESSED: *IKA HANDS*

Among other things I have asked is: why didn't I put myself in those films? It would have been so easy. Why did I leave something of such interest to me now out when it would have been so simple to do? I could also have imagery of the people who were with me. I could also have documented a process over time which is not uninteresting in itself about how I worked. But I was ultra scrupulous about leaving myself out, thinking it would compromise my intentions to preserve my objectivity.

ROBERT GARDNER[47]

Forest of Bliss is Gardner's most "objective" film, in the sense that throughout that film we remain comparatively unaware of his presence as filmmaker. It is difficult *not* to be aware of his presence in his earlier feature films, because of his narration most obviously, but also because of the very intimacy of so much of his imagery. In an urban setting like Benares, filming doesn't seem unusual, but in the midst of a battle between Dani groups or during the funeral of a young boy, we can hardly fail to become aware of the fact of Gardner filming, even when the filming doesn't seem to affect the Dani. The irony is that while it is *Forest of Bliss,* more than any other film, that has sustained Gardner's reputation as a film artist, it was completed during a period when Gardner was becoming increasingly dubious about his methods and goals as a filmmaker, a period that would lead to a new motif in his work: his appearance within his films *as a character.*[48]

Before beginning *Forest of Bliss* in 1984, Gardner had already recorded most of the imagery and sound for what would become, two years after the release of the Benares film, *Ika Hands* (1988), his depiction of the Ika, whose "rich and complex culture," as Gardner explains in his opening voice-over, was thought "to be a sur-vivor of pre-Colombian high civilization."[49] He had visited the village of Mamingeka in 1980 and returned with Robert Fulton to shoot in 1981. While he did consider further visits to the village, the only additional footage shot for *Ika Hands* was a conversation recorded in Cambridge in 1985 with Gerardo Reichel-Dolmatoff, whose writing had originally lured Gardner to the Sierra Nevada mountains in northern Columbia. After an opening shot/countershot interchange, Reichel-Dolmatoff's comments on the Ika and on Gardner's footage provide a kind of voice-over narration to the finished film. We see Gardner himself—silver haired and in profile—in two close-ups near the beginning of the film, and Reichel-Dol-matoff once; but Gardner's appearance is suggestive: it is clear that he is unsure how to proceed with his film. He asks Reichel-Dolmatoff what the function of filming the Ika might be—especially since what *he* feels is of interest, their spiritual life, is an internal psychic state; Reichel-Dolmatoff suggests that the justification for making the film is that the way of life of the Ika offers "an option" to those of us living within what Gardner describes, in his early (and only) voice-over, as "the turmoil of a relentless modernity." Gardner's second close-up suggests that he's not entirely convinced by Reichel-Dolmatoff's comments.

Ika Hands is a montage of life in Mamingeka held together by three general motifs: everyday village activities introduced by textual titles ("Greeting in the men's house by/exchanging coca leaves"; "The work of prayer is quotidian"; "Mak-ing rope"; "Fetching water" . . .); the spiritual ministry of Mama Marco, who seems the most influential elder in the village; and the conversation between Gardner and Reichel-Dolmatoff. The montage is punctuated by seven passages of sunrises, clouds moving through the mountains, a distant lightning storm, shot by Fulton— Gardner's way of suggesting both the passage of time in the village and the idea that these Ika live with a more macrocosmic sense of time than most people do. Increasingly the focus is on Mama Marco's spiritual activities within the village as other everyday routines are playing out and on his solo excursions and activities.

Often, Gardner intercuts between daily activities and Mama Marco chanting or doing other ritual actions. While Mama Marco is the primary character in *Ika Hands,* we get little sense of him beyond his spirituality; and while the other Ika men, and the women and children, seem comfortable with Gardner and his camera, they are not distinguished as characters the way Pua and Wayek are in *Dead Birds.*

While in some ways, *Ika Hands* seems of a piece with *Dead Birds, Rivers of Sand,* and *Deep Hearts,* there is a basic difference: the Ika seem to remain more of a mystery to Gardner than the other groups he has filmed (the puzzlement evident in the early close-ups of Gardner is a premonition). There were practical reasons for this: judging from Gardner's journals written during the time he spent in Mamingeka, translation, especially of Mama Marco's chantings, was problematic at best. Since Gardner's original interest in the Ika was primarily their spiritual life and the ways in which a shaman might be serving his community, not being able to know what is being said seriously inhibits understanding. Though Gardner films Mama Marco often, most of the shooting confirms the distance between Gardner and this priest, along with Gardner's respect for him: often Mama Marco is seen in low-angle shots, mostly from behind or from the side; and the final shot of the film shows Mama Marco walking away from the camera into the mountain mist: he, and his spiritual reality, will remain a mystery to Gardner and to the viewer.

The publication of *The Impulse to Preserve* in 2006 made available Gardner's journal entries recorded during his time in Columbia (November 15–30, 1980; May 28–July 24, 1981), and his comments reveal dimensions of *Ika Hands* that force us to see the film both as a depiction of the Ika and as an evocation of a pivotal moment in Gardner's career. That *Ika Hands* is as much about Gardner as about the Ika is obvious two-thirds of the way though the film when this interchange takes place between Reichel-Dolmatoff and Gardner:

> REICHEL-DOLMATOFF: You capture this essential loneliness. In a way, I'm impressed by the absence of your filming social relationships. You don't have people relating to each other, or very rarely you have a scene where someone greets someone or . . .
>
> GARDNER: This says more about me than it does about the Ika. . . .
>
> REICHEL-DOLMATOFF: This is very possible. . . . This shows man alone, man in a tremendous tension, very, very, there's a tremendous anxiety in this film, you know?

Gardner's journals dramatically expand our sense of Gardner's struggle in Mamingeka.

While the primary focus in the film is the pervasive spirituality of Mama Marco and the other Ika, the focus of Gardner's journal entries is the physical challenges of living in Mamingeka. Everything seems difficult, from defecating ("Maintaining a squatting position takes great concentration of mind," even "with no [feces eating] pigs in attendance")[50] to sleeping ("I write lying in a sleeping bag liberally sprayed with insecticide in an effort to resist an invasion of fleas that have kept me awake for the last two nights. Both of my arms are swollen from their attentions and I'm told bedbugs are next. This experience is uncomfortable so far and one for which I admit having wavering enthusiasm").[51] And though Gardner does adjust to these hardships, he must also deal with his flagging spirits; this has to do with "the interminable coughing, retching, spitting, whining, and tantrums I hear from all directions. . . . It is in my face, sitting, standing, or lying down. Mucous and vomit pour forth. Gobbits of expectorate fly in all directions. . . . I wheel and dodge, duck and run. I recoil a hundred times a day. . . . The work suffers as I suffer. I don't feel centered, forgiving, or even interested. . . ." The sickness in the village (it also claims Fulton) is so exhausting that at one point Gardner is led to write, "Why isn't that sick child dead? It should be and will be. The film could use it"![52] And filming itself was bringing its own challenges: "I managed to fall into a substantial torrent rushing past some of the outlying houses of San Sebastian. It might not have happened had I not been trying to cross it carrying a number of things I wanted to keep dry. Twenty years ago in the Baliem Valley I had no difficulty overcoming such obstacles."[53]

That the village's struggle with illness is evident in only a single sequence in *Ika Hands,* as a mother deals with her sick son, and that Gardner's struggle with shooting his footage is not evident in the film says a good bit about Gardner's commitment to the idea of the spiritual. Gardner's fascination with Mama Marco has much to do with the priest's unflagging activity in his spiritual enterprise—"the *mama*'s work never ends"—but Gardner's activity in *filming* Mama Marco and his environment is also unflagging and full of hardship; when Mama Marco makes the exhausting climb to the sacred lakes, Gardner walks with him, carrying a thirty-pound camera. That is, Gardner's own cine-spiritual quest not only reflects on, but mirrors the physical and psychic challenges demanded by Mama Marco's commitment.

That Mama Marco remains quite distant from Gardner (and from us), that he is ultimately a figure walking away into the mist, also implies that shooting *Ika Hands* made clear to the once-indefatigable Gardner that he could no longer commit to making films the way he once did. Even as he was beginning his investigation of the Ika, Gardner had wondered, "But why do I even consider another desolate geography to probe another disappearing remnant of humanity?"[54] And the fact that he could not finish this film for seven years confirms that this particular kind of cinematic quest can no longer be his; in making *Ika Hands* he himself was the man walking into the mist; his earlier ethnographic filmmaking was now a "disappearing remnant" of his cine-humanity.

The triumph of *Forest of Bliss,* occurring midway through the process of making *Ika Hands,* demonstrated the value of eliminating one form of filmmaker presence (narration), and it seems to have opened the way for Gardner's fuller acceptance of his own filmmaking process. While *Ika Hands* does include vestiges of Gardner's earlier uses of narration—Gardner's opening voice-over and Reichel-Dolmatoff's commentary—it also represents a change, because Gardner is present primarily as a character (the filmmaker struggling with his film) in conversation with a narrator who is also a character: we develop a sense of Reichel-Dolmatoff before he becomes an off-screen voice.

The character of Robert Gardner as filmmaker would become a good deal more prominent in the two films that followed *Ika Hands,* both of which focus not on disappearing ways of life but on artistic creation. In *Dancing with Miklos* (1993), his film about filmmaker Miklos Jansco at work on *The Blue Danube Waltz* (1991; the film was produced by Gardner and Michael Fitzgerald), and *Passenger* (1997), a depiction of the artist Sean Scully at work, Gardner is a major character. As the title *Dancing with Miklos* suggests, Gardner's filmmaking is interwoven with Jansco's (which itself portrays the press covering a set of events: there is filmmaking within filmmaking within Gardner's filmmaking); and in *Passenger,* Gardner is simultaneously the director of the film about Scully and the filmmaker depicted shooting footage in Scully's studio.

STILL JOURNEYING ON: UNFINISHED EXAMINATIONS OF A LIFE

I am a great admirer of writers and writing and would have been one had I more talent and courage.

ROBERT GARDNER[55]

During recent years, Gardner's primary energies have been directed to revisiting his career in cinema, a career that, he hopes, can survive his own passing. He has explored his personal archive, bringing into print writings that help us to understand the achievements, challenges, and compromises of his earlier cinematic adventures. And he has produced film experiences that recycle moments from his filmmaking and sometimes from the filmmaking of other filmmakers he has admired as a way of thinking back through the decades. Gardner's exploration of his cinematic past in prose and in film has retrieved moments from his filmmaking career that had gotten lost in the lifelong shuffle of film projects and other obligations—it also seems to betray a deep-seated concern that his filmmaking accomplishments remain underappreciated.

Gardner's history in publishing began with *Gardens of War: Life and Death in the New Guinea Stone Age* (New York: Random House, 1968), the book-length photo essay coauthored with Karl Heider that, along with his own *Dead Birds* and

Matthiessen's *Under the Mountain Wall,* was the most important product of Gardner's first expedition to New Guinea. *Gardens of War* is an inventively organized volume, a compendium of imagery and text about the Dani; both Margaret Mead and Elizabeth Edwards argue that it is a landmark in the history of the anthropological photo essay, largely because of the manner in which the volume's 346 photographs are presented.[56] *Gardens* is structured rigorously, alternating regularly between Gardner's essays about Dani culture and Heider's captions for the photographs, and groupings of photographs, both black and white and color. *Gardens of War* not only includes much the same information as *Dead Birds,* but depicts many of the same people and moments.

During the 2000s Gardner returned to writing and to the writing he had been doing during earlier decades—though his first foray back into publishing was a book-length interview. *Making Forest of Bliss: Intention, Circumstance, and Chance in Nonfiction Film: A Conversation between Robert Gardner and Ákos Östör* was published by the Harvard Film Archive in 2001; it is a sustained, virtually shot-by-shot conversation about *Forest of Bliss,* one of two shot-by-shot discussions of the Benares film (the other is Gardner's conversation with Stan Brakhage, "Looking at *Forest of Bliss,*" included on the 2008 DVD produced by Studio7Arts).[57] *The Impulse to Preserve: Reflections of a Filmmaker* (New York: Other Press) was published in 2006; it is a collection of Gardner's journal entries during the production of many films plus a variety of short essays. *Making Dead Birds: Chronicle of a Film,* published by the Peabody Museum in 2007, is a nonfiction novel, largely made up of journal entries and letters to and from Gardner written during the production of *Dead Birds.* And *Just Representations* (2010), a collaboration of the Peabody Museum and Gardner's own Studio7Arts, is a collection of previously unpublished journals, essays, and other writings focusing on Gardner's films and various aborted filmmaking projects (it includes his adverse reactions to working with Laurence and John Marshall in the Kalahari Desert).[58]

The Impulse to Preserve is Gardner's most elaborate and personal book, a kind of autobiography. Through its unusual organization, the volume provides a creative, and revealing, summing-up of Gardner's then fifty-five-year filmmaking career. The first piece (after Charles Simic's brief foreword) is an essay, "A Human Document," which describes an extremely elderly lady (she is not named in the essay) whom Gardner met while on the 1958 Marshall expedition to the Kalahari Desert. The woman is illustrated with two photographs and described in precise detail ("Often she would be visited by butterflies that always love the sun, especially if there is the simultaneous excitement of some nearby moisture. Wherever two of her limbs had been crossed or where the flap of one of her empty breasts had lain on some other part of her, little patches of moist skin would tantalize the dancing butterflies. They would hover ecstatically in the invisible vapor, drinking in the feeble steam of her being")[59] though for Gardner the old lady seems to

have been important primarily as a metaphor for the long history of !Kung culture and its imminent demise: "I knew, as well as I knew that I would kill her
when I cut the film, that she would die in Nyae Nyae."[60] Within *The Impulse to
Preserve,* however, the essay has a different function: it is a memento mori, an
evocation of Gardner's own mortality, implicitly the fundamental catalyst for
this book. The following sections of *The Impulse to Preserve* review Gardner's life
by focusing on his filmmaking projects ("A Human Document" is the only vestige of his early work with Marshall), beginning with *Dead Birds.* For decades
Gardner was careful to eliminate references to the act of shooting from his films,
and as a result, the journal entries create a fascinating context for anyone who
knows the films.[61]

Gardner's personal retrospective has also produced several film experiences.[62]
In October 2009 Bard College honored Gardner's filmmaking career, and for this
occasion Gardner put together a 50-minute compilation he titled *Nine Forsaken
Fragments.* Since the 1970s the Film and Electronic Arts Department at Bard,
headed by longtime Gardner friend and fellow filmmaker (and March 1977 *Screen-
ing Room* guest) Peter Hutton, has been well known as a place where avant-garde
filmmaking is honored, and I assume the fragments Gardner assembled for the
Bard event were chosen with this history in mind. Since October 2009, *Nine
Forsaken Fragments* has been under revision, though in his comments at Bard
Gardner was quite diffident about the fragments being considered films or *Nine
Forsaken Fragments* being considered a finished work. This is evident both in his
title and in the opening credit, "Filmed by Robert Gardner," which suggests that
the fragments were filmed, but are not films.

However, if one looks at *Nine Forsaken Fragments* from within the context of
avant-garde film history, it can be considered an important contribution to the
avant-garde tradition of the film notebook. Beginning in the 1960s with Marie
Menken's *Notebook* (last version, 1963) and *Go! Go! Go!* (last version, 1964) and
developed by Jonas Mekas's *Walden* (1966) and his later diary films, the notebook
is a loose form that, at its best, allows a filmmaker to sing the diversity of cinematic
possibility. Even if *Nine Forsaken Fragments* was not meant as a finished piece,
within this context it can be understood as one of Gardner's finest works.

The nine short films included in *Nine Forsaken Fragments* include "Tide (1966),"
a lovely portrait of a fisherman in Nova Scotia collecting flounder during low tide,
reminiscent in tone of Flaherty's *Man of Aran* (1934) and Joris Ivens's *Rain* (1929);
"It's Stupid (2003)," a portrait of artist/filmmaker Christian Boltanski during the
installation of a show; "Creatures of Pain (1968)," a record of a Fulani ritual that
takes place annually in northern Nigeria during which young men endure the pain
of being hit by staves (Gardner's prose piece, "Creatures of Pain," which describes
"sharo," is included in *The Impulse to Preserve*); "Healing (1978)," a portrait of a
Nepalese healer, before, during, and after a healing ceremony; "Salt (1968)," a

depiction of salt mining in Africa's Afar Depression; "Policeman (1973)," a traffic cop directing cars, bicyclists, and kids on their way to school at a Cambridge intersection; "The Old Lady (AKA A Human Document) (1958)," a portrait of the aged San woman discussed earlier, filmed while Gardner was with the Marshall family in the Kalahari Desert in 1958; "Finding the Way (1968–1981)," a triptych of men consulting oracles: Hamar men consulting the sandal oracle before hunting ostrich; Gardner, Octavio and Marijo Paz, consulting the *I Ching* (to see if Gardner should be alone), filmed by Robert Fulton, who advises the three on how to consult the oracle; and an Ika man consulting a bubble oracle by dropping beads into a bowl of water. The final fragment is "It Could Be Good It Could Be Bad (Flying in Chile) (1997)," during which Gardner and Fulton are flying over the Andes to see glaciers and Fulton tells a shaggy-dog joke about a student and a master, whose response to the student's happinesses or sadnesses as events play out is always, "It could be good; it could be bad."[63]

While several of these short films—"Tide (1966)," "Salt (1968)," and "Policeman (1973)," most obviously—reveal dimensions of Gardner's filmmaking that even someone familiar with his career might not be aware of, others reference Gardner's better-known films or offer additional insight on earlier work. "The Old Lady (AKA A Human Document) (1958)," for example, is the most electrifying section of *Nine Forsaken Fragments*; it provides a visual counterpart to "A Human Document," the prose piece that begins *The Impulse to Preserve*.[64] In fact, the visual power of "The Old Lady (AKA A Human Document)," combined with its having remained in Gardner's archive for so long, reveals—as does Gardner's decision to begin *The Impulse to Preserve* with "A Human Document"—the considerable significance Gardner's documentation of the Old Lady continues to have for him, half a century later (fig. 14).

Earlier I suggested that the "Old Lady" is Gardner's metaphor for a dying culture. In a 1959 letter to John Marshall (the longest letter in *Making Dead Birds*), Gardner confirmed this idea:

> As I have told you, my interest is focused on the Bushmen in their decline, in their death struggles, which I see as a sign both of demise and, perhaps, rebirth. The struggle in death is also the pang of new life.
>
> In my fascination I seized, somewhat ghoulishly, upon our dear Old Lady. She gave me contact, if only in my mind's eye, with the peace and serenity these people may once have had. "The Gatherers" [Gardner had been considering a sequel to *The Hunters*] began, in earnest, as I sat by her side and tried so unsuccessfully to see into her with my camera's eye. The object (the Old Lady) which I grew to love, grew itself into the central figure of a film which would portray the life of a !Kung woman, this woman, *all gatherers.*[65]

Gardner mentions that Marshall "responded to this letter with what I would call now a mixture of concern and irritation" and conjectures about this response.[66]

FIGURE 14. Photograph of the Old Lady (/Gasa) by Robert Gardner. Courtesy Robert Gardner.

Gardner returned once more to the Old Lady in *Just Representations,* beginning "Kalahari Journal" with a photograph of her and including further comment on her situation.[67]

Marshall referred to the same issue in 1993, in his essay "Filming and Learning": "Bob wanted to make a film called *The Gatherers* to complement *The Hunters.* He planned to follow the life of a typical Ju/'hoan woman beginning in her lissome youth, proceeding through her gathering maternity and ending with /Gasa in the dust.... I knew that /Gasa was exceptional.... In film from the early 1950s, she is seen leading her blind sister around with a digging stick...."[68] It seems clear that Marshall's frustration is with Gardner's interest in /Gasa (Gardner never names her) as a symbol for his interpretation of the !Kung, an "object" he grew to love, rather than as an exceptional individual in her own right and with her own right to privacy.[69] It is not hard to empathize with Marshall's frustration with Gardner.

In fairness to Gardner, it must be said that his in-close depiction of /Gasa, lying in the dust, sleeping, eating sand, crawling to her hut does continue to work as a metaphor, not so much for the death of a culture, but for aging and mortality itself. Gardner's "The Old Lady (AKA A Human Document) (1958)" is electrifying precisely because of its candidness about the aging human body, which remains the fundamental taboo in capitalist media: the process of aging must be hidden at all costs. After all, maintaining a culture-wide horror of physical aging offers virtually limitless opportunities for marketing youth and the products that claim to maintain a youthful appearance. In the Kalahari, seeing the aging body was part of normal reality; in twenty-first-century American it feels shocking. Here, Gardner was in tune with Stan Brakhage's films of the same period. As in *Window Water Baby Moving* (1958), in "The Old Lady (AKA A Human Document) (1958)" the experience of cinema becomes a means of defying a culturally willed blindness.

Nine Forsaken Fragments is held together by a rigorous formal organization: each piece is separated from the next by 10 seconds of darkness, interrupted by the fade-in–fade-out of title and date. The fragments are ordered so as to create maximum cinematic surprise, not merely in the consistent change in subject matter, but in method: "Tide (1966)" is black and white and silent, shot on film; "It's Stupid (2003)" is color and shot in sync-sound video. "Policeman (1973)" is a music video of the policeman as conductor of vehicles and pedestrians (and metaphorically of the rock-blues soundtrack) in an upscale neighborhood. The lengths of the fragments vary considerably: "Policeman (1973)" lasts about a minute; the triptych in "Finding the Way (1968–1981)," more than 10 minutes.

Nine Forsaken Fragments is also coherent thematically. In "It's Stupid (2003)," the most recently filmed fragment, Christian Boltanski verbalizes a central theme: the paradox of the importance of human beings and their fragility.[70] This paradox is evident in the Boltanski pieces being installed (they are large photographic close-ups of individuals, printed on what appear to be sheets of gauze), and it is evident throughout *Nine Forsaken Fragments*. The importance of human beings is evident in Gardner's continual focus on them; and their fragility is evident in the many ways in which particular individuals and groups challenge their fears, and mortality itself. Boltanski makes art, the Fulani demonstrate their endurance of pain, a woman goes to a healer, a policeman protects children on their way to school, an old lady barely stays alive, men consult oracles, and Gardner and Fulton risk taking a tiny plane above the Andes to look at glaciers. Even in "Tide (1966)," where the fisherman seems hale and hearty, the film's lack of a soundtrack evokes the silent cinema and the scratches in the print suggest the fragility of the cinematic record itself. At one point in "It's Stupid (2003)," Boltanski says, "What you are and what I am is a lot of small memories"—a perfect description of *Nine Forsaken Fragments.*

Nine Forsaken Fragments creates a representative montage of Gardner's filmmaking, illustrating both the longevity and diversity of his career and his two primary interests: ritual and the making of art. Further, the montage mirrors his recent dedication to revealing himself as filmmaker and retrieving the history of his work: Gardner himself appears in both "Finding the Way (1968–1981)" and "It Could Be Good It Could Be Bad." *Nine Forsaken Fragments* concludes with what amounts to a combined dedication and a final memento mori, a text superimposed over a final shot of the nose of Gardner's Cessna flying over the Andes: "On May 30th, 2002 Robert Fulton/encountered a hellacious storm cell/that cost him his prodigious life." The fundamental theme of Gardner's work, that the inevitability of death inspires creativity, and that creativity can transcend mortality, at least for a time, is confirmed still again. Gardner has continued to return to his earlier work, to "forsaken fragments," and to document artistic process: in 2010 he completed *Deus,* a video of Christian Boltanski installing a large piece, *Personnes,* in the immense Grand Palais in Paris; and *Still Journey On: An Unfinished Examination of a Life,* something like a revised version of *Nine Forsaken Fragments* with a tighter structure (Rebecca Meyers worked on the editing with Gardner)—although a version of *Still Journey On* was completed in 2010, as recently as October 2012, Gardner has said it is unfinished.[71]

While *Nine Forsaken Fragments* is a formally organized cine-notebook, *Still Journey On* is, in its current form, a dense montage of recycled imagery and sound from several different sources: bits of home movie imagery of Gardner as a child, allusions to his own films and to films by others (Ingmar Bergman, Luis Buñuel, Vitali Kanevsky, Akira Kurosawa, and Andrei Tarkovsky), excerpts from some of the same films included in *Nine Forsaken Fragments,* plus several cinematic memories of his interactions with his friends Robert Fulton and Richard P. Rogers—all held together by imagery of Gardner waltzing with himself (or really with the fact of mortality) in a gallery full of Sean Scully's paintings and by a network of subtle interconnections between image and sound.

As in *Nine Forsaken Fragments* it is implicit throughout *Still Journey On* that this is Gardner's life passing before his eyes as he nears ninety. The Harry Lauder song, "Keep Right on to the End of the Road," which includes the film's title, is simultaneously defiant of mortality and (the song was written after Lauder's son was killed in World War I) a recognition of its sting: on one level *Still Journey On* is Gardner's homage to Fulton and Rogers, two younger men whose friendship Gardner misses. This cinematic dance of death also allows Gardner to answer some of his critics: during a passage of Gardner talking with Fulton, recorded when they were in Niger to shoot *Deep Hearts,* Fulton claims that by their presence in this Niger village, they are breathing their own culture into the one they are try-ing to represent, and Gardner responds, "By breathing into it . . . you're affirming the fundamental precept that humanity *is* humanity, and that without breathing into it, what you're doing is setting up a whole lot of individualistic sui generis straw societies, which seem, in Lévi-Strauss's terms, to be the wrong-headedness of anthropology." In the end, the montage of *Still Journey On* demonstrates that this one life is made of interactions with men and women from around the globe and perhaps that all lives now are simultaneously particular and transcultural.

STUDIO7ARTS: SHARON LOCKHART'S *DOUBLE TIDE* AND ROBERT FENZ'S *CORRESPONDENCE*

During the years he ran the Film Study Center at Harvard, Gardner functioned essentially as a producer, allocating funding to projects he thought worthwhile; and in 2010 he registered his studio, Studio7Arts, as a 501(c)3 nonprofit that "produces, promotes and supports work that interprets the world through the creation of nonfiction media."[72] Associates of the studio include a range of film-makers and photographers: Kevin Bubriski, Robert Fenz, Peter Hutton, Sharon Lockhart, Susan Meiselas, Samina Quraeshi, and Alex Webb; Rebecca Meyers is Gardner's creative assistant.[73] Through Studio7Arts Gardner has worked to pro-mote a range of films and photographic work, sometimes projects that can be understood as a continuation of his own work. In January 2012, for example, the studio funded Peter Hutton to fly to Ethiopia to shoot footage for a film on salt mining in the Afar Depression: that is, a film that would essentially fulfill the mis-sion of Gardner's "forsaken" fragment, "Salt (1968)." Unfortunately, Hutton was unable to shoot the footage he had hoped to because the murder of several Euro-pean visitors to Ethiopia just before his arrival made further travel and the planned filming impossible.

Other filmmakers supported by Studio7Arts, including Sharon Lockhart and Robert Fenz, have produced impressive work. In 2009 Lockhart finished *Double Tide,* a 90-minute digital film made up of what seem to be two continuous, tripod-mounted, 45-minute shots of a woman (Jen Casad) clamming in Seal Cove, Maine (near Gardner's residence there), on July 22, 2008 (fig. 15). The first "shot" (actually, each of the two 45-minute sections of *Double Tide* is composed of multiple 16mm shots, but the transitions between one shot and the next are virtually invisible) was filmed in the morning; the second, in the evening.[74] The experience of *Double Tide* is evocative of nineteenth-century-landscape painting, especially the work of Americans Martin Johnson Heade, John Frederick Kensett, and Winslow Homer, as well as of the Europeans Jean-François Millet, Édouard Manet, Gustave Cour-bet, and J. M. W. Turner. *Double Tide* was shot in-sync, though during postproduc-tion, Lockhart worked with several audio tracks in order to communicate not

FIGURE 15. Jen Casad clamming in the evening, from Sharon Lockhart's *Double Tide* (2009). Courtesy Sharon Lockhart.

simply the sounds made by Casad as she trudges through the mud and digs for the clams, but the environmental soundscape created by various birds, by animals in the distant woods, and by nearby (though invisible) buoys and lobster boats.

By any conventional measure, little happens in *Double Tide*. In both morning and evening, Casad arrives on screen from the left foreground and gradually works from the foreground of the image into the background. The considerable stamina necessary for walking in the deep mud of the cove and reaching into the mud to collect the clams quickly becomes obvious, and on one level *Double Tide* is a paean to a traditional form of physical labor. Casad is hardly an exotic, but having the opportunity to see and hear her at work can seem as novel, especially within the near-hysterical distractions of modern life and modern media, as a San gathering bitter melons. Casad is also a performer: it is increasingly evident during *Double Tide* that her movements are defined by the space revealed by the unmoving film frame and that this constriction of her movement can only have been arranged in advance with Lockhart.[75]

The experience of *Double Tide* is an exercise in patience, a form of cine-perceptual training that, on one level, is analogous to the clammer's work, which requires both stamina and perceptiveness. As Casad gradually moves away from the camera, continually searching for the tiny air holes that reveal the presence of the clams, the viewer's attention tends to shift from the particulars of Casad's actions to other, more subtle changes in each of the two overall scenes. Early on during the morning shot, Seal Cove is misty, though gradually the mist burns off, revealing more and/or less of the cove and the forested hills that descend to the water in the distance to the left of the image. Sometimes visibility is confined to the space in which Casad is working; at other times, people—perhaps other clammers—can, just barely, be seen in the distance. A description of *Double Tide* might suggest that the experience of the film is boring, but when I have presented it to audiences (both classes in film studies and general audiences), the luxury of being able to engage this lovely scene at length and the discovery of the many particulars and tiny transformations that occur throughout the two extended moments seem to have been both engrossing and pleasurable for most of those in attendance.

Robert Fenz's *Correspondence* (2011) is an overt homage to Gardner himself and to particular Gardner films, as the film's introductory text and images suggest. The introductory text reminds viewers of Gardner's filming *Dead Birds* in West Papua, *Rivers of Sand* in southwestern Ethiopia, and *Forest of Bliss* in Benares and is followed by the dedication, "To Robert Gardner" then by two color shots. The first shot reveals the Maine bay near Gardner's home where Lockhart filmed Jen Casad clamming in *Double Tide*; the second, Gardner himself, sitting outdoors in a chair, his white hair ruffled by a breeze, looking toward the bay, filmed through a window so that he is seen in double reflection. The shots of Gardner are followed by color imagery filmed in some of the West Papua locations Gardner documented in *Dead Birds*, then by a color sequence filmed in Benares—followed by the film's title.

The remaining 25 minutes of the 30-minute, silent, 16mm film is composed of black-and-white imagery recorded in four locations: three extended sequences— one filmed in West Papua; another in Ethiopia; the third in Benares—are framed by pairs of images of windows during the winter months in Cambridge: the misty, sometimes frosty glass reveals and/or obscures the activity outside the windows. During the years when he was conceptualizing and then shooting what became *Correspondence,* Fenz lived and worked in Cambridge in order to be near Gardner—"I thought it would help me to understand him better and to understand his approach to filming in the places he chose to film"; the Cambridge-in-winter images were shot from Fenz's apartment on Walden Street, not far from the original Studio7Arts location at 7 Standish Street in Cambridge, and "were meant to represent his window or my window or both."[76] The three pairs of framing images—they separate the introduction up through the title from the body of the film; then, each of the three sequences—seem meant to suggest how Fenz's (and by implication, Gardner's) travels to far-flung locations were in part escapes from the long New England winters.

FIGURE 16. New Guinea man in Robert Fenz's *Correspondence* (2011). Courtesy Robert Fenz.

Correspondence revisits locations familiar from Gardner's films, but Fenz engages these locations in a manner quite distinct from the way Gardner engaged them—while at the same time creating many particular moments that are evocative for anyone familiar with Gardner's work (fig. 16). During the West Papua sequence, the Warabara—the hill where battles take place in *Dead Birds*—is recognizable, and Fenz also filmed at the salt well recorded by Gardner and includes brief portraits of several individuals who appeared in *Dead Birds* (one man reveals an arrow wound in his thigh). But whereas *Dead Birds* is interpretive, Gardner's reading of an ancient way of life, *Correspondence* is a form of nostalgia, not so much for earlier ways of life, but for what Gardner's films (and the implicit courage, labor, and creativity they embody) seem to have meant for Fenz.

Although Fenz mentions in his opening text that *Rivers of Sand* was filmed in southwestern Ethiopia, he traveled instead to northeast Ethiopia to film in the Afar Depression—the location where Gardner recorded the imagery in "Salt (1968)" and where Peter Hutton had hoped to film, during January 2012—though the opening images of a woman collecting water in a sandy riverbed is an obvious allusion to *Rivers of Sand,* as are later images of a man with a whip.[77] Both Fenz's black-and-white evocation of Benares and the earlier color sequence are full of allusions to *Forest of Bliss,* from the shot of the stray dog that closes the color sequence (Gardner's film begins with a pack of dogs attacking another stray, and dogs are ubiquitous throughout the film) to the sequence's, and the film's, final shot, of a man rowing a boat on the Ganges—one can almost hear the rhythmic sound of the creaking oarlocks from *Forest of Bliss.*

One of the ironies of *Correspondence* is that although Fenz sees himself "in correspondence" with Gardner and although the locations he records do "correspond" to locations familiar from the Gardner films, Fenz's compositions and editing and his overall structure are less resonant of the Gardner films than of the work of Peter Hutton and other filmmakers identified with the avant-garde (sometimes Marie Menken, sometimes James Benning).[78] As in Hutton's silent and for decades black-and-white films, Fenz's silent, black-and-white compositions are often relatively minimal and shots are sometimes long enough (more than 40 seconds) to verge on the meditative. Like Hutton, Fenz is intrigued with filming in low-light conditions: several of the most interesting shots and sequences in the Benares section of *Correspondence* were filmed at night and play inventively with the camera's limitations. Fenz's structuring of *Correspondence* is a bit more complex than the structures of Hutton's films but has little in common with the complex visual and auditory pyrotechnics in *Forest of Bliss.*

As he did at the Film Study Center, at Studio7Arts Gardner provides financing and facilities for work he finds interesting, work that he sees as closely related to his own, at least philosophically, by people he has come to know and trust— often people who have demonstrated their admiration of and commitment to his own work. Gardner has known Fenz since 1998, and in 2003 invited Fenz to work with him at the Film Study Center, where Fenz oversaw the 16mm to 35mm blow-ups and DVD transfers of *Dead Birds, Rivers of Sand,* and *Forest of Bliss*—work that seems to have instigated *Correspondence.*[79] And to make *Double Tide,* Sharon Lockhart was able to borrow Gardner's Aaton camera, which had been donated to the Film Study Center. She remembers, "The week before we shot I had to drive down to Cambridge to pick up the Aaton and we [Lockhart and Gardner] spent an afternoon in the Carpenter Center watching *Forest of Bliss* by ourselves. (A brand new 35mm print.) It was magical and, thinking back now at how perfect that was— the fog in the beginning of FOB [*Forest of Bliss*] and in DT [*Double Tide*], that I was shooting with Bob's camera (the one he made FOB with and how influential his work has been to me), [that] was kind of perfect."[80] If Studio7Arts is something of a mutual admiration society, there is, of course, much to admire in the work Gardner has supported and continues to support.

3

Timothy Asch

In the films he completed in Cambridge during the 1970s, Timothy Asch rigorously avoided reference to his personal experiences in the interest of foregrounding the experiences of those he documented. Ed Pincus remembers a visit Asch made to his filmmaking class at MIT:

> Asch came to show some Yanomamo films to my class at MIT—this would have been some time before 1975. We had lunch before going to class (Tim was an old friend; I'd known him for years), and he was describing his experiences filming the Yanomamo. Maybe you remember how the Yanomamo tribesmen tie a string around their foreskins so that their penises are belted up on their belly? Well, Tim told me that it was so hot in the jungle that he had to go naked, and since he was circumcised, his penis couldn't be tied up, and as a result, it flopped around. The Yanomamo men thought this was funny, disgusting, even sexually threatening, and there was a hostile relationship between him and the tribesmen from then on. Tim said they would take him into the woods and try to lose him, or they would climb a tree and spread their cheeks and fart down on him—stuff like that. Incredible stories.
>
> So when we went into class, I said, "Tim, tell them about what you were telling me at lunch," and he looked at me blankly, as if we'd not had this conversation. He had put on his ethnographic hat. At that time it was not okay for ethnographers to talk about their process of interacting with other peoples; they were supposed to remain detached. But the conflict Asch described was more revealing than anything we would understand from just observing the Yanomamo.[1]

While Asch avoided revealing how working with the Yanomamo affected him personally and what these experiences might have taught him about himself, he was increasingly clear about what the process of making ethnographic film was teaching him about the cinematic depiction of other cultures. Further, while he joined with John Marshall in presenting himself not as a film artist but as a filmmaker in the service of anthropology, even his earliest films reveal his earlier training as an artist, and his *The Ax Fight* is a masterwork of film art that demonstrates how each new experience of a cinematic record of events can reveal something new about subject, filmmaker, and viewer.

DODOTH MORNING AND THE
ETHNOGRAPHIC DEADPAN

Unlike John Marshall and Robert Gardner, Timothy Asch was not a Boston-area native, and he spent most of his life in other parts of the world. However, his presence in Cambridge during the late 1950s and the 1960s, when he helped John Marshall come to terms with the immense backlog of Marshall family footage about the Ju/'hoansi, was formative both in his own development as a filmmaker as well as for John Marshall's. Further, the first film Asch completed, *Dodoth Morning* (1963), developed from his experiences working with Elizabeth Marshall Thomas, who was doing the research that would result in *Warrior Herdsmen,* her book about the Dodoth herdsmen of northeastern Uganda (Asch supplied photographs for the book).[2] *Dodoth Morning* was produced by the Peabody Museum in collaboration with John Marshall and Elizabeth Marshall Thomas and completed while Asch was teaching in the anthropology department at Brandeis University. Beginning in 1968, his collaboration with John Marshall in the founding and formation of what became Documentary Educational Resources (DER) made a crucial contribution to the distribution of ethnographic cinema that has lasted for more than forty years. And while a research fellow in the anthropology department at Harvard from 1973 to 1979, he finished the films he is best known for, a series of collaborations with anthropologist Napoleon Chagnon on the Yanomamo people living around the headwaters of the Orinoco River in southern Venezuela and northern Brazil.

Having become fascinated with still photography as a student at the Putney School in Vermont, Asch studied with Ansel Adams, Minor White, and Edward Weston at the California School of Fine Arts (now the San Francisco Art Institute), then did seven months of photographic fieldwork on Cape Breton Island before working as a photographer for *Stars and Stripes* during military service in Japan. He was continually in communication with White during these years.[3] Asch received his B.A. in anthropology from Columbia University in 1959, and when Robert Gardner contacted Margaret Mead, looking for someone to assist Marshall at the Film Study Center at Harvard, Mead suggested Asch. Beginning in 1959, Asch examined the Marshall footage, providing screening notes and sound annotations for material shot during the early Marshall expeditions. This led Asch to pursue his studies at Boston University, where he majored in African studies (with a concentration in anthropology at Harvard) and earned his M.A. in 1964. Beginning in 1968 and continuing into 1975, he traveled with anthropologist Napoleon Chagnon to document the lives of Yanomamo tribesmen. The films Asch is best known for were a product of these expeditions, though beginning in 1979 and through the 1980s he (and Patsy Asch) worked regularly in Bali, documenting Balinese spiritual teachers and healers. In 1982 he was named director of the Center for Visual Anthropology at the University of Southern California, where he mentored young anthropologists-filmmakers, among them Ilisa Barbash and Lucien Castaing-Taylor, subjects of a later section of this book.

Jay Ruby's chapter on Asch in *Picturing Culture* begins, "Tim Asch has a unique place in the development of ethnographic film. Unlike most filmmakers, he was not primarily concerned with producing 'memorable' films to enhance his reputation as an 'auteur' or to further some sociopolitical agenda. He was not an anthropologist who conducted field research, analyzed, and published the results. He was not very concerned with large theoretical issues. In a remarkably single-handed fashion, Asch devoted more than thirty years of his life to discovering ways in which he could produce films in collaboration with anthropologists."[4] Nevertheless, despite and to some extent because of Asch's commitments as filmmaker and anthropologist-teacher, his films are, like Marshall's, frequently artful and sometimes of interest well beyond the field of anthropology. In fact, Asch produced one of the most remarkable of all films about film. As he makes clear in his interview with Douglas Harper, Asch's experiences studying with some of the past century's most accomplished photographic artists never left him; his photographic training is evident in much of his best work, and near the end of his life he would turn to writing poetry and return to still photography, having "finally got confidence in myself as an artist."[5]

Even in his earliest film, Asch seems to have been concerned to present the information he hoped to convey in an artful manner. *Dodoth Morning* (1961), which Asch would later call "a terrific film . . . one of my best films," begins with a series of eight still photographic landscape images of Dodoth territory, each held on screen for 20 seconds.[6] These still images are ordered so as to gradually bring viewers from expansive, panoramic views that emphasize the importance of cattle in Dodoth society into a Dodoth family compound. The landscape imagery itself is beautiful, and the slow dissolves from one shot to the next, engaging. Surprisingly, Asch's use of these photographs embroiled him in legal action with Elizabeth Marshall Thomas, who had stipulated in the contract they signed before the Uganda expedition that "no time on this expedition shall be devoted to motion pictures by Timothy Asch without the express consent of either S. M. [Stephen M. Thomas] or E. M. Thomas" and who seems to have felt that Asch's use of the eight photographs (of the 10,000 shot during the expedition) for his own project was in excess of their agreement. In the end Asch apologized and paid $600 for the use of the eight slides.[7]

Superimposed over these shots are three texts providing context for what will follow, including the information that "this film was made one morning during harvest time in the family compound of Lomori and his four wives."[8] Live action, accompanied by Asch's narration, begins 3 minutes into the 17-minute film. As Lomori's compound comes to life, Asch draws attention to some of the specifics of family life, including the fact that Lomori is particularly attentive to his oldest wife, Napuyo, because of her intelligence. We see Napuyo's power near the end of the film when she refuses to allow Lomori to berate his son, Kubal, for being slow to take the cattle to pasture.[9] During the brief brouhaha, Asch records what the family members are saying to each other in a manner that communicates the passion of what seems to be rather typical friction between a father and his adolescent son:[10] as Lomori moves angrily toward Kubal, Asch's struggles to get out of the way cause his handheld camera to express the volatility of the moment.

In general, the lovely landscape shots that open *Dodoth Morning* and the activities in the Lomori compound at the beginning of the day create a sense of normalcy: Lomori's wives are having a spartan breakfast before going to work winnowing grain. The men are talking together around a fire. The women go to work sweeping the grain into piles and winnowing the millet, all the while talking and apparently bantering (none of these conversations is translated; Asch provides brief bits of narration to contextualize what we're seeing).[11] This may be a vastly different culture from our own, the film seems to suggest, but this quiet morning doesn't seem all that unfamiliar. And then, not long after a shot of Napuyo spreading liquid cow dung over the earth surface of the compound with her hands—it will make a base on which the millet will be threshed—Asch shows Lomori's older sons seeing to the bleeding of an ox: an arrow is shot into the neck of the ox, the resulting fountain of blood is caught in a bowl and given to Napuyo to cook.[12] The moment of friction between Lomori and Kubal interrupts this activity (Kubal is hoping to have some of the blood to eat), and immediately following Kubal's clearing mucous from a nostril, a series of close-ups reveals Napuyo preparing the bowl of blood (working it with her hands and mixing in a bit of milk) and pouring the clotted mixture into a large gourd.[13]

Within the field of anthropology, the activities and events depicted in ethnographic films are generally unsurprising, at least for trained anthropologists. At most, these films provide data to be explored, much of it already experienced by anthropologists in their field research and recorded in textual form within anthropological literature (much of the information in *Dodoth Morning,* and a good bit more besides, is available in Elisabeth Marshall Thomas's *Warrior Herdsman,* in which Asch himself is a character). When seen outside the context of a course in anthropology, however, the activities revealed in many ethnographic films can be shocking, especially when presented in what one might call "ethnographic deadpan"—that is, the narrator presents this shocking imagery *as though nothing unusual is happening.* For many viewers, such moments can seem at least as surreal as they are scientific.

Asch's deadpan narration in *Dodoth Morning,* his performance of the detached, unfazed, mature researcher simply providing facts,[14] has much the same effect as those juxtapositions within surrealist films that are meant to take viewers by surprise: the slicing of the eyeball early in Luis Buñuel and Salvador Dalí's *Un Chien andalou (An Andalusian Dog,* 1929) is a famous instance. Buñuel and Dalí meant to confront conventional bourgeois society and forms of cinema that sustain mindless convention;[15] Asch means to confront our cultural biases and resistances by revealing practices that will seem to most filmgoers bizarre, even shocking.[16] While as narrator, he does not treat the bleeding and the blood as anything out of the ordinary, Asch's close-ups of the coagulating blood provide a visual emphasis that goes beyond simple scientific detachment. Whether *Dodoth Morning* is seen by students of anthropology, who we may assume were the intended audience, or by moviegoers in some other context, his depiction of the bleeding of the ox and the preparation of the blood can be seen as an effective form of shock value—one that perhaps was made, at least in part, to demonstrate the distinction between trained anthropologists and other filmgoers.

ASCH AND THE YANOMAMO

Asch's earliest collaborations on films about the Yanomamo, first with James V. Neel and Napoleon Chagnon on *Yanomamo: A Multidisciplinary Study* (1968), then with Chagnon on *The Feast* (1970), resulted in relatively conventional documentaries, though the focus in *Yanomamo: A Multidisciplinary Study* on the expedition itself—fully as much a subject as the Yanomamo—is unusual within ethnographic filmmaking of the time: the sequences of the researchers doing tests on the affable Yanomamo men, women, and children and collecting saliva, blood, and stool samples are revealing of both cultures.[17] The most unusual formal element in *Yanomamo: A Multidisciplinary Study* is its use of two narrators: Neel narrates the opening, describing the makeup and purposes of the expedition and the journey from Caracas to Patanowä-teri; then, during the center section of the film, Chagnon narrates, reviewing a range of particulars about Yanomamo culture; finally, Neel takes over again, explaining the various activities of the expedition, particularly the attempt to forestall a measles epidemic by inoculating the Yanomamo and the gathering of information for further research.

By the time Asch finished *The Feast,* his approach to presenting information about the Yanomamo had changed. *The Feast* begins with a an extended précis during which Chagnon explains the purposes of Yanomamo feasting and the way this particular feast unfolds, as we see a series of still images illustrating Chagnon's comments (and hear appropriate sound). A visual text, "The following film elaborates the events just described," is followed by live action footage of the feast. No further narration is used—though a few superimposed texts indicate time of day and distinguish between hosts and visitors when that might be unclear. Subtitles translate some of what is said. That this structure is reminiscent of John Marshall's *N/um Tchai: The Ceremonial Dance of the !Kung Bushmen* (1969), *An Argument about a Marriage* (1969), and *N!owa T'ama: The Melon Tossing Game* (1970) is no accident, since *The Feast* was edited during the period when Asch was working with Marshall on the editing of those films.[18] As in Marshall's early work (and Gardner's ethnographic films as well), the presence of the filmmakers and the filmmaking is generally suppressed in *The Feast*.

The majority of the Yanomamo films were finished in 1974–75. All the films are credited to Asch and Chagnon, but it is clear that Asch was the filmmaker (he did the shooting and editing) and Chagnon the Yanomamo expert.[19] During the two years that passed between *The Feast* and *Magical Death* (1973), Asch's approach changed again, and he seems to have become committed to two kinds of films. In *Magical Death* and *A Man Called "Bee": Studying the Yanomamo*, the focus is on Chagnon interacting with the Yanomamo, and in a more general sense on the process of doing participant observation. In the bulk of the Yanomamo films, however, Asch employed the approach that had come to typify Marshall's films of the late 1960s and early 1970s; as Asch would explain:

> It is common in documentary filmmaking to only make one general . . . one hour film out of as much as 30 hours of exposed film. . . . In an effort to make the best use of his Ju'/hoansi (!Kung) footage, the filmmaker John Marshall developed a new approach: the sequence film method. After I had worked with Marshall on such sequence films as *The Meat Fight* and *An Argument about a Marriage,* I was eager to apply this approach to filming the Yanomamo. Thus, whenever I turned on the camera, I tried to film long sustained shots of social interaction that comprised a sequence. We [Asch and Chagnon] produced these sequences, each as an independent film, and then made more general films out of them, like *Man Called "Bee": Studying the Yanomamo.* . . .[20]

Asch credits Margaret Mead with first teaching him about sequences when he was her student at Columbia, in her field methods course and in her book, *Balinese Character:* "I was very impressed with the idea of sequences of photographs, which tell you a story that single photographs don't."[21]

Further, Asch's first paper, when he had become a Ph.D. student in Harvard's anthropology department—"A Proposal for Making Ethnographic Film"—focused on the use of sequences. The essay begins, "The following proposal for making ethnographic films is an outgrowth of my work with John Marshall on the Peabody Museum Bushman Film Project and my current anthropological studies";

"the term 'Film Sequence' as used here, was initiated by John Marshall."[22] Not surprisingly, particular Asch sequence films often recall specific Marshall films. The sensuality of Asch's *A Man and His Wife Weave a Hammock* (1974), for example, is reminiscent of *A Joking Relationship* (1962). Asch's *A Father Washes His Children* (1974) and *Weeding the Garden* (1974) evoke the Marshall idylls *A Group of Women* (1961) and *Men Bathing* (1973). And *Arrow Game* (1974), *Children's Magical Death* (1974), and *Tug of War* (1975) evoke Marshall's *Baobab Play* (1974).

Unlike the Marshall sequence films, however, the Asch films make no effort to suppress the presence of filmmaker/filmmaking. After *The Feast* Asch seems to have decided that the Yanomamo ways of responding to his presence were as fully a dimension of Yanomamo culture and personality as their ways of responding to anything else. In *A Man and His Wife Weave a Hammock* Möawä and his favorite wife Daeyama banter, clearly to amuse Asch; and throughout Asch's sequence films Yanomamo adults and children glance at the camera and sometimes speak to Asch. In *Children's Magical Death*, one child says, "Brakiwä! That cameraman looks horny!"[23] And at one point during *Firewood* (1974) Kaösarama asks Asch, or someone behind the camera, to pass her the belt she wraps around her forehead to carry the wood, and the belt is handed to her older child. When the little wood-gathering group returns to the village, a dog barks at the camera/filmmakers.

The text that introduces *A Father Washes His Children* reveals Asch's presence in other ways. After explaining that Dedeheiwä's wife has been sick, the text continues, "Unlike many men, Dedeheiwä willingly assumed the task of fetching the drinking water and bathing the children—including a granddaughter *[sic]*. He had earlier obtained a small quantity of soap from the anthropologist which he used to wash the children." Clearly the event documented in this lovely film was, in part, inspired by Asch's (or one of the anthropologist visitor's) giving Dedeheiwä soap. Further, the patience and gentleness of Dedeheiwä as he washes the children—the young ones cry continually—seems to have impressed Asch. The introductory text suggests that Dedeheiwä has the confidence and decency to break with conventional gender assumptions—something that was on the mind of many American men during the early 1970s as a new wave of feminism took hold.

THE AX FIGHT

The import of the difference between pragmatism and rationalism is now in sight throughout its whole extent. The essential contrast is that for rationalism reality is ready-made and complete from all eternity, while for pragmatism it is still in the making, and awaits part of its complexion from the future. *On the one side the universe is absolutely secure, on the other it is still pursuing its adventures.*

WILLIAM JAMES[24]

> *Just as the ethics of filmmakers are experienced as aesthetics by the viewer, so the anthropologist's objectivity translates into ambiguity: and the "real-life" density commonly attributed by viewers to such film is our experience of active engagement in the generation of meaning.*
>
> DAI VAUGHAN[25]

In at least one instance, *The Ax Fight* (1975), Asch produced a work of consummate cinematic art, a fascinating exploration of the filmmaking and film viewing processes. It is hardly surprising that an anthropologist who made ethnographic films, especially one as responsible to the idea of anthropological research and teaching as Asch seems to have been, would at some point cinematically explore the issues surrounding the making of such films. *The Ax Fight,* completed near the end of Asch's years working with the Yanomamo footage, is his attempt to come to terms with the process he had become so adept with. However, while *The Ax Fight* does deal with issues of particular interest to anthropologists and other ethnographic filmmakers, its value and significance goes well beyond the field of anthropology.

The multipartite structure of *The Ax Fight* distinguishes the film from all of Asch's earlier work and from all other ethnographic films I am aware of. The nearly 30-minute film is divided into four major sections, each of which provides a different kind of information about the events depicted in the film. The first section (a bit less than 13 minutes) is a sync-sound record of a fight that took place in the village of Mishimishimaböwei-teri (fig. 17). Before the live action visual record of the events begins, the sounds of ongoing activity in the village are audible, and Craig Johnson, Asch's sound person on the shoot, is heard saying, in a quavering voice, "February 28th, 1971, afternoon, ten minutes after three." Napoleon Chagnon adds, "Two women are fighting with each other." As the sounds of the village are dropping viewers *in medias res* into a situation of considerable tension, the imagery is showing a series of color terrain maps that indicate approximately where these events are occurring. The maps are followed by two visual texts, one of which describes the background of this fight.[26] Then, after Napoleon Chagnon is heard telling Asch, "Bring your camera over here. It's gonna start," a second visual text explains, "You are about to see and hear the unedited record of this seemingly chaotic and confusing fight, just as the field workers witnessed it on their second day in the village."

During the following minutes Asch records several women, presumably the beaten woman and female relatives, crying in their living quarters, then the resulting fight, which begins in the center of the compound as one man attacks another with a large club and is then confronted by the wounded man's supporters. A momentary stand-off is followed by the parties to the attack dispersing and a moment of quiet. Then two men carrying axes jog across the compound to make a second attack within the living quarters of the visiting group. A large crowd of

FIGURE 17. Early in the confrontation in Timothy Asch's *The Ax Fight* (1975). Courtesy Documentary Educational Resources.

hosts and guests quickly assembles. A fight ensues and a young man is injured and falls to the ground. He is quickly surrounded by other men who protect him from further danger. Finally, when the young man is able to stand and walk away, the crowd disperses. The section ends with two women yelling insults across the compound at the visitors.

It is clear that Asch is filming this volatile moment as best he can, though the events are unpredictable and confusing. As is true in many of his Yanomamo films, in *The Ax Fight* Asch makes frequent use of his camera's manual zoom lens, which allows him to witness, in close-up, events that are a considerable distance from him (and do not seem to have anything to do with his presence). In *Climbing the Peach Palm* (1974), a film that records a young man climbing a palm tree covered with thorns to collect the peaches at the top, Asch first films the man using the two wooden frames that allow him to climb up the trunk without injury in medium shot, then dramatically zooms back, revealing that the camera is in the middle of the village compound, recording an event that is taking place a considerable distance away, just outside the compound. After providing this visual context, Asch returns to closer views of the man in the tree.[27] In *The Ax Fight* Asch's camera is continually on the move, zooming in and out, as the action seems to dictate, and panning to reframe what he sees as the crucial visual activity during any given moment. Viewers are witnessing the fight between several Yanomamo, *and* they are witnessing a filmmaker struggling to make sense of what he's seeing and hearing: the camera movements and adjustments express the excitement of the situation. The changing levels of excitement evident in the visuals are confirmed by changes in the volume of the sound—though the volume levels may have been adjusted during the editing.

While the fight is dramatic and frightening, the concluding comments of the two women are comic.[28] After the first woman complains, "Why the hell did your shiftless son insult us that way? He said we had blemishes! We don't take that kind of talk from a bunch of visiting bastards like you" (Chagnon supplied these translations), the second chimes in: "It's your goddam son that has all the filthy blemishes on his ugly face. He's an ass of the first order! His ugly skin is so blemished that he looks more like a pimple than a person. And it's clear to us why all your children are so foul and ugly! We know! We know! It's their ugly mothers that made them that way! You're all descended from pus and pimples! You all come from the Village of Pimples!" These women have the final word in the sequence. Their comments are particularly emphatic since this is the only moment when we hear and can understand what someone involved in the event is saying. Unlike those directly involved in the fight, who are filmed from a considerable distance, the camera is close to these women, and they seem to be performing not only for their kinsmen and the visitors but for the camera.

The sound of the events continues even once the visual record of the fight has ended; as a result, the audience is privy to a somewhat startling conversation among Asch, Chagnon, and Craig Johnson:

JOHNSON: Sound reel 14; February 28, 1971; finish to wife-beating sequence.

ASCH: Did you get sync on that?

CHAGNON: Wife-beating sequence, my foot.

JOHNSON: Okay, what *is* it?

CHAGNON: It was a club fight.

JOHNSON: What was first?

CHAGNON: Well, two women were in the garden, and one of them was seduced by her *son*. It was an incestuous relationship, and the others found out about it, and that's what started the fight.

ASCH: No kidding!

JOHNSON: About 3:30 in the afternoon.

CHAGNON: No, about 3:00 it started. One guy was hit on the back from behind with an ax and just about knocked unconscious with the blow.

ASCH: So this is just the beginning of lots more?

CHAGNON: Well, when you get a village this big, things like this are bound to happen.

ASCH: Did you figure out how many there were in the village?

CHAGNON: No, I haven't counted them yet; there are over two hundred. *[Speaks to Moäwä in Yanomami],* Ah, that's about the tenth person today that's asked me for my soap.

ASCH: Tell him I'll give him my soap. . . .

CHAGNON: No, you won't give him your soap!

ASCH: . . . when I go home.

CHAGNON: They're going to make damn sure we leave in a hurry if we keep promising them everything when we go home.

ASCH: Shotiwa ["brother-in-law" in Yanomami], living in your Village must be tiresome.

CHAGNON: Thought I was shitting you about the fierce people, eh?[29]

This interchange makes obvious that Chagnon is the person in charge and the one with the most expertise about the Yanomamo; and the touch of glee evident in Asch's response to the idea that the fight was caused by incest seems to expose a somewhat immature excitement.

The conversation among the filmmakers is immediately followed by a text that causes us to revise whatever conclusions we have formed on the basis of seeing the events and hearing the filmmakers' subsequent comments: "First impressions can be mistaken. When the fight first started, one informant told us that it was about incest. However, subsequent work with other informants revealed that the fight stemmed from quite a different cause." A second text explains that the fight began because visitors refused to work in the garden. After Mohesiwä demanded plantains from Sinabimi and she refused to supply them, he beat her, after which "she ran into the village screaming and crying." This leads immediately into the second major section of the film, a review of the ax fight narrated by Chagnon and presented using a variety of visual effects, including slow motion and stop motion and arrows to identify individual participants. This review shortens the original documentation of the fight to about 8½ minutes but reveals a level of understanding of the events that suggests that the anthropologist-filmmakers did a good bit of research after witnessing the fight.

During the past twenty-five years, I have taught *The Ax Fight* regularly, both in courses in documentary and in general introductions to the history and theory of cinema, and in every instance students have felt that the review of the fight dramatically changes their understanding of the Yanomamo. The original recording of the incident seems entirely chaotic; these seem to be "violent savages out of control." The review of the fight, however, reveals that this conflict is quite nuanced, and compared with much of the violence in our own culture, rational and civilized. It becomes obvious that the Yanomamo restrain themselves on several levels. Most obviously, the women are not attacked, even when they exacerbate the situation with their biting comments (one woman is chased away from the fight during the most volatile moment, so as not to inflame the situation further), and the children seem in no danger. But even the violence itself is clearly conducted according to a complex system of rules. Machetes are not used, even though they are handy, and though the club fight becomes a more dangerous ax fight, the axes are used with considerable care. When one man turns his ax so that the blade is up, a woman comes up behind him and turns the ax head over, so that, whatever action the man takes will not involve his use of the ax to chop into an opponent's body. Ultimately, the fight is brought under control by a man who carries no weapon at all. A young man is injured as a result of the fighting, but after a few moments he is able to walk away from the altercation and no further violence occurs.

What the anthropologists seem to have learned from their research, and what viewers understand from the review of the fight, is more than that "first impressions can be mistaken." The original documentation of the fight allows most viewers to impose their own cultural assumptions about "primitive," "savage" societies onto the confusing situation they witness. This promotes a kind of blindness, an inability to notice particulars. The review reveals details of the event that, while visible, are not noticed by most viewers during the unedited recording (or at least not consciously recognized): the sister's changing a small club for a larger one, for example, and the mother's stroking the arm of the man who was struck by the club. Indeed, by titling the film "The Ax Fight," Asch can be said to have promoted such a response. While "ax fight" might be the correct anthropological term for what we have seen, to most American filmgoers the title implies something a good bit more violent than what actually occurs in the film: not, perhaps, quite as violent as *The Texas Chainsaw Massacre,* released the year before *The Ax Fight,* but a violent altercation according to the then-current conventions of cinema violence. As a result, the discovery that in fact the Yanomamo violence is less gruesome than viewers were expecting, even less gruesome than what they might have imagined they saw, confirms the general sense that during their first viewing of the fight, they were blind to what was occurring right in front of them.

Within the history of documentary, the second version of the ax fight can be said to provide a critique of the truth claim made by early cinema verite filmmakers: that on-the-spot recording from within events resulted in a more realistic, honest cinema than the older documentary approach that had relied on narration to explain what was important to see and what it meant. *The Ax Fight* demonstrates that while the approach promoted by Frederick Wiseman and D. A. Pennebaker, among others during the 1960s, may work within a given culture for film viewers who understand the context within which the filmic events are recorded, it is less useful—indeed, it may be entirely misleading—within an unfamiliar culture. Clearly, without the explanations provided by Chagnon during the review of the ax fight, the spontaneously recorded events would tend to confirm not merely ignorance but cultural prejudice. The candid revelation of this event, by itself, would create only obfuscation.

Of course, Chagnon's explanation of the details of the fight during the review of the events is inevitably contextualized by the conversation heard at the conclusion of the original documentation of the ax fight and immediately before the review. While the text that introduces the review indicates that "one informant told us that it [the fight] was about incest," we know that in using "us," Asch is being kind, or at least professionally respectful: it was Chagnon, after all, who confidently asserted that the fight was about incest. As a result, while Chagnon's subsequent analysis of the fight seems generally confirmed by the particulars of the imagery revealed by Asch's reworking of the original footage on an optical printer and with the use of an Oxberry animation stand (the Oxberry allowed Asch to enlarge portions of the imagery for the review), our confidence in the explanations provided by Chagnon and Asch is, or should be, tempered by our awareness that these are experts *and* fallible human beings.

This ambiguity is confirmed by the third major section of *The Ax Fight,* Chagnon's explanation of how the history of kinship within Mishimishimaböwei-teri and neighboring villages helped to create the tensions that resulted in the fight. Chagnon's review of kinship is relatively brief (a bit less than 2½ minutes) and almost entirely male centered.[30] A three-color diagram of three Yanomamo lineages is presented, and using black lettering for residents of Mishimishimaböwei-teri and red lettering for visitors (plus white arrows, to draw our attention to one or another section of the diagram), Chagnon explains that the ax fight is a result of tensions among members of Moäwä's lineage that have been developing for some time. While Chagnon's explanation may be sensible and clear to those familiar with the Yanomamo, I have never talked with an audience that was not confused by it. Yanomamo kinship is quite complex—the kinship chapter of Chagnon's *Yanomamo: The Fierce People* (New York: Holt, 1968) is nearly half the book—and at most, the only thing most viewers understand from the kinship section of *The Ax Fight* is that kinship probably had something to do with the conflict. Asch himself was concerned about this: "When I asked Chagnon to do the kinship diagram (his only responsibility) for a third time to show the marriage alliances between the combatants—which somehow didn't get into the first two attempts. . . . He had done it twice and would not do it a third time. I was flabbergasted."[31]

The fourth section of *The Ax Fight* is announced by a brief text: "A final edited version of the fight follows." This final version shortens the review of the fight to a bit under 5 minutes. No narration or textual information is used in this version and all vestiges of the filmmaking process (the conversation among Asch, Chagnon, and Johnson, a brief moment during the original shooting when Chagnon, pipe-in-mouth, is visible and when one Yanomamo boy pretends to be attacking them) are eliminated. The "final edited version" does communicate a good bit of what happens in the fight, but more quickly than either of the two earlier versions, by using shorter shots and more abrupt transitions. It also allows viewers to re-see the various stages of the fight with Chagnon's explanation in mind and perhaps congratulate themselves on now being aware of aspects of the events they were blind to during the original, unedited version.

However, this version also foregrounds several distortions of the original events. The most obvious of these is Asch's movement of the first woman seen yelling at the visitors at the conclusion of the unedited version to a position much earlier in the fight, so that her taunts (in this version they are not translated) seem to be directed at the original confrontation of the two men in the center of the village. What is a single, continuous shot of this woman in the unedited version is presented here as three brief shots that are intercut with shots of the confrontation of the two men. This change may be, as Bill Nichols has suggested, a way of foregrounding the beating of Simibimi and her resulting anger as the instigation of the fight, or it may an attempt to make clear that the women's insults were a continuous part of this altercation, not an afterthought.[32] The second taunting woman concludes this version, as she concludes the original version, though here, only the second half of her rant is included. When the imagery fades out, a text explains, "Several days after the fight, some of the visitors began leaving. Tensions were temporarily relieved," and the film ends.

As Bill Nichols suggested long ago, the final version both reveals and obscures.[33] Like the earlier versions, it does reveal a good bit about the Yanomamo, including what they look like, how they move, what weapons they use, what they wear, how they sound, how they arrange their villages, and something of how gender roles play out, especially in body language, during a volatile moment. Further, it makes clear that the production process used by ethnographic filmmakers (and documentary filmmakers in general) involves collecting raw footage, researching this material (looking at what has been collected and doing whatever research seems necessary to understand it), and then proceeding through a series of edited versions until a "final edited version" is decided on. The implication is that what viewers are seeing in this final version, what Asch would later call "the slick version," is "all they get ordinarily" in an ethnographic documentary about a particular practice or event.[34] Here, however, because viewers have seen both the original version (including the entire audio recording of the events) and the second, explanatory version of the fight, they know, in a way they normally do not, how much information is *not* included in the "final edited version," information about both the Yanomamo and the filmmakers. Most obviously, the final version betrays no sense that the filmmakers are fallible, even capable of immaturity; and it suppresses all evidence of the process that has been used to produce what viewers see and hear and whatever distortions have occurred during this process.

The final version of the ax fight is not, of course, the final version of *The Ax Fight*. It is merely an illustration within a larger structure—and one of several possible final edited versions of the event (Asch calls it "*a* final edited version," not "*the* final edited version"). Once Asch had decided on the four sections he would include in the film, and the order in which these sections should be arranged, he produced a series of textual transitions to guide the viewers through this meta-film experience. These six transitional texts represent Asch's final conclusions about the ax fight and are the final stage of his cinematic rendering of it. While these texts feel definitive and are literally the final word both in the experience of *The Ax Fight* and in the process that produced the film, like every other element of *The Ax Fight* the feeling of closure they provide must be understood as tentative. As Asch told Jay Ruby, "I was feeling . . . halfway into making the film, this great suspicion of the whole field beginning to fall apart before my eyes. . . . But now I would love to put on an introduction to it [*The Ax Fight*] that says, 'About Realism.'"[35] In the final analysis, Asch recognizes that "realism" in ethnographic cinema, and in cinema itself, is always partial, always inclusive of distortion, worth pursuing perhaps, if we are to understand *anything* about the world we live in, but inevitably tentative.

On at least two levels, *The Ax Fight* is a remarkably pragmatic film, in the Jamesian sense. First, it reveals how the filmmaker develops a tentative understanding of a complex situation as he experiences it, and then, as further experiences reveal more information, comes to a new, still tentative, but more complete understanding. In other words, Asch's understanding of the Yanomamo and of his own process is part of the flow of events; it is always in transition, always "in the making," to use James's phrase. In fact, during the year or so when he was editing the material used in *The Ax Fight,* the film was in a continual state of transition, as Asch showed various parts of the film in various orders to his students at Harvard and to groups at Wellesley College and Boston University: "I changed *The Ax Fight* twenty-five times in the course of that semester."[36]

Second, the finished film, the version Asch decided on after a long period of working with the material, continually examining the footage itself and learning how various versions of the material affected audiences, provides a continually changing experience that requires that viewers reevaluate their assumptions and conclusions again and again as they experience the film, and then come to whatever tentative final understanding seems warranted by this film-viewing process. What viewers are left with once *The Ax Fight* has concluded is a sense of the complexity and flux of experience and of the resulting ambiguity and tentativeness of all cinematic representations of it. Viewers learn something of what happened at a particular moment in a specific Yanomamo village, but they are also reminded that understanding others (Yanomamo, documentary filmmakers . . .), understanding their relationship to representations of the experiences of others, and understanding themselves is an ongoing adventure. As Asch would later tell Jay Ruby:

> This whole notion of truth and making an accurate representation blew up in my face. . . . My whole life and commitment to anthropology got really shattered. I had put myself out to make this film, and in so doing, it completely undercut years and years of training. . . . At that moment, I saw *The Ax Fight* as a subtle commentary about the end of an era. But that didn't mean it still wasn't fun to do. That is where a lot of the irony is; I mean, that is why I didn't make things explicit about the way I felt, because I really didn't feel that way until I was a third of the way into it. And then I thought, let the others figure it out for themselves.[37]

4

Ed Pincus and the Emergence of Personal Documentary

The social turmoil of the late 1960s and early 1970s brought with it a wholesale reevaluation of many of the institutions that had seemed to define American culture for the previous generation. The federal government had involved the nation in a war during which the American military perpetrated shocking, inhumane brutalities against a humble underdog—to many young people coming of age, America seemed the new Third Reich. State governments that had condoned generations of American apartheid came under attack from their own disenfranchised citizens and from "outside agitators," including a president and attorney general educated at Harvard. Under pressure from students and faculty, colleges and universities were beginning to rethink their economic and ethnic exclusivity. And a new wave of feminism was questioning the nature of male–female relationships, the institution of marriage, and one of the central assumptions of the American nuclear family: a belief in privacy. Indeed, the broad green lawns that surrounded the new suburban homes springing up during the post–World War II years were a visual emblem of the idea of privacy; they kept auditory evidence of family problems away from the ears of potentially prying neighbors.

Within this volatile social climate, it is hardly surprising that for a new generation filmmaking became a means for investigating problematic traditions and promoting cultural change. Newsreel and other filmmaking collectives made it their business to confront mainstream depictions of international events and national policy. Many avant-garde filmmakers confronted the fundamental assumptions of moviegoing and television watching, inventing new formal strategies that redefined the nature of spectatorship. And in Cambridge and other locations, documentary filmmakers began to carry 16mm cameras and video camcorders into the inner sancta of family and personal relationships in order to see what might be learned about the ways in which the unfolding of daily experience reflected problematic ideas and social patterns.

In Cambridge this new interest took two different forms. In some instances, filmmakers directly confronted family members, recorded the results of these confrontations, and shaped these records into new understandings of family life and their own positions within it. In other instances, filmmakers reexamined the previous generation's records of family interaction—stories frequently retold within the family, home movies, family photographs—to see what these records might tell us about the ways in which the traditional family had functioned and how changes in technology and social organization were affecting what had seemed essential to an earlier generation and its concept of family.

THE MIRIAM WEINSTEIN QUARTET
AND RICHARD P. ROGERS'S *ELEPHANTS:*
FRAGMENTS OF AN ARGUMENT

Some filmmakers in this new generation, directly or indirectly influenced by the women's movement which began to find significance in what was called the personal, began to avoid famous personalities, newsworthy events, and the obviously lofty subjects. . . . Everydayness for the first time became a possible subject. Ordinary people in ordinary situations, no longer defined by a social role that was their entrée to being the subject of a film—race car driver, actress, prisoner, poor person, politico. Their justification for being a film subject was often only that they had a relationship with the filmmaker or were somehow accessible to the filmmaker. Like any possibility, this one has been abused and there have been a rash of sentimental personal films. But in the most interesting, people divorced from their social definitions became interesting in new ways.

ED PINCUS

Also, previous to the women's movement, there was a branch of SDS, the Weathermen, whose slogan was "The pig is in us." We were supposed to look inside.

IDEM[1]

In the general introduction to this study, I suggest that ethnographic film and what came to be called personal documentary are the inverse of each other. This seems obvious to me in the same way that it seems obvious that during the dawn of documentary filmmaking, the two major forms—what Erik Barnouw called "films of exploration" (*Nanook of the North, Grass, Moana*) and the City Symphony: that is, films about the industrial centers of modern nations (*Berlin: Symphony of a Big City, The Man with a Movie Camera*)—were the inverse of each other: the explorations of far-flung locations and peoples in Flaherty's and Cooper-Schoedsack's films were tied to the industrial center of modern life by a celluloid umbilical cord. In Cambridge, however, this connection was more than theoretical conjecture; it was (and remains) a fact of everyday experience. Alfred Guzzetti, who would complete his landmark personal documentary, *Family Portrait Sittings,* in 1975, was a student in the first class in filmmaking Robert Gardner taught in the Carpenter Center and remembers admiring Gardner tremendously: "I was in awe of *Dead Birds* and then *Rivers of Sand.*"[2] Guzzetti thought of these films as very "Other," but his own rebellion in *Family Portrait Sittings* against cinema verite filmmaking's tendency to base films on short-term explorations of high-profile events in favor of a more in-depth look at quotidian family life may owe something to the in-depth explorations of everyday experience that produced Gardner's first ethnographic features. Another instance: between the time Ross McElwee began shooting the footage that would find its way into *Backyard,* his first personal documentary, and the completion of that film in 1984, he accompanied John Marshall to the Kalahari Desert to assist in the shooting of what became *N!ai, the Story of a !Kung Woman* (1978).

While the emergence of personal documentary was an important new development in the 1970s, it was preceded both by a considerable body of personal cinema produced by American avant-garde filmmakers and by what remains the most interesting satire of personal documentary. Among the most important figures in this earlier exploration of the personal are Stan Brakhage, Jonas Mekas, Carolee Schneemann, and Andrew Noren. Much of Brakhage's early filmmaking was centered on his family life with Jane Brakhage and their children. The "personal" for Brakhage, and for these other filmmakers, however, meant more than a focus on the activities of self, family, and friends; the filmmakers' personal events and activities were recorded by handheld, often gestural camerawork, and presented within idiosyncratic editing strategies that were intended to express the filmmakers' psychic experiences and aesthetic interpretations of the events and activities depicted. In *Window Water Baby Moving* (1959), for example, we are not simply watching Jane Brakhage give birth to a daughter; we are watching Stan Brakhage's immediate reaction to the birth process—we can feel his excitement, his anxiety, the ways in which the process of birth triggers particular memories—and his subsequent interpretation of what the experience meant to him in an expressive montage.

Much the same can be said of Carolee Schneemann's *Fuses* (1967), the filmmaker's record and interpretation of her lovemaking with composer James Tenney; of *Walden* (1969), Mekas's "home movie" of the emergence of the New American Cinema in New York during the 1960s; and of *Huge Pupils* (part 1 of *The Adventures of the Exquisite Corpse;* 1968), Noren's record of light and love. In all these films, gestural camera movement and new approaches to editing create visceral forms of personal expression roughly analogous to the kinds of personal expressiveness characteristic of abstract expressionist painting. An exploration of the various forms of the "personal" in personal cinema is a challenge for a different book, but roughly speaking, the distinction between this earlier, "avant-garde" sense of the personal and what I am calling "personal documentary" has to do with the use of sound and in particular, of conversation, usually recorded in sync.

The widespread popularity of personally expressive cinema during the 1960s was depicted and satirized by Jim McBride in his *David Holzman's Diary* (1967), though in one of the strange ironies of film history, McBride's satire was largely irrelevant in relation to the personal cinema I've just described—except for the fact that Andrew Noren was the inspiration for David Holzman.[3] It was, however, remarkably prescient. McBride and L. M. Kit Carson, who played David Holzman in McBride's film, had interviewed some of the major proponents of cinema verite ("Ricky Leacock, Pennebaker, Bob Drew, the whole bunch") for a monograph sponsored by the Museum of Modern Art.[4] The monograph was never completed, but their research was incorporated into *David Holzman's Diary*, in which McBride conflated his interest in the immediacy of the on-the-spot sync-sound filmmaking that had emerged during the early 1960s (along with the claims of those who celebrated cinema verite's supposed access to unmediated reality) with the personal revelations of the avant-garde filmmakers who were so visible in New York (McBride and Carson had also interviewed Andy Warhol, Gerard Malanga, and Noren). Though *David Holzman's Diary* is a fiction, and a trick film (even contemporary audiences are shocked when the credits roll), as Jim Lane has said, McBride's film seems, in retrospect, at least a premonition, and perhaps an instigation, for the rise in personal documentary in Cambridge beginning in the decade that followed.[5]

While David Holzman doesn't resemble Andrew Noren in the slightest (nor could *David Holzman's Diary* ever be mistaken for a Noren film), McBride's feature is remarkably close to films that Miriam Weinstein, Richard P. Rogers, Ed Pincus, Ross McElwee, Ann Schaetzel, and others would come to make during the 1970s, 1980s, and 1990s. Further, as Ed Pincus has suggested, the emergence of the form of personal documentary McBride imagined in *David Holzman's Diary* had much to do with the impact of the wave of feminism that was developing at the same time. For the first generation of avowedly feminist filmmakers, both women and men, the idea that in gender relations "the personal is the political" was particularly relevant to filmmaking. Of course, Hollywood, much of the European art cinema so popular during the 1960s, and even a good many avant-garde filmmakers had portrayed women in very limited ways, undervaluing women's labor and fantasizing about women's bodies. A new generation of independent women filmmakers, and particularly documentary filmmakers, envisioned and created a counter-cinema that exposed the realities of women's lives in middle-class American culture. Among the earliest of these feminist filmmakers, and perhaps the

FIGURE 18. Miriam Weinstein
in the 1970s. Courtesy Miriam
Weinstein.

most prescient of the developments in personal documentary that would soon
occur, was Miriam Weinstein (fig. 18).

Between 1972 and 1976, Weinstein completed a quartet of films about her own
life—*My Father the Doctor* (1972), *Living with Peter* (1973), *We Get Married Twice*
(1973), and *Call Me Mama* (1976)—that offered a panorama of crucial developments in the life of a young, middle-class woman and of Weinstein's exploration of
the options available for the personal documentary filmmaker.[6] Ed Pincus was an
important model for Weinstein's filmmaking: "Ed was the elder statesman of the
Cambridge scene (he is probably only a few years older than I am). . . . In 1968,
which was a time of tremendous social upheaval, the young media types would
meet at Ed's house/office. There was a lot of discussion about how we would cover
events that were happening, disseminate information, etc. etc. I remember covering actions by VVAW (Vietnam Veterans Against the War) and similar groups."[7]
Pincus's *Diaries (1971–1978)*, which has much in common with Weinstein's films,
would not be finished until two years after her final personal documentary, but
Pincus often presented early rushes, and Weinstein believes she probably saw
some of these.[8]

In *My Father the Doctor* Weinstein's interview with her father is embedded within still photographs and home movies of her grandparents, parents, and of herself and her sister as children. The interview focuses on Saul Weinstein's pride in his daughter's education (she graduated from Brandeis with honors in painting) and on Miriam Weinstein's interest in how her father became a doctor and how he feels about her being a filmmaker: "Are you surprised?," she asks him. His disappointment is evident; he had imagined that Miriam would find her way into a profession more appropriate to her being a "brain." In *Living with Peter* the focus is Weinstein's anxiety about living with Peter Feinstein without being married, an anxiety evidently not shared by her mother ("I think it's great, because I've done it, long before you did") or Peter's sister. Throughout the film, Weinstein talks with Feinstein about the possibility of their getting married—he doesn't want marriage, she does—and with a pair of friends (Deac Rossell, who ran the film program at the Museum of Fine Arts, Boston, at the time, and his wife, Mickie Meyers) who got married without living together first and are enthusiastic about their choice.

We Get Married Twice documents Weinstein and Feinstein's two weddings, one of them held informally at their home, the ceremony conducted by a Methodist minister friend; the other, a more formal wedding in a synagogue, overseen by a rabbi, and instigated by Weinstein's mother and acceded to by Feinstein, once it was made clear to him that a formal wedding would be economically rewarding: "So being a pragmatist, we decided it would be fun to get married in true style in New York City by the same rabbi who married Saul and Sally Weinstein." *Call Me Mama* focuses on the typical activities of Weinstein's young motherhood: she and her two-year-old son, Eli, are seen at home, in a park, visiting a friend and her young daughter, and reading, as Weinstein in voice-off describes the pleasures and struggles of being a mother. The struggles seem to have included Feinstein's early lack of interest in his young son: "I was having a difficult time being a mother and trying to make sense of my life. Although the women's movement had made it okay for women to work, etc. etc., I did not really believe it. And Peter had very little interest in being around little children, so it was not a happy period, although both my kids were great kids and I loved being with them. But still, I look at that movie and I see claustrophobia."[9]

Each of the four films uses a different filmmaking strategy. In *My Father the Doctor* Weinstein intercuts between recycled photographs and home movies of her family and her interviews with her father: she is never visible, but we hear her behind the camera asking questions; indeed, her presence as filmmaker/interviewer and his responses as subject/interviewee provide the drama of the film.[10] In *Living with Peter* Weinstein is also the interviewer behind the camera, though in this case, the fact of her filming, at least in the case of her conversations with Feinstein, is more directly an issue: Feinstein is clearly annoyed (or pretends to be annoyed) by the filming, and when Weinstein asks him, "Do you feel any pressures to do it [get married]?," Feinstein responds, "Well, I didn't until you started making this movie!"[11] Later, when they are talking about their visits to family over Thanksgiving, she tells Peter, "This film is about you and me and about marriage. Could you please say something about Thanksgiving that's more relevant?" Near the end of the film, Weinstein jumps through time, and in a later conversation with Feinstein, it becomes clear that he has given her a wedding ring for her birthday. Weinstein's interviews with Feinstein are more intimate than those with her father in *My Father the Doctor* or with the other subjects in *Living with Peter;* especially during their conversation in the bathroom as Feinstein is shaving, their conversation is a kind of intimate banter reflected by Weinstein's filming in extreme close-up.

In addition to interviewing Feinstein and the others, Weinstein sits on the bed in their bedroom and addresses the camera in several monologues, first talking about how her unmarried status has caused her to be rejected by an insurance company "for moral reasons" and admitting, "I just wanted to kind of use it [this rejection] as an excuse to get married. . . ." In a second monologue, she reveals that none of the people she's interviewed seem bothered that she is living with Peter: "The whole thing has been a little bit anticlimactic." A final monologue, after Peter has given her the ring, reveals that the idea of marriage has become "less important" to her, though she continues to want marriage more than Peter, "and in a way that's why I'm making the movie too. Because I want to talk about it and I want it to be something I *can* talk about." She has a ring but is not a wife, and "*girlfriend* is getting a bit ludicrous at this point." Weinstein's monologues in *Living with Peter* are, of course, evocative of David Holzman's monologues in *David Holzman's Diary* and a premonition of the monologues in several of Ross McElwee's films— though hers seem a good bit more unrehearsed than McElwee's. Indeed, the intimacy and immediacy of Weinstein's films is generally reflected in, and communicated by, a variety of glitches: the sound of the camera, a visible microphone here and there, sudden changes in sound level and light values.

For *We Get Married Twice,* which was made with the assistance of the Carpenter Center for the Visual Arts at Harvard, Weinstein asked others to document her two weddings: Len Gittleman did camera and sound for the informal wedding at home, and the formal Jewish wedding was recorded by Henry Felt (camera), Marilyn Clayton (sound), and Ed Joyce (lighting). The differences in the weddings are reflected by the differences in the two documentations. The more intimate first wedding is presented in a free-form style, evocative of Brakhage and Mekas. No sync sound is used; at the beginning Weinstein and Feinstein introduce this wedding in voice-over; subsequently we hear the comments of the participants and guests (along with the sound of the camera running), and near the end of this section of the film Weinstein talks about the after-party and the days that followed. We see bits of the events in stills and in handheld motion pictures, often in passages of slow motion and stop action, and very largely in close-up.

The depiction of the first wedding lasts a bit more than 7 minutes; the formal wedding, about twice as long, is presented in a more traditional documentary manner. Nearly the entire event is presented in sync sound and focuses on interviews with various participants and guests who are identified by superimposed titles ("my sister," "my sister's boyfriend," "my father"). Weinstein is told by her mother that filming will not be allowed in the synagogue during the ceremony because of the lights and the distraction (Feinstein asks Sally Weinstein, "God doesn't like extra light?," triggering some barely repressed anger). Despite this restriction, the ceremony is represented in the finished film—as an audio recording; the screen remains dark during this passage (a premonition of a remarkable moment in McElwee's *Time Indefinite*; see p. 217). While the second wedding may have placated her parents, Weinstein herself seems less than enthusiastic about it ("I didn't like the rabbi"), while Feinstein seems to have found it exhilarating.

Call Me Mama was also recorded by others—John Terry (photography) and Pat Lockhart (sound recording)—but directed and edited by Weinstein. Recognizing that she could not mind Eli and make a film (Feinstein is entirely absent from *Call Me Mama*), "I decided somebody else had to be behind the camera and I would have to be in the film with Eli." *Call Me Mama* is recorded sync sound, and Weinstein provides an ongoing voice-off narration about her struggles to be a good mother and to continue to do her own work. The result is reminiscent of Laura Mulvey and Peter Wollen's *Riddles of the Sphinx*, which was finished the same year.

Weinstein's quartet of films may now seem typical of the feminist filmmaking of the 1970s, but her exploration of the possibilities of her own presence in documentations of her own experiences is an early breakthrough that would be developed by many other filmmakers. Further, however personal these films seemed during the 1970s, they seem a good bit more than personal now. Earlier chapters of this book have suggested that in the films of the Marshalls, Robert Gardner, and Timothy Asch, the quest to objectively document long-surviving cultures under the threat of transformation by the relentless spread of modern life led first to idealized fantasies, then to careers in which the personal lives, beliefs, and the filmmaking and teaching activities of the filmmakers themselves became increasingly central. The inverse has tended to be true in the history of personal documentary. What began as a variety of attempts to depict and analyze the filmmakers' most personal feelings and activities has increasingly become ethnographic evidence about life in the United States, including the changing role of filmmaking within family life.

This is certainly evident in Weinstein's films. As is clear in films that have recycled home movies—Alan Berliner's *The Family Album* (1986), the Austrian Gustav Deutsch's *ADRIA, Film—Schule des Sehens 1* (1990), much of the work of Peter Forgács—the home movie was for many decades largely a record of certain forms of performance for the camera. The advent of sync sound didn't entirely change this, of course, but it added the option of interviewing, and as a result, amateur home movie makers and personal documentary filmmakers alike could not only record their family members' antics in front of the camera but could elicit responses to questions asked within the immediacy of family interaction. In Weinstein's *My Father the Doctor* it is obvious that Weinstein's position as filmmaker has given her the reason and the courage to ask her father about his feelings and is the motivation for Saul Weinstein's considered and sometimes revealing answers: when Saul reveals his earlier hope that Miriam might go into the sciences or mathematics, Miriam responds that girls weren't expected to understand about science and math. Saul's startled "Why?" suggests how assumptions about women were changing; Saul has given up a stereotype, even if Miriam continues to be affected by it. Further, his attempt to take his daughter's filmmaking seriously confirms his considerable respect for her intelligence.

The debate about living together versus marriage in *Living with Peter* may seem quaint to a post–sexual revolution audience, but Weinstein's film does document, from within an unfolding relationship, an issue that affected many middle-class American young people and their families during the late 1960s and early 1970s. *Living with Peter* reveals not just the issue itself, but the ways in which young people and their parents articulated their ideas about this issue. During the years when Weinstein was making her personal documentaries, she was in touch with Jane Pincus, who was one of the founders of Boston's Our Bodies, Ourselves collective: Weinstein remembers, "We began to think that maybe personal concerns deserved some attention—a very new idea for women."[12] Weinstein's candidness about her own deviousness in pushing for marriage reveals how women (and men) could identify themselves as feminists while continuing to see themselves in problematic ways and allowing themselves to be patronized by men even within their personal relationships. Weinstein's four films reveal a woman in the throes of personal transformation: on one hand, she is acceding to the conventional by pushing for marriage and later, by taking full charge of her young son; on the other, she is demonstrably a working filmmaker—and she was among the first to carry her camera and tape recorder into her family life to document the ways in which societal changes were affecting intimate relationships in American middle-class lives.[13]

At the beginning of *Elephants: Fragments in an Argument* (1973; the opening title divides *elephants* into its three syllables: *el•e•phants*), and following the credits (which are accompanied by the sound of his father apparently looking at and identifying family photographs), Richard P. Rogers presents a montage of close-up shots of elephants in a zoo: we see skin, a tail, an ear, an eye, the face seen through the bars of a cage, a foot with a chain around it, the top of the head, the back, the trunk, an ear, and skin again. During this montage we hear, first, Rogers's father,

B. Pendleton Rogers, saying that his son, "like anybody else, has to sit down, and do some—as you *are*—weighing the different possibilities. You do have to take some chances; you do have to have some faith; you do have to be a little brave," followed by his mother Muriel Gordon Rogers's first comments (these begin as we see the chained elephant's foot): "I *do* think that possibly Kathy Rogers, Kathy Dodge had *guts*." My assumption is that Rogers means to evoke the well-known story about the blind men and the elephant: asked to touch an elephant and decide what it is, the man who touches the leg decides the elephant is a pillar; the man who touches the tail, believes it's rope, and so on. In its various guises in several cultures the story has usually been thought to illustrate that a single point of view cannot reveal the truth.

The relevance of this story to *Elephants* is multifaceted. Rogers seems to be making the film to try and come to terms with the various forces shaping his life as a young man: near the end of the film, intercut with a second montage of the elephants, we see him cleaning his small apartment as he delivers a brief monologue that begins, "I'm twenty-nine years old; I live at 20 Trowbridge Street, Cambridge, Massachusetts, in this apartment; I teach at Harvard University where I went as an undergraduate and where I went as a graduate student.[14] I wanted to make a movie about anger or about limits and about the forces that limited someone, but they had no control over, like their family and their past and their relationship to power in the society that they lived in." While *Elephants* draws no clear conclusions, the body of the film does explore the forces that seem to be affecting Rogers.

In *Elephants* family is represented in two ways—the same two ways Weinstein uses in *My Father the Doctor*: through family photographs from the past and through conversations with family members (in this instance, Rogers's father and mother). The family photographs and Rogers's parents' comments make clear that both families were rich and powerful, but that for whatever reasons, much of their power and money has vanished—though both parents, now divorced, seem to live quite luxuriously: the father in Manhattan, the mother in the Hamptons. Early in *Elephants,* as Rogers's mother talks about the family's past (sometimes we also hear the father's voice superimposed with hers), Rogers presents a black-and-white photo montage (one image dissolving into the next) that makes clear how luxurious the lifestyle of his recent ancestors was. While B. Pendleton Rogers seems worried about his son's lifestyle and is dubious that Rogers's filmmaking will yield him a decent living, Rogers's mother is downright hostile: she seems entirely self-involved, desirous of being left alone: "I don't like your tripod and your cameras and all your instruments all over my living room; it is my right to tell you to get them the hell out!" For the young filmmaker, family seems largely repellent; indeed, he seems to have foresworn any financial support from them.

The review of family history via photographs ends with a shot of Rogers as a baby, followed by a live action color shot of Rogers as an adult (his face, in close-up, moves across the frame from right to left). As we hear Rogers reading a passage from Karl Marx ("It is not the consciousness of men that determines their being, but on the contrary, their social being that determines their consciousness"), the film transitions from imagery of Rogers's family's past and present, first into a color sequence of close-up images of his cramped and grungy apartment and then into a long sequence of black-and-white imagery photographed on city streets, often in slow motion: kids having their pictures taken by apparently loving parents; porn theaters (Rogers films imagery inside one of the theaters), prostitutes, indigent street people, young women chosen for their erotic appeal. It is clear that Rogers is more at home, at least as a filmmaker, in these lower-class settings than with his angry mother or his vague father.

During the on-the-street sequence, imagery of one young woman (Terry Villafrade) becomes increasingly prominent and leads into the final major focus of the film: Rogers's relationship with her. We see black-and-white film imagery of Villafrade, shot apparently at various moments over a period of four years, contextualized by a sync-sound interview, during which she describes meeting Rogers when she was seventeen (she was in Cambridge alone, with no place to stay, and approached him), and their various, sometimes erotic, interactions over the years (Villafrade is naked in several shots). While this seems an affectionate, if rather haphazard relationship, it is clear, at least to Villafrade, that both she and Rogers interacted out of loneliness and that this relationship has no future. This sequence is interrupted by a long, color shot of Harvard Yard set up for graduation and leads into the closing sequence of Rogers cleaning the apartment and describing what he had hoped to accomplish by making *Elephants*. The film concludes with Rogers's voice-over, "I don't have any way to end this," and as we see end-of-roll perforations, "Why don't you just let it run out?," followed by a brief interchange with his father, who says, "Nothing ventured, nothing lost," and is corrected by Rogers: "It's nothing ventured, nothing *gained*."

While *Elephants* has much in common with Weinstein's earliest films, Rogers's first foray into personal documentary is in some senses quite distinct from *My Father the Doctor, Living with Peter,* and *We Get Married Twice*. Weinstein's films document small but real successes in her life, as a daughter, partner, and wife, as well as in filmmaking. *Elephants,* while technically more adventurous and accomplished than Weinstein's films, is a record of a period of confusion and frustration; the film provides no conclusion and no indication that filmmaking has been useful to Rogers personally, except in the sense that it has given a lonely young man a way of interacting with his family's past and the world around him. *Elephants* feels ragged and a bit out of control—an effective expression of a life in crisis.

Rogers would return to personal documentary ten years later, with *226-1690* (1984)—the title refers to his phone number in New York City. Using only messages left on the answering machine he shared with photographer Susan Meiselas, from New Year's Day 1984 to Christmas of that year, accompanied by imagery shot (by both Rogers and Meiselas) out the windows of their apartment in lower Manhattan, Rogers fashions a fascinating, engaging revelation of the complex life he and Meiselas were living during that year, a life full of work, lovers, the demands of friends and family (we recognize the voices of B. Pendleton Rogers and Muriel Gordon Rogers, neither of whom seems to have changed during the years since they were recorded for *Elephants*), within ongoing political developments.

1973 was a pivotal year in the emergence of the forms of personal documentary that were to become characteristic of Cambridge; and Weinstein and Rogers invoke the two approaches to the cinematic exploration of family that would characterize the feature films that would become the major achievements of Cambridge-based personal documentary: the use of filmmaking as a means of engaging family life as it is evolving around the camera and the exploration of familial past using visual documents of this past and oral history. While these two approaches are combined in Weinstein's films and in *Elephants*, Ed Pincus, Alfred Guzzetti, and Ross McElwee would develop forms of personal documentary that would be characterized by an emphasis on one or the other of the two approaches.

ED PINCUS'S *DIARIES* (1971–1976)

> There is a strange existential experience of seeing oneself on film, seeing oneself as others see you. . . . What a humiliating and humbling experience to appear equally as others appeared before. What is the nature of all our lives and our relations with others, our little lies and pretenses? . . . A new kind of filmmaker has emerged who deals with these questions. They find their material directly around them. They relate to the old traditions of American cinema verité by having a deep respect for the world as it exists independently of the presence of the camera, and although they often participate in different ways in the film, they do not in general manipulate action for the camera. . . .
>
> ED PINCUS[15]

Ed Pincus's career as a filmmaker and filmmaking teacher has been productive, influential, and very unusual. For several of his most productive years he was stalked by Dennis Sweeney, who had threatened his life and the lives of his family and who did kill civil rights attorney and liberal Democratic politician Allard Lowenstein in 1980.[16] Because of this, and because of his personal inclinations, Pincus turned away from filmmaking and remained largely out of the public eye for decades: since 1987 he and Jane Pincus have managed a flower farm in Vermont. Pincus's reemergence in 2007 as co-maker with Lucia Small of *The Axe in the Attic*, a documentary of the Hurricane Katrina disaster and the experience of trying to document it (see chapter 7), made clear that Pincus remained capable of making contributions to modern independent cinema.

Pincus began his career as a filmmaker in Cambridge not long after studying photography at the Carpenter Center at Harvard and telling Robert Gardner that he had absolutely no interest in filmmaking. When two friends, Sweeney and D. J. Smith, who knew Pincus had made a couple of short films, asked him if he'd be willing to go to Mississippi and document the freedom schools that had been established by civil rights activists, he agreed—"I had wanted to go down south and do something in the civil rights movement"—and proceeded first to enlist David Neuman (a Harvard dropout-turned-craftsman friend who would collaborate with Pincus on several films) to do sound; and then, to rent a camera from John Marshall: "I asked John for some instruction [on how to use the camera], and he said, 'Put it on your shoulder and push the button; you'll do fine.' That was all the instruction I had. David had about the same amount of instruction for taking sound. We had to figure things out from scratch."[17] In the end *Black Natchez* (1967) had nothing to do with freedom schools, but it remains a fascinating document of the civil rights campaign in Mississippi.

Pincus's experience shooting *Black Natchez* in 1965 had much in common with the anthropological expeditions discussed in earlier chapters: Pincus and Neuman were venturing into what was, for all practical purposes, a different culture, one in which they themselves were strangers and in which they could not assume they'd be out of harm's way. One important difference, of course, was that whereas Gardner and Asch could remain essentially neutral during the conflicts they documented in *Dead Birds* and *The Ax Fight,* Pincus and Neuman were resolute supporters of black liberation; indeed, that was the reason they were excited to undertake this project. And their presence as young white men living among and filming Natchez blacks announced this ideological commitment.

During their forty days shooting in Natchez, Pincus and Neuman worked in the tradition of Frederick Wiseman's brand of direct cinema, struggling to remain as invisible as possible to their subjects—not all that difficult, since, like the patients in Wiseman's *Hospital* (1969), the people they were documenting were embroiled in a deeply emotional, life-endangering struggle: *Black Natchez* documents the conflict within the black community of Natchez about which approach to the white power structure might be most effective for improving the situation of local blacks. Older, financially more established businessmen were nervous about confrontational strategies; a younger group was committed to large-scale nonviolent marches; and a third group was interested in establishing a secret cadre for taking guerrilla action against the Ku Klux Klan. A second film, *Panola,* not completed until 1970, was also a product of the Natchez shoot.[18] *Panola* is a 21-minute portrait of Panola, a wino who hides his fury about racism within an off-the-wall performance: "He said the only way to be free in Natchez is to make people think you're crazy."[19] Both *Black Natchez* and *Panola* reveal Pincus's fast-developing skill as a cameraman. Throughout *Black Natchez* Pincus's ability to work in-close with those he films is obvious, and *Panola* ends with Panola's astonishing performance of his existential agony, captured in a nearly 2-minute shot filmed with remarkable dexterity, as Panola offers a tour of the small shack where he and his large family live.

Pincus and Neuman's second project also began as an attempt to document a different culture, in this case the hippie commune culture that was developing during the late 1960s: "We chose Harry's commune. One of the reasons was that a lot of people said it was a very good commune, and it represented what people thought was the best happening in San Francisco."[20] Unfortunately, this commune was breaking up just as their shooting got underway, and as a result, they chose to focus on the daily life of a single hippie family—Harry, Rickie, and their son Joshua—and the result was *One Step Away* (1967). Pincus and Neuman were also rethinking their approach to documentary in a direction that would culminate in Pincus's decision to make *Diaries* (1971–1976). While in *Black Natchez* Pincus is at pains to suppress all evidence of his own presence and his own attitudes about the unfolding events, except insofar as the shaping of the footage implicitly reflects these attitudes, in *One Step Away,* his conclusion that the hippie way of life was not really all that different from conventional American life, that in many instances it was only an exaggeration of the conventional, is evoked by his use of the rather sardonic texts that introduce the various sections of the film. In large part, like *Black Natchez* and *Panola,* *One Step Away* reflected the direct-cinema approach Wiseman was developing, but in this instance Pincus's subject was the daily life of a real family, again filmed in-close with considerable intimacy, this time in a manner implicitly revelatory of the filmmaker's attitudes.[21]

Even if in retrospect it seems evident that Pincus's earlier films were gradually becoming more personally revealing, *Diaries* (1971–1976), begun once Pincus was teaching at MIT, represents a radical shift in his approach to filmmaking: a commitment to use portable sync-sound technology not to film a far-flung cultural group or set of sociopolitical events but to record and interpret his own personal life within a period of experimentation and change. During 1971, when Pincus began to shoot what would become *Diaries,* he and Jane Pincus, a committed feminist and one of the founders of the Our Bodies, Ourselves collective (and one of the producer/directors of *Abortion* [1971]),[22] had agreed to transform their eleven-year marriage by opening up the possibility of exploring sexual and emotional relationships with additional partners while remaining married to each other: "The notion that no one person could fulfill another's needs (whatever that meant) was in the air."[23] This decision was made essentially in tandem with Ed Pincus's decision to document what would happen to their marriage and their children over an extended period (fig. 19).

Pincus devised a plan to record footage of his personal life, as uncompromisingly as possible, for five years, then wait another five years before editing what he

FIGURE 19. Ed and Jane Pincus during the shooting of Ed Pincus's *Diaries* (1980) in the early 1970s. Courtesy Ed and Jane Pincus; photograph: Edna Katz.

had shot—though at the outset what editing might entail was ambiguous. Pincus's ten-year plan can be read as a reaction to the tendency of cinema-verite filmmakers to focus on particular events unfolding in a very limited time frame: "A very important part of the *Diaries* project was wanting to see what changes happened over a five-year period in people's lives, in the tenor of their politics, and perhaps in the way a filmmaker shoots."[24] In the end Pincus would adhere to his plan; he would shoot until 1976 and wouldn't finish editing what he had shot until 1980. Because *Diaries* has been out of general distribution since the early 1980s, the following discussion includes more description of what occurs in Pincus's inventive and influential personal documentary than might be necessary were the film better known.

　　Diaries was released as a 200-minute personal epic, divided into five unequal sections. "Part One," subtitled "Christmas eve 1971," is 52 minutes long. It begins in medias res with Ed and Jane dealing with the reality of Ed's filming (JANE: "I feel like I'm sacrificing myself for your film; I don't consider it my film. Get you mad?"; ED: "Doesn't make me happy"; JANE: "Tough shit"), with Ed involved in a romantic relationship with Ann Popkin, and with Jane and Ann working to deal with their discomfort with this situation. When Ed and Jane leave Cambridge to visit David Neuman in California, Jane struggles with feelings of inadequacy that she has apparently been dealing with for years, and though she can joke about Ed's lover— "She's a very nice girl," she tells David—the situation also means "a lot of agony for the wife." When Jane returns to Cambridge to rejoin their children, Ed stays in a cabin owned by Jim and Clarissa McBride, where he takes mescaline: after a shot during which Ed films himself in a mirror (reminiscent of similar shots in McBride's *David Holzman's Diary*), the repeated intertext "sometime between 5:00 and midnight" expresses his loneliness during the mescaline trip. At the end of this sequence Jim McBride films Pincus trying to deal with what seems to have been a long and unpleasant evening.

Once Ed returns from the "trip" within his trip, the remainder of part 1 immerses viewers within the busy-ness of everyday life at work (the office of the Film Section at MIT is introduced briefly, along with Pincus's colleague Ricky Leacock); and *Diaries* cuts directly from one aspect of his life to another: Pincus's son Ben has stitches taken out of a finger; Jane considers a tubal ligation; David Neuman and Ed visit an old friend who works at Simon & Schuster; Jane leaves for Paris to spend time with her lover Bob; Ed spends time with Ann; Jane returns, pregnant, and plans to abort the pregnancy (ED: "So it's like Bob's kid?; JANE: "Yes, but it's not a kid, it's an abortion"); Ed documents anti-war demonstrations, attends a therapy session; and Jane and Ed travel to New York State with their friends Emmanuel and Aliza, who is also aborting a pregnancy; the men talk with each other and, after the abortions, with the women. The abortion sequence is presented without melodrama, indeed as a kind of idyll: flowers are blooming everywhere. Throughout part 1 (and generally throughout *Diaries*), Pincus moves from one part of his life to another via direct cuts—a way of suggesting the simultaneity of all these ongoing, developing relationships and activities.

Near the end of part 1, as Jane is driving Ed to Ann's house, they discuss the fact that they are now living apart (Ed has moved into his office at MIT). Although each of them has had several lovers, both, says Jane, struggle with intimacy; indeed, she has realized that her tendency to sneeze is an expression of her need for more connection than she generally feels with Ed. During Ed's subsequent visit with Ann, she confirms Jane's analysis ("You're seeing a lot of women to escape your real life problems with Jane"). Life goes on for the MIT Film Section (Ed records a meeting in which Ricky Leacock explains how much a planned renovation of the Film Section's building will cost), and part 1 concludes with a monologue by Ed—the only such monologue in the film—during which he speaks to the camera, explaining that he has moved into his office because he feels he cannot live up to Jane's demands and that he hasn't been shooting film recently. He is interrupted by a phone call from Jane, and they discuss seeing a marriage counselor. In the final shot of part 1 Ed films Ben, the Pincuses' daughter Sami, and Jane in their bedroom at home.

While self-revelation (albeit within highly controlled and usually highly synthetic situations) has become the stuff of reality TV, during the five years when Pincus was documenting his and his family's experiences, his and Jane's openness involved a continual confrontation of convention. Ed and Jane Pincus had grown up during the 1950s and early 1960s, an era when secrecy was endemic in middleclass American life (Todd Haynes portrays this quite accurately in *Far from Heaven* [2002]). For their generation (this is also my generation) virtually everything about one's family life, from how much money one made to the nature of one's sexual activities, was "personal." Indeed, one important aspect of the youthful rebellion that characterized the late 1960s and early 1970s was the refusal of many young and middle-aged people to continue being secretive about their beliefs and activities or to accept secrecy about governmental policies that directly affected them: the release of the Pentagon Papers was a macrocosmic version of what was happening within the microcosm of many American families during those years. Two quite different reflections of this determination to be open and honest are evident from the beginning of *Diaries*. One is the frequent nudity, of Jane, of Ann, of Ben, and of Ed himself. In general, this is not exploitive nudity—though clearly Ed takes pleasure in Jane's body. Often it is evident during a particular shot that Jane is nude or partially nude, but there is no effort to expose her. Both Ann and Ed are seen nude in Ed's office loft early in the film, but here the camera is presumably mounted on a tripod on the floor of the loft, angled up, so that we see that they *are* nude together, but there is no attempt to reveal either of them in any detail. And sometimes Ben and his playmates are nude, in a bathtub or playing, but this is the nature of living with young children and, again, receives no undue focus.

A second kind of openness involves the ways in which Pincus makes visible (and audible) the filming process itself. The first conversation in the film reveals Jane's concern about looking beautiful for the camera and that she feels judged by it ("I have a mustache," she laughs, in an early close-up), and Ben's first line in the film is "What's that wheel?" Ed responds, "That's the camera." The sound of the camera running is audible, sometimes more, sometimes less, throughout *Diaries (1971–1976)* and becomes a motif. While there was nothing new in the 1970s about drawing attention to the apparatus of filming—many avant-garde filmmakers had engaged in explorations of the apparatus of the camera and projector—Pincus's decision to maintain the audience's awareness of his process in these ways was still unusual in the world of American documentary filmmaking: in the direct cinema of Wiseman, the Maysles Brothers, and others, the filmmaker's goal was to be as invisible as possible, especially insofar as the camera and sound equipment were concerned.

During the original shooting and within the finished film, Pincus doesn't merely depict the nature of his relationships with Jane, Sami, Ben, David Neuman,

Ann Popkin, and the others included in the footage, or reveal a particular change or transformative moment in a relationship. Pincus's five-year plan allows him to track the continually shifting nature of his relationships with family, lovers, friends, as well as the gradual changes in how his subjects (including Ed himself) interact with the camera and his filming. In other words, the life Pincus is revealing is a reality in continual flux within which he and Jane test, and retest, their marriage and their idea of marriage, adjusting to each other's changes on the basis of what they learn during each new adventure. They exemplify William James's understanding of reality as always "*still in the making*," always awaiting, "*part of its complexion from the future.*"[25]

Part 2 of *Diaries*, the longest in the film (72½ minutes), immediately reveals how much things have changed during the months between Ed and Jane's considering a marriage counselor and the summer of 1972, when they have rented a house in Vermont by a small lake. After the personal (and political) turmoil of late 1971 through early 1972, the opening section of part 2, which takes place in the Vermont landscape, seems idyllic, even Edenic. Early on, after several family scenes, including one in which Jane tells her visiting father how disrespected she feels by his disapproval of her hanging her batiks in the kitchen, we realize that although Ed stands up to her father (FATHER: "Ed, how did you feel about your wife turning your kitchen into a studio?"; ED: "I really liked it"), it has not been clear during the first hour of *Diaries* that Jane *is* a batik artist. Implicitly, Ed has changed since part 1: he's become more accepting of Jane's creativity. A kind of rebirth seems in the air, symbolized not only by this episode but by the Pincuses' new puppy, and by a scene during which Jane, Ann, and a third woman are lying nude in a kiddie pool, enjoying the sun (Ed, nude himself, hovers nearby; it is not clear who is doing the filming). Around this same time, it seems that Ed has been physically involved with both Jane and Ann, together; to Ed's embarrassment, they complain about his "looming" above them during the recent sexual adventure. During this passage—and in fact all through *Diaries*—the presence of Ben and Sami playing and fighting is pervasive, part of the auditory and often visual atmosphere of the film, and evidence not only of the continual change in the children and in their relationships with each other, but of Ed's and Jane's commitment to rethinking their marriage within a commitment to family.

A jump through time brings us to "fall 1972" and a brief passage during which Jane is working on batiks and Ed is filming. Jane, whose relationship with Bob seems in hiatus, explains that she was sexually open with him in ways she has never been with Ed. This is followed by "South by Southwest," a nearly 30-minute interruption in the Pincus family narrative during which Ed and David Neuman travel from California through Arizona (Tucson, where Ed makes contact with a now-married former lover and her newborn), New Mexico (a bridge over the Rio Grande near Santa Fe, and Taos), Arizona again (the Grand Canyon), and Las Vegas. After this interlude, Pincus returns to Cambridge, where Jane is learning the flute, and where Ed films the broadcast of his appearance on Robert Gardner's *Screening Room* and spends time with Christina, apparently a new lover, and Ann. About two hours into the film, *Diaries (1971–1976)* announces an intermission.

Pincus's determination to record the realities of a nuclear family undergoing experimentation and change is quite radical (of course, what is radical here is not simply the couple's taking lovers but their openness about this process, both with each other and with the camera and implied audience), but it is not Pincus's only commitment as filmmaker. His documenting the development of his family life is interwoven with a second commitment, this one specifically cinematic: he means to explore and redefine the relationship between filmmaker and subject within film history, and especially within the history of cinema verite filmmaking. From the beginning of *Diaries (1971–1976)*, Jane (and Ben and Sami) are the objects of Ed's filmic gaze, but he himself is also on screen regularly: twenty-three times during parts 1 and 2. In three instances, Ed films his reflection in a mirror, and in two others he has set up the camera in order to film himself, but in most instances, someone else is holding the camera: Ann, during their conversations; Jim McBride, during Ed's mescaline trip; David, when Ed is driving in Tucson; and other people in other instances. While we are often not sure who is filming Ed, it is obvious that the documentation of his open marriage involved also the opening up of the filming process itself: that is, in *Diaries (1971–1976)* the marital experimentation and the filmic experimentation are analogous to one another.

Subsequent to the intermission, the mood of *Diaries* changes: part 3 (20¾ minutes) opens, just as part 1 does, with a mirror shot in which we see both Ed and Jane, but in this instance, Ed's hand is seen in the foreground giving Jane a ring, as Ed says, "Will you marry me?" The remainder of this section of the film seems to confirm the Pincuses' comfort in the ongoing development of their domestic life, and this development is apparent in a variety of ways: for example, Jane has finally gotten the tubal ligation she considered during part 1, and much of part 3 is focused on Ed's cousin Jill's wedding in New York, a traditional wedding during which Ed, Jane, the children, and Ed's mother function in conventional ways. The adventurousness of the open marriage is alluded to during two passages focused on Christina, but Christina's comments that conclude this section of the film—"Everybody has to learn that they are *alone*. . . . You gotta learn how to be alone!"—seem contradicted by Ed's immersion in both nuclear and extended family.

Part 4 (30 minutes) confirms the changes in part 3; indeed, the opening of part 4 ("winter 1974—a broken leg") seems a further counterpoint to Christina's comments on having to learn to live alone. Pincus, now with his leg in a cast, films the family functioning around him. Jane's batiks are hanging here and there, more visible than at any previous moment in the film; and her developing creativity is also emphasized by the motif of her playing the flute: we can hear how she has improved (the ongoing improvement in her ability as a musician remains a motif). In the following sequence, when Ed visits the MIT Film Section office on crutches, we can see that a romance is brewing, or is underway, with a woman there; and it is evident that an involvement with other lovers continues (near the end of part 4, Ed and Jane talk about Ed's feeling more temptation in the city than in Vermont).

Part 4 also confirms Pincus's increasing openness about himself, his deepening engagement with domesticity; and it marks a change in his thinking as a film-maker. Early in part 4, Ed films (and has someone else film) the process of reha-bilitating his leg; we see various men, nude, undergoing whirlpool treatments in a training room. Also during part 4, Pincus includes a shot (again a shot made by someone else) of himself teaching at MIT (he refers to Rossellini's *Voyage in Italy* [*Viaggio in Italia*, 1953]: "The action . . . is the . . . small moves between couples"), and at a party we see Ed, talking with Ricky Leacock (the conversation filmed by a third person) about the somewhat different costs of being a private versus a public person. In part 4, Ed also seems increasingly appreciative of his family life. Ben's curiosity about filmmaking becomes more obvious, and Sami is developing as a performer; in several instances she and a friend do song and dance numbers for the camera. The obvious intimacy of this nuclear family is encapsulated in one noteworthy composition midway through part 4: parts of Ed's, Jane's, and Ben's bodies are intertwined on a bed; they seem almost a single being.

The change in Pincus's thinking as a cinematographer is evident in a conver-sation he has early in part 4 with Christina, who wonders what Ed is learning about his life from recording footage for *Diaries*. Pincus's response—"It's inter-esting, light's just become more important"—annoys Christina: "That's not what I'm asking! That disgusts me that that's your answer! That's a technical answer to this philosophical question. . . . I mean what about just this nitty-gritty sort of human aspect of your life? It has nothing to do with light!" While, in the end, Pincus does admit that he's found out "a lot about myself; I just don't want to talk about it," his immediate response to Christina's query is, "I don't know if you're right about that," which is implicitly confirmed by his focusing on patches of reflected light on the wall of Christina's loft, and, at the end of the conversation, by his transitioning from the window in her loft to a window in his Vermont home (actually, Pincus's awareness of light is quite evident throughout *Diaries*). This interchange between Ed and Christina reflects a gradual change in empha-sis from the nitty-gritty of Ed's and Jane's working on their relationship to the physical beauty of Vermont and to Ed's increasingly idyllic engagement with his children and Jane so evident in part 5 ("filming every day in January—the small events of days at home"), which begins with an unusual voice-over: "Today is January 1st and I'm going to try to film every day" (unusual because this is the first voice-over in the film spoken within the present, rather than from the dis-tance of the editing process).

While part 5 (22 minutes) is increasingly idyllic, this is not because the Pincuses have retreated from their experimental marriage into conventional monogamy. Early in the section, Ed asks Jane about her upcoming visit to Joe. Jane responds, "It's piquant, it's unusual, it's an adventure, it's a risk; it will not jeopardize our marriage, but it will change it in small ways." When Ed asks why, she responds, "I'm not sure. . . . I somehow feel sexier already, toward *you* . . . and I feel also very thankful that I can have that kind of adventure, and recognize it as some kind of adventure and that there's maybe some dangers, but—and maybe I'm being stupid, I don't know—but I guess I feel pretty good about it." The return to a series of upbeat domestic moments confirms the idea that Jane's adventure not only does not endanger the marriage but may invigorate it.[26] This idea is cinematically confirmed soon after this conversation when Jane, in a flirty manner, says to Ed, who is filming her, "You look cute. Can I take a picture of you?" Ed says, "Sure," and we see that the camera changes hands; Jane pans around to Ed, who is sitting at a desk, naked from the waist down.

As has been suggested, throughout *Diaries (1971–1976)* Ed opens up his process by releasing his camera into many other hands. This, however, is the first instance where we witness the transfer of control from his hands to another's. That Jane has *asked* to make this image (another first in the film—though we assume she is filming in other instances) brings *Diaries* full circle from Jane's voicing concern at the opening of the film about the presence of the camera and being the object of its gaze. And it creates a cinematic "ring" (echoing perhaps the ring Ed gives Jane at the beginning of part 3) that joins the man and woman as co-creators of both a marriage and a family and as makers of the film we are watching.

Part 5 concludes with four distinct but related sequences that function as a coda to Pincus's domestic epic. The first of these, titled "Summer 1975—freeze tag," focuses entirely on Ben (fig. 20), Sami, and some other children playing freeze tag in a lovely, green-glowing Vermont landscape. The very idea of freeze tag evokes the larger project of *Diaries (1971–1976)*, which freezes a series of moments in several intertwined lives; and a shot of Ben trying, without too much success, to freeze in position echoes the nature of the lives depicted in the film: Ed and Jane work to maintain their stability as a couple and as parents within a continually changing social landscape. The freeze tag sequence also confirms the film's increased focus on Ben and Sami. When Ben throws a tantrum because he doesn't want to be "it," Sami functions as his therapist, explaining that being "it" is "part of the playing, part of the whole game, and if you don't be it, it's no fun for anyone else. You gotta be it sometimes, Ben, just *try* it!" I read this interchange as not only a poignant record of the interaction between two siblings (Ben does become involved with the game), but also as a metaphor for Ed and Jane: early in the film, Jane seems the one who is struggling with both the experiment of open marriage and with this experimental film; in the final sections, and despite the strength of their ongoing relationship, Ed is "it" and must deal with Jane's going off with other men.[27]

FIGURE 20. Ben Pincus in Ed Pincus's *Diaries* (1980). Courtesy Ed and Jane Pincus.

The second sequence begins with Ed's voice-over announcing, "That summer, we decided to live permanently in Vermont," followed by a lovely sequence of Jane walking through a snowscape outside of their Vermont home in beautiful winter light. Pincus explains how this move has involved him in commuting from Vermont to MIT and that part of the reason for this change in their lives is that "Dennis Sweeney had become a problem in my life. . . . Dennis had turned vicious and now threatened Jane, Ben, and me"; "Five years later, in March 1980, Dennis walked into Allard Lowenstein's office and shot and killed him." This is followed by a conversation between Jane and Ed—they are in a car; Jane is driving—revealing their anger and frustration with Sweeney and his threats. This is the final instance in the film of what has been a motif throughout: filming conversations in a moving car; and like so many other motifs in *Diaries* this one functions both literally and metaphorically. In a variety of senses, Ed, Jane, Sami, Ben, and their friends and extended family members are continually "on the move." Sometimes one or another person is driving this movement (in this final instance, Jane is driving the car, though Sweeney is implicitly driving the Pincuses into a new kind of life), but as in freeze tag, the lives Pincus portrays are made up of a series of moments of stability within ongoing social, political, physical, psychological, and emotional change.

Immediately after Ed and Jane's conversation about Sweeney, an intertitle, "summer 1976—a friend has terminal cancer" introduces a brief sequence that reveals Ed's visit to his friend David Hancock's home and Ed's subsequent sadness about David's illness. This is followed by a cine-memorial to David, a series of five shots, beginning with David, looking very gaunt, in a bed covered by a blanket with red edging. This bit of red is carried into the shots that follow: a red geranium on a window sill; a view out the window at distant trees with leaves changing that pans to a crayon drawing of the geranium; a ground-level shot of David's burial in which several women have red skirts; and finally, a rainy fall day and a tree with leaves turned red. This "bouquet" of red is Pincus's tribute to his friend and to the passion for life and for Vermont that David had apparently always exhibited.

The conclusion of *Diaries (1971–1976)* is a 3-minute shot of Ed, Jane, and Ben, in the early fall after David's death, outside their Vermont home, on Yom Kippur.[28] As the credits roll, Jane is cutting Ed's hair and Ben is whining about Sami's bothering him (Sami is heard, behind the camera, defending herself, though we never see her during this shot).[29] As Jim Lane has suggested, "The cutting of Ed's hair suggests not only a renewed bond between the couple but also a transformed Ed, an Ed more content with his revised role as husband and father. His unique relationship with the camera (which he warns his children not to knock over during the scene) underpins this realization. This relationship has changed over time, as has his relationship with his family."[30] Throughout this final family portrait, a reflection on the left side of the frame appears rhythmically, a final emblem of cinema itself and of Pincus's decision to embed the filmmaking apparatus within the reshaping of his personal life and the lives of his family. This final image also encapsulates what Pincus knew by 1980, when he finished editing *Diaries:* that he had not only documented a redefinition of marriage and family, and rethought how filmmaking could function within domestic, everyday life, but had exited from filmmaking altogether. Pincus would leave his teaching job at MIT in 1979 and, in concert with Jane, would establish and manage Third Branch Flower, in Roxbury, Vermont. He wouldn't finish another film for twenty-seven years.

Flannery O'Connor's belief in "the possibility of reading a small history in a universal light" seems relevant to Pincus's quest to document the particular changes he and his family went through during a half-decade, for while Pincus's focus is even more intimate than what O'Connor would call "local," this intimacy represents a substantial portion of a particular American generation during an unusually eventful extended moment.[31] During the early 1970s many thousands of young married couples (my present wife and I were among them) experimented with new definitions of marriage, definitions that challenged traditional monogamy and conventional assumptions about privacy. Pincus is one of few filmmakers who has chronicled, from inside the experience itself, this generation's experimentation and the ways in which their experiments affected the day-to-day lives of couples and families.

Ultimately, Pincus's revelations in *Diaries (1971–1976)* have much in common with what John Marshall reveals in *A Group of Women, A Joking Relationship,* and *A Kalahari Family,* what Robert Gardner reveals in *Dead Birds* and *Rivers of Sand,* and what Timothy Asch reveals in *Dodoth Morning, A Father Washes His Children,* and even perhaps in *The Ax Fight.* All these films reveal the lives of families and their attempts to find moments of stability and intimacy in a continually changing environment within which the fact of filmmaking itself is emblematic of both transformation and a hunger for continuity.

During the interim between his shooting and editing *Diaries,* Pincus collaborated with Steven Ascher on *Life and Other Anxieties,* which was shot during 1976–77 and completed in 1977 (the two men would later collaborate on two editions of *The Filmmaker's Handbook,* first edition published in 1984).[32] *Life and Other Anxieties* begins more or less where *Diaries* ends, with a prologue during which Pincus returns to the summer and fall of 1976, when he discovered that David Hancock had cancer of the liver. In voice-over he explains:

> Six months ago I hugged David and he felt strong like an oak tree. The next time I talked to him, his voice was distant: he told me he had cancer of the liver. He had been planning to go to Europe to make a film; and now he wanted to do a film about his dying, about the brutality of the medical establishment. He'd asked me to help him; I was never able to do that. When Steve came to visit, I asked him to shoot for me. I tried to give David's death meaning, but none comes. David was a good friend; what more can I say?

Footage of Hancock at his Vermont home is followed by Pincus's indicating that he has received a grant to make a film in Minneapolis during the following winter: his plan is to attract strangers to the project and to film whatever the strangers indicate they would like him to film. Before he and Ascher travel to Minnesota for the winter-spring, Hancock is filmed one more time (he is on the phone, looking very frail, saying, "Looks like it's all over"); his funeral follows. Ascher and Pincus then travel to Minneapolis, and the remainder of *Life and Other Anxieties* intercuts between the filmmakers trying to convince people to be involved in their project and the various events they end up being a part of.

Except for the sequences involving Hancock (and footage shot when Pincus flew home to Vermont for ten days—Jane, Sami, and Ben make appearances), the personal dimension of *Life* is the personal struggle of Pincus, who did the shooting, and Ascher, who took sound, to get the film made: this involves a range of personal interactions with strangers, evocative in a general sense of Jean Rouch and Edgar Morin's *Chronique d'un été (Paris 1960) (Chronicle of a Summer (Paris*

1960); 1961). At one point, in desperation, Pincus and Ascher follow random people around, filming them; but they do find their way to a variety of willing subjects and are able to weather the brutal Minnesota winter (they film at a party on an evening when there is a −80 degree wind chill). The result is an engaging panorama of men and women, young and old, black and white, working and playing in the Twin Cities area. The film is dedicated to Hancock, who was a Minnesota native.

As this book goes into production, Pincus is at work on what might be considered a further response to Hancock's death, and in particular, to Hancock's asking Pincus to produce a film about his (Hancock's) death—a request Pincus didn't feel he could grant (*Life and Other Anxieties* seems, in a sense, an atonement for this decision). In 2012, Pincus learned that he had AML (acute myeloid leukemia), a rare and dangerous form of leukemia. His response, a response that echoes Hancock's, was to throw himself into a film about facing his own imminent mortality. The tentative title is *The Elephant in the Room*; Pincus is co-making it with Lucia Small.

ALFRED GUZZETTI: *FAMILY PORTRAIT SITTINGS*

Here was a subject (my family) that I already knew a lot about, and I felt that this offered an opportunity to make a film that went deeper, into more detail, than the cinema verite films, including the personal documentaries that were being made. Ed Pincus was committed to a very pure kind of cinema verite; Diaries *is an exploration of that purist point of view. Ed has always been tactful enough not to talk about* Family Portrait Sittings, *but I suspect he didn't like it.*

ALFRED GUZZETTI[33]

Like Ed Pincus, Alfred Guzzetti was drawn to family as a subject for documentary because, like so many filmmakers coming of age in the late 1960s and early 1970s, he believed that the personal is the political, and because a focus on family would allow him to circumvent what he had come to feel was one of the crucial limitations of the forms of documentary that had become popular during the 1960s and early 1970s: "At the time, I felt that cinema-verite documentary, which was all the rage, was nearly always superficial—I sometimes still feel this way. One reason is that people who make cinema-verite documentaries encounter their subjects in the way that Flaherty prescribed: practically without preconception. This is wonderful in one sense—it allows for certain kinds of discoveries—but on the other hand, diving into something new and exploring doesn't take you very deep, given the amount of time you have to learn about your subject and the amount of shooting time you usually have."[34] Making a film about his own family, Guzzetti reasoned, would allow him to come to his subject with long-term experience and considerable knowledge, and it would allow for an extended shooting schedule, enough time to produce something substantive. Unlike Pincus, however, Guzzetti decided to focus not on an ongoing experiment in redefining the experience of family, but rather on the history that had brought his family to its present situation, and in general, on the way in which families come to represent themselves over time.

Family Portrait Sittings divides into three approximately equal parts, each of which has somewhat different emphases and reflects different aspects of what Guzzetti came to understand about his family during his three years of shooting. Part 1 begins with a brief foreword during which we hear Domenick Verlengia, Guzzetti's maternal great-uncle and the oldest surviving member of his family, in voice-over, describing his decision to leave Italy and emigrate to the United States. The excitement of this decision is suggested by a series of forward tracking shots through South Philadelphia streets. The final tracking shot comes to a stop as Verlengia says, "And I arrive here in Philadelphia the thirteen of May, 1921." The film's title is then superimposed over a close-up of hands sewing a man's suit coat (Verlengia was a tailor), which is followed by a listing of those whose voices chronicle the family's history: Guzzetti's great-uncle; his grandmother, Pauline Verlengia; his paternal grandfather's cousins Guido and Savaria D'Alonzo; his own parents, Felix and Susan Verlengia Guzzetti.

During the remainder of part 1, the focus is on the background of the two families. Domenick Verlengia describes the history of his family up until his emigration to America: his focus is the intelligence of his mother, who died young, and brother (Guzzetti's grandfather), who knew how to make a suit by the time he was fourteen years old. His narration of the Verlengia family history is accompanied by forward tracking shots through Abruzzo, Italy, with stops in the locations mentioned. Verlengia's review of his family history is followed by the Guzzetti cousins' voice-over review of their family's history (translated by subtitles), beginning with a story from 1365 and ending with two brothers, Quirino and Nicolino, coming to America. An extended passage of black-and-white photographs of the two families follows, with Guzzetti's parents, grandmother, and uncle describing the families' early years in Philadelphia, years that led to the union of Susan and Felix. Interrupting this photo montage, in two instances, are sync-sound moments from interviews first with Pauline Verlengia and then with Domenick, and finally with Sue and Felix, sitting on a couch in their apartment, talking about their courtship (fig. 21). Black-and-white home movies and photographs of their wedding bring part 1 to a close.

Part 2 focuses on the Guzzettis' early married life: the struggle for jobs during the Depression; Sue's decision to go to teacher's college; Felix's employment by Economical Coal Company and his interest in photography; Domenick's tailoring work; and the arrival of children: Alfred in 1942 and Paula in 1946. The emergence

FIGURE 21. Susan and Felix Guzzetti on couch in family home in Alfred Guzzetti's *Family Portrait Sittings* (1975). Courtesy Alfred Guzzetti.

of Felix and Sue's family is formally signaled by Guzzetti's inclusion of his father's color home movies, which become a subtext of *Family Portrait Sittings* from here on, a kind of secondary chronology of events represented by artifacts produced during this chronology. The motif of Guzzetti's parents sitting on the couch (and Domenick Verlengia sitting in a chair), speaking to Guzzetti behind the camera, becomes central in part 2, as the parents discuss their history and their differences in temperament and attitude over the years, along with some of the sacrifices their family required: most obviously, their move from South Philadelphia to a new neighborhood where the children could have more room and better schools—a neighborhood, it turns out, neither parent is comfortable in, though the children thrived. Sue's and Felix's very different personalities and the resulting mixture of agreement and conflict during their years together are echoed by their changing positions on the couch: sometimes they sit next to one another, at other times, at opposite ends of the couch. Part 2 ends with Sue and Felix discussing their relationship to religious belief (both, in somewhat different ways, make clear their ambivalence) and with a silent, color shot of young Paula eating cereal at the kitchen table.

Part 3 continues the motifs established in part 2: Sue and Felix Guzzetti's commentary on their history together, Domenick Verlengia's reflections on his involvement with his niece's family, accompanied by the color home movie records of the development of the Guzzetti children: like most home movies, these are focused on birthday parties and other family get-togethers. More fully than earlier parts of *Family Portrait Sittings*, however, part 3 reveals struggles with issues that were becoming increasingly important in the 1950s and 1960s, including Sue's emerging as what Domenick Verlengia describes as the "prime mover" of the family and her own ambivalence about her "aggressiveness" (during this section of the film, Sue and Felix are arranged on the couch so that Sue is in the very center of the frame, and Felix to her right). Later in the section, the elder family members discuss the Vietnam War and President Richard M. Nixon (Domenick Verlengia is outspoken in his contempt for Nixon and the war), and various forms of more local political struggle, including Sue on a picket line demonstrating for better working conditions for teachers. In a break from strict chronology, Guzzetti's grandmother asks Domenick Verlengia to "tell Alfred about the story when pop died, how you took over the house," and Verlengia describes the political discussions he once had with his brother.

Part 3 ends with a sequence during which we see both Felix Guzzetti and Alfred shooting film, a kind of shot/countershot between two generations and two modes of filmmaking (Felix is shooting with a small 8mm camera; Alfred in one instance with a CP16 and later with a professional grade Arriflex), followed by Felix's comments on his son's filmmaking:

> I've never seen anybody who's as enthusiastic over making these films that have no commercial value at all, actually have no . . . they *don't*, Alfred. You can never make any money out of it. You know that and I know that, and not once has anyone of us said, "Well, he is crazy, he is doing all this work and he gets no commercial rewards." But we know how you feel about these things and we know you're happy in it, and that remark will never, never come out of me, that you're crazy for doing them. . . .

While Felix's comments can be taken as a well-meaning critique of the film we are seeing (as well as a premonition of Ross McElwee's father's disapproval of his son's choice of filmmaking as a vocation, which becomes something of a motif in McElwee's personal documentaries), I assume Guzzetti's father is referring to the films that his son had completed by the time he was recording imagery for *Family Portrait Sittings—Air* (1971), for example, which is fully within the tradition of the American avant-garde (see Chapter 5). Brief final comments by Guzzetti's parents, uncle, and grandmother conclude the film.

If Guzzetti as filmmaker is virtually invisible during most of *Family Portrait Sittings*—we see him as an adult only once, in the shot/countershot moment just described, and we hear him off camera, from time to time, asking his parents and his uncle questions—several of his formal choices draw attention to themselves and to his filmmaking in unusual ways. The first of these formal choices is evident in the film's prologue. Guzzetti's forward tracking shots through South Philadelphia streets are presented as a series of jump cuts that simultaneously draw attention to this neighborhood and to Guzzetti's editing of these shots. That Domenick Verlengia's memories of the importance of tailoring for him and Guzzetti's father provide the soundtrack during these shots and that these memories are then confirmed by the title shot of Verlengia sewing the collar of a suit coat makes explicit, as Jim Lane has suggested, Guzzetti's belief that his filmmaking has its roots in his maternal family's involvement in tailoring: "Associating film production with the skilled labor of the tailor-uncle demystifies the filmmaking process and brings it to the level of tangible work of a second-generation Italian American. The film acknowledges that it is made and woven together, just as a fine suit might be hand-sewn."[35]

Guzzetti's framing of his mother and father on the couch is another suggestive formal choice. The couch sits against a mirrored wall, so that we see both what is in front of us and what is behind us (a staircase, a table with a vase on it)—*except for* Guzzetti and his camera. While Guzzetti has said that the decision to film his parents in front of the mirror was a simple, practical one that involved altering their small living room as little as possible, it creates not only an obvious metaphor for Guzzetti's project—as William Rothman has said, the mirror serves "throughout the film as a metaphor for the process of reflection"[36]—but a visual mystery: we cannot help asking, through much of the film, where Guzzetti's camera, and Guzzetti himself, are. That is, Guzzetti's physical invisibility is rendered visible, in a manner that recalls, and is the inverse of, what occurs in *David Holzman's Diary* (1967), where the visibility of "David" and his equipment in a mirror seems to prove that the film is nonfiction and that David is alone, filming himself. Here, the mysterious invisibility of the filmmaking process makes us fully conscious of the fact that much is going on beyond the seemingly expansive frame the film offers us. And this expands the metaphoric implications of Guzzetti's composition: clearly, what Sue and Felix tell their son and his camera are particular versions of their history, versions that, as coherent as they have become over time, leave out a good deal not only of what has occurred but also of the ways in which this history has affected and continues to affect their understanding of and their feelings for one another.[37]

In *Family Portrait Sittings* Guzzetti is at pains to balance image and sound as equal contributors to the history he is exploring. He provides both a visual history of his family, as it is recorded in photographs and home movies, and an oral history: "I also wanted the style to acknowledge the gap between what the image could show and the sense the words could make, to claim equal attention for both, to avoid reducing the image to an illustration or the words to a commentary, even where this meant putting unaccustomed difficulties in the way of the viewer."[38] Guzzetti's decision to allow the sync signal provided by his Arriflex—a screech— to remain part of the footage of his parents, great-uncle, and grandmother speaking to him draws particular attention to the sync-sound passages that follow. For anyone not familiar with filming with an Arriflex, these screeches must remain a mystery, though they do offer a dramatic entry into the "present" of Guzzetti's conversations with his relatives, and they inevitably draw attention to the filmmaking process that is underway.

These self-reflexive formal choices ask viewers to factor into their experience of the film their recognition that Guzzetti's presence as filmmaker must be having a variety of forms of impact on the truth of what we see and hear, and that while he doesn't wish to make himself the central character in his film—the history of his family is that—he also does not want to pretend his activity as a filmmaker is irrelevant. One of the revelations of the Watergate fiasco, which concluded with Nixon's resignation from the presidency the year before *Family Portrait Sittings* was finished, was that Nixon had been secretly taping (and more recently, erasing) his conversations with visitors to the Oval Office. Guzzetti may be indirectly referring to this well-known incident, which was disastrous for Nixon's reputation; while he is at some pains to keep his person out of the film, Guzzetti does not hide what he is up to.

Family Portrait Sittings is a landmark personal documentary, one that has had some considerable influence, or at least seems to have charted a territory that others would later explore (think of Alan Berliner's triad of family films: *The Family Album* [1986], *Intimate Stranger* [1991] and *Nobody's Business* [1996]; and Su Friedrich's *The Ties that Bind* [1984] and *Sink or Swim* [1990], all of which recycle family home movies into a narrative of family life during a particular era). We can also think of Guzzetti's film as having ethnographic value on at least two levels. Most obviously, the story of two Italian immigrant families arriving in the United States and making a life for themselves is representative of a good many Americans of their generation. *Family Portrait Sittings* is evidence of the ways in which many families of this generation defined themselves, spoke with each other, decided on practical matters, and how they aged and what aging meant to them and to their understanding of the family life they had lived.

Second, Guzzetti's interweaving of his own filmmaking with his father's home movies reveals how a younger generation learned from their elders and transformed their own thinking about the *representation* of family life. Felix Guzzetti's home movies are generic: they are ritual records of those occurrences that one generation felt were worthy of being documented, occurrences that his generation wanted to remember in this particular way. Not only was there nothing unusual in what these home movies captured, the fathers and mothers (probably mostly fathers) who recorded family events would have understood that their filmmaking was, and was meant to be, perfectly conventional—as much a ritual activity as blowing out the candles on a birthday cake. The generation of their children, however—a generation that includes both Guzzetti and Ed Pincus—had come to deploy movie making in an entirely different way within a family situation. Just as the generation coming to maturity in the late 1960s and early 1970s was reconsidering the nature of American family life, the filmmakers of this younger generation were rethinking how family life could be represented. This difference in generations is evident in the fact that while there is no mystery whatsoever—and only the most basic formal decision making—in what Felix Guzzetti records in his family home movies, his son's filmmaking shows how opening up the family to new kinds of cinematic scrutiny resulted in various formal challenges, including, as William Rothman has shown, combining objectivity and subjectivity.[39]

For Pincus the challenge was how to integrate his filming into the moment-to-moment evolution of his relationships with family members, lovers, and colleagues, and this resulted in his adaptation of the possibility of single-person sync-sound shooting, and at times, the recruitment of his fellow subjects as camera people. In the case of Alfred Guzzetti's first foray into personal documentary, the challenge was how to create a coherent experience from many sources and kinds of information, accumulated over a period of half a century, and how to figure the particular saga of his own family within the larger forces of history. Guzzetti was successful in meeting these challenges; certainly *Family Portrait Sittings* communicates a good bit about a certain generation's experiences as well as about his own family's input into his becoming a filmmaker of a particular kind. That *Family Portrait Sittings* is sometimes confusing and can feel a bit cluttered is itself evidence of the difficulties of rethinking family and reinventing films about family at a certain moment in modern cultural history. Guzzetti would return to the history of Sue and Felix's marriage and its impact on his own filmmaking in a very different form in *Time Exposure* (2012), discussed later in this chapter.

GUZZETTI: *IT'S A SMALL WORLD*

Guzzetti's fascination with family continued to instigate film projects during the decade or so after *Family Portrait Sittings* was finished. This fascination took two directions. In *The House on Magnolia Avenue* (shot in 1975 and 1987, finished in 1989), *Scenes from Childhood* (shot during the summer of 1977 and finished in 1980), and *Beginning Pieces: A Picture of Sarah Ages 2 to 5* (shot from 1981 to 1985, finished in 1986), Guzzetti explored first his and Deborah Fortson's attempt to develop their family within an economically communal context, and then, the nature of childhood. In *Living at Risk: The Story of a Nicaraguan Family* (1985), Guzzetti teamed up with Richard P. Rogers and photographer Susan Meiselas first to document the experiences of a Nicaraguan family dealing with the pressures of the Nicaraguan revolution, then to make *Pictures from a Revolution* (1991), which revisits Meiselas's canonical photographs of the revolution within the context of a postrevolutionary Nicaragua.

The House on Magnolia Avenue is reminiscent of Michael Apted's *Up* series: Guzzetti interviews Deborah Fortson and the five friends with whom they bought a house on Magnolia Avenue in Cambridge, first in 1975, and then again twelve years later (a brief interview with Guzzetti and Fortson's son Ben is included in the first series of interviews; interviews with Ben and their daughter Sarah in the second series). Essentially, the film is a record of the thinking of a reasonably diverse group of young men and women who have been powerfully enough affected by the social ferment of the late 1960s and early 1970s to imagine a new social construct both in their work lives and their living arrangements; and then of how twelve years have affected these earlier ideas and ideals. In general, the passing of time has resulted in changes in location (only feminist psychiatrist Judith Herman had continued to live in the Magnolia Avenue house) and some modifications in outlook and in professional direction, but the group remains committed to living in a manner that they hope can be a progressive model for others.[40]

Scenes from Childhood is a feature-length observational film during which Guzzetti focuses on the play of several young children (the youngest are a bit over three years of age, the oldest, a bit over five). In many ways, *Scenes from Childhood* is reminiscent of Fred Wiseman's work: Guzzetti is able to be the fly-on-the-wall observer as the children interact, and even in those few instances when a child seems to appeal to him for help, he remains entirely detached (Guzzetti was a one-person crew on the film). The film begins with a quote from *Walden*: "Children, who play life, discern its true law and relations more clearly than men . . . ," and whether one concludes that these children are in fact discerning about the nature of their world, the film does allow for an extended focus on their interaction when adults are not involved. For Guzzetti this was an ethnographic film, and it reflects the interest in childhood that seems an important dimension of the ethnographic filmmaking of Marshall (who finished his own film about American childhood, *Vermont Kids,* in 1975),[41] Gardner, and Asch, as well as of earlier personal documentaries, *Call Me Mama* and *Diaries (1971–1976),* most obviously.

Beginning Pieces (currently not in distribution) expands Guzzetti's exploration of early childhood in a more personal way than *Scenes from Childhood:* his focus here is his daughter Sarah, though Ben, who is seen in *Family Portrait Sittings* and in *The House on Magnolia Avenue* and is one of the children in *Scenes from Childhood,* is an important figure in this film as well: indeed, *Beginning Pieces* opens with Ben reading "a dream I had on February 15th, my sister's birthday." As in *Scenes from Childhood,* Guzzetti generally remains invisible during his filming of Sarah and her friends, though, from time to time the children interact with him. Given our present context, what seems most interesting about *Beginning Pieces* is the way in which it provides a record of assumptions about childhood, and the representation of childhood, during a certain era. I am not raising children now and in recent years have not been privy to how young parents deal with their children, but I do remember that both during my own childhood in the 1940s and when I was a young parent in the 1970s, children often played together nude—in the 1970s this seemed part of that generation's commitment to rethinking social convention (this included teaching young children the real names for parts of the body and being responsive to their questions about "how babies are made"). In more recent years, the understandable concern about child pornography has had the unfortunate effect of rendering virtually all representations of the nudity of children problematic. As a result, seeing young Sarah and her young friend Ben (Benjamin Blum-Smith) cavorting around the backyard, singing the "Vagina Dance," a tune Sarah seems to have made up, has come to feel somehow dangerous—something that a Web pornographer might exploit. Like Stan Brakhage's lovely film *Vein* (1965), which focuses on a very young boy taking pleasure in his own body, the experience of *Beginning Pieces* has been corrupted by changes in the social fabric.

During the same period that he was making *Beginning Pieces* Guzzetti was in regular communication with filmmaker Richard P. Rogers and photographer Susan Meiselas (she received her master's in education from Harvard Graduate School of Education in 1971), and all three were concerned about political events in Nicaragua. Meiselas's photographs of the Nicaraguan revolution had become canonical, and her photo book, *Nicaragua: June 1978–July 1979*, had been published in 1981 by Pantheon (it was reissued by Aperture in 2008). When President Ronald Reagan claimed that the Nicaraguan contras were the equivalent of America's founding fathers and that Nicaragua under the Sandinistas was like Nazi Germany in the 1930s, Guzzetti, Meiselas, and Rogers decided to go to Nicaragua and test these claims. Originally they planned to focus on the upcoming election of 1984, but when the logistical difficulties of making such a film became clear to them, Guzzetti suggested that they focus on a particular family during this volatile moment, and Meiselas suggested a family she had gotten to know. The result was *Living at Risk: The Story of a Nicaraguan Family*, which focuses on five children of the Barrios family who agreed to participate in the film: Miguel Barrios and his wife Mary Ann; Federico Barrios and wife Loli; Alberto Barrios; Martisabel Barrios and husband Eduardo Holmann; and Mauricio Barrios (Carlos Barrios, the father; and the eldest brother, Carlos José, who was living in Costa Rica at the time, refused to participate in the film; both had become disenchanted with the Sandinistas). For *Living at Risk* Rogers did the cinematography and Guzzetti took sound; Meiselas, the only one of the three who spoke Spanish, organized the shooting.[42] All three worked together on the editing.

Certain of the editing choices in *Living at Risk* and even some of Rogers's compositions are reminiscent of *Family Portrait Sittings*, but the three makers seem to

FIGURE 22. Susan Meiselas photograph in Guzzetti-Meiselas-Rogers's *Pictures from a Revolution* (1991). Courtesy Alfred Guzzetti.

have emulated the commitment of the younger members of the Barrios family to collaborative, noncompetitive ways of working. The same is true of *Pictures from a Revolution* (1991), in which Guzzetti, Meiselas, and Rogers revisited Nicaragua in order to talk with men and women who had appeared in Meiselas's photographs about their activities during the revolution and their current feelings (fig. 22). There are moments in *Pictures from a Revolution* that evoke Guzzetti's earlier family films: for example, Guzzetti, Meiselas, and Rogers returned to particular spots to record them in the present, juxtaposing this imagery with Meiselas's photographs, creating much the same effect that is created during *Family Portrait Sittings* when Guzzetti embeds within pans of domestic spaces filmed in the present these same spaces as they appeared years earlier in his father's home movies. But in general, *Pictures from a Revolution* is an effective blend of the contributions of the three collaborators.

During the years following *Pictures from a Revolution* Guzzetti was involved in several other collaborative projects, including *Seed and Earth* (1994), an ethnographic depiction of a village in West Bengal, India.[43] For this project, Guzzetti teamed with anthropologist Ákos Östör, the Harvard anthropologist who had worked with Robert Gardner on *Sons of Shiva* (1985) and *Forest of Bliss* (1986), and with Lina Fruzzetti (she and Östör did sound recording) and Ned Johnston (he and Guzzetti did cinematography)—Guzzetti edited the film himself. *Seed and Earth* forgoes all commentary; the filmmakers allow the village of Janta to reveal itself. The result is a lovely, unpretentious depiction of life in an agricultural village—and a premonition of some of the films that would come out of Harvard's Sensory Ethnography Lab during the 2000s (see chapter 9).

Meiselas and Guzzetti (Rogers died in 2001) have remained engaged with the unfolding of Nicaraguan life. In 2006 they collaborated on *Reframing History*, an 11-minute documentation of Meiselas's show of photographs from her book *Nicaragua:* the photographs were enlarged and printed on cloth and exhibited in close proximity to the locations where they were originally shot.[44] During the same trip, Guzzetti recorded the footage he would use in *América Central* (2004), a 7-minute meditation on an intersection in Masaya during which a series of news items are seen as texts that scroll from right to left below the image of the intersection. The implicit focus on the United States in these news items is juxtaposed with Nicaraguans going about their daily business in the wake of the political changes that have occurred in previous decades.[45] On one level, the stories seem unrelated to Nicaragua, even to ignore Nicaragua and its recent volatile history; but on another level, it is clear that for all practical purposes this is *American* news on Nicaraguan media: the implication being that America's role in toppling the Sandinistas was considerable and successful and that American interests continue to dominate this nation.

In 2011, Guzzetti and Meiselas produced a DVD called *A Family in History,* which includes an updated version of *Living at Risk* and a new work, *The Barrios Family 25 Years Later* (2011), a set of twenty short films, all of them interviews with the women and men interviewed in *Living at Risk* and their children—produced, directed, and edited by Guzzetti and Meiselas (Guzzetti shot the footage and recorded sound). The suite of films is both engaging and revealing; it provides considerable insight into how this remarkable family came to terms, first, with their disappointments with the Nicaraguan revolution and with the continued volatility of Nicaraguan politics, and, second, into how they feel now about their part in the revolution itself. *The Barrios Family 25 Years Later* is also a significant addition to Guzzetti's cine-investigations of childhood; the interviews with the children of the revolutionaries reveal that they have internalized their parents' idealism and commitment to service in a wide range of ways. Guzzetti and Meiselas's visits with the family members who participated in *Living at Risk* are supplemented by interviews with Carlos José Barrios, and Father Zubizarreta, who Guzzetti believes was an important inspiration for the family's commitment to the revolution and to postrevolutionary Nicaragua.[46]

GUZZETTI: *TIME EXPOSURE*

In 2012 Guzzetti completed a short video, *Time Exposure,* in which he returned to the world he explored in *Family Portrait Sittings,* this time not to expose the way in which family members mythify the family's past, or to focus on the history of his family as an instance of Italian emigration to America and South Philadelphia, or even to reveal the way in which his mother and father (and his other relatives) respond to each other and to his filming, but in part as an affectionate memorial to his parents—the film ends with an "In Memoriam" to Felix Guzzetti, who died in 1983, and Susan Guzzetti, who died in 2011—and to focus on the element of their history and their parenting that has had the most impact on Guzzetti himself.

The particular instigation for *Time Exposure* seems to have been a single photograph of a South Philadelphia street, taken by Felix Guzzetti in 1938 when he was twenty-two years old (fig. 23): as Guzzetti explains in his voice-over, "My father entered the photo in a Kodak snapshot contest and won honorable mention. My mother and her family were impressed that on a dark, rainy night he could come up with a picture as good as this and then have it win a prize. It was what started him off." Subsequently, Guzzetti explains that when his father died, "I kept the print of his prize-winning photo. To me it showed a generic place in South Philadelphia, a street indistinguishable from all the others. I promised myself that one day I'd find the spot where it was taken."

As brief as *Time Exposure* is, it is remarkably though unpretentiously dense: it charts several histories, some overtly, others implicitly. Most obviously, it reviews the main events in Felix's development as a photographer: his interest in photography from the time he was twelve years old; Susan Guzzetti's giving him a book, *Elementary Photography,* for Christmas in 1933; his taking a course in photography (at Susan's suggestion) from Severo Antonelli at the photography school Antonelli had established. During this course Guzzetti photographed Philadelphia sites: bridges, trees, buildings; as well as still lifes (in the family kitchen-turned-studio) and women models—some of them nude (Susan Guzzetti called this "the famous nude lesson"). Following the Antonelli course, Guzzetti established his own photographic business focusing on weddings and banquets. In time, he also bought an 8mm motion picture camera and filmed in his neighborhood (*Time Exposure* includes black-and-white footage shot at Felix's father's coal delivery business and of Susan Guzzetti during the years when Felix was courting her) and in the years to come, as is evident in *Family Portrait Sittings,* birthdays and other Guzzetti family events.

A second history charted by *Time Exposure* is Alfred Guzzetti's development as photographer and filmmaker. During his voice-over description of the extended Guzzetti family photograph that his father shot in his mother-in-law's living room, Alfred mentions that he can be seen "in the second row with the big white collar,"

FIGURE 23. Felix Guzzetti's Honorable Mention photograph, from Alfred Guzzetti's *Time Exposure* (2012). Courtesy Alfred Guzzetti.

and that "on the table at the left-hand edge of the picture is my first camera, a Brownie Hawkeye." The remembered excitement of this moment is clear in Guzzetti's delivery, and this excitement echoes his earlier memory of his father's calling *his* first good camera "the light of his life." Alfred's recycling of some of the shots that begin *Family Portrait Sittings*—the shots made in a moving car traveling down narrow South Philadelphia streets—not only recalls his first successful feature, it adds a dimension to these particular shots not evident in the original film: Alfred explains that Felix was driving the car—early evidence of the father's support of his son's interest in filmmaking. In a final voice-over, as the viewer contemplates a zoom out from the prize-winning photograph, Guzzetti contemplates its impact on his life: if his father hadn't taken the photograph and won a prize, "Would I have been my father's assistant when he photographed weddings and banquets? Would I have learned to change the film holders and flashbulbs, to focus the camera, to make test strips and enlargements, to burn and dodge, to hand-color with the semi-transparent oils? Would my father have bought an 8mm movie camera and editing equipment and made all the movies of our family that I've inherited? Would I have started making my own photographs and my own movies?" Of course, the implicit history of Alfred Guzzetti's becoming a filmmaker culminates in *Time Exposure* itself.

A third bit of history in the video results from Guzzetti's decision to keep his promise to himself to find the exact location where his father's prize-winning photograph was made. The search for the mysterious location is short-lived, but in the end, poignant, because Guzzetti comes to realize that the photograph was shot not at some out-of-the-way intersection in South Philadelphia but one block from where his father was living during the time he was courting Susan, specifically from in front of Susan's family's row house. For Alfred this photograph now takes on a metaphoric dimension; it represents the place where Felix's fascination with photography and his relationship with Susan came together, opening a new "avenue" into the future, one that would involve not merely an expansion of Felix's involvement in the photographic arts, but the birth of his son, the photographer and filmmaker. The original photograph might have held metaphoric implications for Felix as well: he was seeing his world from a new angle, one conditioned by his feelings for Susan: the photograph transforms a dark, rainy night into a lovely urban nocturne.

Implicit within the histories of Felix's, then Alfred's, developing commitment to photography and cinema is the history that is discussed more fully in the next chapter: that is, Alfred's lifelong exploration of filmmaking and film history. What is evident in *Time Exposure* is that Guzzetti is demonstrating how his practical knowledge and ability to work with the ever-diversifying forms of still and motion photography has evolved since those years when he was learning from his father, is in fact continuing to evolve; and how his many years teaching film production and film history now echo through his work.

In its brief 11 minutes *Time Exposure* includes black-and-white still photography, black-and-white 8mm and 16mm footage, high-definition digital video in color and sync sound, as well as a variety of manipulations of this material. Guzzetti zooms in and out from photographs, and from stills of the digital footage of Emily Street in the present day; he reformats the wide-screen digital image so that it conforms to Felix Guzzetti's vertical nocturne, and at the end of the video, creates a magical moment first by changing the present-day color image of Emily Street to black and white, then returning to the cover of the book, *Elementary Photography,* with Susan's inscription—"To Felix/from Sue/Christmas 1937"—then digitally fading the book cover out and leaving the inscription, which was in fact written inside the book.

Throughout *Time Exposure,* viewers familiar with the history of independent cinema will notice echoes of this history, some of them presumably conscious, others just a function of Guzzetti's long tenure as a teacher. His contextualizing a particular still photograph or a series of photographs with narration is reminiscent of the mini-history of such films: Chris Marker's *La Jetée* (1962), Hollis Frampton's *(nostalgia)* (1971), Jean-Luc Godard and Jean-Pierre Gorin's *Letter to Jane* (1972), Morgan Fisher's *Standard Gauge* (1984); and the nature of Guzzetti's voice-over evokes Morgan Fisher's quiet, informal, but rigorously controlled narration in *Standard Gauge,* especially the frequent use of silence. The series of questions Guzzetti asks himself at the end of *Time Exposure* recalls Su Friedrich's narrator's questions about her father at the conclusion of *Sink or Swim* (1990). And of course, Guzzetti's voice-over recalls the various voice-overs of Ross McElwee, and especially his comments about three photographs of himself and his father that form the précis of *Backyard* (see chapter 6).[47]

Film, as Guzzetti suggests at the end of *Time Exposure,* is an art of time—he is "endlessly fascinated by the way film puts before us the endless flow of time"—but it is also an art of *exposure,* and not just in the photographic sense. *Time Exposure* is more than a memorializing of Guzzetti's parents and more than a heartfelt thank you for their support of his becoming an independent filmmaker. Its revisiting of the historical and psychological territory explored in *Family Portrait Sittings* seems at least partly a way of making amends for exposing these supportive parents in that earlier film. It is clear in *Family Portrait Sittings* that Guzzetti is dealing with his parents as instances of a particular cultural tendency, or as William Rothman has put it, "as living artifacts of a historical America."[48] Fundamentally, Guzzetti was exploring how families mythify themselves and the ways in which this process can function to disguise or suppress particular tensions between family members. Felix and Susan Guzzetti, as depicted in Guzzetti's first film about them, reveal more about themselves and the various tensions in their relationship than they might have meant to—revelations that sometimes create wry humor for the audience and that also distort certain realities. In the earlier film Susan Guzzetti sometimes seems to downplay Felix's talents and accomplishments, and Felix's comment that he's never called his son "crazy" for making the kinds of films he makes is easily read as ironic, as a reflection of Alfred's feeling that his father found his work strange and impractical.

My conjecture is that over the years, Guzzetti has felt some embarrassment about his willingness to expose his parents in this way, and in making *Time Exposure* decided to return to his earlier depiction of Felix and Susan to "expose" how fully nurturing of his talents and ambitions they were (and how clearly supportive Susan was of Felix's interest in photography). Further, while Felix Guzzetti's accomplishments as a photographer are nowhere in evidence in *Family Portrait Sittings,* they are quite evident in *Time Exposure;* indeed, Guzzetti has said that he could not have made *Time Exposure* before high-definition, since earlier film or video formats could not have done justice to his father's work.[49] Within this context, we can understand Alfred Guzzetti's decision to work with voice-over—for the first time in his fifty years as a filmmaker—as implicitly an act of *self*-exposure, both personal and professional: not only is he present in *Time Exposure* in his words and delivery, but he is working in an environment that has produced some of the most remarkable work with voice-over in the annals of cinema—no one knows this better than Guzzetti, who got "some good advice from Ross" as he was making *Time Exposure!*[50] Of course, even the self-exposure in *Time Exposure* is limited, just enough to be recognized *as* self-exposure. Guzzetti remains his modest self, embodying his reticence in the video's conceptual density and modest length: *Time Exposure* is the haiku of personal documentary.

5
———

Alfred Guzzetti and Personal Cinema

Looking back at the 1960s and 1970s from half a century later, few transformations that were occurring at the time now seem more significant than the emergence of new image-making technologies: attempts to devise inexpensive sync-sound film-making gauges led in the end to videotape and camcorders and then to the emergence of a series of digital technologies that have taken the difficulty out of the process of recording image and sound, have simplified editing, and have made darkened theaters unnecessary for the experience of motion pictures. While most of those who were developing independent filmmaking careers during that era remained satisfied with 16mm filmmaking, there were others who were frustrated by the most crucial limitation of 16mm: optical sound. Alfred Guzzetti, whose interest in film developed along with a passion for music—Guzzetti began composing music as a teenager and studied music composition at Harvard for his first two years—was one of those, and, once he had experienced the way in which 16mm optical sound impoverished the experiences he had hoped to create in his first important avant-garde film, *Air* (1971), and in *Family Portrait Sittings* (1975), he became increasingly interested in the potential of video: if the image quality of early videotape couldn't compare with the image quality of 16mm (much less 35mm), video's sound quality was quickly becoming substantially better than what 16mm could offer.

By 1975 even the image quality of video had become acceptable; video imagery might not be able to hold the big screen, but on good-quality monitors it was adequate, and the sensitivity of magnetic sound allowed for increasingly complex image-sound-text experiences. While he was continuing to make various kinds of film using 16mm cameras, Guzzetti also made it part of his ongoing work as an artist to explore the possibilities of new video technologies in order to see how the various advances might affect his ability to express his sense of the world and himself in the world. Between 1995 and the present, Guzzetti's experiences with the new technologies taught him what he could effectively express for viewers, and the advent of high-definition video has finally made it possible for him to bring his newest video work into theatrical situations. With the exception of *Time Exposure* (2012, discussed in the previous chapter), Guzzetti's video art is personal in a manner quite distinct from personal documentary and more in tune with approaches to the personal by avant-garde filmmakers.

AIR

Out of what is in itself an undistinguishable, swarming continuum, *devoid of distinction or emphasis, our senses make for us, by attending to this motion and ignoring that, a world full of contrasts, of sharp accents, of abrupt changes, of picturesque light and shade.*

WILLIAM JAMES, *THE PRINCIPLES OF PSYCHOLOGY*[1]

In the fall of 1965, Fred Camper, who is best known as a leading scholar of the work of filmmaker Stan Brakhage, joined with several of his MIT freshman classmates to form a film society that would offer regular screenings of avant-garde film—in those days more often called "underground film," "experimental film," and, after Jonas Mekas, "the New American Cinema"—along with some foreign language features and classics by under-recognized Hollywood auteurs (Douglas Sirk, Edgar G. Ulmer).[2] Camper had found his way into avant-garde film in Manhattan, and when he matriculated at MIT, immediately looked around for avant-garde screenings. He discovered Robert Steele, a Boston University professor who was presenting films at the Cambridge Adult Education Center and from time to time would include an avant-garde feature. Camper remembers that when Steele's plan to show Jack Smith's *Flaming Creatures* (1963) fell through, Gregory Markopoulos filled in and showed one of his films.

And there was Tom Chomont, a filmmaker and avant-garde aficionado who had dropped out of Boston University when he felt constrained by what he perceived as the film department's predilection for social documentary and had begun hosting screenings, beginning with Markopoulos's *Twice a Man* (1963), at the Odd Fellows Hall in Cambridge.[3] In 1965 Brakhage came to the Odd Fellows Hall to present a show of his 8mm *Songs;* subsequent presentations included films by Robert Nelson, Bill Vehr, Andy Meyer, the Kuchar Brothers, Jack Smith (the *Normal Love* rushes), and Bruce Baillie. The screening of Vehr's *Brothel* (1966) confirmed the Cambridge police's suspicion that Chomont was showing "dirty movies," and when they quarantined the Odd Fellows Hall three days before Gregory Markopoulos was to screen the original rolls of *Galaxie* (1966),

Chomont mimeographed maps of how to get to MIT, where Camper had agreed to host the event.

Camper and his MIT colleagues had begun their screenings with a program that included Kenneth Anger's controversial *Scorpio Rising* (1963), along with a Brakhage film and Stan Vanderbeek's *Breathdeath* (1964), which drew a crowd of three hundred people (a second screening that evening presented the films to another hundred who hadn't been able to get into the first screening). During the fall of 1965 the MIT Film Society began presenting monthly shows, and by the following spring had expanded their schedule to weekly Monday evening screenings, sometimes adding a second weekly event. Camper saw himself as an evangelical missionary for avant-garde film, and if he didn't quite believe the 1960s mantra of "Change your consciousness, change the world," he was convinced that opportunities to see the full range of cinema experiment and accomplishment was worth his dedication. Although the regular presentations of the MIT Film Society were primarily screenings (accompanied by Camper's program notes), Camper did host filmmakers from time to time. Brakhage presented one of the first screenings of *Twenty-Third Psalm Branch* (1966) in April 1967; Warren Sonbert visited the series twice, and Peter Kubelka presented a program of his work in 1968.

While Camper remembers no specific interaction between the MIT Film Section and his series (Camper hosted screenings until 1971), he does remember being invited to a party hosted by MIT philosophy professor Mark Levensky, who, Camper thinks, may have wanted to convince Ed Pincus of Brakhage's merit: "I remember that Pincus was totally unconvinced and had a kind of nasty expression on his face, about how he didn't like Brakhage." On the other hand, Alfred Guzzetti, then in his early years teaching at Harvard, was a devotee of Camper's series: "I went all the time. I saw Brakhage and Peter Kubelka, Warhol, Bruce Baillie—I loved Bruce Baillie—and crazy stuff that I liked but didn't seem to have anything to do with me: for example, I knew I'd never make anything like George and Mike Kuchar's films."[4]

Guzzetti's fascination with what Camper was showing, particularly with Kubelka and Baillie, helped to instigate *Air,* an 18-minute rumination on the psychic complexity of an era that seemed to many of us both exhilarating and frightening. *Air* opens with an extended black-and-white shot (73 seconds) filmed on an escalator ascending from a subway station to the street (it is the old Harvard Square T stop); when the camera nears street level, the image becomes overexposed, almost blinding, as a "Danger" sign (warning subway travelers against running up and down or sitting on the handrails) passes overhead. At the end of this shot, the first of two voices is heard: a woman talks about generational changes, and a black preacher proclaims that when a government fails to protect its citizens, it is the citizens' obligation to "abolish that government." These voices are heard simultaneously, and the resulting auditory challenge is characteristic of the film; indeed, unlike nearly all avant-garde filmmakers before 1971 (Kubelka is the obvious exception), Guzzetti was, from the beginning, committed to the idea that a film's soundtrack should be as complex as the image track.

While we hear these two voices, and subsequently, several voices recorded from radio broadcasts of world news, we see, first, a montage of slow motion color shots of traffic, and then sequence that intercuts between black-and-white shots of a woman, blindfolded, walking slowly through an indoor lightscape, and color shots of another woman with a gun walking with confidence in an outdoor space. Then, a radio reporter describing methods of torture used by the military government in Brazil is accompanied by an elegant, slow, black-and-white, leftward tracking shot through the rooms of a city apartment, then by color street scenes in slow motion: the serene pace of the pan and the slow motion traffic shots match, even as the content of these shots is light years away from the horrors of the torture being described. During the following 2 minutes, the image track intercuts between very brief, nearly subliminal color montages of street scenes shot from moving vehicles and moments of darkness; and the soundtrack is a collage of three voices: one talking about the troubled situation in the Middle East, a woman's voice talking about the fragmentation of "the Movement," and a second woman's voice talking about the difficulty of knowing enough about diverse issues to make sensible decisions about how to act in relation to them. The juxtapositions of mundane activity and quiet spaces with the disturbances of world news—expressed through collisions of sound/image, color/black and white, image/no image, clarity/obscurity, montage/extended shots—continue throughout *Air* and provide an engrossing sense of a societal moment characterized both by political and moral challenges on all sides and a commitment to new forms of art-making, including the expansion of cinematic possibility.

While Guzzetti does not seem to be consciously alluding to the avant-garde filmmakers whose work he was seeing, many dimensions of *Air* recall important earlier contributions to independent cinema. Guzzetti's editing of sound and image—not merely his evocative juxtapositions, but the careful editing that allows the particulars of visual motion to intersect with the specifics of spoken articulation or other sounds in a wide variety of subtle ways—is reminiscent of Kubelka's legendary editing precision in *Unsere Afrikareise* (*Our Trip to Africa*, 1965) and prescient of the intricate editing of Su Friedrich's personal films, *The Ties That Bind* (1984) and *Sink or Swim* (1990).[5] The brief, nearly subliminal bits of montage used in two extended sequences evoke Kubelka's experimentation with "metric cinema" (construction of sequences not shot by shot, but frame by frame) in *Schwechater* (1958).[6] Guzzetti's combinations of color and black and white and the layering on his soundtrack (of voices and of music and environmental sound) are reminiscent of Bruce Baillie's *Castro Street* (1966). And the series of four extended (each is 30 seconds long), close-up portraits of two women and two men midway through the film, recall Andy Warhol's *Screen Tests*—though Guzzetti's depictions of Deborah Fortson, Ned Block, Susan Carey, and William Rothman are accompanied by Schoenberg's *Sechs kleine Klavierstücke, Op. 19—No. 2*, which provides a romantic aura around these four friends, quite different from Warhol's apparent detachment in the *Screen Tests* (this difference is also evident in the fact that Guzzetti subtly engages with the portraits by making slight adjustments in his zoom lens).[7]

The most important influence on *Air* and, in some ways, on Guzzetti's later experimental video work, however, was Jean-Luc Godard, and in particular his 1966 feature, *2 ou 3 choses que je sais d'elle* (*2 or 3 Things I Know About Her*). Guzzetti's participation with a group of Harvard faculty in an informal seminar on the film ultimately led to his *Two or Three Things I Know about Her: Analysis of a Film by Godard* (Cambridge: Harvard University Press, 1981), an exhaustive, shot-by-shot analysis of the film, "the most complex and profound work of the most interesting and inventive filmmaker of our time . . . one of the masterpieces of the sound cinema."[8] The influence of Godard, and *2 ou 3 choses que je sais d'elle* in particular, is evident in the general complexity of *Air,* in Guzzetti's way of envisioning the urban environment in the film, and to some extent in Guzzetti's combinations of visual text and photographic imagery in his later experimental videos.

During the second half of *Air* several kinds of imagery closely related to what is seen earlier in the film (two slow motion shots filmed from a car moving through tunnels into bright light; a sequence of brief color montages filmed from moving vehicles; a 95-second shot of a blindfolded woman, lit only by a flashlight, feeling her way along a wall in the darkness . . .) are juxtaposed with audio collages of multiple voices that speak, in various modes, of events in Lebanon, of the struggles of women within traditional relationships, of African Americans fighting for their civil rights (Malcolm X is one of the voices near the end of the film). Guzzetti concludes *Air* with a 2-minute sequence of Roberta Collinge (who we have seen earlier walking along city streets) observed through a window from what appears to be an adjoining apartment, trying on outfits in front of a mirror. Actually Guzzetti's frame includes two windows into the same room: Collinge is visible (and sometimes nude) in the right-hand window; a television airing NBC news is visible through the left-hand window. As Collinge puts on one outfit after another, and the television reveals a stream of news stories, Guzzetti uses camera position and his zoom lens to create different compositions of and within the scene. On the soundtrack, a piano is being tuned—though this process seems to create its own music. It is as if the outer world of international struggle (seen through the little television), the inner world of coming to terms with how to determine and represent one's personal identity (enacted by Collinge), and Guzzetti's attempt to find a meaningful cinematic articulation of his place in the world are emblematic of a single wildly complex and contradictory cultural moment.

EXPERIMENTAL VIDEO: "LANGUAGE LESSONS"

The personal cinema mode Guzzetti explored in *Air* lay dormant for nearly twenty-five years, or at least was sublimated into other kinds of filmmaking, until good-quality video (with its superior magnetic sound) became available,[9] but since the mid-1990s it has been Guzzetti's primary fascination and has produced much of his most remarkable work. The structure of *Variation* (1995) demonstrates the approach that would dominate the suite of videos—*Rosetta Stone* (1993), *The Curve of the World* (1994), *The Stricken Areas* (1996), and *What Actually Happened* (1996)—that he came to call "Language Lessons."[10] In the twelve numbered sections of *Variation* Guzzetti explores the myriad compositional and editing possibilities of sound-to-image, image-to-image, and sound-to-sound juxtaposition, along with the ways that verbal and visual text can weave disparate audio and video imagery into an experiential whole.

Guzzetti's inspirations for *Variation* seem to have been both poetic and musical.[11] *Variation* is divided into a series of brief, numbered "stanzas" (the longest around 40 seconds, the shortest a bit more than 15 seconds). Each stanza is introduced by a number, presented as an active part of the visual experience: some numbers fade in, others move into the frame or across the frame. Within a given stanza, Guzzetti organizes several visual and auditory images into a brief montage. For example, part 3 begins with "3" fading in at the center of the frame, accompanied by bird sounds. After about 4 seconds, a shot of clouds against a blue sky is seen for around 20 seconds, as deep, reverberant symphonic music fades in and then dissolves into the sound of a plane. The cloud shot fades to white, just as the plane sound becomes primary, and a brief superimposition reveals a man and woman walking from right to left. There is a sudden cut to an explosion of fireworks at night in black and white; another direct cut, to people walking on a city street, accompanied by traffic sounds; and the sequence ends with a second cloud shot, this one with two birds flying through the frame while the slowly fading sound of a plane is heard (this sound continues into part 4). The subtle audio-visual composition of the diverse elements of part 3 are evocative of certain forms of modern poetry—John Ashbery's work, for example. Another obvious inspiration for *Variation,* however, is musical: it is a modification of the variation form, the most famous example being Bach's *Goldberg Variations* (Guzzetti rejects this particular comparison).[12]

Each of Guzzetti's brief montages in *Variation* is distinct from the others, though each replays several of the elements of earlier sequences. For instance, part 4 includes scenes of people walking on a city street, and the same shot of fireworks that is seen in part 3—here, followed, after a shot of clouds in a reflective sky-scraper, by a shot of a full moon positioned so as to echo the circular fireworks explosion; the final sound of part 4 is the sound of a plane. During subsequent parts of *Variation,* these and a good many other elements become familiar, though they are always seen within differing contexts, moods, and rhythms. It is as if each visual and auditory element is a musical instrument in an orchestra, and each numbered section, a different orchestration. Guzzetti's compositions could hardly be more different from the filmmakers identified with "visual music" (Oskar Fischinger, Len Lye, Norman McLaren, Jordan Belson) or from Bruce Conner and Kenneth Anger, all of whom create imagery to accompany musical compositions, but they offer an inventive and engaging variation on how sound and image can be combined within cinema experiences that have the adventure and the coherence of experimental musical pieces.[13] *Variation* and the "Language Lessons" videos make "music" out of the cacophony of modern life.

Guzzetti's calling the suite of four videos he began in 1993 "Language Lessons" is obviously a reference to the language lessons heard sometimes in the videos, but also presumably to the lessons he himself was learning as he explored the possibilities of video. Like *Air*—but here with the expanded flexibility and quality of magnetic sound—each of the four videos combines complex, highly edited soundtracks with visual montage. And each of the videos works with visual text, though in varying ways. In *Rosetta Stone* and *The Curve of the World* in particular, Guzzetti also explores the possibilities of formatting one image within another, sometimes so that the inner image is quite different from the outer and sometimes so that for a moment the composite nature of the image is not immediately obvious; sometimes one double image is followed by a very different double image.

The visual track of each "Language Lessons" video juxtaposes active images with serene images, images of natural spaces with city scenes, indoor and outdoor shots, complicated compositions with simple images, motion in one direction with motion in another; and on each soundtrack, moments of loud, even abrasive sound "collide" with moments of silence, or of very subtle natural sounds; voices recorded from radio are juxtaposed with traffic noise or with the sound of rain, or of fireworks—sometimes we are hearing what we are seeing, often not. Within this audiovisual variety, however, a sense of developing structure is always evident: details of sound and image seem to be evolving into a formal and ideological continuity.

Each of the four "Language Lessons" uses both visual and auditory text. In addition to the literal language lesson heard on the soundtrack, *Rosetta Stone* provides a visual text, a translation of a bit of museum lecture we see early in the video: "WITHIN A SHORT TIME ALL KNOWLEDGE AND CONSCIOUSNESS OF THIS FORM OF WRITING WAS LOST." This entire text is seen first, in green typeface superimposed within the shot of the lecture; then, bits of the sentence are seen within other, very different contexts, and the film ends with the entire text, in white and in a different typeface, rolling through the frame from bottom to top. The idea of the passing of both a form of writing and of human awareness of it that is emphasized by Guzzetti's repetitions helps to establish the essential theme of *Rosetta Stone* and the videos that would follow: the apparent inevitability of mortality and the human and artistic challenge of dealing with it. It is clear that within Guzzetti's evolution as an artist this video is working with a new visual-auditory "language," but, like everyone working seriously with video as an art form, the issue of its durability was much in question during the 1990s. For Guzzetti, the excitement of the new possibilities was accompanied by concerns about whether the works he was so carefully constructing could last even a lifetime.

In *The Stricken Areas* and *What Actually Happened,* the gems of the "Language Lessons" suite, Guzzetti continues to return to elements and motifs developed in *Rosetta Stone* and *The Curve of the World* (with the exception of composite double images), including the use of visual text—in these later videos the texts recount dreams. In fact, *The Stricken Areas* presents, in poetically arranged textual form, the very dreams heard in voice-over in *The Curve of the World.* The imagery in *The Stricken Areas* is often beautiful, and is sometimes juxtaposed with texts that implicitly reorient our sense of the beautiful: a lovely shot of a marina late in the video, for example, includes a language lesson presented in texts that move across the frame from right to left (in Spanish at the top of the frame, English at the bottom). The English version: "We see / that man lives on earth / a few years / and then / dies" (my slashes represent the temporal pauses between the movement of individual elements of the sentence across the screen; we must construct the sentence gradually a phrase or a word at a time). Guzzetti composes the various elements of *The Stricken Areas* so that the variety of life itself and our continually changing moods in relation to it are evoked within a structure that suggests that making these videos is his way of holding on to what matters to him within the continual flux of his life.

What Actually Happened is a travel video in which visual and auditory records of Guzzetti's experiences traveling in Italy—images and sounds of an outdoor sculpture garden, of a gallery in a museum, of a space inside an old church, shots taken from the rear window of a train speeding through Italian landscape—are interwoven with a series of four dreams that presumably occurred during these travels, or later were evoked by them. In the first dream, presented in yellow print over images and sounds of water from the Tiber River flowing powerfully through the frame, Guzzetti imagines he and "Deborah" (presumably his wife Deborah Fortson) are in India, where they are taken up in a glider, powered in some mysterious way by their host; the glider flies over a river full of sharks and other sea life. The second dream, also presented in yellow text, is superimposed over imagery and sound shot from the train. This dream focuses on Guzzetti's attempt to find a theater where he and presumably Deborah are expecting to attend a performance. The third dream is superimposed over shots of a narrow Italian street. It reads as follows (in *What Actually Happened,* as in *The Stricken Areas* and in later videos, dreams are presented in what amounts to poetic form; here, sentences appear at the bottom of the frame—my slashes indicate line breaks; each sentence is a new text, separated from the previous text by a temporal pause):

A chartered train.
The engineer is a woman.
The train goes fast through a town / where trains normally stop.
She blows the whistle to warn / that we're coming through.
Ahead I see another train / stopped on the track.
I realize she will have to slam on / the breaks.
I don't know if we can stop in time.
I shout a warning.
My father is thrown forward.
I put my hands out to catch him.

At the end of this dream the image of the street fades to white, causing the final lines of text to seem particularly emphatic. In the fourth dream (presented in texts that cross the bottom of the frame from right to left, and superimposed over left-to-right tracking shots past the faces of marble sculptures in a museum), it is the final night of Guzzetti's trip; he is lost and worried about finding his way back to his hotel in time to retrieve his suitcase. This dream concludes with a sudden jump in geography (emphasized by a change in the color of the dream text, to white); Guzzetti tells a man, "I'll always remember my moment in Central America with you," as music evoking Central America fades in; the dream text is followed by a shot of a palm tree, now also evoking Central America. Of course, for those familiar with Guzzetti's earlier career, this dream reference may suggest how the pleasures, difficulties, and fears of his work on *Living at Risk* and *Pictures from a Revolution* continued to haunt his subconscious.

Guzzetti's inclusion of dreams in *The Curve of the World, The Stricken Areas,* and *What Actually Happened* provides a dimension of the personal rarely evident in the personal documentaries discussed in this study—though as Luis Buñuel would remind us, our dreams are as real as anything else we experience. In general, the freeform logic of the dreams in the "Language Lessons" and the videos that followed provides a contrast to Guzzetti's formal rigor as a video artist. Guzzetti's memory of the pleasures and discoveries of travel (as represented by the imagery and sounds he captured on his Italian trip) are combined with the subconscious fears that attend his moving out of his routine.[14] The precise compositional creativity of a conscious artist is conjoined with the ongoing, free-form, creative logic of what William James named the "stream of consciousness."

SCYLLA AND CHARYBDIS

The "Language Lessons" suite was followed by a series of accomplished experimental videos, including *Under the Rain* (1997), *A Tropical Story* (1998), and *The Tower of Industrial Life* (2000), each of which combines Guzzetti's reworkings of the cinematic records of immediate perception with textually presented memories of dreams. *Under the Rain* is a travel video, shot while Guzzetti was traveling in China. *A Tropical Story* and *The Tower of Industrial Life* are the most expansive and inclusive of Guzzetti's digital videos, and both work off an awareness of the earlier videos. *A Tropical Story* is partly about travel (the sound of a Chinese language lesson opens the piece, and there is visual imagery of China and Spain), though here travel is seen as one experience among others. Like *Variation, A Tropical Story* is presented as numbered parts, four in this case, and is punctuated by dreams, presented textually, the first two of which seem to reflect on Guzzetti's filmmaking (in the first dream, complete sentences move across the image from right to left at the bottom of the frame: a new sentence begins once the last word of the previous sentence exits left; in the second dream, full sentences, one immediately after another, fade in and out at the center of the frame—in my rendering, slashes indicate line breaks):

> I go into a large house.
> Someone tells me that the owner's ambition was to fill it with beautiful things.
> The windows do not open onto the outdoors but instead onto paintings of the
>   outdoors.
> I get close to one.
> I see an image of the sky.

And:

> I go down a corridor.
> To the left there is a door / leading to a cinema.
> I look inside and see a marquee / at eye level.
> The title of the film is / one word beginning with M.
> The letters are dried, dark leaves.
> I imagine it must be / a tropical story.[15]

The implicit self-reflexivity of these two dreams sets the tone for *A Tropical Story.*

By the time he completed *A Tropical Story* Guzzetti seems to have recognized that he had developed a new way of representing his life, a mode of personal cinema that is neither a way of exploring the familial past and its relation to the present, as in *Family Portrait Sittings,* nor, as in *Scenes from Childhood* and *Beginning Pieces,* a way of trying to capture the present before it disappears. In *A Tropical Story*—and in *The Tower of Industrial Life,* the masterwork that would follow—Guzzetti's new mode allows him to focus on *where he is* at a particular extended creative moment, as a person and as an artist.

The Tower of Industrial Life is in most ways similar to the videos discussed so far, though it elaborates the use of visual text: excerpts of news stories are presented in most ways like the dream texts in this and earlier videos, but also with a difference: unlike the dream texts, which are always presented with poetic phrasing, the news texts are graphically justified in a manner that evokes newspaper columns, and sometimes words and lines are broken awkwardly. Guzzetti seems to mean to keep the distinction between dreams and news stories clear, while also suggesting their parallels. After all, what really happens in the world, or at least what we read in the papers or see on television about world events, can seem as surreal as what occurs in our dreams: for instance, the second news text in *The Tower of Industrial Life* is (slashes indicate breaks in lines of text, which fade in and out, one immediately following another), "Then the night sky turned orange / over this southern suburb of Bel- / grade, and on a hill just a mile or so / away, where a radar antenna sits, / a NATO missile or bomb exploded. / Sara's father, Mile, ran to his balco- / ny, a little stupidly, he admits. / 'I told Sara, "Where are our Ninja / turtles to help us now?"'"

One of the video's more evocative juxtapositions is an image of a fire, shot apparently from a television set (perhaps during coverage of the Russia–Chechnya conflict). The image forms a horizontal oval within the frame, which then dissolves into a woodsy landscape. The image of the fire is seen three times, and each time dissolves into the same landscape, seen in the first instance, in summer, then in fall, and, during the final sequence of the film, in winter. This motif suggests the way in which mediated imagery of world violence and other forms of crisis, events that have a claim on our attention and often on our engagement, are superimposed in our consciousness with our personal experiences of the physical world around us, including our experience of aging through the changing seasons of our lives.

The title of *The Tower of Industrial Life,* like the titles of *What Actually Happened* and *A Tropical Story,* seems in one sense a random choice: it is the English translation of the name of a Montreal skyscraper ("La Tour L'Industrielle-Vie") seen in two brief shots that do not seem any more crucial than any of the other myriad elements of image and sound.[16] However, the phrase, "the tower of industrial life," and *The Tower of Industrial Life* itself can also be understood as a metaphor for Guzzetti's life, and for all lives in modern industrial nations (does anything represent modern life more clearly than a skyscraper?). The video's juxtapositions of city and country; of moments of visual serenity and of sudden, dense montage; of the mysterious and the mundane; of advertising icons and real people, of noise and silence and music, represents Guzzetti's commitment, as video artist, to navigate the Scylla of violence in the world at large and the Charybdis of personal mortality (as expressed in his dreams) by acknowledging the wonder and mystery of modern experience and by demonstrating, again and again in video after video, the artist's ability to provide opportunities to contemplate, even take pleasure in, the frenzy and complexity of our day-to-day experiences in our particular "towers."

Throughout the 2000s, Guzzetti continued to produce intricate, engaging, often remarkable videos. *History of the Sea* (2004), like *The Tower of Industrial*

tell her that he could at last breathe

FIGURE 24. Urban scene and dream text from Alfred Guzzetti's *History of the Sea* (2004). Courtesy Alfred Guzzetti.

Life, combines complex, beautifully composed and edited imagery and sound, as well as visual texts of both news items (here, focusing on executions) and dreams that reflect the inevitable anxieties of Guzzetti's life as an academic (fig. 24).[17] The title comes from the second dream: "T shows me a sheet of printed questions. It is an exam for an evening course he is taking on the history of the sea"; the subsequent dream, related to the first, is probably familiar to most teachers and students (the dream is presented in hand-printed white letters against black at the bottom of the frame; slashes indicate line breaks):

> I am taking the final test in a long room with / high windows to the right and gray
>   woodwork.
> I have not prepared.
> Everyone begins writing.
> But no questions have been given out. / There are no questions on the blackboard.
> Perhaps knowing the questions is part of / the exam.
> Should I try to find out what the / questions are?
> Have they been omitted from my papers / by mistake?

I stop an attendant in a gray cloth jacket and / ask in a whisper where I can find the
   questions.
He replies at some length in what sounds / like French but I understand nothing.
I think that if I concentrate I will / recognize something, a word at least.
But I do not.

STILL POINT

In my view, the most interesting development in avant-garde film and video during the 2000s and early 2010s has been the continued emergence of a meditative or
contemplative cinema of place that has taken two roughly distinct forms. Some
filmmakers—Nathaniel Dorsky is the preeminent instance—create complex, subtle (and in Dorsky's case, silent) montages, organized according to what Dorsky
has called "polyvalence": "I want successive images to be disparate *and* connected,
and I want each shot to link back to earlier shots. The connection can be as simple
as the return of a certain red or of a particular pattern. Sometimes it's the iconog-
raphy. There are various levels where your mind can make connections. They say
the grandchildren are actually more like their grandparents than their parents; my
method feels something like that. I want each shot to continue to play a role, after
the next shot, and the next, have passed."[18]

Guzzetti's videos from the "Language Lessons" through *History of the Sea* are,
with Dorsky's films of the 1990s and 2000s, the quintessential works of "polyvalent
montage"—though there is an irony in this comparison. Dorsky has been resolute
in his commitment to traditional, silent, 16mm filmmaking, going so far as to
expect his films to be shown at "silent speed," that is, at sixteen frames per second
(he calls it "sacred speed")—something few current exhibitors other than film
archives can now manage. Guzzetti has been equally resolute in working with new
video and digital technologies and with the sound (and visual text) options video
provides—though with projection equipment continually changing, this has created its own exhibition challenges. Indeed, his commitment to video has tended to
keep Guzzetti away from the audiences most likely to enjoy his work. That Dorsky
has become widely regarded as a major force in avant-garde filmmaking (in a
recent *Film Comment* poll, he was named the most important avant-garde filmmaker of the 2000s), while Guzzetti's videos remain obscure becomes more ironic
the more familiar one grows with his work.

The other approach to a meditative/contemplative cinema of place is exemplified by the films of Peter Hutton, the films and high-definition videos of James
Benning since 1995 (most obviously, *13 Lakes* and *Ten Skies,* both 2004), and Sharon
Lockhart's *NŌ* (2003) and *Double Tide* (2009). These films and videos are committed to rigorous composition, shots of extended duration, and visual (and auditory)
subtlety—and to the use of cinemagoing as a form of perceptual retraining away

from the hysterical consumption (of imagery, of products) promoted by the commercial media. In 2009 Guzzetti, now working with high-definition digital video, produced *Still Point*—at once a literal expansion of his vision (his earlier videos were designed for presentation in art gallery situations on monitors; *Still Point*, for first-rate, large-scale, wide-screen digital projection) and a meld of the aesthetics represented by Hutton/Benning/Lockhart and Dorsky.

Still Point is made up of thirty-two shots, many recorded in and around the Boston area (three of them in Guzzetti's backyard in Brookline), but others at Walden Pond, on Cape Cod, at Mount Desert Island, Maine, in Philadelphia, and in various locations in New Mexico—and all of them accompanied by what appears to be sync sound (in fact, the audio for nearly all the shots was composited from more than one source). Compared with the complex montage of earlier videos, the editing of *Still Point* feels straightforward: in most instances, one shot is followed by a direct cut to the next, though at times fades out and in are used; and the individual shots are substantially longer than in the earlier videos (the shortest shot in *Still Point* is 11 seconds; the two longest, 56 and 52 seconds; most shots last 20 to 30 seconds). Over time, each image reveals a different set of subtleties and mysteries.

The tenth image, for example, focuses on an outdoor advertisement on Boylston Street in Boston: a photographic image of a woman covering her ears is centered in the frame. During the shot, this framed space is subtly expanded in three ways: the surface of the ad reflects tiny bits of light; at the top left, there is the moving shadow of the branch of an otherwise invisible tree; and the visual imagery is accompanied by a variety of street sounds. The woman's covering her ears may be a metaphor for Guzzetti's long-held and continuing assumption that most commercial film and video makes little use of the full range of audio possibility. In *Still Point* the soundtrack is full of subtle mysteries, and though the sound feels consistently realistic, we are frequently hearing sounds recorded in disparate locations. Shot 29, a nocturne of Walden Pond in winter, is accompanied by the sound of wind recorded in Reserve, New Mexico; and a sunset recorded at White Sands, New Mexico, is accompanied by the sound of wind recorded in Zanzibar.[19]

While the individual images in *Still Point* feel meditative, they are arranged in the "polyvalent" manner championed by Dorsky (figs. 25, 26). Often, successive images are simultaneously quite disparate *and* subtly linked to each other. Images 18, 19, 20, for example, are a color shot of a portion of a billboard with a gorgeous red and yellow peach, arrayed against a deep blue sky (the sound is air handling at an MIT building seen earlier in the video, mixed with close-up recording of an electrical transformer on a telephone pole on a street near Guzzetti's home); a black-and-white landscape shot of a slag heap near a mine somewhere in New Mexico (a sunny spot on the side of the mountainous pile gradually disappears as the sound of an airplane grows more intense); and a black-and-white street-level

FIGURES 25 AND 26. Landscape in El Malpais National Monument, New Mexico *(top)*, and street advertisement in Boston *(bottom)*: images 6 and 7 in Alfred Guzzetti's *Still Point* (2009). Courtesy Alfred Guzzetti.

photographic advertisement of a beautiful young woman in Post Office Square in Boston, flanked on the upper left by a green branch blowing in the breeze and on the bottom right, by a man and a woman (wearing a red jacket) reflected on the surface of the ad: they walk into the image from the right , disappearing, it seems, "behind" the sign (sound recorded in Post Office Square is mixed with a low-level recording of a crowd at a railroad station).

Some connections between these three images are obvious, others subtle. The first and third images focus on advertisements and in both these cases the product being advertised is unclear. The middle image is evidence of the result of industrial mining; the slag heap is impressive, even grand, but its implications are sobering: producing the products advertised commercially, after all, often has problematic environmental results, and this is subtly emphasized by the way in which the industrial sounds in the previous shot lead into the second image and reconfirmed by the sound of the jet plane growing louder, as the sunny area on the side of the heap disappears. While the peach billboard shot and the slag heap shot are relatively simple compositions, the third shot is complex and subtly dynamic (and immediately evocative of shot 10, described earlier); it draws the viewer's eye first to the ad in the center of the image (bits of reflected color tease the attention), then to the upper left where the green branch moves, and finally to the bottom right, as the couple moves into the image.

Still Point can be understood as reducing Guzzetti's experimental videos to an essence: the kinds of image and sound he uses are familiar from earlier work, but the experience is slowed down, "stilled/distilled," for our more careful examination (in *Still Point* Guzzetti forgoes text, both visual and audio).[20] At the same time, however, as short as *Still Point* is (14½ minutes), the individual shots, and the video as a whole feel epic, not only as a result of being shot in high definition and projected wide screen, but because of Guzzetti's expansive compositions, the video's elegant pacing, and the startling variety of spaces included. While earlier Guzzetti videos engage the often overwhelming qualities of modern life, *Still Point* is consistently meditative. Like Hutton/Benning/Lockhart, Guzzetti seems to have returned to the "still point" where cinema began, to the approach to filmmaking instituted by the Lumière Brothers and their excitement with capturing extended, well-composed 50-second images of the familiar and unfamiliar world around them.

6

—

Ross McElwee

As of the new millennium, no personal documentary filmmaker had become better known than Ross McElwee. Despite what we might imagine was the influence of Ricky Leacock and Ed Pincus at MIT and of Alfred Guzzetti, McElwee's teaching colleague at Harvard since 1986—all of whom abjured or at least avoided voice-over narration in documentary film—McElwee has become the most inventive explorer of voice-over in the history of personal documentary. Indeed, if his approach to narration no longer seems as distinct as it once did, that is because so many working in personal documentary in recent years have been under his influence. McElwee is also among the few filmmakers who have entirely devoted themselves to personal documentary. Aside from youthful experiments and from his earliest feature films—*Charlene* (1977) and *Space Coast* (1979, co-made with Michel Negroponte)—and one collaboration with Marilyn Levine (*Something to Do with the Wall*, 1991), McElwee has been devoted to personal documentary for going on thirty years.[1]

McElwee's seven personal documentaries reveal a filmmaker exploring, on one hand, the nature of his personal relationships with family members and with friends and colleagues as they have developed over time, and on the other, the continually evolving ways in which McElwee's self-identification as a filmmaker has affected these relationships. Further, since each new McElwee personal documentary builds (explicitly and implicitly) on the previous films, those who continue to follow his career are involved with his work on a meta-level: each new experience with McElwee's life and filmmaking causes us to rethink the long chronicle of McElwee's experiences and our reactions to it over time. As spectators, we are learning not only from McElwee's experiences but from our own experiences with him. Indeed, on a certain level, McElwee as filmmaker seems more intimate with us than he is with those he films. Decade after decade we have been his trusted confidants, continually learning not only about McElwee, but about our ongoing, always evolving "relationship" with him.

FINDING A MUSE: *CHARLEEN*

In a way, by having made The Blue Angel, *the most widely circulated German film, I had made a German woman the toast of many lands, and, if nothing else, had spread good will for the Germans at a time when they were not very popular.*

JOSEF VON STERNBERG, *FUN IN A CHINESE LAUNDRY*[2]

Ross McElwee has become synonymous with autobiographical filmmaking, and his mentoring of filmmakers and films during his many years teaching at Harvard has probably had nearly as significant an impact on the field as his films. At MIT both Ed Pincus and Ricky Leacock were crucial influences. Ed Pincus's *Diaries* was important for McElwee—"I'm sure I was influenced by it in all kinds of ways"[3]— and when he graduated with his master's degree in 1977, he worked as Pincus's teaching assistant for an additional year and a half. Ricky Leacock, especially his *Happy Mother's Day* (1963) and his general attitude toward filmmaking, were also important. McElwee implicitly pays homage to Leacock by having him speak the opening narration in *Sherman's March* (1986) and by having him appear in *Time Indefinite* (1993), and he has made his appreciation explicit: "When I was at MIT, Ricky was always irreverent, always encouraging us to do films for ourselves, to do films that were not conceived of as commercial entities. This is not what you hear in a lot of film schools, where you're encouraged to produce films that will get you jobs in public television, or in commercial television or Hollywood. Ricky was always very caustic and irreverent about those reasons for making films."[4]

Both Pincus and Leacock seem to have agreed that their job was to see that those men and women who wanted to make films got to make them (often whether they were matriculated at MIT or not), and by the time he left MIT, McElwee had shot footage for the three films that would, each in its own way, provide him with the cinematic approaches and elements that, combined, would make his films distinctive and memorable: *Charleen* (1979), which was McElwee's thesis film; *Space Coast* (1979, co-made with Michel Negroponte); and *Backyard* (1984), McElwee's breakthrough autobiographical documentary.[5]

If it took some years before McElwee settled on the combination of cinematic elements that we now recognize as his distinctive approach to autobiographical filmmaking, one of his central themes—the American South—was evident from the beginning. Though *Charleen* focuses on McElwee's good friend, Charleen Swansea, he had originally envisioned the project as a portrait of the South, or at least of Charlotte, North Carolina, with Charleen as a witty tour guide. I wasn't at all sure that the film would be an intimate portrait of Charleen herself, though I hoped this would be the case. As it turned out, Charleen enjoyed being filmed and was a natural performer, in the sense that even though it was simply her own life that she was performing, she always performed it with a certain élan that was very "film-able." She enjoyed revealing her life to me and the camera. As a result, much of the Southern detail simply got eclipsed by Charleen herself.[6]

As McElwee would explain later, in *Backyard,* his move to the North, and in par-ticular, New England—first, to Providence, Rhode Island, where he was an under-graduate at Brown, then to Cambridge, to attend MIT and later to teach at Har-vard—was seen by some members of his family as a kind of abandonment of his heritage; and while McElwee has often made comic use of his subsequent differ-ence from his relatives, his films, at least up through *Time Indefinite* (1993), seem to have as an implicit goal a confrontation of certain prejudicial assumptions that northerners often have about his native region.

This confrontation is evident from the beginning of *Charleen,* as McElwee pro-vides information about Swansea's unusual background, and his own relationship to her, in a scrolling text:

> Charleen Swansea Whisnant taught poetry in the schools of Charlotte, N.C., where I grew up. I first met her when I was a high school student and we have since become good friends.
>
> When Charleen was quite young, she ran away from home to find a new father, preferably a famous one. She was in turn "adopted" by Albert Einstein, e. e. cum-mings, and Ezra Pound.
>
> She now publishes a literary journal and teaches in the Poetry-in-the-Schools Program.

McElwee's reference to Swansea's impressive (and somewhat mysterious) connec-tion with three famous northern intellectuals is followed by a remarkable sequence of Swansea at work in the Poetry-in-the-Schools Program: remarkable, because of her obvious ease and effectiveness at working with African American young people.[7]

In order to model the direct expression of feeling that poetry demands, Swan-sea asks a young man, Fred, to stand beside her while she pretends to be someone in love with him. "I *luv* ya, Fred!," she says to Fred; then, explaining to the class that a sure way to win the attention of a beloved is to enunciate specifically what one loves about him, she says, "Freddy, you smell like a melted Hershey bar, and every time I look at you, Fred, and look into your laughin' black eyes, it makes me feel like it's the middle of the night and ain't nobody in the world but me and you in the dark." That all this is done in very close physical proximity with Fred, and to the amusement of Fred and the apparent delight of the class, represents a crossing of racial barriers in a manner that, even thirty years later, can seem surprising in any sector of the United States (indeed, for those overly concerned with decorum in the classroom, Swansea's teaching might seem dangerously "inappropriate" because of the erotic innuendo implicit in her performance of passionate attraction). If we can assume that the fear of miscegenation remained alive in the South of the late 1970s, Swansea's teaching is a high-spirited defiance of this fear.

At least as we witness it in *Charleen,* the Poetry-in-the-Schools Program seems dedicated to offering young people, African American young people in particular, an opportunity to broaden their horizons. And judging from what McElwee shows us, Swansea's mission is to move both the black and the white South in a progressive direction. This is evident during the second sequence of *Charleen,* when Swansea is the guest at a Bible study gathering at her mother's home, attended entirely by older white women. Swansea describes an incident that occurred when she was trying to give a group of young people the tools to ask for what they need. When she challenged a quiet, resistant, formidable-looking young man named Peanut, sitting in the back of the class, to "tell me what you want; talk me out of my money!," he walked up to her, pulled out a knife, and said, "Give me your money!" A fellow classmate tells Peanut, "Nigguh, put up that knife! That's why we tryin' to teach you to talk, so you don't *have* to use that knife!," and Swansea explains to the women's group, "I realized that Jasper had said it better than I'd ever said it, and I think it's really true, that those youngsters who can't read, who can't talk, who can't talk you into giving them or society into giving them what it takes to live, are gonna click that knife open." Swansea's story doesn't simply confirm her skill at working with African American youngsters, it demonstrates her willingness to educate an older generation of southern white women by sharing what she feels she has learned through her teaching.

That McElwee begins *Charleen* with these two incidents reveals his admiration of Swansea's courage and commitment as a teacher and makes clear at the outset that he means to document Charleen Swansea within a context of the problematic racial history of the South as this history reveals itself in the present. The two sequences make clear that southerners (Swansea, McElwee, and implicitly Swansea's mother) are aware of this history and engaged in confronting the problems it continues to pose. Much of what follows in *Charleen* involves Swansea, her boyfriend (we learn early on that she is separated from her husband and is living with their two children), and a racially integrated group of young people preparing, then presenting what might now be called a noncompetitive poetry slam to students in a rural school (the group at the school seems with a single exception white). Throughout *Charleen* it is obvious that the city of Charlotte and the area around it remain largely segregated, but it is equally obvious that there are southerners, old and young, who, with persistence, courage, and good humor, are working to confront the imbalance of power and opportunity that segregation has created.

Having demonstrated Swansea's commitment to using poetry and her teaching abilities in the interest of progressive cultural change, McElwee focuses increasingly on Swansea's day-to-day life, and in particular on her relationships with Ezra Pound (she is in the process of selling her Pound memorabilia in order to fund her daughter's and son's college education), her boyfriend Jim, her father, her children, friends, and acquaintances, and on her interactions with McElwee and the filmmaking process he has instigated. The racial issue is evident, often subtly, within each of the situations McElwee documents, though it is Swansea's effusive, engaging personality that becomes the foreground of *Charleen*. During the time when McElwee was documenting Swansea's experiences, her relationship with Jim was in flux. She and Jim argue, try to work together on the poetry slam, and following the event, break up, seemingly for good—we learn in *Time Indefinite* (1993) that she and Jim later married. It is also clear that Jim's living with Swansea creates some tension with her children, Tom and Ena; Ena in particular, while part of the crew for the poetry slam, enjoys rebelling against both Swansea and Jim.

McElwee's documentation of Swansea begins as fly-on-the-wall observation, and whatever information McElwee provides is presented in a series of brief visual texts. However, from the beginning, and increasingly as the film unfolds, Swansea engages the camera and even McElwee directly. The first instance occurs during the drive to Swansea's mother's home—she talks to McElwee and Michel Negroponte, who took sound for the film, about Tom being ill the previous evening and how excited she is to be visiting her mother. The camera follows Swansea to the door of her mother's home, and Swansea holds the door for McElwee and Negroponte. Later, Swansea provides a tour of some of the Pound material directly to McElwee and Negroponte, and during later scenes often addresses the filmmakers. Midway through the film, when Swansea says that she doesn't think she'll stay in her job, McElwee can be heard asking, "Why not, Charleen?," and later, after she drives her maid to the bus stop, she expresses her discomfort with her relationship with the woman ("*the* only person I know in my life who, when I talk to her, I don't look in her eyes"), then, as the maid gets on the bus, asks McElwee, "Can I go?" McElwee says, "Sure." In other words, McElwee is "present" within the film in two distinct ways: as the implicit narrator of the visual texts and as an invisible character within the scenes documented. Of course, McElwee would continue to explore and expand this combination of detachment and engagement.

Charleen concludes with two events, one professional, the other personal. The poetry concert is presented successfully in Piedmont: McElwee documents the cast and crew gathering to travel to the concert, the concert itself and the audience's response, and the trip back. Then, following a final visual text, "After the concert, Charleen said she wanted to be alone. Several days passed. Finally, she asked us to come to her house. She had been in the hospital and now she wanted to talk to us" The film concludes with an extended conversation with Swansea, who has injured her hand by smashing it through glass panels on Jim's door—after

FIGURE 27. Charleen Swansea and Ross McElwee in the early 1990s. Courtesy Ross McElwee.

finding out that Jim had been "off for the weekend with a girl younger than me." Swansea seems devastated by his leaving, but says she recognizes the realities of having a boyfriend much younger than she and claims to be excited about moving on and seeing where life will take her: "I'm gonna *love* it," she laughs. The final shot reveals Swansea alone in a classroom, singing "Georgia on My Mind" backed by a limited pianist on an out-of-tune piano.

In the sequence in her home, Swansea's lying across her couch, her melodramatic assessment of her embarrassing situation, and her final attempt to put a positive face on the situation come across as instances of Swansea's typical candidness, but also as a kind of melodramatic comedy, even perhaps an evocation on McElwee's part of Scarlett O'Hara's final lines in *Gone with the Wind*. And this comedic edge is confirmed by Charleen's singing with the out-of-tune piano. What is clear, especially from our perspective several decades later, is that in *Charleen*, McElwee had found one of his primary topics—the American South—as well as his Marlene Dietrich, an attractive, highly intelligent and accomplished natural performer, who seemed to defy the conventions of her place and time and who would continue to be a crucial figure in nearly all of McElwee's most successful films (fig. 27).

It would be five years before McElwee would develop the more complex kind of presence that makes his later films distinctive, in the remarkable *Backyard*.[8]

FINDING A VOICE: ANN SCHAETZEL'S *BREAKING AND ENTERING* AND McELWEE'S *BACKYARD*

In the Diaries *[Pincus's* Diaries*] McElwee discovered the basic elements of a first-person observational cinema that he would develop further to the point of transforming the conventions of direct cinema: long-term solo filming; observation of one's familiars; presence of the filmmaker behind and in front of the camera (he becomes not only a character apart, but he also created a genuine cinematographic* persona, *a Keaton-like screen double); confessional monologues addressed to the camera (abandoned in his later work); and, most importantly, a subjective and partial commentary in the first person.*

DOMINIQUE BLUHER, "ROSS MCELWEE'S VOICE"[9]

For most of those filmmakers who were excited about the potential of observational cinema, one of the advantages of the new options afforded by sync-sound, on-the-spot filmmaking was the chance to avoid the forms of narration that had come to seem inevitable in documentary filmmaking. Both Ricky Leacock and Ed Pincus avoided narration, as did Alfred Guzzetti. By the end of the 1980s, however, filmmakers working in personal documentary were exploring the possibilities of new forms of narration: not the voice-of-god expert narrator so common in informational documentary, and still quite common today (in nature documentary, for example), but voice-over narration by the filmmaker, commenting on the personal activities represented in the sync-sound imagery. McElwee has become the most famous and the most adept filmmaker with this kind of voice-over, at least within the history of personal documentary—within the more general annals of personal filmmaking, Jonas Mekas's voice-overs in such films as *Walden* (1969) and *Lost Lost Lost* (1976) are also remarkable and memorable. But McElwee's first major experiment with this form of narration, *Backyard* (1984) was preceded by Ann Schaetzel's *Breaking and Entering*, which was made at the MIT Film Section and finished in 1980.[10]

Schaetzel's voice-over carries *Breaking and Entering*; without it, the imagery would have little impact. Her narration is sporadic through most of the film, but her opening comment—heard over a sync-sound, first-person shot made by Schaetzel on an airplane—frames the entire film: "I've come home in a state of anger. I came back to hurt my parents; I came back to hurt them because they hurt me. It's really that simple." Her comments are presented in a quiet, intimate voice, as if she is speaking to a friend. This opening is followed by a brief shot of her arrival at the airport gate, where her smiling father approaches her and apparently hugs her while she is filming: he seems to have no consciousness of his daughter's anger.[11] In fact, at no point in *Breaking and Entering* is Schaetzel's anger ever evident to her mother and father (or to her sister and her husband). We are the only ones within the context of the film who know that more is involved here than a family visit.

Schaetzel's anger is a result of events that took place when she was sixteen and seventeen—that is, fourteen years before this visit to her parents and sixteen years before the release of *Breaking and Entering*.[12] Early in the film, she mentions that when her father found out she had made love when she was seventeen, he was furious, and "he threatened to kill Bob. Later he modified it and was only going to charge him with statutory rape"—the end of this voice-over coincides with her father's saying, apropos of an entirely different subject, "I just have a continual feeling that there's a conspiracy to make life difficult." Schaetzel does not reveal the full story of this past event until nearly the end of the film:

> When I was eighteen . . . no, when I was sixteen, I met a boy who I guess he was a man then; he was twenty-one, who was very, a very sexual person. I met him on a bus because I was working during the summer at a magazine office . . . and I knew *nothing*, really one of the amazing things: I knew *nothing* about sex. My mother had told me when I was pretty young that sexual intercourse took place when a man put his penis in a woman's bottom. I didn't like the sound of that.
>
> But I fell in love with this guy, I fell in love with him, passionately in love with him and my parents forbade me to see him because they, they thought he was too old. . . . So I saw him anyway, daily, for two years, and . . . on my seventeenth birthday, I made love with him for the first time, and it was from the beginning extraordinary love-making. It was simple and powerful.
>
> My parents discovered at one point I think about the time I was seventeen-and-a-half, that I'd been seeing him and that we'd made love. And they sent me to a farm in Belgium for the summer. . . . My mother wrote me letters everyday in which she told me my deception of them was proof that I didn't love them and that my affair with Bob was sordid.
>
> When I went back to Washington, I couldn't stop seeing Bob. From then on, I was terrified of sex.

The effect of this event is evident throughout *Breaking and Entering*, not simply in what Schaetzel says, but in the rather depressive tone of her voice and in the nature of her cinematography.

Once she has landed in Washington, D.C., where her parents live (her father worked in the State Department much of his life and at the time of the filming was a consultant for Honeywell), Schaetzel documents everyday events: her parents reading the newspaper, a dinner party with their friends, her father pontificating about this and that, a small anniversary party thrown by her sister (during which barely suppressed friction between the parents is obvious), conversations with her mother and sister, her father's visit to the dentist, her mother's getting dressed to go out. . . . Ann, filming, generally does not play an active role in these conversations, and while the parents seem much involved with appearance (throughout Schaetzel's description of the incident with Bob, her mother is ironing handkerchiefs), they seem quite oblivious to Ann's filmmaking. Though neither parent evinces the slightest discomfort in front of the camera, this seems less a form of acceptance than an implicit indication of a smug obliviousness not merely to their daughter's real motive for recording them but to the revelatory potential of the camera and to Ann's seriousness as a film artist.

Breaking and Entering concludes after Schaetzel's mother leaves the house, having told her daughter, "Don't forget to baste." After a few brief shots of the now-quiet house, Schaetzel cuts to a close-up of a chicken roasting on a rotisserie, and the sound of the turning rotisserie continues to be audible once the screen goes dark and the credits roll. This sound has several levels of implication: the revolving chicken seems to represent the boring repetitiveness of her parents' marriage; it suggests the way in which the parents' intervention in Ann's love life has continued to affect their daughter and produce the anger (the heat) that they are so oblivious to; and it confirms with subtle humor that Schaetzel's revenge on her parents is complete: they have been "cooked" by their daughter's filmmaking without having any sense of what their normal activities and conversations have revealed about them.

In a very real sense, *Breaking and Entering* is *about* Schaetzel's narration. Her implicitly depressive voice-over helps us understand that Schaetzel's thoroughly anti-romantic black-and-white cinematography is an expression of suppressed anger and depression. The film seems an instance of what Laura Mulvey once called "scorched earth filmmaking": that is, feminist filmmaking that "consciously denied spectators the usual pleasures of cinema."[13] *Breaking and Entering* shares an implicitly grim, shell-shocked mood with Su Friedrich's films up through *Gently Down the Stream* (1981) and with Sally Potter's *Thriller* (1979).

McElwee's *Backyard*, finished four years after *Breaking and Entering*, depicts another trip home by a filmmaker who feels alienated from his family, and it expands on the narrative strategy developed by Schaetzel. After handwritten credits, *Backyard* begins with a brief précis, spoken by McElwee and illustrated by a series of three still photographs of his father and himself, camera in hand (each photograph separated from the next by one second of darkness):

[first photograph: long shot of the father and son in the McElwee backyard in Charlotte, North Carolina]

Before this film begins, I have to tell a story about my father and me.

When I was eighteen, I left my home in North Carolina to go to college in New England, and ended up living in Boston. Ever since then, my father, who was born and raised in the South, and I have disagreed about nearly everything.

[cut to second photograph: McElwee and father in medium shot, looking at each other]

When I graduated from college, my father, who's a doctor and conservative Republican, asked me what I planned to do with my life. I told him I was interested in filmmaking, but that there were also several other alternatives, such as working

FIGURE 28. The third photograph of Dr. McElwee and Ross McElwee from the opening précis of Ross McElwee's *Backyard* (1984). Courtesy Ross McElwee.

with black voter registration in the South, or getting involved in the peace movement, or possibly entering a Theravadan Buddhist monastery.

My father thought this over for a moment and said, "Son, I think your concept of career planning leaves something to be desired. But I've decided not to worry about you anymore. I've resigned myself to your fate."

[cut to third photograph (fig. 28): the McElwees in medium shot, but closer to the camera than in the previous image, looking at the camera]

I didn't know exactly how to respond to this, but finally I said, "Well, Dad, I guess I have no choice but to accept your resignation."

This opening sequence reveals several major changes in McElwee's approach to documentary and several distinctions from Schaetzel's approach in *Breaking and Entering*. For one thing, McElwee makes it immediately clear that this voice-over means to do more than provide contextualizing information about the action within the film. *This* voice-over posits a relationship between the filmmaker and the viewer that supersedes the film itself ("Before this film begins . . ."). Further, it seems evident in McElwee's monologue that he has carefully written and practiced speaking his comments; McElwee's pun on "resignation" feels more literary than anything in his previous films, and his delivery is carefully modulated: when he recalls what his father said to him, he subtly imitates his father's speech. This commentary is not in service of the visuals, but vice versa; the use of the three photographs is clearly (and humorously) illustrative of what McElwee says, and the changes from one photograph to the next provide a subtle and witty punctuation for the monologue. Further, McElwee's review of his "other alternatives" not only demonstrates a youthful rebellion against Dr. McElwee and what he represents, it suggests that McElwee can be the butt of his own humor: his listing of alternatives seems amusingly typical of the often self-righteous pretension of youth—pretension that, judging from the fact that we are watching a finished film, seems, even to McElwee in the "present" of the voice-over, a thing of the past.

The most obvious change in approach, of course, is the humor of this précis, humor evident not only in what McElwee says and in his delivery of the monologue but in the way in which the three photographs reveal the two men. McElwee's father is dressed in a suit and tie, arms folded over his chest, while McElwee is casually dressed and holding his camera, which is pointed at his father as if it were a gun. The wry humor of the précis is confirmed in the opening sequence of the film proper, when McElwee himself is seen playing the beginning of Beethoven's "Moonlight Sonata" on the family piano (playing badly, on a piano that is out of tune); in voice-over he indicates that the one thing his father and he *do* agree on is the unlikelihood of Ross's having a musical career.

McElwee cuts directly from the piano playing to a hospital operating room where his surgeon father is cutting off a growth, and McElwee's voice-over comments, "In the past I've felt queasy when I've seen my father's scalpel cut through warm living flesh, but I discovered that, as long as I was filming my father operating, this problem disappeared completely." He adds, "Unfortunately, I had other problems," just before his camera malfunctions—the conceit is that his father's presence has the power, or more precisely used to have the power (the voice-over implicitly postdates the shooting), to interfere with McElwee's equipment. The film's third sequence is also comic: McElwee films his stepmother Ann and his father, sporting a yarmulke, listening to a couple singing "Silent Night" to them on the phone, a ritual that "occurs every Christmas." "For some reason," McElwee comments, again in voice-over, "my father is wearing a yarmulka, despite the fact that he's a staunch Presbyterian."

While *Backyard* begins with repeated instances of McElwee's deadpan humor, it is soon clear that the film is about a good deal more than family foibles and a son's oedipal struggle with his father. During the first piano-playing shot (he returns to this shot twice during the first half of *Backyard*), McElwee indicates that he had come home "to make a film about the South, which for me meant making a film about my family." That this is the second mention of the South as a region (the first is Ross's apparent interest in working with black voter registration), and that it is followed by his introduction of Melvin and Lucille Stafford, African Americans who have worked for the McElwee family since Ross was a child ("As I grew up, I never questioned the fact that black men were taking care of the yard, while their wives were taking care of *me*"), makes clear that *Backyard* is about the specific issue of race in the South. If, growing up, he never questioned the fact that blacks helped his family to function, McElwee is certainly questioning this now—or at least using the making of this film to see the reality more clearly than he could as a child.

As McElwee is introducing the Staffords in his voice-over, Melvin Stafford is seen raking leaves, with neighboring dogs barking at him, and McElwee asks whether the dogs always act this way. Melvin says yes and evinces surprise that the dogs never seem to get used to him, before McElwee moves in for a closer shot of the dogs, barely visible through the brush that separates the two yards. Within the context McElwee has created, the implicit evocation of slavery is obvious. Then, we see Lucille Stafford working in the kitchen, asking Ross if he wants some soup, as McElwee's brother Tom and his friends come in and leave the kitchen (Tom hugs and kisses Lucille). After further shots of Lucille and Melvin Stafford working (Melvin and Ross also discuss Ross's childhood treehouse), McElwee concludes the sequence with the third shot of him playing the piano: the awkwardness of his playing on the out-of-tune piano now suggests McElwee's discomfort with his recognition that while the McElwees and the Staffords seem very comfortable, even affectionate, with one another, their relationship is nevertheless an instance of the history of the problematic racial politics of the South and the resulting economic disparity between the two "races."

During the remainder of *Backyard* McElwee confirms his awareness of some of the obvious and subtle ways in which racial history has affected the present-day South, and he does this within a particular cine-historical context. By the early 1970s, film scholars were beginning to explore the representation of African American characters in American cinema and to recognize that a relatively predictable set of stereotypes accounted for most roles African Americans had played in commercial films. The first edition of Donald Bogle's *Toms, Coons, Mulattoes, Mammies, and Bucks* appeared in 1973 and, with its provocative title, established what Bogle, and most scholars after him, understood as the most prevalent stereotypical film roles available to African American actors.[14] Two of these stereotypical figures, the tom and the mammy (and her offshoot, the aunt jemima), were conventionally depicted as loyal domestics whose lives were defined by the white families they worked for.[15]

It cannot have escaped McElwee as he was editing *Backyard,* and it does not escape those who have learned about ethnic stereotyping, that Lucille and Melvin seem, at least at first, to fit these roles. In a very general sense, Lucille and Melvin Stafford look like the mammy and the tom in D. W. Griffith's *Birth of a Nation* (which of course is set in the Piedmont region of the Carolinas, where Charlotte is located); and we see them almost entirely within the context of the McElwee household (McElwee never depicts the Staffords in their own home—though he does visit the backyard of Clyde Cathey, a beekeeper who does yard work for the McElwees and their neighbors, and he goes with the Staffords to visit Lucille's hospitalized brother).[16] Further, even though it is obvious that the McElwees are financially well off—they live in an elegant neighborhood, near a country club—Melvin must struggle to start the McElwee's old lawnmower but doesn't offer the slightest complaint about this.

Of course, although McElwee's depictions of the Staffords evoke two of the stereotypes Bogle defined, the Staffords are not actors playing scripted stereotypical roles in a fiction film. They are individuals who are documented doing their jobs and living their very real lives. They are, of course, instances of the southern class system, the twentieth-century inheritance of the history of slavery, but they are neither caricatures nor sociological data; they are living individuals not only in McElwee's film but in his life. The stereotypes defined by Bogle are normally understood within the history of the representation of blacks in literature and the visual arts, but they must also be understood as exaggerations of particular social roles that real African Americans have played in southern society: while many African Americans have in fact worked as domestics and as domestic laborers in and around white southern homes, and may have acted or even felt grateful to have these jobs, for viewers to conflate Hollywood stereotypes with real individuals, that is, to understand the Staffords merely through the lens that Bogle and other scholars of African Americans in cinema have provided, is to reduce the Staffords to caricatures and to participate in precisely the kind of reductive thinking that produced these racist stereotypes in first place.

Within *Backyard* the most obvious distinction between whites and blacks, other than the differences in social class, is the way in which the two groups react to McElwee's filming. It is evident from the beginning of the film that Dr. McElwee is dubious about his son's involvement in filmmaking and is uncomfortable in front of the camera (though it must be said that he does give his son entry to the operating room and allows Ross to join him in visits to recovering patients). At one point, he looks at the camera and says, "I'll be glad when that big eye's gone." In another instance, as he is being filmed putting up a volleyball net for a party, he expresses puzzlement about what his son uses his "expensive film" to record. Even at the end of the film, McElwee follows his voice-over explanation that he and his father are "getting along pretty well these days" with a final instance of his camera jamming in the operating room—confirming the earlier suggestion that his father's proximity (and implicit hostility to his son's career choice) causes his equipment to malfunction. Tom McElwee is also uncomfortable around the camera and hides behind a newspaper when Ross is filming him at the breakfast table. And when McElwee visits the country club kitchen, the (white) man in charge (most of the other employees in the kitchen are black) asks, with a wry, uncomfortable smile, whether McElwee is filming "all the dirt here."[17]

McElwee's stepmother and grandmother do seem supportive of his filmmaking. McElwee tells us that during his visit Ann suggested various activities for him to film and that his grandmother offered to sing some old songs for the camera, but in general McElwee indicates that "I had many contradictory feelings about being home again, and I felt very awkward about filming members of my family." These contradictory feelings are certainly confirmed when his grandmother sings for him and he mentions that he "was especially struck by the lyrics to one of her songs":

> Lilac trees are blooming in the corner by the gate,
> Mammy in her little cabin door,
> Curly headed pickaninny coming home from school
> Just crying 'cause his little heart was sore.
> All the children round about have skin so white and fair
> None of them with him will ever play,
> But mammy in her lap takes this dusty little chap
> And she croons in her own kind way:
> "Now honey, don't you mind what them white childs do,
> And honey, don't you cry so hard.
> Go out and play as much as you please,
> But stay in your own backyard."

McElwee was struck enough to use the lyrics as the source of his title, and I would guess that most viewers are struck by this elderly woman's apparent obliviousness about the implications of the lyrics she sings so beautifully. Her smile when she finishes the song is both endearing and a vestige of the South's troubling past, as is suggested by the faded quality of this imagery.[18] However, even if we think of the way of life emblemized by the song as fading, the lyrics come through loud and clear and continue to have more relevance in McElwee's life, and in ours, than we might wish.

Generally, the African Americans filmed by McElwee betray little discomfort with his camera. Melvin and Clyde seem completely at ease with McElwee's filming, and Clyde is happy to recall stories about his beekeeping. When Ross is filming Tom McElwee in the kitchen, hiding behind the newspaper, Tom asks, "You like the camera, Lucille?" And Lucille responds, "It don't bother me." Indeed, Lucille seems to accept that filmmaking is part of Ross; she laughs the first time she sees Ross filming her, but she goes about her business, asking him if he needs anything, even as he films. Early in the film, McElwee explains that his mother "died the year before I moved to Boston; my father has since remarried," and even if Ross gets along with Ann she seems to be something of a stranger to him, as in fact are his father and brother: early in the film McElwee explains that "since moving away,

I felt I'd become a kind of stranger to my own family. My brother had even taken to calling me 'the Yankee.'" If his family considers him a stranger, however, there is no evidence in the film that Melvin and Lucille feel this way. Early in *Backyard,* we see Lucille Stafford transferring boxed shoes to a bag, and in voice-over McElwee comments, "Lucille was given the last of the clothing that belonged to my mother." I read this moment as a suggestion that McElwee sees Lucille not exactly as a replacement for his mother but as what she has always been: one of the women who has helped raise him, and someone who continues to support the person (and the filmmaker) he has become.

An exception to the pattern I've described occurs when McElwee joins Lucille and Melvin when they visit Lucille's brother in the hospital. On one level, this suggests that McElwee feels himself a part of the Stafford family, though in the hospital sequence it seems clear not only that Lucille Stafford's brother is uncomfortable with Lucille and Melvin but also with McElwee's camera. After Lucille and Melvin leave the room, McElwee remains for a moment filming, and the brother's discomfort with his presence becomes obvious. As McElwee later explained:

He makes a gesture, a sideways move of the hand that's right on the border between being a wave, a perfectly innocent good-bye, and a somewhat hostile shooing me away. This man is very depressed, and a lot of the reason he's depressed is because he's oppressed. For whatever reason (I don't know the specifics of his history), his alcoholism, growing up black in the South, never having had anything of material value, starving himself—that's what Lucille said; he's suffering from malnutrition—that gesture is very important; it's emblematic of an anger that blacks in the South want to express, but can't really because of the mutual interdependency between blacks and whites, and because of an odd sense of family. And I don't mean "family" in a sentimental way: it's not a good situation.... Certainly there's the implication in that scene of the cameraman as one more white exploiter of the black class. I am victimizing the helpless, using them for fodder for my film. If I'd cut the shot before the gesture, I would have cleaned the scene up as far as implicating myself in this idea of white domination of blacks. But then it would have been dishonest. Godard's comment about every cut being political is very true.[19]

The conclusion of *Backyard* reconfirms McElwee's nuanced exploration of the issue of race in his own backyard. First, he returns to his father in an operating room visually, as his voice-over defines the temporal distance between the footage we've been looking at during the film and his commentary about it: he mentions that he goes down to visit his father whenever he can, "and I continue to make films. My brother is now a surgeon and Lucille continues to keep the house in order while Melvin keeps mowing the lawn. And basically, things go along smoothly, pretty much the way they always have." Immediately after this voice-over concludes, McElwee's camera malfunctions as his father passes near it, and the last we see of the hospital is a brief blurry image of a black orderly leaving the operating room. Things may seem to be moving smoothly, but clearly the tensions that McElwee experienced during the time when he was shooting are still in evidence.

Of course, "smoothly" for whites is different than it is for blacks: Tom McElwee has become a surgeon and Ross an accomplished filmmaker, so accomplished that he can *use* those moments when his camera malfunctioned as humor within the accomplished film we've been watching. But Lucille and Melvin have gone nowhere. During the film's final shot we see, from inside the McElwee home, a window that looks out onto the backyard, as Melvin, on the old McElwee lawnmower, rides by. McElwee's composition of the small window inside his film frame suggests the constrictions of black life in the South, even within households like his own; and the fact that we see Melvin through the metal grid of the window guard suggests that, for all his family's good will toward the Staffords and African Americans in general (McELWEE: "I'm told that when my father set up his practice in Charlotte . . . he was the first doctor in the city to have a desegregated waiting room"),[20] life in the McElwee backyard remains a kind of prison for them.

DOPPLEGÄNGER: *SHERMAN'S MARCH*

He said, "You can't be in love and be in this business."
UNNAMED FILM DIRECTOR, AS REPORTED BY PAT RENDLEMAN[21]

In his canonical meta–short story, "The Snows of Kilimanjaro," Ernest Hemingway uses an unusual narrative strategy.[22] "Snows" charts the demise of Harry, a writer whose African hunting safari has been interrupted by a serious infection that has developed from an untreated scratch; as he lies in his tent on an African plain, he is dying of gangrene. As Harry drifts in and out of consciousness, he remembers a series of events that he had never gotten around to writing about, and he realizes that he has failed as a writer because he has allowed himself to become distracted (by wealth and fame) from doing justice to his gifts. Of course, most readers of "Snows" will remember that Hemingway himself was a devotee of hunting in Africa, and a good many of those who have written about the story have drawn comparisons between Harry and Hemingway. What is unusual about the story's narrative strategy, however, is the way in which it offers Harry as an example of literary creativity gone awry within a story that demonstrates its author's literary creativity going full bore. Hemingway uses italics to present the various events that Harry feels he *should have written about*, not so much as a way of calling attention to these events as memories (other memories, memories implicitly not worthy of becoming literature, are not italicized), but rather calling attention to the fact that while Harry did not write about these events, *Hemingway* did; indeed, for anyone familiar with Hemingway's career, the italicized passages in "The Snows of Kilimanjaro" evoke the italicized chapters that separate the longer stories in his first important book, *In Our Time* (1925). As Hemingway said in *Green Hills of Africa* (1935), the nonfiction account of his own 1933 safari, "The hardest thing" for a writer, "because time is so short, is for him to survive and get his work done."[23] In "The Snows of Kilimanjaro" Hemingway uses Harry to dramatize the dangers that time can pose *and* demonstrates, through his completion of "The Snows of Kilimanjaro," that it is possible to resist the moral and aesthetic corruption that destroys Harry's career. Harry is the writer Hemingway might have become but has not.

In *Sherman's March: A Meditation on the Possibility of Romantic Love in the South during an Era of Nuclear Weapons Proliferation* (1985), McElwee uses a similar strategy, but for a documentary comedy. He creates a Ross McElwee character, a character obviously based on his own experiences, who seemingly fails to achieve his goals, but within a film in which McElwee demonstrates, as director, that this Ross McElwee character is not the only Ross McElwee we need consider. McElwee's double presence as director and character is set up as the film begins. First, we see a map of the American South and hear what seems to be a traditional voice-of-god narrator who provides a brief description of Sherman's "march to the sea" during 1864, leaving "a path of destruction sixty miles wide and seven-hundred miles long." That some aficionados of documentary will immediately recognize that this is Ricky Leacock's voice provides an in-joke: Leacock, as McElwee has explained, "pioneered a kind of filmmaking in which narration, didactic narration at any rate, was to be avoided at all costs."[24]

At the conclusion of Leacock's opening narration, we hear McElwee himself ask Leacock, "Do you want to do it once more?," and Leacock's response: "Do it again. Yes." This has a variety of effects. First, it reveals that the supposedly disembodied, voice-of-god narrator is in fact an actor, performing the role of expert; and second, it makes clear that McElwee is in charge of this process. As a result, when McElwee subsequently begins his own narration, with "Two years ago, I was about to shoot a documentary film on the lingering effects of Sherman's march on the South," we understand both that this is the voice of the film's director and that, like the immediately previous Leacock narration, this one is a performance by an actor (McElwee himself) who is implicitly directed. That this is the case is evident in McElwee's suggestion that he was working on a documentary on Sherman "two years ago." At first we may understand the Leacock narration (and the map and photographs that follow it) as vestiges of this earlier project,[25] but even as we imagine that this is the case, we cannot *not* realize that, whenever this material was recorded, it has become the beginning of the film we are watching. The fundamental reality of *Sherman's March,* of course, is that the film that begins to unfold (or has already begun to unfold) as the McElwee character heads South to see his family "to try and begin my film" has already been completed by McElwee, the director. Clearly, whatever frustrations and failures McElwee will be documenting have been recycled into the completed film we are watching (McElwee's indication that he has gotten a grant to make his film confirms these implications; obviously not everyone is successful in getting financial support from grant agencies).

In his opening narration McElwee explains that the woman he'd been seeing has decided to go back to her former boyfriend and that he is staying in a friend's currently vacant studio loft, as he is seen in extreme long shot in an empty New York loft, first pacing back and forth in front of very large windows, then sweeping up, then looking into what appears to be an empty refrigerator. This moment provides deadpan humor, in part because it is obvious that McElwee has either directed someone else to film him or he has somehow figured out a way to film himself in long shot as he reenacts activities that he may have originally performed when he came into this loft or, more likely, that he has decided will be adequate to evoke whatever that original experience was. Already, McElwee is present in this scene not only as an actor, and as the person telling us about his situation, but as the person who set up this amusing composition (McElwee seems tiny in this huge space, as "tiny" as his character supposedly feels) and as the director who, much more recently, has edited the film we are watching so that we hear his character's comments as we watch him. This prelude to the body of Sherman's March— the title and director credits appear immediately after McElwee's first voice-over concludes—has much the same function as the prelude to Backyard. In both cases, McElwee's introduction of himself creates a larger (implicitly directorial) context for the actions of McElwee as character.[26]

In the sequence that follows the opening credits, McElwee develops both his McElwee character and our consciousness of him as director, confirming the comic mood evident in the scene in the New York loft—and beginning the articulation of the complex approach that made Sherman's March a breakthrough not only for McElwee but for autobiographical filmmaking. In voice-over McElwee introduces us to his family as they walk through the woods to attend a picnic and Scottish festival at a resort. McElwee films his sister and brother, then his father, and sets up the basis for the action that follows in a voice-over: "For a long time, the consensus among family members is that what I really need to do is find what they call 'a nice southern girl'. . . . They're on vacation in the mountains of North Carolina and they've invited me to go with them to a picnic and festival. They've also invited a number of family friends and their sons and daughters—mostly, it seems, daughters." This voice-over, like the earlier one, has a doubling effect, first, because McElwee refers to his family as "they," even though he is with them on this vacation (he could of course have said, "We are on vacation"—though, as a filmmaker Ross is not); but also because the voice-over is superimposed with McElwee's sync–sound recording of the family walking through the woods: we hear his voice-over just after he says, "Hi, sis!," and "Where's dad? Oh, he's way back there."

That is, McElwee is present simultaneously as a character within the action and as a commentator on the action.

Further, as Dominique Bluher has said, this and subsequent voice-overs add a doubling effect as a result of McElwee's unusual use of the present tense: "Whereas McElwee writes and records the commentary during editing . . . the commentary is written in the present tense"—what Bluher calls a "past-present": "More shrewdly, the manner of dating or using temporal deixis, creates an effect of coexistence, as if he were commenting on the images for viewers during the projection of the film in a movie theater. . . . In this manner, three presents superimpose themselves one on top of the other: the past-present (images), the present-present (speech utterance), and the future-present (projection); or, from another perspective, two pasts (shooting and the recording of voice-over) actualize themselves in each new projection."[27] I would add an additional "present": the present when McElwee brought the images and the speech utterances together in the editing. Precisely at the statement, "mostly, it seems, daughters," McElwee cuts to a line of young women walking through the woods, which is amusing because of McElwee's precise timing. If, on one hand, we see McElwee, within the present of the film's action, somewhat at the mercy of his family, the obvious wit of his cut to the young women filing past his camera is evidence of his total directorial control over what we are seeing and hearing.

The deadpan survey of the almost ludicrously phallic Scottish games, "various demonstrations of strength and virility," that follows at the picnic seems to confirm the idea that McElwee himself is *not* strong or virile. But again, regardless of the self-effacement he performs in the action or draws our attention to in his voice-overs, it is clear that ultimately McElwee is in complete control of what we are seeing and how we are seeing it. This simultaneous development of the McElwee character as a bit of a sad sack about whom his family is concerned and of McElwee's considerable wit as director continues throughout *Sherman's March* and evokes a certain tendency in 1920s American film comedy, and in particular— as Bluher has suggested—Buster Keaton, who, like McElwee, often played self-effacing roles within films over which he had virtually total directorial control. The embarrassments and dangers Johnny Gray experiences in *The General* (1926), for example, are funny because, and only because, we understand that Buster Keaton created these experiences for the character he plays and that he survived his dangerous stunts and completed this remarkable film.

During the sequence after the Scottish games, McElwee takes advice about his love life from his sister Dede and subsequently attends a fashion show with his stepmother Ann, where one of the women modeling clothing is "a childhood sweetheart of mine, someone I haven't seen in over twenty years." These two events introduce another subtle but crucial aspect of McElwee's approach. The conversation with Dede takes place in a canoe, as Dede paddles while making suggestions about how McElwee might "tidy up" and dress more carefully to attract women. Dede wears sunglasses so that it is difficult to see precisely where she is looking, and we understand the conversation as Dede talking with McElwee-as-the-camera. However, during the next two conversations—the first with his stepmother Ann; the second, with Mary, the childhood sweetheart—McElwee is holding the camera so that it is to the right (and slightly below) where we assume his face is, so that when Ann tells McElwee that she has planned to attend the fashion show, she looks to the left of the camera, at McElwee. That is, the gaze of McElwee's camera is quite distinct from his gaze as a character within the action. The same is true, but even more dramatically, when he meets Mary at the fashion show: Mary looks to the left of the camera at Ross, who judging from her gaze, is standing up, and the camera captures the excitement of the reunion from below. After they greet each other, Mary asks what McElwee is doing, and he responds, "I'm making a film about Sherman's march to the sea." Mary sees this as a joke, but they agree to meet each other later. During their subsequent conversation, the same visual situation is created: Mary talks with McElwee, looking to the left of the camera, which provides us with an oblique angle onto the interchange.

This unusual strategy has a variety of effects, the most obvious of which is to create humor through the very awkwardness of McElwee's conducting a social interaction (including a hug at the beginning of the reunion and kiss good-bye when Mary leaves the resort) while carrying a camera and recording equipment. But there are more subtle and suggestive implications as well. That the camera literally provides an angle on these situations different from the one experienced by the McElwee character confirms the doubling effect evident in other ways earlier in the film: there is McElwee the character and McElwee the filmmaker—a filmmaker who knows as he is shooting that, whatever else is going on, he is in the process of making a film. That is, McElwee is automatically somewhat detached from the emotional involvements that his character seems to be experiencing. The separation of the McElwee character's gaze from the gaze of McElwee's camera remains obvious in nearly every important interchange in *Sherman's March,* and the few exceptions to this pattern prove the rule. Of course, many filmmakers who have filmed within events have carried their cameras on their right shoulders, and during interviews their subjects have looked slightly to the left of the camera's gaze. McElwee's distinctive exploitation of this device, however, gives it a complex psychological dimension.

McElwee's use of the split gaze confirms the implicit doubling evident in the voice-overs, when McElwee seems to be speaking to us even while he is engaged in the film's action. While we understand that it is McElwee's *camera* that is viewing his conversations from a different angle than he himself has, the effect is that *we* seem to be present at these events, experiencing them from the camera's position. Like his speaking to us in voice-over, this positioning of the camera creates the sense that we are McElwee's confidants (as we are Schaetzel's confidants in *Breaking and Entering*), intimates who are present during his experiences, and in many cases, closer to him, both physically and emotionally, and often politically, than those we see him speaking with. This becomes particularly evident during McElwee's subsequent interactions with Pat Rendleman and Dede's friend Claudia, the next two women McElwee meets on his march through the South.

This sense of the two Ross McElwees and the film's positioning of the viewer as director McElwee's confidant and partner are confirmed during several extended monologues that McElwee delivers to the camera in voice-over and in person. After Pat Rendleman leaves for Hollywood, McElwee, lying in a motel room bed, complains to the camera about his situation("Having two large empty beds is twice as depressing as having one large empty bed") then, as we see a shot of the moon, he remembers his experience in Hawaii as a child, when he and his family saw the white flash of the Crossroads nuclear test from eight hundred miles away: "We could see the ocean sparkling for miles out on the horizon, and behind us, Honolulu was as visible as if it were broad daylight. This flash gave way to a lingering lime green which then faded to a sort of deep dark red, and then finally, the stars and moon started to come back out through the redness. No one on the beach said anything." The bedroom scene, of course, presents the sad sack McElwee, but the memory of the nuclear flash functions on a different register: McElwee's elegant, sobering description suggests the immensity of the Crossroads test; whatever humor is created by his bedroom scene complaint is overshadowed by this memory, and it sets the stage for his complex response to events that occur later in *Sherman's March*.

McElwee's most memorable on-screen monologue occurs the night after a costume party McElwee attends with Claudia and her daughter Ashley. Dressed as a Union officer, McElwee talks about the good time he had at the party, then provides some history of Sherman, revealing the complexity of the general's feelings about the South (he had lived in the South before the Civil War, then at the end of his campaign offered the South very generous terms at the surrender).[28] At the beginning of the monologue, McElwee says, "I have to be quiet . . . because my father is asleep upstairs, and I think he already has enough questions about the validity of my film project without seeing me dressed up like this, talking to my own camera, so I have to be quiet." McElwee repeatedly looks over his shoulder while he is speaking to the camera, as if afraid of being interrupted, and the effect is that we seem to be taking part in a secret conversation with him. Within the action of the film, he is speaking to the camera, but within the larger context of the finished film, he *is* in fact speaking to those of us who are watching this scene: even as he plays the role of the nervous son, McElwee is fully aware that he is speaking not just within the present but to the future viewers of the film he is directing.

McElwee's development of a complex relationship with the viewer occurs just as his tour of the South in search of love (and for the remnants of Sherman's military campaign) is getting underway. The first potential girlfriend is Pat Rendleman, whose narcissism and apparent inability to imagine how she might appear to those who will watch McElwee's film make her a comic character. Rendleman's performing her cellulite exercises for the camera (and saying that "I'd do them a lot better if I had on some underpants") keeps the McElwee character awake that evening ("I keep wondering how I should have responded to Pat's comment about not wearing any underpants; I mean, that's not like telling someone that you're not wearing any socks"), and provides the *Sherman's March* audience with laugh-out-loud humor. Rendleman's remarkable ability to make a fool of herself on camera is confirmed when she describes the screenplay she plans to write: in the movie she imagines, she becomes the best actress in the world in a love scene "comparable to *Romeo and Juliet*"; she moves to a South Seas island where she founds a think tank and cures cancer, and when her jealous "Tarzanlover" beheads her, her head arrives in Hollywood to address the planet. The doubling of McElwee as actor and director is nowhere more obvious than during the Rendleman sequences. As a character, McElwee pretends to be fascinated, even infatuated with Pat—and while this may be the case, it is only in the sense that Rendleman is the perfect subject for the comedy McElwee the director is making. As inventive as McElwee is as a writer (his voice-overs are consistently witty, intelligent, and carefully researched), he could never have written the lines that Pat Rendleman provides him with. It is a tribute to his abilities as an actor, in fact, that he can listen, seemingly with serious interest, to Pat's description of her screenplay and stay engaged with her as she subsequently pursues her career in Atlanta and leaves for Los Angeles.

McElwee's interactions with Claudia and her daughter Ashley are not material for the kind of humor that Rendleman creates, but the people Claudia introduces him to (an evangelist who sees the coming destruction of the planet as a temporary stage on the way to the Second Coming and several survivalists who are in the process of setting up a compound in the mountains where they'll be able to weather a nuclear holocaust—it includes a tennis court) are material for grim amusement (fig. 29). Again, the McElwee character pretends interest in what these men (and Claudia herself, who provides McElwee with a tour of her fallout shelter) believe, in the service of director McElwee's determination to make these people part of his portrait of the modern South. The description of the Crossroads test that precedes McElwee's visits to Claudia suggests the immense scope of even a single nuclear detonation, rendering these survival plans as childish as Ashley's dollhouse. During *Sherman's March,* McElwee's creation of his often diffident character is more than a means for creating humor; it allows him to function as a kind of spy within what would otherwise be hostile territory for a northern intellectual. Obviously, it would be something of a stretch to call *Sherman's March* an ethnographic film, and yet, McElwee's lovelorn character is in large part a disguise that allows him to

FIGURE 29. Claudia's survivalist friend speaks with McElwee as he films, in Ross McElwee's *Sherman's March* (1986). Courtesy Ross McElwee.

create a memorable and intimate panorama of a region of the country and the people who live there that can seem as surreal as the worlds we visit in Robert Gardner's *Dead Birds* and *Deep Hearts*.

During the remainder of *Sherman's March,* McElwee's interactions with southern women vary a good deal, both in terms of his feelings for these women and in the ways in which the film depicts these relationships. None of the young women we meet after Pat Rendelman is absurdly comic in the way Rendleman is, and in certain instances McElwee does in fact develop feelings, or revisits earlier feelings, for these women. His visit to Winnie on Ossabaw Island, for example, is full of humor, but not at her expense. Unlike the other women McElwee has met, Winnie is an intellectual, a linguist working on her Ph.D. When McElwee asks her to discuss her work on camera, she responds, "I can't explain the theory of linguistics in two and a half minutes; that's ridiculous!" But she and McElwee talk at some length about linguistic concepts (a series of jump cuts humorously suggests both Winnie's willingness to talk at length about her work and McElwee's growing interest in Winnie), leading to his asking her how it is that she always got involved with her instructors and professors. Winnie, embarrassed, replies, "You're really fascinated by someone who can talk well and think well about the things that you find most interesting. For a very long time I thought the most important things in life were linguistics and sex. It's easy to see how one would get involved with a linguistics professor." McElwee moves in for an extended stay, and soon is describing to Winnie his own research on Sherman, which Winnie engages, just as he has engaged her linguistics research. Not surprisingly, McElwee soon feels that he's "stumbled into Eden."

During McElwee's conversations with Winnie, his camera doesn't take a separate angle from the McElwee character.[29] Here, character and director merge, and a real relationship is formed. We learn later—when McElwee returns to Ossabaw Island after an extended stay in Boston where he has taken an editing job—that Winnie has moved on from the sexual relationship they had been sharing by the end of his first visit. In other words, even when McElwee has achieved a relationship, his commitments as a filmmaker have taken precedence.

McElwee next visits ex-girlfriend Jackie. Like Winnie, Jackie is not material for McElwee's humor, in part because her commitment to antinuclear work seems a more sensible response to the threat of nuclear war than building fallout shelters or mountain hideouts and also because she is clearly a committed and energetic art teacher at a public school in Hartsville, South Carolina, where her students seem to be primarily African American. Jackie is reluctant to talk with McElwee about whatever their former relationship has, or has not, meant to her, and when they do have a moment alone together, it is clear that Jackie is in no particular hurry to fall in love: "I think it's all more trouble than it's worth." When McElwee suggests that she's "become cynical in her middle age," Jackie replies, "Yeah, haven't you?" If Jackie is more fully involved in her political concerns and her teaching, and in her plans to move to California, than with her love life, McElwee is more fully involved with his filmmaking than with searching for a mate, even when he pretends that he is searching, which is, in fact, not far from cynicism.[30]

After a brief interlude when McElwee talks with a would-be Burt Reynolds stand-in and a visit to a historical exhibit that emphasizes that the Civil War was a testing time for a breed of new and deadly weapons, McElwee travels to Charleston, South Carolina where he reunites with Charleen Swansea, who professes to be bored with his "singleness" and advises him to "forget the fucking film and listen to DeeDee," a young woman she believes is the perfect partner for him. The meeting with DeeDee reestablishes the split gaze situation, and Swansea speaks probably the most memorable, and most ironic, line in the film. "Would you stop!," she says to McElwee, and covers the camera lens with her hand; when McElwee says, "Don't touch that lens!," she replies, "I can't help but touch it. This is important. This is not art, this is life!" A moment later, when McElwee films Swansea explaining to DeeDee that McElwee is no longer filming, just turning the camera from one person to another, Swansea's delusion about what is happening is underlined: in fact, this meeting with DeeDee is, at least for McElwee, art, not life, something that DeeDee may understand more fully than Swansea does.

Throughout this visit to Charleston, the potential relationship with DeeDee seems less McElwee's focus—both McElwee and DeeDee are humoring Swansea—than Swansea herself. Swansea's considerable accomplishments as an intellectual and as a teacher, so obvious in *Charleen,* are invisible in *Sherman's March.* Indeed, here, Swansea plays a role closer to Pat Rendleman. Further, unlike Winnie, Swansea seems not only disrespectful of McElwee's filmmaking, but uninterested in his research on Sherman, even when McElwee tells her that Sherman "painted portraits of his friends in Charleston; he did still-life watercolors of the landscape"—clearly one of the aspects of Sherman that McElwee relates to: he too is creating portraits of people and landscape imagery of the South. What seems implicit throughout the Charleston visit becomes clear when DeeDee and McElwee talk about her commitments as a Mormon and her desire "to bring the priesthood into her home."[31] The Charleston visit ends when Swansea announces she has found still another perfect woman for McElwee, and filmmaker McElwee conveniently runs out of film: what appears to be end-leader creates a kind of cinematic ellipsis.

A visit to Sheldon Church, torched by Sherman's troops in November 1964, leads to the McElwee character's assessment of his filmmaking process: "It seems like I'm filming my life in order to have a life to film, like some primitive organism that somehow nourishes itself by devouring itself, growing as it diminishes. I ponder the possibility that Charleen is right when she says that filming is the only way I can relate to women. I'm beginning to lose touch with where I am in all of this. It's a little like looking into a mirror and trying to see what you look like when you're not really looking at your own reflection." As he delivers this voice-over, McElwee is visible in successive long shots, in each of which he is further from the camera, as if to say that for McElwee the director, the value of the lovelorn character McElwee has been playing, this particular reflection of himself, is beginning to diminish. But McElwee's subsequent visit to Columbia, South Carolina, quickly reveals that he will be staying with the character awhile yet. After McElwee, standing by the Congaree River, delivers a monologue about Sherman's destruction of Columbia, he steps back and seems to lose his footing in the weeds by the river, then apparently "loses his footing," when he comes upon Joyous Perrin, an attractive, sexy nightclub singer, performing Aretha Franklin's song, "Respect," in a parking lot. As with Winnie and Jackie, McElwee provides no laughter at Perrin's expense; and while she is certainly attractive, he seems less interested in Joyous as a possible mate than in her commitment to her artistry.[32] When Joyous leaves for a nightclub tour in preparation for her planned move to New York City to further her career, McElwee decides to visit one more old flame before returning north himself.

Of McElwee's relationships with women he knew before beginning what would become *Sherman's March,* his involvement with Karen seems the most substantial, though there is no evidence that for Karen their relationship was ever more than an affectionate friendship. Like Joyous, Karen is not material for humor; she is a lawyer and a feminist (we see her marching in support of the Equal Rights Amendment). Nowhere in *Sherman's March* does McElwee himself, or at least the McElwee character, seem less mature and a less likely mate: as McElwee says in voice-over, "Bumbling around with my camera, I don't really know how to film these things and I'm ruining our friendship." Nowhere in the film is McElwee as filmmaker more evident: after his first conversation with Karen, he films himself with his filmmaking rig in a full-length mirror, the only time this happens in *Sherman's March* (a premonition of this self-portrait has occurred earlier: as he hugs Joyous Perrin good-bye, we see McElwee's back in long shot in a mirror).

Further, during his final conversation with Karen, she confronts McElwee's filmmaking. Just after McElwee asks, "Why aren't you in love with me?," he snaps his fingers in front of the lens to make a slate for this roll of film, and Karen tells him to stop filming. "That's cruel," she says. McElwee replies, "No, it's not cruel," but Karen is adamant: "It *is*. Stop." A moment later he resumes filming, but it seems clear that this is the end of the road, not only for this relationship, but for McElwee's use of his camera to instigate (or to pretend to instigate) relationships. Our last glimpse of Karen is at a lake, where she turns her back to the camera, saying "Stop it. You stop it." McElwee's visit with Karen suggests that his commitment to the role of lovelorn sad sack is running out of gas (like his sports car and the leaky container Cam, Karen's boyfriend, brings to get the car started), while his acceptance of himself as a filmmaker is becoming more complete.

What remains is an extended denouement that includes McElwee's visit to the spot in Charlotte where the Confederacy officially died; the serendipitous discovery that Burt Reynolds is in Charlotte and McElwee's unsuccessful attempt to make contact with the actor ("The production staff informs me that I'll be arrested if they catch me on the set again"); his visit to the General Sherman statue at the southeast corner of Central Park (filmed by Michel Negroponte); and his return to Cambridge, where he explains that he has gotten a job teaching filmmaking (we see Sever Hall on the Harvard campus, where filmmakers-teachers still have their offices). At Harvard McElwee begins auditing courses, one of them a music history course taught by a young musician, Pam, who McElwee finds attractive. *Sherman's March* ends during a concert at Boston's Symphony Hall where McElwee watches an orchestra and chorus (including Pam) perform Beethoven's "Ode to Joy."

That McElwee's travels through the South conclude with his visit to a monument to the death of the Confederacy is suggestive on several levels. The Civil War involved the dividing of America into two distinct entities and the separation of American history into two eras: before the war, when, as historian Shelby Foote suggests in Ken Burns's *The Civil War* [1990], the United States was a plural noun, and after the war, when "the United States" became singular. As he travels the South, McElwee is of two minds: he remains a child of the region he travels, seemingly quite comfortable with his personal history and the people he meets, *and* he has become a northern intellectual, visiting his native region and exposing its sometimes engaging, often bizarre dimensions. This schizoid identity is expressed in the doubling of McElwee as a character–voice-over and in the doubled gaze of his character–camera. Further, in planning, shooting, and editing *Sherman's March,* McElwee was engaged in two separate but related activities: the apparent desire for a romantic relationship and the quest to complete his first feature-length film, a new kind of documentary.[33] While, at first glance, McElwee's concluding *Sherman's March* with "Ode to Joy" may seem simply an amusing ellipsis that suggests that his quest for a mate continues, a closer reading suggests that the film's mock-triumphant conclusion is a confirmation of McElwee's maturation *as a filmmaker:* he has been hired by one of the most prestigious universities in the world to teach filmmaking and he has completed the film we have just finished watching.

In her canonical novel, *O Pioneers!* (1913), Willa Cather depicts two fundamentally different kinds of passion. The romance between Marie Shabata and Emil Bergson, who fall in love and are murdered by Marie's husband in the midst of their first erotic encounter, represents a form of youthful passion distinguished by its fierce necessity, its sharp desire, and its inevitable brevity. The novel's other form of passion is represented by protagonist Alexandra Bergson's creativity in transforming wild land into productive farmland (her relationship with the land is described in more erotic terms than any other relationship in the novel). At the end of *O Pioneers!* Alexandra does find a human mate, her old friend Carl Linstrum, but it is clear that their friendship is based in large measure on Carl's recognition that Alexandra's fundamental commitment is to her creative urge, expressed in her passionate relationship with the spirit of the land. *O Pioneers!* and *Sherman's March* are, of course, worlds apart, but McElwee's articulation of himself as a double character throughout his film suggests a very similar understanding of the complex nature of passion. In frustration after her failure to instigate a relationship between DeeDee and McElwee, Charlene Swansea complains, "How can you be a filmmaker if you never have any passion!" McElwee answers with his only heated comment in *Sherman's March:* "I have plenty of passion." This passion, however, is not for the women he meets during the film, but, like Alexandra's, for the creative urge that is fueling the making of this film.

The pretense of McElwee's search for romantic love in the South is really a vestige of the filmmaker's youth (at the time when McElwee was completing *Sherman's March* he was the same age—thirty-nine—as Cather was when she was writing *O Pioneers!*). On the other hand, McElwee's creative passion for making *Sherman's March,* which throughout the film always takes precedence over his enacted desire to find a romantic partner, is evidence of his adulthood: McElwee's "march" through the South is ultimately a rumination on the experience of filmmaking itself as well as a testament to McElwee's recognition that, whatever else he may be or may become, fundamentally he is determined to be defined, to define himself, not by his family, his native region, his education, or his mate, but through his creative passion as a film director and its results.

NESTING DOLLS: *TIME INDEFINITE*

While at Brown University, I studied with John Hawkes, a novelist (Blood Oranges, The Passion Artist) who taught literature and creative writing there. I was very influenced by his writing, and by his emphasis on developing a voice in writing. Hawkes's prose—dark, intense, sardonically passionate—was powerful, and you had the unmistakable sense that it arose from his own life experience. Hawkes's voice could not be mistaken for anyone else's. I remember that one assignment he gave us was to write an autobiographical essay, but to write it in a style that intentionally mimicked Hemingway's style. I remember how uncomfortable it was to try someone else's voice on for size, and yet how interesting it was to try writing from my own experience. I began keeping a journal that year.

ROSS MCELWEE[34]

What is relevant is what he himself believed. And there the answer is clear. He believed our life-stories are ours to construct as we wish, within or even against the constraints imposed by the real world. . . .

"SOPHIE," ON JOHN COETZEE, IN HER INTERVIEW WITH THE "COETZEE SCHOLAR" IN J. M. COETZEE'S *SUMMERTIME*[35]

I framed my discussion of *Sherman's March* with allusions to Hemingway and Cather, in order to draw attention to the literary quality of McElwee's use of narration and to provide a context for his expanded commitment to narration in his masterwork, *Time Indefinite*. McElwee's voice-over in *Time Indefinite* (1993) is not only more obviously *written* than the voice-overs in his previous films, it evokes the history of the novel, where a first-person narrator in the "present" begins by recalling the events leading up to the action of the narrative and introducing the characters who will be its central figures. This is, for example, how Hawkes's *Blood Oranges* (1970) begins, and in that novel Hawkes creates a narrator, Cyril, whose view of the events he describes seems quite distinct from what one imagines was Hawkes's own. If the narrator of *Time Indefinite* is far less morally problematic than Cyril, his relationship with the viewer is equally complex. Few documentaries, few films of any kind, have used narration in more interesting ways and with more subtlety than *Time Indefinite*.

During the opening moment of the film, a continuous 37-second shot of a North Carolina beach, shot from a pier, it is clear that in *Time Indefinite* McElwee's voice-over narration will be even more significant than it is in *Backyard* and *Sherman's March*. The image of the beach is the background for McElwee's introduction, and only begins to take on meaning as we listen to what McElwee says. He explains, "Every summer since I was a kid, my family has gathered here on the coast of North Carolina for a weeklong reunion," as we see two young boys pushing bicycles up the beach, and by the time McElwee indicates that his family has never known "what to think of the fact that I moved north, and even more strangely, took up documentary filmmaking," we have noticed the tiny shadow of the filmmaker, visible within the larger shadow of the pier—his shadow seems to image the isolation he has often felt because of his filmmaking.

On the other hand, *Time Indefinite* makes clear from the outset that, however detached from his family he may have felt in the past, McElwee has accepted himself as filmmaker (the considerable success of *Sherman's March* probably had much to do with this), and he has come to understand that filmmaking is a crucial part of family itself. His presence as filmmaker is explicit from the start, and it is clear that his family has accepted his filmmaking (his father for the first time seems interested in using McElwee's camera, presumably to record his granddaughter, Ross's brother Tom's child). While McElwee's visual portrait of himself as filmmaker in a mirror might be said to begin the denouement of *Sherman's March,* here we see him with his filmmaking equipment during the film's opening sequence, being videotaped by his stepmother, Ann: "I'm sure I must look a little strange to Ann as she frames me in her viewfinder. I mean, at this particular moment, I'm not exactly blending in with the rest of my family" (not only is McElwee outfitted in a professional sync-sound rig, he is dressed entirely in black, his "negative wardrobe," as McElwee's father calls it). However distinct from his family McElwee may be as a professional documentary filmmaker, however, it is clear that motion pictures have become an essential element in these family reunions. This may be the first family reunion McElwee has filmed, but even if he were not present, it is clear that this family ritual would be recorded by Ann's video camera and by McElwee's uncles, Fred and "Super-8 Nate."

From the beginning of *Time Indefinite* McElwee's voice-over relationship to the viewer, like his presence as filmmaker, is more complex than in *Backyard* or *Sherman's March*. As is true in these earlier films, the viewer is McElwee's implicit confidant, but during the opening sequence of the film, he withholds information from us. After bringing us to the family reunion and introducing his immediate family members, he comments, "I guess in some ways I've always felt more comfortable *filming* the family, rather than starting one myself, and in fact today I've decided to begin shooting a new movie—sort of a home movie—and my filmmaking partner, Marilyn, has come down south to help me." That Marilyn is already a good bit more than his filmmaking partner becomes evident almost immediately, but for the moment we, like his family, are in the dark about this. McElwee assembles the family for a group shot, calls for their attention, and says, "As long as we have you all gathered here, I thought we'd make this announcement that Marilyn and I are getting married!" That we are finding out about his engagement to

Marilyn at the same time as the family suggests that we are intimate with this McElwee narrator, but in a different way than we are with the McElwee narrator in *Sherman's March*: intimate in a more familial sense.

That McElwee has come to see filmmaking as a crucial dimension of family is confirmed not only by his assembling the family so he can film their reaction to his announcement but by what happens when his camera battery dies immediately afterward: McElwee presents excerpts from Ann's decision to videotape "background information on how her stepson actually took the momentous first step on the road to marriage." Ann too is using the act of filming to create family history—perhaps even to become more intimate with her in-laws and in particular to her somewhat distant stepson Ross.

As director of *Time Indefinite*, McElwee does not assume that viewers are familiar with his earlier work (even though in several instances his introductory comments will have special meaning for those who have seen *Backyard* and *Sherman's March*); after introducing his family, he proceeds to review his history as a filmmaker by recycling excerpts from earlier films, beginning with shots of Tom McElwee, then Lucille and Melvin Stafford, and (after a shot of his father and Ann watching a tennis match that was not used in those earlier films) Dr. McElwee, from *Backyard*, followed by several excerpts from *Sherman's March*—his sister giving him advice on how to dress, Charleen introducing him to DeeDee.[36] This introductory review of McElwee's cinematic depictions of his life up until he begins to shoot this new "home movie" continues with imagery recorded during the time McElwee was getting to know Marilyn and shots recycled from the film he and Marilyn subsequently made together about the Berlin Wall: *Something to Do with the Wall* (1990). As Marian Keane has said, McElwee's films have come to "compose an oeuvre and call for being studied as such, for their connections and revelations of each other," and by the completion of *Time Indefinite* this process is well underway.[37]

Having created a general context for the action of *Time Indefinite*, McElwee reviews the series of events that followed his marriage proposal to Marilyn. *Time Indefinite* breaks down into to three general sections: the buildup to the marriage and the couple's first pregnancy; the miscarriage and the sudden deaths of McElwee's grandmother and father and McElwee's attempts to deal with his loss; and the final recovery from loss. During the first section, McElwee combines on-the-spot recording of events (getting the marriage license and the blood test, Marilyn's gynecological exam, talking with the printer who will do the wedding announcements, visiting Ricky Leacock, the bachelor party, talking with the wedding florist, the marriage itself, McElwee's visit to his grandmother to tell her about his marriage, the announcement of Marilyn's pregnancy to her parents, the move to a larger apartment, and the couple shopping for baby furniture) with recyclings of filmed imagery (old home movies of Ross McElwee and his parents, shot by

Uncle Fred, and Super-8 film of McElwee's first kiss, shot by Super-8 Nate; a shot from *Something to Do with the Wall*; imagery of a graveyard for children that McElwee recorded on a trip to Mexico with Marilyn).

Humor is provided by the reactions of people to McElwee's filming and sometimes by the very fact of his filming (during Marilyn's gynecological exam, for example), and foreshadowing, by the imagery of the children's graveyard; but McElwee's narration consistently elaborates on what we see, providing context and insight. It is clear that filmmaking has become the way McElwee engages the life around him, as well as his family history. He focuses on his uncles and stepmother, who, like him, are dedicated to recording the family; his wife is a filmmaker and his collaborator; and his friends are filmmakers: his bachelor party is "mostly other filmmakers" (including Robb Moss and Steven Ascher). During the moments before the marriage, McElwee negotiates with Marilyn for a few more minutes of filming, and the wedding itself is documented by McElwee's friends (Ascher shot the imagery and Moss took sound). The only important event not filmed is the honeymoon to Italy, but even this Edenic moment is represented in *Time Indefinite*, by a continuous photograph of an Italian landscape and McElwee's voice-over—"Edenic" not only because Italy "seemed the most beautiful place on earth" and because McElwee "felt incredibly happy to be there with Marilyn," but because the use of the still photograph instead of a motion picture image evokes the Edenic timelessness that preceded Man's "fall" into time with the knowledge of life and death.

The grandmother's death, Marilyn's miscarriage, and Dr. McElwee's funeral are represented only indirectly—by a moment of the grandmother's singing, from *Backyard;* by voice-over and television imagery of Times Square on New Year's Eve; and by television imagery of the blizzard that hit Charlotte at the time of the funeral, respectively—but McElwee's attempts to come to terms with mortality are dealt with in detail, and combine on-the-spot recording with periodic recyclings of representations of the past. McElwee visits the family home in Charlotte and talks with Lucille Stafford; he visits Charleen Swansea, who has recently lost her ex-husband (Jim died in a fire he had set in the home they had shared), then his sister Dede in Key West, and finally his brother Tom in Charlotte. In several instances, McElwee's commentary moves *Time Indefinite* to a level of complexity and subtlety beyond anything in his earlier work. One of these moments occurs during the visit to Charlotte, when a Jehovah's Witness comes to the door of the McElwee home. McElwee uses this moment to provide a bit of humor during what is otherwise a dark moment: as the man talks to him about the end of days, McElwee films the conversation, and in voice-over complains that religious witnesses of various faiths find him wherever he is and that by now he "could almost qualify for the Federal Witness Protection Program." For the most part, we cannot hear precisely what the Witness says, but during a pause in the voice-over we hear the man describe how God's kingdom "in itself will stand to time indefinite," and how "that time is very near, in the near future, when this God's kingdom will start to rule"—and recognize immediately that the man's words have provided this film with its title. The voice-over continues, and McElwee talks about how his attention is on capturing the lovely light playing across the face of the man and his little daughter, "when suddenly, something he said about thirty seconds ago catches up with me, something about 'time indefinite.' It's such a beautiful phrase, but what exactly does this mean, 'time indefinite'? I mean the remarkable thing is that while I'm standing here, pretending to be Monet with a movie camera, this man is trying to save my soul. I mean he's not even asking of for money, or for anything . . . except my attention."

Implicitly, this moment posits three "Ross McElwees": the filmmaker focused on getting the exposure right and responding to the conversation with his subtle camera movements; the voice-over McElwee, who is several seconds behind us in realizing the importance of "time indefinite" and who can comment on his own self-involvement and pretension ("pretending to be Monet with a movie camera"), and, of course, the filmmaker who edited *Time Indefinite* into its present form and knew as he did so that we would hear the phrase before the first McElwee seems to and wonder why this phrase was thought significant enough to be the source for the title. This moment makes clear, or clearer, that time is a fundamental issue for *Time Indefinite* on two different, but related levels. As a person, McElwee is trying to come to terms with mortality, with the finiteness of all lives and the many forms of loss that result; and as a filmmaker, he is working to understand how cinema might function in regard to mortality, how it can be useful in dealing with loss. His presentation of his conversation with the Witness implies that, while cinema cannot change the fact of mortality, it can allow both filmmaker and viewer to return to what has passed, to reconsider its meaning, and to be attentive to the moment-to-moment incarnation of experience: the physical light on the man's face, the emotional sweetness of his daughter, and the spiritual sacrifice and generosity that McElwee sees in this man's actions.

McElwee, continuing to struggle with his multiple losses, leaves Charlotte to visit Charleen and then Dede, neither of whom seems to offer him much relief (neither seems able to put the deaths of their loved ones in the past, and Dede can barely speak about her father for the camera). He returns to Charlotte, more obsessed with death than ever, but still "thinking there must be some way for me to deal with this through my filming." At the family home, McElwee, for the only time in *Time Indefinite*, speaks directly to the camera, while simultaneously speaking in voice-over about *his own* comments.[38] McElwee, speaking to the camera, says:

> Everything begins and ends with family. I don't know, some part of me resists that idea. I mean, there's so much conflict in family, especially between the generations. You drive your parents crazy, they drive you crazy, and then suddenly they're dead

and you're stunned. First, you're twisted by their lives, then you're twisted by their deaths. And then you get to grow up and do the same thing to your own kid.

His voice-over comments:

> So, as I'm sitting here, talking to my camera, my mind starts to wander and I begin worrying that I've gotten off on the wrong track. I mean, sure, my family and I had our differences, but we did all love one another. That's actually the problem. You get bound up in family and everyone in it starts to die. The pain just goes on, generation after generation. But I can't just sit here and talk about all this. It's too depressing.

Here, we have four "McElwees," one inside another, like nesting dolls. There is the McElwee who is talking to the camera; there is the McElwee who is thinking about what he is saying to the camera as he is saying it; there is the voice-over McElwee who is remembering his debate with himself at a later time; and there is the fourth McElwee who constructed this image-sound form of shot-countershot dialogue after recording the voice-over.[39]

The voice-over McElwee continues to counter the McElwee who is recording himself, seemingly increasingly frustrated with the morbidity of the latter's monologue; and the sequence comes to a close with his voice-over observation that "sitting here staring at my camera, I've somehow gotten trapped in a morbid metaphysical feedback loop, and to say the least, I need to break out of it. But still there are these questions that won't go away. It's all very complicated," which is immediately followed by the McElwee who is speaking to the camera, saying, "It's all very complicated." What is complicated is not only the issue of mortality, the limited time of all lives, but the complexity of time itself, and of cinematic time in particular, and the ways in which any present includes not only memories of the past but imaginings of the future, and perhaps, imaginings of the past (did McElwee really have this debate with himself during his monologue to the camera?)—even possibly, memories of imaginings of the future (McElwee seems to have thought that talking and filming with his family and Charleen would be of more use than the voice-over McElwee now believes it has). It's all very complicated.

McElwee's "morbid metaphysical feedback loop" takes final form, first, in the humor of his discovery of a nest of dead and dying bees and the arrival of the exterminator, and then, during his visit with his brother, who is dealing with an unusual patient: a woman who has lived with a malignant breast cancer for years, but has ignored this gruesome reality because, as she says, "I don't want to think about myself; I'm Scarlett. . . . I don't like to worry people." Tom McElwee explains that, though the woman claims the tumor had only been bothering her for a few months, in fact she must have ignored it for years: "The tumor ulcerated and started draining pus, and you could not be in the same room with her, it was so infected and it smelled so bad." McElwee asks his brother about their father's death, about which Tom has no information, then returns to the issue of the woman's tumor. For 75 seconds we stare at a slide of the tumor, as McElwee explains that

> she simply denied she had this thing on her body, pretended it wasn't there. I mean it's kind of like death itself. This huge grotesque thing that stares us in the face, but somehow we manage to deny it, to abstract it, which is what happens when I stare at this photograph long enough. And it's what's beginning to happen with my father's death too. I came down here hoping to face directly his death, and death in general. I wanted to somehow corner death with a camera and prevent it from becoming abstract, but now, ironically, this filming of my family is all beginning to feel like a distraction, just another form of denial, and I need to stop.

This momentary visual caesura and McElwee's use of the tumor as a metaphor for the deaths he's been trying to come to terms with, and death itself, is the final turning point in the film: a shift from a focus on death to a focus on life (the fact that Tom's patient actually is *not* dead but will be going home the next day is a premonition of this shift).

The tumor shot is followed by the most upbeat sequence in *Time Indefinite:* McElwee's documentation of the remarriage, on their fiftieth wedding anniversary, of Lucille and Melvin Stafford. For the first time in all of his films, McElwee's filmmaking is done at the request of someone else ("Lucille asked me if I would do her a favor; she wants me to make a video of her wedding anniversary"). As Lucy Fischer has suggested, this "reverses the pattern of Southern race relations," allowing McElwee to become "part of *their* family instead of they becoming part of his."[40] The following sequence reverberates on several levels, not only within *Time Indefinite*, but within McElwee's autobiographical filmmaking in general. The Staffords' elegant remarriage event could not be more upbeat, and it ends with the happy couple, amidst their cheering family, leaving in a limousine. The union of the Staffords, of course, is a model of longevity, a temporary defiance of mortality; but the fact that the Staffords are a southern black family suggests a larger reference: the long, painful, courageous, persistent struggle of African Americans with slavery, lynching, Jim Crow, and in the ongoing present, racism and economic disenfranchisement. That the Staffords' celebration of life, despite all the reasons a southern black family might have for bitterness, lifts McElwee's spirits is made clear in the direct cut from the departing limousine to a view out the window of the plane taking McElwee back to Boston. As McElwee is flying home, the film presents a final sequence of early home movies of his parents, and McElwee returns to "time indefinite," redefining it in cinematic terms: "Maybe I've been trying to preserve things in the present, somehow keep everyone alive in some sort of 'time indefinite,' as my Jehovah's Witness friend likes to say."

McElwee's return home, and "overwhelming desire to be with Marilyn again" results in a second pregnancy and then, a suggestive "filming" of the birth—

"suggestive" for its implications for McElwee's maturation and within the modern history of American independent cinema. Even before the birth, it has become clear that *Time Indefinite* is McElwee's attempt to do precisely what his brother's patient, and his own family members, have not done: refuse to deny disease and death, crucial and inevitable parts of aging. But once this process has become, as McElwee says, "just another form of denial," he returns to Cambridge; desire is reborn and produces a new life. The "filming" of Adrian McElwee's birth is a radical departure from virtually everything else in McElwee's oeuvre: the birth is presented entirely in sound, and the film is without an image for 39 seconds. McElwee explains, "I didn't film the birth because I wanted to help the midwife deliver him." For the first time in the film since his honeymoon with Marilyn, McElwee forgoes image making in order to be an active participant in a crucial moment in his, and Marilyn's and Adrian's, lives—but in this instance, the only "image" is the empty film frame.

The fact that, despite our not *seeing* the birth, we are present for it has another level of implication for anyone familiar with American independent cinema. The moment of Adrian's birth is preceded by a shot of Marilyn, nude, lying on a bed, representing the couple's anxious wait for this pregnancy to come to term. Marilyn's distended belly is close to the camera and at one point her hand caresses her belly; as she does so, McElwee's hand enters the frame and covers her hand in a loving gesture. The birth immediately follows. Within the annals of independent cinema, the most famous film about birth is, of course, Stan Brakhage's *Window Water Baby Moving* (1959). *Window Water Baby Moving* could hardly be more different from *Time Indefinite*: Brakhage's commitment to silent cinema, montage editing, gestural camerawork, and the repetition of particular motifs is evident throughout *Window Water Baby Moving*. Perhaps the most memorable motif is a close-up of Jane Brakhage sitting in a bathtub, framed so that we see only her pregnant belly, with her hand resting on it. During this repeated shot, Brakhage's hand enters the frame and covers her hand in a loving gesture that is virtually identical to McElwee's gesture in *Time Indefinite*.

Of course, the presentations of the births in the two films are the inverse of each other. *Window Water Baby Moving* uses visceral visual imagery, depicting virtually the entire process: labor, the baby's crowning, the baby emerging from the vagina, the cutting of the umbilical cord, and the expulsion and examination of the placenta. In fact, although the directness of the film must have been a good bit more powerful for audiences in the 1950s and early 1960s, when absolutely nothing like Brakhage's film had ever been seen by film audiences, *Window Water Baby Moving* continues to be a shocking film for many viewers. It communicates not merely the facts of the birth but also Brakhage's heightened emotional state: his excitement, his amazement at what birth actually *is,* and his terror that things might go wrong. Indeed, while Brakhage's happy face is seen at the conclusion of *Window Water*

Baby Moving (Jane took the camera from Brakhage to record his response), for most first-time viewers this finale is lost in the shock of the preceding imagery.

Brakhage's commitment to cinema as a visual art and his abjuring of sound in nearly all of his films produced the most remarkable body of work in the history of avant-garde cinema (and a good many contributions to the history of documentary). And while *Window Water Baby Moving* remains a wondrous and beautiful film, it is also true that it transforms Jane's body and the birth into a spectacle. Brakhage's use of close-up magnifies much of what we see, bringing us closer to the particulars of this birth than would be possible even for someone actually present. This magnification reveals and communicates Brakhage's astonishment and his commitment to our really *seeing* what had been for so long visually suppressed—but there is a paradoxical dimension to this intimacy. Brakhage has explained that filming the birth was a practical necessity as well as a cinematic challenge: "I really didn't know if I could go through the birth without fainting. Every time they drew blood on me I used to pass out . . ."; "There was a strong desire on Jane's part that I be present during the childbirth, and I wasn't really wanting that burden. I thought I might faint. I rather think I would have had I not been making a film, and something in me knew that."[41] During *Window Water Baby Moving* Brakhage is both intimately present *and* detached, by virtue of his use of the camera as a kind of visual protection: as close as it allows *us* to be to the birth, the camera remains between Brakhage and the birth itself. His subsequent decision to present the birth as a complex, deeply metaphoric montage intellectualizes his visuals, implicitly creating a second form of detachment.

Though McElwee has told me that he was not thinking of *Window Water Baby Moving* when he made *Time Indefinite*, I read his presentation of Adrian's birth as an implicit response to Brakhage's film. Like Brakhage, McElwee had had his problems with experiencing the physicality of the body. Early in *Time Indefinite*, as Marilyn and Ross are having their blood tests, McElwee indicates that he is beginning to feel nauseous, and explains, "I've actually found that it's easier for me to watch blood being drawn when I'm filming it, because for some reason if I watch it through a lens, then it seems less real to me, like I'm watching a movie." Whatever concerns he may have had about being in the delivery room, however, it is clear that McElwee had decided not only to be present at the birth, but to participate directly with it. His decision to tape-record the birth, rather than to film it, allows him to function simultaneously as an artist and a participant-father. Further, by tape-recording the birth, McElwee avoids turning this moment into spectacle; Adrian's birth is not presented as shocking, but as a normal and fundamentally thrilling experience: we can hear the excitement and happiness of the parents as Adrian is born. Of course, it is only fair to acknowledge that in 1959, the visual depiction of birth could not help but be shocking within a culture that had repressed all elements of the body-as-process: this repression included fathers not

being allowed to see, much less participate, in the births. McElwee is the benefi-
ciary of the change in attitudes about birth that *Window Water Baby Moving*
helped to create.

McElwee's decision not to film the birth sets the tone for the conclusion of *Time
Indefinite:* "I don't have much other footage from the first six months of Adrian's
life, partially because I felt so amazed by him and so connected to him in such a
deep way that I haven't been able to bring myself to pick up a camera and film
him." And even when Ross, Marilyn, and Adrian attend that summer's family
reunion, McElwee doesn't shoot film, but instead presents imagery from the
reunion that Super-8 Nate's daughter has made, imagery of family members and
the "great wall of babies" with Adrian in the back . It is clear that whatever estrange-
ment McElwee felt during the reunion that opens *Time Indefinite* is long gone. The
reunion is followed by a visit to Charleen, who is seen, for the first time since *Charleen,* as her intellectually engaging self—she, and Ross and Marilyn, discuss the
implications of parenthood in a world where so many babies are starving. For the
second-to-last shot of the film McElwee returns us to the pier on the Carolina
coast with which *Time Indefinite* begins; this shot is virtually identical to the one
that opens *Time Indefinite,* except that here, instead of two young boys leaving the
beach, we see a man and a woman arriving. The two beach shots are an implicit
synecdoche for the maturation that McElwee, as a man and as a filmmaker (again
we see his tiny shadow) has experienced by facing mortality. He explains, "So as
the first year of Adrian's life goes by, I film him now and then. It's a pleasure now,
something I enjoy doing, and he even seems to like it. Maybe I'll eventually make
some sort of film about him growing up in the world." The film ends with a 35-
second shot of Adrian, the first image McElwee recorded of his son when he was
one week old, and McElwee imagines, "Maybe the film can begin with that first
shot of him." McElwee's meditation on his son represents an escape from the "morbid feedback loop" he struggled with earlier, and at least a momentary end to the
obsessive engagement with his own pain that for a time shattered his identity into
multiple, conflicted selves.[42]

ON THE ROAD AGAIN: *SIX O'CLOCK NEWS*

By the completion of *Time Indefinite* McElwee had mastered all aspects of the
approach that has continued to characterize his work—his complex narration,
his deft amalgam of deadpan humor with poignancy and pain, his reliance on
subjective camera, and his use of his friend Charleen, his family, and himself as
characters—and in recent decades has deployed this approach in several features,
the first of which was *Six O'Clock News* (1996). While *Six O'Clock News* does in
fact begin with the "gerbil shot" with which *Time Indefinite* ends (it also concludes
with a sequence focusing on Adrian, three years later), the film is not really about

Adrian's growing up but rather the ways in which being married and becoming a father of a young child have affected McElwee's life—most obviously the fact that "since the baby's been born, we're home a lot more now and we've ended up watching more TV than we used to, especially the local news." Of course, the preponderance of television news stories, especially local news stories in larger cities, reflect an "if it bleeds, it leads" assumption about what the public will watch; and from the beginning of *Six O'Clock News* McElwee uses excerpts of horrific stories, filmed off television screens, as a motif and as the motivation for a new set of filmmaking adventures.

Like *Time Indefinite, Six O'Clock News* begins by creating a context for McElwee's autobiographical approach that functions simultaneously as background for any viewer unfamiliar with his earlier work and as a reconfirmation of the cinematically intimate relationship he has created with those familiar with his earlier films. The first of the film's many brief montages of horrific news stories ends with brief coverage of the damage hurricane Hugo has done to the Isle of Palms off the coast near Charleston, South Carolina, where Charleen Swansea lives. After presenting an excerpt from *Charleen,* McElwee documents his trip to South Carolina to be with Swansea as she confronts and deals with the damage to her new home. It turns out that, while many homes on the island, including many in her neighborhood, have been leveled, her home has been damaged but not destroyed. Even her papers are intact; she can continue to work as a teacher and editor.

McElwee returns to Cambridge, where the film's introduction of his approach continues: he records his neighbor and landlord, Barry, who is obsessed with taping episodes of *Twilight Zone* and other similar fantasy TV series; and McElwee is taped by a local television crew interested in "this guy, meaning me, who was always filming his own life." McElwee meets Debbie Shapiro and her crew with camera running, and their conversation provides first-time McElwee viewers with some sense of his thinking as well as a demonstration of how television news reporters restage reality to suit their needs: the scene of the news crew arriving at McElwee's apartment is repeated three times. McElwee, in voice-over, wonders, "Is it any less real that they're filming themselves coming into my apartment a third time? Ultimately, what difference does it make? I'll edit this scene for my purposes, just as they'll edit it for theirs." McElwee's unusual work with cinematic time, so crucial in *Time Indefinite,* is evident again here: his voice-over, obviously recorded after this scene, suggests what the McElwee character may be thinking to himself during the "present" of the television shoot, but the wit of this moment is in our recognition that in fact filmmaker McElwee already has edited the sequence we are watching.

McElwee decides to "somehow punch directly into the territory held by the six o'clock news," by taking his camera on the road. Suddenly he is at a motel in Mississippi, where he sees a news story about the sentencing of the murderer of

Gloria Im and the reaction of her husband, Steve Im. McElwee decides to make contact with Im, who moved to Arkansas after the murder. In one sense, McElwee's decision to film a person who is a stranger to him (and who is not introduced to him by a friend or family member) is reminiscent of *Space Coast* (1979), his early collaboration with Michel Negroponte about several residents of Cape Canaveral, Florida, in the wake of the Apollo moon missions (see n. 8), but the tragic loss Im has experienced offers an implicit challenge: certainly the news focuses on such tragedies, but for an independent documentary filmmaker to decide to enter this man's life in order to cinematically mine this tragedy is evidence of some considerable chutzpah.

McElwee does find his way to Im and the two explore the implications of Im's tragic loss. At the conclusion of McElwee's visit, the self-made, successful businessman (remarried, to a former Miss Korea) asks for a final conversation with McElwee, without the movie camera. Im explains to McElwee and his tape recorder that the loss of Gloria Im has shaken his religious faith: Im still goes to church, still believes in God, but has concluded that "God [is] out of control [of] this world; He cannot control the world." Both McElwee's interest in finding his way to victims of some of the tragedies he sees on the news and the fundamental issue raised during this first experiment—the rather surreal relationship between tragedy and belief—determine the trajectory of the rest of *Six O'Clock News,* which is organized into a series of episodes (the film's earlier reference to *The Twilight Zone* seems a premonition—especially since McElwee continually finds himself transported to new, and sometimes bizarre situations).

McElwee is next seen in the outskirts of Phoenix, where a devastating storm has destroyed parts of a trailer camp while leaving others intact. McElwee visits the site, talks with several residents, and observes the ubiquitous local news crews recording sound-image bites—McElwee's ambivalent sense of the news is evident in his voice-over: "If you view enough local news, you sense that there really are thousands of people out there waging battles against their own demons, against fate, even against God. And for better or worse, it's only the six o'clock news that really acknowledges them, tells their stories." Unlike Steve Im, the survivors McElwee talks with in Phoenix are grateful to God for sparing them. The sequence ends with McElwee's wry observation, "I guess life's easier if you believe that, in fact, God is in control of everything. Or maybe life's only easier if your house trailer is the one that's spared."

A story he sees on cable TV news about an out-of-control brush fire threatening a grove of sequoias sends McElwee to California, where he attempts to join a cadre of firefighters. His Forest Service guide, who explains that "fire really doesn't know any rules"—one tree may be destroyed while the one next to it is spared—is amusingly optimistic, though by the time they catch up with the firefighting crew, this part of the fire is under control and McElwee reports that subsequently he and the guide were lost for five hours on their way back. McElwee halts his cross-country excursion at this point, disappointed that his trip did not end "with some sort of epiphany, an epiphany about fate and news gathering and reality," because he needs to return to his family and his teaching job.

During the following months, McElwee teaches at Harvard (a pan of the class reveals a young Nina Davenport, who was an assistant editor on *Six O'Clock News*) and one day receives a communication from Hollywood producer Michael Peyser, expressing interest in McElwee's directing a fictional version of an autobiographical film. The major earthquake that hit the L.A. area in 1994 occurs soon after he begins to take Peyser's offer seriously, and during the news coverage of the disaster, he sees a story about Salvador Peña, who was seriously injured in the quake. When, eight months later, McElwee flies to California to meet with Peyser and to continue his interrupted trip, he tracks down Peña, who becomes McElwee's next subject.

The use of strange, often absurd juxtapositions of disparate dimensions of reality is a characteristic strategy of surrealist art, and the deadpan surrealist quality of *Six O'Clock News* is evident throughout the visit to L.A. McElwee intercuts between his conversation with Peyser and Josh Kornbluth (whom Peyser has chosen to play the McElwee character in the proposed film) and his observation of a shoot for *Baywatch* near the Santa Monica Pier, and his visits with Peña, who is continually described as "lucky," despite his considerable injuries and difficult economic situation, and whose religious faith seems to have been strengthened by his misfortune. Peña explains, "I think of it as a test that God gave me to see how I would react to the experience. Definitely, it's the most beautiful thing I now see in myself, that it's made me believe more in God." As *Six O'Clock News* develops, McElwee comes to seem more, rather than less puzzled by the mysterious and often absurdly comic interplay of tragedy and belief. This puzzlement is confirmed in McElwee's subsequent conversation with Adrian "three years later."

Adrian asks about McElwee's microphone—McElwee is filming on Adrian's fourth birthday—then takes his father on a tour of the "serious picture of God" that he's just painted. McElwee asks Adrian, "Who is God?," and Adrian replies, "Up there"; McElwee asks, "Have you ever seen him before?," and Adrian shakes his head no but responds, "I talk to him though." For McElwee, whose mixture of puzzlement and skepticism has been a motif throughout *Six O'Clock News,* this sudden incarnation of belief within his own home seems to be a disconcerting, even chilling discovery, nearly as disconcerting as the tragedy that occurs in the film's final television news story montage, which begins with "Chaos on Beacon Street in Brookline," where two abortion clinics have been attacked and several people killed (at the time Brookline was McElwee's home), followed by an attempted bank robbery and a shootout in Harvard Square, "less than a hundred yards from where I've been working every day, editing this film." The juxtaposition of an intimate, if disconcerting, family moment with the sudden death and destruction revealed in these news stories is the final demonstration of the chaos that, for McElwee, seems to underlie experience.

The implicit angst McElwee feels sends him back to Charleen Swansea for the final sequence of *Six O'Clock News*, where he films "some *good* news for a change": the first visit of Charleen's granddaughter to her grandmother, on Easter weekend. This is followed by the church service Charleen and her family attend at the predominately black Markham Chapel Baptist Church, where a gospel choir sings a rollicking version of "Ain't Nobody Do Me Like Jesus." However frustrating and mysterious the continual interplay of tragedy and belief remains for McElwee, he cannot ignore that the relationship between them is more than just absurd. The exhilaration of the gospel music is intoxicating—though within the context of the film and McElwee's thinking, it is difficult not to notice the ambiguity of the phrase "do me"!

McElwee's one place of security within this surreal world seems to be filmmaking—though in *Six O'Clock News,* one feels McElwee's increasing sense of marginality and confusion, even as his reputation as a filmmaker is growing. At the conclusion of his visit to L.A., McElwee visits the camera obscura overlooking the Santa Monica Pier (fig. 30). Once a more substantial tourist attraction, the camera obscura building now houses a senior center, and there is little evidence that anyone in the center, or anyone else, visits the camera obscura on the second floor (McElwee must remove a box before he can enter). Within the quiet semi-darkness of the camera obscura room, McElwee senses the wonder of the device and its long history—it's "the camera obscura of Aristotle and Kepler . . . the concept has been around for centuries"—and his own connection with it: "People don't realize, the first photographic image was made with a camera obscura. I mean this is how it all began!" After briefly describing how the device works, he films the camera obscura screen, commenting, "This is so beautiful. It's like looking at some strange planet. There's the pier where they were shooting that TV show a few days ago. The image is so strange, off axis, and it all seems so fragile, the people and palm trees, the buses and buildings." This description is as relevant to *Six O'Clock News* as it is to the camera obscura image itself, and the subtle poetic flourish at the end of this voice-over is subtle evidence of McElwee's passion for the cinematic history of which he is part.

That filmmaking *is* McElwee's deepest "belief," his way of coming to terms with the surreality of his world, is revealed at least twice more as *Six O'Clock News* concludes: first, in his comment during his conversation with Adrian that a spider-like black shape within Adrian's painting of God "looks like a movie camera"—perhaps only someone fixated on cameras would see this; and finally, in the film's unusual credit sequence, during which the gospel choir's performance is intercut with the extended listing of those who have worked on, appeared in, and/or provided

FIGURE 30. Ross McElwee at the camera obscura in Santa Monica. Courtesy Ross McElwee.

support for the film. That this is the most high-spirited moment in *Six O'Clock News* is suggestive: the credits list virtually the entire community of filmmakers working in Cambridge during the years when *Six O'Clock News* was being shot and edited, including Steven Ascher, Nina Davenport, Robert Gardner, Alfred Guzzetti, Jeanne Jordan, Dusan Makavejev, Robb Moss, Michel Negroponte, and Richard P. Rogers. This use of the credit sequence evokes the extended credit sequences in Peter Watkins's *The Journey* (1987) and Yvonne Rainer's *Privilege* (1990), both of which suggest that the experience of independent filmmaking is as close to utopia as one can find in this endlessly troubled and troubling world.

OCCUPATIONAL HAZARDS: *BRIGHT LEAVES*

The seven-year hiatus between *Six O'Clock News* and *Bright Leaves* (2003) was the longest in McElwee's career to that point, and given the considerable importance of the filmmaking process to McElwee, one can only wonder what accounts for it. In most ways *Bright Leaves* is of a piece with McElwee's other autobiographical work—though its particular focus on the history of the tobacco industry in the Carolinas (the "bright leaves" of the title are tobacco leaves)—places the film more fully within the tradition of informational documentary than earlier McElwee films. Beautifully shot, *Bright Leaves* combines his ongoing fascination with his

North Carolina family and his friend Charleen with an exploration of dimensions of the culture of the American South, all communicated through a carefully tuned and timed narrative strategy that positions the viewer as McElwee's friend and confidant. Like the earlier autobiographical films, *Bright Leaves* is generally engaging and has a good many memorable moments, especially for those who have become familiar with the McElwee saga.

As William Rothman has suggested, one particularly memorable sequence occurs midway through the film, after McElwee decides to track down some of his father's patients, part of an attempt to come to terms with the combination of his family's early involvement in the tobacco business and a later generation's commitment to medicine.[43] He finds his way first to Dooley Strange, whom Dr. McElwee treated for mouth cancer and other ailments; then to a man named Whytsell whom Dr. McElwee operated on the day before he died; and finally to an African American woman who tells how Dr. McElwee "knelt down beside my father's bed in the hospital. And he prayed with my dad. My father is a praying person. And your dad and my dad were together that night." McElwee says he has never heard this story, though, as the young woman explains, it accounts for why her parents, Mr. and Mrs. Masseys, called Dr. McElwee every Christmas day to sing "Silent Night" to him. McElwee then cuts first to the Masseys singing "Silent Night," *now* for *him*, then to the sequence of his father (wearing the yarmulke) and stepmother listening to the Masseys singing on the phone that originally appeared early in *Backyard*. The impact of the sequence is a function of the way in which a present moment seems to transform not only McElwee's sense of his own past, but—again, for those familiar with his earlier autobiographical films—our sense of *our* cinematic past. In his best work, McElwee's sense of time has often evoked a line from Faulkner's *Intruder in the Dust*: "Yesterday today and tomorrow are Is: Indivisible: One. . . . 'It's all *now* you see. Yesterday wont be over until tomorrow and tomorrow began ten thousand years ago'"[44]—and never more clearly than here.

Another, humorously memorable moment (this one also interesting because of McElwee's complex sense of time and timing) occurs during a voice-over monologue about filmmaking: "I feel it's such a pleasure to film—especially down south—that it almost doesn't matter what I'm filming. Even just shooting around a motel can be an almost narcotic experience—I mean I don't want to force an analogy, but come to think of it, for me, filming is not unlike smoking a cigarette. When I look through a viewfinder, time seems to stop. A kind of timelessness is momentarily achieved." McElwee's voice-over is accompanied by a shot he is making inside his room at a cheap motel, using a mirror so that we can simultaneously see the filmmaker behind the camera, filming into the room, and, through the window to McElwee's right, the outside of the motel. The voice-over continues, "I mean I'm so immersed that I don't even notice the large rat that's about to slip by in the background there," as a rat scuttles along the opposite side of the motel. McElwee concludes, "I guess next time I should consider upgrading my accommodations." Here, the voice-over, recorded sometime after the imagery was shot, and presumably after McElwee returned north and discovered the rat when he was exploring the North Carolina footage, is perfectly timed to contextualize the rat's creepy cameo.

The presence of McElwee's immediate family is minimal in *Bright Leaves*—there are a few shots of Adrian, a brief sequence of a family reunion on the North Carolina coast, and home movie footage, some of it recycled from earlier films—but the film is held together by McElwee's interest in his family's direct and indirect involvement with the tobacco industry, and in particular, by his interest in a film that his cousin John McElwee, a collector of film prints and memorabilia, introduces Ross to: the Michael Curtiz film *Bright Leaf* (1950), starring Gary Cooper, Lauren Bacall, and Patricia Neal.[45] John McElwee believes that the original 1949 novel by Foster Fitzsimons and the Curtiz adaptation were based largely on the life of McElwee's great grandfather, John Harvey McElwee, who competed with rival James B. Duke over the rights to the Bull Durham brand of smoking tobacco. Ross becomes excited over the possibility that his grandfather was played by Gary Cooper, and this excitement instigates an exploration of the McElwee–Duke rivalry and of the tobacco industry in general. The disparity between John Harvey McElwee's ultimate failure to win the rights to Bull Durham tobacco (though he did amass fortune enough to construct his own mansion and smaller mansions for each of his children) and James B. Duke's immense success is material for typical McElwee wit: the Duke homestead, a state historical site; the remnants of the Duke tobacco empire in Durham; and Duke University and medical center are presented in contrast to "McElwee Park," a tiny grassy space with two benches and a broken-down sign that McElwee visits during the film.

There is much to like in *Bright Leaves*. Its panoramic survey of North Carolina is as effective in revealing the diversity of the South as *Sherman's March;* and McElwee's exploration of the tobacco industry is not only informative but confronts the somewhat surreal paradox that many of those who keep the industry running are passionate Christians who refuse to see a connection between the health disaster caused by smoking and the Golden Rule. As engaging and informative as *Bright Leaves* is, however, it suffers, especially in comparison with *Time Indefinite,* from a lack of the personal intensity that is at the heart of the earlier film. Indeed, since McElwee's references to his nuclear family are primarily to Adrian as a young boy, filmed years before the film was finished (Adrian does appear as a young adolescent in two instances—in one case, assisting his father as he films), one can only conjecture that it had become part of McElwee's working process *not* to reveal his family life in his films. McElwee's parallel between being addicted to smoking and to filmmaking is subtly confirmed near the end of the film during a visit to a tobacco museum when a cigarette-rolling machine, the key to James B. Duke's success, is seen in operation. The strips of paper look rather like reels of film, and the machine itself looks remarkably like a motion picture projector, implying perhaps that for McElwee autobiographical filmmaking had begun to have more than pleasurable results in his life.

It seems an occupational hazard of autobiographical documentary that at some point what has seemed both an engaging and convenient subject for cinema—the filmmaker's personal and family life—becomes a limitation. This can happen in several different ways. In some cases, personal documentary filmmaking functions as a kind of cine-therapy, a way for the filmmaker to work through—or at least to seem to work through—difficult times and relationships, as is evident, for example, in *Time Indefinite* and to some degree in McElwee's other films. But once the problems with parents, love life, or personal loss have been dealt with cinematically, what then is the autobiographical filmmaker to do?

Su Friedrich's most powerful films were generated by her concerns about the nature of her mother's involvement in the rise of the Third Reich (*The Ties That Bind*, 1984), by her father's leaving the family when she was a young adolescent and its aftermath (*Sink or Swim,* 1990), and by what turned out to be the temporary demise of her relationship with Cathy Quinlan (*Rules of the Road,* 1993), but once she had come to terms with her parents and she and Quinlan were reunited, the interpersonal tension and/or trauma that had energized those films largely disappeared from her filmmaking. *From the Ground Up* (2007), during which Friedrich explores the process that provides her with her morning cup of coffee, has much in common with McElwee's investigation of the tobacco industry in *Bright Leaves*. In both, the relatively intense therapeutic process is replaced by a somewhat less engaging educational process.

Filmmakers may also decide they no longer want to film the difficult relationships and painful events in their lives. Once Alan Berliner had come to terms with his troubled relationship with his father—an implicit subject in *The Family Album* (1986), more explicitly a subject in *Intimate Stranger* (1991), and the primary focus of *Nobody's Business* (1996)—his next foray into personal documentary was *The Sweetest Sound* (2001), a film about the name "Alan Berliner." The result was a well-made, engaging film, but one with a good bit less energy than *Intimate Stranger* and *Nobody's Business.* Berliner's frustration that he isn't the only Alan Berliner seems a kind of fabrication of the personal, especially because at the time when he was making *The Sweetest Sound,* he was going through a divorce: in effect the film seems to have been an evasion of the more deeply painful personal. Hidden underneath *Bright Leaves* is the mystery of why, despite the film's ostensible engagement with family, so little of McElwee's current family life is evident in the film; might his supposed excitement about *Bright Leaf* in *Bright Leaves* be a similar evasion?

A final difficulty for autobiographical filmmaking can come from the filmmaker's family, who might object to being filmed or to having their lives revealed in a film that has a public life. Alfred Guzzetti has pulled his *Beginning Pieces* (1986) from distribution because his now-grown daughter is uncomfortable with the film; and Robb Moss rarely shows *The Tourist* (1991) because of his concern about what his daughter, who hasn't seen the film, might feel about its depiction of her adoption. McElwee's recent film, *In Paraguay* (2009), a lovely and deeply personal film about the adoption of his daughter Mariah, was pulled from distribution after a single screening at the Venice Film Festival, apparently because of the objections of his now–ex-wife, Marilyn Levine.

Unlike the late performance artist Spalding Gray, whose work has much in common with McElwee's, McElwee seems, at least for a time, to have accepted the idea that his filmmaking was not more important than whatever consternation his revelations might cause within his family.[46] Gray defiantly continued to expose his personal feelings and experiences even after it seemed obvious that his monologues, his "talking cures" as he often called them, must have created frustration, embarrassment, and anger among those he loved or had loved. The movement away from a focus on family in *Six O'Clock News* and even more fully in *Bright Leaves* suggests, at least to me, that after *Time Indefinite* and the birth of Adrian McElwee, either McElwee himself or Marilyn Levine began to feel uncomfortable with his filming within the family circle and that this resulted in McElwee's decision to separate his filming from his home life.

ORPHEUS: *IN PARAGUAY* AND
PHOTOGRAPHIC MEMORY

In Paraguay, finished in 2009, six years after *Bright Leaves,* was a return to the deeply personal, but it is in large measure an act of nostalgia: it revisits events that occurred during the 1990s, beginning with shots of Adrian McElwee's fifth birthday party. McElwee explains that he and Marilyn want Adrian to have a sibling and are in the process of adopting a baby girl from Paraguay; they have already named her Mariah. An early sequence of Marilyn, Adrian, and Ross shopping for the things Mariah will need is shot in the same store visited by Marilyn and Ross during *Time Indefinite,* and Adrian's curiosity about breast pumps recalls his parents' discussion about breast pumps in that earlier film, when Marilyn was pregnant with Adrian. The trip to Asunción is at first uneventful, though Adrian's discovery that the oranges growing on the hotel grounds are bitter is a premonition that the family's expectation of staying briefly in Paraguay is to be disappointed. The process of adopting Mariah turns out to be complicated; the Paraguayan bureaucracy works slowly, and the family is forced to adjust to a new sense of time. A second premonition occurs as McElwee is changing Mariah's diaper; he wonders, "Maybe I'll begin experiencing a more, I don't know, transcendental way of seeing the world, a way to see things more vividly, you know, a sort of Blake-ian intensification of vision. And anyway, I'm thinking these somewhat rarified thoughts when Mariah suddenly reminds me of the task at hand": Mariah pees before Ross can get the diaper on her.

As the family's stay in Asunción lengthens and daily life becomes routine, the film develops a set of thematic and formal motifs. Soon after their arrival, McElwee explains that he senses "a shadow hanging over much of daily life here": "Maybe it's because I feel a little awkward being an American here, because I know the U.S. has meddled in the internal affairs of several countries in this part of the world, with disastrous results." As *In Paraguay* continues, McElwee periodically adds to a chronological, thumbnail history of the country, which turns out to be "one oppressive dictatorship after another." A second motif begins just after the incident of McElwee changing Mariah's diaper, when nondiagetic music is heard (the first instance of nondiagetic music in all of McElwee's films), and McElwee explains that the piece we are hearing is "The Dream of the Doll" by Agustín Barrios, a gifted Paraguayan musician and performer he has come to admire both for his music and for his dedication as a performer to celebrating Paraguay's historical roots. Barrios's lovely, melancholy music is heard periodically during the rest of *In Paraguay*.

Various dimensions of contemporary life in Paraguay provide other motifs. Early on, McElwee films several young boys selling candy on the streets, and during the remainder of the film, he records (or in his historical overview describes) the many struggles of Paraguayan boys. *In Paraguay* is as much about Adrian McElwee as Mariah, and McElwee is fully aware of the disparity between Adrian's privileged upbringing and the poverty of the Paraguayan boys he films and reads about. As the weeks pass, McElwee explores the poorer neighborhoods of Asunción, often talking with the people who live and work there (McElwee speaks serviceable Spanish), conjecturing in voice-over about the obvious class disparities in Paraguay and in so much of the Western Hemisphere. These class disparities are implicit within the film's many birthday cakes: Adrian's birthday cake is the first image of *In Paraguay*, and there is the relatively humble birthday cake at the celebration of the hotel manager's son's birthday, the wildly extravagant birthday cake at the July 4 celebration the family attends at the immense American Embassy in Asunción, and the cake in honor of Mariah and the family's return from Paraguay at the end of the film (in the film's penultimate sequence, when the family meets with a judge to make Mariah a U.S. citizen, McElwee explains that they "learned a lot about patience in Paraguay," and the judge responds that this current bureaucratic episode must be "a cake walk" by comparison).

As in earlier McElwee films, the subject of filmmaking itself is part of *In Paraguay*. As he is filming some boys selling candy to drivers on a crowded street, he wonders to himself whether his presence is helping or hindering the boys' success; one young woman working in an office good-naturedly tells him, "Don't film this!

I'm embarrassed"; and later in the film it is clear he is filming surreptitiously in the Asunción courthouse. As the weeks in Paraguay drag on, McElwee mentions that his filmmaking is adding to the tension: in one instance, Marilyn says, "Ross, that's enough! Bye!," as he is filming dinner preparations (McElwee puts the camera down, but with it running). Near the end of the family's stay in Asunción, Adrian is badly scalded when he spills hot water on his feet, and a few days later, assuming that Adrian is on the road to recovery, McElwee takes the camera to the hospital to film Adrian's dressings being changed. Adrian's screams of pain and the horrific close-up of the boy's burned feet come as a shock to both McElwee and the viewer. In a strange way, the remembered trauma of this moment for Adrian and presumably for Ross filming is demonstrated by the sudden interpolation of a shot from *The Wizard of Oz* (1939) of Dorothy clicking the ruby slippers together and chanting "There's no place like home." Within the larger history sketched by *In Paraguay* the shot of Adrian's burns is an expression of the historical agony of boys in Paraguay and the culmination of the frustration and repressed anger the family's stay in Asunción has produced.

In at least one instance, the frustrating routine of life in Paraguay without phones, computers, and many of the other accoutrements of modern life in a wealthy nation also seems to instigate a productive boredom—and the loveliest sequence in *In Paraguay*. About an hour into the 78-minute film, McElwee explains, "Maybe I'm losing it, but I begin experimenting, filming very long shots in which not much is happening"—as we watch a beautiful minute-long shot of light and shadow on a wall. This shot is followed by close-ups of Mariah holding a toy hourglass, light playing on her face, then by a series of lovely images of light and shadow on the walls of the hotel, as McElwee's voice-over describes a dream that Agustín Barrios had about how god gave him the gift of music by transforming moonbeams into the strings on his guitar.[47] For anyone familiar with Stan Brakhage's theory of child vision, this sequence is resonant; it is as if McElwee's deepening engagement with Mariah frees his perception for a moment, producing the "Blake-ian intensification of vision" he described earlier and allowing him to experience what Brakhage would call "an adventure of perception," a moment of seeing that recalls the world "under childhood," again to quote Brakhage, "before the beginning was the word."[48]

For the most part, however, the amusing drama attending McElwee's filming, so crucial in *Backyard, Sherman's March,* and *Time Indefinite,* is absent here—partly because McElwee himself is rarely visible in *In Paraguay,* but perhaps also because in Paraguay, he seems just a foreign tourist with camera in hand. One of the motifs in McElwee's voice-over is his indicating that he asks the people he films if they mind if he films them, and again and again he is moved by the good humor with which so many of his subjects face the camera. In one of the final sequences before the Paraguayan judge signs the decree allowing Mariah to leave the country, McElwee focuses on a beggar near a church in Asunción. This beggar can only crawl from one place to another, "and yet," McElwee notes, "he smiles." It is easy to read the beggar as an emblem for Paraguay, especially since this sequence is immediately followed by a montage of some of the faces we have seen in the film and the McElwees' return trip to the United States.[49]

Earlier, I mentioned the ways in which *In Paraguay* refers back to *Time Indefinite,* but though *In Paraguay* acknowledges dimensions of McElwee's past (and though his review of Paraguay's history evokes a substantial past that concludes not long before the family arrives in Asunción), the film is otherwise locked into the time of the family's stay in Paraguay: that is, in his voice-over, McElwee speaks from within the present of his day-to-day life in Asunción and environs, generally without reference to the future during which *In Paraguay* was edited. The only exceptions are his comment during his introduction of Agustín Barrios that "this music will always remind me of Paraguay" and two instances when McElwee imagines Mariah seeing his footage as she grows up. During a montage of imagery of a band on an Asunción street, he wonders "what Mariah will think when she sees these images someday. Will she feel connected to Paraguay? Will she be naturally drawn to the people who live here? Will she want to find her birth mother?"; and he takes footage of Iguazu Falls, "so Mariah can see them when she's older."[50] McElwee also wonders how he will explain to his daughter the complicity of the U.S. government with Paraguayan dictators and Paraguayan poverty—complicity that "enables us to come down here and adopt Mariah."

Since *In Paraguay* was completed in 2009, when Mariah would have been fourteen years old, a viewer cannot help but wonder why McElwee provides no sense of what, indeed, Mariah *does* think of McElwee's footage or, if she has not seen the footage, why she hasn't seen it.[51] Once the family has returned from Paraguay, the film does jump ahead eight months to the meeting with the American judge, but the filmmaking present, the period when McElwee edited the film and recorded his voice-over, remains virtually invisible throughout the film. For those familiar with McElwee's work, this invisibility is a kind of narrative black hole, even a kind of inverse visibility. That *In Paraguay* was completed during the extended moment when McElwee and Marilyn Levine were divorcing suggests that by making the film, McElwee was paying homage to his marriage by revisiting events that demonstrate the impressive level of family unity that had been achieved by the time of the adoption of Mariah—a level of unity that has now disappeared, along with (at least for the present) McElwee's affectionate representation of it.

Photographic Memory (2011) is another exercise in retrieving the past, this time with a double focus: McElwee is at pains to reconnect with his son Adrian from whom he feels alienated; and in an attempt to understand how Adrian's life as a young man compares with his own, he returns to the tiny town of St. Quay on the Brittany coast, where he lived, made photographs, and had a love affair during

1972. As is typical in earlier films, McElwee begins by creating a familial context for the action that will follow, beginning with home movie footage of Adrian and Mariah as young children playing at boxing; Adrian announcing "Okay, round 2, ready?," is the first sound we hear—a metaphor for the struggle Ross and now twenty-one-year-old Adrian are currently involved in. It is also round 2, perhaps, because round *1* was *In Paraguay: In Paraguay* is dedicated to Mariah; *Photographic Memory,* to Adrian. During a conversation with Eric Béranger, a photographer he meets in St. Quay, McElwee asks Béranger why his photo shop is named Morgan'Photo, and Béranger tells him that they'd named their home after their son, so they named their business after their daughter: "You have to make it even between the kids, you know?"[52]

As in *Sherman's March* and *Time Indefinite,* in *Photographic Memory* McElwee develops a complex Ross McElwee character, in this case whom viewers are likely to identify with *and* resist. A few minutes into the film, Ross films Adrian lying in bed, sipping coffee and working at his laptop . Ross is frustrated with Adrian's ignoring him and complains, "It's sometimes hard to talk to you when you're communicating with people via your computer; I feel like your attention is always divided among several technical tasks." Ross then expands his complaint, confiding to the viewer in voice-over, "At times it's so clear to me that he's in a constant state of technological overload; I'm not sure how I would have handled it if all this had been available to me when I was his age." While it is easy for people of a certain generation (I include myself) to identify with McElwee's frustration, the irony here is obvious: McElwee is *filming* Adrian during this moment: that is, his own attention is as divided as Adrian's and implicitly Ross also is involved in what will become a communication with people (us) via his video camera. Adrian is entirely aware of this, of course, since his young life has been regularly involved with his father's filming, and while the McElwee-as-parent character doesn't seem to see the irony, at least in this instance, director McElwee surely does.

The McElwee-as-parent character does recognize similarities between Adrian and his younger self; he recalls and the film flashes back to moments from *Backyard* during which Dr. McElwee registers disapproval of *his* son's choices, including the shot of Dr. McElwee saying, "I'll be glad when that big eye's gone" (in *Photographic Memory* the words are subtitled so we cannot miss their import). The very fact that McElwee has repeatedly recycled this particular moment into his work suggests its continuing power for him, and not surprisingly he recognizes that his frustration with Adrian is very similar, and must be having a similar effect, or really, ineffect—though this does not seem to keep him from continuing to exacerbate the situation. The similarities between Adrian and Ross are also made clear by McElwee as filmmaker. Ross asks Adrian to film him perusing the journals from his year in Brittany: the journals are stuffed with ideas for stories, drawings, thoughts on photography, memories. This sequence is immediately followed

FIGURE 31. Adrian McElwee on his computer and Ross McElwee in reflection, in Ross McElwee's *Photographic Memory* (2011). Courtesy Ross McElwee.

by Ross's review of Adrian's multifaceted creativity: "He has almost too many ideas; he's making a fiction film, doing graphic design, designing t-shirts to sell on his website, shooting and performing in ski videos, writing a novel. . . . " Nevertheless, McElwee as parent continues to vent his frustrations with his son, telling Adrian that despite his creative interests, "you're undermining yourself by all of this other behavior [Ross is referring to Adrian's losing a tape from an experimental documentary at a party]. . . . You're gonna hurt yourself"—clearly hurting his own relationship with Adrian.

The complex interplay between Ross and Adrian as both antagonists and collaborators is encapsulated in the remarkable shot that forms the transition into McElwee's return to St. Quay (fig. 31). As he and Adrian sit at a café, McElwee films Adrian so that his and his father's reflections in the café window are superimposed. Adrian's amusement at whatever he is seeing on his computer at this moment is implicitly imbricated with what must have been Ross's amusement at seeing and capturing this shot.[53]

From this point on, *Photographic Memory* intercuts between McElwee's return to St. Quay and his exploration of the town (and his own past, including his memories of 1972 and his photographs from that year) and his more-or-less regular Skype contacts with Adrian and accompanying ruminations about their troubled relationship. It is immediately clear that St. Quay is not the town that has lived in Ross's memory; he himself has changed (he's seen enough of the world now that St. Quay no longer seems exotic), as has the town, which has modernized and become more involved with tourism. Indeed, McElwee struggles to locate even the place where he lived and worked with the wedding photographer, Maurice, whose life and passion for Merleau-Ponty made him for a time McElwee's mentor. As McElwee explores St. Quay, Brittany, and his past, it becomes increasingly clear that his frustrations with Adrian are in large measure a function of his own discomfort with change, and not just the changes in Adrian and in the places he is seeing, but in photographic technology.

At the time of McElwee's original stay in St. Quay, he was focused on still photography (a passion that has remained evident throughout McElwee's films, especially during those moments when he has allowed himself the indulgence of recording the nuances of space, light, color, and texture), and *Photographic Memory* is punctuated with still imagery from this earlier visit: indeed the title credit is superimposed over an early photo (one that he considers a mistake, as becomes clear later). Soon after he arrives in St. Quay, he expresses his slight anxiety with using memory cards (for the first time) to record his imagery—"I mean, what if the camera's memory fails?" Still later, a conversation with a local photographer about the change from emulsion-based photography to digital imaging ("Where *are* the photos?," they laugh) is followed by this voice-over: "What happened to film? 16mm film, that you can actually hold in your hand? There was something wonderful about working with film. Its warmth. Its luminosity."

This monologue segues into perhaps the most nostalgic moment in *Photographic Memory:* warm, luminous imagery of Adrian as a young boy, digging for sand fleas on a Carolina beach. When his father asks what he will do with the sand fleas he catches, Adrian says, "I heard you can make a sand flea sandwich," and Ross, reminiscing in voice-over, responds, "Sand flea sandwich. If he had offered me one, I'd have eaten it on the spot." This memory is obviously precious to McElwee, because of the earlier relationship with his son, of course, but also because this was the period of Ross's early exploration of filmmaking, with all its excitements and pleasures—and no doubt forgotten frustrations. The sequence ends with Adrian asking Ross to help him dig for more sand fleas and Ross agreeing—but continuing to film the hole Adrian has finished with: he tells Adrian he's watching in case a sand flea comes out, but it is clear that he wanted to conclude the little sequence effectively. Whatever McElwee's sense of this moment is now—during a time when his relationship with Adrian has changed—his primary focus at that moment was cinematic.

The interplay between McElwee's revelation of the parallels between his youth and his son's and his difficulty in resisting the kind of contempt and frustration Dr. McElwee showed for what has become Ross's remarkable filmmaking career peaks just after Ross reviews his many mistakes as a young photographer and his being fired by Maurice for reasons he never understood. McElwee returns to footage of Adrian extreme skiing and hanging out with his friends; and then, after admitting that his worrying about Adrian's risky behavior has led him to do things he's not proud of, he plays a phone message from Adrian, furious that Ross has apparently searched his room: "I can't understand," Adrian complains, "what all of this stuff over the last five years is doing. . . . I'm not getting in trouble with the police. . . . Think about it for a second. I'm not being rude. Just think about it for a second. Close your eyes and say, 'What is this accomplishing? What evil have you prevented him from doing?' Just think about it."

While McElwee as parent within the action of *Photographic Memory* seems to ignore the intelligence of Adrian's phone message (Ross responds in voice-over, "So I've made mistakes, lots of mistakes, in trying to protect my son, protect him from himself," then discusses how the beloved young child is hidden within the obnoxious teenager), McElwee as filmmaker presents Adrian's message during an extended shot, presumably made by Adrian riding on a ski lift; the message ends as the lift delivers Adrian into the darkness of the lift terminal—but seems also, at least in the long run, to have delivered Ross into a new sense of his son.

Throughout the next (and final) sequence during which Ross in St. Quay films Adrian on Skype, Ross listens patiently as Adrian expresses some sadness and frustration and resists the kind of negative feedback he has offered earlier. A voice-over recorded after his visit to St. Quay has ended, and, presented as the Skype interchange is occurring, expresses something of what Ross was feeling at that moment and something of what he has learned: he admits that his own young experience in France included moments like those Adrian is experiencing now, and explains, "I also know that in trying to give you encouragement, I only end up adding to the pressure you feel. . . . But it seems clear to me now that the reason I went to France was to get out of the house and find my own way to live. It's so obvious, but despite the fact that I worry about you a lot, I really do need to let you carve out your own terrain, figure out your own path"—this last, accompanying a shot of Adrian skiing, presumably down the slope he previously ascended on the lift, a shot that fades to white.[54]

That this is the first voice-over in all of McElwee's oeuvre directed not to the viewer but to someone else is also suggestive of his movement into a new sense of himself as both parent and filmmaker. It is as if Ross has seen the light about this dark time in Adrian's life—and his own: it seems clear that his marriage is over and he needs "to find his own way to live" (which of course for McElwee means a new film to make). McElwee's recognition that he needs to give Adrian the space to create a life for himself also sets Ross free (a sudden close-up of a baby pig, frightened perhaps by McElwee's camera, may confirm Ross's concern with facing the realities of his *own* life); and it is at this point that McElwee's somewhat detached, nostalgic *reminiscences* about his year in Brittany become reembodied into new *experiences*: Hélène Landouar, the former wife of the photographer Maurice tracks McElwee down, and as they review their shared past with the

FIGURE 32. Maud Corbel in Maurice's photograph, in Ross McElwee's *Photographic Memory* (2011). Courtesy Ross McElwee.

deceased photographer—including their realization that Maurice lived a double life as a wedding photographer and a secret photographer of nudes—they discover that McElwee's one good photograph of his former lover, Maud (fig. 32), was taken by Maurice. Further, it turns out that Landouar knows that Maud is still alive, living in a nearby town, and is able to find out how to contact her. McElwee's sudden visit to Carnac in southern Brittany to see its megalithic stone formations suggests his fear of actually meeting the woman of his memory, but of course, he does go to see Maud and discovers that while their former love affair was significant to both of them, each has a very different sense of why it ended: McElwee has remembered that *he* broke off the relationship, Maud believes it was *her* doing: "Clearly one of us is wrong, or perhaps both of us are right." The fact that it is raining throughout McElwee's visits to Carnac and Maud Corbel-Rouchy evokes, at least for me, William Faulkner, in whose fiction rain often accompanies changes in the lives of the characters.

The visits with Hélène Landouar and Maud Corbel-Rouchy transform romantically mysterious but solid ("megalithic"?) memories into living realities with complex pasts, and lead to the final two sequences of *Photographic Memory*. The first is the annual celebration of Saint Quay himself, the Irish monk who founded the town—once a year his cranium is removed from the reliquary and paraded once around the church. McElwee records the ceremony, then follows the caretaker as he returns the cranium to the reliquary, where it is covered in a garbage bag—McElwee in voice-over ruminating about how he now knows two Mauds: the lover of his memory and the real woman; and two Maurices: the mysterious mentor of his memory and the more complex and less impressive Maurice as remembered by his ex-wife. Memory has come to seem a set of relics, as limited as they are unchanging, as problematic as they are comforting.

During the final sequence, Ross and Adrian are visiting the Carolina coast, on a not particularly successful fishing trip, but Ross has discovered that in his absence Adrian's life has also begun to transform: he is applying to film schools and has an idea for a film. *Photographic Memory* closes with what Ross explains are the opening shots of Adrian's film, Ross acting as cinematographer and Adrian as director and performer. The protagonist, "a hipster," wakes up, has breakfast (a beer), and leaves his hotel to go out for a run. The closing shot, of Adrian running into the distance along the beach, is deeply poignant. Adrian, the protagonist of his own film, *is* moving away from Ross and Ross's nostalgic memories of Adrian as a child and yet is maintaining his relationship with his father by becoming a filmmaker and by having Ross film him: they are simultaneously separating and coming together.

But the final shot is more complicated than this, because throughout it, Ross's shadow is visible, first on Adrian's body, then once Adrian runs off, in the bottom left of the frame. For anyone familiar with McElwee's long career, that shadow is an emblem not merely of the past within this film, but of the many similar shadows in Ross's long cinematic chronicle of the McElwee family.[55] Did Adrian ask Ross to include his shadow as an emblem of the fact that Adrian cannot entirely leave Ross behind, or is this a final, somewhat sardonic suggestion by Ross that he simply cannot stay entirely out of Adrian's life? However one understands the shadow, what does seem clear is that through the making of *Photographic Memory*, the implicit stasis emblemized in the superimposed shot of Adrian and Ross at the café early in the film has been transformed into the complex synergy of two men struggling to retrieve what they can from their shared, lost past and working creatively together to move their lives forward.

7

Robb Moss

Like Ross McElwee, Robb Moss earned his M.F.A. in filmmaking from MIT, studying with Ed Pincus and Ricky Leacock, and he became McElwee's colleague in the Visual and Environmental Studies Department at Harvard in 1983 (Moss is now Senior Lecturer in the Visual and Environmental Studies Department, as well as a creative advisor for the Sundance Documentary Labs). Further, like McElwee, Moss established his reputation with films—*The Tourist* (1991) and *The Same River Twice* (2003)—in which he appears as a character. In 2004 Moss described his relationship with McElwee:

> People who don't know anything about us sometimes write to me as Ross. They don't even mean to reference Ross; they're just conflating *Robb* and *Moss*. And we're not only colleagues, we're close friends, who look enough alike that we could be brothers. And we were in Africa about the same time in the early Seventies. Our families often vacation together. Our wives are very good friends. It's bizarre. . . .
>
> Ross was a year or so ahead of me at MIT. The fact that our films seem related to each other probably has less to do with each other's films as such, and more to do with whatever originally drew us to MIT and our initial influences there—the people that we knew and the autobiographical films that were the dominant trope of the place.[1]

The commitment of the two men to personal documentary may be, as Moss suggests, a function of their early development and their influences at MIT, but their filmmaking careers have in certain instances seemed to be in conversation with each other. Moss is one of several friends who get together for a low-key bachelor party just before McElwee's marriage to Marilyn Levine in *Time Indefinite* (1994), and we see Moss at the wedding; and in the final scene of Moss's *The Tourist,*

McElwee and Levine and their infant son Adrian are seen with Robb and Jean Kendall and their adopted daughter, Anna—the climax of each film is the arrival of a longed-for child.[2]

The considerable interplay between Moss's and McElwee's lives and careers can, however, obscure the distinctions between them. While McElwee has been consistently devoted to personal documentary for decades, Moss has always explored a variety of approaches to filmmaking. *The Tourist* is a personal documentary in the McElwee mode, but it is the only film in which Moss uses voice-over; and Moss's other films reveal a wide range of interests and procedures. In 2008, for example, Moss and Peter Galison, professor of the History of Science and of Physics at Harvard, completed *Secrecy*, a feature about the recent history and the dangers of governmental secrecy; and as this is written, Moss and Galison are in the early stages of a film about the only licensed, operating, underground permanent nuclear waste facility in the world.[3] Moss's most remarkable film, *The Same River Twice*, is a personal documentary, but it is not focused on Moss himself or his family. Like *Secrecy*, it reveals Moss's ongoing propensity for using filmmaking as a means of educating himself, in this instance about how a number of the close friends of his youth have changed during the interval of twenty years—as measured by how they respond to the imagery of their younger selves in Moss's earlier film, *Riverdogs* (1982).

RIVERDOGS: A POSSIBLE EDEN

By the time he arrived at MIT in 1977, Moss had finished one film: *The Snack* (1975), an exercise in surrealism made when Moss was an undergraduate at University of California-Berkeley (where he studied film with William Rothman). In 1978, he took the fall semester off to shoot *Riverdogs*, which was his thesis film (he graduated from MIT in 1979). Moss had spent a number of years working as a river guide on western rivers, and *Riverdogs* is a 30-minute record of a thirty-five-day, 280-mile pleasure trip through the Grand Canyon by Moss and a group of river guide friends (fig. 33), or, as he says in one of the introductory texts in *The Same River Twice* (2003), which recycles imagery from the earlier film, "one of my first films about one of my last river trips." *Riverdogs* is a poetic evocation of a particular experience shared by Moss and a group of friends, but not an overtly personal film. Moss does not appear as a character at any point (though in one instance, a river rafter addresses a comment to him); generally he functions as the invisible observer characteristic of early observational cinema.[4]

Riverdogs begins with a visual text—"I used to be a river guide. My friends and I worked for a rafting company, lived in things like tepees and tree houses, and spent close to six months of each year out of doors. In our spare time we took our own river trips. I used to think I would always live on rivers"—as we first hear, then see cars arriving at the Colorado River before dawn (a text indicates that it is

FIGURE 33. The "tribe" of Riverdogs, with Robb Moss on far left, holding the camera. Courtesy Robb Moss.

"MILE 0 / Lee's Ferry, Arizona"). The film ends once the river trip has concluded, as the group packs up and gets back on the road. In between, we see the group making their way down the river, playing games, hanging out, scoping out the more difficult rapids, cooking, hiking into side canyons, talking, singing, sunning, reading, kayaking, and in some instances conversing about aspects of the trip. In general, *Riverdogs* alternates between sync-sound passages during which the rafters interact and montages accompanied by the sound of the river, and in a few instances by extradiagetic music.[5]

While the trip down the river *is* the plot (Moss is careful to reveal the gradually changing terrain), several distinctive characters emerge: Barry Wasserman provides some humor, for example, and our attention is regularly focused on Danny Silver and Cathy Schifferle hiking and talking. By the end of the film, we have become familiar enough with some members of the group that when Wasserman and Jim Tichenor vocalize the group's debate about whether to stay on the river for one extra day, as Tichenor urges, or conclude the trip, as Wasserman is suggesting, their personalities, even their positions in the debate, seem familiar. This is not to say that these individuals are the protagonists of the film; Moss's focus remains consistently on the group working together. Our growing to know some individuals better than others reflects the realities of any group activity and helps to energize the film, the way the periodic rapids in the Colorado energize the river trip itself.

By the time Moss shot the footage that he would edit into *Riverdogs,* he was already a capable cinematographer: the film is consistently gorgeous, and Moss is adept at filming activities both on land and from inside boats, rafts, and kayaks. On one level, *Riverdogs* is a contribution to the considerable history of outdoor sporting activity filmmaking (films by and about skiers, and so on) that remains generally under the radar of serious film study. But to see it as merely a celebration of river rafting is to miss the point. This is implicit in the opening minutes of *River-dogs,* when, once the river trip is underway, we realize that suddenly the rafters seem to be going about their activities nude. It is during the precise moment of this realization that Moss reveals the title of his film. The word *riverdogs* seems to designate not simply a group of people on a river rafting trip, but *this* group who, for a time, are leaving their more conventional lives and selves behind.

As *Riverdogs* develops, the nudity of the rafters comes increasingly to seem both a metaphor for getting back to basics and evidence of a kind of spiritual engagement with the natural world. Indeed, this spiritual dimension of the trip seems implicit from the beginning of the film, in the particular imagery Moss uses of the group assembling at Lee's Ferry. The arrival of the vehicles is presented so as to emphasize the headlights of the cars, which create circular reflections and circles within circles suggestive of mandalas and eye-of-god cathedral windows, that is, of the traditional emphasis on circularity of so much religious and spiritual imagery. Further, Moss's indication that he "*used to be* a river guide" and that he used to think he "would always live on rivers" frames this particular river trip as not simply a pleasure excursion but a special experience that brought an earlier way of life to a close, at least for Moss.

While there is nothing in the action of *Riverdogs* to suggest that, as a group, the participants in the river trip saw themselves a part of anything like a spiritual ritual, the importance of this adventure to Moss is reflected throughout the film. The fact that he is filming the trip at all, of course, suggests its importance to him; and Moss has explained, "When I shot *Riverdogs* . . . I wanted to evoke the *experience* of a river trip, which was what we went back for again and again and again, and what our small community of river guides had fallen in love with. We were like a small tribal group. The film was a bit like salvage anthropology: this way of life was passing, at least for me, and I was trying to get hold of it with a camera."[6] That this river trip is one of many for the participants seems evident in the way that all the members of the excursion seem to know their roles and in the fact that the group seems entirely comfortable with one another (fig. 34). That these sixteen men and women had become something of a "small tribal group" is also suggested by a ritual they perform as they prepare to tackle the final major rapid: they paint each others' faces in a way that evokes the face painting in Gardner's *Deep Hearts* and, of course, in other, more conventional depictions of native peoples.

FIGURE 34. Several Riverdogs play a circle game (the one in the front of the "snake" tries to catch the one in the rear) in Robb Moss's *Riverdogs* (1982) and in *The Same River Twice* (2003). Courtesy Robb Moss.

At the conclusion of *Riverdogs,* as the roped-together flotilla of rafts and boats drifts toward the point of disembarkation, Moss provides a final echo to the circular reflections that begin the film and their implications: a tracking (or, really, floating) shot circles entirely around the flotilla and the rafters relaxing on it. The "way of life" Moss is depicting is, on one level, quite specific, but on another level, it represents more than just this group of friends. Moss has said that *Riverdogs* "was an homage to the Sixties, a Seventies film that grew out of Sixties values,"[7] and few films do a better job of capturing the spiritual idealism that was such a crucial part of the early moments of the American cultural revolution. As an artifact of a particularly hopeful moment in American culture, at least for a good many young people, *Riverdogs* stands with D. A. Pennebaker's *Monterey Pop* (1968) and William Greaves's *Symbiopsychotaxiplasm: Take One* (1972); and as clearly as either of those two films, it focuses on a group of young people who demonstrate, throughout the film, a commitment to communal activity, a respect for the environment, a rejection of conventional notions of proper dress, and even—this, being more characteristic of the late 1970s than the 1960s—a commitment to gender equality so fundamental that it seems automatic: women and men participate equally in virtually every aspect of the river trip without the slightest bit of rhetoric or self-congratulation.[8]

Recent decades have produced a host of critiques and satires of 1960s idealism; T. C. Boyle's novel, *Drop City,* is representative of this tendency, as is Ed Pincus's *One Step Away.* Moss's idyll makes clear that, however silly or problematic we may now find this brief idealistic moment, it was not the property simply of hippies and hypocrites, but in some instances, of women and men who were, at least for a time and in a particular circumstance, capable of living these ideals. That these women and men were river guides suggests a considerable level not merely of skill but of the maturity and responsibility necessary for ensuring the safety of those they guided down rivers. In *Riverdogs* the physical beauty of these remarkably fit young people and their ability to work and play effectively together evokes a golden age, a possible (if momentary) Eden.

THE TOURIST: "FREELANCE EDITING"

Moss's first autobiographical documentary, *Absence* (1981), which is not in distribution—it exists currently as a single 16mm print—was completed in 1981. It is a series of vignettes of family and friends, recorded during a single trip home at the end of 1980. As Moss explains in the film's introductory text, "I had been living in the East and flew home to California for the holidays. My high school ten-year reunion comes and goes, my mother and I take walks, my father tells jokes. I am still not used to the idea that things change." *Absence* communicates something of Moss's feeling of being a stranger in his own life—and it does so entirely without narration, though the vignettes do provide enough background information for viewers to make sense of events. Several people who would become characters in Moss's later films are introduced, including his (divorced) parents and Barry Wasserman, who appears in a scene in a men's steam room—the nudity here a premonition of *Riverdogs.* As would be true in *The Tourist* (1991) and *The Same River Twice* (2003), we can hear Moss behind the camera as he interacts with his classmates, friends, father and mother; like McElwee in *Sherman's March,* Moss holds the camera on his right shoulder, so that it observes his conversations from a detached position to screen right of where those he is talking to are looking, and as in the McElwee film this tends to create a kind of detachment, an implicit "absence," as if Moss is now part of another life, a filmmaking life in the East, and is watching himself visit a world he has left behind.

During the ten years after leaving MIT, Moss supported himself as a freelance cameraman for a variety of projects produced in Ethiopia, Belize, Nicaragua, Liberia, Hungary, and Japan, as well as in the United States; and one of the two main topics of *The Tourist* is these experiences filming, as a "tourist," in far-flung locales. *The Tourist* begins with the sound of children singing a song ("sardines and pork and beans" is a repeated phrase; the song suggests that the singers are tired of eating the same thing every day),[9] and images of Liberian children pretending to be filmmakers, using "cameras," "microphones," and other equipment made from bamboo and revealing in their actions and posture how carefully they've been watching Moss and his colleagues. Moss, in voice-over, then explains, "When I was a kid, I loved the movies. Growing up, it seemed a perfect life to travel and to make movies. Filming other people *is* how I make my living. Sometimes I shoot my own films; sometimes people hire me to shoot theirs. In either case, certain problems arise." While the children's pretending to shoot film is funny, it is also the first instance of many in the film during which Moss reveals how the presence of the camera transforms and exploits what it captures.

After the opening directorial credit, a second sequence reveals the film's other main topic. After shots of the wedding of Moss and Jean Kendall (at Ed and Jane Pincus's farm in Vermont), Moss, again in voice-over, explains that he and Kendall have been struggling to have a baby: "We don't know why it's not working. Jean suspects it's her, and I think it's me." Moss's comments are accompanied by Kendall playing on their bed with a cat, continuing to tease it even though it bites her hard enough to make her shriek. The scene is quite funny, though as the film develops, these playful cat bites come to seem a premonition of some real physical and psychic pain. The film's prologue concludes with a single shot of an oil rig pumping, made from a moving car—a wry metaphor for Moss and Kendall's sexual activity—followed by the film's title credit.

Early on, *The Tourist* seems to be intercutting between episodes relating to issues raised by Moss's experiences as a freelancer and the problems he and Kendall are having with pregnancy. After the title credit, Moss is in Texas, shooting material for a film on hunger in America; then, in Ethiopia where he is working as a cameraman for what would become *Faces in a Famine* (1985) by Robert H. Lieberman: we see moments from the finished Lieberman film on television (including a mother with a starving child) interspersed with shots Moss made in Ethiopia for himself, including a fight. This sequence concludes with Moss in voice-over explaining, "It *is* often the case that the worse things get for the people you are filming, the better that is for the film you are making." This statement seems relevant not only to the starving baby and the fight, but in a very different way, to the sequence that follows: Moss's documentation of a trip he and Kendall and his mother, Laurie Moss, take to Death Valley. Moss explains that his mother, recovering from a car accident, wanted to go somewhere level where she could walk; "Jean, someplace where nothing could grow." During the following sequence Kendall and Moss's mother get the giggles and whatever psychic "low points" led to the Death Valley trip seem for a moment to disappear.

As *The Tourist* continues, the personal and the professional become increasingly imbricated. For one thing, Moss's professional visits to Africa, Europe, Central America, and Asia are interwoven with several personal trips Kendall and Moss take: to Portugal on a delayed honeymoon before another pregnancy is due to come to term; to Belize when they accompany a friend who is writing an article for *Travel and Leisure;* and to the island of St. Martin, a gift from Laurie Moss who has won the trip in a raffle. Midway through the film, Moss explains in voice-over, "The thing about freelancing is that the phone can ring anytime and take you any-place to make a film about anything." This description is implicitly relevant to the course of any pregnancy, and of Kendall's pregnancies in particular: the trip she and Moss take to Portugal as a "postponed honeymoon" is interrupted by Kendall's first miscarriage. Moss's comment is also an explanation of the seemingly chaotic editing strategy of *The Tourist.* Any particular cut can provide a new view of what was recorded in the previous shot or an image from a world away.

Within the continual movement from one place to another, certain motifs develop. For one thing, Moss's way of seeing is increasingly affected by his concern with Kendall's getting pregnant, by her miscarriages, and at the end of the film by the experience of adopting a daughter: whether he is working as a freelancer or record-ing his own material in off hours, children are much in evidence. Another motif involves the way in which film imagery can obscure as much as it reveals. At the end of the sequence of the Death Valley trip, as Kendall and Moss's mother are giggling together, Moss indicates that sometimes, when he is not really a part of what he is filming, "I begin to look around and film what I imagine is the poetry of the situa-tion." At the word *imagine* Moss cuts to a sequence of images shot in Liberia, begin-ning with young girls walking along a jungle path, followed by "poetic" imagery of a woman nursing a baby on the porch of a cabin as she speaks with a neighbor. At the end of the sequence, Moss indicates that, when he had the woman's comments trans-lated, he learned that she had been complaining to the neighbor about "what a pain in the neck we were." A "poetic" moment is immediately transformed into irony.

Still another motif reveals the limitations of spoken language. During a fact-finding trip to Nicaragua, Moss wanders into an earthquake-destroyed church in Managua and gets into conversation with a young soldier. In voice-over, he explains that his Spanish is very limited (as a swimming stroke, the dog paddle), then describes his attempt to mine the soldier's feelings about this picturesque ruin: "I more or less asked him what he felt here, and he more or less told me that he felt a breeze." During a taxi ride with Percival Usher in Belize, a conversation about Nicaraguan dictator Anastasio Samoza seems to lead to Percival's saying that Samoza is a "liar"—apparently a political judgment—though Moss and we soon realize that "liar" is simply Percival's way of pronouncing "lawyer."

Such amusing misunderstandings are often part of the quite serious issue of the sociopolitical power implied by the camera and the exploitive nature of filmmak-ing. Even the opening sequence of the Liberian kids playing filmmaker suggests a disparity between the haves and the have nots: the American crew can shoot real film; the Liberian children can only pretend to. This disparity is powerfully evident in the footage of starving Ethiopians recorded for *Faces in a Famine,* especially the imagery of a starving, fly-covered baby and the child's mother: the Lieberman film is obviously an attempt to bring needed attention to a human disaster; nevertheless, its emotional power comes from its imagery of people who not only cannot represent themselves but are at the mercy both of a terrible drought and of cameraman Moss and the rest of the filmmaking crew. The issue of exploitation seems evident in nearly all of the episodes Moss presents, often in complex and subtle ways.

During the visit to Managua, Moss films George, a member of their group who wants to take a snapshot of a young girl who sells watermelon. Though the girl is embarrassed by the attention, George takes her arm and positions her for some picturesque Polaroids. While George means no harm, he seems oblivious to the fact that this young girl apparently must work to survive. George does plan to give the girl one of the snapshots but is quickly surrounded by a group of mostly young Nicaraguans all of whom now want a picture, and George becomes concerned that a fight will break out. The medium is the message here; whatever the value of the snapshot George takes of the girl, Moss's record of this moment reveals the power of the photographer and his camera within this economically challenged society—and of course, the significance of George's interaction with the young Nicaraguan girl has been made obvious to the mostly young people on this Managuan street by the presence of Moss with *his* even more visible sync-sound rig. As Moss says in voice-over, "In the group I've noticed that as soon as any of us wants anything, then this wanting seems to invoke this chasm of inequality."

Moss seems aware of this issue even during what might seem to be innocent moments. For example, during a taxi ride in Percival Usher's car, the passengers (Moss, Kendall, and their friends) ask Usher how many siblings he has. When he replies twenty-four, the women ask if he can name all his sisters and brothers, and Usher does. Usher's naming his siblings provides amusement for his momentary employers (and for us), while revealing a pattern that distinguishes First World and Third World peoples: the size of Usher's family, given this family's limited economic resources, is the inverse of the lives of the visiting Americans, and implicitly of viewers of *The Tourist,* who have found their way to the kinds of screening rooms likely to exhibit an experimental documentary. This moment in the taxi with Usher concludes with shots of Jean Kendall looking pensively out the window of the cab, revealing Moss's awareness of the irony of Usher's wealth of siblings and Kendall's frustration at not being able to produce a single child. But here too, the camera is subtly exploitive. A few moments earlier, as Moss is creating context for the trip to Belize, his voice-over indicates that "though I'm sure Jean would prefer I hadn't, I brought my camera." The amusing but poignant irony of the distinction between Usher's situation and Kendall's may be a pleasure for viewers engaged with the themes Moss is developing in *The Tourist,* but it depends on Moss capturing and revealing his wife's subtle discomfiture.

Of course, filmmaking isn't *only* a form of one-way exploitation; it can also be a means of connecting disparate realities, not simply within the editing but during the filming. This, too, is evident in that opening sequence of the Liberian kids imitating Moss and the rest of the filmmaking crew. The kids are clearly enjoying their mimicry of a Western obsession, even if they don't have access to the real equipment. And this idea of connection is developed and comes to a kind of conclusion in two different ways during the second half of *The Tourist*. First, the original meeting with Percival Usher, recorded in the ride in the taxi, leads to something more than a business arrangement. Moss asks Usher if he might spend a day hanging out with him, and Usher agrees, and while, "of course, everyone, especially myself, is a little too polite," Moss, Usher, and his neighbors seem to take pleasure in their time together and in Moss's filming.

Later, after Kendall has experienced a second miscarriage, and once she and Moss have begun the process that will lead to their adopting a baby girl, Moss returns to Belize for a freelance job and goes to visit Usher. During this visit, Moss learns that while Percival and Minerva Usher do have two young children, Juni and Monica, they too have had experiences with miscarriages. They have lost two pregnancies, and Minerva is pregnant again and is having difficulties. This final conversation between Moss and Usher includes the usual subtle miscommunications; nevertheless, it is clear that whatever their differences, the two men have an important experience in common, and when they say good-bye, both hoping that Usher will have the son he hopes for and that he and Moss will meet again, it is clear that something like a real friendship has formed between these two men from very different societies and social classes.

Moss's meeting with Usher occupies much the same position in *The Tourist* as the wedding of Lucille and Melvin occupies in McElwee's *Time Indefinite*: it heralds the resolution of the struggle of Moss and Kendall to become parents, though this resolution has already begun to develop before Moss's last trip to Belize. After their trip to St. Martin, where on a whim Moss and Kendall tour a new time-share complex, Moss includes a photo montage of Kendall's postcard collection (all the postcards we see are of idealized families and children). This is the second of three photo montages in the film—the first is the visual accompaniment to Moss's description of Kendall's painful miscarriage in Portugal—and in both instances still photography seems to suggest an interruption of the organic motion of life, the experience of life breaking down, the stilling of hope. The postcard montage is followed by Moss's voice-over revelation that he has virtually given up on becoming a father: "As time went by, I too stopped believing and in so doing, also stopped being able to conceive the future."

Without a sense of the future, life ceases to make sense, and Moss's subsequent visit to Japan ("one of the only places on Earth where I not only don't stick out because I'm filming, but where I fit in—this is not to say I feel at home") feels surreal and seems to suggest that without the possibility of family, Moss is psychically lost. He spends his final night in Japan wandering the streets of Tokyo, filming this and that: a kind of dark night of the soul. Now that conceiving their own child and bringing a pregnancy to term has come to seem hopeless, Moss and Kendall have considered adoption, and Moss confesses, "At first the whole idea of adoption seemed strange to me"; "I had this awful thought that I might reject an adopted child as foreign, as an immune system can reject an organ transplant."

In the following sequence *The Tourist* returns to the Death Valley footage in which Moss and his mother are goofing around with Moss's camera ("No matter how old my mother and I get, her face is always ridiculously familiar"), then introduces his father on a visit to Boston, where the two search for the graves of the Moss family in a Jewish cemetery. Filming his long-divorced parents leads to Moss admitting that he is "finding that my desire to parent is overcoming my desire to mix my genes with Jean's genes," and this realization leads to Moss and Kendall's "auditioning to become parents." They work with an adoption agency that sends biographies and pictures of prospective parents to pregnant women who have decided to give their babies up for adoption. This new direction, with its new kind of hope and its own mystery, involves Moss for the first time becoming a photographic subject rather than the man with a camera, which is emblemized by the film's third and final photo montage: still photographs of Moss and Kendall in *all* of which Moss has his eyes closed. This is both very funny and a revelation of how fully Moss himself feels the power of the camera.

During the final sequences of *The Tourist*, Moss intercuts between his and Kendall's meetings with "Lee" and references to Moss's life as a freelancer, which in a serendipitous conjunction of events includes his filming for a videotape manual about caring for newborn babies. In the final sequence, we see Anna, two hours old; Kendall speaking with "Lee" just before she leaves to go home; and, to the accompaniment of the "sardines and pork and beans song," a shot of Anna in close-up as Moss is saying, "One of the secret pleasures about becoming a parent, a pleasure at least kept secret from those of us too distracted by our lives to know better, is falling in love with your children." The final shot of the film is from a home movie made the day before Anna turns fourteen months old; sitting on the floor in a circle are Ross McElwee, Marilyn Levine, and Adrian McElwee, and Kendall and Anna, who, seeing that Moss is filming, toddles toward the camera, smiling.

VOYAGE OF LIFE: *THE SAME RIVER TWICE*

> *His historical researches, however, did not lie so much among books, as among men; for the former are lamentably scanty on his favourite topics, whereas he found the old burghers, and still more, their wives, rich in that legendary lore, so invaluable to true history.*
>
> WASHINGTON IRVING, ON DIEDRICH KNICKERBOCKER IN THE "HISTORICAL" NOTE THAT PRECEDES "RIP VAN WINKLE" IN *THE SKETCH BOOK*

Is there a more American story (and in our relentlessly globalizing, digitizing world, a more *human* story) than "Rip Van Winkle"? The tale of a man who falls asleep for twenty years, then returns to his home town to find everything changed, remains as relevant to our understanding of our experience as Americans as it was nearly two centuries ago. Of course, there is much to recommend the Irving story: it is engagingly written, witty and amusing; and it evokes the changes from Dutch colony to British colony to American nation that must have seemed fascinating to its original readers. Further, it suggests the hunger of an earlier generation of Americans to have a mythic national past like the citizens of other great nations— even if American writers needed to create the requisite legendary tales themselves, tongue in cheek. But what has always made "Rip Van Winkle" most powerful is the idea of a man, long absent from his family, friends, and home town, walking back into his previous life and trying to make sense of the changes two decades have wrought, both in his surround and in himself.

The drama of returning home after long absence was certainly not invented by Irving (perhaps Homer can take credit for it), but it seems particularly relevant for the citizens of a nation that during several centuries was in the throes of geographic expansion and the movement of a western frontier, and that during the past hundred years has experienced a population explosion and endless transformations in technology and thought. Not surprisingly, the drama of Rip's return home has been reexperienced by a good many characters in the American literary canon. The most dramatic moment in Willa Cather's *O Pioneers!*, for example, occurs between parts 1 and 2 of the novel: at the conclusion of "The Wild Land," Cather's protagonist, Alexandra Bergson, realizes that she is committed to the land of the Nebraska Divide and has come to believe that she can transform a wilderness into productive farmland: "Under the long shaggy ridges, she felt the future stirring." The turn of a page jumps the reader thirteen years into the future, causing readers to play Rip Van Winkle: we reenter the farm where Alexandra lives and discover the remarkable changes that have occurred "in our absence." Of course, the very suddenness of this change, at least for readers (we had expected to see the process of the transformation), like the sudden change that occurs in "Rip Van Winkle" between the moment when Rip falls asleep and wakes up—twenty years disappear between paragraphs—is suggestive of the way in which aging in any society, and perhaps particularly in ours, always seems, at least in retrospect, to have occurred very quickly: the older we get, the more quickly durations of time seem to have flown by.

The drama of a return after long absence is also the subject of Robb Moss's *The Same River Twice,* though here, the return takes place on several different levels.[10] To make the new film, Moss returned to *Riverdogs*, which had virtually disappeared soon after it was made, and recycled substantial portions of that film into a personal documentary during which he and five of the original Riverdogs return to Moss's cinematic memory of their 1978 river trip through the Grand Canyon and confront the implications of the twenty-year gap. To the extent that, as suggested earlier, *Riverdogs* has become an artifact of the worldview of a particular generation (or at least of one subculture within a generation) and a demonstration of a set of social ideals, the return of Moss and his five friends to an earlier time is not simply the story of six individuals; it is emblematic of the experience of that generation, and perhaps to some extent of the experience of most generations in moving from youth to middle age.

By the time of *The Same River Twice,* Moss had found a way to be a character in a personal documentary virtually without being visible and entirely without using vocal narration. It is clear throughout *The Tourist* that Moss is not entirely at ease either in front of the camera (every time we see him, and then only in still photographs, his eyes are closed) or as narrator: his discomfort, subtly evident in his voice, confirms the theme of Moss being a "tourist." In *The Same River Twice* Moss is a presence throughout, but he is visible only in two very brief instances: early in the film during a sequence when Barry Wasserman is giving Moss a tour of his medicine cabinet (we see Moss momentarily in the medicine cabinet mirror); and late in the film, again with Wasserman and again in a mirror, when Wasserman is getting dressed after a final radiation treatment for testicular cancer; in this instance, Moss's response to Wasserman's realization that saying thank you and good-bye to the radiation nurses was more emotional than he had expected it to be is visible (and audible). Throughout *The Same River Twice,* however, the five friends (as well as Wasserman's spouse Deb and Danny Silver's husband, Peter) speak with Moss as he films. In *The Tourist,* the people Moss films are usually responding to the presence of a motion picture camera; in *The Same River Twice,* they are generally responding to the presence of Moss himself, often to his questions and comments, and in general willingly collaborating with the record he is making of their shared past and present.

Moss is also implicitly present in *The Same River Twice* through brief visual texts. Three of these, in conjunction with visual images from *Riverdogs,* introduce the action of the film. "1978" temporally locates the action we see in the recycled images, and two longer texts, "We used to be river guides. For many years my friends and I lived an unscheduled, communal, outdoor life" and "I spent most of this trip [that is, the trip in *Riverdogs*] behind the camera, shooting one of my first films of one of my last river trips," confirm the gap between the 1978 river trip and Moss as veteran filmmaker "now" (twenty-*five* years later: *The Same River Twice* was shot from 1996 to 2000 but was not finished until 2003). Often during *The Same River Twice* visual texts are used as segues between then and now, and to provide context for the lives Moss is reintroducing us to. Soon after the opening images of several nude Riverdogs and the introductory texts, Moss presents the sync-sound sequence from the earlier film during which Barry Wasserman and

Jim Tichenor debate whether to stay one extra day on the river. A direct cut from Barry in *Riverdogs* to Barry in 1998 fixing a medicine cabinet and the text, "Barry," followed by "20 years later," confirms the gap in time that is evident in Barry's face, as well as the distance between an earlier "unscheduled," "outdoor" life and his current domestic circumstances.

As *The Same River Twice* continues, Moss uses visual text as a means of creating subtle ironies. For instance, during the opening documentation of Barry's domestic life with Deb and his children, Moss superimposes three successive texts: "Barry is finishing his fourth year as Mayor of Placerville, California"; "He is running for re-election"; and "Barry works full-time as an administrator of a psychiatric care facility." A few minutes later, we learn that Cathy Shaw (originally Cathy Schifferle, then Cathy Golden) "is serving her 9th year as Mayor of Ashland, Oregon," as we see her at what appears to be a city council meeting. Since we have already met Wasserman and Shaw as young people, nude, on the 1978 river trip, the information about their mainstream jobs is amusing. This idea is confirmed when Wasserman mentions that a fellow worker expressed surprise at seeing him in shorts, and Moss cuts from Wasserman in his office to a shot of him, naked, walking into a canyon along the Colorado.[11] On one level, these texts help to demonstrate how the intervening twenty years have changed Wasserman and Shaw; but on another, more subtle level, they also reveal that less has changed than meets the eye: the fact that both worked as river guides in 1978 is evidence that, however unmoored their lives in *Riverdogs* might look to a later generation, they were then, as they are now, fundamentally capable and responsible individuals on whom others can depend.

These and subsequent context-setting visual texts allow Moss to function in a double role. He is, on one hand, an informative, sometimes ironic "narrator," who exists at a several-year temporal remove not only from the events of *Riverdogs* but from the events documented during the shooting of *The Same River Twice*. And he is on the other hand an engaged participant in the lives of his friends during the period from 1996 until 2000. He films them; we hear him ask them often-intimate questions and respond to their answers; and sometimes (in a manner that evokes a particularly McElwee-ian form of presence), one or another of his friends will reveal his physical presence *as filmmaker*: Cathy Shaw dances with Moss as he is filming during the party after her marriage to Rick, and Danny Silver laughs and says, "Excuse me!," as Moss passes close to her while she is leading an aerobics session.

It is crucial for *The Same River Twice* that we feel not only the temporal gap between 1978 and the late 1990s but that we are aware that the lives of Moss's friends are continuing to evolve. As Moss has explained, "The now had to generate its own past, so that when you come back into people's lives, you know them and you can refer to the things that have been happening to them; you have enough dots along that trajectory so that you can graph it emotionally. This happens, that happens; people are getting married, are finding out they have cancer, are being treated, are having children. That's how our lives are. And that becomes the past *of the film.* Otherwise, it would be *The Same Stagnant Pond Twice.*"[12]

The Same River Twice does demonstrate clear distinctions between the different speeds at which lives transform. While Wasserman's and Shaw's lives seem comparatively full of change (Wasserman's bid for a second term as mayor fails, he completes radiation treatments for his cancer; Shaw is first bidding a formal good-bye to a man who has conducted concerts in Ashland; she explains that she has quit her job at Planned Parenthood and is looking for less mind-draining work; she gets married and goes on a honeymoon), Jim Tichenor's apparent aversion to change is part of the humor of the film. Early on, he shows Moss the site of the home he plans to build. Later, we see Tichenor explaining to Moss that the dimensions of the home (the foundation is now dug) are based on the Fibonacci series of numbers; but after a text, "1 year later," Moss returns us to the same spot where nothing seems to have changed: we laugh at what seems Tichenor's stasis—though we realize that things have been changing, however slowly, when men arrive to pour the concrete foundation.[13] Life *is* change—as the title's reference to Heraclitus's famous line suggests—though its velocity varies. The character in *The Same River Twice* whose life seems closest to stasis is Wasserman's mother who, as her son explains to Moss, can't find a way to enjoy her old age but also cannot die; when Wasserman visits her, the mother and son are seen on the Pacific coast where Mrs. Wasserman draws her son's attention to a tiny boat out in the ocean; Moss cuts to the distant boat, seemingly stationary in the water.

Moss uses the filming of *The Same River Twice* not merely to document how the individual lives of the once-Riverdogs are changing during the period from 1996 to 2000 but to show how their relationships with each other have continued to evolve as part of their current experience: Danny Silver, for example, provides the toast at the party following Cathy Shaw's marriage to Rick, and Moss records the moment. A different form of interchange can be understood to take place both within *The Same River Twice and* during an implicit extra-filmic moment. During one of the sync-sound excerpts from *Riverdogs,* the group is meeting to decide something (perhaps how to negotiate the final major rapids) and Wasserman says, "Let's present our plan, Pep [this person is not identified], and then Cathy can present her plan." Shaw says she really doesn't have a plan to present, and Wasserman responds, "Okay, well, you can just criticize ours." Moss presents this moment twice: first, to Shaw, who responds, "Well, fuck you, Barry!" She glances toward Moss, then says, "I didn't say it then, but I thought it." Moss then repeats the excerpt and reveals Wasserman's response: he is clearly ashamed to have embarrassed Shaw and points out how a wave of Shaw's hand subtly reveals her frustration with him: "Look at her hand; the last thing on earth she wants to see right now is my snide face"; then, clearly moved, he says, "Oh god. Sorry, Cathy." This apology, decades after an implicit insult, is poignant partly because we can infer that Shaw will, at some future date, see this sequence and hear Wasserman's apology.[14] In this instance, Moss uses his filmmaking to resolve (or to attempt to resolve) the friction between Shaw and Wasserman that Shaw clearly still feels so many years later.

The twenty-year gap between *Riverdogs* and the action in *The Same River Twice* is also significant in a cinematic sense for Moss for at least two reasons. First, making *The Same River Twice* allowed him to return to *Riverdogs*, which had never had the attention it deserved, and recycle much of its imagery and what that imagery represents to Moss into a new form for a possible new audience. The original decision to film the Grand Canyon rafting trip was one of Moss's first extensive attempts to function as a serious filmmaker, and editing the film involved considerable time and labor. The fact that *Riverdogs* was not widely appreciated does not mean that the experience of making it wasn't important for Moss.

Second, *The Same River Twice* charts the change from shooting in 16mm, still standard for independent filmmakers in the late 1970s, to shooting in video, which Moss uses for all the material shot in the 1990s—a change that is continuing to transform the process of filmmaking for many filmmakers. There is nostalgia in *The Same River Twice* not only on a personal level (clearly Moss has fond memories of his life as a river guide and his experiences with his friends on their Grand Canyon trip, even if the particular trip documented in *Riverdogs* was, as he has explained, "a miserable trip for me; my girlfriend and I were fighting the whole time"),[15] but on the cinematic level. The particular color palate and visual textures of 16mm seem increasingly a thing of the past, and for Moss, who came to love working with 16mm, this represents a considerable loss. Indeed, the look of *Riverdogs* seems more akin to the films of Peter Hutton or Bruce Baillie than to *The Tourist* or to the 1990s imagery in *The Same River Twice,* and there are filmmakers—Hutton is perhaps the best example—for whom what 16mm offers visually is simply not worth giving up for the increased convenience in production and distribution offered now by digital video.

Moss's recycling *Riverdogs* into *The Same River Twice* also involves a transformation in our sense of the earlier film. In *The Same River Twice* Moss's focus on the few sync-sound episodes in the earlier film causes *Riverdogs* to seem far more "talky" than it is; indeed, the sync-sound sequences of the group playing games; Barry's joking with the group about "competitive eating"; a conversation with Cathy Shaw and Jeff Golden, lying in their sleeping bags; the conversation between Wasserman and Shaw about the plan for running the rapids; and the debate about whether to stay on the river an additional day are exceptional within *Riverdogs,* moments of intimacy within a more detached, more mythic, experience: as Moss has said, "I think of *Riverdogs* as a kind of mural; it has a mural kind of narrative."[16] Further, in *The Same River Twice* Moss makes no attempt to echo the order of sequences in *Riverdogs,* choosing instead to use the earlier material to emphasize and clarify what is happening in the present of *The Same River Twice* and what has happened during the interim between the two films.

What Moss has gained as a filmmaker during the twenty-plus years since he shot *Riverdogs* is a dexterity with the camera that allows him to film in-close with his friends in a comfortable, intimate way that maintains our attention on them, rather than on Moss and his filming. While the most amusing moments in McElwee's films tend to be created by the fact of his filming and his complex narration, the most amusing moments in *The Same River Twice* are more fully a product of what Moss notices and/or of the ingenuity of those with whom he talks. For example, the sequence in *Time Indefinite* when the Jehovah's Witness comes to the door of the McElwee home in Charlotte would not be of particular interest were it not for McElwee's complex relationship, as filmmaker and narrator, to the man and his daughter: particularly his mock complaint about being eligible for the Federal Witness Protection Program because of all the Witnesses that have found their way to him, and his voice-over reflection on what this Witness has said about "time indefinite." In *The Same River Twice* Moss asks Barry Wasserman whether he is in a support group for testicular cancer, and Wasserman responds, "Yeah, but they can't relate; they lost their *right* testicle. It's completely different. It's like the opposite end of the scrotum." In *Time Indefinite* we laugh mostly at what McElwee says; in *The Same River Twice,* we tend to laugh, often with Moss himself, at what Moss's friends say or do. There are, of course, obvious exceptions to this pattern.

Moss's maturation as a filmmaker is also evident in his editing (done in collaboration with Karen Schmeer). While *Riverdogs* is edited in a rather straightforward manner so as to accurately document the trip down the Colorado, *The Same River Twice* moves inventively between past and present and from one site in the west to another, using sound and image in subtle and evocative ways, sometimes condensing complex events into relatively brief sequences that nevertheless reveal the subtleties of human relationships over time. A particularly inventive sequence midway through the film explores events that led to the now-defunct marriage of Cathy Shaw and Jeff Golden, who, in the interests of their two children, continue to live across the street from one another.

Moss presents an image of Shaw in 1978, climbing, nude, up a rope ladder, as a ringing phone is heard and Golden tells Moss, "I'd better get this" (fig. 35). It's Shaw. Golden mentions that when the phone rang, he and Moss were watching *Riverdogs* and that the tape is now paused on a shot of her "frozen, flickering butt." Moss then cuts to Shaw on the phone, as if she is talking with Golden, and she seems to respond with a vaguely embarrassed "Mmmm"—though it is quickly obvious that Shaw is not on the phone with Golden but on mayoral business.

FIGURE 35. Jeff Golden looks at nude image of Cathy Shaw in *Riverdogs*, in Robb Moss's *The Same River Twice* (2003).

During the following minutes, Moss intercuts between Shaw doing various mundane tasks, one of which is describing and offering Moss "our favorite" breakfast (toast of some kind, cottage cheese, and fresh tomato and basil from her garden), and Golden cooking a meat and egg breakfast as he talks with a business colleague on the phone. At one point, Moss superimposes his own conversation with Shaw over imagery of Golden cooking just as Shaw is describing moments during the breakup when she and Golden felt tenderness for "what was passing" (here, Moss fades in a brief image from *Riverdogs* of Shaw and Golden in sleeping bags, with the sound of the river superimposed, then returns to sync-sound imagery of Golden cooking and talking on the phone). When Golden, now off the phone, offers Moss some of what he's been cooking, Moss demurs, and Golden says, "You're all cottage-cheese-and-tomato-basil-and-English-muffined out, huh?" Moss: "You know that dish . . ." GOLDEN, sardonically: "Six . . . days . . . a week, over there." Then, as Golden continues his preparations, Shaw's auditory story continues, until, following a more distant long shot of Golden framed by his kitchen doorway, Moss cuts to a close-up of Shaw, who enacts a kind of shot-countershot, describing the moment in a movie theater when she asked Golden if he were having an affair and, after several evasions, Golden said, "Yes"—and the sequence fades out.

This passage, which I have only begun to unpack, deftly encapsulates a series of emotionally complex moments in the intertwined lives of two people over twenty years. Moss reveals the subtle mix of friendship, affection, nostalgia, disappointment, frustration, annoyance, respect, and self-awareness that continues to characterize their ongoing relationship with each other—as well as their continuing intimacy with him.

Because of Moss's embrace of change throughout *The Same River Twice,* the film abjures the kind of resolution that McElwee's *Time Indefinite* and Moss's *The Tourist* provide. Instead, the film concludes by offering viewers a more expansive version of the choice that is the subject of the opening debate between Wasserman and Tichenor about whether to stay on the river one more day (we see this debate three times during the film). Wasserman wants to move on ("I'm ready to go"), while Tichenor wants to stay ("Look where we are; we're in the Grand Canyon, and we can be here one more day"). The subsequent lives of these two men, as Moss depicts them, have confirmed these opposing positions. Wasserman *has* moved on, and being a river guide seems at most a fond memory. At the conclusion of the film, he explains his understanding of his life:

> I don't know how I would make sense of my aging if I wasn't a father. It is *so* basic to the way I think of myself and my temporary place in the world. It's just as simple as, my father was a kid, and then he was a father, and then he was old, and then he died. And now it's my turn to be a father, and soon I'll be old and soon I'll die, and then it will be my son's turn and my daughter's turn.
>
> And when I look at people in their twenties, I think sometimes am I envious of their youth and their healthier bodies and maybe I am, but I really don't think I am, because it's their *turn* to be young.
>
> If they're lucky, they'll have a turn to be middle-age, and if I'm lucky, I'll have a turn to be old. But we all just get one turn at each.

Tichenor, however, has not moved on: indeed, as a text explains earlier in the film, "Except for the six months when he tried to become a dentist, Jim has worked continuously as a river guide since 1973," and in several instances Moss includes shots of Tichenor on the river during the 1990s. *The Same River Twice* concludes with Tichenor's final comments: "Actually, what I've realized is what I want to do, and I don't know if I can do this really for a living, but what I want to do is plant perennials in the fall, trim trees in the winter, mulch in the spring, and water in the summer. It sounds like a possible, attainable goal." Unlike Wasserman, who is conscious of approaching mortality, Tichenor still sees his life as something beginning, still to be determined.

These two views of experience, of course, are not mutually exclusive, and Moss's presentation of the two comments as the conclusion of the film suggests that they are interwoven in all our lives. The implication here is that life is in some measure an attempt to effect a balance between the recognition that any given moment in our experience is part of a larger, ongoing development from youth to age within which we deal with our responsibilities to the broader circle of family, society, environment, *and* the desire to enjoy our momentary incarnation as physical beings in the world, day to day, one day at a time, year round.

All of the now aging Riverdogs reveal one or another form of this balance. Danny Silver seems dedicated to enjoying music and exercise, just as she enjoyed them in 1978—but she is also raising two daughters and wants to raise them well. Cathy Shaw has her responsibilities as mayor of Ashland, as well as a daughter and son to raise, but she is passionate about enjoying the tomatoes from her garden every morning; Jeff Golden, whose earlier married life was focused on his being a mover and shaker in Oregon politics, continues to work at being an accomplished man (early in the film we see him on a book tour for his novel, *Forest Blood*), even as he works at being a good father to his son and daughter and longs for a partner with whom he can share his daily experience. Even the free spirit Jim Tichenor is, however slowly, carefully creating a home, the very image of stability. And Robb Moss is making a film that he hopes will have a public life and meaning for the audiences that see it, and that will enhance his career as a professor at Harvard—though in order to make *The Same River Twice,* he has left his professional and family responsibilities behind, at least for a time, to continue (as Tichenor does) to do what he realized he loved doing as a young man: "Growing up, it seemed a perfect life to travel and to make movies." Indeed, the overall structure of *The Same River Twice*—its attempt to create a balance between the *Riverdogs* imagery and the video documentation of the then-current ongoing moment—models this double sensibility.

In my estimation, *The Same River Twice* is, along with Pincus's *Diaries* and McElwee's *Time Indefinite,* one of the three masterworks of Cambridge personal documentary. And at least as fully as these other two films, *The Same River Twice* demonstrates what autobiographical filmmakers have always hoped to accomplish: the aging Riverdogs' decency, intelligence, and personal accomplishments make them "characters" not only at least as interesting and engaging as those we see in even the best fictional films, but far more believable and often, considerably more worthy of admiration and imitation.

The Same River Twice can also be understood within the broader context of the American visual arts, as a twenty-first century version of Thomas Cole's four-part painting, *The Voyage of Life* (1839–40), one of the canonical works of the Hudson River School (figs. 36, 37).[17] Like Cole, Moss uses a river journey to represent the experience of a life and, also like Cole, sees the transformation from youth to adulthood as the central action of life's journey. But as a documentary filmmaker, Moss can do what Cole couldn't: the painter could only create visual emblems of childhood, youth, manhood, and old age; Moss creates a film experience that provides us entry into the developing lives of real individuals as they navigate the rapids and calms of aging and respond to what they've experienced and learned.

FIGURES 36 AND 37. Thomas Cole's *The Voyage of Life: Youth* (1840), oil on canvas, 52½" × 78½"; and *The Voyage of Life: Manhood* (1840), oil on canvas, 52" × 78"; Munson-Williams-Proctor Arts Institute, Museum of Art, Utica, New York, 55.106 and 55.107.

Cole asks us to understand his representations of what he has come to understand; Moss asks us to make our own deductions about the lives we are witness to.

It remains to be seen if Moss can successfully overcome a weakness of Cole's four-part painting; Cole died at forty-nine, and his painting demonstrates that he did not experience the final "age": the individual in *Old Age* seems to have no life other than a longing for immortality. Moss has begun shooting footage for another river film, and though he has joked that he might entitle it "The Naked and the Dead," one can hope that he will face the complexities of old age with his fellow Riverdogs and will find a way of creating another film experience that he, they, and we, can learn from.[18]

Panorama

Other Approaches to Personal Documentary

While interest among American (and Cambridge) filmmakers in producing eth-nographic film, at least in the modes pioneered by the Marshalls, Gardner, and Asch, diminished by the 1980s, or at least was redirected into a broad-ranging critique of the myth of detached, objective observation both among those who were interested in ethnographic cinema and within the discipline of anthropology in general, the successes of personal documentary, both aesthetic and commercial (Pincus's *Diaries* had a theatrical run, and McElwee's *Sherman's March* was some-thing of a hit), emboldened a good many aspiring documentary filmmakers to try their hand at exploring the autobiographical mode. If classic ethnographic (or proto-ethnographic) filmmakers from Flaherty through Asch had often failed to take adequate account of how their depictions of Other cultures were filtered through their own cultural conditioning, personal documentary offered a route into the study of culture that allowed this very conditioning to be explored. Pincus had been inspired by the slogan, "The personal is the political"; personal docu-mentary was demonstrating that the personal was the cultural.

Pincus, through his teaching at MIT and Harvard (he taught at Harvard from 1980 to 1983); and McElwee, Moss, Guzzetti, and Steven Ascher, through their teaching at Harvard, nurtured a good many prospective filmmakers, including some who soon followed in their personal documentary footsteps. While interest in autobiographical filmmaking has spread far and wide, Cambridge has contin-ued to be a nexus for an exploration of both the formal and practical possibilities of documenting the personal. Some filmmakers—Ascher (and his partner Jeanne Jordan), Michel Negroponte, Nina Davenport, and Alexander Olch, for example—have produced engaging, inventive feature autobiographical work for broadcast on public television; others—John Gianvito, Jeff Daniel Silva, and Amie Siegel—have assumed a smaller, more experimentally inclined audience for films that are more demanding formally. Even Ricky Leacock, teaming up with Valerie Lalonde, found his way into openly personal documentary; and in the wake of Hurricane Katrina, Ed Pincus returned to filmmaking after twenty-five years, teaming up with Lucia Small to explore the ways in which a national tragedy affected the personal lives of those who experienced it and of the filmmakers themselves.

This chapter is a survey of some of the contributions of documentary filmmakers working in the personal mode, arranged more or less chronologically and highlighting several distinct thematic and formal tendencies evident in the films. The particular nature of each of these filmmakers' connections with Cambridge differs considerably: some live and work in Cambridge; others who work elsewhere have maintained and continue to make considerable use of their connections to the Cambridge filmmaking scene. The films discussed must be understood to stand in for a good many other worthy contributions to personal documentary produced and/or instigated in Cambridge but not discussed in what is already an extensive study.

STEVEN ASCHER AND JEANNE JORDAN: FAMILIES IN TRANSITION

A summa cum laude Harvard graduate, Steven Ascher was hired by Ed Pincus in 1975 to help with the editing of *Diaries (1971–1978)*. During the time when *Diaries* was being edited, the two men collaborated on *Life and Other Anxieties* (see chapter 4) and subsequently on *The Filmmakers Handbook* (New York: Penguin, 1984), the canonical guide to making films that Ascher has revised several times.[1] From 1978 through 1982, Ascher taught filmmaking at MIT and more recently has taught at Harvard. He has worked on a wide range of projects, mostly for public television, nonprofit organizations, and government agencies. Jeanne Jordan, a midwestern native, arrived in Boston in 1978 and forged a connection with WGBH, where she worked as an editor on a wide variety of projects, including two episodes of the first series of *Eyes on the Prize* (episode 3: *Ain't Scared of Your Jails [1960–1961]*) and episode 5: *Mississippi: Is This America? [1962–1964]*—both 1986). Ascher and Jordan married in 1989 and have worked together to produce, write, and direct three feature documentaries about American families under stress: *Troublesome Creek* (1995), which was nominated for an Academy Award; *So Much So Fast* (2007) and *Raising Renee* (2011). Ascher has done the cinematography for these films, and Jordan the editing.

In *Troublesome Creek* the focus is Jeanne Jordan's parents during the months after they were faced with the prospect of losing their Iowa farm near the town of Wiota, which had been in the family for 125 years: Norwest, the corporation that had acquired their local bank in 1990, did not have faith that they would repay their loans. Four times during 1991, Ascher and Jordan traveled to Iowa to film her parents' struggle to keep their land, then spent years raising the funds to finish the film, which aired on PBS's *The American Experience* in 1996. In *Troublesome Creek* (the film is named for the stream that winds through the Jordan property), Russel and Mary Jane Jordan believe their only chance at paying off their loan is to sell their cattle and auction off everything else they own and move into town, allowing Jim Jordan, Jeanne's younger brother, who has been renting a farm not far from the Jordan homestead, to move to the Jordan homestead and use his own equipment to farm it—that way, the land will stay in the family. *Troublesome Creek* focuses on the family's reaction to Norwest's decision to place the Jordan farm on the endangered accounts list, the family's plans for the auction, the auction itself, and the aftermath.

Troublesome Creek is a personal film—the film is about Jordan's family (and Ascher's in-laws); it frequently evokes her personal memories of growing up in southwest Iowa, and she herself is often on screen—but it is quite distinct from the tradition of autobiographical filmmaking represented by Pincus, McElwee, and Moss. In *Diaries, Time Indefinite,* and *The Tourist,* the filmmakers' personal struggles are the focus of the action; in *Troublesome Creek* Jordan's and Ascher's personal feelings are largely beside the point, or at least are not a focus of the film. Of course, Jordan and Ascher are concerned about the elder Jordans, the farm, and at the end of the film, Jim's long-term capacity to keep the farm during an era when many farmers are going bankrupt, but the focus of the film is a larger issue.

It is clear throughout *Troublesome Creek* that the choice of the Jordans as the film's focus has to do with the fact that their experiences have become typical of American family farmers (a final visual text dedicates the film not only to "our families," but to "all the Russ and Mary Janes"). Ascher and Jordan portray the Iowa Jordans with much affection and with considerable attention to their particulars as individuals, but the filmmakers and the Iowa Jordans recognize that what is happening with the Jordan farm is a familiar story: like a good many of their midwestern neighbors, they are victims of the consolidation of economic power in the hands of people who have no personal connection to individual family farms or farmers. Of course, the fact that their story is not unusual has not meant that it is usual in cinema—and it is this that presumably motivated Ascher and Jordan to make *Troublesome Creek.*

The film is also formally distinct from the kinds of personal documentary that have been the subject of previous chapters. Beautifully shot and edited, *Troublesome Creek* was made less to exemplify the notions about documentary purity that informed so many of the cinema verite films of the 1960s and 1970s and to some extent Pincus's and Leacock's teaching at MIT, than to make emotional, and perhaps political, contact with a substantial audience. In *Troublesome Creek*—and subsequently in *So Much So Fast* and *Raising Renee*—Ascher and Jordan frequently use musical accompaniment (composed by Sheldon Mirowitz) as an emotional trigger, and both films make considerable use of informational voice-over narration: Jordan narrates *Troublesome Creek*; Ascher, *So Much So Fast*; visual text is used to narrate *Raising Renee*.

As much as the use of narration might seem a concession to the conventional, in *Troublesome Creek* Jeanne Jordan's matter-of-fact, often wryly humorous voice-over is an appropriate reflection of the Jordan family, who are "midwestern" not merely by virtue of living in Iowa but in their largely deadpan response to their plight. While certain sequences are emotionally taxing, especially for Mary Jane Jordan (seeing their cows sold, for example), tearful moments are exceptions: insofar as the film allows us to understand them, the Jordans respond to their financial challenge with consistent good humor, little self-pity, and no overt anger. Jordan's voice-over explains that "Steve and I had dreaded coming back to Iowa for the auction. This wasn't exactly the high point of my family's history, and we were expecting people to be in pretty grim moods," but in fact the family seems in good spirits and is generally amused by the ironies of their situation and the absurdities of how some of the locals are dealing with the auction. Indeed, when Russel Jordan calls his contact at Norwest to tell him that the auction was a success and that they will be able make good on their debt, his cheerfulness causes Jeanne Jordan to complain on-camera, "You were too nice. You don't have to give him so much help assuaging his guilt!" When Ascher and Jordan return to Wiota six months later, they find that the historically taciturn Russel has become the "family optimist," though the struggle for the farm continues: Jim wryly suggests that the supposed freedom of farm life has mostly to do with choosing which bill to pay.

It is implicit from the beginning of *Troublesome Creek* that while the Jordans' story will be poignant, it will not be tragic. This is evident in Jordan's first voice-over: "My husband Steve and I are here filming, because it's no ordinary spring; it's looking like it could be my parents' last on the farm." The fictional device of her saying "could be"—by the time she writes and records this voice-over, Jordan knows that while it *was*, strictly speaking, her parents' last spring on the farm, the Jordans did not lose their land—combined with the quality of her delivery makes clear that while this story will be moving, it will not be a downer. This also seems evident in the film's trope of referring to the history of classic Westerns (*Red River, High Noon,* . . .) and to itself as a "*Mid*western." It's an unusual Western that doesn't have a successful resolution, even if it's a bittersweet resolution like that in *High Noon,* where Will Kane is victorious over the Miller boys despite the town's failure to help him, images from which are intercut with the elder Jordans' watching the Zinnemann film on television during the final sequence of *Troublesome Creek.*

Troublesome Creek is a paean not only to family farming, but to traditional heterosexual marriage. Mary Jane and Russel are depicted as a perfect match, happy and comfortable collaborators in maintaining the farm and raising six children. Though little time is devoted to them, the marriages of the children also seem amicable. And the relationship of Jeanne Jordan and Steven Ascher implicitly mirrors the marriage of the elder Jordans. Ascher and Jordan are partners, working together simultaneously to assist Jeanne Jordan's parents and siblings *and* to produce a film that will be as representative of their own life together, their own creative collaboration (in her voice-over Jordan always uses "we" or "Steve and I" to refer to the filmmaking) as the farm is for Mary Jane and Russel.

During the film, Jeanne Jordan's childhood is surveyed by means of photographs, and she is often on screen. Ascher's cinematography does not detach him from family events: he engages his in-laws from behind the camera (when Ascher and Jordan visit the homestead during the summer after Jim Jordan and his family have moved in, we can hear Steven's excitement about the changes Jim's family have made), and Ascher's affection and admiration for his wife are evident in his cinematography. From time to time he and Jordan exchange an affectionate glance. Ultimately, *Troublesome Creek* models the idea of a marriage of equal and equally productive partners.

So Much So Fast is far less autobiographical than *Troublesome Creek,*but is personal in a manner similar to the earlier film. After a poetically resonant prelude and the opening title and director credits, the filmmakers provide a "1993 prologue" during which several shots are recycled from the sequence near the end of *Troublesome Creek* when Ascher and Jeanne Jordan leave the elder Jordans after the auction, accompanied by Ascher's voice-over: "This is my wife Jeanne and her parents, just before we found out her mother had something called ALS. Also known as Lou Gehrig's Disease, it destroys nerves, then your muscles. Most people die in two to five years, but Russ and Mary Jane decided that they'd be one of the exceptions." In the following sequence, Russel Jordan explains that "eventually, we found out we had to play by the rules," and Ascher's voice-over continues, "We learned the rules of ALS the hard way. Actually, back then there was only one rule: there was nothing you could do, no treatment, no surgery, no drug. We never got over the feeling there was something more we should have done."

The abrupt cut to a *60 Minutes* story about the quest of Jamie Heywood and his brother Stephen Heywood (who has been diagnosed with ALS) to find a cure for the disease before Stephen succumbs to it reveals the implicitly personal motivation behind *So Much So Fast*: if Ascher and Jordan couldn't do something for Mary Jane, they can at least honor the Heywoods' efforts and bring increased attention to the disease. During the following four years, Ascher documents the progress of Jamie's efforts to find a cure and the progressive effects of ALS on Stephen—and during this process Ascher himself becomes good friends with the Heywoods, Stephen in particular. As in *Troublesome Creek,* in other words, a family incident

FIGURE 38. Stephen Heywood as young father, in Steven Ascher and Jeanne Jordan's *So Much So Fast* (2007). Courtesy Steven Ascher and Jeanne Jordan.

motivates a film about an issue that is larger than the filmmakers' family, or even family itself, an issue that presents a dramatic challenge to a particular family as they attempt to come to terms with the changes facing them.

So Much So Fast intercuts between Stephen's struggle with ALS and Jamie's attempt to battle the disease by establishing a foundation and assembling a group of "guerrilla scientists" to find an effective treatment. Jamie's efforts are impressive and, if not successful in the sense that they do not save Stephen (who died in 2006 at the age of thirty-seven when his respirator accidentally detached during the night), they do bring expanded efforts to the search for ways to eliminate the disease or at least to soften its effects: the ALS Therapy Development Institute remains active. But it is Stephen's remarkable disposition throughout his ordeal that is the heart of *So Much So Fast*. Despite his diagnosis and the onslaught of the disease, Stephen marries, renovates a home, and, when he and Wendy Stach have a son (fig. 38), becomes a hands-on father (he is even engaged enough in the lives of those around him to recognize that Jamie's obsession with his work at the ALS Therapy Development Institute is endangering Jamie's marriage: Jamie and Melinda separate partway through the film). Though he cannot defy the effects of ALS, Stephen is quick to embrace those technologies that can keep him active and in touch with his family; and, as Ascher and Jordan portray him, Stephen's bravery, utter lack of self-pity, and astonishing good spirits in the most challenging of circumstances make the troubles of most cinematic protagonists, including most of those in personal documentaries, seem laughable.

As the years pass, Ascher's relationship with the Heywoods and especially Stephen evolves to the point where their friendship can be endangered. After Stephen has lost the ability to make himself clear vocally, Ascher is not able to talk with him for six months—"I missed it and imagined he felt the same"—until Stephen accesses E Z Keys, a computer program that allows him to type what he wants to say and be heard through "Microsoft Paul," a computer voice that speaks what Stephen types. His first words to Ascher are curt: "Don't tell me how to ride my wheelchair!" Ascher admits he is hurt. A phone call from Wendy follows; she relays a message from Stephen, who is embarrassed: "If Steve likes Steve, can you have him mark yes or no on a card and send it to us?" Near the end of the film, in-depth conversations between the two men reveal Stephen's determination to live on a respirator long into the future. And a final visual text indicates that in fact, "in the year before his death, Stephen helped pioneer BrainGate, a technology that controls a computer with thoughts."

In many ways, both *Troublesome Creek* and *So Much So Fast* are the perfect films for public television—they are heroic, emotionally engaging stories about American families, beautifully, if conventionally, shot and edited—and for some of those who make and chronicle independent cinema, this can be a problem. In March 2011 I served as a programmer for part of the annual Stan Brakhage Symposium in Boulder, Colorado. After Bill Nichols, another of the programmers, presented Peter Forgács's *The Maelstrom: A Family Chronicle* (1997), I was astonished when James Benning, among the most accomplished and influential of avantgarde filmmakers, indicated during the discussion that followed the Forgács video that he had felt little sympathy for the Peereboom family (nearly all of whom perished at Auschwitz) because of their status as a relatively wealthy bourgeois family, a status reflected in their ability to document their lives in the home movies from which Forgács fashioned the film.[2]

I can imagine that a similar objection might be leveled at both *Troublesome Creek* and *So Much So Fast*. In both films we are asked to sympathize with the plight of families who are relatively well-off economically. The Iowa Jordans are able to raise $200,000 and keep their land; and the Heywoods have the economic resources to provide considerable technological support to Stephen—in a way, the films are a reflection of the economic status of the two families and are aimed at television audiences who in most cases probably share that status. The plights of both families do not go unnoticed—not only are they are documented by Ascher and Jordan, but Stephen Heywood's case instigated a *60 Minutes* story, a feature in the *New Yorker*, and much Boston-area publicity. Further, while *The Maelstrom* is highly experimental, in the Ascher–Jordan films there is no formal edge or any obvious attempt to expand the documentary form.

Benning's objection to *The Maelstrom* seemed deeply cynical to me. I am proud to have spent much of my life defending and supporting the work of experimental and avant-garde moving image artists; it is true, as Andrew Sarris suggested long ago, that "someone has to man the outposts of culture," to work at the edges, expanding cinematic possibility.[3] However, the purity, even the nobility of cinematic experiment, should not blind us to the fact that compelling human struggles can happen to families of all social classes and that these struggles are legitimate subjects of cinema. Fortunately, there seem to be accomplished filmmakers willing to place their abilities, even their excitement about exploring the possibilities of filmmaking, at the service not just of cinema itself, but of those whose dignity in facing struggle and tragedy can function as models for the lives of others. And it is a facile, even a rather mean-spirited form of conventionality, to deny the value of such films or to ignore the cinematic accomplishments within them.

For example, earlier I mentioned the poetically resonant prelude to *So Much So Fast*. It begins with a still photograph of what I assume are the three Heywood brothers climbing a sand dune; then, as we begin to hear the opening stanza of Underworld's song, "Born Slippy," the shot dissolves to a 53-second live action shot beginning at the feet of a young man (Stephen Heywood) floating in a swimming pool. The shot pans from Heywood's feet, slowly up his body to his hands clasped at his chest (surprisingly, there are children's "swim floaties" on his arms); then to his face. His eyes are closed; he seems to have abandoned himself to the pleasure of floating in the water. The particular position of Heywood's feet, the tilt of his head, and the film's gradual revelation of his body distorted by the water evoke something between an El Greco crucifixion and a Pietà.

The serenity of the visual imagery is contrasted by the energy of Underworld's rock beat and the high-speed lyrics of "Born Slippy": "Drive boy dog boy dirty numb angel boy in the doorway boy she was a lipstick boy she was a beautiful boy and tears boy and all in your inner space boy you had hands girl boy and steel boy you had chemicals boy I've grown so close to you boy and you just groan boy she said come over come over she smiled at you boy." As the film subsequently reveals, the lyrics suggest the speed with which Heywood's life experiences pass (to some extent they also suggest Steven Ascher's experiences filming him: "I've grown close to you boy"), but even during this opening moment, as Stephen floats in the water, the lyrics seem to suggest the astonishing mental energy inside this peaceful man. The shot fades slowly to black, a premonition, of course, of Stephen Heywood's early demise. The prelude is a lovely, memorable moment, a kind of haiku that opens the door to a fascinating story.

The Ascher–Jordan family films are consistently thoughtful and moving, deeply committed, and resonant with craft: their considerable gifts as filmmakers include their ability to make what is complex and difficult to film and edit seem easy.

In 2011 Ascher and Jordan completed the third film in what is now a trilogy of family films, this one focused on painter Beverly McIver and her mentally disabled sister Renee. The focus of *Raising Renee* is Beverly's struggle to make good on the casual promise she made to her mother that she would take charge of her sister after her mother's death. When Ethel McIver dies of cancer, Beverly is faced with the challenge of integrating her sister into her busy life as a successful painter and teacher at Arizona State University. The family is African American, and *Raising Renee* places Beverly's (and Ethel's and Renee's) struggles within the historical context of race and class in the South (the KKK killed several anti-Klan demonstrators outside the McIver's apartment when Beverly and Renee were children). After her husband left her, Ethel supported her three girls by working as a maid in the homes of wealthy Greensboro, North Carolina, whites (Beverly has a different father than her two sisters—the result of her mother's affair with a Greensboro taxi driver). *Raising Renee* was filmed over a period of six years, as Beverly reluctantly takes charge of Renee who indeed does grow up and, at age fifty, begins to live on her own with the support of her sisters and her church community in Greensboro.

There is no indication in *Raising Renee* of the personal connection among Ascher, Jordan, and Beverly McIver that instigated this project (in fact, Jordan and McIver met when both had Radcliffe Fellowships in 2003); and no reference to Ascher's and Jordan's personal and family life is included in the film. *Raising Renee* gives considerable attention to the overtly autobiographical dimensions of Beverly McIver's painting (her production of paintings and their relationship to the events we witness is a motif throughout the film), but even more fully than in *So Much So Fast* in *Raising Renee* Ascher and Jordan channel their autobiographical urge into the larger theme of family struggle and into their "familial" collaboration. Especially early in the film, visual texts provide a kind of narration, and we hear both Jordan and Ascher asking questions from behind the camera from time to time, but for the most part, Beverly "narrates" her own story. *Raising Renee* intercuts between Beverly's experiences with Renee and the historical narrative of Beverly's life growing up in a racially divided city.

It *is* evident in *Raising Renee*, as it is in *So Much So Fast*, that, during the years of shooting, the relationship between filmmaker and subject—here, not just Ascher, Jordan, and Beverly McIver, but Ascher and Renee McIver—evolves, becoming increasingly intimate: when Renee finally moves into an apartment of her own, Ascher films her going to bed on her first night—he seems to be the only one present and takes care to be sure that everything is in order before he leaves. It is clear that while *Raising Renee* was instigated by a personal connection between Jordan and Beverly McIver at a particular moment, during the six years when the film was being shot and edited, the project became personal for the filmmakers more in the way family relationships become intimate: that is, as a result of an ongoing commitment to these relationships over time.[4] In other words, the transition in Beverly and Renee McIver's lives, recorded in the film, is mirrored by what has to have been something of a transition in Ascher's and Jordan's lives and in their relationships with the McIver sisters. Of course, like so many of the personal documentaries discussed in this volume, *Raising Renee* can also be understood as an implicit exploration of a certain class of people in a certain geographic area during a particular era: that is, as an implicit, informal ethnography of African American life in North Carolina and a cinematic report on the long-term collaboration between a southern black family and two northern white filmmakers.

MICHEL NEGROPONTE: GETTING INVOLVED

Michel Negroponte was part of the cohort of students who studied with Leacock and Pincus at MIT during the mid-1970s, and his first films—*Space Coast* (1979), *Resident Exile* (1981)—were collaborations with Ross McElwee (his brother Nicholas Negroponte was cofounder, with Jerome B. Wiesner, of the MIT Media Lab, which in 1980 replaced the Film Section, and served as its director for many years). Like Ascher and Jordan, Negroponte has worked on many film projects produced and directed by others, but he has also found ways of developing his own feature documentaries.[5] Beginning with his breakthrough film, *Jupiter's Wife* (1994; it won a Special Jury Prize at Sundance and an Emmy), Negroponte developed a process of filming in and around his native New York that has allowed him to explore in an intimate way the lives of individuals and groups living on the edge economically and psychically. While his films are not about his own family or even his own life as an artist, Negroponte becomes friends with his often troubled subjects for the duration of his filming, and this friendship factors into his and our understanding of them.

Like Ascher and Jordan, Negroponte is comfortable using the wide range of options available for documentary filmmakers. Each of his films develops a set of unusual, interesting characters and a story that has something like a resolution. He narrates each of his films in an informal, engaging, informative voice, relying on the present tense (the present, that is, of his witnessing of his subjects' experiences) to guide us into the lives of his subjects and his evolving thoughts about them. Negroponte's films are full of talking heads (people speaking for themselves, though not noticeably in response to an interviewer's questions). He employs music as a means of confirming the emotional tenor of scenes, and he often makes use of archival materials. Like the Ascher-Jordan films, Negroponte's find audiences on public television.

Jupiter's Wife begins with Negroponte's explanation that while his parents were immigrants who longed for the Europe of their youth, he and his twin brother have always identified as Americans, and Central Park "is where my bother and I found native soil." Negroponte is an impressive cinematographer, and *Jupiter's*

Wife is full of beautiful images of New York, Central Park in particular. Indeed, like Jonas Mekas, for whom Central Park was an urban "Walden" (in Mekas's *Walden,* 1969), and William Greaves, for whom the park is the very emblem of independent creativity, including creative filmmaking (in *Symbiopsychotaxiplasm: Take One,* 1972), Central Park seems for Negroponte the essence of New York, and Maggie, the middle-aged homeless woman who is the focus of *Jupiter's Wife,* the park's spirit of place.

Maggie is first seen walking a group of dogs and carrying an immense backpack. She seems comfortable, even reasonably happy with her life—though she lives in what appears to be a fantasy world: she claims to be psychically in touch with Jupiter, says that Robert Ryan was her father, claims she has children and that she herself resides in Erebus. Her actual "address" is the steps of St. James Church at 865 Madison Avenue. Negroponte is fascinated with Maggie; her stories intrigue him and he quickly becomes directly involved: "When Maggie invites me to go to the ASPCA with her to get a license for Sterling [Sterling Silver, a new stray dog she has adopted], I offer to pay for it. She accepts"—Negroponte's increasing involvement is confirmed by a subtle drum roll within the musical accompaniment on the soundtrack.

For much of the first hour of *Jupiter's Wife,* the focus is on Maggie's life in and around the park through the seasons, along with Negroponte's attempts to decide how fully, if at all, Maggie's stories are based in fact. The changes in season and weather are reflected by Maggie's moves first to a tunnel in the park, then during an unusually cold winter to a shack. Negroponte explains that he tries to convince Maggie to leave the park and find an apartment and that he has contacted homeless groups for assistance, but gradually, he comes to recognize that Maggie, who is an engaging, attractive person, has many friends and a considerable support system. After six months he learns her family name—Cogan—and discovers that her parents live in New Hyde Park, New York. When Negroponte contacts them, he learns that she stays away from them by choice and that they are unaware that Maggie is homeless. The developing mystery of Maggie Cogan's family is contextualized by the relative conventionality of Negroponte's own: his experiences filming Maggie are interrupted by brief sequences of the filmmaker, his wife, and his son Peter in the Catskills on vacation and in California with family at Christmastime.

After Christmas, Negroponte returns to New York to find that the city has intervened in Maggie Cogan's situation, has destroyed her "Sugar Shack" in the park, moving her to an apartment in Long Island City; and during the remainder of the film, Negroponte reveals more of Maggie's history. It turns out that after graduating from New Hyde Park High School and attending several colleges, Maggie became the first woman carriage driver in Central Park, an accomplishment celebrated in a 1967 Universal Pictures Newsreel item narrated by Ed Herlihy, and later in an appearance on the television show *What's My Line?* It also turns out that

Maggie knew Robert Ryan during the late 1960s, was his daughter's roommate for a time at the Dakota, across from Central Park at 72nd Street (in an apartment building now owned by Yoko Ono). During the Vietnam War years, Maggie seems to have let her financial independence slip through her fingers; she had sons with two men, one a Harvard M.B.A. who paid child support before disappearing; the other, "Jupiter," a fellow carriage driver who abandoned her while pregnant and in love, after which she began to hear voices, lost custody of the children, and was institutionalized.

As Negroponte is finding his way into Maggie Cogan's history, he is also watching her deal with her new life in Long Island City, and in time he becomes frustrated with the fact that the move doesn't seem to represent a real change: "A year ago, the adoption of Mickalittle's puppies filled me with optimism, but Maggie has collected more strays. One of them has a litter; the cycle repeats." If on one hand, his patience with the mysteries of Maggie's personal mythology has worn thin, he comes to recognize that her involvement with the dogs and her sense that she lives in a world inhabited by Jupiter, Hera, and Saturn allow her to survive the pain and trauma of losing her children; and he is also frank in admitting that, as Maggie suggests, she and Michel do seem to have some sort of psychic connection: as we see images of Negroponte's newborn daughter, Ramona, he explains that Maggie had accurately predicted the day and time of Ramona's birth: "Had I taken her more seriously, I would not have had to deliver my daughter in the back seat of a taxicab." He wonders if perhaps fate might "orchestrate a family reunion" between Maggie and her sons, "but *I* can't. I decide to go no further."

During the two years when he was filming Maggie Cogan, Negroponte became part of her extended support system, and over time, a confidant. At the conclusion of *Jupiter's Wife,* Maggie remains a mystery in many ways, but Negroponte has demonstrated that much of what may seem her fantasy has its roots in fact and that the unusual figure he spotted in Central Park in 1992 is a fascinating part of the park's complex history, and therefore, of his own as a New Yorker.

Negroponte's second feature, *Methadonia* (2005), is similar to *Jupiter's Wife* in its general approach; this time, the focus is drug addicts struggling to free themselves not only from addiction to heroin and other hard drugs but from their dependence on methadone, which was developed as a cure for heroin dependency but has become a powerful addiction in its own right. Negroponte narrates the film, again in an engaging, personal voice, but otherwise, *Methadonia* is less personal than *Jupiter's Wife*—though the film was partially instigated by the death of Negroponte's sister-in-law from a heroin overdose. Negroponte does not become directly involved with the group of addicts he observes at the New York Center for Addiction Treatment Services, often at twelve-step meetings coordinated by recovered addict Millie Correa. As in *Jupiter's Wife,* however, he is an intimate observer and sounding board for their troubled lives,[6] and he contextualizes the events he documents within a subtly reverential depiction of New York City. While Negroponte indicates late in *Methadonia* that "a lot of recovery doesn't unfold like a story," in fact, the film has a relatively upbeat ending: addicts Susie and Eddie, on methadone maintenance, are allowed to keep their baby daughter, and Steve, the most prominent of the addicts in the film, ultimately frees himself from methadone and is reunited with his family.

I'm Dangerous with Love, finished in 2009, combines the subject matter of *Methadonia* (*I'm Dangerous* focuses on the hallucinogen ibogaine, which allows drug addicts to escape addiction within a few days—ibogaine is derived from the iboga tree) and the personal engagement of *Jupiter's Wife*. Negroponte's opening narration—"I've started hearing sounds; it's like a swarm of bees inside my head"—begins a sequence during which we see the filmmaker in bed, being administered a dose of ibogaine, as he explains in voice-over, "I've been working on this film for awhile now, and I've seen what ibogaine does to other people, so I know that soon I'll be almost paralyzed. That's when the visions start. But Dimitri still has to give me a few more doses of ibogaine before I get there." Later he calls this experiment "taking my research to a new level." After the opening credits, Negroponte jumps back three years, to when he originally met Dimitri Mugianis. It is implicit in this opening that Negroponte survived his experience with ibogaine and that his involvement with Dimitri is the subject of the film.

Dimitri is a passionate and charismatic "ibogaine provider," working underground in New York City—ibogaine is classified as an illegal drug in the United States—to make what he has come to call a "sacrament" available to those willing to use ibogaine to free themselves from drug dependency (Dimitri freed himself of multiple addictions in Holland in May 2002, and until the time of Negroponte's filming had remained clean). During the first hour of *I'm Dangerous*, Negroponte, fascinated both with the drug and with Dimitri's commitment and courage, follows him to one location after another where he guides individuals through the ibogaine experience. Negroponte learns about the history of ibogaine (long used by shamans in Gabon as a sacrament in the Bwiti religion); about Dimitri's previous life as front man for the rock band "Dimitri M. and Leisure Class"; and about the nature of the hallucinogenic experience ibogaine provides. Twice we return to Negroponte's own experience with the hallucinogen, which is filmed by Dimitri. Negroponte's experience, and the experiences of some of Dimitri's other patients, are visualized in animated psychedelic sequences (Lisa Crafts did the animation)—in Negroponte's case, the experience includes Super-8 home movies of his own childhood that he sees playing in his head and visions of him and his twin brother in their mother's womb.

When Dimitri travels to Canada ("My head has been broken so wide open that I'm going to Canada with Dimitri") to guide two North Carolina men through ibogaine-instigated withdrawal from complicated addictions, Negroponte films the process, which nearly ends in disaster (one of the men goes into seizure and, for a moment, seems to be dead)—leading Dimitri to confront problematic aspects of his own attitude about working with ibogaine. He realizes he needs to do more to educate himself and decides to travel to Gabon to meet with Bwiti shamans with deep knowledge of iboga, the source of ibogaine. Negroponte records the visit: "Dimitri and I have spent a lot of time together and become friends; I'm glad to be with him on the next part of his journey." The final third of *I'm Dangerous with Love* focuses on Dimitri's initiation into Bwiti, which involves a sustained experience with iboga. Though Negroponte's focus is on Dimitri, his involvement continues to go well beyond observational filmmaking: as an attendant at the initiation ritual, he must eat some iboga: "I had my spoonful and someone behind me is whispering instructions about how to film the ceremony, but when I look over my shoulder, there's no one there."

I'm Dangerous with Love concludes back in New York, where Dimitri now offers patients the option of either the original ibogaine treatment or the Bwiti ceremony with iboga. Negroponte briefly reviews the current situations of some of the addicts Dimitri has treated in the film, most of whom have turned their lives around, and concludes this review by explaining, "I relapsed a year after taking ibogaine and I'm chewing nicotine gum again, but I'm okay with it. The Bwiti have a sacred chant for their initiates that ends with something like this: 'The troubled life of the born ones is finished; everything is clean; all is new; all is bright. I have seen the dead and I do not fear.'" While Negroponte's relapse seems amusing, given the physical and legal seriousness of the addictions Dimitri's other patients have struggled with, his inclusion of himself here is one last confirmation of Negroponte's refusal to see himself as detached from his subjects.

During his review of the current state of the (mostly) former addicts near the end of the film, we see the George Washington Bridge through a network of trees—an implicit metaphor for the change in the lives of all those documented in *I'm Dangerous with Love*: ingesting the ibogaine or the bark from the iboga tree has functioned as a bridge to recovery from addiction. Negroponte has been changed by these experiences on two levels. Like the others, he has experienced the power and effects of the hallucinogen, but he has also changed his stance as filmmaker. By becoming friends with Dimitri and filming his ministrations of an illegal hallucinogen, by experiencing both ibogaine and iboga himself and depicting his own hallucinations—that is, by becoming one of the central characters in *I'm Dangerous with Love*—Negroponte has "crossed over" into a new, more immersive and collaborative filmmaking process.

The final scene of *I'm Dangerous with Love*—Dimitri and several other men in an apartment, in face paint, performing the Bwiti ritual—is introduced by the visual text, "Astoria, New York," as if to say that this strange scene, like the life of Maggie Cogan and the lives of the recovering and nonrecovering addicts in *Methadonia*, is just another event in the immense, unfathomably complex life of New York City. Negroponte's feature documentaries are full of impressive imagery of New York—imagery sometimes reminiscent of Peter Hutton's New York portraits—and Negroponte's love of the city is the ground against which the lives of his subjects are figured. For Maggie Cogan, Central Park is, on at least one level, the mythological land of Erebus; for Negroponte New York City is the mythical land that, as a filmmaker, he is committed to explore, and the experience of making *I'm Dangerous with Love* has taught him that real exploration is not possible without his becoming, at least for a time, part of the experiences he records and interprets.[7]

LEACOCK AND LALONDE

I make home movies, therefore I live; I live, therefore I make home movies.
JONAS MEKAS, IN *WALDEN* (1968)

Ricky Leacock is a legendary figure in the development of observational cinema and, as is evident in several of the discussions in this volume, a crucial figure in the development of documentary filmmaking in Cambridge. By the time he became Ed Pincus's colleague at MIT, completing the formation of the MIT Film Section, he had had considerable experience. His first film, *Canary Island Bananas* (1935), made when Leacock was fourteen, was accomplished enough—and presumably Leacock himself impressive enough—to cause Robert Flaherty to tell the boy that they would work together someday, which, of course, they did—after Leacock had worked as an editor at Frontier Films (on Leo Hurwitz and Paul Strand's 1942 polemic, *Native Land*); as a cameraman on *To Hear Your Banjo Play*, a 1947 documentation of a folk festival on a mountaintop in West Virginia; and as a combat photographer during the Second World War—on Flaherty's 1948 feature, *Louisiana Story* (Leacock was Flaherty's cameraman for fourteen months in 1946–47).[8]

During the following years, Leacock worked as cameraman for John Ferno, for Willard Van Dyke, for the United Nations; and, using a small handheld 35mm camera, as a cameraman on Roger Tilton's *Jazz Dance* (1954) before completing *Toby and the Tall Corn* (1954), for which he did the writing, directing, camerawork, and editing. In 1960 Leacock joined Drew Associates, along with Donn Alan Pennebaker, Albert Maysles, and Terence Filgate, to collaborate in producing a series of early canonical observational cinema breakthroughs, including *Primary* (1960) and *Crisis: Behind a Presidential Commitment* (1963). *Happy Mother's Day* (1963), Leacock's collaboration with Joyce Chopra, soon followed, as did *A Stravinsky Portrait* (1965, co-made with Rolf Liebermann) and his work on Pennebaker's breakthrough rock documentary, *Monterey Pop* (1966). Leacock's particular gift was to be able to work in-close from inside personal events and public performances without being disruptive and without drawing undue attention to himself. He once described cinematography as "a form of dance. The way you move with the camera, rising and the knees bending, going up and down, is a dance"[9]—the goal of this dance, as he often said, was to create "the feeling of being there."

At the time Leacock joined Ed Pincus at MIT, virtually all the films on which Leacock's reputation currently rests had been completed. At MIT he put considerable energy into developing a small, inexpensive Super-8mm sync-sound rig that he hoped would allow a far broader range of individuals and groups to document and explore the events occurring around them (Leacock demonstrated a version of the rig for Robert Gardner in a June 1973 *Screening Room*). Leacock's involvement with MIT seems to have diminished his energy for making his own films—though he did complete a number of films during his tenure: *Isabella Stewart Gardner* (1977), a tribute to Boston's Gardner Museum, brainchild of Isabella Stewart Gardner (Robert Gardner's great aunt by marriage), for example, and *Community of Praise* (1981, co-made with Marisa Silver), a contribution to Peter Davis's *Middletown* series. In these films, as in his earlier, better-known work, Leacock's distinctive approach to cinematography is obvious. Nevertheless, during the decade after he joined MIT, Leacock's filmmaking career seemed on the wane.

And then, in 1989 Leacock retired from MIT and moved to Paris, where he met Valerie Lalonde, who became his life partner and his collaborator on a series of films shot with inexpensive video cameras, films that are overtly personal in ways that Leacock's canonical early works never were—beginning with *Les Oeufs à la coque de Richard Leacock* (1989), apparently the first feature "shot with a Video-8 Handicam to go on prime-time television in France."[10] Leacock would describe his approach to these new films in "The Art of Home Movies" in 1993: "For me, the act of filming or, as we are working in video, let's invent a new verb, the act of Videoing is a delight, a pleasure, like singing or sketching with pencil on paper, capturing the essence of places, people, situations, tragedies, comedies . . . life as we see and hear it around us. Then to go home, not to a studio; home, and edit, creating a bridge to one's friends and yes, people you don't even know who might be interested in this evocation of what was experienced."[11]

If the films made with this "home movie" approach generally seem far less formal than Leacock's approach in the films that established his reputation, they are in fact continuations of aspects of his filmmaking and demonstrations of dimensions of his thinking that have long been evident. Most obviously, shooting in inexpensive video formats and editing at home is the fulfillment of Leacock's earlier quest to make Super-8 sync-sound shooting widely available, itself a fulfillment of what he understood as the essential value of the breakthroughs in on-the-spot 35mm and 16mm sync-sound cinema verite shooting during the late 1950s and early 1960s. Further, his "home movies" are collaborations—Leacock has regularly collaborated with others—made not by a detached observer but by an insider, someone who has gotten to know his subjects well enough to "dance" with them.

These qualities are nowhere more in evidence than in *Hooray! We're Fifty!* (1994), the 38¼-minute video he and Lalonde made on the occasion of Leacock's fiftieth class reunion at Harvard in 1993. At first glance, *Hooray! We're Fifty!* (the title is borrowed from a banner used during the reunion) seems so informal that it is hard to take seriously—it is little different from the kinds of home videos many students and their parents make at graduation ceremonies. As one gets to know *Hooray!*, however, Leacock's shaping of the footage taken at the reunion becomes evident. *Hooray!* opens in medias res, as Leacock films and converses briefly from behind the camera with a man carrying a manikin of a woman; the man is celebrating the fact that the "Class of 1968 has been liberalized; we're bringing women directly into the dorm" and admits that he wasn't so lucky back in the '60s. This is followed immediately by a long shot of Leacock filming the man and the manikin, recorded by Lalonde—on one level, Leacock's way of demonstrating that he too is in the process of bringing a woman into a Harvard dorm (this occurs literally a few minutes later in the video); and on a more subtle level a kind of celebration—perhaps, a kind of one-upsmanship—since Leacock's woman is not only real but a real filmmaking partner.

This opening sequence is followed by Leacock and Lalonde registering for the reunion; Lalonde films Leacock putting on his name tag (and asking whether Lalonde has remembered to turn on the microphone) and explaining to two women working at the registration table that he and Lalonde are "making a video film" of the reunion, in part because "I love absurd rituals. There's no shortage of them here." What follows are the various elements of the absurd ritual of the reunion: checking into the dorm, attending an outdoor gathering under a tent, meeting for the evening meal, followed by a talk, apparently by an administrator, about the importance of undergraduate education. Presumably the next morning, Leacock and Lalonde join other men and their wives at the Harvard boathouse and a reunion of those 1943 crew members still alive, who take a boat onto the Charles where they are filmed from a motorboat—apparently by Leacock (Lalonde films the activity around the boathouse). A gathering of the Class of '43 follows, during which they are addressed by a panel of successful alums, introduced by John Blum: Al Casey (one-time chairman and CEO of American Airlines and postmaster general of the United States during 1986), Ben Bradley, and Norman Mailer. As Mailer arrives for the panel, Leacock films him as the two men hug—Leacock was cinematographer for Mailer's film *Maidstone* (1969). Mailer then introduces Leacock to his wife Norris Church Mailer. Excerpts of the panelists' talks are presented, including Mailer's joke about two buffalo in North Dakota, old and grey like the landscape, who are told by a cowboy that they are "a sorry mess"; one buffalo tells the other, "Well, uh, I guess we just heard our first discouraging words!" A church service in Memorial Church and a photo session on the steps of Widener Library are followed by the graduation ceremony in Harvard Yard.

Throughout the events, both Leacock and Lalonde are filming, allowing for multiple visual perspectives on various elements of the reunion and graduation ceremony. Leacock marches with the Class of '43, filming the Class of '93 soon-to-be-graduates lining the walkways—and the usual graduation ceremony follows: honorary degrees are awarded (to Ravi Shankar and Julia Child, among others); Colin Powell is the main speaker. The scene is visually punctuated by pink balloons with "LIFT THE BAN" printed on them (Powell had recently upheld the military's ban on gays). Powell begins his talk, and an abrupt cut to the Harvard Yard, now empty of people, but full of chairs and bird sounds, brings the video to a close.

As my description suggests, there is nothing particularly novel about *Hooray! We're Fifty!* What *is* revealed is something that may seem obvious in retrospect: that the annual rituals of college and university graduation and class reunions, held across the country every spring, are essentially the same everywhere. The Leacock–Lalonde video records many individuals, some of whom are identified and famous, and many of whom, presumably people of distinction, are not identified; nevertheless, the ritual they are part of and the way they play their parts within it, at least in all instances documented in the video, are precisely conventional—and except for the fact that we know this is a *Harvard* graduation-reunion, indistinguishable from any other.

From the time when he was a teenager, impressing Robert Flaherty himself, Leacock's gift was always a consummate charm that allowed him to be accepted by famous and accomplished people who trusted him to represent them in film (and for nearly twenty years to represent filmmaking itself within the nation's foremost institute of technology). He seems always to have understood that, insofar as they play their roles in societal rituals, the accomplished, the rich, the famous are, to rephrase F. Scott Fitzgerald's famous line, *not* all that different from the rest of us. It is this understanding that is communicated by *Hooray! We're Fifty!* When Colin Powell begins his address by promising not to talk much longer than the presumably elaborate introduction that has brought him to the dais (Leacock–Lalonde include nothing of the introduction), the audience responds enthusiastically—instigating a smile from Powell that evokes not Powell's political power or his accomplishments as a military man, but the inevitable embarrassment such a response would create for any speaker at any of the "absurd rituals" of graduation, anywhere in the country. For Leacock, the tendency of documentary, of virtually *all* professional filmmaking, to mythify is full of potential danger; not surprisingly perhaps, his final creative efforts were resolutely in service of de-mythification and a healthy humanization of his subjects and of filmmaking itself.

There is, of course, a paradox here. Leacock and Lalonde have become home movie makers in the sense that their movies are homemade and formally unpretentious and that they propose merely to create "a bridge to one's friends" and perhaps to "people you don't even know who might be interested in this evocation of what was experienced." Nevertheless, these are home movies made *by the legendary filmmaker Ricky Leacock*. Virtually the only reason *Hooray! We're Fifty!* is more interesting than whatever records were made of my fiftieth high school reunion in 2010—I found that reunion a bore and would have no interest in seeing visual records of it—is because of *Leacock's* involvement and because several other famous people appear. In a certain sense, in other words, despite its effective evocation of an "absurd" American social ritual, *Hooray! We're Fifty!* depends on a kind of star system to engage its audience; its "unpretentiousness" is dependent precisely on our recognition of the cultural significance of its makers and subjects.

In "The Art of Home Movies," Leacock quotes Flaherty as saying that "films would eventually be made by 'amateurs,'" meaning, "by people who loved the act of filming; who loved creating sequences that did justice to their subjects, that conveyed an exquisite sense of seeing and hearing, of being there." While *Hooray! We're Fifty!* conforms to this description in some ways, it would be an exaggeration to claim that it employs an "exquisite sense of seeing and hearing." By comparison, the "home movies" of Jonas Mekas (who visited MIT during Leacock's tenure there) *do* have artistic pretensions, but they earn our attention by their commitment to style; Mekas's *Walden* records a good many "important" people, mostly filmmakers who have made significant contributions to cinema; but Mekas doesn't depend solely on his knowing and filming these men and women, on his being part of an in-group, to interest us. *Walden* is a landmark because of Mekas's innovative—often "exquisite"—ways of revealing these people and his evocative but thoroughly unconventional approach to structure. Perhaps I am being unfair to Leacock and Lalonde; few of their personal films have become available as of this writing—*Hooray! We're Fifty* is an exception and may be uncharacteristic of their body of work; as the other films do make their way toward a wider audience, they will be subjects for further research.

THE SUBJECT REBELS: NINA DAVENPORT'S FILMS AND ED PINCUS AND LUCIA SMALL'S *THE AXE IN THE ATTIC*

As fully as any filmmaker to come out of the Harvard filmmaking program, Nina Davenport has taken the baton of personal documentary filmmaking from Ed Pincus, Robb Moss, and especially Ross McElwee. Her *Always a Bridesmaid* (2000) is an exploration of her personal relationships, reminiscent of Pincus's *Diaries* and McElwee's *Sherman's March;* and both *Always a Bridesmaid* and *Parallel Lines* (2004) have much in common with McElwee's *Six O'Clock News* (1996), which Davenport worked on and in which she appears. However, her *Operation Film-*

maker (2007) explores the relationship between documentary filmmaker and subject in manner unusual even within the history of personal documentary. Before she made any of these films, however, Davenport completed *Hello Photo* (1994), an impressive film quite distinct from her more recent work. In 1990 Davenport was awarded a Gardner Fellowship that allowed her to live and travel in India for a year. For about fifteen months between the fall of 1990 and the spring of 1992, she shot silent black-and-white and color footage with a 16mm Bolex and collected sound; and when she returned to Cambridge, worked (again, with the financial support of Robert Gardner) to create a faux-sync experience that reflected and reflected on her experiences as a young woman traveling alone across the subcontinent.

As she herself has said, the strongest influence on *Hello Photo* was neither Robb Moss, with whom she had studied film at Harvard before embarking on her Indian adventure, nor Robert Gardner, whose *Forest of Bliss* she did not see until after her return, but Peter Hutton, whose films she saw in Moss's class.[12] While Hutton's films, like those of some other filmmakers traditionally identified with the American and continental avant-garde—Stan Brakhage, for example, and Peter Kubelka—have increasingly been understood as a contribution to documentary as well as to avant-garde film history, at the time when Davenport saw Hutton's work, it was understood as part of a fundamentally different tradition. Hutton's films were still consistently black and white,[13] and they were then, as they have remained, silent and meditatively paced. Further, Hutton's approach has always reflected his lifelong interest in still photography: it is typical in his films for an image to seem to be a still photograph, then, gradually, to reveal that it is, in fact, a motion picture. Davenport's decision to work in a mode she understood as related to Hutton's was, in a sense, a vestige of the interest in photography that had engaged her during her early years at Harvard; nevertheless, *Hello Photo* cannot be confused with Hutton's work.

The first sequence in *Hello Photo* was shot on the site of the Indian commercial film industry in Mumbai; it focuses on men carrying large, brilliantly colored images of film stars. The sequence creates something like an optical illusion; because the reproductions of the stars are more visually engaging than the street-level reality they are being carried through, they almost seem to be moving on their own. Davenport's immediate nod to the Indian film industry and implicitly to its drawing power in India is followed by the first of many brief sequences, shot in black and white, of people, in this case children, looking into Davenport's camera, crowding into the frame, as we hear voices of both children and adults saying, "Hello," "Photo," "Do you have permission?," "What are you doing?" These opening sequences reveal the power of two distinct modes of cinema: the visual and psychological power of popular cinema and the icons it creates, on one hand; and the more intimate drawing power of a simple motion picture camera filming at street level, on the other. It seems clear that Davenport recognizes the fundamental connection between industrially produced popular cinema and the forms of cinema that provide alternatives to it: without a film industry the cinematic apparatus that makes a range of cinematic approaches possible would never have existed. This introductory diptych is followed immediately by a shot of Davenport filming, seen in a mirror on the outside of a building. The simplicity of her equipment, in contrast to the Mumbai industry's, is obvious.

Following the title credit, *Hello Photo* develops a form of non-narrative organization that is relatively consistent throughout the remainder of the film. Mostly color sequences continue to document the film industry in Mumbai. Each of the other, always black-and-white sequences focuses on a particular dimension of Indian life: the presence of water buffalo and cows on city streets; men and women doing basic labor with rudimentary tools (crushing rock with a sledge hammer, carrying soil and stones); individuals involved with Hindu religious observances; polo (young men in training, polo horses being attended to, a polo match); a jute factory where burlap bags are made (this is a remarkable and beautiful—and Hutton-esque—evocation of large scale, assembly line, industrial production); a man and woman making preparations for a wedding and getting married; the erotic sculptures at Khajuraho; a circus (performers and performances: elephants, trapeze artists, contortionists); a mosque that serves as a retreat for women and men inhabited by spirits; country scenes; a school for the blind; evening prayers at a mosque; and a kite festival. Each of these sequences is accompanied by sounds that seem appropriate, most of them recorded in the same or similar locations. Altogether, *Hello Photo* provides something between a panorama and a phantasmagoria of India as witnessed at street level by an outsider.

Davenport's explorations of particular dimensions of Indian life are separated by the comparatively brief street scenes that dramatize the reactions of Indian men, women, and children to her filming in their midst. These scenes function both as transitions and as a consistent reminder of a crucial dimension of Davenport's commitment as a filmmaker. She never seems to have been interested in the idea of cinematic detachment but has always been fascinated with the interplay between filmmaking and those who are filmed—and though in *Hello Photo* this fascination takes a different form from what we see in her later, more overtly autobiographical work, it also creates an entirely different experience from Peter Hutton's films.[14]

Davenport's street scenes continually demonstrate the paradox of her experience filming in India: the presence of a lone young woman with a motion picture camera continually draws the excited attention of children and the more wary attention of men and women. At the same time, however, both the friendly stares of the children and the sometimes seemingly hostile stares of many of the adults demonstrate the gap between this visitor and the world she witnesses, a gap confirmed by the fact that, while *Hello Photo* includes many voices, there is no sync-sound communication between Davenport and the Indians who are drawn toward her camera or who cannot avoid it. And in at least one instance, during Davenport's visit to the mosque where she films people inhabited by spirits, a woman, apparently furious with the presence of Davenport and the camera, makes her hostility quite clear. All in all, *Hello Photo* is a form of personal filmmaking distinct from both its avant-garde inspiration and from the autobiographical filmmaking world that nurtured her in Cambridge.

When Davenport returned to filmmaking at the end of the 1990s, she did so in the hope that an openly autobiographical form of sync-sound filmmaking might find its way to a more extensive audience than had been possible for *Hello Photo*, to an audience substantial enough to help Davenport make a living with her film-making—the success of McElwee's autobiographical films in the 1990s suggested that such a hope was not entirely unfounded. Indeed, *Always a Bridesmaid* (2000) seems to have been conceived as a female version of *Sherman's March* (1986), and it exploits many of the cinematic strategies McElwee developed for that film. In *Always a Bridesmaid* Davenport is both filmmaker and a character like the McEl-wee character in *Sherman's March*, someone struggling with her relationships to the opposite sex. Davenport explains that she makes her living as a wedding pho-tographer and videographer and uses this as the central irony of the film: she, who attends and records wedding after wedding, cannot achieve marriage herself. She also films her personal conversations with boyfriend, Nick, about their relation-ship, as well as conversations about love and marriage with her parents, her friends, clients and prospective clients, and several elderly women who never married. Near the conclusion of *Always a Bridesmaid*, Davenport also uses a strategy from McElwee's *Six O'Clock News* (1996): frustrated about her inability to find a com-mitted relationship, she sees a newspaper story about a couple in their nineties who have just married, the woman for the first time, and flies to California to visit the newlyweds.

Formally, Davenport's methods also echo McElwee's. She sometimes creates comic moments by filming people during normally private situations and she physically engages people while festooned with her equipment. Those she inter-views look offscreen to our left at Davenport, while we see them and hear her from a position to the right—implicitly reflecting the schizoid quality of Davenport as character and as filmmaker. And she uses narration in some of the ways character-istic of McElwee: for example, while talking with Nick early in the film, she pro-vides a voice-over that expresses her frustration and embarrassment with what she is saying to Nick and what it reveals about her. Just as McElwee's visits to the sites of General Sherman's march through the South provide an alternative narrative to the McElwee's character's "march" through the South in search of love, Davenport's visits to elderly women and her inclusion of photographic imagery from their lives as children, adolescents, young women, mature adults, provides a kind of alternative history to Davenport's own struggles. And perhaps most fundamentally, Davenport reconfirms the distinction in *Sherman's March* between the McElwee character's foibles and McElwee's achievement as filmmaker: Davenport's considerable skill as a cinematographer and her deft editing continually remind us that whatever her failures at relationship (she seems no closer to what she wants at the end of the film than at the beginning), she has been able to transform these failures into a capably made feature film.

While *Always a Bridesmaid* is not as successful as *Sherman's March*—Davenport lacks McElwee's wry, complex wit—both films now seem a bit frivolous, both filmmaker-protagonists embarrassingly self-involved (Davenport is at times annoyingly self-pitying as a character and a bit cloying as narrator). McElwee and Davenport seem to have sensed this problem: McElwee followed *Sherman's March* with the more serious and powerful *Time Indefinite*; and Davenport followed *Always a Bridesmaid* with *Parallel Lines*, her tribute to September 11, 2001. Indeed, just as *Always a Bridesmaid* echoes *Sherman's March*, *Parallel Lines* echoes *Time Indefinite*, especially in its central theme: both McElwee and Davenport use the process of filmmaking in an (ultimately successful) attempt to recover from loss.

On 9/11, Davenport, whose apartment was (and is) in lower Manhattan within sight of the World Trade Center, was freelancing in San Diego. Two months later, her freelance work finished, she was afraid to fly and nervous about returning to New York City. She decided to direct her anxiety into a filmmaking project of her own: she would rent a car and take a six-week road trip across the country, talk with those she met on the trip about their reactions to 9/11, and arrive in New York in time for the New Year's Eve celebration in Times Square. Of course, the cross-country road trip is one of the clichés of American culture and American cinema in particular—though journeying west toward open spaces, freedom from convention, and a new life has been far more common than journeying east.

Traveling east has often been understood as a way of responding to the disappearance of the frontier and of American dreams of finding and/or creating a new Eden. Within modern popular cinema, *Easy Rider* (1969) is probably the most famous cinematic road trip east, and of course it ends in disaster for Wyatt Earp (a.k.a. Captain America) and Billy the Kid. Within the annals of American independent cinema, James Benning's *North on Evers* (1991) may be the most interesting road movie; it too begins with the journey east—like the protagonists of *Easy Rider*, and implicitly in reference to them, Benning travels by motorcycle, beginning in Val Verde, California (his home near the California Institute of the Arts where he teaches filmmaking), and journeying eastward through New Mexico and Texas and into the deep South (the "Evers" in *North on Evers* refers to Medgar Evars), then up to Washington, D.C., and to New York City (Benning's journey continues north and west through New York State, then across the Midwest to

FIGURE 39. Sign on the road somewhere in New Mexico in Nina Davenport's *Parallel Lines* (2004). Courtesy Nina Davenport.

Chicago and westward through Michigan and South Dakota, ultimately back to Val Verde by way of Utah and Nevada).[15] Both *Easy Rider* and *North on Evers* were filmmakers' attempts to consider and come to terms with the current state of America, the same goal Davenport had in making *Parallel Lines* (fig. 39).

Davenport's trip east, like Wyatt and Billy's, is punctuated by encounters with a wide variety of men and women, though in *Parallel Lines* these encounters are never with actors playing locals, but entirely with locals.[16] In this, *Parallel Lines* is most similar to Ellen Spiro's *Roam Sweet Home* (1996), in which Spiro travels the American Southwest visiting elderly Americans living largely away from standard tourist locations and outside of the conventions of American old age, to document a new kind of "Old West." Like Spiro, Davenport alternates regularly between candid conversations with locals and voice-over narration.[17] However, Davenport seems more willing than Spiro to entrust her safety to strangers, particularly men (*Roam Sweet Home* is primarily about older women), even in isolated circumstances. It is as if the shock of 9/11 has freed her, at least for a time, from what would otherwise be perfectly understandable fears—though, of course, Davenport's willingness to work alone in uncomfortable circumstances was already evident in *Hello Photo*.

Within American road movies certain locations seem inevitable: like *Easy Rider* and *North on Evers*, *Parallel Lines* includes a visit to Monument Valley, that portion of Navajo country that John Ford made synonymous with the American West; to New Mexican sites involved in the Manhattan Project (in *North on Evers*, the site of the Trinity atomic tests; in *Parallel Lines,* a museum at Los Alamos that documents the development and use of the atomic bomb); and a visit to the rural Deep South, emblematic of the ongoing American struggle with racism.[18] All in all, however, *Parallel Lines* includes a greater range of human encounters than *Easy Rider* or *North on Evers,* even than *Roam Sweet Home.*

Early in Davenport's trip east, it becomes clear that for some of those she meets, what has happened to New York City is of no concern. Indeed, the first two men Davenport talks with on the road—at the Baghdad Café on Route 66—provide somewhat surprising responses to her questions. When she tells a young trucker that her destination is New York City, he responds, "Why would you want to go there?"—not because of the attacks but because he and New Yorkers "don't get along"; he claims not to have even heard about 9/11 until four days after the attacks, though his motivation for saying this seems to reflect his desire to defy what he sees as Davenport's interest in hearing how important the attacks on New York were for non–New Yorkers. A second man, who identifies himself as General Bob, is more overtly hostile to Davenport; after making fun of her questions, he ends the conversation with "You don't listen; you hear what you *want* to hear"—a charge he has no basis for—and an angry "That's it!"

Many of those with whom Davenport speaks do admit that 9/11 was important for them, but in a good many instances Davenport's questions (and perhaps the presence of Davenport and her camera) trigger stories of personal loss. Indeed, while *Roam Sweet Home* is an encomium to the pleasures of old age, much of *Parallel Lines* is a dirge to broken dreams and painful memories. By the time Davenport reaches Shanksville, Pennsylvania, the site of the crash of Flight 93, she has experienced a good many pleasant surprises—in some instances, gentle thoughtfulness in instances when one might have predicted hostility—but the portrait of America that has emerged is hardly uplifting. Just after she leaves Chikasaw, Alabama, after speaking with two racist farmers, she admits that she's "afraid we'll never be united," and her depression is confirmed by a black-and-white sequence during which she sees the ubiquitous road kill as a reminder of the continual loss she's witnessed during her trip.

On the road to Washington, D.C., Davenport admits that "just hearing other people tell their stories has helped give me the courage to go home," and, after visiting the Pentagon and being pulled over by police as a suspected terrorist while filming near the Capitol Building, she makes the drive to New York City. Like *Time Indefinite, Parallel Lines* ends with a pleasant surprise: on reentry Davenport finds New York changed but not in the way she has expected; the doorman in her apartment building happily explains that the attacks brought people "*so* close": "I never knew people could have been *so* loving here!" While the America Davenport sees during her travels seems a place of mostly sad, isolated souls, New York City seems upbeat, welcoming, and empathetic.

The conclusion of *Parallel Lines* begins with Davenport's reentry into her apartment on New Year's Eve and a mirror shot of the filmmaker and her gear. We have seen her in the car, driving and sometimes eating; and of course, indirectly we have felt her presence all through the film. But this shot of herself as filmmaker suggests that, whatever repressions of her own ideas have been necessary during her six-week cross-country trip in order to accurately record the feelings of others, home is the place where she entirely accepts herself, and is accepted, *as a filmmaker*. Davenport walks to her window and faces the view of lower Manhattan that once included the World Trade Center (she dissolves to the view before the attacks and back to the present); then takes the subway to Times Square (a jubilant group of men are singing in the subway car), where she attends the celebration at midnight.[19]

Operation Filmmaker, which did not begin as a personal documentary, ended by expanding on Davenport's interest in the interplay between filmmaker and subject, and in particular, between a resistant subject and the filmmaker. While this interest is intermittently evident in the earlier films, in *Operation Filmmaker* the growing distrust and hostility between Davenport and a young Iraqi, Muthana Mohmed, becomes the focus of the film.[20] Originally, Davenport was hired as a freelancer to work with Kouross Esmaeli on a piece recording the experiences of Mohmed, who had been invited to the set of the production of *Everything Is Illuminated* (2005) by producer Peter Saraf and director Liev Schreiber. Saraf and Schreiber had been moved by a story on MTV about the destruction of a Baghdad film school that featured an interview with Mohmed during which he claimed that his dream was to become a filmmaker. They decided to offer the young man a chance to realize his dream by working on their film.

Davenport presents the decision of Schreiber and Saraf to help Mohmed and its aftermath as a metaphor for the war in Iraq. Mohmed's arrival in Prague, where he is met by Schreiber and Saraf, is exuberant, in the way the American military's lightning drive to Baghdad and the toppling of Hussein seemed (early in the film Mohmed claims to love George W. Bush for changing his life). Soon, however, friction develops between Mohmed and the producer, director, and support staff of *Everything Is Illuminated* as he fails to complete the (often menial) jobs he is assigned, including, most important, the editing of the "gag reel" for the wrap party. Mohmed's increasing resistance to doing the jobs he is asked to do, along with his consistent need for financial and emotional assistance, becomes a metaphor for what gradually became the Iraq insurgency and the ongoing American struggle to rebuild the Iraqi infrastructure.

Davenport's use of the interaction of the Americans making *Everything Is Illuminated* and Mohmed as a metaphor goes further than these general parallels, however: as *Operation Filmmaker* develops, Davenport increasingly questions not just what was done and its results but the complexities of the motivations of those involved, including her own. The ostensible purpose of the American invasion of Iraq was to find and defuse the mythical "weapons of mass destruction" and, later, to help free the people of Iraq by defeating Saddam Hussein and creating a democracy—though it was widely recognized that essentially the war was about American access to oil, as well as the security of Israel, America's primary ally in the Middle East. It becomes clear early in *Operation Filmmaker* that however self-less the original motivation to help Mohmed may have felt, more was involved than an altruistic urge. Schreiber and Saraf may hope that reaching out to the young Arab will exemplify their concern for human decency and their wish that Jews and Arabs might work together, but they don't simply want to help Mohmed; they want to document themselves helping him—that's why Davenport is in the Czech Republic filming the events. As Mohmed fails to live up to their expectations, Saraf and Schreiber become increasingly frustrated and, when the *Everything Is Illuminated* shoot is over, leave without him.

Of course, as *Operation Filmmaker* makes clear, this same combination of a naïve desire to help someone and implicit self-interest motivates Davenport's decision to continue filming Mohmed. During the sequences focused on the *Everything Is Illuminated* shoot, Davenport is Mohmed's confidant, but the longer she is with him, the more troubled their relationship becomes (fig. 40). The first indication of what becomes a rift occurs during a river trip on the Danube in Prague, when Davenport asks Mohmed to talk about his life in Iraq during the war. Mohmed says that she is ruining a beautiful day by asking him to talk about things he doesn't want to remember, then complains, "You just want the stories. That's it. That's it. You just want an interesting story to watch on the television. . . ." Davenport's sudden cut to news of the insurgents mounting a major attack in Iraq confirms her recognition that her original assumptions about the film she's shooting are being altered by Mohmed's resistance.

After the wrap party for *Everything Is Illuminated,* Mohmed films Davenport and Esmaeli, sitting on a couch, and asks them for help, promising that "I'm gonna change myself." The following text (*Operation Filmmaker* uses no voice-over, but white-on-black intertitles regularly provide contextualizing information) indicates that two months have passed, that Esmaeli has quit working with Davenport on her film (presumably in frustration),[21] and that Mohmed has been taken on as a gopher on a Czech Republic shoot for Andrzej Bartkowiak's *Doom* (2005, with Dwayne Johnson, "the Rock"). The implication is that no real change in Mohmed's way of dealing with his "benefactors" has occurred.

Davenport creates a startling transition from news coverage of a suicide attack in Baghdad to the set of *Doom*, where actors, covered with fake blood and entrails, are performing for Bartkowiak's zombie film—a metaphor, presumably, for the increasing difficulty Davenport is having figuring out what is "real" about Mohmed and what is not, and what the nature of her relationship with him is and should be. It is clear that Davenport continues to be equally surprised by what she sees as

FIGURE 40. Nina Davenport and Muthana Mohmed during the shooting of Nina Davenport's *Operation Filmmaker* (2007). Courtesy Nina Davenport.

Mohmed's deviousness and unwillingness to work and by the way in which others seem to take Mohmed at face value and buy into the idea that they can and should help him—though she herself continues to provide Mohmed with money and assistance in dealing with immigration authorities. During the time between Mohmed's request to Dwayne Johnson for tuition for the London Film Academy and Johnson's response (like Saraf and Schreiber, Johnson is careful to see that the announcement of his generosity is recorded, and in the best lighting), Mohmed for the first time refuses to allow Davenport to film him, claiming that her presence is impeding his efforts to get help. He also makes clear that if he cannot get an extension on his visa and is forced to go to a refugee camp, he will not allow filming there; and further, that since Davenport is not helping him get to the United States, he is quitting her documentary. He returns her microphone and walks away.

Davenport returns to New York, and as she indicates in an intertitle, "Despite serious reservations, I decide to proceed with the visa application," though when she returns to Prague, she finds Mohmed angry at her: "Why do you assume I'm depending on you?," and later, "Do you think you make me a favor? I make *you* a favor: I'm giving you my life!" The irony here, of course, as Davenport is well aware, is that she is as dependent on Mohmed as he is on her: his explicit demands are mirrored by her implicit demand that he continue to be the protagonist of her film.

After Johnson provides Mohmed with tuition to the London Film Academy, Davenport follows him there, gives him money again, and in exchange is allowed to film him at the school and at home. Finally, Mohmed announces on-camera, "Ladies and gentlemen, I'm happy to tell you that I'm quitting this documentary," and tells Davenport, "You don't give a shit about Iraqis, about Iraq; you just want to make your documentary and show how good you are as an American and how bad we are as Iraqis." He demands $10.000 for the next three months of shooting, "because you do know you're going to make lots of fuckin' money from this fuckin' documentary." At his apartment, Davenport wrestles with Mohmed in order to retrieve a tape he has taken out of her camera—though she is not able to get it back.

It is unusual for a filmmaker to be as open as Davenport about the ethical complexities of the work she does. Her use of the Iraq war as a metaphor for her experiences with Mohmed makes clear that she understands that her motivations are as problematic as the American motivations were in invading Iraq. Even though she often feels powerless over Mohmed, it is obvious that hers is the more powerful position: she has resources that he doesn't. In fact, basically Mohmed is right that Davenport will make "lots of fuckin' money from this fuckin' documentary"—not "lots of money" in the Hollywood sense, of course, but enough to keep Davenport's career as an independent filmmaker afloat. Her original motivation for accepting the freelance job of documenting Mohmed's involvement with *Everything Is Illuminated* was economic, as was her decision to continue to film Mohmed once that freelance work was completed. Like Saraf and Schreiber and Johnson, every time Davenport "helps" Mohmed, she is helping herself.

Davenport tries to revive her project by helping Mohmed get accepted to the New York School of Film and Television, but though he does get accepted, he cannot pay the tuition and decides to stay in London, where he is now being supported by the London Film Academy. Mohmed agrees to allow Davenport to film one more time. For her, this meeting provides an adequate conclusion to her film and for Mohmed, an opportunity to justify himself (of course, he knows she will have final control over how he comes across in her film). He describes a film he plans to make

> about the royal family dog, who is escaping from the palace and going down to the city to play in the park, play with the children, going to the cash machine, taking a lot of money, dressing up, smoking weed, going to McDonald's, going to the nightclub, chased by women, another female dog, dancing over the tables, getting drunk, but at the end of the film he just stopped in one situation or in one position. He was just passing a shop with a big screen in television store or television screen and he was watching a BBC report about the suicide bombs, and that's how the palace find him again.

A news report about Iraq sliding into chaos follows this description, leading to one final interchange between filmmaker and subject. Mohmed tells Davenport that he

FIGURE 41. Muthana Mohmed in Nina Davenport's *Operation Filmmaker* (2007). Courtesy Nina Davenport.

"will make it" in the film world: "Do you know why?" "Why?" she asks. "Because I'm real."

The ironies during this final meeting are complex. The narrative of Mohmed's proposed film reflects his tendency to indulge in fantasy—though its obviously autobiographical qualities, its implicit expression of a young person's desire to enjoy youth and to postpone commitment to a profession, make it poignant, especially given Mohmed's experiences in and away from Iraq. And Mohmed's assertion that he "is real" is both an obvious irony (his "being real," insofar as we see it in *Operation Filmmaker,* is largely a form of manipulation) *and,* as Davenport must admit (she has made a film about Mohmed!) he *is* real, a real person interesting enough to have sustained her documentary (fig. 41).

Davenport concludes with a text: "I had hoped for a happy ending. . . . Now I'm just looking for an exit strategy." Again the ironies are complex: if Davenport didn't get the happy ending she may have naïvely imagined early on, her final conversations with Mohmed do provide her with a fitting and effective conclusion, an ending simultaneously less happy and more interesting than a simple success story might have been. Her including the final news story about Iraq seeming to be sliding toward civil war suggests, on one level, the way that a simplistic sense of the filmmaker's identity and of filmmaking ethics has been sliding toward chaos within this film; and on the other, the way that media (both news and independent documentary) tend to thrive on violence and disasters of all kinds. As Robb Moss says in *The Tourist,* "It *is* often the case that the worse things get for the people you are filming, the better that is for the film you are making."

In addition to *Operation Filmmaker,* 2007 also saw the release of *The Axe in the Attic* by Ed Pincus and Lucia Small—Pincus's first completed film in twenty-seven years; and Small's first since her personal documentary about her father, *My Father the Genius* (2002). *The Axe in the Attic* is the filmmakers' attempt to use the film-making process to deal with their outrage about how the Hurricane Katrina disaster was handled and to document its impact on New Orleans and those who survived the storm and the flood. The first half-hour of the film bears comparison to Davenport's *Parallel Lines:* Pincus and Small document their cross-country trip from Vermont (where Pincus lives) to New Orleans, via Pittsburgh; Cincinnati; Murray, Kentucky; Joe Wheeler State Park in Alabama; and Waveland, Mississippi—the film shifts between voice-overs by the filmmakers (Pincus and Small alternate) and inter-views with displaced New Orleanians. And like *Operation Filmmaker, The Axe in the Attic* foregrounds the personal complexities and the ethical issues raised when film-makers, motivated both by a desire to do something positive *and* to produce a film that serves their own needs, inject themselves into the personal crises of others.

The Axe in the Attic is an engaging and moving record of the aftermath of the Katrina disaster. The film recycles the still-startling news footage of the disaster itself and offers its own powerful imagery of the damage caused by the storm and flood; and the filmmakers' interviews with survivors reveal the frustrations, the resilience, and the psychic fragility of those working to cope with losing every-thing. What seems most relevant about *The Axe in the Attic* in this context, how-ever, is the way in which the filmmakers' experiences of meeting and talking with the survivors destabilize their working relationship. It is clear early in the film that Pincus and Small have somewhat different attitudes about their work: Small, in voice-over, describes her "nagging feeling . . . that I'm not doing enough for the people we film. . . . Ed . . . jokes that for him the camera lens observes; for me it absorbs. It's not that he's unsympathetic, but as filmmaker he thinks it's enough to witness and document." Later, when Joseph Griffin, whose family is living in Renaissance Village, a large FEMA trailer park, asks Small for money for a bus pass so he won't need to walk more than two hours each way to get to his night-shift job, Small refuses, acceding to Pincus's belief that giving money to the subjects of a documentary is unethical. Soon after this, when Pincus himself is moved to give $10 to Reverend Charles Jackson, who, like Griffin, has been deeply shaken by the disaster and is miserable living in what appears to be a dangerous situation, Small walks off, embarrassed and confused, and confesses, "I feel so fake now."

Once in New Orleans, the filmmakers make their way through the Lower Ninth Ward, interviewing people faced with what seems the superhuman task of reviving destroyed neighborhoods. While visiting with Ruth and Milton Creecy, who are assessing the damage on their home, they record the arrival of several volunteers, one of whom (Carlton Brown) says, "It would be nice if you would ask us if you could take our picture," and, after telling the Creecys that he and a group of volunteers will return the next day to help them clean up their home, Brown proceeds to vent his frustration with the filmmakers' unethical behavior in filming victims of a trauma. He questions Small about why the release form for *The Axe in the Attic* says nothing about paying anything to the Creecys for their trouble. Both filmmakers are disconcerted, and Small is particularly upset by Brown's apparent contempt.[22]

Obviously, the frustrations and embarrassments experienced by Pincus and Small are nothing compared with the loss and trauma the Gulf Coast residents are dealing with, and, as they edited *The Axe in the Attic* the filmmakers could not have ignored the fact that by seeming to turn the disaster into *their* story they would be accused of exploiting the powerless and minimizing the realities of the disaster and its aftermath. However, as in *Operation Filmmaker*, it is precisely their openly sharing the ways in which making this film affects their professional relationship, their professional ethics, and the filming itself—that is, their *not* suppressing the ways in which this filmmaking process personally affects *them*—that makes the film interesting. Like *Operation Filmmaker*, *The Axe in the Attic* may have been conceived as a detached witnessing of events, but like Davenport's film, Pincus and Small's evolved into a personal film, one that witnesses the human impact of Katrina on the survivors *and* the human impact of the survivors on the filmmakers who documented them.

THE POLITICAL IS THE PERSONAL: JOHN GIANVITO'S *PROFIT MOTIVE AND THE WHISPERING WIND* AND JEFF DANIEL SILVA'S *BALKAN RHAPSODIES*

Having earned a B.F.A. at California Institute of the Arts, John Gianvito came to Boston in 1979 to study at the MIT Film Section. As he remembers, "Louis Massiah and I were the only new grad students that year and when I suddenly realized that they only focused on documentary, and Ricky Leacock found out I hadn't come to do cinema verite, the response was, 'Well, that's odd. What do we do? I suppose if you want to stick around and be our experiment with a fiction filmmaker you're welcome to.'"[23] Upon graduating, Gianvito was offered the opportunity to teach with Leacock, "for which I remain ever grateful,"[24] and in 1982 he completed *The Communicant*, a video portrait of Leacock discussing the making of his film, *Community of Praise* (1981). Gianvito has continued to live and work in the Boston area. He was a guest curator at the Harvard Film Archive from 1996 to 1998 and teaches filmmaking at Emerson College.

Thirty years later, it seems clear that it was not only Gianvito's interest in fiction filmmaking that seemed a strange fit at MIT, but his commitment to filmmaking in which the open expression of his own political views is accepted as part of both process and product. Gianvito's feature *The Mad Songs of Fernanda Hussein* (2001), for example, is reminiscent of Haskell Wexler's *Medium Cool* (1969) and the work of Peter Watkins in its mixture of dramatization and document. Gianvito dramatizes a story about a New Mexican Chicana mother whose children are murdered because of their Arab names, using non-actors within the real landscape where the story unfolds.[25] *Mad Songs* interweaves scripted scenes with documentations of local events to suggest the ways in which the Gulf War affected American communities.

In 2007 Gianvito completed *Profit Motive and the Whispering Wind*, an engaging and deeply personal homage to the history of the struggle by American men and women for social justice. From 2004 until 2007, using Howard Zinn's *A People's History of the United States* (New York: Harper and Row, 1980) as inspiration, Gianvito visited the gravesites of more than a hundred individuals who dedicated their lives to abolishing slavery and overcoming racism, to the struggle for better working conditions for laborers and the right to unionize, and to a more peaceful, more equitable, more ecologically conscious world. Gianvito filmed at these sites, documenting gravestones and historical markers and the environments around them, and then organized the results into a historical progression based on the date when the individuals died, beginning with Anne Marbury Hutchinson, a "courageous exponent of civil liberty and religious toleration" who was "Killed by the Indians at East Chester New York 1643," as her gravestone says; and Mary Dyer, a "Witness for religious freedom" who was "Hanged on Boston Common 1660"; and concluding with the death of Philip Frances Berrigan in 2002.

Profit Motive opens with a prelude: first, a quotation from Claire Spark Loeb ("The long memory is the most radical idea in America"); then, a transcription of an 1894 recording of "Kiowa Ghost Dance No. 12," which is heard on the soundtrack: Gianvito presents the text of the original language in conjunction with the chanting, followed by a translation that reveals that this is a chant-dance to welcome travelers "coming on the march" by offering them berries.[26] The recording and translation is followed by a sequence of berry bushes near the ocean, filmed as if we are Native Americans looking out for arriving ships. This evocation of what would become the continual western march of the European settlers and the near-destruction of Native American peoples and cultures leads immediately into the two forms of "march" recorded during the body of *Profit Motive*: Gianvito's travels across the nation in search of significant gravesites (his travels tend to echo the settlers', of course, since the westward expansion of the nation brought with it both a series of injustices and those who fought against them); and the montage of marches by those demonstrating against injustice in contemporary America that serves as the film's finale.

FIGURE 42. Close-up of Haymarket Martyrs' Monument in Forest Home Cemetery, Chicago, a National Historic Landmark, in John Gianvito's *Profit Motive and the Whispering Wind* (2007). Courtesy John Gianvito.

While we never see or hear Gianvito in *Profit Motive and the Whispering Wind,* the film is personal in the sense that the films of James Benning are personal; indeed, Gianvito's video (the imagery was shot on film, but *Profit Motive* was completed on video) is often reminiscent of such Benning films as *North on Evers* (1991), *Four Corners* (1997), and especially *Deseret* (1995), in the kinds of imagery Gianvito includes and in the film's formal organization, as well as in its politics. Just as Benning surveys the history of the state of Utah in *Deseret,* Gianvito provides a historical panorama of a particular dimension of American history. And as is true in the Benning films, where it is always evident that the filmic journeys are of personal import to Benning, in *Profit Motive* it is obvious that Gianvito's travels to the gravesites are personal pilgrimages, ritual demonstrations of his own political commitments. This is clear both in the nature of the imagery itself and in Gianvito's cinematic approaches to the sites, which often recreate—in his editing, and sometimes in his use of handheld camera—what must have been his original, sometimes halting exploration of cemeteries and other sites to locate the relevant gravestones and historical markers (fig. 42).

Filmmakers who make work that is openly political run the risk of having their films underestimated, as if forthright admission of a political commitment negates the possibility of subtlety or beauty; but *Profit Motive and the Whispering Wind* is more meditation than polemic and is full of deft touches and arresting, often beautiful imagery. For example, early on, Gianvito commemorates Metacomet (King Philip), whose resistance to abuse and treachery at the hands of the English settlers in Massachusetts resulted in King Philip's War. Gianvito films the marker at the spot where Metacomet's head was impaled on a pike for more than twenty years, now next to a sign advertising the Girl Scouts ("Girl Scouts Join Now!")—in this context, the idea of "scouts" seems ironic, and the sign, oblivious. Also, it is a Sunday and a worship service is in progress, presumably in the church in the background— Gianvito's reminder of the early settlers' use of religion as a justification for betraying and brutalizing Native American communities. Later in the video, the inscription on the gravestone of labor organizer Frank Little is difficult to read, until the sun comes out from behind a cloud for several seconds—a metaphor for the illumination that the lives of so many of the women and men memorialized in *Profit Motive* provided during dark times. The order of the various sequences often suggests the cultural diversity and class differences of those who stood up to injustice and of the kinds of respect they seem to have received after their deaths. The monumental memorial to Elizabeth Cady Stanton in Bronx's Woodlawn Cemetery, for example, is followed by the much humbler gravestone of fellow women's suffrage leader, Susan B. Anthony.

While *Profit Motive and the Whispering Wind* focuses viewers on a series of honorific and informative texts, some of which we struggle to read (one is reminded of Hollis Frampton's remark, "Once we can read, and a word is put before us, we cannot not read it"),[27] these texts are contextualized by street-level documentations of many rural and urban spaces, as well as much striking imagery of landscapes from east to west. The considerable range of locations represented in the video makes clear that those who have fought for social justice and social progress have been nurtured by all kinds of environments, but the many differences among Gianvito's honorees are united—as his title suggests—by the wind that blows across all the sites included in the film. This "whispering wind" has many implications. It recalls British Romantic poetry, where wind was often understood as the creative spirit. It also represents "the winds of change": the fundamental contention of *Profit Motive* is that in the long run these women and men played a significant role in making American life more humane, that these are men and women whose ideas have become widely accepted, and in some cases, are now understood as what America stands for, or should stand for (the gravesites are full of American flags). Of course, the wind that rustles leaves and shakes branches throughout *Profit Motive* is meant to "whisper" to viewers, to rustle our consciences and draw us into a stronger connection to the history represented by the men and women whose lives Gianvito celebrates.

Profit Motive is also a documentation of the personal on a more fundamental, more subtle cinematic level. Earlier, I suggested that Gianvito's film has much in common structurally with James Benning's *Deseret*, but the formal similarities between Benning's film and Gianvito's video can also be seen as a ground against which particular differences can be figured. *Deseret* uses the spoken texts from a series of *New York Times* stories about what became the state of Utah—one story per year from 1852 (the year when the *Times* was founded) until 1992—as a soundtrack. The implicit history charted by these stories is accompanied by sequences of imagery that document the current geography of Utah. These sequences relate literally and formally to the stories read in voice-over: each shot in each sequence lasts as long as the corresponding sentence in the accompanying *New York Times* story, and one shot in each sequence was filmed at the site described in the news item.[28]

At first glance, Gianvito's structuring of *Profit Motive* may seem not only similar but comparably rigorous: like Benning, Gianvito follows a timeline through American history; as in *Deseret,* recycled texts comment on the visual imagery; and the texts have both obvious and subtle relationships to the imagery and sound.[29] Gianvito's deviations from this otherwise rigorous structure are therefore all the more suggestive.

The first deviation occurs soon after the prelude, in an item about "The Great Swamp Fight," a crucial battle in King Philip's War: a close-up of a Rhode Island historical road sign indicates that "three-quarters of a mile to the southward on an island in the Great Swamp, the Narragansett Indians were decisively defeated by the United States Forces of the Massachusetts Bay, Connecticut, and Plymouth Colonies. Sunday, December 19, 1675." Eleven seconds into this 17-second shot "massacred," printed by hand on what looks like cardboard, replaces "defeated" on the sign, providing a tiny, homemade intervention into the approved history represented by the historical marker.

The formal rigor of the film is broken again in the 1882 item. Every other informational text to this point in *Profit Motive* is read on signs and gravestones seen within their visual and auditory environment, but here, Gianvito provides information about Uriah Smith Stephens, who cofounded the Knights of Labor, "the first national labor union in the United States," as a white-on-black silent intertitle. Stephens's remains are unmarked (there is no environmental text about Stephens to film), which in one sense accounts for this interruption in the overall structure; nevertheless Gianvito's decision to include Stephens required a textual intervention.

The 1915 item, dedicated to Joe Hill, contains no visual text at all; over a shot of an open grave, Paul Robeson is heard singing "Joe Hill." Again, this is an appropriate choice—Hill was a songwriter as well as a labor organizer—but it required an obvious change in strategy in the form of the extradiagetic music performed by Robeson (the open grave relates to the lyrics: "'I never died,' said he; 'I never died,' said he").[30] Much the same is true for the 1927 Sacco and Vanzetti item: extradiagetic music accompanies Gianvito's pan over the death record for Vanzetti and the following shot of the container housing the ashes of Sacco and Vanzetti.

The most radical break from the otherwise highly formal structure of *Profit Motive and the Whispering Wind,* however, takes the form of five brief black-and-white rotoscoped animations of scenes recycled from other films, located at irregular intervals during the video. The first (an 8-second image of arms panning for gold, recycled from *The Treasure of the Sierra Madre* [1948]), occurs just before the Stono Rebellion item; the second (a 4-second image of arms panning for gold, also from *The Treasure of the Sierra Madre*), just before the 1854 entry on Thomas Wilson Dorr; the third (a 7-second animation of arms gesticulating, perhaps in a commodity market), before the 1893 entry about women's rights activist Lucy Stone; the fourth (6 seconds of men gesticulating, perhaps on the floor of the stock market), just before the 1930 item on Mother Jones; and the fifth (4 seconds more of men on the floor of the stock market), just before the 1976 Paul Robeson item.[31] These animated sequences, all of them direct references to the enemies of social justice who are indirectly referenced by the gravesites and historical markers, are obvious formal abrasions.

I understand these deviations from Gianvito's otherwise rigorous structure as a personal rebellion against the implications of the very formalism he invokes in *Profit Motive and the Whispering Wind.* Revolutions, rebellions, strikes, all the forms of resistance commemorated by Gianvito are interruptions within the otherwise smooth continuities sought by capitalist culture, continuities implicitly reflected within the predictable forms and convenient resolutions of most commercial films and television shows. Indeed, to a considerable extent, even the audiences for independent media, including those for avant-garde film and video, have a tendency to expect certain predictable articulations within specific genres of cinema.

Benning and Gianvito, in *Deseret* and *Profit Motive,* are children of the formalism that seemed so revolutionary to many aficionados of avant-garde film during the 1960s and 1970s—what P. Adams Sitney termed "structural film"—but while Benning's generally radical politics are confined within highly systematic, and therefore highly predictable, cinematic structures, *Profit Motive* expresses Gianvito's discomfort and distrust of systemization and the tendency of systems to oppress difference and defiance, not only in his honoring of those who have stood up to unjust traditions and conventions, but in his refusal to allow the structuring of his own video to provoke too much aesthetic complacency in viewers. Gianvito's desire to produce a coherent video is not allowed to suppress his personal political feelings, and specifically in the moments of animation, his fear of, anger with, and contempt for those devoted to greed and to the hysterical consumption marketed so effectively by modern commercial culture.

The 2002 Philip Frances Berrigan item (and the superimposed text, "and all the others") is followed by images of berry bushes that seem to bring the video back to the opening imagery, and full circle to closure. However, these images and the shots of woodlands that follow are gradually transformed from pristine nature shots to emblems of modern America. Through the foliage, we see a person, then distant traffic, and finally signs for Shell, Walmart, and McDonald's. Suddenly, the sound of drums is heard—very loud after *Profit Motive*'s generally quiet soundtrack—and there is a cut to a montage of demonstrators in the streets of various cities (New York, Washington, D.C., Cambridge), in support of a variety of social justice causes. This 4½-minute montage is still another response to the formal design of the body of *Profit Motive*. It is loud, densely edited, with sequences of single framing and moments of metaphor (a brick wall being demolished) and makes clear that the history charted in the video is very much alive. The montage is a call to arms.

Throughout the first 50 minutes of *Profit Motive,* Gianvito expresses his admiration of those he celebrates by functioning as a cine-historian and as a teacher (that many of the names on the gravestones are unfamiliar suggests that some research on the part of the viewer would be useful). With the finale, Gianvito expresses a more activist commitment; he becomes a participant in (as well as a witness for) street-level, grassroots political activity in the present—and he offers a final, implicit confrontation of the avant-garde cinematic tradition evoked by the structure of *Profit Motive*.[32]

In *The Man Who Envied Women* (1985), Yvonne Rainer confronts the "radical" gesture of Luis Buñuel's slicing of a woman's eye at the beginning of *Un Chien andalou* (1929), a metaphor presumably for surrealism's attack on conventional ways of seeing. When the Buñuel–Dalí sequence is relocated into a feminist context—it is, after all, a *woman's* sight being metaphorically destroyed, a woman being attacked by a man—the gesture doesn't seem so radical! In *Profit Motive and the Whispering Wind* Gianvito offers a similar kind of re-contextualization. The conclusion of *Profit Motive* confronts the way in which the radical formalism of structural film has generally refused to acknowledge its own tendency to reconfirm the conventional "virtues" of consistency, conformity to accepted patterns, predictability within a system, and the suppression of personal political views within an attitude of aesthetic detachment. In a political sense, the rigorousness that characterizes so many of the canonical structural films may be as much avoidance of commitment as it is confrontation of the conventional.

Like John Gianvito, Jeff Daniel Silva has been an important contributor to the Boston and Cambridge film scene. In 2000 Silva was the co-creator and has been programmer (with Alla Kovgan) of the Balagan Film Series, a nomadic exhibition project that focuses on independent and experimental cinema; he worked with

Lucien Castaing-Taylor during the early years of Harvard's Sensory Ethnography Lab (see chapter 9); and his input on documentary works in progress in Cambridge is widely sought. And like *Profit Motive and the Whispering Wind*, Silva's *Balkan Rhapsodies: 78 Measures of War* (2008) involved a personal pilgrimage, in this case visits to Serbia and Kosovo between 1999 and 2005, beginning soon after the seventy-eight days of NATO bombing of Serbia between March 24 and June 10, 1999 (the DVD jacket of the film claims that Silva was the first American civilian allowed entry into Serbia after the bombing).[33] Further, just as the structure of *Profit Motive* is figured against the formal organization of structural film, the form of *Balkan Rhapsodies* seems figured against the history of avant-garde film notebooks and diaries, and in particular Jonas Mekas's *Reminiscences of a Journey to Lithuania* (1972), the second section of which promises "100 Glimpses of Lithuania"—though there are only ninety-one numbered sections.[34] Silva begins *Balkan Rhapsodies* with passages of imagery that are numbered, though the numbering is not rigorously adhered to—or at least not rigorously announced—throughout the 55 minutes of the film.[35]

Unlike both *Profit Motive* and *Reminiscences*, however, *Balkan Rhapsodies* is a collage of many kinds of imagery and sound: recycled news footage of events in the Balkans; on-the-street interviews conducted by Silva in Serbia, Kosovo, and in Cambridge; landscape and cityscape imagery; a recycled music video based on the Beach Boys' song "Kokomo," produced and performed by Norwegian soldiers; visits with Balkan families, and with young men and women hanging out drinking and talking (sometimes Silva is visible); a passage of flicker film that accompanies a sound recording of a NATO air strike on Belgrade on April 8, 1999; clips from various Hungarian Rhapsodies by Franz Liszt (performed by Michelle Campanella); an interview at MIT with Noam Chomsky, and another with Howard Zinn, about the Balkan war; an excerpt from a May Day military parade in Belgrade in 1964. . . . This eclectic mixture of images and sounds is held together by Silva's crafting of a web of motifs—incidents, particular comments—that appear in various forms and contexts.

Early on, Silva provides an in-close look at a postcard he finds in his mailbox—clearly a reenacted scene—that advertises the Balkan plum liquor, Slivovitza: it includes the rhyme, "Fuck the Coca, fuck the pizza, all we need is Slivovitza." The postcard seems a wry comment on the ineffectiveness of international (and especially American) intervention in the Balkans, as well as a mordant recognition that the only thing one can do about the terrible situation there is to get drunk. Various elements of this jingle figure throughout the film. For example, "Coca"—that is, Coca-Cola—is present in various forms of advertising during the film; and two different men at two different times are filmed in Harvard Square trying to say the rhyme for Silva's camera (neither man knows what Slivovitza is, an implicit metaphor for American ignorance about the Balkans). *Balkan Rhapsodies* concludes with an extended close-up of a coffee table with a bottle of Slivovitza, as Silva (only his hands are visible), drinks glass after glass, apparently getting drunk—presumably his final response to the complex chaos he has experienced in the Balkans and his inability to make sense of it.[36] The imagery in this shot grows increasingly out of focus.

While in many instances people are seen only once in *Balkan Rhapsodies,* a set of particular characters is developed. They include a twenty-year-old philosophy student who is first identified as a founding member of the Serbian Student Resistance Movement (each of the people who appear more than once is identified in a new way during each appearance—presumably Silva's way of suggesting the complexity of these lives); a young Serbian man who hid from military service, hoping the conflict would quickly blow over, then served as a soldier; Ivan Nedeljkovic, who is first identified as a musician, then later, when he plays American blues on his guitar, as a car mechanic; still later, as a UN driver, and finally, as a displaced person;[37] and Silva, who films himself in several sequences, is filmed by others from time to time during his visits to the Balkans and is often heard speaking from behind the camera during interviews and other conversations. Indeed, one can identify three distinct Jeff Silvas: the man who journeys to a dangerous part of the world soon after his native country has bombed the people there and returns for subsequent visits; the discouraged Silva who seems so appalled by the destruction he has seen (and the complicity of his own country in what seems to have been a refusal to allow a more peaceful settlement of the problems there) that he can find no way to respond other than to get drunk; and the experimental filmmaker who in time finds a way to transform what he has seen and the cinematic evidence he has collected into an engaging film. The fact that the "second Silva" is most fully revealed during the credit sequence suggests that if working to finish the film was a useful distraction, it was not powerful enough to solve the psychic struggle the project produced.

As fully as any other filmmaker discussed in this book, Silva has brought an inheritance of avant-garde cinema into a personal documentary. Indeed, while Gianvito in *Profit Motive* seems to rebel against the seemingly apolitical formalism of much American avant-garde film, Silva seems in rebellion against the traditional history of documentary. For all the human change and struggle depicted in Gardner's and Asch's films about indigenous cultures and in McElwee's and Moss's personal documentaries, their best films provide a sense that life does make sense, that struggles do get resolved. In *Balkan Rhapsodies,* however, the complex interplay of elements, and the considerable skill with which Silva manipulates sound and image, does not suggest that the world he is depicting makes sense or that the struggles he has witnessed are likely to be resolved before further struggles begin. Indeed, Silva seems to accept his own powerlessness in relation to the events he witnesses.

Silva's use of *rhapsodies* in his title seems at once descriptive and ironic. As a musical term "rhapsody" refers to a composition of irregular form with a dramatic, improvisatory character, usually performed solo—a reasonably accurate description of the structure of *Balkan Rhapsodies* (which is, more than other films discussed in this chapter, full of both diagetic and nondiagetic music). Silva has said that

> *Balkan Rhapsodies* was always intended to be a fragmentary and fluid series of films (or fragments) within the container of the film and that (in theory) the video segments and text inter-titles could ideally be presented in any random order. I did however create what I considered an optimal master for festivals, but in actuality have about 4 different versions that I have shown. But now that technology has caught up to the film I'm actually at a place where I'll be able to author a DVD and possibly online version that will allow for this "random access" viewing.[38]

Yet to the degree that the film evokes the more general sense of "rhapsody," as an exalted or ecstatic expression, the title seems mordantly humorous—except perhaps as a measure of Silva's implicit pleasure in having come to know the many interesting people his filmmaking brought him into contact with and in having, after nine years, finished a film about his experiences. The credit sequence of *Balkan Rhapsodies* is unusually detailed; Silva thanks an extended list of people in the Cambridge and Boston film community who have been supportive of his efforts with the film over the years—a final irony, perhaps, given the destruction of Balkan community caused by the events he has documented.[39]

ALEXANDER OLCH'S *THE WINDMILL MOVIE*: "THIS LITTLE SÉANCE OF FLICKERING LIGHT"

In 2002, a year after the death of Richard P. Rogers, one of his Harvard teachers, Alex Olch was asked by photographer Susan Meiselas, Rogers's widow, to see whether some sort of cinematic memorial to Rogers might be possible, given the wealth of footage Rogers had left behind. Much of the filmed material in Rogers's archive involved a project he had had often shot material for but could never finish. This project seems to have been focused on his relationship to Wainscott, a small town in the Hamptons where Rogers's family had a home, and the private resort at nearby Georgica Pond to which Rogers's family belonged (the resort includes an old wooden windmill). Though Rogers seems to have been obsessed with this project, he was also reticent about it, and about the idea of personal documentary in general—despite his own contributions to the form (see chapter 4). Early in *The Windmill Movie*, Olch includes footage that Rogers shot of himself reflected in a mirror, during which Rogers enunciates what has long been an issue

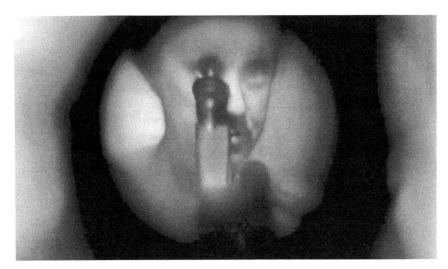

FIGURE 43. Richard P. Rogers filming himself in mirror, in Alexander Olch's *The Windmill Movie* (2008). Courtesy Alexander Olch.

for personal documentary (fig. 43): "This shot is a cliché. It's the filmmaker confronting himself in the mirror, the stock material of a personal documentary. The question is always whether there is anything to say, whether any of this *means* anything. Or is it just a kind of voyeurism, a kind of auto-eroticism, as some would have it, just a kind of jerking off."

Rogers' failure to finish the windmill film (since he never finished, there is no formal title, but the relevant tapes in his archive are labeled "Wind Mill") seems to have been a reflection of his doubts about this kind of project, especially as conceived by someone with his advantages. In an interview shot by David Grubin and excerpted in *The Windmill Movie,* Rogers explains:

> There was no center to the film because the center in some way had to be me, and I was not willing to put myself in the film. Not willing to put myself in the film because it's so stupid to be this privileged, this white, this rich, and be sort of bitching about it, around all of this beauty. And I just couldn't do it and I still think it's stupid. I mean it must be infuriating for somebody to complain in the Hamptons or to be jealous that one is not Steven Spielberg. Why is it hard to make the film? Because probably I have to face myself and I don't want to.[40]

Whatever his self-doubts, Rogers was an accomplished cinematographer and director who finished a variety of films, including two experiments in autobiography, *Elephants* (1973; see chapter 4) and *226-1690* (1984); two features about the Nicaraguan revolution, collaborations with Meiselas and Alfred Guzzetti (see chapter 4); portraits of writers William Carlos Williams, Wallace Stevens, and William

Kennedy (*William Carlos Williams*, 1986; *Wallace Stevens*, 1987; *William Kennedy's Albany*, 1993); and a variety of other documentary and fiction projects, including *A Midwife's Tale* (1996), an adaptation of Laurel Thatcher Ulrich's novel *A Midwife's Tale: The Life of Martha Ballard, Based on Her Diary, 1785–1812* (1990). Rogers taught at Harvard, off and on, from 1970 to 1985 and from 1989 to 2001 (and at the State University of New York at Purchase from 1974 to 1983). He was associate director of Harvard's Film Study Center during the 1989–90 academic year, and again from 1992 to 1997, and director from 1998 to –2001. In 2003, Meiselas donated Rogers's films and outtakes to the Harvard Film Archive.

From the beginning, there were certain ironies in Olch becoming involved in a documentary project, particularly this one. Olch had been frustrated by the obvious commitment of the Harvard filmmaking program to documentary and with what he saw as its resistance to narrative fiction, and he had a tendency to defy class assignments, redirecting them so that they served his interest in making fiction films;[41] and his thesis film, *Artemin Goldberg: Custom Tailor of Brassieres* (2000), was a faux documentary.[42] Of his Harvard professors, Rogers was the most supportive of Olch's interest in fiction. But whatever his reservations about working in nonfiction, Olch committed himself to finding a way to document Rogers's life. By the time *The Windmill Movie* was finished in 2008, Olch had spent seven years on it—and it had become "personal" in ways he could not have predicted.

Certainly, *The Windmill Movie* is not the first instance when someone close to a director has completed a documentary that the director did not live long enough to finish. The most celebrated instance is the Tom Joslin, Peter Friedman project, *Silverlake Life: The View from Here* (1993), which Joslin began and Friedman, Joslin's student at Hampshire College, completed.[43] Both films confront the issue of mortality: Joslin dies of AIDS, Rogers of cancer, though the films are very different in tone. *Silverlake Life* was conceived as a confrontation of what was then the widespread ignorance about AIDS and the marginalization of those suffering from it; that is, Joslin and his lover Mark Massi were to be understood both as individuals and as instances of a major cultural injustice.[44] In *The Windmill Movie* Rogers's life is far from an example of a larger injustice—though his experiences and personality, his very imperfections and failures, his self-doubt resonate with many viewers. Further, both Friedman and Olch use raw material shot by their mentors to make films different perhaps from what Joslin and Rogers had in mind—though Olch's approach is very different from Friedman's. Although Friedman finished *Silverlake Life* for Joslin and Massi, he is not a major presence in the film: the original focus on the relationship of Joslin and Massi is maintained. In *The Windmill Movie* Olch *is* an important presence: indeed, he attempts to channel Rogers by means of a fictional diary that proposes to imagine what Rogers might have written at various points in his life had he kept a diary.

FIGURE 44. Wallace Shawn performs as Richard P. Rogers, in Alexander Olch's *The Windmill Movie* (2008). Courtesy Alexander Olch.

The Windmill Movie begins with several brief sequences that function as a précis. A montage of images of Rogers through the years, from the 1940s until 1999, seen forward, then in reverse, is followed by a shot of Rogers in his editing room a year before his death, telling Susan Meiselas that he doesn't want her to be filming him right now. Then, after an opening credit, we hear Olch in voice-over: "Dick Rogers was my film teacher at Harvard," immediately followed by Rogers speaking to the camera, apparently held by Olch when he was Rogers's student in 1997, asking, "Is something wrong with the cameraman?" Olch's voice-over review of Rogers's career is followed by the shot recorded by David Grubin of Rogers questioning personal documentary, then by the title credit.

The mixture of times and points of view in this précis—we see Rogers from the point of view of his father (and whoever else was involved in making the home movies that open the film), and from the points of view of Meiselas, Olch, and Rogers himself—is a fitting introduction to the first half-hour of *The Windmill Movie*, during which Olch provides a panorama of insights into Rogers's life, family, friends, and career, shot in various ways by Rogers and by his friends and colleagues. He also tells the story of how he himself became involved in making the film we are watching: we see Olch and Meiselas working through Rogers's archive, as well as some of the results of Olch's early interest in having Rogers's friends enact elements of his life. For example, Wallace Shawn performs the speech, quoted earlier, during which Rogers explains his resistance to making the Wainscott film (fig. 44).

After a sequence describing Rogers's bus trip to Palm Beach where he met up with Robert Gardner, who flew the two of them to Haiti, Olch includes an excerpt from Gardner's *Screening Room* episode featuring Rogers, recorded in June 1975,[45] during which Gardner says to Rogers, "You once told me that you started out making this film [*Elephants*] in a very different way than you ended up making it." In *The Windmill Movie* this is followed by film records of Rogers shooting *Elephants*, at a point when he was using actors to play himself and Terry Villafrade (in the end Rogers and Villafrade played themselves). In voice-over we hear Olch reading an excerpt from the imagined "director's diary," during which "Rogers" wonders what an actor might add to the film: "How does his *not being me* help to tell a story about *me*?" Soon after this passage, Olch's voice-over provides context for a new strategy:

> At this point we're running out of narration. The scenes with Richard's voice are working, but I have nothing like that for the story of his life with Susan. . . .
>
> But remembering his director's diary, "How does not being me help tell a story about me," I start thinking maybe there's a way to build on that. . . .
>
> So, using the boxes we can find, what his friends have told me, what *he* had told me, the things Susan will reveal to me, I begin to write a kind of script in Dick's voice. A way to take this footage and tell the story for him.

It is a sleight of mind worthy of Ross McElwee that Olch, speaking for himself, gives credit to Rogers for writing a diary that instigated Olch's voice-over, a diary that Rogers in fact never wrote but has been imagined by Olch. From this point on, Olch uses a fictional version of what Jim Lane has called the "journal entry" approach to autobiographical documentary as a means of structuring *The Windmill Movie* and bringing Rogers's life into focus.[46]

It is remarkable how quickly the viewer adjusts to the fiction of Olch-as-Rogers voice-over, especially given that Rogers's and Olch's voices are quite distinct and that Olch begins the film by making clear that he is Rogers's student. In large measure this is a function of the engaging quality of Olch's voice, of his skillful writing of "Rogers's" thoughts, and of his clear sense of Rogers as a person. It is also, of course, a testament to what can only be called the film viewer's will to believe: that hunger, intrinsic to so much of film pleasure, to pretend that what is clearly a fiction is nevertheless believable, a (temporally limited) alternative reality.

Early in *The Windmill Movie*, during the passage when Rogers speaks to the camera about the personal documentary he hopes to make, he wonders "whether it will be interesting to make a film that deals with the difference between documentary filmmaking and fiction filmmaking." What quickly becomes clear in *The Windmill Movie*, once Olch has become Rogers's voice, is that however one understands the difference between documentary and fiction film*making*, the viewer's experience of these two categories of cinema is remarkably similar. This is particularly true in the case of personal documentary, where most voice-overs are closer in impact to the first-person narrators of novels and short stories than to the voices-of-god so typical of informational and polemical documentaries, from *The Plow That Broke the Plains* (1936) and *The River* (1937) to *March of the Penguins* (2005).

The magic of *The Windmill Movie* is that while it creates a convincing and engaging mixture of documentary and fiction, it never hides the reality of what is occurring. Even once Olch has taken over as Rogers's voice, we continue to see and hear Rogers speaking within events and to hear him offscreen, talking to his mother and to a man interviewing him about the film he hopes to make about Wainscott (in one instance near the end of the film, we hear Rogers in voice-over). Indeed, Olch regularly creates wry humor by documenting the real-life relationship between Rogers and himself: I have mentioned the moment in the précis when Rogers speaks to Olch as he is shooting Rogers; and in two instances later in the film, Rogers holds the door for Olch, who is shooting, as they leave or enter Rogers's Mott Street loft. Late in the film, as they are filming at Wainscott Beach, Olch's voice-over (Olch as Rogers) tells us, "I get a student of mine, Alex Olch, to come out to the beach and help shoot some material for me in the ocean.... He keeps saying there should be more footage of me. What does *he* know?" Here, we are experiencing documentary and fiction simultaneously. The visuals document the real-life relationship of Olch and Rogers, while the voice-over is Olch's fictional rendering of what he imagines are Rogers's thoughts about him; in a sense, the sequence documents Olch's voice-over as the fiction it is.

Olch's experiment of working between fiction and documentary in *The Windmill Movie* is successful in part because Rogers is a compelling character—the beauty of his cinematography, his obvious intelligence, his complex personal life, his nagging doubts about himself, and his struggles with injury and disease form a fascinating mix that is easy to relate to—but also because of the illusion of intimacy created by Olch's voice-over. Olch imagines Rogers's thoughts about his womanizing ("Valentines Day, Susan back from the Philippines, living in my loft. I told her I just broke up with Noni. I've always told Noni that I am single. These are both lies") and even his thoughts about Susan's feelings after an abortion ("Undated. The one page that should be blotted out. May there be no record of this. We just got back from the clinic. I don't think I've ever seen Susan this still. She's still in pain"), as well as his own feelings a month later, as we see a room full of floating balloons each with its own string: "It's Susan's birthday, and I surprise her with a party. The next morning I keep staring at the balloons. Seeing my ... thwarted sperm floating, happily frozen, useless and unrealized, from now to eternity. Note: think about similarities to my film, my aborted film."

Olch's willingness to imagine Rogers's thinking about the most personal dimensions of his life is confirmed by his ways of engaging Rogers's friends and lovers. Rogers's holding the door for the camera to enter his loft leads into a sequence filmed in Noni Pratt's apartment, during which Olch (inadvertently?) seems to be echoing what we might assume was Rogers's interaction with Pratt. When she learns that the camera Olch is using was Rogers's, Pratt says, "So Dick lives on. Or the poltergeist around him." Following imagery of Pratt shot by Rogers on a boat trip they took the day after Rogers told her he was going back to Susan (Pratt, obviously upset, tries to be a "good sport" in front of Rogers's intrusive camera), we are back in Pratt's loft, where she is suddenly uncomfortable with Olch's filming her. "Just stop that!," she says, though when Olch hesitates, Pratt continues, "No, no, no, you could do whatever you want. It's like the same thing. You know it's like it's really irritating and kind of strange, and you could just go on ahead and keep doing it, but just let me walk away from you and that's fine. God, Dick, the things we do for you!" It's as if for Noni, the past and the present, Rogers and Olch, are momentarily conflated. Near the end of *The Windmill Movie,* Wallace Shawn, dressed as Rogers is dressed in David Grubin's interview with him, performs Rogers's original comments about the filmmaker confronting himself in the mirror, then continues, speaking comments that Olch wrote, as if they were part of Rogers's original speech: "I actually feel rather good about the moment that I'm going through, because my problem in life has always been about the future. What are you going to accomplish? What are you going to *do?* What's going to happen to you in the *future?* Well, I don't have a future now and this solves most of the problems!"

During the final moments of *The Windmill Movie* the interrelationship of Rogers and Olch reaches an extended climax. Olch, in voice-over, imagines Rogers's thoughts about losing his mind and memory as cancer destroys his brain: "When I used to go to the dentist, I would think about how I'm separate from the pain in my tooth. I thought this about losing my toes, about cancer in my leg, thought this all my life when something hurt. . . . But I *can't* say I'm separate from my *brain.* My brain *is* me. My brain *is* these memories. The things that I photographed *are* my memories. Therefore they are me." These words are accompanied by footage of Rogers as a young child, imagery that his father shot. Whose memories are these home movie images now that Rogers and his father are dead? They, and the voice-over we are hearing, have been transformed into Olch's memories—and are becoming ours as we experience the film. Early in the film, we hear Rogers speaking to a woman about a film he has in mind: "It's about memories," he says, "and how those memories interface with now. But you know, I'll do lots of things. I might even reconstruct some things, sort of the things that I remember." Whether Rogers would have approved of *The Windmill Movie,* Olch has clearly taken direction from Rogers.

The Windmill Movie ends at Wainscott Beach the year before Rogers's death, with the sync-sound imagery Rogers and Olch shot together. An extended shot begins with Olch shooting his feet in the shallow surf, then we hear both Olch and Rogers off camera as Rogers directs Olch to walk into the surf with the camera, shooting, and to dive the camera into one wave, which Olch does, then, as a second wave approaches, to "dive in, stay in." The camera is again submerged, and the film concludes. This sequence confirms the film's complex interface of past and present, of memory and perception, of Rogers and Olch. The shot of Olch's feet reminds us of the earlier, rather jolting shots of Rogers's injured foot after he had lost toes in an accident in France, clearly distinguishing Olch from Rogers; but the camera's dive into the waves conjoins the teacher and student one final time, both literally (they are collaborators in this extended shot) and metaphorically: obviously, the dive into the wave is a final emblem of Rogers's demise after breasting a series of "waves" of psychic and physical struggle; and it is a final emblem of Olch's dive into Rogers's film archive, and his life and death, in order to make *The Windmill Movie.*

Olch's tribute to Rogers's life is personal in an unusual sense. All we learn about *Olch* from *The Windmill Movie* is who he is as a filmmaker, or really, who he has become as a filmmaker in order to do justice to Rogers's life, personality, and filmmaking. In voice-over Olch speaks to us in much the same way that Ross McElwee speaks to us in *Backyard, Time Indefinite,* and *Six O'Clock News*—that is, intimately, as if we are his confidants. But he is speaking *as Rogers,* not as himself—though on some level what he understands about Rogers and how he articulates this understanding *is* certainly part of who Olch is. Of course, nearly all of what is actually "personal" in Olch's film *was* personal for Rogers—though this is Rogers's personal life as filtered through and fictionalized by Olch's understanding.

Ultimately, *The Windmill Movie* is less a personal documentary about either Rogers or Olch than a kind of cine-séance between documents of the past and fictional imaginings in the present, and, as Olch makes explicit in his final voice-over as Rogers before the camera dives into the wave, between a supportive teacher and a grateful student who became friends and collaborators, making possible the transformation of the teacher's death into the ongoing life of the student's film: "Part of me thinks that I should be filled with regret. That I was doomed by my own politeness, doomed by my own home, to make a failure of no proportion, embraced and swallowed back up by the land where I was conceived. Would that I could say there are ghosts, spirits where I will lurk, but there is only this, this movie, where just for an instant, I will be alive in this little world, this little séance of flickering light. And no one—not even the heavens—can take that away from me."

AMIE SIEGEL'S *DDR/DDR*

Still another exploration of the personal in Cambridge documentary filmmaking is evident in the essay film, *DDR/DDR* (2008), by Amie Siegel,[47] who has taught filmmaking in the Visual and Environmental Studies program at Harvard since 2008. *DDR/DDR* is a rumination on the passing of the Deutsche Demokratische

Republik (the German Democratic Republic, what Americans call "East Germany"), which was established in 1949. The construction of the Berlin Wall in 1961 in order to impede emigration out of the country (the population had dropped by 3,000,000 to 16,000,000 by 1960) made Berlin and the DDR a focal point of the Cold War and a fascinating topic for artists. Surrounded by the DDR, West Berlin became an increasingly extravagant outpost of Western capitalism and artistic freedom. Many artists lived in West Berlin or were awarded grants to work there, among them Yvonne Rainer, whose approach to filmmaking—*Journeys from Berlin/1971* (1979) and *Privilege* (1990) are especially relevant—seems one of the foundations for Siegel's approach in *DDR/DDR*. Another is Jean-Luc Godard, whose films of the late 1960s early 1970s—*Deux ou trois choses que je sais d'elle* (*Two or Three Things I Know about Her;* 1966) and *Sympathy for the Devil* (1968), for example—seem an important inspiration for both Rainer's and Siegel's work.

Siegel's film examines the ways in which moving-image technologies (particularly surveillance activities and commercial movies) were fundamental to the cultural fabric of East German society, to the rigorous enforcement of the nation's underlying Stalinist ideology, as well as to incipient resistance to this ideology. Further, it asks viewers to consider the degree to which all forms of cinema, including depictions of distant cultures and of filmmakers' personal lives, can be understood as instances of surveillance and exertions of political power.[48]

Siegel herself is a presence throughout *DDR/DDR*. She appears as director within the film in several instances. In voice-over, Siegel comments on various dimensions of several surveillance films and tapes she presents. *DDR/DDR* also includes her interviews with men and women, some of them actors, who discuss the East German experience of "the *Wende*," the extended moment when the dismantling of the Berlin Wall led to German reunification. Siegel talks with former functionaries of "the Stasi" (Ministry for State Security), the massive surveillance program that with 91,000 full-time staff was East Germany's largest employer; with Detlef Vreisleben, who provides a tour of Stasi surveillance equipment; and Annette Simon, Jochen Schade, and Hans-Joachim Maaz, who became psychoanalysts after the *Wende* (psychoanalysis was forbidden in the DDR). All in all, *DDR/DDR* is Siegel's personal rumination on a fascinating history and its demise, after-effects, and implications for twenty-first century Americans.

Siegel has come to understand the DDR as a kind of mirror image of its supposed opposite: West Germany and Western capitalism in general. This is suggested by the film's title, as it appears in the film itself, where the first "DDR" is presented as a mirror image of the second—though this cannot be rendered by conventional keyboards (a detail that itself seems suggestive).[49] Siegel's sense of the DDR as a mirror of the West is made explicit in a dream presented by a young girl (and translated into English): "I had a dream. A pair of twins walked along a forest path. They hadn't seen each other in forty years. When they saw each other again, neither recognized the other. They had grown up separately. They tried to remember their parents and grandparents but it was difficult. The twins were East Germany and West Germany."

This doubling is reflected in Siegel's intercutting in some sequences between a male and a female psychoanalyst (Schade and Simon), and in others between two former Stasi functionaries who took somewhat different roles within the surveillance system. Indeed, *DDR/DDR* is full of obvious and subtle doublings: for instance, two pieces of music ("Rabatki," a rock song, and "The Internationale") are heard during the film, each of them twice: "Rabatki" is performed live by Los Trabantos, then is heard as background at a bar where actor Kurt Nauman orders a beer; "The Internationale" is heard as a tune on a child's toy at the end of Siegel's interview with the young girl, then in an East German orchestral version as accompaniment to a montage that traces a chair being bought in Germany and shipped to a store in New York City.

The idea of East Germany (and communism) and West Germany (and capitalism) as mirrors of each other is also evident in Siegel's discussions of the popular East German westerns produced at the DEFA Film Studio.[50] The twelve DEFA westerns, while imitative of American westerns, were distinct from this tradition in particular ways. The DEFA films depict the Native Americans as the good guys and the European American settlers as money hungry imperialists: the "redskins" were understood as "reds"—people living within a democratic, communal system.

The popularity of these westerns helped to fuel a (still active) subculture of East Germans who, during vacation time, would don Native American dress and live in teepee villages in the countryside (fig. 45). Siegel talks with several of these back-to-Native-America enthusiasts within a teepee village about how their activities functioned within the DDR (and about the impact of the *Wende* on this still popular but now transforming subculture), revealing that while overtly the teepee villages seemed in concert with East German ideology, they were also a space in which DDR citizens could escape or could feel momentarily released from the strictures of East German surveillance and the system it maintained. Siegel's discussions with the Native American enthusiasts function as a kind of postmodern salvage ethnography of an *imitation* of a set of cultures that were overwhelmed by the arrival of new technologies and the rapacious capitalism these technologies made possible. Further, judging from the comments of the enthusiasts, the *Wende* has instigated an echo of this transformation within the "culture" of Native American hobbyists.

Other than the idea of East and West Germany being mirror images, the most fundamental doubling in *DDR/DDR* is between the Stasi's activities and Siegel's own. The explicit and implicit parallels between Siegel's filmmaking process and the forms of filmmaking that were important in the DDR include both shooting and editing. Throughout *DDR/DDR*, Siegel is careful to perform surveillance on

FIGURE 45. Native American enthusiast in German encampment, in Amie Siegel's *DDR/DDR* (2008). Courtesy Amie Siegel.

her own activities as filmmaker. This begins during her opening interview with a woman (played by actress Christiane Ziehl) who misses the security of the DDR, when there was little anxiety about finding work and supporting a family. At one point Ziehl wants to take the microphone from Siegel, who along with her sound man is standing with Ziehl, to answer a question. There is a bit of a wrestle over who is to hold the mike; Siegel retrieves it and continues the interview. It is not clear within *DDR/DDR* whether this momentary awkwardness is candid, scripted, or reenacted (according to Siegel, it was an improvised gesture during a roughly scripted moment),[51] though the woman's reaching for the mike and being denied it occurs just as Siegel is asking about her experience after the *Wende*. What at first seems a glitch works as a subtle metaphor that reflects, on the one hand, what the woman tells Siegel about the feeling of freedom and new possibility that immediately followed the *Wende*, which was quickly followed by widespread insecurity about the future; and, on the other, Siegel's understanding that as filmmaker she, not her subject, makes the final decisions about what is filmed and seen. Similar "accidents" occur periodically throughout *DDR/DDR*—drawing attention to the constructedness of *DDR/DDR* and implicitly of all cinema, including, of course, all forms of documentary.

In general, Siegel's examination of the DDR through her conversations with one-time citizens and her voice-over commentary on aspects of DDR history is also a self-examination. The Stasi's fascination with surveillance equipment is clearly reflected in Siegel's own: we not only see the equipment used, but see it

demonstrated as part of Siegel's film: when she interviews an unnamed Stasi oper-
ative about his work as an interrogator, she films him with both a modern video
camera and a Stasi camera with one of the meter-long lenses presented by Vreisleben earlier in the film, intercutting between the two technologies so that both their
differences and their similarities are evident. A third camera records Siegel and her
crew filming the Stasi interrogator.

In a number of instances Siegel reveals approaches to editing in Stasi surveillance footage, either soon after recording the material, or once it was placed in the
archive where Siegel was able to access it. Ironies abound. In one instance, a record
of a man confessing in an interrogation apartment is presented, but with the man's
face electronically blocked out: clearly, the man's privacy was invaded in order to
obtain information about his activities and to make a record of his confession, but
the tape provided to Siegel by the Stasi archive is *anomisiert* ("anonymized")—
seemingly in order to protect the very privacy the video reveals the man didn't
have! And the anonymizing doesn't entirely work; at times the man's face is quite
visible.

Siegel herself re-edits material in order to reveal dimensions of it that would
have been ignored by the Stasi. In one instance, during what are presumably outtakes in a surveillance project, a Stasi cameraman seems to become entranced with
the aesthetics of a shot, revealing more about himself than about whoever was the
subject of the surveillance project, and in a sense about Siegel's cinematic background as an experimental filmmaker: Siegel earned her B.A. from Bard College
and her M.F.A. from the School of the Art Institute of Chicago, institutions widely
known for their focus on experimental media, including forms of filmmaking
focused on texture and chiaroscuro.

At one point, a tracking shot follows a truck from which various pieces of
equipment are being thrown to the side of the road—a metaphor that is explained
late in the film in one of Siegel's voice-overs: "The history of the Stasi is simultaneously a history of media technology in the second half of the twentieth century.
Their surveillance efforts begin with silent, small-gauge film, 8mm then 16mm,
throughout the '60s. In the '70s black-and-white video is introduced, accompanied by silence. In the '80s, 16mm film is abandoned entirely for sound color video.
And this lasts until 1989. The Stasi are entirely analog, encapsulating the period
before digital, the wall falling before the advent of digital video, mini-DV, HDV,
and HD." This historical review can hardly fail to suggest the modern history of
American avant-garde film and experimental video, a pair of cultural projects that
have always been understood by creators and most audiences as demonstrations of
free expression.

As *DDR/DDR* moves toward its conclusion, Siegel reveals aspects of her own
editing process that would normally be suppressed in a finished film. A brief passage when she is working on translation with Millay Hyatt—they are seated at a

computer editing console—is followed by a sustained conversation with a group of Germans about how to translate *Wende* for non-German speakers. The heavy editing of this discussion, especially in contrast to the relatively serene pace of the rest of *DDR/DDR*, draws attention to itself as editing, making clear that either the conversation was scripted or reenacted or that Siegel's editing transformed whatever candid conversation actually occurred.

Near the conclusion of *DDR/DDR* the idea that the East and West were mirror images of each other is given a more specific application by Frank Döbert, filmed standing in front of the Zeiss headquarters in Jena (Zeiss, the legendary German, then East German, now once again German manufacturer of optical equipment) who suggests that, during the years since 9/11, America has become like the DDR: "I think the DDR was a dictatorship. A socialist dictatorship with security and surveillance and little personal freedom. And I think America has become like that.... After 2001 things have changed. I think personal freedoms are being twisted and the system seems very familiar to us. And we're really sorry, here in the GDR, that America has gone in that direction. And as a tourist it's very stressful and complicated, the whole state control—biometrics, surveillance: you can't believe it." Siegel asks Döbert whether traveling to the United States gave him "a feeling like in the DDR," and he responds, "Yes, very strong."

Early in the history charted by this volume , the exploration of distant, preindustrial cultures in ethnographic cinema seems to have instigated its apparent inverse: in-depth cinematic examinations of the filmmakers' personal experiences. As each of these approaches evolved, however, it began to incorporate the other: ethnographic film has increasingly recognized the personal, and personal documentary is increasingly recognized as ethnographic. Here, Siegel's examination of an Other culture is implicitly an investigation of her own; and her discussions with ex-Stasi operatives and citizens about DDR surveillance becomes the ground against which *her* "surveillance" of her subjects is figured, revealed, and considered. A crucial difference, of course, is how these two filming projects are situated within history: the Stasi operatives interviewed in *DDR/DDR* are being candid (or more or less candid) *now* about what they did in secret *then*, whereas Siegel is being candid now about what she is doing now.

Siegel's survey of life in the DDR is interrupted several times by a symbolic motif of Kurt Nauman, star of *The Architects* (1989, directed by Peter Kahane), the final film produced in the DDR: it was begun before the Berlin Wall came down, finished afterward. Nauman is seen in various locations walking along the line that indicates where the wall was, as if he is on a tightrope or trying to keep his balance after drinking too much (at one point Nauman is seen ordering a beer); his balance seems to grow more precarious as the film proceeds. If we see the "line" Nauman walks as the border between the one-time East and the West of then and now, this motif suggests Siegel's own attempt to come to an understanding of the distinctions and the similarities between the DDR and post–9/11 America. Early in *DDR/DDR* Hans-Joachim Maaz describes the wall as a "projection screen" that allowed East Germany to portray the West as evil Fascists and the West to portray East German society as an oppressive, poverty-stricken failure. *DDR/DDR* is a projection into the present of an important moment in the modern history of Germany, and while it confirms much of what the West has always assumed about the DDR, it also holds the DDR up as a mirror to contemporary America, explicitly and implicitly suggesting a very wide range of questions of cinema: Is our use of media technology less problematic than the uses of media in the DDR? Is our fear of the Other less socially and politically formative, less *ironic,* than the DDR's fear of Fascism? Further, is the emergence of personal filmmaking (and personal documentary in particular) during the past half-century something more than a confirmation of modern America's increasing invasion, through all sorts of audio-visual and digital means, of what we used to call "privacy," of the *personal* itself?

9
_____

Lucien Castaing-Taylor and
Sensory Ethnography

Harnessing perspectives drawn from the human sciences, the arts, and the humanities, the aim of SEL is to support innovative combinations of aesthetics and ethnography, with original nonfiction media practices that explore the bodily praxis and affective fabric of human existence. As such, it encourages attention to the many dimensions of social experience and subjectivity that may only with difficulty be rendered with words alone.

FROM THE WEBSITE OF HARVARD'S SENSORY ETHNOGRAPHY LAB[1]

If, at first, intelligent people could imagine that, when representing Other cultures, a picture is worth a thousand words, it was not long before those with a serious interest in anthropology and ethnographic filmmaking saw that, whereas written ethnography generally condensed months or years of study into a more or less accessible verbal form, whatever film imagery of preindustrial cultures was recorded and then edited into "complete" films—by men and women finding their way not merely into anthropology, but filmmaking—was little to be trusted. If even a written text compiled on the basis of long periods of research was limited in what it could reveal about Others, film, often recorded on the fly and/or quickly dramatized, tended to be not just limited, but superficial and prone to obvious distortions. This problem was quickly evident in the films of Lorna and John Marshall, Robert Gardner, and Timothy Asch, even to the filmmakers themselves: John Marshall was increasingly embarrassed by *The Hunters, Bitter Melons,* and his other early films about San peoples; and Asch's *The Ax Fight* directly addresses dimensions of this issue.

The problem, of course, was that from the beginning too much was expected of cinema. The fact that film could combine image, sound, and even visual and spoken text suggested to some that film could tell us more about the world than could just the written word or the written word plus still photography. A generation of filmmaking and anthropological critique was necessary before it became clear that what cinema *can* do is reveal something *different* from what gets revealed in even the most intelligent and engaging prose. A written text on a culture or cultural practice can tell us what the writer has come to understand about that group or activity, can even help us imagine what it might like to be in a certain place and live a certain way, but a carefully made film can offer its audience a *sensory experience* that reflects and reflects on the actual experiences of others (including the filmmakers themselves) as they occurred in a specific place during a specific time.

As is suggested by the description on the Sensory Ethnography Lab's (SEL) website, "sensory ethnography" does not assume that the process of filmmaking or the work that results from it need be limited by the conventions of the theatrical history of cinema, or even that SEL productions need involve images. "Original nonfiction media practices" are to be encouraged as long as they offer hope of providing more interesting and revealing experiences of "the bodily praxis and affective fabric of human existence." One of the distinctive qualities of the films produced in conjunction with the lab has been a commitment to sound. It is typical of SEL films that we hear before we see (and after we see), and that sound is conceived not as an adjunct to image, an accompaniment, but as a complex, often intense auditory surround within which the imagery unfolds. The sound designs for SEL films are often created in collaboration with Ernst Karel, whose contributions to this body of work would be difficult to overestimate, and whose own sound works—CDs include *Heard Laboratories* (and/OAR, 2010) and *Swiss Mountain Transport Systems* (Gruenrekorder, 2011)—have opened new documentary territory and have been an important influence on SEL filmmakers.

By the end of the first decade of the new millennium, the Sensory Ethnography Lab had revived interest in ethnographic cinema in Cambridge by instigating the production of engaging, revealing, immersive sync-sound films, video installations, and sound works by young anthropologists-artists committed to using media as a means of communicating the broadest range of human experience.

ILISA BARBASH, LUCIEN CASTAING-TAYLOR, AND *SWEETGRASS*

More than any other medium or art form, film uses experience to express experience.

ILISA BARBASH AND LUCIEN CASTAING-TAYLOR[2]

By the time they arrived at Harvard in 2003, Ilisa Barbash and Lucien Castaing-Taylor had established themselves as important contributors to current thinking about ethnographic filmmaking. Both had earned master's degrees in visual anthropology at the University of Southern California (USC), where they studied with Timothy (and Patsy) Asch, among others (while Castaing-Taylor was earning his Ph.D. at UC Berkeley, Barbash taught anthropology at Berkeley and San Francisco State). Castaing-Taylor had been founding editor of *Visual Anthropology Review*; and he had edited *Visualizing Theory: Selected Essays from V.A.R. 1990–1994* (New York: Routledge, 1994). He and Barbash had collaborated on *Cross Cultural Filmmaking: A Handbook for Making Documentary and Ethnographic Films and Videos* (Berkeley: University of California Press, 1997)—like Pincus and Ascher's *The Filmmakers' Handbook,* a basic reference, in this case specifically for nonfiction filmmakers—and they had collaborated on two films: *Made in USA* (1990), a film about sweatshops and child labor in the Los Angeles garment industry, and *In and Out of Africa* (1992), a video about the transnational market for African art.

As Castaing-Taylor worked to establish what came to be called the Sensory Ethnography Lab (early on, it was called the Media Anthropology Lab), he and Barbash (who began working as assistant curator of media anthropology at the Peabody Museum in 2003) were also completing a project they had begun during their tenure at the University of Colorado in Boulder, where both had taught film and anthropology from 1998 to 2003. The project, a record of the last cowboys to lead herds of sheep into Montana's Absaroka-Beartooth mountains for summer pasture, took various forms over several years and ultimately produced the feature documentary *Sweetgrass* (2009); nine installation pieces, each with five channels of sound; and four large photographic works.[3] *Sweetgrass* and its satellite films represent a significant transition in Castaing-Taylor's and Barbash's thinking about anthropology and ethnographic cinema, and it is this thinking that became the theoretical foundation for the Sensory Ethnography Lab.

In and Out of Africa, Barbash and Castaing-Taylor's thesis film at USC, is formally a relatively conventional documentary. It forgoes a voice-of-god narrator but relies very largely on interviews with Muslim art dealers (especially Gabai Baaré, a Hausa from Côte d'Ivoire), with artisans who produce and reproduce various forms of African art, and men and women in Europe and North America who buy and resell the work. The hour-long film intercuts between the interviews and shots of the locations where the art is made, shipped, and sold (the interviews function as narration for the location shots). African music often accompanies African scenes; classical European music is used for scenes at art galleries. *In and Out of Africa* is well shot and informative, both about the trade in African art and about the absurdities of art markets in general and especially those dealing in "indigenous" art. Bill Nichols has argued that, as an ethnographic film, *In and Out of Africa* is a breakthrough because it reveals how various cultural groups and histories are imbricated in the African art trade by means of "editing, or juxtaposition, in which situations, behavior, and comments amplify one another and prompt perceptions that may otherwise lie dormant. . . . Its mode of cinematic argumentation clearly provides the basis for an anthropology that is not a discipline of words."[4]

By the time they began to explore Montana sheep ranching in 2001 for their next film project, Barbash and Castaing-Taylor had redefined the kind of film they felt was worth making. Both were well aware of the theoretically problematic aspects of even the canonical films that had pretended to document Other cultures; both were suspicious of the demonstration of expertise that ethnographic film seemed to require, and Castaing-Taylor in particular had grown increasingly disenchanted with academic writing.[5] As Anna Grimshaw has suggested, the new project became an extension of, but also an escape from, typical academic life and what had become conventional academic thinking about anthropology and cinema.[6] Barbash and Castaing-Taylor immersed themselves in the experiences of the sheep ranchers of Big Timber, Montana, and Castaing-Taylor accompanied the cowboys as they herded thousands of sheep into the mountains. Though the sheepherding project began before Barbash and Castaing-Taylor's move to Harvard, the various parts of the project evolved along with the Sensory Ethnography Lab, and *Sweetgrass* became the first critical success related to the lab.

Throughout the shooting of the various elements of the sheep ranching and during the subsequent editing of the film and the various installation pieces, the filmmakers were less interested in recording and presenting information or demonstrating anthropological expertise than in conveying the experience of being present in a certain place and time as particular events (events with a considerable history and no apparent future) unfolded. For Castaing-Taylor in particular, who worked as a one-man crew shooting video and recording sound, *Sweetgrass* involved forms of labor analogous to what the cowboys were doing: carrying a heavy camera, climbing into the upper reaches of the Absaroka-Beartooth range (Castaing-Taylor largely on foot), and once there, keeping to the cowboys' schedule. Editing the film was a question of creating a sense of the life of these cowboys as Castaing-Taylor had experienced it: that is, creating an intensified, engaging film experience based on and analogous to what seemed the essential elements of the experience of sheep ranching.

Sweetgrass is structured into a composite year-in-the-life of the sheep and sheep ranchers, beginning in winter and ending at the end of the summer pasturing, as John Ahern, one of the two cowboys who become the central focus of the film (Pat Connolly is the other), considers what he'll be doing in the fall. The decision to begin the film during the winter, when the sheep are sheared and when ewes give birth to lambs (a process carefully manipulated by the sheep ranchers to ensure maximum productivity of lambs), and then to present the cowboys herding the sheep into the mountains at the beginning of summer came relatively late during the editing of the film. Shifting the shearing and the birthing of lambs to the beginning of *Sweetgrass* seems an attempt to resist seeing sheep ranching simply as an entrepreneurial activity, a process that produces saleable commodities. Barbash and Castaing-Taylor were committed to foregrounding the experiences of the people and animals involved in this process, or more specifically, to creating a sense of the ways in which humans and animals interrelated within the activity of sheep ranching as it had been practiced on the Raisland-Allestad Ranch for a century.

Castaing-Taylor shot the film insofar as possible in the classic observational documentary manner exemplified by Frederick Wiseman: that is, without intruding into the various sheep-ranching activities; and in the completed film Barbash and Castaing-Taylor rigorously avoided narration and extradiagetic music. However, while Wiseman sees himself as an essentially detached and neutral observer, both politically and in the sense that his decision to explore a particular institution is instigated by general curiosity rather than by detailed research,[7] no one who has heard Barbash and Castaing-Taylor talk about *Sweetgrass* (or who has listened to the filmmakers' gloss of the film on the commentary track on the *Sweetgrass* DVD) can be in any doubt about the extent of the historical, sociological, anthropological, and biological research that went into this project. Barbash and Castaing-Taylor educated themselves about the history of the domestication of sheep (it is thought that sheep were the first animals domesticated by humans), about the human communities across the planet that have supported sheep ranching, about the history of sheep ranching in general and this American instance of it, and about the physical environment of the area of Montana and Wyoming within which the events depicted in *Sweetgrass* take place. This research is not reported in *Sweetgrass*, but it is often subtly evident within the action of the film.

Further, as cinematographer, Castaing-Taylor sees himself as both a witness and a person sharing the experience he is recording. This is evident in the film's fifth shot, a 45-second close-up of the head of a single bellwether ewe in a winter landscape (fig. 46): the ewe is first seen in profile, chewing (the previous shot is a close-up of several sheep jockeying for the solid feed that has been put out for them), then gradually she seems to become aware of the camera and looks generally in its direction, still chewing, and finally stops chewing and looks directly into the camera. For an extended moment Castaing-Taylor and this sheep are sharing the experience of observing each other. The moment is startling and funny, partly because the ewe seems to be looking not only at Castaing-Taylor but at *us* and at the entire project of documentary cinema. Often, Castaing-Taylor is literally immersed in the activities he films. For example, at the end of the "sheep wreck" passage ("sheep wreck" is the filmmakers' name for the moment when an overgrown trail has stopped the progress of the herds into the mountains [fig. 47]), he films the sheep from sheep-butt level; throughout this 48-second shot, it is as if Castaing-Taylor is one of the sheep and we experience something of how it might look and sound to be part of the herd.

FIGURES 46 AND 47. Bellwether ewe looks at camera *(top)* and a moment of "sheep wreck" on the trail *(bottom)* in Ilisa Barbash and Lucien Castaing-Taylor's *Sweetgrass* (2009).

It is clear throughout *Sweetgrass* that Barbash and Castaing-Taylor were committed, insofar as was practical, to the unedited single shot. In general, the individual shots are unusually lengthy; more than a hundred of the film's 148 shots are longer than 20 seconds; several are more than two minutes long; and many are in effect mini–motion pictures, full of subtle drama and suggestiveness. Early in the film, for example, the camera is filming from the bed of a truck that is driving through a pasture so that the roll of grass mounted on the back of the truck can unspool onto the ground for the hungry sheep; the shot lasts more than two minutes and ends soon after the last part of the bail falls off the truck. The unspooling grass seems a metaphor for the traditional cinematic apparatus of camera and projector—even perhaps for this film's consistent use of extended takes.

Barbash and Castaing-Taylor were also committed to a highly experimental use of sound. Working with Ernst Karel, they found a way of generating an immensely complex environmental soundscape for *Sweetgrass* (among Cambridge filmmakers and films, the most obvious premonition of this aspect of *Sweetgrass,* and of other Sensory Ethnography Lab films, is Gardner's *Forest of Bliss* [1985]). Since the arrival of sound-on-film at the end of the 1920s, the history of cinema, documentary as well as fiction film, has always privileged the human voice, and in particular, dialogue. *Sweetgrass* does include human dialogue—some of it engaging and funny—but this dialogue is but a small part of the auditory experience of the film. We hear the cowboys making a variety of sounds during the shearing and birthing sequences and during the sheep drive; and often we hear the cowboys talking or singing to themselves and to the sheep, the dogs, and the horses. The primary sound during most of *Sweetgrass,* however, is the bleating of the three thousand ewes and lambs, often a loud and intricate din within which indecipherable human voices can be heard yelling to one another or using walkie-talkies. Since lambs and ewes bleat in order to remain in communication with one another amid the mass of other sheep, these moments are emblematic of the complex reality of intra- and interspecies communication that has developed within the cultural activity of raising sheep. Once the herd and Ahern and Connolly have settled into the mountain pasturing, the environmental sounds of birds and other animals, and especially the sound of wind, become important. The relative quiet in the mountains—particularly in contrast to the deafening shearing sequence and after the relentless bleating of the sheep during the drive into the mountains—seems to be one of the factors that over the years has helped draw men into this demanding work.

Frequently in *Sweetgrass* the filmmakers (and Karel) explore what Castaing-Taylor calls the "aesthetic tension" between auditory and visual perspective (close-up sound is used in conjunction with distant action, and vice versa).[8] For example, after Ahern and Connolly have been alone in the mountain pasturing area caring for the sheep for some weeks, the strenuousness and stress of their labor begins to tell, at least on Connolly. At one point, he discovers that the sheep have wandered down into an area that makes protecting them difficult, and he is furious. During a shot nearly two minutes long, recorded from a position far above the action, Connolly can be seen trying to drive the sheep back up to the pasturing area. Two developments occur simultaneously within the shot: Connolly launches into an extended barrage of obscenity, which is heard in auditory close-up; and after a moment, Castaing-Taylor begins a slow zoom back from the already distant view of the sheep and Connolly. The longer Connolly's rant lasts, the funnier it becomes (funny in large measure because we can easily empathize);[9] and the further Castaing-Taylor zooms out, the more impressive is the mountain vista the shot reveals. The combination of Connolly's private fury and the increasingly expansive landscape demonstrates one of the ironies of this form of labor, and perhaps of labor in general: workaday stresses often blind us to the beauty that surrounds us. All in all, the sound experimentation in *Sweetgrass* recalls Peter Kubeka's experiments with dialectic sound and image in *Unsere Afrikareise* (*Our Trip to Africa*, 1966), though often in *Sweetgrass*, Barbash, Castaing-Taylor, and Karel are working dialectically with *synchronized* sound.[10]

Another aspect of the unusual balance in *Sweetgrass* between the visual and the auditory involves the use of "long takes" of two kinds. During the longest shot in the film proper (2 minutes, 36 seconds; a final shot during the credit sequence is a few seconds longer), a woman works to entice an ewe to join her lamb in a pen separate from the rest of the flock. This process involves various actions on the part of ewe and woman, all included within the continuous shot, the length of which creates an implicit tension that reflects the considerable patience demonstrated by the woman. In other instances it is the sound that's continuous. One of the film's most memorable sequences takes place in the mountains: as evening sets in, Ahern prepares the sheep for the night. He is heard gently talking and singing to the sheep and to himself, working to calm the ewes and lambs. His sweet monologue—it is clear that, unlike Connolly, he loves the sheep and this work—is continuous, while we see Ahern in various contexts and from various distances in a series of shots, one of them a 36-second long-shot of Ahern on horseback crossing the horizon—a canonical image from western movies.

On the commentary track for *Sweetgrass*, Castaing-Taylor describes the bell around the neck of the bellwether ewe recorded in the fifth shot, as "made . . . in Switzerland by a Finnish-German American sheepherder who ended up marrying a French shepherdess and moving to the Alps. So it's [*Sweetgrass* is] already culturally syncretic and hybrid." Though this is information that most viewers would not deduce from a screening of the film, it is a clue to an important dimension of the thinking behind *Sweetgrass*. A certain strand in the weave of ethnographic film—originated by Flaherty in *Nanook of the North* and *Moana* and epitomized by John Marshall's *The Hunters* and Robert Gardner's *Dead Birds*—has proposed to offer a representation of a traditional culture "uncorrupted" by modernization. For

Barbash and Castaing-Taylor the quest to represent this kind of cultural "purity" is pointless, because culture by its very nature is always in transition, and every particular cultural practice is regularly confronted by, even formed by, influences from outside itself. This is suggested in a variety of ways during *Sweetgrass*.

As the sheepherders move the sheep down the main street of Big Timber, on the way to the mountains, we see what looks like the traditional town in a classic western—though the Radio Shack store across the street from the camera undercuts what at first seems a romantic evocation of the past. The gorgeous mountain vistas where the sheep are grazed evoke the paintings of the Rocky Mountain School, as well as the western, and yet, even when Ahern and Connolly seem most isolated from the "impurities" of civilization, Connolly uses his cell phone to call home and whine about the difficulty of his job to his mother. As the sheepherders bring the sheep back down from the mountains near the end of the film, we see a sign on a tree indicating that these events have been recorded in Gallatin National Forest, reminding us of the long history of debates about land use and preservation that, in this particular instance, have directly affected the sheepherding depicted in the film: pressure from environmentalists to keep the Yellowstone area entirely wild (within the national park's legal boundaries!) is one of the reasons why the history of pasturing sheep in the mountains near Big Timber is coming to an end.

Sweetgrass includes a number of reflexive moments. From time to time, the ranchers speak to Castaing-Taylor or refer to him. For example, when the Allestad family and friends leave Ahern, Connolly, Castaing-Taylor, and the sheep to return to Big Timber, two of the Allestads yell, "See ya', Lucien!" Later on, the camera is positioned within a tent; Connolly is washing dishes in front of the tent and Ahern is sitting inside. They are chatting about this and that, when Ahern looks toward the back of the tent and says, "Kinda warm in here; Lucien went to sleep." The sheep, too, sometimes respond directly to Castaing-Taylor's presence; he and his camera make them nervous when he's too close. It would have been an easy matter to eliminate these moments the way Fred Wiseman does and the way most nature films do, in order to sustain the illusion of an invisible observer; but it is precisely because such invisibility *is* an illusion that Barbash and Castaing-Taylor avoid it. Castaing-Taylor's presence is in fact part of the experience he is documenting, as in a sense our seeing the film is as well: *Sweetgrass* is about the transformation of a way of life and about the cultural practice of memorializing it within the history of cinema.

Barbash and Castaing-Taylor's interest is in the nuances of hybridity and transformation; they do not view change as corruption, but as an inevitable dimension of all cultural practices. Though *Sweetgrass* is an instance of salvage ethnography, it is not a film about "how things were," in the sense that things had been a particular way since time immemorial. It is a record of how things were changing in a particular environment at a particular moment in history. This is emphasized by

FIGURE 48. John Ahern (on left) moving onto the next job at the conclusion of Ilisa Barbash and Lucien Castaing-Taylor's *Sweetgrass* (2009). Courtesy Ilisa Barbash and Lucien Castaing-Taylor.

the two final shots of the film. Immediately following the herding of the sheep into the Big Timber stockyard, the film cuts to a close-up of Ahern in the passenger's seat of a truck being driven by another man (fig. 48). The driver asks him what he has planned for the fall; Ahern responds, "I wasn't gonna worry about it for a week or two," and the shot continues visually for another minute, as the truck speeds down the highway, the landscape whizzing by out the driver's window; when the screen goes dark, the sound of the truck on the road continues, accompanying the first set of closing credits. More than anyone else in the film, Ahern has come to represent the tradition of sheepherding in the American West, and seeing him sitting quietly in the truck, looking ahead, simultaneously prolongs our sense of Ahern's serenity about the work he does and presents him as a man in motion, being carried away from the past and into a fast-approaching future that remains beyond his ken, and ours.

    The final image of *Sweetgrass* is a vista of the Beartooth range in early fall. The shot is devoid of human presence, but the sounds of animal life can be heard. Over this stationary, 2-minute, 40-second shot, extensive rolling credits thank the people from the Allestad Ranch and from the Big Timber area who contributed in one way or another to the production of the film, as well as a considerable number of people with whom Barbash and Castaing-Taylor conferred during the editing. This concluding moment can be read in various ways. The mountain vista suggests perhaps that wildness remains at least part of the reality of the American West and that the demise of sheep ranching will enhance this wildness, transforming this environment once again. That this landscape is visible behind the extensive rolling credits (surprisingly extensive for a film that involved a one-person crew, two editors, and a sound designer) is a final reminder that we always see the natural world within the context of human society and its history of exploiting natural resources for what have been defined as the necessities of life—including, in our transforming moment, the "necessity" of cinema.

"SHEEPLE": CASTAING-TAYLOR'S
AUDIO-VIDEO INSTALLATIONS

Sheep and humans have existed uneasily with each other since we first domesticated them in Mesopotamia ten-thousand-odd years ago in the Neolithic Revolution; sheep were quite possibly the first domesticated livestock animal. They gave humanity our first staple proteins: milk and meat. Not to mention their skins, for shelter—and a couple of thousand years later, also their wool. They wouldn't exist without us, and couldn't survive without us, because of the way we've bred them (to maximize both birth weight and the number of live births) over the millennia. So I don't think you can distinguish between "people" and "sheep." It's more that we're so many variations of sheeple.

LUCIEN CASTAING-TAYLOR[11]

In the spring of 2009, I was invited to speak at a conference sponsored by the graduate students in the Department of Comparative Literature and Film at the University of Iowa called "Avant-Doc: Intersections of Avant-Garde and Documentary Film." The focus of this conference was what was coming to seem a liminal zone between the two film histories, evidenced by the more and more frequent production of films that fit both categories or that function somewhere between them.[12] The fact that an "Avant-Doc" conference could be organized suggests that what in earlier decades may have seemed a set of intermittent and unrelated crossovers within the relatively distinct histories of documentary and avant-garde film is increasingly understood as an evolving tradition. The proliferating combination of social and environmental anxieties during recent years seems to have energized a desire on the part of some filmmakers to combine cinema's ability to create representations of cultures and subcultures (long considered the focus of documentary) with its capacity for retraining perception and providing experiences akin to meditation (generally identified with certain forms of avant-garde film). While *Sweetgrass* can be said to rest more fully on the documentary side of this zone, the short installation videos that emerged from the project, and most especially, *Hell Roaring Creek* (2010), seem closer to the work of filmmakers generally identified with the American avant-garde (Castaing-Taylor is credited as the sole author of the installation videos).

In *Hell Roaring Creek* the sheep and sheep ranchers mass at Hell Roaring Creek at dawn, then cross the creek. The piece is composed of three sustained sync-sound shots (6 minutes, 42 seconds; 8 minutes, 21 seconds; 4 minutes, 11 seconds, respectively), filmed by a tripod-mounted camera set up in the middle of the creek facing the rushing water so that when the herd and herdsmen cross the creek they move into the frame from screen right and out of the frame to screen left. The first and second shot, and the second and third are separated by 10-second moments of darkness. Each successive shot involves a slight change in the composition: for the second shot, Castaing-Taylor zoomed in slightly; for shot three, he zoomed back out. As in *Sweetgrass,* sound is very important in *Hell Roaring Creek;* indeed, its importance is dramatized by the fact that we hear the creek for 42 seconds before we see it; then, at the end, we continue to hear it for 30 seconds after the screen goes dark (the sound seems continuous through the 10-second moments that separate the shots).

There are three general forms of movement within *Hell Roaring Creek:* the continuous motion of the water of the creek rushing toward the camera; the real-time arrival of dawn, gradually lightening the scene; and the motion of sheep, cowboys, horses, and dogs arriving at the creek, then crossing. At the beginning, the film seems to be about the creek itself. After about a minute, slight movements begin to be visible and sounds other than the creek begin to be faintly audible, and just after two minutes, we hear a dog bark and soon realize the herd is nearby. The most dramatic action in the video, of course, is the herd and herdsmen negotiating the shallow rushing water, a process that begins 4 minutes, 36 seconds into the video. As he shot footage for *Sweetgrass* and the shorter videos, Castaing-Taylor was careful to look at the sheep as both a collectivity and as a group of individuals, even intelligent individuals (on the commentary track for the *Sweetgrass* DVD, he says, "For the proverbial dumbest animal, they [sheep] have an amazing kind of intelligence"), and the double nature of sheep is dramatically evident in *Hell Roaring Creek.* No two sheep seem to cross the creek in the same way. The lambs often hurry across; the ewes tend to move more slowly and with more dignity. Some sheep are content to cross by themselves; some cross in small clusters; some negotiate the crossing in a series of leaps; others, at a run; still others, slowly and carefully. Some are quiet, others vocally expressive.

For anyone familiar with the full range of film history, including the developments that led to cinema itself, *Hell Roaring Creek* is evocative of Eadweard Muybridge's motion studies. Castaing-Taylor uses the rigorously framed, only very gradually changing image of this mountain landscape, as the "grid" against which to measure the movements of the animals—though he goes Muybridge one better by allowing us to study the sheep as they move through a natural environment (fig. 49).[13]

As a cinematic meditation on a particular place and moment, *Hell Roaring Creek* is an accomplished instance of what has become in recent decades a tradition in American avant-garde filmmaking, exemplified by Larry Gottheim's breakthrough

FIGURE 49. Hell Roaring Creek as the "sheeple" begin to cross, in Lucien Castaing-Taylor's *Hell Roaring Creek* (2010). Courtesy Lucien Castaing-Taylor.

Fog Line (1970) and much of the work of Peter Hutton, James Benning, and Sharon Lockhart, all of whom have worked with rigorously organized, extended shots of landscape and cityscape.[14] The most obvious distinction between the *Sweetgrass* installation videos and the work of these "avant-garde" filmmakers is the nature of Barbash and Castaing-Taylor's commitment to the animals and people recorded. Gottheim, Hutton, and Benning often use the presence of people in their films as a generalized marker of human presence and an indication of scale rather than as their focus. This is analogous to the way in which human beings and animals are positioned within nineteenth-century American landscape painting, especially in the work of the Hudson River School, Rocky Mountain School, and Luminist paint-ers. In *Sweetgrass* and in *Hell Roaring Creek* (and the other installation videos) human and animal activities within the landscape *are* the focus, and Castaing-Taylor's extended shots allow for a deeper awareness of the particulars of the experi-ences of individual animals and people. Like Benning and Hutton, Barbash and Castaing-Taylor are committed to landscape, but—to return to nineteenth-century American landscape painting—more in the manner of Winslow Homer than of Thomas Cole, Thomas Moran, or Martin Johnson Heade.

Except for *Hell Roaring Creek,* all the installation pieces Castaing-Taylor edited from the Sweetgrass footage are reworkings of events depicted in *Sweetgrass.* In some cases, the differences between what is included in *Sweetgrass* and the rele-vant gallery piece are relatively few. For example, the primary difference between *Daybreak on the Bedground* (2010) and the comparable sequence from *Sweetgrass* is the inclusion in the former of a coughing fit John Ahern has before riding down to join the herd. In other instances, the differences are considerable.

The High Trail (2010) involves the most elaborate reworking of a sequence from *Sweetgrass,* specifically a portion of the movement of the herd down from the high mountain pasture at the end of the summer. In *Sweetgrass* this portion of the descent is depicted in a single, 80-second shot that begins as a wide mountain vista; after about 20 seconds, during which we hear the distant sound of sheep, but cannot see where in the image the sheep might be, the camera begins a slow zoom into the scene, revealing that in fact the sheep are winding along what appears to be a precarious drop-off. This shot is followed by a brief shot of the moon and a bit of treetop. In *The High Trail* the movement of the sheep down the mountain along the drop-off involves nine shots, beginning with an expanded version of the extended shot used in *Sweetgrass.* Here, the shot lasts nearly 2½ minutes, and the zoom doesn't begin for 75 seconds, extending the mystery of the location of the sheep. During the final 30 seconds of the shot, we hear the sheepherders talking on walkie-talkies and the quiet voice of Lawrence Allestad complimenting his dog on doing a good job; Allestad's voice continues through the next seven shots, as Castaing-Taylor intercuts between often beautiful compositions of the sheep in motion, all of these shots filmed closer to the herd than the original shot, and two shots of a wild mountain goat who seems fascinated with the sheeple. The sequence concludes with the shot of the moon and treetop from *Sweetgrass.*

Castaing-Taylor's sequence films (to use John Marshall's term) offer an opportunity to consider how editing strategies vary depending on context. For Barbash and Castaing-Taylor to finish a coherent feature about sheep ranching, much detail needed to be eliminated; but for a short video about a particular moment within this process to be coherent, more detail was necessary. Of course, though the short videos certainly work as theatrical projections, their ultimate context, so far as Castaing-Taylor was concerned, was as art gallery installations. I have not, so far, had the opportunity to see any of these pieces presented as installations,[15] but I imagine that within a gallery (and here I'm thinking of galleries as primarily an urban phenomenon), the subject matter of these videos would have a more powerful impact than seeing them projected. It is not unusual to see expansive imagery of the American West in a movie theater: *Brokeback Mountain* (2005), which also includes spectacular imagery of sheepherding, is a case in point. But to walk into an urban gallery space and find oneself immersed in the sound and imagery of any of the scenes depicted in Castaing-Taylor's installations could be fascinating and powerful—indeed, for those familiar with nineteenth-century American landscape painting, the experience might evoke the dramatic ways in which some of the epic paintings of the American West by Albert Bierstadt and Thomas Moran were originally presented to the public.[16]

THE SENSORY ETHNOGRAPHY LAB:
J. P. SNIADECKI, STEPHANIE SPRAY, VÉRÉNA
PARAVEL, AND *LEVIATHAN*

The approach to filmmaking that instigated and informed the making of *Sweetgrass* was institutionalized as Castaing-Taylor developed the Sensory Ethnography program, and it has been absorbed by the students in the program. As Barbash and Castaing-Taylor were struggling to find a satisfactory final form for *Sweetgrass*, Castaing-Taylor was showing various versions of the edited footage to students and colleagues at and beyond Harvard. Like Ed Pincus, whose early screenings of rushes and early edits of portions of *Diaries* helped give other filmmakers the confidence to make personal documentaries, Castaing-Taylor's screening of early edits of *Sweetgrass* and its satellite installations helped open what seemed a new avenue for aspiring filmmakers interested in documenting the ways in which human beings function within their environments. The Sensory Ethnography Lab is a young program, but it has been productive of impressive films by several filmmakers, among them J. P. Sniadecki, Stephanie Spray, and Véréna Paravel.

Sniadecki's *Chaiqian (Demolition)* (2008) makes clear both the continuities between the *Sweetgrass* project and Sniadecki's work and several distinctions. The first shot of *Chaiqian (Demolition)* ends with a 360-degree panorama that reveals the contours of a particular landscape—a city block in Chengdu, China, that is being redeveloped—that most of the remaining film will explore and provides a subtle metaphor for both the film and the world it is exploring: before the extended pan begins, Sniadecki records a man, one of the managers of the demolition site, relaxing on what appears to be a broad steel surface that rests on the ground. Nearly two minutes into the shot, another man, visible far below the plane on which the relaxing man is sitting, walks into the image from the bottom left, then seems to walk *under* what we now realize is the top of some kind of steel structure.[17] The arrival of the second man instigates the panning that subsequently follows his walk through the space, but Sniadecki's initial revelation that what seems a simple, level space is actually multilayered prefigures the issue of social class, which becomes increasingly evident as *Chaiqian* proceeds.

During the 62 minutes of *Chaiqian*, Sniadecki documents the labors of a group of migrant workers who are combing through the rubble from whatever structure has previously been on this space for rebar.[18] The process involves several backhoes that work at shaking the rebar loose from the cement that encases it; and men working with a variety of tools finish the job of cleaning the strands of rebar, piling them together, and finally loading them onto trucks. Sniadecki often films in close proximity to these events, sometimes mimicking the workers' actions in his style. In one particularly elaborate shot (it lasts 4 minutes, 26 seconds)—as in *Sweetgrass, Hell Roaring Creek,* and Sniadecki's earlier film, *Songhua,* the shooting pace throughout *Chaiqian* models patience—Sniadecki follows a man who is carrying a tank up the main pile of rubble, where a second man connects this tank to a compressed air tank, then walks to a position past a man pounding cement with a sledgehammer, lights the nozzle of his blowtorch, and goes to work, apparently dividing the rebar pieces into manageable lengths: the continuity of the several actions is reflected in Sniadecki's continuous shot, and each new portion of the workers' actions necessitates an obvious readjustment of Sniadecki's position.[19]

As *Chaiqian* develops, Sniadecki's relationship with the workers seems to evolve. For approximately the first half of the film, he is just a close observer of their labors, but soon the workers begin to wonder about him: about 15 minutes into the film, one man asks, "Where did you film these last few days?," and Sniadecki tells him, "I was resting and taking care of things." He is invited to eat with the workers, though he refuses, apparently preferring to continue filming, and later is the subject of a meal-time conversation among the managers that reveals some of the particulars of his filming process:

"He gave a pack of cigarettes to each worker."
"Who?"
"The foreigner."
"Everyone got a pack."

At the end of the work shift, the laborers use a hose to wash their clothes and make plans for the evening (some of them joke about calling a "little sister"—a prostitute); the day ends when several of the workers and Sniadecki walk to the central square of Chengdu, where the workers pose for a portrait in front of a statue of Chairman Mao and are subsequently accosted by a young woman police officer concerned about a group of migrant workers not only being in this public place but being filmed. An 8-second moment of darkness brings the film to what is apparently the next morning. There is less activity than on the previous day, and Sniadecki learns that most of the workers have left the site: "I didn't get a chance to say good-bye," he complains. "It's a little sad."

In the implicit analogy between the laborers' work and Sniadecki's filmmaking, *Chaiqian* evokes *The Man with a Movie Camera* (1929), though, of course, the social transformation evident in China in July 2007, when *Chaiqian* was shot, was (and remains) quite different from, in some ways the inverse of, the transformation into an industrialized communist state celebrated in the Vertov film. *Chaiqian* (and *Songhua*, Sniadecki's exploration of life along the Songhua River in northern China as it flows through the city of Harbin) can be understood as inventive contributions to the tradition of the city symphony (that form of film about urban life that depicts a composite day in the life of a city); both films are synecdoches: that is, a relatively limited portion of each city is used to represent a larger urban space.[20]

The fact that Sniadecki focuses on the harvesting of the rebar rather than on the destruction of the buildings that were originally in this space or the construction the demolition has made way for suggests his commitment to the labors that change involves rather than the particulars of before and after. For Sniadecki, this process is worthy of attention, primarily because of his respect for the laborers, but also because the workers' considerable efforts are productive and make possible the conservation of an important resource. Near the end of the film, Sniadecki asks Mr. Deng, one of the managers of the operation, how much rebar has been taken from the site and Deng says he thinks it's more than 200 tons. Sniadecki is interested in what can be saved as the past transitions into the future—both as an environmentally political person and as a filmmaker.

Ethnographic film has traditionally functioned, and in the work of the filmmakers associated with the Sensory Ethnography Lab, continues to function, as a form of salvage ethnography. Traditionally, however, the disappearing way of life has involved the arrival of modern industry within a non-urban setting. *Chaiqian* focuses on a dimension of urban experience that is itself transitional, ephemeral, continually disappearing, then appearing again somewhere else. The need to demolish a building requires the formation of a community of men (mostly men, but some women: near the end of *Chaiqian*, Sniadecki shares a moment with a woman laborer who is reminded of her own son by some bicycling boys).[21] These men and women grow to know each other, but when the job is done, this community moves on or disperses, is "demolished" along with whatever physical structure was involved. Sniadecki's sadness at not having had a chance to say goodbye to the workers he has gotten to know, and in a sense has worked with, is a modern, urban vestige of the poignant loss implicit in so many salvage ethnography projects.

Though her films have much in common stylistically with Barbash and Castaing-Taylor's and Sniadecki's—like them, she uses extended shots and complex soundscapes—Stephanie Spray's decisions about what to film and how to function in relation to what she films reveal a somewhat different sensibility. Spray seems less concerned with finding a reason to film what she films—the salvage ethnography reason evident in *Sweetgrass* and in *Chaiqian*, or the environmentally political reason in *Songhua* (where one of the themes is the pollution of the river)—than in recording the experience of simply being present with families in rural Nepal during their day-to-day activities over long periods of time.[22]

Perhaps the most unusual dimension of Spray's films is the way in which she positions herself and her camera in relation to events. In her earliest films, *Kale and Kale* (2007) and *Monsoon-Reflections* (2008) the camera is handheld by Spray, often as she sits on the ground. Even when she is following someone walking, her camera generally records from a position below waist level. In *Monsoon-*

Reflections, a depiction of the labor of several women, Spray establishes this ground-level position within the film's opening 2-minute shot, during which we see a young woman (Bindu Gayek) kneeling to grind peppers and garlic with a stone, recorded indoors and in-close, at the level of Gayek's hands. In combination with the shot's length, Spray's physical position as cameraperson, or at least the position that seems implied by the position of her camera, seems the essence of humility, a meditation pose. Although Castaing-Taylor and Sniadecki accept their status as "foreigners" within the worlds they film, Spray attempts to achieve an unusual kind of inclusion, where she can meditate on the moment-to-moment realities of Nepalese daily life as if she were a member of this family. Indeed, in *As Long as There's Breath* (2009), the Gayek women often refer to Spray as "daughter" and sometimes talk with her at length, asking questions about her family.

Like Barbash, Castaing-Taylor and Sniadecki (particularly in *Songhua*), Spray expands the limited space revealed by the frame of her video camera with highly complex sound environments (Ernst Karel did Spray's and Sniadecki's sound designs). Her films often use image and sound in a kind of dialectic, where what we are seeing is not what is most evident in the sound. *Untitled* (2010), a single, continuous 14-minute shot—recorded as usual, from a position close to the ground—focuses on a man and woman sitting on the steps of a small village temple. The man is quietly drunk and the woman, who has also been drinking, teases him, pulling hairs out of his face and chest, playfully slapping him; and their little daughter and son ring a bell next to the dwelling, seemingly to have fun annoying their father. The man and woman face both the camera and another road: several people who pass behind the camera are acknowledged by the couple, and the noises of motorized vehicles seem to pass close to the scene but, again, behind the camera. On one level Spray's way of working with sound in relation to her imagery recalls the sound-image games James Benning plays with viewers in films like *11 X 14* (1976) and *13 Lakes* (2004); but it is also a visual way of demonstrating that she is not a detached observer, but someone *within* the circle of the action, interested not so much in providing us with information as in being immersed, and immersing viewers, within another way of life.

As Long as There's Breath, another film about the Gayek family, and in particular Bindu and Chet Kumari, is stylistically consistent with Spray's earlier work, but it has a more dramatic structure and is more cognizant of the political realities of Nepalese life than the earlier films. The drama of *As Long as There's Breath* is evident on two levels. As we watch daily activities and listen to the conversations among the Gayek family, it becomes clear that they are waiting for a visit by Kamal Gayek, the oldest son of Bindu and Bhakte Gayek, who has joined the YCL (the Youth Communist League), an illegal Maoist group. Nearly every conversation in the film at some point refers to Kamal and the family's expectation that he will visit, and though Bindu and Chet Kumari are told that Kamal has just been seen in the village while they've been working in a rice paddy and Bindu leaves to find her son, Kamal never makes an appearance. In the film's concluding shot, Bindu expresses her worry about her son's safety. On this level, *As Long as There's Breath* is reminiscent of *Waiting for Godot,* and though the family's concern for Kamal seems more serious than the action in Beckett's comic play, in fact, Spray's film is also full of humor, which provides the film's other dramatic level.

As Long as There's Breath is punctuated by a series of conversations among Bindu, Bhakte, and Chet Kumari, and in other instances, among groups of women; and these conversations are often, at least for an American audience, surprising in their candidness. At one point, a group of women sitting on a porch discuss sexuality: first, Bindu talks about a wife who would "climb trees and then spread herself out for her bother-in-law"; then the women talk about dildos. One neighbor apparently has a wooden one, and Bindu remarks how smooth it is and that using it doesn't make you itch. Apparently, this neighbor asked her husband to get it for her before he left to work in India. Then the conversation turns to a widow, who received a rubber dildo when she went to get her pension: a pump is "attached to it that makes it big and erect" and it has two "potatoes" underneath; "you lie down and put it in. Then you tell it how long you want it to run . . ."; "When you're satisfied, it turns off and shrinks to a little wad."

While Spray's films and Sniadecki's early films resulted from the filmmakers' immersion over substantial periods of time in far-flung locations, Sensory Ethnography Lab filmmakers have also explored cultural experiences closer to home, in several instances in New York City. Indeed, these films exemplify the commitment of the SEL to a sense of culture as continuous transformation, interpenetration, and imbrication at least as obviously as any of those discussed so far. Of the New York City films, *Foreign Parts* (2010), the feature-length collaboration of Sniadecki and Véréna Paravel, has been the most successful, achieving a level of visibility comparable to that of *Sweetgrass.*[23] An exploration of the automobile junkyard at Willets Point, Queens, *Foreign Parts* was originally Paravel's idea, and a spin-off of an earlier film, *7 Queens* (2008), during which Paravel walked through some of the neighborhoods along the Number 7 subway line in order to experience the myriad ethnic communities that are serviced by the line.

As Paravel has explained, the moment she first saw Willets Point she knew that this environment would be the subject of her next film, and also that, because Willets Point can be a dangerous environment, the project would profit from a male collaborator.[24] It is easy to imagine what made the first sight of Willets Point so powerful for Paravel: its 250 shops, dealing with every aspect of automobile maintenance and repair, and its location near Citi-Field (the new home of the New York Mets) and LaGuardia Airport as well as the Number 7 subway line offer an unusually complex visual and auditory field, a phantasmagoria of image and sound

(Ernst Karel would be responsible for the sound edit and mix). Sniadecki came on board in the summer of 2008, and the two shared in the filming of the junkyard, soon to be a casualty of redevelopment by the city of New York: *Foreign Parts* captures the routine of Willets Point during what appears to be one of its final years.

The primary focus of *Foreign Parts* is a set of interesting individuals: Luis and Sara Zaplain, a couple who live in a van (Luis freelances at the junkyard and is often in prison); Julia, an elderly woman who has lived in a small van much of her life and seems to be Willets Point's resident beggar; and Joe Ardizzone, the lone legal resident of the junkyard, who has lived in Willets Point for all of his seventy-six years. And like *Sweetgrass, Chaiqian (Demolition),* and several of Spray's films, *Foreign Parts* is much involved in depicting labor and the spaces in which labor takes place. Paravel and Sniadecki also seem particularly concerned with revealing the ethnic complexity of Willets Point. Early in the film, two men sitting in a doorway sing along with a Spanish-language song about Puerto Rico on the radio, and in the following shot, two Hassidic men maneuver around the ubiquitous puddles to a shop where a man is studying Judaism.

As is true in their earlier films, Paravel and Sniadecki do more than observe. They become part of the life of the junkyard, interviewing a range of individuals who work there and following the lives of the Zaplains, Julia, and Ardizzone across the months. At one point, Julia is recorded dancing with whoever is holding the camera or perhaps with the camera itself; when Ardizzone goes to City Hall to find out information about the city's plans for his neighborhood, the filmmakers follow him; and when Luis Zaplain goes to jail upstate, the filmmakers remain in touch with Sara during the lonely months and are present when Luis returns—indeed, Sara finds out about Luis being released on Paravel's cell phone, and as he and Sara are reunited, Sniadecki tells Luis, "You look good! Mind if we film?," and Luis answers, "No, go ahead," and greets Paravel on camera, hugging her, before he and Sara walk off together (fig. 50).

Paravel and Sniadecki shot at Willets Point off and on for two years, and the film is arranged as a seasonal cycle, beginning and ending in summer. The cyclic structure suggests the considerable history of this junkyard—the work of junking and repairing cars has been going on year-round in Willets Point for decades. Paravel and Sniadecki's frequent wide-angle framing of the activities in the junkyard evokes Robert Gardner's compositions in *Forest of Bliss* (1986): we see many layers of activity at various distances from the camera simultaneously and hear many layers of sound, all conditioned by the natural environment as it is affected by the seasons (Willets Point, next to an inlet of Flushing Bay, is often partially under water and is home to many birds). During the 80 minutes of *Foreign Parts,* the rhythms of the junkyard and the panorama of the many men and women who work there (a text at the conclusion of the film estimates the number of workers at two thousand) become familiar.

FIGURE 50. Luis and Sara Zaplain, reunited at Willets Point after Luis's release from prison, in Véréna Paravel and John Paul Sniadecki's *Foreign Parts* (2010). Courtesy Véréna Paravel and John Paul Sniadecki.

As depicted in *Foreign Parts*, Willets Point is a sensuous place. In the earliest sequence in the film, a man on a forklift shakes a car apart, revealing its innards; he cuts hoses and tubes so that fluids run out. This sequence creates a context for both the "intimacies" these workers have with automobiles and for the filmmakers' intimate engagement with the place and the people who work there. Essentially, the junkyard becomes a metaphor for the process of filmmaking: Paravel and Sniadecki "take Willets Point apart"—recording images that represent one or another dimension of the place and warehousing the results—then, during the editing process, they put the usable parts together into a piece they hope can move those who see the results.

In this age of hysterical consumption and endless distraction, it has become commonplace for people, especially young people, to escape from sensory awareness of their daily surround by reducing their focus to the miniature screens of their smart phones. These screens offer the panoply of codifiable information that seems necessitated by the demands of social interchange and the pressures of education and work within an economically precarious society. Implicitly the phones reduce the world, or at least those aspects of the world necessary for practical life, to what seems a manageable size. The sensory world is increasingly understood as a distraction from the electronic environment within which smart phones (and all our other digital devices for accessing information and communicating with others) function. As a result, it is hardly surprising that a new generation of motion picture artists would become interested in confronting this tendency toward the miniaturization of sensual experience, that Castaing-Taylor and his SEL filmmaker colleagues would dedicate themselves to the production of motion picture experiences that evoke the power and fascinations of the sensory world.

Nevertheless, Castaing-Taylor and Véréna Paravel's *Leviathan* (2012) *is* surprising—its immersion of its audience within the audio-visual surround created from the filmmakers' experiences on fishing boats shipping out of New Bedford, Massachusetts, feels not only overwhelming, but quite new in the annals of modern theatrical cinema. While the film's title seems to be a reference to the biblical leviathan (the film's opening quotations from the Book of Job confirm the biblical reference), the leviathan in *Leviathan* is the film itself. Made to be shown on the big screen with surround sound, *Leviathan* swallows *us*—regurgitating us out of the theater at the end of 90 minutes, exhausted and happy to have lived through what is as close to a sensory trauma as any documentary in recent memory.

Of course, there are precedents for *Leviathan*. The nineteenth-century maritime paintings of Winslow Homer and J. M. W. Turner, for example, and on a different register, the action painting of Jackson Pollock and Willem de Kooning: Castaing-Taylor–Paravel's digital cameras-in-motion seem at least as close an approximation to the procedures of action painting as Stan Brakhage's gestural 16mm filming of the late 1950s, which has often been compared with the action painters' gestural brushwork. There are cinematic precedents as well, including Georges Franju's *Le Sang des bêtes* (*The Blood of the Beasts,* 1949), as well as Stan Brakhage's *The Act of Seeing with One's Own Eyes* (1971), which is regularly shown to Sensory Ethnography Lab students, and Robert Gardner's *Forest of Bliss* (1986).

What will most powerfully strike most viewers of *Leviathan* is the soundscape of the film, designed first by Ernst Karel, then re-engineered by Hollywood sound designer Jacob Ribicoff (*The Wrestler, Revolutionary Road*). In *Leviathan*, as in most of the films to come out of the Sensory Ethnography Lab, sound comes before image and has sensory impact at least as powerful and complex as the imagery. In this case, the near-deafening noise of the fishing boat and of the processing of the fish and shellfish creates an aural "nest" within which human speech can rarely be made out. If the film's spectacular imagery completes the experience of the film, it does not deflect attention from the sound. Even as we sometimes struggle to *see* what we're seeing and to understand how it fits within the daily round of the fishing boats, we continue to struggle, as the filmmakers must have, to become accustomed to the din of the industrial process of harvesting the ocean.

The endless motion of the boat, buffeted by waves and wind, is continually visceral: severed fish heads float toward us, then away, toward us, then away; the view out the side of the boat reveals a nearly black ocean—much of *Leviathan* was shot at night—that seems to move one way as boat and camera roll another and as the inevitable flock of seagulls floats above the fray, waiting for fish scraps to be washed overboard. Often, we are (literally) immersed in the film, as the camera (thanks to some modifications by Leonard Retel Helmrich) reveals what's going on around the boat under the surface of the sea. Throughout *Leviathan,* the intense demands of the dangerous work being done on these boats—some of the most dangerous work on the planet—and the stamina and skill of the men who are dedicated to it are obvious. Throughout *Leviathan* we are experiencing not only the labor of the fishermen, but the labor of the filmmakers themselves, from *inside* their experience as we feel rocked to and fro, continually astonished that the theatrical experience of documentary cinema, even after more than a century, can still powerfully reinvigorate our awareness of the sensory world.

Earlier in this study, I described what I called the "occupational hazard" of personal documentary—the fact that as family dynamics change, a personal documentary filmmaker can find that what was once an admired and appreciated film has become a familial problem. Ethnographic filmmaking, too, has its occupational hazards. What may at one time have seemed obvious to ethnographic filmmakers about a cultural group, that is, what they assumed was "true" or important according to their understanding of then-current anthropological research, has often been rendered misguided and false by subsequent research. Indeed, decisions that may have been made with the best intentions—for example, John Marshall's deciding for his first major film, *The Hunters,* to portray the !Kung San as an isolated communal band of hunters, noble and peaceful, a people with much to teach us—have often come to seem, even to the filmmakers themselves, a myopic romanticizing of history that ignored the broader realities of that moment. In a sense, a fictional film is freed from the need to be accurate, but a documentary, especially an ethnographic documentary (to *be* ethnographic) must be true to its subject—and yet this is virtually impossible because both the filmmakers and those depicted are in continual transformation (the presence of the filmmaking itself is evidence of this).

However, even if we were to agree that Marshall, Gardner, and Asch often didn't "get it right" in anthropological terms, that they sometimes substituted their own romantic assumptions for what now seems reality, there seems little question that their initial motivations, at least those they were conscious of, were decent and humane, and that their willingness to devote themselves to observing and recording ways of life distant from their own, even if this meant putting themselves in harm's way, and to make these ways of life familiar to others, is evidence of a deep commitment both to a broader understanding of human experience and to an expanded vision of what is possible for cinema. Further, their very failures to recognize that their envisioning of others was largely a projection of themselves allows their films to function for us in a new way—as emblems not of the Truth of other cultures, but of the complex realities of limited, fallible human beings working to understand each other. If ethnographic film has often been more about the filmmakers than their subjects, then ethnographic film becomes, if not another form of personal documentary, at least another form of personal expression. And the experiences of these films, like the experiences of any other form of personal expression, can continue to be fascinating and valuable—just in different ways within a new context.

The Sensory Ethnography Lab and the films coming out of it have built on the experiences of an earlier generation. Do the SEL filmmakers "get it right"? Inevitably, as time passes, we will learn more about the realities surrounding the experiences they document, realities that may, probably will, throw the apparent assumptions and implicit conclusions of their films into question. But this is inevitable for anyone searching for Truth or even just truth. The alternative, to *not* care about reality, is hardly to be preferred, and in any case, modern film history is deluged with big-budget fictional fantasies, made by men and women with little concern for anything but enhancing the financial bottom line by feeding viewers the most obvious and dangerous clichés about "us" and "them." Whatever their failures, the SEL filmmakers working (as Marshall, Gardner, and Asch themselves did) to learn, as best they can, from their cinematic forebears' successes and mistakes, and from their own, are at least willing to invest themselves in "getting it right" in their filmmaking, and often at considerable personal sacrifice. If they are doomed by the continuing transformations of culture and knowledge to fail, there is, as Faulkner might say, a "splendor" in their failures. And by taking account of these failures, they and we will learn from what they *do* achieve both as observers of human experience and as filmmakers.

Epilogue

Personal histories are processes of change in time, and the change itself is one of the things immediately experienced.

WILLIAM JAMES, *ESSAYS IN RADICAL EMPIRICISM*[1]

Both of the documentary histories that have been nurtured in Cambridge continue to develop and to be productive. Indeed, in recent years they have become increasingly imbricated with each other in large measure because so many of the major contributors continue to be part of a small, regularly interactive, generally mutually supportive filmmaking community. The passing of Ricky Leacock in 2011 instigated a coming together of much of the Cambridge documentary community and those with connections to it, as well as a useful body of new information about Leacock (Leacock's *The Feeling of Being There: A Filmmaker's Memoire,* edited by Valerie Lelonde [Paris: Semeïon, 2011], for example) and attempts by Documentary Educational Resources to make available Leacock's extensive body of work, including at long last the many personal documentaries he and Lelonde produced during his final years.

Of course, some of the early pioneers of both ethnographic filmmaking and personal documentary continue to be productive and to play a role in contemporary thinking. Robert Gardner has been working to be sure that his films, and the information about them that he himself is privy to, will be available to the next generation of programmers, critics, and historians; and those who have followed his work have rallied to honor it with retrospectives and with cinematic homage. When it became clear that Ed Pincus's health was in serious danger, the Harvard Film Archive hosted a full retrospective of his films, accompanied by discussions with Pincus and his various collaborators. Much of this work had not been publicly screened for decades, and it was clear that Haden Guest, the archive's director, was excited about the possibility of working with Pincus to see his work onto DVD and back into general circulation. A retrospective at Lincoln Center followed in November, 2012.

Instigated by the Sensory Ethnography Lab (SEL), Cambridge filmmakers continue to reinvigorate the history of ethnographic cinema. As I write this, new SEL films are in progress, including Stephanie Spray and Pacho Velez's *Manakamana*, filmed on the aerial tramway that takes the Nepalese (some of them familiar from earlier Spray films) and visitors from other places to a mountaintop temple dedicated to the goddess Manakamana; and J. P. Sniadecki and Libbie Cohn's China-cliché–killing *People's Park*, a single 75-minute, hip-level dolly shot through a busy park in Chengdu, China, on a Saturday. The early versions of these films suggest that in each instance, the new work will reconfirm not only the talent of the SEL filmmakers but their ability to incorporate into their process not simply earlier ethnographic work (and the history of critique of that work) but also aesthetic breakthroughs normally identified with avant-garde cinema. *Manakamana*'s 8-plus-minute, single-take portraits are reminiscent of James Benning's 10-minute shots in *13 Lakes* (2004; Spray: "His films made a strong impression; *13 Lakes* was the first that I saw, and is a favorite") and Sniadecki's willingness to try a 75-minute shot in *People's Park* may owe something to Sharon Lockhart's 45-minute "shots" in *Double Tide* (2009; Sniadecki did a sound workshop with Lockhart in Maine during her making of that film).[2]

The Boston area, and Cambridge in particular, also continue to nurture personal documentary. The major early contributors to the genre persist in exploring new avenues into the personal. Ross McElwee's recent films—*In Paraguay* and *Photographic Memory*—are engaging and insightful contributions to his cinematic chronicle. Robb Moss continues to revisit those friends who were the subjects of *Riverdogs* and form the nucleus of *The Same River Twice*, filming them for a third "river film" that he sometimes jokingly refers to as "The Naked and the Dead." And Alfred Guzzetti has returned to family portraiture in *Time Exposure*, in a manner that recontextualizes his breakthrough feature, *Family Portrait Sittings*. Even Ed Pincus has teamed up with Lucia Small to produce what they are calling "The Elephant in the Room," a feature about Pincus's confrontation with imminent mortality. Small describes it this way: "*Elephant in the Room* is an intimate portrait about friendship, collaboration, loss and legacy in the face of terminal illness and death. Made by two filmmakers of different generations, it interweaves footage they have filmed of each other and of their own lives over the course of a ten-year artistic relationship. A meditation on the wonder and complexities of life, it walks a tightrope inherent in autobiographical filmmaking—how to capture life and live it simultaneously, especially when each moment of time feels more precious than ever."[3]

There are also newcomers to Boston-Cambridge personal documentary, including Chico David Colvard, who received his law degree from Boston College, was filmmaker-in-residence at WGBH, and has been a moderator for the DocYard Series at the Brattle Theater (sponsored by the LEF Foundation); Lyda Kuth, executive director at LEF; and Jason Steeves, office assistant in the Visual and Environmental Studies Department at Harvard. In *Family Affair* (2010), his harrowing exploration of incest, Colvard uses methods akin to McElwee (Robb Moss was an advisor on the film), attempting to come to terms with the history of his and his three sisters' deeply troubled relationship with their father. In *Love and Other Anxieties* (2011)—the title is a reference to Ascher-Pincus's *Life and Other Anxieties* (1977)—Kuth candidly explores her concerns about empty-nest syndrome and aging as her daughter leaves for college (Lucia Small edited the film). And in *The Lost Year* (2012—Moss was an advisor here too) Jason Steeves unapologetically reviews the history of his love life, his experimentation with drugs and immersion in rave culture, his struggles with his bigamist father, and the events leading to his second marriage and the birth of his triplet daughters. If these films cannot be called breakthroughs—all three recycle approaches familiar from the history this volume explores —each in its own way is a serious attempt to come to grips with personal issues, and together, they reconfirm the way in which personal documentary has come to reflect the astonishing variety of the human experience, even within what might seem to be a single locale.

Of course, in large measure because of the innovations and successes of the filmmakers working in Cambridge, the personal documentary approach has become ubiquitous across the country. In fact, by the new millennium the earlier sense among some cineastes that personal documentary had become passé, a cine-cliché, was itself becoming untenable. Success—aesthetic success as well as financial success—breeds imitation, and a good many young and not-so-young filmmakers have demonstrated that personal documentary continues to offer filmmakers and cineastes new insights and pleasures. The personal documentary (and Cambridge's formative influence on it) seems here to stay.

The very ubiquity of the personal documentary and the other forms of personal filmmaking that have proliferated during recent decades has become a topic for cultural studies, demonstrated, for example, by Michael Renov's placing the emergence of the personal into a contemporary media-cultural framework: "The journalistic standards of objective reportage have been so eroded by the news gatherers and high-profile TV anchors, the emergence of the digital has so undercut our faith in the indexicality of signs, irony as master sensibility of our time has become so pervasive that objectivity has become an empty shell of a construct, kept alive by a vocal minority. Given the waning of objectivity as a compelling social narrative, there appear to be ample grounds for a more sustained examination of the diverse expressions of subjectivity produced in nonfiction texts."[4] No one has as yet stepped forward to fashion a history of the full range of personal filmmaking as it has evolved during the past century, but that seems only a matter of time.

As has been evident in the foregoing chapters, the histories of ethnographic filmmaking and personal documentary have begun to merge: each of these ongoing cultural projects increasingly reveals the influence of the other. This is evident in several ways. At various points in the foregoing discussions, I've suggested that individual personal documentaries and/or the work of particular personal documentary filmmakers can be understood as generally reflective of certain groups within American society or of particular generations—that is, at least in a loose sense, "ethnographic." It is equally clear that many ethnographic filmmakers have come to agree with those committed to personal documentary that the personal need not be suppressed in nonfiction cinema, that indeed, its suppression is a fictionalizing of the experience they are documenting. All the filmmakers I am aware of who are veterans of the Sensory Ethnography Lab reveal their presence within the events and the communities they depict and often include various forms of personal interchange between those they record and themselves.

The interplay between ethnographic filmmaking and personal documentary, especially in Cambridge, has also been functioning on a more informal level for half a century. Filmmakers living, studying, working in and around Cambridge have created a mutual support system that is obvious in virtually every final credit sequence of one of the Cambridge films. At the end of *Sweetgrass,* Lucien Castaing-Taylor and Ilisa Barbash thank Alfred Guzzetti, Ross McElwee, Robb Moss, and Amie Siegel (among many others). In the credits for *The Same River Twice,* Moss acknowledges the critical support of Robert Gardner and Richard Rogers at the Film Study Center, and thanks Barbash, Castaing-Taylor, John Gianvito, Guzzetti, McElwee.... And in the credits for *Photographic Memory,* Ross McElwee thanks Steve Ascher, Barbash, Castaing-Taylor, Guzzetti, Jeanne Jordan, Moss, Jeff Silva.... A good many of these acknowledgments have resulted from the fact that the Cambridge filmmakers show their works in progress to their colleagues when they feel the need for feedback. This kind of interchange, experienced regularly over years and in some instances over decades, cannot not help but bridge what might otherwise seem the gaps between different approaches to documentary. Within the annals of film history the community that has developed in Cambridge among ethnographic and personal documentary filmmakers seems unusual, both in its longevity and in its extent—and it has been, and I hope will continue to be, unusually productive of fascinating cinema that has considerable "cash value," to return to William James's provocative term, for the ever-transforming lives of those who have the good luck to experience it.

I have used William James's Pragmatism as a frequent reference throughout *American Ethnographic Film and Personal Documentary: The Cambridge Turn* because of the ways in which the filmmakers discussed use the making of documentary films as a process of coming to understand their subjects', and their own, place in the world. Not only are most of the films I've discussed records of the unfolding experiences of particular peoples or people in time; but in making records of these unfolding experiences as they were happening, the filmmakers themselves were having experiences that changed *them,* both as individual men and women and as filmmakers. It is particularly clear in many of the careers that have been nurtured in Cambridge that each new adventure of perception and each successive filmmaking process has developed out of the previous one, as a result of the inevitable questioning—of their subjects, of themselves—that the filmmakers did during and after the production of their films in their determination to be honest and communicative about what they've come to understand from those they've filmed and from their filming. For these filmmakers, coming to know something is a result of sharing the process of filmmaking itself with their subjects, with colleagues, and with audiences, both within particular films and during life-long filmmaking careers.

My hope is that *American Ethnographic Film and Personal Documentary: The Cambridge Turn* will be understood as an invitation to experience the films and the careers I've discussed. If cineastes, film history teachers, students, people interested in the ever-proliferating possibilities of cinema should find their way to this book and decide to accept that invitation, I shall feel well rewarded.

Sources for Films

This listing reflects the sequence of the discussions in *American Ethnographic Film and Personal Documentary: The Cambridge Turn*. The films of Lorna and John Marshall and Timothy Asch, some of the films of Robert Gardner, Alfred Guzzetti, Ricky Leacock, J. P. Sniadecki and Stephanie Spray are available through Documentary Educational Resources: www.der.org. All of Gardner's work is available through his studio: www.studio7arts.org. Robert Fulton's *Reality's Invisible* can be seen on Gardner's *Screening Room* episode (at www.studio7arts.org); Sharon Lockhart's *Double Tide,* through Blum and Poe: www.blumand-poe.com and the Gladstone Gallery: www.gladstonegallery.com, as well as through Lockhart: sharonlock@earthlink.net; Robert Fenz's *Correspondence* through the Harvard Film Archive (hcl.harvard.edu/hfa) and robertfenz@gmail.com. Ed Pincus's work, through Pincus: epincus@tds.net; Guzzetti's videos and personal films through Guzzetti: guzzetti@fas.harvard.edu; Miriam Weinstein's films through Weinstein: miriamw@att.net; and Richard P. Rogers's short films through the Harvard Film Archive: hcl.harvard.edu/hfa. Ross McElwee's films are widely available; see his website: rossmcelwee.com. Ann Schaetzel's *Breaking and Entering* is available through Schaetzel: aschaetzel@earthline.net. Robb Moss's films are available through Moss: robbmoss@fas.harvard.edu; Steven Ascher and Jeanne Jordan's films, through West City Films: www.westcityfilms.com; Michel Negroponte's films, through Negroponte: www.michelnegroponte.com; Nina Davenport's films, through Davenport: nina.davenport@gmail.com; John Gianvito's *Profit Motive and the Whispering Wind,* through Gianvito: john.gianvito@verizon.net; Jeff Silva's *Balkan Rhapsodies* through Silva: jeffdanielsilva@gmail.com; Alexander Olch's films at olch@olch.com; Amie Siegel's *DDR/DDR* at amie@amiesiegel.net; Barbash and Castaing-Taylor's *Sweetgrass* and Paravel and Castaing-Taylor's *Leviathan* through Cinema Guild: info@cinemaguild.com; Castaing-Taylor's installations: lgtaylor@fas.harvard.edu; J. P. Sniadecki's films, at jpsniadecki@gmail.com; Stephanie Spray's, at stephaniespray@gmail.com; Véréna Paravel's, at verenaparavel@fas.harvard.edu.

NOTES

INTRODUCTION

1. William James, "A World of Pure Experience," in *Essays in Radical Empiricism,* in Bruce W. Wilshire, ed., *William James: the Essential Writings* (Albany: State University of New York Press, 1984), 187.

2. Obviously, documentary is made in a variety of locations, and New York and the Bay Area have been productive of much important nonfiction work, but no American metropolitan area deserves to be called "fountainhead" as clearly as the Boston area.

3. Two exceptions need to be mentioned. The film theorist-historian-critic William Rothman, who graduated from Harvard and spent many years teaching there, has regularly noted the importance of Cambridge. In both his "Eternal Verités," in Charles Warren, ed., *Beyond Document: Essays on the Nonfiction Film* (Middletown: Wesleyan University Press, 1966), and in the introduction to his own *Documentary Film Classics* (New York: Cambridge University Press, 1997), Rothman surveys the early evolution of documentary filmmaking in Cambridge. In fact, *Beyond Document* itself is, at least implicitly, a paean to this history: many of the contributors to the volume have, or have had, Cambridge connections.

The other crucial exception here is the LEF Foundation, a private foundation that, through its Moving Image Fund, provides support for a wide range of film projects by filmmakers based in New England and sponsors "programs that highlight the rich history and ongoing legacy of innovation within New England's independent film community" (LEF website). The Moving Image Fund, established in 2002, has provided substantial financial support to many of the films discussed in this volume, and LEF's exhibition program in the Boston area has generally highlighted Boston, and Cambridge, documentary history.

4. The term *cinéma vérité* was invented by Jean Rouch and Edgar Morin as an homage to Dziga Vertov, particularly *The Man with a Movie Camera* (1929) and Vertov's term *kino-pravda* (film-truth). In English the term is sometimes printed in the original French,

sometimes as "cinema verité," and more usually as "cinema verite," without italics or accents, which is how it is used in this study.

5. In his seminal *Documentary: A History of the Non-Fiction Film,* in several editions since 1974 (New York: Oxford University Press), Erik Barnouw distinguished between what he called "direct cinema"—that is, fly-on-the-wall observational documentary—and "cinema verite," documentary in which the filmmakers provoke situations that they then record. This terminology quickly became confusing, since many filmmakers continued (and continue) to use "cinema verite" for any form of sync-sound filmmaking from within events. In *Representing Reality* (Bloomington: Indiana University Press, 1991), Bill Nichols proposed to avoid the confusion by using "the observational mode" to refer to fly-on-the-wall shooting and "the interactive mode" for provocational documentary filmmaking. In general, scholars have followed Nichols's lead, as I have here—though "direct cinema" and "cinema verite" continue to be in common use.

6. Drew Associates produced a number of other important early experiments in observational cinema. P. J. O'Connell has tracked the history of Drew Associates in *Robert Drew and the Development of Cinema Verite in America* (Carbondale: Southern Illinois University Press, 1992).

7. Gardner in an interview with Ilisa Barbash, in Barbash and Lucien Castaing-Taylor, *The Cinema of Robert Gardner* (Oxford: Berg, 2007), 106.

8. The third modern ethnographic film to be included in the National Film Registry, *Uksuum Cauyai: The Drums of Winter* (1989) was made by Leonard Kamerling and Sarah Elder. Kamerling studied with Leacock at MIT and worked with Marshall and Asch at Documentary Educational Resources (DER); and Elder, while a student at Brandeis, also took courses at MIT.

9. Bujalski's breakthrough film, *Funny Ha Ha* (2002), was shot in Cambridge. Bujalski:

> The Harvard program was hugely influential on how I've been working ever since I got out of there. It's impossible to untangle in retrospect how much I was naturally a good fit for what they were doing there & how much I was just highly impressionable—perhaps I'd be a crusader for USC methodologies if I'd studied there, though that's hard to imagine. Though about half of the work I did in school was, as they called it, "fiction," the backbone of that program was quite evidently not just in documentary practice but also, I think, a documentary way of looking at the world—essentially, an awareness of the camera and Nagra as tremendous tools for capturing something of the pulse of life, and the Steenbeck as a station where we searched for the story that that material was trying to tell us. As opposed to a more traditional American notion that filmmaking is a process of taking a vision from one's mind and using technology to force the world into the shape you'd imagined. (E-mail to author from Bujalski, May 2011)

10. According to the Balagan website (www.balaganfilms.com), the Balagan series is named for a type of traveling theater troupe common during the eighteenth to early twentieth centuries in Russia. As this is written, curators Kovgan and Silva have been joined by Stefan Grabowski and Mariya Nikiforova.

11. Dewey, *Art as Experience* (New York: Perigee, 2005), 58–59, 59.

12. Ibid., 94.

13. Louis Massiah, a veteran of the MIT Film Section, who has gone on to produce and direct such films as *The Bombing of Osage Avenue* (1987) and *W. E.B. Du Bois: A Biography in Four Voices* (1997) and is founder and executive director of the Scribe Video Center in Philadelphia, has suggested that the emphasis on personal documentary, as he witnessed it at MIT, involved problematic power relations: personal documentary was

> people with power—meaning the cameraperson, the filmmaker—making a film about someone who has much, much, much less power, and who either because they are media-starved, or out of love, agrees to be a subject. . . . There was this huge power differential that was never really talked about. . . . By the 1970s people are much too knowledgable about what it means to allow [themselves to be filmed] so that the type of subjects that student filmmakers are getting are basically people . . . who are poor; people who are darker; women; or people who are mentally disturbed; the other group are family members who love you, who want to help you get your degree. (Unpublished interview with the author, recorded September 4, 2011)

Much the same might be said about ethnographic filmmaking, of course. While there is truth in Massiah's view, as is often evident in the films themselves, the power relations between independent filmmakers and their subjects are often complex, and indeed, as will be clear in the discussions that follow, these power relations are often the subject of personal documentaries and ethnographic films.

14. Carolyn Anderson and Thomas W. Benson, "Put Down the Camera and Pick Up the Shovel: An Interview with John Marshall," in Jay Ruby, ed., *The Cinema of John Marshall* (Philadelphia: Harwood Academic Publishers, 1993), 136.

15. The establishment of the Film Section involved the hiring of Ricky Leacock, by the late 1960s one of the best-known of observational filmmakers (Ed Pincus was already teaching film at MIT, and graduate student John Terry was much in evidence and would soon join Pincus and Leacock on the faculty). According to Gerald O'Grady, "Wiesner perceived Ricky [Leacock] as a documentary maker and asked, as part of his original contract, that he film the demonstrating anti-Vietnam-War students who were swarming across campus." From "'Ricky' by O'Grady," in Robert Haller and Victoria Leacock Hoffman, eds., *Richard Leacock Memorial Journal,* published on the occasion of MIT's memorial to Leacock in June 2011.

16. Cavell's statement:

> Because I know that the books whose reading I teach are better than anything I say about them; and because I believe that it is one, perhaps after all the fundamental, value of a teacher to put such books before students and to show that an adult human being takes them with whatever seriousness is at his, or her disposal; and because I know, furthermore, that the gift for teaching is as rare as any other human gift; my question is this: Is film worth teaching badly? And this is meant to ask: Does one believe that there are films the viewing of which is itself an education. ("Film in the University," in *Pursuits of Happiness: The Hollywood Comedy of Remarriage* [Cambridge: Harvard University Press, 1981]: 270)

17. Rothman was the first to write about Alfred Guzzetti's *Family Portrait Sittings;* his *Documentary Film Classics* (New York: Cambridge University Press, 1997) includes a detailed discussion of *Happy Mother's Day;* and *Three Documentary Filmmakers* (Albany: SUNY Press, 2009), edited by Rothman, focuses on Errol Morris, Ross McElwee, and Jean Rouch (whose visits to Cambridge had considerable influence on other filmmakers): in his essay on McElwee, "Sometimes Daddies Don't Talk about Things Like That," Rothman is at pains to evoke the larger cinematic and cultural context of Cambridge.

18. Stella Bruzzi, *New Documentary: A Critical Introduction* (London: Routledge, 2000), 8.

19. Dai Vaughan, *For Documentary* (Berkeley: University of California Press, 1999), 198.

20. Bruzzi, *New Documentary,* 3.

21. Kreines and Joel DeMott refused to make their earliest work available to me, to tell me anything about how I might access it, even to help me understand why they were refusing their support. In the end I found my way to some of their films—but I regret that work that would surely have been discussed here could not be included as part of this project. I apologize both to those who find their way to these pages and to Kreines and DeMott for my failure to find a way to engage them. My hope is that another scholar will have more success.

My communications with Mark Rance were friendly, but in the end, for whatever reasons, he did not make his films available to me.

22. Unpublished conversation with Wiseman at the Brattle Theater, July 19, 2010—an event sponsored by the LEF Foundation.

23. Unpublished interview with Gardner, 2011.

24. I interviewed Abigail Child for *A Critical Cinema 4* (Berkeley: University of California Press, 2005).

CHAPTER 1

1. "!Kung," as Lorna Marshall explains in *The !Kung of Nyae Nyae* (Cambridge: Harvard University Press, 1976), "has been traditionally used in the literature on Bushmen for the group of Bushmen to which the Nyae Nyae !Kung belong—both for the people and their language" (15). The !Kung language uses several clicks, and the exclamation point in "!Kung" is, as Marshall explains, one of these, an alveolar-palatal click; others incorporated into this discussion include the dental click, "/"; the alveolar click, "≠"; and the lateral click, "//" (xix–xx).

Ju/'hoansi means "people." John Marshall: "People call themselves Ju/'hoansi the way Germans say they are Germans, speak German and live in Germany." Marshall used "the term San for all the peoples classified as 'Bushmen' by the South African government as well as many writers and scholars." See John Marshall, "Filming and Learning," in Jay Ruby, ed., *The Cinema of John Marshall* (Philadelphia: Harwood Academic Publishers, 1993), 126n. Marshall explains, "Seven peoples speaking different San languages and dialects were the original inhabitants of the colony [of South Africa]" (1).

The reader will notice that the names of San individuals and places are sometimes spelled differently in quotations than they are in my text. Over the years, decisions on how to render San names in English and in other languages have resulted in considerable variation in spelling. In my text I have tried to remain consistent in using the spellings Lorna and John Marshall used.

2. Marshall, "Filming and Learning," 25.

3. These expeditions were of various sizes. The 1951 expedition, the first that all four Marshall family members were part of, included twenty other people; the 1952–53 expedition was thirty-five strong, including the Marshalls, and director of the Peabody Museum, J. O. Brew; the 1957–58 expedition included John and Laurence Marshall, Robert Gardner, and eleven others. Of course, not all the members of an expedition stayed the entire time. The expeditions were also of varying lengths.

4. Carolyn Anderson and Thomas W. Benson, "Put Down the Camera and Pick Up the Shovel: An Interview with John Marshall," in Ruby, *The Cinema of John Marshall*, 136.

5. The online filmography for John Marshall, compiled by the Smithsonian for their John Marshall Ju/'hoan Bushman Film and Video Collection website, indicates that these are the same film—though John Marshall's description of *!Kung Bushmen of the Kalahari* in the Anderson–Benson interview seems to refer to imagery not in *First Film*: "It really shows the Tshumkwe people, a thousand of them, in this Nyae Nyae area," in Ruby, *The Cinema of John Marshall*, 137. I am assuming that two different cuts of the original 1951 footage were made. John Bishop indicates that "a sixty-minute program, *First Film*, was cut from the original. The first two-thirds was found as a single strand conformed original (83.11.2–1)"—in "Hot Footage/Cold Storage: The Marshall Ju/'hoan Bushman Archive," in Ruby, *The Cinema of John Marshall*, 221.This might also help to account for the fact that several sources list *First Film* as 60 minutes, when in fact the version currently distributed by DER is a bit under 45 minutes (despite the indication on the DVD cover that it is 60 minutes).

6. Lorna Marshall, *The !Kung of Nyae Nyae* (Cambridge: Harvard University Press, 1976), 3.

7. Marshall, "Filming and Learning," 19.

8. E-mail to the author from John Bishop, March 3, 2010.

9. Lorna Marshall's extensive diary is at the Peabody Museum at Harvard University. This comment is from p. 138.

10. David MacDougall, "The Fate of the Cinema Subject," in Lucien Castaing-Taylor, ed., *Transcultural Cinema* (Princeton: Princeton University Press, 1998), 27–28.

11. The extent of Gardner's input into *The Hunters* has long been a topic for debate. See chapter 2 for details.

12. Bill Nichols, *Ideology and the Image* (Bloomington: Indiana University Press, 1981), 260.

13. Anderson–Benson interview, 139.

14. Marshall, "Filming and Learning," 39.

15. Anderson–Benson interview, 137.

16. Ibid., 140.

17. Marshall, "Filming and Learning," 20.

18. The approximate lengths (in seconds) of the shots in *A Group of Women* are 7, 8, 14, 11, 19, 21, 11, 50, 7, 15, 4, 8, 5, 6, 5, 16, 11, 25, 7, 10, 17, 5, 17.

19. David MacDougall sees Marshall's subtitling in *A Joking Relationship* (and presumably in *A Group of Women*) as a breakthrough: "Subtitles propelled ethnographic films into a new phase. Audiences no longer listened to spoken information *about* people in these films [as, for instance, in *The Hunters*] but began to watch and listen to them more directly."

David MacDougall, "Subtitling Ethnographic Films," in Castaing-Taylor, *Transcultural Cinema,* 165.

20. This text is not included on the DVD of *A Group of Women,* but I am assuming that here, too, sound was recorded at the time of the filming and reconstructed later.

21. I am indebted to Harvard student Lily Erlinger, who suggested this idea to me in the fall of 2007.

22. The moment under the baobab tree did become an issue for N!ai, as she explains in an unpublished interview: "I used to play and the Marshalls would film me. One time, when my breasts had just begun to develop, when I still hadn't menstruated, an older man kept grabbing me and he filmed. That older man grabbed me, we grabbed each other. That's when my breasts were just standing out a little"; "When we played like that, my heart was happy because he was my grandfather and not someone else. If it were someone else, I would be shy. . . . We played with each other and we both felt good"; "But because my grandfather held me like that, my husband was jealous. He wouldn't talk to us. When we lay down that night, he didn't talk to me"; "One day, we went somewhere else with John Marshall. He wouldn't talk to me." John Marshall collection at the Human Studies Archive of the Smithsonian Institution, Series 5; Sub-series: Expedition VIII [translation: 1975 Interview with N!ai], circa 1975. I assume "grandfather" here simply means older man.

23. An earlier film, *The Lion Game* (1970), has much in common with *Baobab Play;* in it several boys play a game in which one is a lion and others are prey and vice versa. There is no narration or translation. It's another golden moment—though less implicitly serene than *Baobab Play.*

Editing *Baobab Play* may have instigated Marshall's decision to make *Vermont Kids* (1975). The three sections of the film reveal three groups of Vermont children of different ages involved in forms of play that seem relevant to their particular stages of development. Like *Baobab Play, Vermont Kids* can be understood as an idyll.

24. See Kenyan G. Tomaselli and John P. Homiak, "Powering Popular Conceptions: The !Kung in the Marshall Family Expedition Films of the 1950s," *Visual Anthropology* 12: 2–3 (1999): 153–84.

25. Scott MacDonald, *The Garden in the Machine: A Field Guide to Independent Films about Place* (Berkeley: University of California Press, 2001).

26. John Marshall, "The Arrow Makers," unpublished description, in collection at the Human Studies Archive of the Smithsonian Institution, Series 6; Sub-series: !Kung projects John [Treatments and Notes], circa 1958–61.

27. Marshall, "Filming and Learning," 23.

28. This is reported by Edwin N. Wilmsen in his essay "Knowledge as the Source of Progress: The Marshall Family Testament to the 'Bushmen,'" part of a special issue of *Visual Anthropology* 12: 2–3 (1999): 219—though Wilmsen's own citation for the comment I've quoted is confusing.

29. Much the same form, a précis, using still imagery, followed by "the film proper," is used in Timothy Asch's *The Feast* (1969), and Jay Ruby argues that Asch's use of this structure was an innovation (see Ruby, *Picturing Culture: Explorations of Film and Anthropology* [Chicago: University of Chicago Press, 2000], 121). This seems to have been a simultaneous innovation in both Asch's and Marshall's work. Asch (and Frank Galvin) made shot-by-shot lists of the Marshall footage during the 1960s—see John M. Bishop, "Hot Footage/

Cold Storage," in Ruby, *The Cinema of John Marshall*, 216—and there may have been discussions between Asch and Marshall about film form around this time. However, Galvin, not Asch, is listed as editor on most of the Marshall films of the late 1960s that use this format (Asch and Joyce Chopra are listed, along with Frank Galvin, as editors of *A Rite of Passage* [1972]).

30. David MacDougall, "The Fate of the Cinema Subject," in Castaing-Taylor, *Transcultural Cinema*, 31–32.

31. The explanatory voice-over has made clear that some of this joking is homophobic, just the sort of joking that many American men do when they're together in a similar circumstances.

32. Elizabeth Marshall Thomas, *The Harmless People*, rev. ed. (New York: Vintage, 1989), 169.

33. Wilmsen, "Knowledge as the Source of Progress," 246.

34. The University Film Study Center was, I believe, based in Cambridge.

35. Oukwane's name is spelled differently in different places. Elizabeth Marshall Thomas uses "Ukwane," and in their brochure, Documentary Educational Resources uses "Ukxone" I am using "Oukwane," since that's the spelling Marshall uses in his essay, "Filming and Learning" (though he sometimes used "Ukxone," as well).

36. Marshall, "Filming and Learning," 56. The end credits list Nicholas England, ethnomusicologist, as musical director.

37. "Gai, for example, went into trance during the dance, suddenly flinging his arms into the air "and with a piercing shriek crashed to the ground. He landed stiffly with a bounce, his head cracking. On the ground he writhed and groaned and Ukwane pulled him by the arms to remove his body from the dance circle. Gai was in deep trance." Elizabeth Marshall Thomas, *The Harmless People*, 131.

38. Edwin N. Wilmsen makes the point that the film's conceit that Oukwane must search for the bitter melons his song evokes required that Marshall suppress the fact that the particular melons that are seen in the film were not wild but were grown in a large garden by a !Kung woman, so that the film could play "on primitive themes common to old myths and an emerging epistemology of Euro-American ontology: man engaged in a primordial struggle against nature." Wilmsen, "Knowledge as a Source of Progress," 242, 241. Marshall had in fact photographed such gardens.

39. Thomas, 130. I am assuming this is the same dance, since her description of the Marshalls' stay in the Okwa valley intersects with *Bitter Melons* in so many instances.

40. Marshall, "Filming and Learning," 57.

41. *Bushmen of the Kalahari* is a National Geographic Society Special, finished in 1974, directed and photographed by Robert M. Young, written by Bud Wiser, and edited by Hyman Kaufman and David Saxon. There are several narrators, including Leslie Nielson and Marshall himself. The 50-minute show focuses on Marshall's return to the Kalahari in 1972, where he meets up briefly with ≠Toma, N!ai, /Qui, and others at the new border fence between Namibia and Botswana, and then visits a group of Khwe bushmen from the band that had been the focus of *Bitter Melons*. These visits are the narrative center of *Bushmen of the Kalahari;* they are contextualized by flashbacks to earlier periods, often using imagery from early Marshall films, including *The Hunters* and *Bitter Melons*.

42. Marshall, "Filming and Learning," 57–58.

43. Wilmsen sees *N!ai* as evidence that Marshall had become far less naïve about modern !Kung history but argues that, nevertheless, the film remains committed to the idea of the "idyllic, mythic past of *The Hunters.*" In the presentation of N!ai's reminiscences, "nothing intrudes of the stress of coping with hunger, with material poverty and illness, with the complexities of wage, or wageless, labor, with sometimes abuse by dominant neighbors. Nothing, that is, of the lived reality of the 1950s." Wilmsen, "Knowledge as a Source of Progress," 244.

44. In "Filming and Learning" Marshall spells the location Tshumkwe, as I have done in this chapter. In *N!ai, the Story of a !Kung Woman* it is spelled "Tshum!kwi."

45. N!xau's name is sometimes spelled "N!Xau," and in "Filming and Learning" (31), Marshall refers to him as "/Gao." Since he is identified as "N!xau" in *The Gods Must Be Crazy,* I have used that spelling.

46. The absurdity of the situation for Marshall was exacerbated by the fact that N!xau "was a cook in a school when Jamie found him." Marshall, in Anderson–Benson interview, 162.

47. Of course, *An Argument about a Marriage* (1969) provides an early transition from the idyll of *The Hunters* to *N!ai, the Story of a !Kung Woman:* the conflict between /Ti!kay and /Qui in that film is a premonition of the disintegration of !Kung life instigated by white interference.

48. Marshall, in Anderson–Benson interview, 148, 152. However Marshall felt about this episode, suspicion remains that he was refused his just credit for *Titicut Follies;* I have heard that Ricky Leacock believed it was really Marshall's film.

49. Ibid., 146.

50. The other fifteen titles: *After the Game, $40 Dollar Misunderstanding, A Legal Discussion of a Hit and Run, Manifold Controversy, Nothing Hurt but My Pride, $20 or 21 Days, Two Brothers, Wrong Kid, You Wasn't Loitering, Youth and the Man of Property, Henry Is Drunk, Appitsch and the Drunk, T-Group,* and *The 4th, 5th, & Exclusionary Rule.* All of these films except *Appitsch and the Drunk* and *T-Group* are available from DER (in some cases, the titles of the DER DVDs are slightly different from the titles in the Sue Marshall Cabezas filmography I am using. Cabezas's "Filmography of the Works of John Marshall from 1951 to 1991" is included in Ruby, *The Cinema of John Marshall,* 231–67.

In a strange accident of film history, the credits of *Inside/Outside Station 9* and *Three Domestics* indicate that Dennis Sweeney worked on the sound of the two films: Sweeney would later terrorize Ed Pincus and his family and assassinate Allard Lowenstein (see chapter 4).

51. *Inside Outside Station 9,* for example, begins with versions of *$40 Misunderstanding* (1973), *Wrong Kid* (1973), *Nothing Hurt but My Pride* (1973), and *You Wasn't Loitering* (1973); and *901/904* begins with versions of *$40 Misunderstanding, Henry Is Drunk* (1973), and *Nothing Hurt but My Pride.*

52. There is considerable discrepancy in listings of the lengths of Marshall's Pittsburgh Police films. For example, both Sue Marshall Cabezas and Documentary Educational Resources list *Inside/Outside Station 9* as 90 minutes long, when in fact, the film, at least as it appears on the DER DVD, is a bit under 78 minutes. *901/904* is listed as 65 minutes, when in fact it is a bit over 69 minutes.

53. Marshall: "Thickness and thinness are as old as literature. The stories of Gilgamesh and Beowulf are thin. The heros are motivated by conventions rather than by their person-

alities and inner conflicts. . . . Events are elaborated in thick films. Supporting characters are given a suggestion of independent life. Main characters are endowed with enough inner life for autonomy and the power of choice. . . . To be useful in education, and worth the time and effort of discussion, the content of documentaries has to be thick." Marshall, "Filming and Learning," 107, 108.

54. Marshall, in Anderson–Benson interview, 150. Marshall goes on to say, "I had a very good friend in that film. A strange guy, cop *extraordinaire*. He was a terrible cop and I'd tell him so and he'd argue with me. We'd go get drunk together"; during the celebration following the Pittsburgh Pirates World Series victory in 1971, this policeman lost an eye, and later that year "smoked his .38. But those were friends. That was the purpose of that film."

55. Marshall, "Filming and Learning," 73–74.

56. Brakhage in Scott MacDonald, *A Critical Cinema 4* (Berkeley: University of California Press, 2005), 93.

57. Independent filmmaking has long had a strong presence in Pittsburgh, from the work of Sally Dixon in hosting filmmakers at the Carnegie Institute beginning in the early 1970s and Robert Haller's work at Pittsburgh Filmmakers, to George Romero's working-class zombie films filmed in and around Pittsburgh. See Robert Haller, *Crossroads: Avant-garde Film in Pittsburgh in the 1970s* (New York: Anthology Film Archives, 2005) and Peggy Ahwesh's comments on the Pittsburgh film scene, in Scott MacDonald, *A Critical Cinema 5* (Berkeley: University of California Press, 2006), 116–21.

58. Marshall, "Filming and Learning,"106.

59. Cynthia Close, e-mail to author, February 23, 2010.

60. These include *Fighting Tooth, (Nail) and the Government* (1988), a video update of *Pull Ourselves Up or Die Out,* and two videos that Documentary Educational Resources produced with Marshall as a service to Massachusetts schools: *!Kung San: Traditional Life* (1987) and *!Kung San: Resettlement* (1988)—both of which recycled earlier footage of the !Kung.

61. *Pull Ourselves Up or Die Out* is directly informational and polemical in a manner more like documentaries of the 1930s and 1940s.

62. The arrival of Marshall's truck with the cattle feed echoes the shots of the military vehicles arriving at Tshumkwe in *N!ai,* as well as the arrival of the Marshall family's early expeditions into Nyae Nyae, which left those tire tracks that contributed to the demise of the Ju/'hoansi gatherer-hunter way of life.

63. Marshall, "Filming and Learning," 124. Marshall goes on to say, "The members of a family from Calcutta who take their grandmother to Benares to give her a funeral they cannot afford would have been interesting if Gardner had allowed us to meet them in *Forest of Bliss* (1985). Events in the intensive care unit of Beth Israel Hospital in Wiseman's *Near Death* (1989), and the people involved in the Kennedy-Wallace confrontation on the steps of the University of Mississippi in Leacock-Pennebaker's *Crisis* (1962) are very interesting."

64. Throughout *A Kalahari Family* Rena Baskin provides the voice-over for events that John Marshall was not a witness to: the extermination of bushmen, the war between South Africa and what was to become Namibia, for example.

65. William James, from "A World of Pure Experience," a chapter in *Essays in Radical Empiricism,* included in Bruce W. Wilshire, ed., *William James: the Essential Writings* (Albany: State University of New York Press, 1984), 187.

66. Flannery O'Connor, "The Regional Writer," in *Mystery and Manners* (New York: Farrar, Straus & Giroux, 1961), 54.

CHAPTER 2

1. From the Studio7Arts website: www.studio7arts.org.
2. From "Biographic Timeline" on Gardner's website: http://robertgardner.net.
3. Unpublished interview with Gardner.
4. This phrasing recalls Pare Lorentz's poetic narrations for *The Plow That Broke the Plains* (1936) and *The River* (1938).
5. Letter from Laurence Marshall to J. O. Brew, dated March 26, 1953.
6. Letter from Robert Gardner to Laurence Marshall, dated April 16, 1953.
7. John Marshall, "Filming and Learning," and "Put Down the Camera and Pick Up the Shovel," in Jay Ruby, ed., *The Cinema of John Marshall* (Philadelphia: Harwood Academic, 1993), 36, 140. I assume the award Marshall is referring to is the Flaherty Award given to Gardner in 1957. During the discussion of *The Hunters* at the 1958 Robert Flaherty Seminar, Gardner seems the primary spokesman for the film, though Marshall is present.
8. Jay Ruby, *Picturing Culture: Explorations of Film and Anthropology* (Chicago: University of Chicago Press, 2000), 107. The article Ruby is referring to is "Anthropology and Film," which appeared in *Daedalus* 86 (October 1957): 344–52. In this essay Gardner seems to be speaking for the Peabody Museum Film Study Center; as Ruby indicates, John Marshall's—indeed the Marshall family's—involvement in the !Kung material is not mentioned. Gardner describes what must have been *his* plan for the !Kung material as of 1957:

> It is probable that the series of Bushmen films will provide a fairly broad sum-mary view of !Kung culture, though this is not an objective that is foremost in the minds of the project members. We have chosen, instead, five dominant aspects of this culture with the intention of making each the subject of a rela-tively long work, each somewhere between sixty and one hundred minutes in length. Along with these five major films, we intend to make fifteen or twenty others that will be shorter and more narrowly conceived. . . . The five major films will be concerned with the following themes: *The Hunters, The Gather-ers, The Players, The Rhythms,* and *The Seasons.* . . . The special skills and activities involved in the expression of hunting, gathering, and playing in this culture will be given fuller treatment in the shorter films while their signifi-cance and meaning will be explored in the longer films. . . . In the period since the Film Study Center was started, there has been time to produce only one, *The Hunters.*" (350)

9. Robert Gardner, *The Impulse to Preserve: Reflections of a Filmmaker* (New York: Other Press, 2006), 102; "Introduction," *Making Dead Birds* (Cambridge: Peabody Museum, 2007), 7. In this introduction Gardner describes the collaboration: "At [J. O.] Brew's sugges-tion, I was asked in 1955 to help Marshall's son John, who was still an undergraduate, to review the available footage and develop a longer film from an existing 45-minute version of what would become *The Hunters.* Eventually the film grew to more than 70 minutes and,

when it was publicly released, quickly began to enjoy wider than usual attention as a nearly feature-length nonfiction account of a small, delicate, and vivid hunting-and-gathering society in the Kalahari Desert of southwest Africa" (6–7).

10. In his *Just Representations,* published by the Peabody Museum and Gardner's Studio7Arts in 2010 (edited by Charles Warren), Gardner includes his "Kalahari Journal," which details his experiences with the Marshalls in 1958 and offers a somewhat jaundiced account of Laurence and John Marshall:

> Marshall senior is a man of such impetuosity and disregard for any but his own convictions that things go quickly to hell, only to be partially corrected after considerable damage and expense. Marshall junior is in such awe of his father he cannot exercise independent judgment, even if his mind is working in that direction. I watch quite stunned by the amount of wealth and energy expended with no clear purpose or goal in mind. Common sense is subordinate to whim and chance. We are in possession of an elaborate medical kit and there is no one to use it correctly. We have five different and complex vehicles in which we fling ourselves about, and no one who can give them proper attention. Everything is conducted on the basis of trial and error and, unfortunately, error seems almost inescapable given the confusion of premises and intentions. . . .
>
> Traditional Bushmen life is clearly at an end. Some may weather the storm of change better than others. As I see it, the only reason there are any !Kung at all is that a few may never have had contact with the Marshalls. For the others, there is the payoff of staying Bushmen as long as the Marshalls are around. (17, 21)

11. See the Brakhage interview in Scott MacDonald, *A Critical Cinema 4* (Berkeley: University of California Press, 2005), 63.

12. Published in 1974, *Film as a Subversive Art* (New York: Random House) surveys a wide range of cinema that could be considered subversive for reasons of content or form or both—though ethnographic film seems not to have been one of Amos Vogel's otherwise wide-ranging cinematic interests.

13. Gardner in an interview with Ilisa Barbash, in Barbash and Lucien Castaing-Taylor, eds., *The Cinema of Robert Gardner* (New York: Berg, 2007), 102.

14. Peter Matthiessen, *Under the Mountain Wall: A Chronicle of Two Seasons in Stone Age New Guinea* (New York: Viking, 1962), xiii.

15. Matthiessen, *Under the Mountain Wall,* 3, 255–56.

16. Gardner, Barbash interview, 109.

17. The fact that Pua rolls a stalk of grass into a moon shape soon after Weaké's death as he is thinking about his dead friend suggests his developing maturity. Pua's little moon, like Weyak's rolled-up shell band, evokes a film reel.

18. Gardner, Barbash interview, 106.

19. Gardner, *The Impulse to Preserve,* 82.

20. Gardner's *Just Representations* includes "Mark Tobey Journal," Gardner's notes on his experiences filming Tobey during December and January 1971–72. The journal creates a somewhat different sense of Tobey, whose increasingly mental frailties could be frustrating, and of the experience of shooting the film than is evident from seeing the film itself.

21. Gardner, Barbash interview, 105.

22. Peleshian describes "distance montage" in my interview with him in *A Critical Cinema 3* (Berkeley: University of California Press, 1998), 93–103. In the case of *Nash Vek,* the subject is the international space program as a metaphor for the human drive to transcend mortality.

23. Gardner, Barbash interview, 104. *N!ai, The Story of a !Kung Woman,* of course, was shot several years after *Dead Birds* and may have been influenced by it.

24. See Ruby, *Picturing Culture,* 108. Ivo Strecker, in "Filming among the Hamar," *Visual Anthropology* 1: 4 (1988): "I was also frustrated because I remained barred from the process of conceptualizing the film as a whole. In 1971, Bob and I knew very little about Hamar culture . . . and I found it extremely difficult to make any generalizations. I sensed that Bob was planning a grand and explanatory film about the Hamar" (372). Ruby traces the reception of the film in anthropological circles on pages 107–9 of *Picturing Culture.*

25. In his critique of *Rivers of Sand* Jay Ruby argues that Gardner's acceptance of Omali's (Ruby spells her name "Omalleidna") comments as gospel is evidence of Gardner's failure to recognize "an anthropological cliché: What people say about themselves is not the truth but data." And he also questions Gardner's obvious disapproval of the whipping: "Gardner employs slow-motion shots of women running up to men, thrusting their breasts toward their 'oppressors,' and apparently taunting the men to beat them. Omalleidna claims she and all women in her group are oppressed, yet they appear to provoke the beatings." Ruby, *Picturing Culture,* 109. Here, Ruby seems naïve: in circumstances when oppression is systemic, the oppressed often look, and are expected to look, content with their situation.

When I was a student at DePauw University (1960–64), I was a member of the Lambda Chi Alpha fraternity, and as a pledge, I was expected to ask the brothers to whack me on the buttocks with a wooden paddle, and not only to thank them, once they had done so, and had signed their names on the paddle, but to ask them if they wanted another whack. During this ritual, it was de rigueur to pretend to enjoy the process.

26. Gardner, Barbash interview, 107.

27. This description is from Gardner' website: robertgardner.net/, under the listing for *Deep Hearts* in "Films & Videos."

28. Gardner, *The Impulse to Preserve,* 210.

29. Thomas W. Cooper, *Natural Rhythms: The Indigenous World of Robert Gardner* (New York: Anthology Film Archives, 1995), 63–64.

30. Ibid., 64.

31. *Altar of Fire* (1976), made shortly before *Deep Hearts,* is longer than that film, but receives no attention in *The Impulse to Preserve,* presumably because Gardner considers it too conventional. *Altar of Fire* records what at the time Gardner and his co-director J. F. Staal believed was the final performance of a 3,000-year-old Vedic ritual of sacrifice. The twelve-day ritual is filmed in some detail, and Gardner's imagery is described and explained by continual, and quite conventional, voice-over narration. While it is obvious why Gardner might have agreed to document this event, it seems equally obvious that nothing in the ritual struck Gardner as having a relevance to his own thinking comparable to what he filmed in *Dead Birds* and *Rivers of Sand.*

32. Gardner talks about his uses of narration in the Barbash interview, 101. He admits that *Forest of Bliss* was a breakthrough in this regard and indicates his admiration of Mar-

shall's narration in *The Hunters*: "I started doing my own 'voicing' with *Dead Birds* which came fairly fast on the heels of *The Hunters* which I helped John Marshall complete. He did the writing and the voicing as you know, and I always thought that made perfect sense inasmuch as the story was so much his own personal odyssey. I thought he put tremendous feeling into that track despite what he might more recently be thinking" (101).

33. See Angerame's comments on Fulton on the Canyon Cinema website: www.canyon-cinema.org.

34. I've not been able to find much detail, including credit listings, for any of these films.

35. This is Fulton's claim in his unpublished filmography.

36. I'm thinking in particular of Child's *Prefaces* (1981). During her undergraduate years at Radcliffe/Harvard—1970–74—Child studied filmmaking at the Carpenter Center with animator Derek Lamb. Child: "I was eighteen, and to the extent that I was thinking about filmmaking, my intention was to become a documentary filmmaker. I took anthropology at Harvard, in a program that took you to Chiapas. That was an important experience for me, and for a while I thought I would become an ethnographic filmmaker. I never did take a course with Robert Gardner, who was already at Harvard—he scared me—but I did take an animation class with Derek Lamb and sat next to Caroline Leaf, who discovered sand animation." From the interview with Child in my *A Critical Cinema 4*, 202. In fact, Child did begin her filmmaking career as a documentary filmmaker.

37. For some years Documentary Educational Resources distributed the *Screening Room* episodes available on DVD, but Gardner now oversees distribution at Studio7Arts.

The original *Screening Room* episodes lasted 90 minutes; the DVD versions have been edited and are a bit shorter.

38. During the early years of *Screening Room*, Gardner often invited another guest to join him and the filmmaker. Animator Eric Martin with John Whitney Sr., for example; philosopher Stanley Cavell with Standish Lawder; film theorist Rudolf Arnheim with Robert Fulton (the 1973 show); Gerald O'Grady with Bruce Baillie. In general, these additional guests tended to clutter up the shows rather than to add anything of importance; and in time Gardner's confidence in his ability to create useful conversations with filmmakers led to his abandoning the use of additional guests.

39. Unpublished interview with Robert Gardner.

40. Gardner: "Nobody programming independent film had much of a budget in those days. I had something like a thousand dollars to pay each filmmaker, plus money for their travel expenses; they were put up in a hotel, and they were paid a per-foot rental fee for the films we screened. They could usually walk away with fifteen hundred or two thousand dollars." Unpublished interview with Robert Gardner. In the 1970s a thousand dollars was a considerable honorarium for most independent filmmakers.

41. Of the first generation of City Symphony filmmakers, only Cavalcanti seems not to have been interested in the city as industrial center. His Paris is large and complex, but its excitement is not a function of new mechanical technologies.

42. The controversy created by *Forest of Bliss* is best illustrated by the September 1988 (4: 2) and the March 1989 (5:1) issues of *Visual Anthropology Review* (*VAR*); indeed the March 1989 issue, as editor Daniel Marks explains, was "our largest ever"). Two reviews in the September 1988 issue, one by Alexander Moore, the other by Jonathan P. Parry, see *Forest of Bliss* as "an irresponsible, self-indulgent film" (Moore, 3), largely because Gardner

does not subtitle the people heard speaking in the film and does not use narration to provide information about what we are seeing. Gardner's brief letter to *VAR* dismisses these complaints and Moore's review. In the March 1989 issue, Radikha Chopra defends *Forest of Bliss*, as does Ákos Östör (who collaborated with Gardner on the film); and Jay Ruby offers a sustained attack on both the film and Gardner's career, arguing that because Gardner is not a true anthropologist—"In addition to displaying a lack of interest in or knowledge of contemporary thinking in anthropology, Gardner has never learned the language of any of the people he filmed, nor has he stayed in the field long enough to do adequate ethnography" (10)—his films are not only "irrelevant to anthropology," but by being identified by Gardner and others as ethnographic help to maintain the marginality of visual anthropology. Ruby's credibility and integrity are attacked in the same issue by Edmund Carpenter.

43. Gardner discusses the "Forest of Bliss" in *The Impulse to Preserve*, 286.

44. *Making* Forest of Bliss *(Intention, Circumstance, and Chance in Nonfiction Film): A Conversation between Robert Gardner and Ákos Östör* (Cambridge: Film Study Center Harvard University, 2001), 38.

45. Brakhage: "I just think it was tremendously courageous of you to be able to do this. Doing my autopsy film, I had to get a lot of courage together to do that; but these burning grounds are so much more so, as I say, I *feel* them from your film as not just observing the privacies or the forbidden, but observing something that really is holy ground; it feels holy." This DVD was supervised by Gardner at his workshop, Studio7Arts; Robert Fenz saw to the transfer (and the adding of Dolby Stereo). The DVD was finished in 2008; it is distributed by Documentary Educational Resources.

46. Gardner's comment appears in Walter Goodman's review of the film, "Screen: Daily Life in India," in the *New York Times*, May 14, 1986, section C, p. 24. Paul Henley has suggested much the same idea: "It seems that Gardner intends this to be not so much a film *about* a rite of passage as *to be* a rite of passage." See Henley's "Beyond the Burden of the Real: An Anthropologist's Reflections on the Technique of 'A Masterful Cutter,'" in Barbash and Castaing-Taylor, *The Cinema of Robert Gardner*, 52.

47. Gardner, Barbash interview, 115.

48. Actually, the earliest instance when Gardner appears as a visual character in one of his film occurs, I believe, in *Mark Tobey Abroad*: at one point in that film, Tobey works on a charcoal sketch; gradually it is clear that he is sketching Gardner, who is then seen posing for the portrait.

49. From Gardner's voice-over at the end of the opening sequence of *Ika Hands*, just before the opening title and director credits.

50. Gardner, *The Impulse to Preserve*, 224.

51. Ibid., 223.

52. Ibid., 267.

53. Ibid., 222.

54. Ibid., 237.

55. Gardner, Barbash interview, 101.

56. Mead sees *Gardens of War* as a landmark in collaborative anthropology. In her introduction to the volume, she says, "It is unique. Never before has such a diverse group, with such diverse interests and skills, on a complex and lengthy expedition into primitive territory, taken so many pictures that it became possible to select from among thousands a

set of pictures which fit together so well that the identity of the individual photographer is almost obscured" (vii). Elizabeth Edwards argues that *Gardens* "was intended as serious ethnography but one that sought to project anthropological statements for a general audience rather than an exclusively academic one," and that because of Gardner and Heider's use of clusters of imagery, photo montages, arranged in a variety of organizations, "The book therefore has the character not of traditional documentary film, but of expressive, subjectively engaged and experimental filmmaking." See Edwards's "*Gardens of War*: Materiality and the Photographic Narrative," in Barbash and Castaing-Taylor, *The Cinema of Robert Gardner,* 176, 192.

Susan Meiselas's *Recent Encounters with the Dani* (New York: International Center of Photography; Göttingen: Steidl, 2003), which grew out of Gardner's first return expedition to the Dani in 1989, provides an update not only on the Dani, but on the book-length photo essay about the Dani.

57. R. Bruce Jenkins, then director of the Harvard Film Archive, oversaw the production of *Making Forest of Bliss*—an endeavor that seems to have been somewhat controversial, at least within the Harvard community.

58. For Gardner's comments on John and Laurence Marshall, see note 10.

Just Representations also documents Gardner's involvement with a project to make Nobel Prize–winner J. M. Coetzee's *Waiting for the Barbarians* (1980) into a feature narrative film starring Tommy Lee Jones and Ben Kingsley. The year-long process of interviewing possible actors, scouting locations from Morocco to China, and assembling a crew ultimately came to naught (in part because Jones summarily dropped out of the project), and Gardner's journals reveal the philosophical and practical difficulties faced by an accomplished independent filmmaker trying to find his way through the complexities of producing even a small-budget feature. Gardner wonders "what is really at stake. *Waiting for the Barbarians* is a powerful story still living its life as an exquisite short novel. We are proposing to give it another life, on the screen. Why? Is this what the screen is really for?"; "Why simply transpose to another idiom something that flourishes already in its initial form?" (107–8).

59. Gardner, *The Impulse to Preserve,* 3. The "Old Lady" is also briefly described in Gardner's *Just Representations,* 13–4.

60. Gardner, *The Impulse to Preserve,* 5.

61. The same is true of *Making Dead Birds,* which is made up of letters to and from collaborators and friends, including John Marshall and Timothy Asch, during the months leading up to the expedition, throughout the expedition itself, and during the editing of *Dead Birds* and the reception of the finished film. The letters are supplemented by excerpts from Gardner's journals and camera notes and Gardner's later interpolations within the general chronology traced by these documents; plus Gardner's memoranda of conversations and meetings with various people involved in the project, and excerpts from Michael Rockefeller's sound-recording notes. (It is interesting to compare the journal entries presented in *Making Dead Birds* with those included in the *Dead Birds* section of *The Impulse to Preserve.* The journal entries in the later volume are often excerpts from the often much longer journal entries included in *The Impulse to Preserve*—I assume because Gardner wanted, insofar as possible, to avoid sustained repetition in the two books.)

Half-epistolary, half-graphic novel, the volume is engaging and beautifully designed, by Jeannet Leenderstse.

62. Gardner's recent mining of his archive has also produced several limited edition photographic books, including *Beauty Contest* (2009), which presents fifteen Polaroid photographs of Bororo men at Gerewol, introduced by an entry from Gardner's journal; and *In & Out* (2009), which presents fifty-five Polaroids of the doorway to an Ika dwelling "taken from a fixed position every twenty seconds for one half hour," accompanied by musings by the poet Fanny Howe. Both books were produced by Gardner's Studio7Arts in editions of 250. Michael Hutcherson supervised both projects.

63. Gardner's trip with Robert Fulton to southern Chile was far more extensive than this brief moment of flying footage in *Nine Forsaken Fragments* would suggest; "Chile Journal," a detailed account of the journey and the many flights Gardner and Fulton shared is included in *Just Representations,* 138–61.

64. "A Human Document" originally appeared in *Daedalus* 89: 1 (Winter 1960): 144–50.

65. Gardner, in letter to John Marshall, November 5, 1959, reprinted in *Making Dead Birds,* 14.

66. Ibid., 15.

67. Gardner's discussion of the Old Lady in "Kalahari Journal" suggests that he was humane toward the woman when others were not, and the journal's depiction of John Marshall is less than flattering. Could this be a result of Marshall's apparent disapproval of Gardner's way of thinking about the !Kung?

68. Marshall in "Filming and Learning," in Ruby, *The Cinema of John Marshall,* 71. In this essay Marshall references the original publication of "A Human Document."

69. Marshall's concern was also more general. In "Filming and Learning" he makes clear that he was concerned with Gardner's interest in using the proposed *The Gatherers* to focus on women's lives, when in fact, he had come to realize how much the Ju/'hoansi "suppressed sexual roles in the interest of subsistence" (71): "I opposed making another narrative film like *The Hunters* that used many women in a concocted story ending with /Gasa eating sand. Ju/'hoansi are not like that. The fantasy that 'Bushmen' abandon their old and sick was used against Ju/'hoansi and is still widespread. The film record is a testament to the facts. In 1978 the record shows a woman with leprosy who was carried around in a blanket by her family for fifteen years" (71).

Gardner's comment to Marshall that he had become involved with /Gasa "somewhat ghoulishly," suggests that he himself was uncomfortable about exploiting her for his own purposes. In "A Human Document" Gardner admits that the "noise of the camera troubled her for quite a while. Her long periods of rest were interrupted by times when the one or two inescapable physiological activities that had not ceased had to be performed. . . . At first she lay back, hoping the noise would stop and she could have privacy. But the camera was more constant than her taunting young relatives, and perhaps, because the camera never raised its voice, she detected in it no malice or contempt. Later she talked to the camera, asking it for water, or tobacco, or some fire. It nearly always responded with what she wanted" (*The Impulse to Preserve,* 2). Gardner's combination of intrusion, detachment, and connection here means to demonstrate his fascination, his "love" of this cinematic subject, but it also evokes a guard in a prison or a visitor to a zoo: the old lady seems Gardner's captive.

70. In his remarks about *Nine Forsaken Fragments* at Bard College, Gardner suggested that the nine fragments were held together by two concepts: human fragility and the human need to "find the way," to determine the right way to move into the future.

71. In an e-mail to the author on October 21, 2012, Gardner indicated that *Still Journey On* is "most certainly not finished"—though the DVD version I studied concludes with "© 2010." This 2010 version premiered at the Harvard Film Archive, was part of a 2011 Gardner retrospective at Film Forum in New York, and has been shown at several festivals.

72. From the Studio7Arts website. The description continues, "To this end the organization provides support—in the form of monetary contributions and the use of its facilities—to individual artists pursuing projects in keeping with its mission. It also initiates work (including small-press artist books and DVDs) that explores the potential of still and moving image-makers to give visible evidence that testifies to our shared humanity."

73. See the Studio7Arts website: www.studio7arts.org/.

74. Lockhart's film encapsulates the transition from celluloid-based cinema to digital filmmaking: it was shot in 16mm, then transferred to high-definition video. *Double Tide* has been exhibited as both a 90-minute projection and as an installation in which the two shots are presented simultaneously on two screens. It is available from Blum and Poe, Lockhart's gallery: www.blumandpoe.com.

75. In this sense, *Double Tide,* like some of Lockhart's other work, evokes Yvonne Rainer, whose fascination with the choreography of labor and of everyday activities has informed her performance work and films.

76. Unpublished phone interview with Fenz, 2012.

77. Fenz: "Ethiopia was the last country I filmed in for the project. Due to economic and time constraints, I had to choose between traveling south (where the Hamar live) and going north to the Afar in the Danakil Depression where Gardner had made images for an unfinished film. My Ethiopian guide informed me that the Hamar had many visitors. It was now standard practice for them to charge money and pose for the camera. I decided that such formal and posed images would not be appropriate for the film and decided to travel north to the Danakil Depression." Ibid.

78. This is hardly surprising. Fenz studied with Hutton at Bard College and went on to earn an MFA at California Institute of the Arts, where Benning teaches; both Bard and CalArts are widely recognized as nurturing grounds for avant-garde and experimental forms of cinema.

79. For *Correspondence,* Fenz "was given frequent flyer miles to travel to all locations. I had full access to editing equipment and materials at Studio7; some film stock and processing costs were supplemented. I was also able to review Gardner's finished and unfinished projects (sound and image) as much as I desired." Unpublished phone interview with Fenz, 2012.

80. E-mail from Sharon Lockhart to the author, August 28, 2011.

CHAPTER 3

1. Unpublished interview with the author, recorded in 2009.

2. Elizabeth Marshall Thomas, *Warrior Herdsmen* (New York: Knopf, 1965); a paperback edition, with a new introduction by Marshall, was published by Norton in 1981. Earlier on, in 1960, Asch had shot footage for a film that was never completed, focusing on a family making a life for themselves on a farm on Cape Breton Island. This had also been the site of an earlier photographic project that resulted in Asch's photographic book

Cape Breton 1952: The Photographic Vision of Timothy Asch, published by the International Visual Sociology Association in 1952.

3. The Timothy Asch collection at the Human Studies Archive of the Smithsonian Institution includes a fascinating folder of letters between Asch and White, who seems to have taken Asch quite seriously both as a photographer and as a theorist about photography.

4. Jay Ruby, *Picturing Culture: Explorations of Film and Anthropology* (Chicago: University of Chicago Press, 2000), 115. Ruby's Asch chapter comes immediately after his chapter on Robert Gardner, with whose work he has substantial problems; the seeming contempt for "auteurs" interested in producing "'memorable' films" is, I would conjecture, a reference to Gardner in particular.

5. See Douglas Harper's interview with Asch, "An Ethnographic Gaze: Scenes in the Anthropological Life of Timothy Asch," in E. D. Lewis, ed., *Timothy Asch and Ethnographic Film* (London: Routledge, 2004), 53.

6. Harper interview, 48.

7. Documents in the Timothy Asch files in the Human Studies Archive at the Smithsonian help to detail this conflict. In a January 2, 1975, letter to Edward Ginsburg, Elizabeth Marshall Thomas's lawyer, Asch explains:

> Mrs. Thomas said, before she went, that she did not want me to make a movie, for fear that I would not do a proper job with the still photographs. I respected her concern by concentrating on taking still photographs for her book until the very morning that we broke camp to leave the field. It is rare that anyone could make a successful film in three hours. When I discovered that, by using eight color slides to provide general introduction to the film I did have a publishable film, I was very excited. Mrs. Thomas knew that I was in training to become an ethnographic filmmaker; indeed, I was given leave from the Peabody Museum at Harvard, for whom the film was made, and therefore, thought that she would be excited by my use of eight slides to complete the film.

Asch's claim to have made the film on the morning he broke camp may be something of an exaggeration; in his "Notes on a Trip to Uganda—January 10," he explains:

> At one time, while making a movie, I had asked that an ox be bleed *[sic]* so that I could photograph it. The blood was given to Napuo [Asch's spelling of names here is different from what he would use later on; see note 7] who was not going to cook it or eat it that day because she was winnowing grain.... The beginning of the movie started late one evening when I photographed the cows (afternoon) going into L.'s [Lomori's] from a high rock. The next morning I photographed the grain being winnowed....

8. The names mentioned in *Dodoth Morning* differ from the names of the same people when they're described in Elizabeth Marshall Thomas's *Warrior Herdsmen,* where Lomori is called Lopore. This discrepancy came about because Thomas was concerned that if she identified particular Dodoth men and women, the identification might be used later to the detriment of these people; she invented names for each of the characters in the book. Telephone conversation with Thomas, June 19, 2010.

9. I am guessing at the spelling of these names, based on my hearing Asch say them in his narration.

10. In an early review of *Dodoth Morning* Ronald C. Simons makes the same point: "When the old man scolds and threatens his adolescent son, he is interrupted by the wife, who carefully balances her chastising the father with some words of reproach to the son concerning proper respect. The impression given is of a scene which in its most significant aspects might be repeated in other times and settings anywhere in the world." See Simons's review in *AAAS* (the journal of the American Association for the Advancement of Science) 13: 2 (September 1977): 104.

11. In fact, the sounds of the Dodoth speaking were not recorded during this expedition: "We didn't have a tape recorder. But David MacDougall gave me sound from the tribe next door that speak quite the same language. I dubbed his sound onto this film. It worked perfectly terrible." Harper interview, 48–49.

12. Asch asked that this ox be bled so that he could film it. See n. 6.

13. Elizabeth Marshall Thomas provides her own version of this process:

> Oxen give their blood. A man wishing to bleed an ox tightens a cord around its neck until its eyes and veins are bulging. While his sons hold the ox by the tongue, tail, and horns, he shoots its bulging neck vein with a blocked arrow. Blood pours in a steaming arch and is caught in a basin. When a quart or two is in the basin, the cord around the ox's neck is jerked away, the vein collapses, the bleeding stops as the ox runs off shaking its head and the blood is eaten. People drink the blood raw, after squeezing it with their fingers to break the clots, or cook it with green millet flour into a delicate, delicious pudding, as airy as soufflé. (Thomas, *Warrior Herdsmen,* 7)

14. There are, of course, comparable instances in films by other ethnographic filmmakers: Jean Rouch's *Les Maîtres Fous* (*Mad Masters,* 1954) provides particularly good examples, and there are instances in Gardner's *Dead Birds* and in several of Marshall's films about the San.

15. In *The Man Who Envied Women* (1985), Yvonne Rainer relocates Buñuel/Dalí's gesture into a feminist context, reminding viewers that, in its depiction of apparent violence to a woman for the sake of shock value and/or surrealist humor, *Un Chien Andalou* is rather less rebellious toward cinematic convention than its makers might have assumed.

16. Dai Vaughan sees the power of such moments differently. In *For Documentary: Twelve Essays* (Berkeley: University of California Press, 1999) he explains, "The horror of a documentary can lie in our being required to conceptualise (or—if there were such a word—perceptualise) the world in a certain way and being, at least for the duration of the film, powerless to intervene in it" (118)—the assumption being that seeing such an event in person, where the "perceptor" would have the power to become involved or leave is different from the implicit imprisoning of vision in the movie theater.

17. The focus on the doctors may have had a tactical economic instigation. Chagnon, in an early letter to Asch about preparations for the Yanomamo project, is excited that the budget he has submitted for the expedition to Venezuela has been granted, and explains that "the 16mm film is a sort-of tacked-on afterthought to the major interest of the department [the Department of Human Genetics at the University of Michigan Medical School], and

regarded as illegitimate issue to some extent. In fact, one of the selling points I harped on was the possibility of documenting 'modern medical scientists at work', something that the department viewed with somewhat more enthusiasm." Letter from Chagnon to Asch, dated October 30, 1967, Timothy Asch collection at the Human Studies Archive of the Smithsonian Institution.

18. Also, while *The Feast* is made up of both précis and live action material, Asch identifies the live action material in as the film itself, which is merely introduced by the précis, just as in the Marshall films the live action material that follows the précis is called "the film proper."

19. Asch told Jay Ruby:

> Well, he [Chagnon] had very little input in editing the films. It wasn't necessary, as the work was pretty straightforward. Much of the film had already been edited in the camera while I was shooting. However, when I asked for translations, he gave them. And when I got stuck and I asked for advice and whatnot, he was always helpful. . . . He never really had a role in any of the editing because he never really wanted it. . . . I was very good about showing him what I was doing, and he was always very praiseworthy, and then we would go out and drink beer. But at heart, he wanted to make didactic, self-contained films with heavy, long narration. I mean the first script of *The Feast* was something like thirty-five pages that I had to cut down to four pages. (*Picturing Culture*, 123)

Ruby indicates that his interview with Asch began in October 1993 "in a New York City hotel and later by phone. The interviews were edited and combined into their present form. All 'constructed' quotations were approved by Asch as representing his point of view. In some cases, he added material and revised his own words" (116).

20. I am quoting from the Timothy Asch brochure produced by Documentary Educational Resources.

21. Harper interview, 44.

22. In his essay Asch explains "film sequence" in some detail: "The filming commences with the initiation of interaction between individuals, it continues through the period of meaningful exchange and it dissipates when this phase of interaction ceases: two people see each other from a distance, they meet and discuss, perhaps the need for a sacrifice, they conclude and part." The paper was submitted in September 1964.

23. On all the Asch–Chagnon Yanomamo films, Chagnon is listed as translator.

24. The quotation is from the 1907 lecture, "Pragmatism and Humanism," available in William James, *Pragmatism and Other Writings* (New York: Penguin, 2000), 113.

25. Vaughan, "The Ethics of Ambiguity," in *For Documentary*, 83. By "such film," Vaughan is referring to forms of documentary made possible by the new equipment developed during the 1960s (sync-sound rigs, better film stocks, etc.); this equipment has recovered "the plenitude" of actuality, increasing that "margin of 'excess' whereby the film outstrips its makers' intentions: and it is by this argument—by this argument alone—that they [observational documentaries] may be justified [as documentaries] within the viewer's frame of reference" (83).

26. The first text: "Large Yanomamo villages are volatile, and the slightest provocation can start a violent outburst. On February 28, 1971, a fight erupted in the village of Mishi-

mishimaböwei-teri, with some 270 inhabitants. The fight began when a woman was beaten in the garden. She fled into the village, where her brother challenged the assailant to a club fight. The contest rapidly escalated to an ax fight."

27. This shot is reminiscent of, perhaps Asch's homage to, the famous shot of Pe'a climbing a coconut palm in Robert Flaherty's *Moana* (1926).

28. In his analysis of *The Ax Fight*, "What Really Happened: A Reassessment of *The Ax Fight*," in *Timothy Asch and Ethnographic Film* (229–37), Bill Nichols mistakenly conflates these two women. They do look and sound alike, but if one looks at their bodies, they cannot be confused.

29. I am grateful to Jay Ruby, who transcribed this conversation for his chapter on Asch in *Picturing Culture* (125–56). My listening to the sound led to a few minor changes in his transcription, but Ruby was able to make sense of several comments I couldn't understand.

30. Linda H. Connor and Patsy Asch discuss the gender orientation of *The Ax Fight* in their essay, "Subjects, Images, Voices: Representations of Gender in the Films of Timothy Asch," in Lewis, ed. *Timothy Asch and Ethnographic Film*, 176–78. As they make clear, the only woman named on the lineage chart is Sinabimi: "A careful examination of *The Ax Fight* reveals a contrast between the male focus of the analysis and visual evidence that women were active participants who provoked and sustained the fight" (177). In fairness to Asch, it must be said that the two women who hurl insults are the only characters in the film whose comments are translated (and their diatribes are amusing and engaging). Further, during the analysis of the fight, Chagnon's narration draws viewers' attention to the activities of women.

31. Asch, quoted in *Picturing Culture*, 129.

32. Nichols argues that the narrative structure of the final, edited version "gives us an explanation of the event: a woman provokes visitors, a fight breaks out, the woman gloats over vanquished visitors [see note 10]; therefore, the provocations of women cause men to fight" (Nichols, "What Really Happened: A Reassessment of *The Ax Fight*," 231).

33. Nichols has described the final, edited version of the event as Asch falling back on a "narrative explanation" of what the viewer has seen that "flirts with an ethnocentric essentialism—an assumption about the 'given' nature of women that is peculiar to our culture, namely, the notion of the eternally feminine as bitch. . . . The narrative sequence requires no further explanation: that's the way women are (as we all know, it seems to say in its complicity of silence)" (Bill Nichols, *Ideology and the Image* [Bloomington: Indiana University Press, 1981], 273). This seems a stretch on several levels (indeed, Nichols himself seems to be participating in something akin to the essentialism he describes: I see these women as performers, poets, not "bitches"). And it also underestimates Asch's intelligence. The final section is not meant as an *explanation;* it's a demonstration of the way in which what had come to be the accepted form of an anthropological film involved the transformation even of its own records of lived experience, with all the attendant distortions this transformation required. I see Asch's emphasizing the position of women in this final version as, on one hand, a (self-aware) confirmation of the gender assumptions of the anthropologists and, on the other, his recognition of the cinematic magnetism of these two particular women.

34. Asch, quoted in *Picturing Culture*, 128.

35. Ibid.

36. Ibid.

37. Ibid., 129.

CHAPTER 4

1. Ed Pincus, "New Possibilities in Film and the University," *Quarterly Review of Film Studies* 2: 2 (May 1977): 172; Pincus, in an unpublished interview with the author, 2009–11.

2. Scott MacDonald, "An Interview with Alfred Guzzetti," *Millennium Film Journal* no. 55 (Spring 2012): 72.

3. See L. M. Kit Carson's comments in the introduction to the published screenplay for *David Holzman's Diary* (New York: Farrar, Strauss & Giroux, 1970).

4. Jim McBride, in Scott MacDonald, *A Critical Cinema 4* (Berkeley: University of California Press, 2005), 185.

5. In his *The Autobiographical Documentary in America* (Madison: University of Wisconsin Press, 2002), Jim Lane argues, "By intermingling recorded moments, albeit scripted and acted for the camera, with the larger narrative frame of the autobiographer, *David Holzman's Diary* established a narrative model for the journal entry documentary. Despite its fictional status, *David Holzman's Diary* created a simulated, intimate mode of narration that proved viable for actual autobiographical documentarists" (45).

The increasingly fuzzy distinction between fiction and nonfiction filmmaking is especially evident in *David Holzman's Diary,* since McBride's fictional story of David Holzman, which is largely based on his own experiences, is shot on location in New York City. Indeed, *David Holzman's Diary* continues to seem real to most first-time viewers largely because much of what we see in the film and hear on the sound track is a faithful and evocative documentation of New York City during a volatile decade. Further, "David" introduces viewers to his recording equipment—his Arriflex camera, Nagra tape recorder, and his Angineux lens—making visible in detail, perhaps for the first time in an American film, the equipment typically used during that era in making both observational documentary and films in which the filmmakers instigate events.

6. Two other personal documentary filmmakers whose work is closely related to Miriam Weinstein's are Amalie R. Rothschild and Maxi Cohen, whose films *Nana, Mom, and Me* (1974) and *Joe and Maxi* (1978) have had considerably more exposure than the Weinstein films. Rothschild's *Nana, Mom, and Me* explores the relationships among the filmmaker's grandmother, her mother, and herself and the ways in which the three women's lives both fulfilled and defied the assumptions of their moment. *Nana, Mom, and Me* mixes Rothschild's interviews with her grandmother and mother, home movie footage and family photographs of all three women, along with narration by Rothschild to provide an engaging film that remains an emblem of early 1970s feminism. *Joe and Maxi,* made when Maxi Cohen was twenty-three, is her attempt to come to terms with her father, who is dying of cancer (Cohen's mother had died earlier). Joe Cohen is a cantankerous junkyard owner whose relationship with his daughter is fraught with conflict, and Maxi Cohen for her part struggles to use filmmaking as a way of knowing her father, though in the end, he banishes her from his presence—presumably because he doesn't want a record of his succumbing to the disease.

7. Weinstein, in e-mail interview with author, July 23, 2010.

8. Ibid.

9. Ibid.

10. I asked Weinstein about her strategy of talking with her subjects from behind the camera: "I think that Ed Pincus talked from behind the camera. Although you say his diaries weren't released until much later, I probably would have seen excerpts. Also, given that I worked on two-person crews with Al Fiering [at Polymorph Films], I was familiar with this style of shooting. For educational films, we would mostly cut out the off-camera questions, but they were definitely part of the process." Ibid.

11. I say Feinstein may be pretending to be annoyed by Weinstein's filmmaking because by the time Weinstein was shooting *Living with Peter,* Feinstein had developed considerable familiarity with independent cinema. For a time, he functioned as Hollis Frampton's agent; and if my memory is correct, he introduced a screening of three of Frampton's films (*(nostalgia)* (1971), *Poetic Justice* (1972), and *Critical Mass* (1971)—the first three sections of his *Hapax Legomena* series—at the same summer institute at Hampshire College where *Living with Peter* was also presented.

12. Miriam Weinstein, e-mail to the author, February 11, 2010. Weinstein was not a member of the Our Bodies, Ourselves (OBOS) collective: "As part of my work at Polymorph Films, I was involved with films on natural childbirth and breastfeeding. I took sound at a couple of hospital births. When OBOS needed photos of births, they called me. Now, I can't remember if I had a series of stills that I had taken for some other reason, or if I took them for OBOS. I think my work was in a couple of editions [of *Our Bodies, Ourselves*]. I was never part of the collective." E-mail interview with author, July 23, 2010.

13. In 1969 Weinstein was one of the first women to earn an M.F.A. in filmmaking from Boston University:

> I have to say that I did not enjoy my time at BU, and was very happy to be done with it. Coming from Brandeis, I was disappointed with the intellectual quality [of the courses there]. I'm not sure if it was place or the subject at the time. Also, being a technophobe did not help. The production courses seemed to be all about the machinery. There was little or no attention paid to structure/tone/creative aspects of the films we were producing. (Later, I taught film production at the Carpenter Center at Harvard, and at Mass College of Art and I must say that we gave those students a much better experience.) The film history courses at BU were nowhere near as rigorous as the art history courses I was accustomed to. It was a poor fit for me. The professor that I liked was Evan Cameron.

After graduation from Brandeis and before matriculating at Boston University, she worked for a time at WGBH before joining Al Fiering at Polymorph Films.

14. Rogers taught more or less regularly at Harvard from 1970 to 1985, and then again, from 1989 to 2001. Depending on the year, he taught as few as one or as many as three courses. Rogers was associate director of the Film Study Center for the 1989–90 academic year, then again from 1992 to 1997; and director of the Film Study Center from 1998 to 2001.

15. Pincus, "New Possibilities in Film and the University": 172–73. In this essay Pincus distinguishes American from European (and Canadian) cinema verite filmmaking: "The Americans, unlike the French and the Canadians, thought that the filmed reality should be

unmanipulated. People were never requested to do anything, even repeat actions, and in general the interview was eschewed as a form of camera-created reality" (165).

16. Dennis Sweeney and Pincus were friends early on in Cambridge; indeed, Sweeney's interest in and involvement with the civil rights movement in the American South helped to instigate Pincus's decision to make a film in Mississippi; and Sweeney appears in Pincus's *Black Natchez* (1967). In time, Sweeney seems to have become psychically unhinged and began to threaten some of those who had been his comrades in working to end American racism, including Pincus. After he killed Allard Lowenstein, Sweeney was caught and served eight years in the Mid-Hudson Psychiatric Center, New York State's maximum security mental hospital, and later was moved to a lower security facility. He was released in 2000.

17. Unpublished interview with Ed Pincus.

18. *Panola* was not finished for five years because Pincus and Neuman had grown uncomfortable about being "white people making a film about a black wino" in an era of Black Power. Pincus, in G. Roy Levin's interview in *Documentary Explorations* (New York: Doubleday, 1971), 360. Levin's interview includes conversation about several Pincus projects that were never completed.

19. Ibid.

20. Ibid., 361.

21. *One Step Away* was followed by *Harry's Trip* (1967), in which Harry, tripping on hallucinogens, talks to the camera in a single, continuous shot; and *Portrait of a McCarthy Supporter* (1968), in which Pincus and Neuman recorded Pincus's father-in-law as he talks politics. That there is no evidence in *Portrait* of Paul Kates's relationship to Pincus makes obvious the change in Pincus's approach that would be evident in *Diaries (1971–1976)*, where Kates makes an appearance and Pincus records the friction between his father-in-law and Jane Pincus and his own response to it.

22. *Abortion* is a landmark in its own right—one of the first, if not *the* first, to openly discuss and polemicize for abortion rights. Shot in 1970–71, as a collaboration between Jane Pincus, Catha Maslow, Mary Summers, and Karen Weinstein, it combined testimony from women who had experienced illegal abortions with various kinds of information about abortion and the feminist struggle to legalize it.

23. Unpublished Ed Pincus interview. Jane Pincus: "I don't remember whose idea it was. I think what happened is that each of us became attracted to other people, and then at a certain point in the midst of the ferment that developed after 1965, we made what we thought was a conscious decision to open our marriage. Right now, I'm not sure how conscious it was, and I'm not sure how smart it was—but I remember it as a mutual decision." Unpublished interview with Jane Pincus, October, 2010.

24. Ibid.

25. James, from the lecture, "Pragmatism and Humanism," in William James, *Pragmatism and Other Writings* (New York: Penguin, 2000), 113. The italics are James's.

26. A bit further on in part 5, we witness another conversation presumably about another lover Jane is planning to meet. This time, Ed seems uncomfortable: "Why are you doing it with somebody who's like almost a stranger?" Jane explains, "I'm kind of testing out my own strength by going, my own contours, my own solidity, you know what I mean?"; "It throws things into relief somehow." This passage too is followed by a series of upbeat domestic images.

27. A brief sequence soon after a conversation about Jane going to meet a new lover (see note 23) reveals that Ed may be struggling with his feelings about Jane's adventure. Ed is also struggling to decide what to do with his professional life; a sequence of Ed walking through a Vermont winterscape, just after his conversation with Jane about her going to see Joe, reveals that he has come to Vermont "to be alone" and "to think of what I want to do: do I want to teach at MIT, do I want to go back to philosophy?"

28. As Jim Lane has suggested, the mention of Yom Kippur concludes the motif of Jane's becoming more interested and more involved in her Jewish heritage: "The conclusion also connects Ed to this religious identity and family. Attempting to comfort a whining Ben, Ed says consolingly, 'My book is different than your book,' noting that if their 'books' were the same, they would be the same person. This statement, uttered by father to son, affirms Ed's new-found identity and reassures Ben of his identity and place in the family. Moreover, this metaphorical statement is spoken on the day when, according to Jewish tradition, God closes the Book of Life until Rosh Hashanah of the following year" (Lane, *The Autobiographical Documentary in America* [Madison: University of Wisconsin Press, 2002], 57–58).

29. Throughout *Diaries* Sami is, at least compared with Ben and Jane, reticent about being filmed. She conquers her shyness by learning to perform when Ed is shooting, but this final moment confirms her tendency to avoid being filmed, except when she can control her appearance within arranged performances.

30. Lane, *The Autobiographical Documentary,* 58.

31. Flannery O'Connor, "The Regional Writer," in *Mystery and Manners* (New York: Farrar, Straus & Giroux, 1969), 58.

32. As this is written (January 2012), *Life and Other Anxieties* exists as a single 16mm print in the Harvard Film Archive.

33. Guzzetti, unpublished interview with the author, 2011. In fact, Pincus liked *Family Portrait Sittings,* "didn't love it. Family too glued to their seats." On the other hand, "I loved *Scenes from Childhood* on the big screen (the small writ large)." E-mails to the author, November 9, 2012.

34. Ibid.

Willliam Rothman argues that *Family Portrait Sittings* was important as an early response to the tendency in direct cinema documentaries to make the filmmaker and the filmmaking invisible. See his "Alfred Guzzetti's *Family Portrait Sittings,*" in *The "I" of the Camera: Essays in Film Criticism, History, and Aesthetics* (New York: Cambridge University Press, 2003), 189–90. Along with Jim Lane's discussion in *The Autobiographical Documentary,* Rothman's remains the most substantial discussion of *Family Portrait Sittings.*

35. Lane: 100. This connection between tailoring and filmmaking, especially editing, is also central in Alan Berliner's *Nobody's Business* (1996), another film that traces the history of the filmmaker's family and makes considerable use of the filmmaker's interviews with his parents.

36. See Rothman, *The "I" of the Camera,* 312.

37. Rothman explores the ways in which repressed, or at least suppressed, resentments are expressed in the subtle gestures of Guzzetti's parents as they speak to him and respond to each other. See Rothman, *The "I" of the Camera,* 199–200.

38. Alfred Guzzetti, program notes for John Stuart Katz, ed., *Autobiography: Film/Video/Photography* (Toronto: Art Gallery of Ontario, 1978), 50.

39. William Rothman sees one of the crucial dimensions of *Family Portrait Sittings* as Guzzetti's development of a double role:

> In presenting its family as, at one level, a "case," the film establishes an "objective" authorial perspective that appears radically separate from that family's historical situation. Yet, at another level, the film constitutes the filmmaker's own acknowledgment that, despite everything, he is himself a member of this family, and dedicated to it. . . . Hence, the author implied by the film has a problematic duality. He is the analytical investigator, armed with a Marxist interpretation of history, presenting this family as a case, but he is also Alfred, son of Susan and Felix, husband of Deborah, and father of Benjamin: a major character in the film's story. (*The "I" of the Camera*, 308)

40. As in *Family Portrait Sittings*, Guzzetti remains generally absent from the frame: we hear him ask questions of his subjects and in a single instance we see him on screen, filming himself filming (in a mirror): first in 1975, then in 1987 (the direct cut from Guzzetti "then" to Guzzetti "now" dramatizes the passage of time); he also provides a brief context-setting narration at the beginning of each of the film's two parts.

One of the things that seems to have instigated the changes in outlook and in living arrangements is the arrival of children and the need to support them, and Guzzetti represents this by including interviews with Ben and Sarah. These interviews, while charming, do not quite make sense within the context of *House;* they seem a somewhat self-indulgent expression of Guzzetti's excitement and pride in his children.

41. *Vermont Kids* is made up of four short films shot by Marshall as part of Roger Hart's research on children's outdoor play: *Sandbank,* about a large group of boys and girls playing on a large mound of sand near to what appears to be a warehouse; *Playing House,* about two teenage girls pretending to design a house in the woods (their little brother hovers nearby); *In the Dirt,* about several young boys playing with model cars in the dirt, and later on, making "airplanes" out of clothespins; and *Treehouse,* about several boys and girls constructing a plywood treehouse in the woods. From time to time Hart speaks with the children about what they're doing.

42. Images from Meiselas's *Nicaragua* are used in order to provide background context before the title credit; these are presented as an echo of the implicit narrative line of the book, which begins with conditions before the revolution, then the revolution itself, its hardships and victory.

43. For two other collaborative projects, *Khalfan and Zanzibar* (1999), a portrait of Khalfan Hemed Khalfan, who established and runs a disability center in Zanzibar, and *Songs of a Sorrowful Man* (2009), a documentary portrait of a scroll painter in West Bengal, Guzzetti again teamed with Ákos Östör and Lina Fruzzetti.

44. *Reframing History* is available on the commercial DVD (from Docurama) of *Pictures from a Revolution.*

45. *América Central* is reminiscent of Ernie Gehr's *Signal—Germany on the Air* (1985); both films explore an urban crossroads (a generally nondescript intersection in Berlin, in Gehr's film) and the obvious and subtle "intersections" between the news (and "news") stories we see and hear on television and radio and these particular locations.

46. *A Family in History* seems both an echo and a fulfillment of the urge that instigated Guzzetti's earlier *The House on Magnolia Avenue,* which has never been released because of the objections of one of the participants. The idea of seeing how a familial group evolves through time seems an ongoing fascination for Guzzetti, and the unpretentious idealism and willingness to allow ideals to structure practical life that is obvious in both the older and younger generations of the Barrios family seem meant as an antidote to the cynicism that currently pervades American political life.

47. E-mail from Guzzetti to the author, May 1, 2012:

> I do admire Morgan's [Morgan Fisher's] work. . . . I've known Morgan a long time. I went to college with him [at Harvard]. I've seen *Standard Gauge* only once, quite a while ago, but did respond to it and do remember it. And yes, I think that *Sink or Swim* is a strong, rich film. Likewise *(nostalgia).* I wasn't thinking of any of these while working on *Time Exposure.* I was thinking nearly exclusively of the history I recount, struggling with writing, and struggling with the V.O. [voice-over], which I've never done before (I got some good advice from Ross). I did think a bit about *Letter to Jane* and even more of *Ulysses* by Agnès Varda. I thought also about *La Jetée,* because it's nearly all still photographs and V.O. . . . with a single moment of movement. I thought of this moment in relation to the single moment of color and sync sound that I use, though I use movement three times. And of course of all the work I've done with Susan Meiselas, especially in *Pictures from a Revolution.*

In a November 9, 2012, e-mail, Morgan Fisher told me that he has vivid memories of Guzzetti at Harvard and that he held Guzzetti and his various activities in the arts—including a production of a Greek play, his programming of avant-garde music by Christian Wolfe, John Cage, and David Tudor, and his accomplishments in English literature—in high esteem.

48. Rothman, *The "I" of the Camera,* 307–8.

49. Guzzetti said this to me in April 2012.

50. See n. 45.

CHAPTER 5

1. William James, "The Stream of Consciousness," excerpted from *Psychology: Briefer Course,* in William James, *Pragmatism and Other Writings,* ed. Giles Gunn (New York: Penguin, 2000), 187.

2. My information in this and subsequent paragraphs about Camper's activities is based on a telephone interview conducted on August 12, 2010.

3. I interviewed Tom Chomont in the spring of 1980, and all the information about his presentation of avant-garde film and filmmakers is from that interview: see my *A Critical Cinema* (Berkeley: University of California Press, 1988), 157–59. Chomont also organized a showing of Andy Meyer's *Match Girl* (1966) and Jean Genet's *Un Chant d'amour* (1950) at the Swetzoff Gallery in Boston: "Sure enough, at the second showing two plainclothesmen tried to get in the door. Mr. Swetsof was very clever: he just stepped outside the door and slammed it. (He had locked the door on the inside so when he shut it he couldn't even get in himself.)

It was very exciting. I'm sure the bravado was inspired by reading about Jonas Mekas and *Flaming Creatures*."

4. Scott MacDonald, interview with Alfred Guzzetti, *Millennium Film Journal* 55 (Spring 2012): 73.

5. Guzzetti explains:

> I came to film after composing music off and on for more than ten years. *Air* is a film opera that, like musical operas, includes passages of vocal counterpoint. Mike Figgis published a couple of pages of his scenario for *Time Code* [2000], which was written on music staffs—I think he's a jazz musician as well as a film-maker. The same thing is all but true in *Air*. . . . I would hold the strips of paper next to one another and think, "If I move the second phrase of voice B five frames later, then *that* phrase will have a relationship with *this,* and it will fall into another relationship *here*." I made the rule for myself that the rhythms of these passages would be composed so that you would have an ensemble, the way you have an ensemble in Mozart when people are singing different texts at the same time, with the music bringing them together, harmonizing them. (Ibid., 74)

6. Kubelka explores the idea of metric cinema in "The Theory of Metrical Cinema," available in P. Adams Sitney, *The Avant-Garde Film: A Reader of Theory and Criticism* (New York: Anthology Film Archives and NYU Press, 1978), 139–59.

7. Warhol's *Screen Tests* were, like his other early films, shown at 16 frames per second, so his portraits are essentially in slow motion, whereas the four portraits in *Air* are not slowed down—though to a 1971 audience, they might still have seemed unusually long and slow-paced.

8. Alfred Guzzetti, *Two or Three Things I Know about Her: Analysis of a Film by Godard* (Cambridge: Harvard University Press, 1981), 4.

9. Recently, Guzzetti made a video copy of *Air* and remixed the soundtrack in order to make it stereo and to eliminate a lot of the compromises he'd had to make for 16mm optical sound. A Dolby 5.1 version of *Air* is now available: contact guzzetti@fas.harvard.edu.

10. Two other notable early experiments are *Evidence* (1972), an experimental road movie Guzzetti shot while on a cross-country trip with Richard P. Rogers, and *Chronological Order* (1982), a lovely landscape film. Guzzetti and Rogers devised a way of mounting a camera on the front of their car and another on a metal arm mounted within the car (so they could shoot out a side window) and filmed along the road in a variety of locations, including Louisiana, St. Louis, and across Texas, New Mexico, and Arizona into California. Guzzetti edited the film and devised a soundtrack made up of music of his own composition, recordings made from the car radio (they fed the radio into their tape recorder) of preachers, and of other more abstract sounds. The result is an engaging, strange, 16-minute experience that has much in common with James Benning and Bette Gordon's *The United States of America* (1975). Looking back from Guzzetti's recent video work, the element of *Evidence* that seems most prescient of what would come later is the matching of Guzzetti's editing of the visuals to the particulars of sound during several sequences.

Chronological Order is a continuous view of a woods framed so that a white birch on the right identifies the particular space, filmed intermittently over several seasons for several seconds each time: the film begins in the summer, moves through fall, winter, spring, summer, and into a second fall (environmental sounds, mostly of birds, sometimes of weather, make up the soundtrack). Like J. J. Murphy's *In Progress* (1972, co-made with Ed Small), Guzzetti's 4-minute film demonstrates the stability and continual variety of a familiar natural space.

11. No doubt there are other influences. Part 6 of *Variation* includes a shot of a beach that seems a conscious homage to John Frederick Kensett's *Coast Scene with Figures* (1869).

12. When I spoke to Guzzetti in August 2010, he explained that in *Variation* he was trying to make something that had no words but just was purely a sound and image relationship and that worked on some kind of musical principle of variation: "But not *variations*, because there isn't any theme; it's like variation without a theme."

13. Guzzetti's digital videos are quite distinctive, though at times their experimentation with sound-image possibilities does evoke Kubelka's *Unsere Afrikareise*, Alan Berliner's *Everywhere at Once* (1985), and some of the films of Abigail Child: *Prefaces* (1981) and *Mutiny* (1983), for example.

14. The dreams Guzzetti includes in any given digital video often make reference to people and events that are the subject of his earlier, more conventionally personal films. The third dream's mention of Guzzetti's father is a poignant reminder of Felix Guzzetti's death, which is part of the introductory context for *Beginning Pieces;* the narrow Roman street that forms the backdrop of this dream is reminiscent of the Italian streets Guzzetti walks in *Family Portrait Sittings.* Deborah Fortson is referred to directly here (in other dreams in other videos, she's sometimes identified as "D."); and, as I've suggested, the sudden shift to Central America at the end of the fourth dream evokes Guzzetti's work on *Living at Risk* and *Pictures from a Revolution.*

15. The first dream is presented as a black text that moves quickly across the bottom of the frame from right to left, superimposed with a shot of a lone tree; the second dream, in yellow text, superimposed over a shot of leaves in a pond; a distant storm is barely audible. In both cases, each sentence is separated from the next by a temporal pause. Line changes in the first dream indicate temporal pauses as sentences move through the frame from right to left; in the second dream, the texts are still and centered in the frame—slashes indicate line breaks.

16. The title of *What Actually Happened* refers to a comment heard on the radio: "I want to recount what actually happened"; the title of *A Tropical Story* is the final phrase of one of the dreams presented textually: "I imagine it must be a tropical story."

17. According to Guzzetti, the locations included in *History of the Sea* are "(in no particular order): Grand Canyon (first shot), New Mexico Roads; train, Northeast corridor; train station Sanford, CT; White Sands, NM; house in Jamaica Plain, MA; Cape Cod ocean; lake surface, NH; rooftops, Back Bay, Boston; sea at Halibut Point, MA; forest on Mt. Desert Island, Maine; escalator at Los Angeles County Museum of Art; billboard in Hollywood; Pacific Ocean from California Route; very Large Array, NM; roads in CA and MA; stop sign, wires, clouds in rural NM; black and white 16mm of sea at Cape Cod; South Station, Boston." E-mail to the author, August 25, 2010.

18. Nathaniel Dorsky, in my interview with him in *A Critical Cinema 5* (Berkeley: University of California Press, 2006), 95.

19. Guzzetti described the sound design and the sources of his visual imagery for *Still Point* to me in an August 2011 e-mail.

376   NOTES TO CHAPTER 6

20. The title of *Still Point* is from T. S. Eliot's *Four Quartets:* "At the still point of the turn-ing world. Neither flesh nor fleshless; / Neither from nor towards; at the still point, there the dance is, / But neither arrest nor movement" ["Burnt Norton," part 2, lines 16–18].

CHAPTER 6

1. There is also the 30-minute collaboration with Michel Negroponte, *Resident Exile* (1981).

2. Josef von Sternberg, *Fun in a Chinese Laundry* (San Francisco: Mercury House, 1965), 275.

3. McElwee in Scott MacDonald, *A Critical Cinema 2* (Berkeley: University of Califor-nia Press, 1992), 269. In "Mirror Shot," an essay written for *Landscapes of the Self: The Cinema of Ross McElwee/Paisajes del yo: El Cine de Ross McElwee* (Madrid: Ediciones Inter-nacionales, 2007), the catalog that accompanied a retrospective of his work, McElwee goes on to say that *Diaries* "is a profound and disturbing work . . . technically brilliant and emo-tionally courageous" (246).

4. McElwee, in MacDonald, *A Critical Cinema 2*, 275.

5. McElwee had made two films before *Charleen: 20,000 Missing Persons* (1974) and *68 Albany Street* (1976). When I inquired about these films, McElwee told me:

> There are no surviving copies of *20,000 Missing Persons* nor *68 Albany Street*. The latter was made (under Ricky's guidance) for a lab at MIT as a student film commissioned by Draper Labs. Not so sure it would be all that interesting now. But it was shot in 16mm, and somewhere at MIT there may be a print—perhaps in the archives of Draper Laboratories. It featured Phil Bowditch, an engineer who perfected the inertial guidance system that led to the success of the Apollo Moon Landing Program. I remember trying to track the film down for someone years ago and having no luck. You're welcome to try, but I think it is probably not worth your time. *Missing Persons* was commissioned by a NC [North Carolina] television station (WSOC-Charlotte) and no existing copies of it exist. Frankly, it was not a very good film—I had to work with a TV staff cameraman—and I am rather relieved that it has disappeared. I took it off my resume at least a decade ago, so you must be working from an ancient document. (E-mail to the author, September 7, 2010)

6. McElwee, in *A Critical Cinema 2*, 268.

7. Swansea's accomplishments include the founding in 1964 of *Red Clay Reader,* an annual magazine that published the work of southern authors and artists, which Swansea edited until 1970. Subsequently she founded Red Clay Publishers to publish books by women writers. Swansea's papers are in the Southern Historical Collection at the University of North Carolina. These papers include a substantial collection of correspondence and memorabilia from her friendship with Ezra Pound.

8. In retrospect, *Space Coast*, the collaborative project by McElwee and his MIT colleague Michel Negroponte, completed the year after *Charleen,* seems a side trip for McElwee, an exercise in direct cinema. An opening visual text tells us "Cape Canaveral, Florida several years after the phasing out of the Apollo moon landing missions," but while

the history of Cape Canaveral's involvement in the space program may form the general background for the action in *Space Coast,* the film's focus on three individuals and their families seems motivated less by the space program or the economic results of its downsizing than by a fascination with the quirkiness of these individuals and the humor and/or repugnance they seem meant to provoke.

Space Coast seems a step back (at least for McElwee) in its articulation of the filmmakers' presence within the film. Like *Charleen, Space Coast* provides brief bits of voice-over context about the characters and their activities (spoken by Negroponte), imitative of the voice-overs in the early classics of direct cinema (Drew Associates' *Primary* [1960] and *Crisis: Beyond a Presidential Commitment* [1963], for example). And like *Charleen, Space Coast* reveals some interplay between the filmmakers and the protagonists and their relatives. But there is nothing in *Space Coast* like the developing relationship between Charleen Swansea and McElwee in *Charleen.*

9. Dominique Bluher, "Ross McElwee's Voice/La Voz de Ross McElwee," in *Landscapes of the Self,* 138.

10. Joel DeMott's *Demon Lover Diary,* finished the same year as *Breaking and Entering* at MIT, is also relevant here. DeMott creates a narrator who confides in the viewer as the events of the film unfold (*Demon Lover Diary* chronicles the aborted attempt by Jeff Kreines and Mark Rance to assist with the production of a low-budget horror film, *Demon Lover*). DeMott's narrating voice differs from both Schaetzel's and McElwee's in that she pretends to be speaking to the viewer during the events she is commenting on, when in fact, her comments were, at least according to Jim Lane, recorded during postproduction. See Jim Lane, *The Autobiographical Documentary in America* (Madison: University of Wisconsin Press, 2002), 165–66.

11. In his discussion of *Breaking and Entering,* Jim Lane sees this shot as nightmarish: "The blurred image of Ann's father quickly advancing toward the camera and filling the frame graphically suggests a monstrous figure who will try to consume the film and filmmaker." Lane, in *The Autobiographical Documentary in America* (Madison: University of Wisconsin Press, 2002), 159. This seems an exaggeration to me. Schaetzel's family seems entirely banal and self-involved, and Schaetzel's father's affectionate welcoming of his daughter demonstrates the irony that her father seems entirely oblivious to her anger.

12. During *Breaking and Entering,* Schaetzel's mother and Schaetzel converse about the age of a friend of the family; Schaetzel mentions that she is thirty-two and her mother confirms that she knows Ann was born in 1946.

13. Mulvey discusses "scorched earth filmmaking" in my interview with her, in Mac-Donald, *A Critical Cinema 2,* 334. Mulvey names her and Peter Wollen's *Penthesilea* (1974) as their scorched earth film.

14. Donald Bogle, *Toms, Coons, Mulattoes, Mammies, and Bucks: An Interpretive History of Blacks in American Films* (New York: Continuum, 1973). The fourth edition of the book appeared in 2006.

15. Bogle's definition of "the tom": "Always as toms are chased, harassed, hounded, flogged, enslaved, and insulted, they keep the faith, n'er turn against their white massas, and remain hearty, submissive, stoic, generous, selfless, and oh-so-very kind" (5–6); and "the mammy": "Mammy is distinguished . . . by her sex and her fierce independence. She is usually big, fat, and cantankerous. . . . Mammy's offshoot is the aunt jemima. . . . Often aunt jemimas are toms blessed with religion or mammies who wedge themselves into the

dominant white culture. Generally sweet, jolly, and good-tempered—a bit more polite than mammy and certainly never as headstrong" (9).

16. For those geared to spotting stereotypical black roles, several of the young men McElwee films at the local country club might also seem to fit, at least roughly, the role of "the coon," the black character who functions essentially as a clown.

17. In the *A Critical Cinema 2* interview, McElwee has suggested that the black employees in the country club kitchen are subtly rebelling against their situation: "I read some hostility in those black kids. They're seventeen or eighteen years old, washing dishes for the white folks, and they're really banging those dishes around" (272). Of course, this hostility may have something to do with McElwee's filming them.

18. McElwee's use of faded imagery here to suggest a fading way of life and perhaps his own increasing distance from it is reminiscent of John Marshall's use of low-grade video imagery from his early idyllic films about the !Kung in his later work to suggest the decay of their lifestyle and his increasing embarrassment about his participation in films that distorted their reality. See chapter 1. Also, McElwee's beginning *Backyard* with a photographic précis and voice-over that, he suggests, is not part of the real film ("Before this film begins") is reminiscent of John Marshall's similar tactic in several of his !Kung films.

19. McElwee in MacDonald, *A Critical Cinema 2*, 271–72.

20. McElwee's complete statement:

> The fact that they [McElwee's family] don't talk about it doesn't mean they don't think about it, or act upon it. I'm told that when my father set up his practice in Charlotte, after finishing medical school and his residency in New York City, he was the first doctor in the city to have a desegregated waiting room. There was no fanfare, no newspaper story. (I was not told this by him but by other people.) It seemed absurd to him that black people had to sit in one room and whites in another when he was going to be operating on all of them sooner or later. He's quietly done things like that all his life. I saw them throughout my childhood. (McElwee, in MacDonald, *A Critical Cinema 2*, 273–74)

21. This comment is reported by Pat after her interview with her agent, half an hour into *Sherman's March*.

22. I detailed my reading of the narrative perspective in "The Snows of Kilimanjaro" in *Studies in Short Fiction* 11: 1 (Winter 1974): 67–74.

23. Ernest Hemingway, *Green Hills of Africa* (New York: Scribner's, 1935), 27.

24. McElwee, in MacDonald, *A Critical Cinema 2*, 275.

25. McElwee's inclusion of the map can be understood as a reference to the many ethnographic and proto-ethnographic films (*Nanook of the North, The Ax Fight*) that begin with maps, suggesting that *Sherman's March* will have, like *Charleen, Space Coast*, and *Backyard*, ethnographic dimensions.

26. In her "Documentary Film and the Discourse of Hysterical/Historical Narrative," Lucy Fisher reminds us that the elaborate full title of *Sherman's March* evokes the title of Kubrick's *Dr. Strangelove or: How I Learned to Stop Worrying and Love the Bomb* (1964)— a hint on McElwee's part, perhaps, that the events he will portray are to be taken with

more than one grain of salt. Fischer's essay is included in Barry Keith Grant and Jeannette Sloniowski, eds., *Documenting the Documentary* (Detroit: Wayne State University Press, 1998), 333–43.

27. Dominique Bluher, "Ross McElwee's Voice," 144–46. Bluher's astute comment about how McElwee seems to be present talking with us during the projection of the film reminds me that during the era when McElwee was a child, presentations of records of family excursions and vacations, on slides or on film, often included "voice-overs" by whoever recorded the imagery. McElwee's films evoke this familial intimacy. We are part of a "cinematic family," confidants with whom he shares his thoughts about himself and his nuclear family.

28. As Lucy Fischer has suggested, "the Civil War becomes a multivalent metaphor not only for McElwee's divided self, but for American political discord. . . . The work's focus on regional antagonism also invokes the fissure of race, both in contemporary and historic contexts." Fischer, "Documentary Film and the Discourse of Hysterical/Historical Narrative," in *Documenting the Documentary*, 340.

29. Another, rather different, instance occurs during McElwee's conversation with a mechanic and longtime friend of the McElwee family while he and his son are working on McElwee's brother's sports car, which will become Ross's means of transportation for a time. The two reminisce about the man's son, Philip, who now works with him, and they share their feelings about the deaths from cancer of the mechanic's daughter and McElwee's mother. During this conversation, the mechanic looks at McElwee to the left of the camera *and* at the camera, equally. Once again, though in a different way, the two McElwees become one: the real McElwee, the mature *filmmaker*, takes precedence and our sense of the McElwee *character* momentarily disappears.

30. The scene of Jackie teaching at her school is one of the more candid in *Sherman's March*. The children's interest in engaging McElwee and his camera, and McElwee's enjoyment of their interest, is obvious. Indeed, Jackie herself seems to enjoy the pedagogical opportunity McElwee's presence creates and the attention her students are getting from him.

31. McElwee recalls this particular comment at the end of a monologue he records in a tunnel at Fort Moultree: he has positioned himself so that he appears as a distant silhouette, though it is clear that the monologue is recorded in sync. The effect is similar to the shots of McElwee in the New York loft at the beginning of *Sherman's March;* as in that earlier sequence, McElwee as filmmaker and the McElwee character are quite separate.

32. Compared with DeeDee's rather melodramatic singing at the Ashley Hall School for Girls, which is seemingly irrelevant for the little girls she's singing to, Perrin is an engaging performer, and like Jackie, a woman who is comfortable crossing racial lines; McElwee films her preparing for an upcoming tour with African American pianist Grady, in Grady's home. Like the children in Jackie's school, the neighborhood children are fascinated with McElwee's filmmaking.

33. This new kind of documentary conflates two dimensions of film history. The McElwee character's quest for a romantic relationship is an inventive incorporation of one of the central dimensions of traditional commercial melodrama; and McElwee's following the route of Sherman's march through the South, visiting various historical sites along the way and providing information about Sherman's experiences, is an inventive incorporation of the informational documentary.

34. McElwee, "Mirror Shot," *Landscapes of the Self,* 241–42.

35. From J. M. Coetzee, *Summertime* (New York: Penguin, 2009), 227.

36. The fact that McElwee concludes this review of his earlier filmmaking with the observation that "being single definitely had its ups and downs, but overall I had decided that I kind of liked the freedom" seems to confirm my reading of McElwee's quest for a mate in *Sherman's March* as merely a performance for the film. That Marilyn Levine is a filmmaker also provides an amusing confirmation of this reading: it was not until he found a partner who shared his respect for and commitment to filmmaking that he could end his search for true love.

37. Marian Keane, "Reflections on *Bright Leaves,*" in William Rothman, ed., *Three Documentary Filmmakers: Errol Morris, Ross McElwee, Jean Rouch* (Albany: SUNY Press, 2009), 73.

38. As Jim Lane has suggested, McElwee is "referencing *Sherman's March* by using the same scene set up. . . . This reference within a self-reference creates a continuity of tension and resolution between father and son. . . . In *Time Indefinite,* with his father truly absent and the house apparently vacant, Ross assumes the off-camera presence himself in voice-over, transferring his father's critical point of view onto his present point of view." See Lane's "Drifting in Time: Ross McElwee's *Time Indefinite,*" in Rothman, *Three Documentary Filmmakers,* 89.

39. Not surprisingly, a number of those who have commented on *Time Indefinite* have focused on this remarkable moment, including Jim Lane (see note 35), Charles Warren ("We do not get the whole Ross, and sometimes see and hear a Ross on-screen in counterpoint with rather another Ross speaking in voice-over"—in Rothman, *Three Filmmakers,* 96), and most perceptively, at least by extension, Rothman himself, in his discussion of *Bright Leaves,* "Sometimes Daddies Don't Talk about Things like That," in *Three Filmmakers:*

> The moment he is invoking is one in which he is viewing this shot, as we are, not the moment when he filmed the shot. So this line marks a significant shift. Ross is no longer speaking about what he was imagining when he was looking through the viewfinder. By "these images and reflections" Ross can only mean this sequence itself. In other words, the experience Ross is now invoking pertains to the time of his speaking of these words, not the time of his taking of these shots. His words testify to his sense of the uncanny power of these "images and reflections" as they are used in *Bright Leaves.* (117)

40. Fischer, in Grant and Sloniowski, eds., *Documenting the Documentary:* 341.

41. Brakhage, in Scott MacDonald, *A Critical Cinema 4* (Berkeley: University of California Press, 2005): 66, 65.

42. In 1996 Marilyn Levine completed *Life, Death & Baseball,* an autobiographical film focusing on her loss of her older sister, Adrienne, to an osteo-sarcoma during their childhood. Levine's hour-long film echoes *Time Indefinite* in a variety of ways. Her interviews with her parents and friends are generally similar to McElwee's: she too holds the camera so that her interviewees speak to the left of our viewing position, and we hear her asking questions and responding with an "um hum" from behind the camera. The film is Levine's attempt to cinematically come to terms with what losing her sister has meant in her life (it seems to have confirmed a childhood tendency toward angst) so that she can feel capable of becoming a mother.

McElwee is introduced at Levine's father's seventieth birthday party: "And this is my husband Ross, whose strategy for keeping his emotional equilibrium is to place himself behind a movie camera as often as possible," and he appears intermittently during the remainder of the film. He is also credited with additional camera and sound.

Levine's revisiting of her sister's life—e.g., she tracks down former Yankee pitcher Roland Sheldon (before her death, Adrienne Levine had formed the Roland Sheldon fan club) in Kansas City—is interwoven with her pregnancy, and the film concludes with Adrian's birth—presented here, as in *Time Indefinite,* so that we hear the birth as we watch a black screen (we first see Adrian as a Polaroid photograph)—and with a scene recorded four years later of Adrian planting corn with his grandmother and, sometime later, carrying produce from the garden into the grandparents' home.

The story of Adrienne Levine is moving, and at times the film is effective (Levine's interview with her neighbor and physician, Susan, is engaging, and the visit with Sheldon interesting), but *Life, Death & Baseball* is poignant primarily in its failure to achieve the mix of emotion and intellect, the wry humor, and the lovely cinematography so characteristic of McElwee's films. Levine's narrative voice does not approach the complexity of McElwee's narration or his exquisite timing. Indeed, Levine's film seems a largely ineffective attempt to make a McElwee film rather than to develop a distinctive form of autobiographical documentary.

43. See Rothman's "Sometimes Daddies Don't Talk about Things like That"—Rothman's title is a reference to this scene; it's what the Masseys' daughter tells McElwee—in *Three Documentary Filmmakers,* 111).

44. From William Faulkner, *Intruder in the Dust* (New York: Vintage, 1991), 190. This passage is from Chick Mallison's stream of consciousness, which includes his own rumination on time interwoven with that of his uncle Gavin Stevens.

45. For a film historian John McElwee's collection of 35mm prints, trailers, posters, and photographs is one of the most remarkable dimensions of *Bright Leaves.* That a southern lawyer, living in a modest country house, could have this collection and be so aware of (commercial) film history seems remarkable, and it seems strange that, until the time of shooting *Bright Leaves,* Ross had never met him.

46. In their best work, both artists use their personal struggles as the subject matter of engaging narratives, and great films have resulted from both their efforts. Gray's performance of *Swimming to Cambodia,* documented by Jonathan Demme in his wonderful *Swimming to Cambodia* (1987), has much in common with McElwee's films. Like *Sherman's March* and *Bright Leaves, Swimming to Cambodia* interweaves information about historical events—about the Vietnam War, the fall of Cambodia, and the making of Roland Joffé's *The Killing Fields* (1984), in which Gray had a small role—with personal reminiscences. Both Gray and McElwee create personae that seem intimately engaged with the viewer, and each creates an engaging mix of seriousness and humor about both themselves and the wider world.

Their particular modes of address to the viewer are, however, somewhat different. Gray faces us directly, revealing himself through his storytelling. When McElwee addresses the camera, his performances do resemble Gray's; but McElwee's primary means of engaging viewers is through voice-over. He seems to speak privately to us, quietly and discretely, as if we were close friends standing beside him, sharing his interests and concerns.

47. A comparable sequence occurs in *Six O'Clock News.* As McElwee's visits with Salvador Peña become less revealing, McElwee begins observing the particulars of Peña's environment with a cine-poetic eye. Filmmaking is not only McElwee's way of dealing with

tension and trauma but with boredom: his camera allows him to transform emptiness into engaging visuals.

48. I am referring to Stan Brakhage's canonical essay, "Metaphors on Vision," originally published as a special issue of *Film Culture* in 1963 and excerpted in Bruce R. McPherson, ed., *Essential Brakhage: Selected Writings on Filmmaking by Stan Brakhage* (Kingston, NY: Documentext, 2001). I once asked Brakhage about his sense that small children are more perceptive of the phenomena around them than adults; Brakhage's response: "But that's exactly, from my viewpoint, what you *do* with boredom. You sink into it; you begin to be aware of the slight subtleties that are left in the gray field. The only thing that can be done with the dull civilization we are now having is to be fascinated by the *endless* riches of variance within the dullest, greyest field." Scott MacDonald, *A Critical Cinema 4* (Berkeley: University of California Press, 2005), 86.

49. At the Society for Cinema and Media Studies in Boston in March 2012, as part of a panel organized by William Rothman called "Documentary Filmmaking in Boston and Beyond," Diane Stevenson (during her presentation of "Internal Exile: What Edward Said Has to Teach Us about Ross McElwee") noted that this sequence of portraits recalls Walker Evans's photographs for his and James Agee's *Let Us Now Praise Famous Men*—an astute connection.

50. This moment in Paraguay echoes the moment in *Bright Leaves* when, as William Rothman has suggested in "Sometimes Daddies Don't Talk," Ross is imagining (as he films random imagery in and around his cheap motel room), what "Adrian—some time in the future, when Ross is no longer around—looking at what Ross has filmed, that is, looking at what he is now filming," will think of his filming and this film (116).

51. In an unpublished interview conducted in 2012, McElwee discussed this issue with me:

> For reasons I will never fully understand, Marilyn changed her mind about wanting the film to be made. She consented to the film being premiered at the Venice Film Festival, but did not consent for it to be shown anywhere else. . . . The adoption was never a taboo topic in our family. We discussed it openly with Mariah as soon as she was able to understand the concept. Mariah has talked often about wanting to go back to Paraguay someday and try to find her birth mother and her siblings. She has a brother and a sister who have also been adopted by American families living in Pennsylvania and New Jersey, and she likes to joke about her adopted siblings possibly being "Yankee fans," and how that might create friction in a family that adores the Red Sox. Mariah has been totally in acceptance of the reality of her adoption, and would, I am sure, love the film. I have promised Marilyn that I would not show it to her for another year, until she turns eighteen.

52. Might "round 2" be a subtle reference to the battle McElwee had with Marilyn Levine over the release of *In Paraguay?* Is *Photographic Memory* the second round in McElwee's attempt to get back to his particular brand of truly *personal* personal documentary?

53. Indeed, that Adrian never comments on the irony of his father's regularly filming him as he complains about Adrian's being distracted suggests to me that he and his father are not only similar to one another, but in a deeper sense in cahoots.

54. McElwee's reference to finding "his own way to live" is the most overt reference in *Photographic Memory* to the McElwee/Levine divorce, which though never mentioned directly, seems implicit throughout: Adrian seems to be living in Ross's apartment, and at one point Ross tells him to not break a glass teapot, "It's Mom's." Later, when he is preparing to meet Maud, Ross mentions that his interest is not romantic, explaining, "I'm married with kids and she's probably married too," but this seems mostly a way to avoid bringing the divorce into the film and perhaps suggests understandable anxiety about admitting that there could be some romantic energy in the meeting: after all, just before he goes to see Maud (and immediately after his visit to the prehistoric ruins at Carnac), McElwee faces the camera in extreme close-up, wondering how he will look to Maud, concluding with, "Seriously, how did I get to be this old!"

55. This conclusion echoes the conclusion of *Bright Leaves,* where Adrian runs to the surf to save the tiny fish he has caught. Rothman, in "Sometimes Daddies Don't Talk": "Ross, filming Adrian, is at once 'tying the knot,' strengthening his bond with his son, and letting Adrian go, embracing his son's freedom, blessing him on his way. This is expressed by the camera's remaining behind, so that, visually, Adrian recedes further into the distance until he is finally enveloped in the dreamy calm of the shot" (120). In a context of *Bright Leaves,* the ending of *Photographic Memory* takes on an irony: what may seem, and be, a breakthrough for Adrian (and thus for McElwee as well) is—or at least is *also*—evidence that things have not changed all that much.

CHAPTER 7

1. Interview with Robb Moss, in Scott MacDonald, *A Critical Cinema 5* (Berkeley: University of California Press, 2006), 194.

2. That we see Adrian McElwee in *The Tourist,* finished two years before *Time Indefinite,* which concludes with his birth, suggests that while Moss may have been emboldened to use his own voice-over narration in *The Tourist* after seeing McElwee's *Backyard,* McElwee's knowledge of *The Tourist* may have had something to do with his decision to end *Time Indefinite* with the arrival of his first child—both Jean Moss and Marilyn Levine suffer miscarriages early in *The Tourist* and *Time Indefinite.*

3. *Secrecy* was broadcast on the Sundance Channel and was widely seen—in an unusually varied set of venues—here and abroad. See the *Secrecy* website: www.secrecyfilm.com. *Secrecy* and the new project have grown out of Moss's and Gilason's collaboration as teachers. Moss:

> We began teaching "Filming Science" in the fall of 2000; it's a hybrid class: people read books, see movies, write papers, and then make small videotapes in laboratory settings (broadly construed). We explore what happens to science when you film it, what happens to film when science is its topic; and we ask all kinds of interesting questions like what can you *see* with a camera, what strategies do you need in order to get underneath what's going on in a laboratory, how do people's personalities affect the kind of work that they do, is the *sociology* of a laboratory *science?* We've taught the class every other year since 2000, and a whole group of people have come through, mainly from the history of

science side rather than the filmmaking side, who have then gone on to get Masters and Ph.D.s that include filmmaking as a part of what they're doing. It's been fun to be part of that process. (Unpublished interview with Moss, 2011)

4. Moss:

I could have been in *Riverdogs,* and I do think of it as an autobiographical piece, just not as explicitly as *The Tourist.* Of course, even in *The Tourist* it's not like you see me on camera all that much. I do turn myself into a character through photographs at one point. But I didn't want to be in *Riverdogs.* It's funny because even when I was shooting, there were people around me saying, "Why don't you make it about fighting with your girlfriend?" And that might have been kind of interesting, but it wasn't what I was after. (Moss, in MacDonald, *A Critical Cinema 5,* 186–87)

The "trip members" are listed at the end of the film: Gary Berlant, Rick Brenner, Don Flasher, Bosco (actually Jeff—"Bosco" was Schifferle's name for him) Golden, Lyn Harlan, Teal Kinamun, Sparky Kramer, Ed Maloney, Roxanne Maloney, Davia Lee Nelson, Cathy Schifferle (later Cathy Golden, then Cathy Shaw), Danny Silver, Jim Tichenor, Steve Tichenor, Barry Wasserman, and Gayle Wilcox. Cathy Shifferle seems to address Moss at the end of a conversation midway through the film when Cathy and Jeff decide to go back to sleep, since no one is in a hurry.

5. As of the completion of *The Cambridge Turn* (spring 2013), *Riverdogs* remains out of general circulation, because Moss does not have the rights to use the version of Tom Waits's "Looking for the Heart of Saturday Night," with which the film concludes.

6. Moss, in MacDonald, *A Critical Cinema 5,* 186.

7. Ibid.

8. Some might argue that Danny Silver, who at one point calls the rafters to dinner, is fulfilling a conventional role; but we see her doing this only once during the film; and it is obvious that she takes active part in a very wide range of activities during the trip.

9. Moss: "The Sardines and Pork and Beans song was recorded somewhere in the south, sometime in the 60s. It was sent to me as part of a cassette mix by a former girl friend, and I found it haunting and innocent—somehow both as an early sound of home-made R and B and evocative (somehow) of these West African kids imitating us." E-mail to the author, January 13, 2011.

10. Of course, Ross McElwee's *Photographic Memory* (2011) is a more recent instance of the "Rip Van Winkle effect." See pp. 231–37.

11. Actually the transition here is from Wasserman in his office, to a close-up of a framed black-and-white photograph of him as a young river guide (the photograph is visible, behind Wasserman, in the office shot), to the shot from *Riverdogs.* The photograph seems to represent the way Wasserman has put the past behind him, while Moss's presence and the shots from *Riverdogs* are reviving the past for him.

12. Moss, in MacDonald, *A Critical Cinema 5,* 196.

13. My experience teaching *The Same River Twice* has made clear that for many students Jim Tichenor, who was for the Riverdogs, as Jeff Golden says, "a river deity. . . . We were Jim-ists," now reads as a "hippie"—though Moss is at pains to make clear Tichenor's intel-

lectual qualities (we see Alan Watts's *The Way of Zen* and Noam Chomsky's *Deterring Democracy* in Tichenor's trailer). To the current generation a hippie seems to be a lazy, irresponsible druggie, but it is obvious that Tichenor is certainly neither lazy nor irresponsible. He has not become a family man, and he remains a loner, but he would certainly be the right choice to guide one safely through the Grand Canyon on a raft.

14. This moment in *The Same River Twice* works in much the same way as Su Friedrich's letter to her father in her autobiographical film *Sink or Swim* (1990). Friedrich's letter tells her father of the pain her mother and Friedrich herself felt when Paul Friedrich left the family. We read the letter as Friedrich types it, through the P.S.: "I wish that I could mail you this letter." And yet, since *Sink or Swim* was widely exhibited, and since Friedrich made sure her father was invited to a screening of the film in Chicago, she did in a sense send him the letter. Of course, we can't be sure, as we are watching the films that Paul Friedrich or Shaw did indeed receive this communication—but in fact we know, from Moss and Friedrich, that they did, which conditions subsequent viewings of both films.

15. Moss, in MacDonald, *A Critical Cinema 5*, 186.

16. Ibid.

17. *The Voyage of Life* is composed of *Childhood, Youth, Manhood* and *Old Age*. In each painting, we see a single individual in a small boat on a river. In *Childhood,* a young male child is seen coming out of a cave in the springtime; in *Youth,* a young man in a summer landscape is seen looking toward a distant castle in the sky. In *Manhood,* the man, now in a rudderless boat, is at the mercy of violent rapids and of violent fall weather. And in *Old Age,* the old man rests in a boat in the darkness (presumably of winter) and looks toward the heavens in the hope of salvation. *The Voyage of Life* exists in two versions. The earlier, painted as a commission for the New York banker and philanthropist Samuel Ward, is on exhibit at the Munson-Williams-Proctor Arts Institute in Utica, New York. Cole's frustration that the original version was hidden away in a private collection led him to paint a second version, which was completed in 1842: it is part of the collection of the National Gallery of Art in Washington, D.C.

I have written about the cinematic, or really proto-cinematic, qualities of *The Voyage of Life* in *The Garden in the Machine* (Berkeley: University of California Press, 2001), 23–29.

18. Moss, in MacDonald, *A Critical Cinema 5*: "I would go back in ten or fifteen years and film people's lives over a five-year period. I'd love to do that if the people in the film will allow it; it may be a little scarier because of the kinds of things that may be happening. When I joke with Barry that I'll call the third film, 'The Naked and the Dead,' he cringes; he *doesn't* think it's funny and tells me that *none* of them will think it's funny in ten or fifteen years. I hope I'll be able to find out" (198).

CHAPTER 8

1. The most recent edition, *The Filmmaker's Handbook: A Comprehensive Guide for the Digital Age* (New York: Plume), was published in 2012.

2. I spoke with Benning after the discussion, noting that his refusal of sympathy on the grounds that the Pereebooms were privileged seemed hypocritical to me, since Benning himself is reasonably privileged—as exemplified by his being invited to the symposium. His response: "Well, I hate myself too!" At base, I suspect Benning's reaction to *The Maelstrom*

was a function of his understandable concern about the ways in which Israeli Zionists have created a new instance of fascism with regard to Palestinians. The frustrations of the present had become the lens through which he watched the Forgács video.

3. Actually, Sarris's line was a way of damning with faint praise the accomplishments of what Jonas Mekas had named the New American Cinema. As Sarris says in that same essay, "Finally, the collectivity of Independent Cinema is not worth writing about. Only individual films. . . . Add it all up and you have an interesting footnote to the history of world cinema. Much ado about nothing? Hardly. Someone has to man the outposts of culture." See Andrew Sarris, "The Independent Cinema," in Gregory Battcock, *The New American Cinema: A Critical Anthology* (New York: Dutton, 1967), 56–57.

4. In their artists' statement for *Raising Renee*, their films "begin at a moment of crisis and take a longitudinal approach to uncover meanings that are only visible by filming over years, through an intimacy with our subjects forged by time." See www.westcityfilms.com.

5. Three of Negroponte's films—*Jupiter's Wife, W.I.S.O.R.*, and *No Accident*—were produced, or co-produced, by Jane Weiner, the director of *"On Being There" with Richard Leacock* (2011). Weiner also produced *Silverlake Life: The View from Here* (1993). Weiner was one of a number of young filmmakers who worked with Ricky Leacock and Ed Pincus at MIT during the early 1970s without being matriculated at the university.

6. In one instance, it is clear that Negroponte has taken one of the addicts, Jeff, to breakfast—Jeff tells him, "That was really nice of you to take me out to breakfast; that was very nice. Thank you." But so far as is evident in *Methadonia*, this is the extent of Negroponte's direct involvement—other than his filmmaking.

7. Negroponte has completed one other feature and two short films, all of which explore dimensions of New York City. *W.I.S.O.R.* (2000) documents the engineering project that produced a robot (named W.I.S.O.R.) that could make repairs to New York's century-old system of steam pipes responsible for heating and providing hot water to the city. *W.I.S.O.R.* includes much archival footage of Manhattan during the early 1900s but focuses on the group of engineers at Honeybee Robotics responsible for creating the robot. Negroponte is not a character in *W.I.S.O.R.*—though his direction is energetic and his cinematography full of impressive images of New York. *No Accident* (1996, 22 minutes) is an homage to the New York subway system. Poet John Giorno functions as our guide through the underworld of the system and is the voice of the subway. *The Sightseer* (2003) is a mixture of documentary imagery of the city and a fictional story of a New York marriage—an homage to the city after the terrorist attacks of September 11, 2001. Both these films are available on Vimeo and on Negroponte's website: www.michelnegroponte.com.

8. A complete—or at least the most complete—filmography for Leacock is in Richard Leacock, *The Feeling of Being There: A Filmmaker's Memoir*, ed. Valerie Lalonde (Meaulne, France: Semeïon, 2011).

9. See Jennifer Dunbar interview with Leacock in *Rolling Stock* (Boulder, CO) 11 (1986): 31.

10. See Leacock's website—www.richardleacock.com—under "About Richard Leacock."

11. Leacock's website, under "The Art of Home Movies, or 'To Hell with the Professionalism of Television and Cinema Producers,'" an essay, according to the website, drafted in 1993, but not generally available until the website was up.

It is hard to imagine that Leacock's knowing Jonas Mekas, who was a guest at MIT in the 1970s, did not confirm his developing commitment to home movie–making as an art.

12. Unpublished interview with Davenport, 2012.

13. Actually, the earliest film Hutton lists in his filmography, *In Marin County* (1970), is color; Hutton returned to color in *Time and Tide* (2000) and has continued to explore color—along with black and white—in his recent films, most dramatically perhaps in *At Sea* (2007).

14. Hutton has consistently eliminated any interchange with or between the human beings who appear in his films. Indeed, with few exceptions human beings are rare in nearly all of his work: Hutton's films are overwhelmingly involved with landscape, cityscape, and seascape; there are few close-ups of any kind. Exceptions include one of Hutton's earliest films, *July '71 in San Francisco, Living at Beach Street, Working at Canyon Cinema, Swimming in the Valley of the Moon* (1971) and the recent *At Sea* (2007). For his final sequence in the trilogy of locations in *At Sea* (the first section explores a Korean ship-building operation; the second, a voyage across the Atlantic on a container ship during early spring), Hutton filmed men working on a ship-dismantling operation in Bangladesh; near the end of this sequence several of these men are drawn to Hutton's camera in much the same way as some of the Indians in *Hello Photo* are drawn to Davenport's.

15. Actually, to make *North on Evers* Benning traveled the route twice: a 1989 trip is evoked in a written text that scrolls across the bottom of the frame; a 1990 trip to the same locations was documented in image and sound. The viewer's attempts to comprehend the two trips, presented in two very different ways, can create forms of frustration and fascination not available in *Easy Rider* and *Parallel Lines*.

16. Actually, *Easy Rider* involved locals in a number of scenes, including the visit of Wyatt (Peter Fonda), Billy (Dennis Hopper), and George Hanson (Jack Nicholson) to a restaurant in Louisiana. Indeed, it is relatively difficult to distinguish the actors and the locals in *Easy Rider*.

17. Davenport's voice-over in *Parallel Lines* is relatively straightforward (Spiro's companion, Sam the dog, narrates *Roam Sweet Home!*—Alan Gurganus wrote Sam's monologues); she speaks what purport to be her thoughts at various moments during her journey. There is no direct reference to the fact that the narration was written after the trip was completed—though, of course, we assume all along that she does in fact complete her trip back to New York City.

Both *Parallel Lines* and *Roam Sweet Home*—and *Easy Rider,* but not *North on Evers*—rely on extradiagetic music as transitional device and confirmation of the emotional states of Davenport and those she speaks with. Sheldon Mirowitz, who teaches at Berklee College of Music in Boston, did the score for *Parallel Lines* (as well as for *Always a Bridesmaid* and Ascher-Jordan's Family Trilogy). His music for *Parallel Lines* seems to me a bit too typical for this subject.

18. In Monument Valley, Davenport speaks with a Navajo guide who describes the trauma of being separated from his culture and "civilized" by being sent to a white school where he was not allowed to speak his native language. In Los Alamos, Davenport is surprised to find that no mention of the number of Japanese casualties at Hiroshima and Nagaski is included in the exhibit devoted to the dropping of the atomic bombs. And in Chickasaw, Alabama, when Davenport stops her car to film some cattle, two local farmers pull up beside her; their mean-spirited racism evokes the Louisiana scenes in *Easy Rider*.

Davenport and Benning seem closely allied in one culturally political sense. In *North on Evers* Benning visits several folk artists, two of them African Americans (Alabama painter

Mose T and Georgia fundamentalist preacher turned painter-graphic artist, Howard Finster); in *Parallel Lines* Davenport visits Lee Shanks, who decorates the trees in front of his home as Jesus Christ has directed him to. Both films depict incidents that reveal how toxic the issue of race still is in much of the South so that this folk art is read as a creative response to racism, a way of living on a plane detached from it.

19. The next day, she visits Ground Zero. There, she has one final human encounter, with a Chinese American photographer, who, like Davenport, is refusing to record the destroyed buildings themselves in favor of making a record of people's responses to the tragedy. He provides Davenport with what feels like a final assessment of what *Parallel Lines* has revealed about the United States: "It's like we're standing in the shadow, a big, big shadow, and inside that shadow are our own little shadows." Shadows are a visual motif in *Parallel Lines,* and Davenport's focus on them increases during the voyage east. Often we see the shadow of her car, and the film's final image is her filming her own shadow as she leaves the site of Ground Zero: Davenport's travels in search of responses to the big shadow of 9/11 have revealed the many struggles that shadow her countrymen and have, over time, dispersed the shadow of her own fear of resuming her life as a New Yorker.

20. *Demon Lover Diary* (1980) by Joel DeMott, shot when she was a student at MIT, prefigures *Operation Filmmaker. Demon Lover Diary* chronicles an aborted attempt by Jeff Kreines and Mark Rance—also veterans of the MIT Film Section—to assist Don, a friend of Kreines who is making a low-budget horror film. When DeMott, Kreines, and Rance arrive in Michigan, where *Demon Lover* is to be shot, there is immediate resistance to DeMott's working on *her* project. She does continue to shoot, as the *Demon Lover* project falls apart: Don and his colleagues clearly have no idea how to make a film, and in the end the MIT group flees the scene of the shooting. Both Patricia R. Zimmermann and Jim Lane suggest that DeMott's film offers a feminist critique of both the *Demon Lover* project and the kind of horror film it represents (in the proposed film, women are victimized) and of film as a male-dominated profession in general. See Zimmermann, "*Demon Lover Diary*: Deconstructing Sex, Class, and Cultural Power in Documentary," *Genders* 8 (July 1990): 93–94; and Lane, *The Autobiographical Documentary in America* (Madison: University of Wisconsin Press, 2002), 163–71.

21. Near the end of *Operation Filmmaker,* Esmaeli tells Davenport, "I don't deny the fact that I blew him off, that I stepped away from this project and I didn't want to talk to him."

22. At the end of the film in a series of visual texts, Pincus and Small update the status of those of their subjects they were able to track down, and they mention that "the volunteers do not return the next day." One implication is that these men may have been masquerading as Common Ground volunteers (as the group arrives, Brown is upset with their taking pictures; and later, as he complains to Small, he tells Pincus, "Don't film this."). Just before the visit to the Creecys, Pincus and Small have filmed the executive director of Common Ground, Malik Rahim, and two of his assistants, all of whom seemed pleased that someone is bearing witness to their struggles. Indeed, one volunteer mentions that the presence of NBC may have kept the work crews from bulldozing homes that Common Ground is working with Lower Ninth Ward residents to save. In the surreal environment of post–Katrina New Orleans, it is impossible to know who is trustworthy.

23. Unpublished interview with Gianvito, 2011.

24. Ibid. The courses Gianvito team-taught with Leacock were Introduction to a History of Film; Pabst/Fassbinder; Advanced Aesthetics in Contemporary Film; and New Horizons for Documentary.

25. *The Mad Songs of Fernanda Hussein* is set in New Mexico during the 1991 Persian Gulf War and focuses on three characters: Fernanda Hussein (Thia Gonzalez), a Mexican American mother, separated from her Arab husband (their two children are murdered at the beginning of the film; her grief and anger drive her mad); Raphael Sinclair, a teenage Santa Fe boy (Dustin Scott) who is isolated in his opposition to the war; and Carlos Sandia (Robert Perrea), a Chicano who has returned from military duty in the Persian Gulf and cannot leave the experience behind. Gianvito himself plays Raphael's anti-war high school teacher. The film is shot in and around Santa Fe and Bernalillo, New Mexico, mostly with nonprofessional actors. A performance on the oud by Arab musician Naseer Shamma, recorded by Milan Kohout—the performance was a response to the American bombing of Baghdad—is a motif through the film.

26. The original text: "E'hyuñ'i degi'ata, E'hyuñ'i degi'ata / Tsä'hop ää'he'dal, Tsä'hop ää'he'dal / Na de'gu'anta, de'gu'anta; Na de'gu'anta, de'gu'anta; / Gadal-guñ t'añgya deo'ta, Gadal-guñ t'añgya deo'ta / Go' debi'äta, debi'äta, Go' debi'äta, debi'äta"; the translation, as presented in *Profit Motive and the Whispering Wind:* "I am mashing the berries, I am massing the berries. They say travelers are coming on the march, they say travelers are coming on the march. I stir (the berries) around, I stir them around; I take them up with a spoon of buffalo horn, I take them up with a spoon of buffalo horn. And I carry them, I carry them (to the strangers), And I carry them, I carry them (to the strangers)."

27. Hollis Frampton in an interview in Scott MacDonald, *A Critical Cinema* (Berkeley: University of California Press, 1988), 49.

28. There are other dimensions to Benning's structuring of *Deseret.* The ninety-three newspaper stories evoked in the film—Benning edited the texts of the stories down to manageable lengths—are separated one from the next by a single continuous shot. Each successive transitional shot is shorter than the previous one (a way of suggesting, among other things, the increasingly hectic pace of modern life and of newspaper reporting). *Deseret* is divided into two halves: the first uses only black-and-white shots (often evocative of nineteenth-century landscape photography); the second half, which begins at the point when Utah was granted statehood, is in color. See my discussion of *Deseret* in *The Garden in the Machine* (Berkeley: University of California Press, 2001), 337–45.

29. Benning concludes several of his films—*North on Evers,* for example, and *Deseret, Thirteen Lakes* (2004)—with a listing of locations visited. Gianvito does the same in *Profit Motive.*

30. The full title of the song is "I Dreamed I Saw Joe Hill Last Night." It was adapted from a poem of the same title by Aldred Hayes in 1936 by song writer Earl Robinson. In *Profit Motive,* Robeson sings the opening (and closing) stanza.

31. Gianvito has indicated that these other rotoscoped shots are from Antonioni's *The Eclipse* (1962) and from a documentary on Wall Street. Unpublished interview with Gianvito.

During these animated passages, the sound varies: the first two passages are accompanied by electronic music; the third is presented silent; the fourth uses music; and the fifth is accompanied by the sound of men, perhaps the original sound of the imagery Gianvito rotoscoped.

32. After this exuberant montage, *Profit Motive* is suddenly quiet again; a 27-second shot of a green field with a breeze blowing through some trees in the distance is followed by a text indicating that the video was "Inspired by and dedicated to 'A People's History of the United States' by Howard Zinn," then by the final credits, which are accompanied by an instrumental version of "The Internationale" performed by Ani Difranco and Utah Phillips.

33. Specifically, Silva traveled to Serbia in June and in December 1999 and in August 2005; and to Kosovo in January 2000. Several sequences were filmed in Cambridge, near Harvard Yard, in July 2006.

Silva's involvement with the Balkans and *Balkan Rhapsodies:*

> happened by chance, really, while I was working at MIT as a producer of educational videos. I had no previous relationship to the region, and to be honest, knew very little about the Balkans prior to my visit. By chance, one day at MIT one of my "assignments" was to film a head-shot interview of Noam Chomsky for a presentation that Noam was not able to attend. . . . I was taken by his genuine humbleness and warm-hearted sensitivity and spirit. . . . I was fortunate after that shoot . . . to work with Chomsky regularly . . . doing tapings and sometimes live satellite and ISDN uplinks, so we talked a lot and became friendly. . . . A couple of months later the war in Kosovo started and his talks and our conversations turned to the Balkans. I felt an obligation to read up on Yugoslavia before our next meetings so that I didn't sound like a complete fool, and eventually, through my own research and my conversations with Chomsky I developed a passionate interest in the region and a deep concern about the war, the US involvement, and the mainstream media's one-sided view of the situation. . . . The bombing lasted nearly 3 months . . . when it finally ended I decided rather impulsively to try to go there, in part to bear witness to the situation that ordinary Serbian citizens, who were completely demonized, faced from the war and the Milošević regime and to hopefully be able to add something unique to the discourse surrounding the war. (E-mail from Silva, March 1, 2012)

34. In an e-mail to the author, March 2, 2012, Silva explains that he's "a huge fan" of *Reminiscences of a Journey to Lithuania,* "and I consider it a big influence on the film," along with Jørgen Leth's *66 Scenes from Amerika* (1982), Su Friedrich's *Sink or Swim* (1990), and Abraham Ravett's *The March* (1999).

35. Measure 21, "January 4, 2000—first glimpse of kosovo," seems a direct reference to Mekas's glimpses in *Reminiscences.*

36. This final sequence is itself the culmination of a motif that is first evident about 12 minutes into the film, in a reverse motion shot of a glass with Slivovitza sitting on a table (along with, if one looks closely, a copy of Ilisa Barbash and Lucien Castaing-Taylor's *Cross-Cultural Filmmaking: A Handbook for Making Documentary and Ethnographic Films and Videos* (Berkeley: University of California Press, 1997). In Measure 59, Silva is seen drinking from the glass—from a camera placed underneath the glass—for the first time.

37. Ivan Nedeljkovic would become one of the two protagonists of Silva's *Ivan & Ivana* (2011), which follows the married couple as they immigrate to California, then separate.

38. E-mail from Silva, February 27, 2012.

39. Silva has not adopted what has tended to be the typical minimalist approach to "signing" a work of cinema on the part of many male avant-garde filmmakers: in most cases, the canonical avant-garde filmmakers have been satisfied to sign only their own names or logos—an implicit nod perhaps to the way that painters and poets normally acknowledge only their own authorship. Women filmmakers identified with the American avant-garde— Yvonne Rainer, Su Friedrich, Peggy Ahwesh, for example—often acknowledge a range of supporters and contributors, and in general, the documentary filmmakers I discuss in this volume have been careful to see their work as having developed within an extensive community of makers, scholars, curators, and other contributors.

40. This reticence about himself was not confined to his making the windmill film. In the brochure included with the DVD edition of three of Rogers's early short films, Tom Gunning remembers that "not long after I met Richard Rogers he said to me with the mixture of irony and humility that was one of his characteristics, 'Sooner or later I am going to have to show you my films—which will be a problem.' I looked at him quizzically. He explained, 'I know everyone goes through a period where they hate their work, but right now I even hate the person who made it!'" From "Richard P. Rogers: Three Short Films. Notes by Tom Gunning," on "Three Films by Richard P. Rogers," a DVD produced by Susan Meiselas. The DVD includes *Quarry* (1970), *Elephants* (1973), and *226-1690* (1984), as well as a video recording of Gunning, filmed at the Harvard Film Archive, talking about Rogers.

41. In an unpublished interview, Moss describes Olch to me: "He was in my first-year documentary class and he fought documentary the whole way. The first project in that course is to film light, meaning that you don't *create* the light, you *observe* the light. But Alex got lights and he filmed a woman in a white dress walking down a stairway—that was his interpretation of the project, an interpretation that explicitly defied the instructions and ended up having very little to do with light, at least in the way that I had intended. The whole year was like that."

42. If *Artemin Goldberg: Custom Tailor of Brassieres* doesn't quite work, at least if the goal was to fool viewers into thinking they were watching a documentary, it can be understood as a satire of standard documentary form—and it is prescient of the interest in fashion that would ultimately become Olch's primary focus: Olch has become internationally known for his ties and other accessories, in much the way his character of Artemin Goldberg is famous for his brassieres.

43. Friedman's voice-over introduction of Joslin in *Silverlake Life: The View from Here* is similar to Olch's introduction of Rogers in *The Windmill Movie*. Friedman: "Tom Joslin was my film teacher back in college in the mid-seventies. He was my mentor, and later he and his lover, Mark Massi, became two of my closest friends"; Olch: "Dick Rogers was my film teacher at Harvard. . . . He directed documentaries for PBS, for the BBC, he made eighteen films in places like Nicaragua, Rome, Surinam, New York, but he also spent decades working on one film he could not find a way to finish."

The title of Joslin's previous film, *Blackstar: Autobiography of a Close Friend* (1976), a personal documentary about his coming out as a gay man, its effects on his family, and his struggle to make a life with Mark Massi, seems a premonition of both *Silverlake Life: The View from Here* and *The Windmill Movie*.

44. In his director's statement on the DVD version of *Silverlake Life*, Peter Friedman explains, "I didn't undertake the sad and difficult task of completing *Silverlake Life* as a personal tribute. I did it because I believe in what Tom was trying to do—to make people understand the magnitude of the suffering and loss that people with AIDS and their loved ones face, and also to show the depth of love and commitment that can exist in a gay relationship."

45. A DVD of this episode of *Screening Room* is available through Gardner's Studio-7Arts—as are a good many other *Screening Room* episodes.

46. Lane: "By *journal entry* I mean a type of autobiographical documentary that involves the shooting of everyday events for a sustained period of time and the subsequent editing of these events into a chronological autobiographical narrative. Events appear along a diachronic chain as if they are occurring for the first time in the present tense" (*The Autobiographical Documentary in America* [Madison: University of Wisconsin Press, 2002], 33).

47. The "essay film" has emerged as the newest category of documentary—or at least as a newly popular term for certain types of films roughly analogous to the personal essay in literature. Essay films may include any of the other sources of image and sound used by traditional documentaries, but whereas the information in traditional documentaries is often presented by "voice-of-god narrators" who draw clear and definite conclusions, essay films tend to rely on the filmmaker's personal observations and ruminations on the topic at hand and are less involved with drawing conclusions or creating a sense of resolution than traditional documentaries.

48. *DDR/DDR* is not the first of Siegel's films to deal with the issue of German reunification and to focus on the idea of surveillance in the broadest sense. Her *German People/ Deutsche Menschen* (2006) is a collection of interviews with German men about the experience of the German reunification. And her *Empathy* (2003) explores psychoanalysis as a form of surveillance, and within a formal structure that in many ways predicts the structure of *DDR/DDR*. Mark Rance was the producer of *Empathy*.

49. What Siegel conceives as, originally, a pair of mirror opposites—East Germany and West Germany—were ultimately unified into the current German state, but not of course on the basis of equality. As Hans-Joachim Maaz says at the end of the film, "The enthusiasm after the *Wende* didn't really become a constructive unification. The question, What experience do people in the East have? How can we use them? Is there a so-called 'third way'? Could there be a new constitution that would bring together Easy German and West German elements? This discussion did not take place. Instead, it very quickly turned out that everything just had to be taken over: the entire order, all the laws, the entire economic system." That is to say, East Germany, which had originally been a mirror opposite of West Germany, now became just a (disadvantaged) version, a repetition, of the West; and this is reflected in the technology of contemporary word processing, where "DDR" can only be typed in one direction.

50. Early on, Studio Babelsberg, among the first large-scale film studios in the world, was UFA, where *The Cabinet of Dr. Caligari*, *Metropolis*, and *The Blue Angel* were produced. During the Nazi era Joseph Goebbels oversaw the production of the Nazi propaganda films there. DEFA was established in 1946 and was the only film producer in the DDR. After the *Wende* it became, once again, Studio Babelsberg, in private ownership.

51. Unpublished interview with Siegel, 2011.

CHAPTER 9

1. http://sel.fas.harvard.edu/.

2. Ilisa Barbash and Lucien Castaing-Taylor, *Cross Cultural Filmmaking: A Handbook for Making Documentary and Ethnographic Films and Videos* (Berkeley: University of California Press, 1997), 1.

3. The installation pieces: *Bedding Down, Breakfast, Coom Biddy, Daybreak on the Bedground, Hell Roaring Creek, The High Trail, Into-the-Jug (geworfen),* and *Turned at the Pass;* the photographic pieces: "Sheep Wreck," "Dawn Mist II," "Dawn Mist I," "Bull Moose Crossing."

4. See Bill Nichols, "Dislocating Ethnographic Film: *In and Out of Africa* and Issues of Cultural Representation," *American Anthropologist* 99: 4 (December 1997): 817. Of course, juxtaposition has always been one of the primary techniques in documentary, though Nichols sees its use in an anthropological context as a critique of the tradition of depicting particular cultural groups as distinct and disconnected from other cultural developments, including the developments that have brought anthropologists to study these particular groups.

5. Two exceptions are the books about filmmakers Barbash and Castaing-Taylor edited: a collection of writings by ethnographic filmmaker David MacDougall, *Transcultural Cinema* (Princeton: Princeton University Press, 1998); and a collection of writings about Robert Gardner, *The Cinema of Robert Gardner* (New York: Berg, 2007).

6. Grimshaw: "Barbash and Castaing-Taylor's approach does not proceed according to the conventions of academic argument. Instead it draws on the synesthetic, spatial, and temporal properties of film to open a space of suggestive possibilities between the experiential and propositional, between the perceptual and conceptual, between lived realities and images of the American West." From "The Bellwether Ewe: Recent Developments in Ethnographic Filmmaking and the Aesthetics of Anthropological Inquiry," *Cultural Anthropology* 26: 2 (May 2011): 257–58.

7. Wiseman: "I think the shooting of the film *is* the research. I don't particularly like to hang out in the place I'm planning to make a film about if I'm not prepared to shoot what's going on; at least if I'm not there, I don't know what I'm missing. I like to think that I approach each new subject with an open mind, and one aspect of the editing is thinking through what the experience of being at the place meant to me. My 'notes' about the place *are* the rushes." From an unpublished record of a discussion of *Hospital* (1969) at the Brattle Theater in Cambridge, July 19, 2010.

8. Castaing-Taylor discusses the "aesthetic tension" between sound and image on the commentary track of the *Sweetgrass* DVD.

9. Connolly's obscene rant is reminiscent of the Yanomami woman's rant at the visitors in Asch's *The Ax Fight*. Not only is it similarly humorous, but Connolly's rhythmic fury becomes nearly poetic: "You old whores! Sour cunts! Motherfuckers! You can't leave the cocksuckers five fuckin' minutes! I'm fuckin' tired of it! I need a day off. I just need to get the fuck away from this shit! Fuckin' mountain climbin', goat climbin', cocksucking mother *fuckers!*"!

10. The only comparable use of epic visuals and intimate sounds that I am aware of occurs in Abbas Kiarostami's *The Wind Will Carry Us* (1999)—though in this case Kiar-

ostami is creating the impression of sync sound rather than working with actual sync. In some instances, Kiarostami's fabrication of sync has much the same impact as the use of actual sync in the sequence just described: during the long opening sequence of *The Wind Will Carry Us,* a car negotiates tiny, curving roads in a spectacular Iranian landscape, as we hear what purports to be a conversation within the car between the reporter and his colleagues: their conversation reveals that they are basically oblivious to the beauty of the place through which they are driving, too engaged in their work to see where they are.

11. Unpublished interview with Lucien Castaing-Taylor, 2011.

12. Both terms have become increasingly problematic as categories. *Avant-garde* was adapted to film from the other arts, particularly from modernist painting, to represent the idea that "avant-garde" filmmakers have often devised new approaches to cinema that have subsequently been exploited by commercial movie makers. The logic of "avant-garde" in a cinematic context has always been questionable, because it is obvious that without the early development of commercial film, the means for producing "avant-garde film" would never have been available. Further, the several filmmaking approaches that have come to be identified with avant-garde film have developed their own traditions; makers working in these traditions can no longer claim to be original, no matter how accomplished their work is. The current value of the term is its inclusiveness, rather than its designation of any particular approach, though most "avant-garde" films can be understood as explicit and/or implicit critiques of commercial media and the audience that has developed for it.

Documentary was first used by John Grierson, who said that Robert Flaherty's *Moana* (1926) had "documentary value," meaning, presumably, that Flaherty had successfully documented aspects of the life of a distant culture (the Samoans). Of course, we now know that during the production of *Nanook of the North* and *Moana* Flaherty asked the Inuit and the Samoans to reenact elements of earlier ways of life; generally, though he was working in collaboration with real Inuit and real Samoans in their actual environments, Flaherty was documenting performances, and in some instances, performances of the past. Recent years have seen increased suspicion of documentary's truth claim—though, like *avant-garde,* the term is usefully inclusive of, if not particularly precise about, a range of attempts to represent "the real."

13. Of course, in a certain sense, Muybridge's photo records of animals moving through his constructed laboratory environment are no less "unnatural" than the tradition of developing herds of sheep and moving them into mountain pastures. If the ranchers don't construct the space through which the sheep are herded, they do reconstruct it by their presence.

14. Larry Gottheim's *Fog Line* is an 11-minute, single-shot film of a foggy pasture in outside of Binghamton, New York; during the film, the fog gradually disperses, at one point revealing two horses grazing across the pasture. Throughout his career Peter Hutton's focus has been cityscape and landscape, always filmed silent and for several decades in black and white, using extended shots: *Landscape (for Manon)* (1987), for example, is a black-and-white meditation on Catskill Mountain scenes that begins with shots that last around 30 seconds, then slows down to shots of nearly a minute, before concluding at the earlier pace. Each of the films in James Benning's California Trilogy—*El Valley Centro* (1999), *Los* (2000), and *Sogobi* (2001)—is composed of thirteen 2½-minute shots, each rigorously composed and recorded with a tripod-mounted camera. His *13 Lakes* (2004) and *Ten Skies*

(2004) are composed of 10-minute shots (thirteen and ten, respectively). And Sharon Lockhart's *Double Tide* (2010) is a meditation on a woman clamming in a Maine cove in the morning and in the evening, composed of what seem to be two 45-minute continuous shots.

15. Various galleries have exhibited one or more of the video installations: Marion Goodman Gallery, New York City (*Hell Roaring Creek, Into-the-jug (geworfen)*, and *Coom Biddy*) in 2007; Musée du quai Branly, Paris (*Hell Roaring Creek, Into-the-jug (geworfen)*) in 2009; James Art Gallery, New York City (*Hell Roaring Creek, Into-the-jug (geworfen)*, and *Turned at the Pass*, along with the photographic works, "Sheep Wreck," "Dawn Mist II," "Dawn Mist I," and "Bull Moose Crossing") in 2008; X Initiative in New York City (all eight video installations) in 2010.

16. Thomas Moran's large-scale *Grand Canyon of the Yellowstone* (1872), for example, was the first non-portrait to be exhibited in the rotunda of the U. S. Capitol Building. Its presence there is generally thought to have played a role in the instigation of the American national park system.

17. To be more precise, the man walks into the image 1 minute and 49 seconds into the shot. I am discussing the 62-minute version of *Chaiqian;* in a 60-minute version of the film, this opening shot is more than a minute shorter and the man who walks into the image transforming our sense of the space arrives 48 seconds into the shot.

18. Nothing in *Chaiqian* itself makes clear, at least to an American audience, that these men are migrant workers. Snaidecki has written about the making of the film for the online journal *Media Fields:* see "Beyond the Frame: Personal Testimony as Counter discourse in the Life of Gao Jianqing," www.mediafieldsjournal.org/beyond-the-frame/2011/2/28/beyond-the-frame-personal-testimony-as-counterdiscourse-in-t.html.

19. The man working the blowtorch is Gao Jianqing, "a middle-aged migrant laborer, husband, and father of three" who Sniadecki met at the worksite. Gao Jianqing is the primary subject of Sniadecki's "Beyond the Frame" essay (see n. 21).

20. Arno Danusiri's *On Broadway* (2010), also made in conjunction with the SEL, is similar to *Chaiqian* and *Songhua* in this regard. In four extended shots, each filmed from an identical position providing a wide-angle view of a large basement space, Danusiri documents the preparations for a service and sermon in a makeshift mosque, the service and sermon itself, and the transformation of the space back into what appears to be an informal game room. The five shots are separated by four 12-second moments of darkness, each punctuated by an Italian musical term: *andante, expressivo, animato,* and *affrettando*—a suggestion that this transformation of a nearly empty space into a crowded, spiritual event, then back into an empty space is a city symphony, albeit of a very unusual kind.

21. There were thirty workers at the demolition site documented in *Chaiqian*: twenty-seven men and three women. Sniadecki, "Beyond the Frame": 2.

22. As this is written (January 2012), Spray has finished *Kale and Kale* (2007), *Monsoon Reflections* (2008), *As Long as There's Breath* (2009), and the installation pieces: *Māto* (2008), *Untitled (bed)* (2009), and *The Loiterers* (2010).

23. Like *Sweetgrass, Foreign Parts* had its American premiere at the New York Film Festival; seen widely on the festival circuit, it won major prizes at Locarno, Festival Dei Popoli, Docs Barcelona, and Punto de Vista.

24. Unpublished interview with the author, 2011.

EPILOGUE

1. Bruce W. Wilshire, ed., *William James: The Essential Writings* (Albany: State University of New York Press, 1984), 181. The italics are James's.

2. Unpublished interview with Spray, 2011. Benning's and Lockhart's films have been regularly shown to SEL students for years. Of course the use of the long take and the single-shot film have a long history in avant-garde cinema, beginning most obviously with Andy Warhol.

3. E-mail from Small to the author, May 8, 2012.

4. Michael Renov, *The Subject of Documentary*, Visible Evidence, vol. 15 (Minneapolis: University of Minnesota Press, 2004), xvii. It is a mark of the extent of the cinematic personal in recent decades, as well as of the problems of cinematic categories, that Renov's book makes a single, offhand reference to McElwee, and no mention at all of the personal documentary filmmakers I've discussed in *American Ethnographic Film and Personal Documentary*. In the introduction to his essay on Jonas Mekas's *Lost Lost Lost* (chapter 4), Renov attempts to bridge "the gap between filmmaking that focused on the subjectivity of social actors joined in struggle [that is, for example, Newsreel and Asian-American attempts to rethink America's ethnic past] dominant in the 1960s and 1970s, and the first-person forms that developed in the 1980s and 1990s" (69). One can only assume that *dominant* here means that particular kinds of films have dominated Renov's attention, since his sketch of this history ignores virtually the entire early development of personal documentary.

INDEX

CPSIA information can be obtained
at www.ICGtesting.com
Printed in the USA
JSHW021417101119
2373JS00005B/61